Praise for the Previous Edition

This encyclopedic book is not only a definitive Rails reference, but an indispensable guide to Software-as-a-Service coding techniques for serious craftspersons. I keep a copy in the lab, a copy at home, and a copy on each of my three e-book readers, and it's on the short list of essential resources for my undergraduate software engineering course.

—Armando Fox, adjunct associate professor, University of California, Berkeley

Everyone interested in Rails, at some point, has to follow *The Rails Way*.

—Fabio Cevasco, senior technical writer, Siemens AG, and blogger at H3RALD.com

I can positively say that it's the single best Rails book ever published to date. By a long shot.

—Antonio Cangiano, software engineer and technical evangelist at IBM

This book is a great crash course in Ruby on Rails! It doesn't just document the features of Rails, it filters everything through the lens of an experienced Rails developer—so you come our a pro on the other side.

—Dirk Elmendorf, co-founder of Rackspace, and Rails developer since 2005

The key to The Rails Way is in the title. It literally covers the "way" to do almost everything with Rails. Writing a truly exhaustive reference to the most popular Web application framework used by thousands of developers is no mean feat. A thankful

i

community of developers that has struggled to rely on scant documentation will embrace *The Rails Way* with open arms. A tour de force!

—Peter Cooper, editor, *Ruby Inside*

In the past year, dozens of Rails books have been rushed to publication. A handful are good. Most regurgitate rudimentary information easily found on the Web. Only this book provides both the broad and deep technicalities of Rails. Nascent and expert developers, I recommend you follow *The Rails Way*.

—Martin Streicher, chief technology officer, McLatchy Interactive; former editor-in-chief of *Linux Magazine*

Hal Fulton's *The Ruby Way* has always been by my side as a reference while programming Ruby. Many times I had wished there was a book that had the same depth and attention to detail, only focused on the Rails framework. That book is now here and hasn't left my desk for the past month.

—Nate Klaiber, Ruby programmer

As noted in my contribution to the Afterword: "What Is the Rails Way (To You)?," I knew soon after becoming involved with Rails that I had found something great. Now, with Obie's book, I have been able to step into Ruby on Rails development coming from .NET and be productive right away. The applications I have created I believe to be a much better quality due to the techniques I learned using Obie's knowledge.

—Robert Bazinet, InfoQ.com, .NET and Ruby community editor, and founding member of the Hartford, CT, Ruby Brigade

Extremely well written; it's a resource that every Rails programmer should have. Yes, it's that good.

—Reuven Lerner, *Linux Journal columnist*

THE RAILS™ 3 WAY

The **Addison-Wesley Professional Ruby Series** provides readers with practical, people oriented, and in depth information about applying the Ruby platform to create dynamic technology solutions. The series is based on the premise that the need for expert reference books, written by experienced practitioners, will never be satisfied solely by blogs and the Internet.

THE RAILS™ 3 WAY

Obie Fernandez

✦✦ Addison-Wesley

Upper Saddle River, NJ • Boston • Indianapolis • San Francisco
New York • Toronto • Montreal • London • Munich • Paris • Madrid
Capetown • Sydney • Tokyo • Singapore • Mexico City

The publisher offers excellent discounts on this book when ordered in quantity for bulk purchases or special sales, which may include electronic versions and/or custom covers and content particular to your business, training goals, marketing focus, and branding interests. For more information, please contact:

> U.S. Corporate and Government Sales
> (800) 382-3419
> corpsales@pearsontechgroup.com

For sales outside the United States please contact:
> International Sales
> international@pearson.com

Visit us on the Web: informit.com/aw

Library of Congress Cataloging-in-Publication Data
Fernandez, Obie.
   The rails 3 way / Obie Fernandez.
      p.   cm.
   Rev. ed. of: The Rails way / Obie Fernandez. 2008.
   Includes index.
   ISBN 0-321-60166-1 (pbk. : alk. paper)
   1. Ruby on rails (Electronic resource) 2. Object-oriented programming (Computer science)
3. Ruby (Computer program language) 4. Web site development. 5. Application
software–Development. I. Fernandez, Obie. Rails way. II. Title.
   QA76.64.F47 2010
   005.1'17–dc22   2010038744

ISBN-13: 978-0-321-60166-7
ISBN-10:   0-321-60166-1

Text printed in the United States on recycled paper at Edwards Brothers in Ann Arbor, Michigan.
Second printing, May 2011

Editor-in-Chief
Mark Taub

Executive Acquisitions Edit◄
Debra Williams Cauley

Managing Editor
John Fuller

Project Editor
Elizabeth Ryan

Copy Editor
Carol Loomis

Indexer
Valerie Haynes Perry

Proofreader
Erica Orloff

Publishing Coordinator
Kim Boedigheimer

Cover Designer
Chuti Prasertsith

Compositor
Glyph International

To Dad, thanks for teaching me ambition.

Contents

Chapter 3   REST, Resources, and Rails   55

Chapter 4   Working with Controllers   85

Chapter 17   Caching and Performance   483

Chapter 18   RSpec   501

Foreword

Rails is more than a programming framework for creating web applications. It's also a framework for thinking about web applications. It ships not as a blank slate equally tolerant of every kind of expression. On the contrary, it trades that flexibility for the convenience of "what most people need most of the time to do most things." It's a designer straightjacket that sets you free from focusing on the things that just don't matter and focuses your attention on the stuff that does.

To be able to accept that trade, you need to understand not just how to do something in Rails, but also why it's done like that. Only by understanding the why will you be able to consistently work with the framework instead of against it. It doesn't mean that you'll always have to agree with a certain choice, but you will need to agree to the overachieving principle of conventions. You have to learn to relax and let go of your attachment to personal idiosyncrasies when the productivity rewards are right.

This book can help you do just that. Not only does it serve as a guide in your exploration of the features in Rails, it also gives you a window into the mind and soul of Rails. Why we've chosen to do things the way we do them, why we frown on certain widespread approaches. It even goes so far as to include the discussions and stories of how we got there—straight from the community participants that helped shape them.

Learning how to do Hello World in Rails has always been easy to do on your own, but getting to know and appreciate the gestalt of Rails, less so. I applaud Obie for trying to help you on this journey. Enjoy it.

— **David Heinemeier Hansson**
Creator of Ruby on Rails

Foreword

From the beginning, the Rails framework turned web development on its head with the insight that the vast majority of time spent on projects amounted to meaningless sit-ups. Instead of having the time to think through your domain-specific code, you'd spend the first few weeks of a project deciding meaningless details. By making decisions for you, Rails frees you to kick off your project with a bang, getting a working prototype out the door quickly. This makes it possible to build an application with some meat on its bones in a few weekends, making Rails the web framework of choice for people with a great idea and a full-time job.

Rails makes some simple decisions for you, like what to name your controller actions and how to organize your directories. It also gets pretty aggressive, and sets development-friendly defaults for the database and caching layer you'll use, making it easy to change to more production-friendly options once you're ready to deploy.

By getting so aggressive, Rails makes it easy to put at least a few real users in front of your application within days, enabling you to start gathering the requirements from your users immediately, rather than spending months architecting a perfect solution, only to learn that your users use the application differently than you expected.

The Rails team built the Rails project itself according to very similar goals. Don't try to overthink the needs of your users. Get something out there that works, and improve it based on actual usage patterns. By all accounts, this strategy has been a smashing success, and with the blessing of the Rails core team, the Rails community leveraged the dynamism of Ruby to fill in the gaps in plugins. Without taking a close look at Rails, you might think that Rails' rapid prototyping powers are limited to the 15-minute blog demo, but that you'd fall off a cliff when writing a real app. This has never been true. In fact, in Rails 2.1, 2.2 and 2.3, the Rails team looked closely at common usage patterns reflected in very popular plugins, adding features that would further reduce the number of sit-ups needed to start real-life applications.

By the release of Rails 2.3, the Rails ecosystem had thousands of plugins, and applications like Twitter started to push the boundaries of the Rails defaults. Increasingly, you might build your next Rails application using a non-relational database or deploy it inside a Java infrastructure using JRuby. It was time to take the tight integration of the Rails stack to the next level.

Over the course of 20 months, starting in January 2008, we looked at a wide range of plugins, spoke with the architects of some of the most popular Rails applications, and changed the way the Rails internals thought about its defaults.

Rather than start from scratch, trying to build a generic data layer for Rails, we took on the challenge of making it easy to give any ORM the same tight level of integration with the rest of the framework as Active Record. We accepted no compromises, taking the time to write the tight Active Record integration using the same APIs that we now expose for other ORMs. This covers the obvious, such as making it possible to generate a scaffold using DataMapper or Mongoid. It also covers the less obvious, such as giving alternative ORMs the same ability to include the amount of time spent in the model layer in the controller's log output.

We brought this philosophy to every area of Rails 3: flexibility without compromise. By looking at the ways that an estimated million developers use Rails, we could hone in on the needs of real developers and plugin authors, significantly improving the overall architecture of Rails based on real user feedback.

Because the Rails 3 internals are such a departure from what's come before, developers building long-lived applications and plugin developers need a resource that comprehensively covers the philosophy of the new version of the framework. *The Rails*™ *3 Way* is a comprehensive resource that digs into the new features in Rails 3 and perhaps more importantly, the rationale behind them.

— **Yehuda Katz**
Rails Core

Introduction

As I write this new introduction in the spring of 2010, the official release of Rails 3.0 is looming, and what a big change it represents. The "Merb-ification" of Rails is almost complete! The new Rails is quite different from its predecessors in that its underlying architecture is more modular and elegant while increasing sheer performance significantly. The changes to Active Record are dramatic, with Arel's query method chaining replacing hashed `find` parameters that we were all used to.

There is a lot to love about Rails 3, and I do think that eventually most of the community will make the change. In most cases, I have not bothered to cover 2.x ways of doing things in Rails if they are significantly different from the Rails 3 way—hence the title change. I felt that naming the book "The Rails Way (Second Edition)" would be accurate, but possibly misleading. This new edition is a fully new book for a fully new framework. Practically every line of the book has been painstakingly revised and edited, with some fairly large chunks of the original book not making the new cut. It's taken well over a year, including six months of working every night to get this book done!

Even though Rails 3 is less opinionated than early versions, in that it allows for easy reconfiguration of Rails assumptions, this book is more opinionated than ever. The vast majority of Rails developers use `RSpec`, and I believe that is primarily because it is a superior choice to `Test::Unit`. Therefore, this book does not cover `Test::Unit`. I firmly believe that `Haml` is vastly, profoundly, better than ERb for view templating, so the book uses `Haml` exclusively.

0.1 About This Book

This book is not a tutorial or basic introduction to Ruby or Rails. It is meant as a day-to-day reference for the full-time Rails developer. The more confident reader might be able to get started in Rails using just this book, extensive online resources, and his or her wits, but there are other publications that are more introductory in nature and might be a wee bit more appropriate for beginners.

Every contributor to this book works with Rails on a full-time basis. We do not spend our days writing books or training other people, although that is certainly something that we enjoy doing on the side.

This book was originally conceived for myself, because I hate having to use online documentation, especially API docs, which need to be consulted over and over again. Since the API documentation is liberally licensed (just like the rest of Rails), there are a few sections of the book that reproduce parts of the API documentation. In practically all cases, the API documentation has been expanded and/or corrected, supplemented with additional examples and commentary drawn from practical experience.

Hopefully you are like me—I really like books that I can keep next to my keyboard, scribble notes in, and fill with bookmarks and dog-ears. When I'm coding, I want to be able to quickly refer to both API documentation, in-depth explanations, and relevant examples.

0.1.1 Book Structure

I attempted to give the material a natural structure while meeting the goal of being the best-possible Rails reference book. To that end, careful attention has been given to presenting holistic explanations of each subsystem of Rails, including detailed API information where appropriate. Every chapter is slightly different in scope, and I suspect that Rails is now too big a topic to cover the whole thing in depth in just one book.

Believe me, it has not been easy coming up with a structure that makes perfect sense for everyone. Particularly, I have noted surprise in some readers when they notice that Active Record is not covered first. Rails is foremost a web framework and, at least to me, the controller and routing implementation is the most unique, powerful, and effective feature, with Active Record following a close second.

0.1.2 Sample Code and Listings

The domains chosen for the code samples should be familiar to almost all professional developers. They include time and expense tracking, auctions, regional data management, and blogging applications. I don't spend pages explaining the subtler nuances of the business logic for the samples or justify design decisions that don't have a direct relationship to the topic at hand. Following in the footsteps of my series colleague Hal Fulton and *The Ruby Way*, most of the snippets are not full code listings—only the relevant code is shown. Ellipses (...) denote parts of the code that have been eliminated for clarity.

Whenever a code listing is large and significant, and I suspect that you might want to use it verbatim in your own code, I supply a listing heading. There are not too many of those. The whole set of code listings will not add up to a complete working system, nor are there 30 pages of sample application code in an appendix. The code listings should serve as inspiration for your production-ready work, but keep in mind that they often lack touches necessary in real-world work. For example, examples of controller code are often missing pagination and access control logic, because it would detract from the point being expressed.

Some of the source code for my examples can be found at `http://github.com/obie/tr3w_time_and_expenses`. Note that it is not a working nor complete application. It just made sense at times to keep the code in the context of an application and hopefully you might draw some inspiration from browsing it.

0.1.3 Concerning Third-Party RubyGems and Plugins

Whenever you find yourself writing code that feels like plumbing, by which I mean completely unrelated to the business domain of your application, you're probably doing too much work. I hope that you have this book at your side when you encounter that feeling. There is almost always some new part of the Rails API or a third-party RubyGem for doing exactly what you are trying to do.

As a matter of fact, part of what sets this book apart is that I never hesitate in calling out the availability of third-party code, and I even document the RubyGems and plugins that I feel are most crucial for effective Rails work. In cases where third-party code is better than the built-in Rails functionality, we don't cover the built-in Rails functionality (pagination is a good example).

An average developer might see his or her productivity double with Rails, but I've seen serious Rails developers achieve gains that are much, much higher. That's because we follow the Don't Repeat Yourself (DRY) principle religiously, of which Don't Reinvent The Wheel (DRTW) is a close corollary. Reimplementing something when an existing implementation is good enough is an unnecessary waste of time that nevertheless can be very tempting, since it's such a joy to program in Ruby.

Ruby on Rails is actually a vast ecosystem of core code, official plugins, and third-party plugins. That ecosystem has been exploding rapidly and provides all the raw technology you need to build even the most complicated enterprise-class web applications. My goal is to equip you with enough knowledge that you'll be able to avoid continuously reinventing the wheel.

0.2 Recommended Reading and Resources

Readers may find it useful to read this book while referring to some of the excellent reference titles listed in this section.

Most Ruby programmers always have their copy of the "Pickaxe" book nearby, *Programming Ruby* (ISBN: 0-9745140-5-5), because it is a good language reference. Readers interested in really understanding all of the nuances of Ruby programming should acquire *The Ruby Way, Second Edition* (ISBN: 0-6723288-4-4).

I highly recommend Peepcode Screencasts, in-depth video presentations on a variety of Rails subjects by the inimitable Geoffrey Grosenbach, available at `http://peepcode.com`

Ryan Bates does an excellent job explaining nuances of Rails development in his long-running series of free webcasts available at `http://railscasts.com/`

Last, but not least, this book's companion website at `http://tr3w.com` is the first place to look for reporting issues and finding additional resources, as they become available.

Regarding David Heinemeier Hansson, a.k.a. DHH

I had the pleasure of establishing a friendship with David Heinemeier Hansson, creator of Rails, in early 2005, before Rails hit the mainstream and he became an International Web 2.0 Superstar. My friendship with David is a big factor in why I'm writing this book today. David's opinions and public statements shape the Rails world, which means he gets quoted a lot when we discuss the nature of Rails and how to use it effectively.

David has told me on a couple of occasions that he hates the "DHH" moniker that people tend to use instead of his long and difficult-to-spell full name. For that reason, in this book I try to always refer to him as "David" instead of the ever-tempting "DHH." When you encounter references to "David" without further qualification, I'm referring to the one-and-only David Heinemeier Hansson.

There are a number of notable people from the Rails world that are also referred to on a first-name basis in this book. Those include:

- *Yehuda* Katz
- *Jamis* Buck
- *Xavier* Noria

0.3 Goals

As already stated, I hope to make this your primary working reference for Ruby on Rails. I don't really expect too many people to read it through end to end unless they're expanding their basic knowledge of the Rails framework. Whatever the case may be, over time I hope this book gives you as an application developer/programmer greater confidence in making design and implementation decisions while working on your day-to-day tasks. After spending time with this book, your understanding of the fundamental concepts of Rails coupled with hands-on experience should leave you feeling comfortable working on real-world Rails projects, with real-world demands.

If you are in an architectural or development lead role, this book is not targeted to you, but should make you feel more comfortable discussing the pros and cons of Ruby on Rails adoption and ways to extend Rails to meet the particular needs of the project under your direction.

Finally, if you are a development manager, you should find the practical perspective of the book and our coverage of testing and tools especially interesting, and hopefully get some insight into why your developers are so excited about Ruby and Rails.

0.4 Prerequisites

The reader is assumed to have the following knowledge:

- Basic Ruby syntax and language constructs such as blocks
- Solid grasp of object-oriented principles and design patterns
- Basic understanding of relational databases and SQL
- Familiarity with how Rails applications are laid out and function
- Basic understanding of network protocols such as HTTP and SMTP
- Basic understanding of XML documents and web services
- Familiarity with transactional concepts such as ACID properties

As noted in the section "Book Structure," this book does not progress from easy material in the front to harder material in the back. Some chapters do start out with fundamental, almost introductory material and push on to more advanced coverage. There are definitely sections of the text that experienced Rails developer will gloss over. However, I believe that there is new knowledge and inspiration in every chapter, for all skill levels.

Acknowledgments

A whole new set of players contributed to *The Rails™ 3 Way*, however I still need to thank some of my original supporters first. I can't say enough good things about Debra Williams Cauley, my editor at Addison-Wesley. She is an excellent coach and motivator and oh-so-caring of her authors. I love you, Deb! Also again I have to thank my long-term partner Desi McAdam and my kids Taylor and Liam for being super-supportive and understanding of my time constraints during the heaviest times of writing.

My team at Hashrocket has been an amazing source of encouragement and help during the preparation of *The Rails™ 3 Way*. My partners Marian and Mark made sure I had all the time and help needed, and were always ready with a hug or words of encouragment when the times got tough. Jon Larkowski and Tim "tpope" Pope spent hours with me at my apartment, sometimes every night of the week, to make sure that the book got finished. Eliza Brock and Tim Pope hacked a massive XSLT script that converted the original Word .doc manuscript files into LaTeX, enabling us to put the book into proper source control and make much more rapid progress than would otherwise be possible. Eliza, you are a freaking genius and an inspiration!

My friend Xavier Noria, Rails committer and former textbook reviewer, once again impressed us with his careful technical review and laser-focused feedback. Xavi picked up on dozens of ommissions and errors that would otherwise have gone unnoticed. What a hero!

One of my oldest and closest friends, Durran Jordan, was a late and welcome addition to *The Rails™ 3 Way* team. He's the author of Mongoid, http://mongoid.org—one of the premier frameworks for using Mongo with Ruby and an up-and-coming personality in the NoSQL space. He's currently working on a NoSQL in Ruby title for this series and provided some of the new content in this book concerning Active Model and background processing.

Chicago-based Rocketeers Josh Graham and Bernerd Schaefer also provided late-stage help, contributing material related to XML processing and Ajax. Other folks at Hashrocket that deserve acknowledgment include our director of operations and my longtime friend Sal Cardello, who controls resourcing and allowed me to take people away from billing to help me with the book. I also need to thank everyone else at Hashrocket who played supporting roles, including but not limited to, Rogelio Samour, Thais Camilo, Adam Lowe, "Big Tiger" Jim Remsik, Lar Van Der Jagt, Matt Yoho, Stephen Caudill, Robert Pitts, Sandro Turriate, Shay Arnette, and Veezus Kreist.

Thanks to David Black, James Adam, Trotter Cashion, Matt Pelletier, Matt Bauer, Jodi Showers, Pat Maddox, David Chelimski, Charles Brian Quinn, Patrik Naik, Diego Scataglini, and everyone else who contributed to making *The Rails Way* such a success.

About the Author

Obie Fernandez is a recognized tech industry leader and local celebrity in the Jacksonville business community. He has been hacking computers since he got his first Commodore VIC-20 in the eighties, and found himself in the right place and time as a programmer on some of the first Java enterprise projects of the mid-nineties. He moved to Atlanta, Georgia, in 1998 and gained prominence as lead architect of local startup success MediaOcean. He also founded the Extreme Programming (later Agile Atlanta) User Group and was that group's president and organizer for several years. In 2004, he made the move back into the enterprise, tackling high-risk, progressive projects for world-renowned consultancy ThoughtWorks.

Obie has been evangelizing Ruby on Rails via online via blog posts and publications since early 2005, and earned himself quite a bit of notoriety (and trash talking) from his old friends in the Java open-source community. Since then, he has traveled around the world relentlessly promoting Rails at large industry conferences.

As CEO and founder of Hashrocket, one of the world's best web design and development consultancies, Obie specializes in orchestrating the creation of large-scale, web-based applications, both for startups and mission-critical enterprise projects. He still gets his hands dirty with code on at least a weekly basis and posts regularly on various topics to his popular technology weblog, `http://blog.obiefernandez.com`.

CHAPTER 1

Rails Environments and Configuration

[Rails] gained a lot of its focus and appeal because I didn't try to please people who didn't share my problems. Differentiating between production and development was a very real problem for me, so I solved it the best way I knew how.

—David Heinemeier Hansson

Rails applications are preconfigured with three standard modes of operation: development, test, and production. These modes are basically execution environments and have a collection of associated settings that determine things such as which database to connect to, and whether the classes of your application should be reloaded with each request. It is also simple to create your own custom environments if necessary.

The current environment can be specified via the environment variable RAILS_ENV, which names the desired mode of operation and corresponds to an environment definition file in the config/environments folder. You can also set the environment variable RACK_ENV or as a last resort you may rely on the default being development. Since this environment setting governs some of the most fundamental aspects of Rails, such as class loading, in order to really understand the Rails way you should understand its environment settings.

Bundler is a tool that manages gem dependencies for your Ruby application. It takes a gem manifest file and is able to fetch, download, and install the gems in this manifest, and all child dependencies.

In this chapter, we start by covering Bundler, which is a fairly new addition to the Rails ecosystem and one of the biggest differences about working with Rails 3 versus older versions. Then we move on to more familiar territory by covering how Rails starts up and handles requests, by examining scripts such as boot.rb and application.rb and the settings that make up the three standard environment settings (modes). We also cover some of the basics of defining your own environments, and why you might choose to do so.

Note that this book is not written with absolute newcomers to Rails in mind. To make the most out of this book, you should already be at least somewhat familiar with how to bootstrap a Rails application and the meaning of M.V.C. If you are not, I recommend that you first take advantage of the excellent *Ruby on Rails 3 Tutorial* book and website[1] by Michael Hartl, another Professional Ruby Series author.

1.1 Bundler

Bundler[2] is not a technology that is specific to Rails 3, but it *is* the preferred way to manage your application's gem dependencies. Applications generated with Rails 3 use Bundler automatically, and you should not need to install the `bundler` gem separately since it's a dependency of Rails 3 itself.

Since we believe that you should use Bundler, figuring out how to not use Bundler is left as an exercise for adventurous and/or nonconformist readers.

One of the most important things that Bundler does is dependency resolution on the full list of gems specified in your configuration, all at once. This differs from the one-at-a-time dependency resolution approach employed by Rubygems and previous versions of Rails, which can (and often did) result in the following hard-to- fix problem:

Assume that your system had the following Rubygem versions installed.

```
activesupport 3.0.pre
activesupport 2.3.4
activemerchant 1.4.2
rails 2.3.4
```

It turns out that `activemerchant 1.4.2` depends on `activesupport >= 2.3.2`, therefore when you load it using the `gem` command (from the RubyGems library) like this

```
gem "activemerchant", "1.4.2"
```

it results in the loading of `activemerchant`, as well as the latest compatible versions of its dependencies, including the `activesupport 3.0.pre` gem, since it is greater than or equal to version 2.3.2. Subsequently, trying to load rails itself with

```
gem "rails", "2.3.4"
```

---

1. `http://railstutorial.org`
2. `http://gembundler.com`

results in the following exception at runtime:

```
can't activate activesupport (= 2.3.4, runtime)
for ["rails-2.3.4"], already activated
activesupport-3.0.pre for ["activemerchant-1.4.2"]
```

The exception happens because activemerchant has a broader dependency that results in the activation of a version of activesupport that does not satisfy the more narrow dependency of the older version of Rails. Bundler solves this problem by evaluating all dependencies at once and figuring out exactly the right versions of gems to load.

For an interesting perspective concerning the way that Bundler was conceived and how it contrasts with gem environment managers such as `rip`, make sure to read Yehuda's blog post on the subject.[3]

Xavier says...

Bundler is a strong default in Rails 3, but you can easily opt-out.

The `rails` command has a flag to disable Gemfile generation. If your app already has a Gemfile, it is enough to delete it to stop depending on Bundler. Rails bootstrapping routines check whether the Gemfile exists, and if it does not then Bundler is not used.

1.1.1   Gemfile

Once you need gems other than those belonging to Rails itself, you'll need to introduce a Ruby-based manifest file named `Gemfile` into the root of your Rails project directory. The basic syntax for the `Gemfile` is super simple:

```
gem "nokogiri"
gem "geokit"
```

To load a dependency only in a specific environment, place it in a group block specifying one or more environment names as symbols:

```
group :test do
  gem "rspec"
  gem "faker"
end

group :development, :test do
  gem "wirble"
  gem "ruby-debug"
end
```

---

3. http://yehudakatz.com/2010/04/21/named-gem-environments-and-bundler/

The gem directive takes an optional second argument describing the version of the Rubygem desired. Leaving the version argument off will simply get the latest available *stable* version, which may not be the latest version available. To include a release candidate or a pre-release gem you'll need to specify the version explicitly.

The format of the version argument matches the Rubygem versioning scheme to which you should already be accustomed.

```
gem 'nokogiri', '1.4.2'
gem 'faker', '> 0.3'
gem 'decent_exposure', '~> 1.0.0.rc1'
gem 'rspec', '2.0.0.beta.20'
```

You can find full instructions on how to craft a version string in the RubyGems documentation.[4]

Occasionally, the name of the gem that should be used in a `require` statement is different than the name of that gem in the repository. In those cases, the `:require` option solves this simply and declaratively right in the Gemfile.

```
gem 'sqlite3-ruby', :require => 'sqlite3'
```

Loading Gems Directly From a Git Repository

Until now we have been loading our gems from `http://rubygems.org`. It is possible to specify a gem by its source repository as long as it has a `.gemspec` text file in the root directory. Just add a `:git` option to the call to `gem`.

```
gem 'paperclip', :git => 'git://github.com/thoughtbot/paperclip.git'
```

Gemspecs with binaries or C extensions are also supported.

```
gem 'nokogiri', :git => 'git://github.com/tenderlove/nokogiri.git'
```

If there is no `.gemspec` file at the root of a gem's git repository, you must tell Bundler which version to use when resolving its dependencies.

```
gem 'deep_merge', '1.0', :git =>
'git://github.com/peritor/deep_merge.git'
```

It's also possible to specify that a git repository contains multiple `.gemspec` files and should be treated as a gem source. The following example does just that for the most common git repository that fits the criteria, the Rails codebase itself. (Note: You should never actually need to put the following code in a Gemfile for one of your Rails applications!)

---

4. http://docs.rubygems.org/read/chapter/16

```
git 'git://github.com/rails/rails.git'
gem 'railties'
gem 'action_pack'
gem 'active_model'
```

Additionally, you can specify that a git repository should use a particular ref, branch, or tag as options to the `git` directive:

```
git 'git://github.com/rails/rails.git',
  :ref => '4aded'

git 'git://github.com/rails/rails.git',
  :branch => '2-3-stable'

git 'git://github.com/rails/rails.git',
  :tag => 'v2.3.5'
```

Specifying a ref, branch, or tag for a git repository specified inline uses the same option syntax.

```
gem 'nokogiri', :git =>
  'git://github.com/tenderlove/nokogiri.git',
  :ref => '0eec4'
```

Loading Gems From the File System

You can use a gem that you are actively developing on your local workstation using the `:path` option.

```
gem 'nokogiri', :path => '~/code/nokogiri'
```

1.1.2 Installing Gems

Everytime you modify the `Gemfile`, or more specifically, if you introduce dependencies not yet installed, invoke the `install` command to ensure that all the dependencies in your Gemfile are available to your Rails application.[5]

```
  $ bundle install
  Fetching git://github.com/rails/rails.git
  Fetching source index for http://rubygems.org/
  Using rake (0.8.7)
  Installing abstract (1.0.0)
  Using activesupport (3.0.0.beta4) from git://github.com/rails/rails.git
(at master)
```

---

5. RVM by Wayne Seguin allows you to easily install, manage and work with multiple Ruby environments from interpreters to sets of gems and it's a must-have tool for modern Rails developers. http://rvm.beginrescueend.com

```
Installing builder (2.1.2)
Installing i18n (0.4.1)
Using activemodel (3.0.0.beta4) from git://github.com/rails/rails.git
(at master)
Installing erubis (2.6.6)
Installing rack (1.2.1)
Installing rack-test (0.5.4)
Installing tzinfo (0.3.22)
Using actionpack (3.0.0.beta4) from git://github.com/rails/rails.git (at
master)
Installing mime-types (1.16)
Installing polyglot (0.3.1)
Installing treetop (1.4.8)
Installing mail (2.2.5)
Using actionmailer (3.0.0.beta4) from git://github.com/rails/rails.git
(at master)
Installing arel (0.4.0)
Using activerecord (3.0.0.beta4) from git://github.com/rails/rails.git
(at master)
Using activeresource (3.0.0.beta4) from git://github.com/rails/rails.git
(at master)
Using bundler (1.0.0.beta.2)
Installing factory_girl (1.3.1)
Installing haml (3.0.13)
Installing rack-contrib (1.0.1)
Installing thor (0.13.7)
Using railties (3.0.0.beta4) from git://github.com/rails/rails.git (at
master)
Using rails (3.0.0.beta4) from git://github.com/rails/rails.git (at
master)
Installing rspec (1.3.0)
Installing rspec-rails (1.3.2)
Using sqlite3-ruby (1.3.0)
Your bundle is complete! Use `bundle show [gemname]` to see where a
bundled gem is installed.
```

The `install` command updates all dependencies named in your Gemfile to the latest versions that do not conflict with other dependencies.

You can opt to install dependencies, except those in specified groups using the `--without` option.

```
$ bundle install --without development test
$ bundle install --without test
```

Installation Directory

The default location for gems installed by bundler is directory named `.bundle` in your user directory. To specify a project specific directory simply add the name of the directory like this:

```
$ bundle install vendor
```

Disabling Shared Gems

By passing `--disable-shared-gems`, to `bundle install` you are telling Bundler to install gems even if they are already installed in the system. Normally Bundler avoids that and symlinks to already downloaded gems that exist in your system.

```
$ bundle install vendor --disable-shared-gems
```

This option is especially useful if you're trying to package up an application with all dependencies unpacked.

1.1.3 Gem Locking

Everytime you `install` or `update`, Bundler calculates the dependency tree for your application and stores the results in a file named `Gemfile.lock`. From that point on Bundler will only load specific versions of gems that you are using at the moment that the Gemfile was locked, versions that you know will work well with your application.

1.1.4 Packaging Gems

You can package up all your gems in the `vendor/cache` directory inside of your Rails application.

```
$ bundle package
```

Running `bundle install` in an application with packaged gems will use the gems in the package and skip connecting to rubygems.org or any other gem sources. You can use this to avoid external dependencies at deploy time, or if you depend on private gems that are not available in any public repository.

Making gem dependencies available to non-Rails scripts

Non-Rails scripts must be executed with `bundle exec` in order to get a properly initialized RubyGems environment.

```
$ bundle exec cucumber
```

1.2 Startup and Application Settings

Whenever you start a process to handle requests with Rails (such as with `rails server`), one of the first things that happens is that `config/boot.rb` is loaded.

There are three files involved in setting up the entire Rails stack:

boot.rb sets up Bundler and load paths

application.rb loads rails gems, gems for the specified `Rail.env`, and configures the application

environment.rb runs all initializers

All three are run when you need the whole Rails environment loaded. That's what's done by `runner`, `console`, `server`, etc.

1.2.1 application.rb

The file `config/environment.rb` used to be where many of your application settings lived. In Rails 3, the settings move to a file called `config/application.rb`, and it's the only file required at the top of `config/environment.rb`.

Let's go step by step through the settings provided in the default `application.rb` file that you'll find in a newly created Rails application. By the way, as you're reading through the following sections, make a mental note to yourself that changes to these files require a server restart to take effect.

The next lines of `application.rb` are where the wheels really start turning, once `config/boot.rb` is loaded:

```
require File.expand_path('../boot', __FILE__)
```

Note that the boot script is generated as part of your Rails application, but you won't usually need to edit it.

Getting back to `application.rb` we find the following line:

```
require 'rails/all'
```

A new feature of Rails 3 is the ability to easily cherry-pick only the components needed by your application.

```
# To pick the frameworks you want, remove 'require "rails/all"'
# and list the framework railties that you want:
#
# require "active_model/railtie"
# require "active_record/railtie"
# require "action_controller/railtie"
```

```
# require "action_view/railtie"
# require "action_mailer/railtie"
# require "active_resource/railtie"
```

The main configuration of our application follows, which in Rails 3 gets its own module and class:

```
module TimeAndExpenses
  class Application < Rails::Application
    # Settings in config/environments/* take precedence over those
    # specified here. Application configuration should go into files
    # in config/initializers
    # -- all .rb files in that directory are automatically loaded.
```

The creation of a module specifically for your application is part of the groundwork for supporting running multiple Rails applications in the same process.

Load Path Modifications

By default, Rails looks for code in a number of standard directories such as app/models and app/controllers, referred to collectively as the load path. You can add other directories to the load path using the following code:

```
# Custom directories with classes and modules you want to be autoloadable
# config.autoload_paths += %W(#{config.root}/extras)
```

Note that `config.root` refers to the root directory of your Rails application. Therefore, if you wanted to, for instance, create a separate directory for observers instead of having them in with your models, you might do the following:

```
config.autoload_paths += %W(#{config.root}/app/observers)
```

In case you didn't know, the `%W` functions as a whitespace-delimited array literal and is used quite often in the Rails codebase for convenience.

Xavier says...

Since Ruby has `$LOAD_PATH`, `config.load_paths` of older Rails versions has been renamed to `config.autoload_paths` in Rails 3 so that it is crystal clear to the develooper that the collection is about stuff that can be autoloaded. Those directories are also added to `$:`, but in general that is of little interest, because stuff in `autoload_paths` is usually meant to be autoloaded.

Plugin Load Order

Normally, Rails loads plugins alphabetically by directory name. If you are unlucky enough to run into a problem with the default order, you can use the following code to adjust ordering.

```
# Only load the plugins named here, in the order given (default is
alphabetical).
# :all can be used as a placeholder for all plugins not explicitly named
config.plugins = [ :exception_notification, :ssl_requirement, :all ]
```

Chapter 19, "Extending Rails with Plugins," covers the subject, and a companion book to this one in the *Addison-Wesley Professional Ruby Series*, *Rails Plugins: Extending Rails Beyond the Core* (ISBN: 0-321-48351-0) by James Adam, is an exhaustive reference about authoring plugins.

Observers

Active Record observers are first-class objects in your Rails applications that perform specific tasks such as clearing caches and managing denormalized data. The examples below are just that, examples of classes that you might theoretically be writing in your application as observers. (There aren't actually `cacher` or `garbage_collector` observers provided by Rails, but don't take that to mean that Ruby doesn't do garbage collection!)

```
# Activate observers that should always be running
config.active_record.observers = :cacher, :garbage_collector,
:forum_observer
```

This book covers Active Record observers in-depth in Chapter 9, Advanced Active Record.

Time Zones

The default time zone for Rails 3 applications is UTC. If the business domain of your application is sensitive to knowing exactly what time zone the server is in, then you can use the following setting to override the default:

```
# Set Time.zone default to the specified zone and make Active Record
auto-convert
# Run "rake -D time" for a list of tasks for finding time zone names.
config.time_zone = 'Central Time (US & Canada)'
```

Localization

Rails features localization support via locale files and is covered in great detail in Chapter 11, "All About Helpers" in the TranslationHelper and I18n API section.

The default locale is :en and can be overridden in your configuration.

```
# The default locale is :en and all translations from
# config/locales/*.rb,yml are auto loaded.
# config.i18n.load_path += Dir[Rails.root.join('my', 'locales',
'*.{rb,yml}')]
# config.i18n.default_locale = :de
```

Generator Default Settings

Rails generator scripts make certain assumptions about your tool chain. Setting the correct values here means having to type less parameters on the command line. For instance, at Hashrocket we use RSpec without fixtures and Haml exclusively, so our settings would look like:

```
# Configure generators values. Many other options are available,
# be sure to check the documentation.
config.generators do |g|
  g.template_engine :haml
  g.test_framework :rspec, :fixture => false
end
```

1.2.2   Initializers

Rails 2 introduced the concept of breaking out configuration settings into their own small ruby files under the `config/initializers` directory, where they are automatically loaded at startup. You can add configuration settings for your own application by adding ruby files to the initializers directory. The following five initializers are included by default in all Rails applications.

Backtrace Silencers

Nobody likes really long exception backtraces, except maybe Java programmers. Rails has a mechanism for reducing the size of backtraces by eliminating lines that don't really add anything to your debugging.

The `backtrace_silencers.rb` initializer lets you modify the way that backtraces are shortened. I've found it useful to remove backtrace entries for noisy libraries, but removing all silencers is usually never needed during normal application development.

```
# You can add backtrace silencers for libraries that you're using
# but don't wish to see in your backtraces.
Rails.backtrace_cleaner.add_silencer { |line| line =~ /my_noisy_library/ }

# You can also remove all the silencers if you're trying to debug
# a problem that might stem from framework code.
Rails.backtrace_cleaner.remove_silencers!
```

Cookie Verification Secret

Certain types of hacking involve modifying the contents of cookies without the server knowing about it. By digitally signing all cookies sent to the browser, Rails can detect whether they were tampered with. The `cookie_verification_secret.rb` initializer contains the secret key, randomly generated along with your app, which is used to sign cookies.

```
# Your secret key for verifying the integrity of signed cookies.
# If you change this key, all old signed cookies will become invalid!
# Make sure the secret is at least 30 characters and all random,
# no regular words or you'll be exposed to dictionary attacks.
ActionController::Base.cookie_verifier_secret =
'3419dbd82eefe65c27e71b0...'
```

Inflections

Rails has a class named `Inflector` whose responsibility is to transform strings (words) from singular to plural, class names to table names, modularized class names to ones without, and class names to foreign keys, etc. (Some of its operations have funny names, such as `dasherize`.)

The default inflections for pluralization and singularization of uncountable words are kept in an interesting file inside the ActiveSupport gem, named `inflections.rb`.

Most of the time the `Inflector` class does a decent job of figuring out the pluralized table name for a given class, but occasionally it won't. This is one of the first stumbling blocks for many new Rails users, but it is not necessary to panic. With a little ad hoc testing beforehand, it's easy to find out how `Inflector` will react to certain words. We just need to use the Rails console, which by the way is one of the best things about working in Rails.

You fire up the console from your terminal with the `rails console` command.

```
$ rails console
>> ActiveSupport::Inflector.pluralize "project"
=> "projects"
>> ActiveSupport::Inflector.pluralize "virus"
=> "viri"
>> "pensum".pluralize  # Inflector features are mixed into String by
default
=> "pensums"
```

As you can see in the example, `Inflector` tries to be smart, pluralizing *virus* as *viri*; but if you know your Latin you have already noticed that the plural *pensum* should actually be *pensa*. Needless to say, the inflector does not know Latin.[6]

However, you can teach the inflector new tricks by adding new pattern rules, by pointing out an exception, or by declaring certain words unpluralizable. The preferred place to do that is inside the `config/initializers/inflections.rb` file, where a

---

6. Comically, the Rails inflection of virus is also wrong. See `http://en.wikipedia.org/wiki/`
`Plural_form_of_words_ending_in_-us#Virus`

commented example is already provided:

```
ActiveSupport::Inflector.inflections do |inflect|
  inflect.plural /^(ox)$/i, '\1en'
  inflect.singular /^(ox)en/i, '\1'
  inflect.irregular 'person', 'people'
  inflect.uncountable %w( fish sheep )
end
```

The file `activesupport/test/inflector_test.rb` has a long list of pluralizations correctly handled by `Inflector`. I found some of them pretty interesting, such as:

```
"datum"     => "data",
"medium"    => "media",
"analysis"  => "analyses"
```

Custom MIME Types

Rails supports a standard set of MIME types (*/*, text/html, text/plain, text/javascript, text/css, text/calendar, text/csv, application/xml, application/rss+xml, application/atom+xml, application/x-yaml, multipart/form-data, application/x-www-form-urlencoded).

Short name	respond_to symbol	Aliases and Explanations
text/html	:html, :xhtml	application/xhtml+xml
text/plain	:text, :txt	
text/javascript	:js	application/javascript, application/x-javascript
text/css	:css	Cascading style sheets
text/calendar	:ics	iCalendar format for sharing meeting requests and tasks
text/csv	:csv	Comma-separated values
application/xml	:xml	text/xml, application/x-xml
application/rss+xml	:rss	Really Simple Syndication format for web feeds
application/atom+xml	:atom	Atom Syndication Format for web feeds
application/x-yaml	:yaml	text/yaml - The human-readable data serialization format

Short name	`respond_to` symbol	Aliases and Explanations
application/x-www-form-urlencoded	`:url_encoded_form`	The default content type of HTML forms
multipart/form-data	`:multipart_form`	Used for HTML forms that contain files, non-ASCII data, and binary data
application/json	`:json`	text/x-json, application/jsonrequest - JavaScript Object Notation

If your application needs to respond to other MIME types, you can register them in the `mime_types.rb` initializer

```
# Add new mime types for use in respond_to blocks:
# Mime::Type.register "text/richtext", :rtf
# Mime::Type.register_alias "text/html", :iphone
```

Session Store

Session cookies in Rails are signed with a random secret string that's generated along with new Rails apps. You can change that secret string in `session_store.rb` if you're really paranoid.

```
# Your secret key for verifying cookie session data integrity.
# If you change this key, all old sessions will become invalid!
# Make sure the secret is at least 30 characters and all random,
# no regular words or you'll be exposed to dictionary attacks.
ActionController::Base.session = {
  :key    => '_example_session',
  :secret => '70c647f83a15edd9895b86c16...'
}
```

If you want to store user sessions in the database instead of in cookies, which you want to do if your application keeps sensitive data in sessions, then this initializer is the place to do it:

```
# Use the database for sessions instead of the cookie-based default
# (create the session table with "rake db:sessions:create")
ActionController::Base.session_store = :active_record_store
```

This book covers configuration and implications of Active Record session store in Chapter 13, Session Management.

1.2.3 Additional Configuration

That does it for the configuration options for which we get examples in the default `application.rb` and the standard initializers. There are additional options, which you can add in additional initializer files.

Log-Level Override
The default log level is `:debug` and you can override it if necessary.

```
# Force all environments to use the same logger level
# (by default production uses :info, the others :debug)
config.log_level = :debug
```

This book covers use of the Rails logger in-depth later on in this chapter.

Schema Dumper
Every time you run tests, Rails dumps the schema of your development database and copies it to the test database using an autogenerated `schema.rb` script. It looks very similar to an Active Record migration script; in fact, it uses the same API.

You might find it necessary to revert to the older style of dumping the schema using SQL, if you're doing things that are incompatible with the schema dumper code (see the comment).

```
# Use SQL instead of Active Record's schema dumper when creating the
# test database. This is necessary if your schema can't be completely
# dumped by the schema dumper, for example, if you have constraints
# or db-specific column types
config.active_record.schema_format = :sql
```

Remember we said that the value of the `RAILS_ENV` environment variable dictates which additional environment settings are loaded next? So now let's review the default settings for each of the standard Rail modes.

1.3 Development Mode

Development is Rails' default mode and the one in which you will spend most of your time as a developer. This section contains an in-depth explanation of each setting.

```
# File: config/environments/development.rb
Example::Application.configure do
  # Settings specified here will take precedence over those
  # in config/environment.rb
```

1.3.1   Automatic Class Reloading

One of the signature benefits of using Rails is the quick feedback cycle whenever you're working in development mode. Make changes to your code, hit Reload in the browser, and Shazam! Magically, the changes are reflected in your application. This behavior is governed by the `config.cache_classes` setting:

```
# In the development environment your application's code is reloaded on
# every request.  This slows down response time but is perfect for
development
# since you don't have to restart the webserver when you make code
changes.
config.cache_classes = false
```

Without getting into too much nitty-gritty detail, when the `config.cache_classes` setting is `true`, Rails will use Ruby's `require` statement to do its class loading, and when it is `false`, it will use `load` instead.

When you require a Ruby file, the interpreter executes and caches it. If the file is required again (as in subsequent requests), the interpreter ignores the require statement and moves on. When you load a Ruby file, the interpreter executes the file again, no matter how many times it has been loaded before.

Now it's time to examine the Rails class-loading behavior a bit more in depth, because sometimes you won't be able to get certain things to reload automatically and it will drive you crazy unless you understand how class loading works!

The Rails Class Loader

In plain old Ruby, a script file doesn't need to be named in any particular way that matches its contents. In Rails, however, you'll notice that there's almost always a direct correlation between the name of a Ruby file and the class or module contained within. Rails takes advantage of the fact that Ruby provides a callback mechanism for missing constants. When Rails encounters an undefined constant in the code, it uses a class loader routine based on file-naming conventions to find and require the needed Ruby script.

How does the class loader know where to search? We already covered it earlier in the chapter where we discussed the role of `initializer.rb` in the Rails startup process. Rails has the concept of load paths, and the default load paths include the base directories of just about anywhere you would think of adding code to your Rails application.

Want to see the contents of your project's load path? Just fire up the console and type `$LOAD_PATH`

```
$ rails console
Loading development environment.
```

```
>> $LOAD_PATH
=> ["/usr/local/lib/ruby/... # about 20 lines of output
```

I snipped the console output to save space. A typical Rails project load path will usually have 30 or more items in its load path. Try it and see.

Xavier says . . .

Note that files in `lib` are no longer autoloaded. The `lib` directory is added to `$LOAD_PATH`, but not to `autoload_paths`. You'll have to require files in `lib` manually where they are needed or add `lib` back to `autoload_paths` in `config/application.rb`.

Rails, Modules, and Auto-Loading Code

Normally in Ruby, when you want to include code from another file in your application, you have to include a require statement. However, Rails enhances Ruby's default behavior by establishing a simple convention that enables Rails to automatically load your code in most cases. If you've used the Rails console at all, you've already seen this behavior in action: You never have to explicitly `require` anything!

This is how it works: If Rails encounters a class or module in your code that is not already defined, Rails uses the following convention to guess which files it should require to load that module or class:

If the class or module is not nested, insert an underscore between the constant's names and require a file of this name. For example:

- `EstimationCalculator` becomes `require "estimation_calculator"`

- `KittTurboBoost` becomes `require "kitt_turbo_boost"`

If the class or module is nested, Rails inserts an underscore between each of the containing modules and requires a file in the corresponding set of subdirectories. For example:

- `MacGyver::SwissArmyKnife` becomes `require "mac_gyver/swiss_army_knife"`

- `Example::ReallyRatherDeeply::NestedClass` becomes `require "example/really_rather_deeply/nested_class"` and if not already loaded, Rails would expect to find it in a file called `nested_class.rb`, in a directory called `really_rather_deeply`, itself in the directory `example` of which can be found somewhere in Ruby's load path (e.g., one of the `app` subdirectories, `lib`, or a plugin's `lib` directory).

The bottom line is that you should rarely need to explicitly load Ruby code in your Rails applications (using `require`) if you follow the naming conventions.

1.3.2 Whiny Nils

Rails attempts to help newbie developers figure out what's wrong with their code with extensions to Ruby's `NilClass`. The flag `config.whiny_nils` determines whether this feature is enabled. By default it is on in development and test modes, and it is off in production mode.

```
# Log error messages when you accidentally call methods on nil.
config.whiny_nils = true
```

The complete behavior of whiny nils is covered in Appendix B, "Active Support API Reference."

1.3.3 Error Reports

A couple of settings govern Rails error reporting. Requests from localhost, like when you're developing, generate useful error messages that include debugging information such as a line number where the error occured and a backtrace. Setting `consider_all_requests_local` to true causes Rails to display those developer-friendly error screens even when the machine making the request is remote.

```
config.consider_all_requests_local = true
```

The `config.action_view.debug_rjs` setting governs whether RJS responses should be wrapped in a try/catch block that alerts errors before re-raising them.

```
config.action_view.debug_rjs = true
```

1.3.4 Caching

You normally do not want caching behavior when you're in development mode. The only time you do want it is if you're actually testing caching.

```
config.action_controller.perform_caching = true  # for testing in
development mode
```

Remember to set it back to `false` when you're done testing. Unexpected caching behavior can be very tricky to figure out.

1.3.5   Raise Delivery Errors

Rails assumes that you don't want Action Mailer to raise delivery exceptions in development mode, so based on the `config.action_mailer.raise_delivery_errors` settings, it will swallow them. Mailing capabilities don't necessarily work in an average development workstation, particularly on Windows and other platforms that lack `sendmail`.

```
# Don't care if the mailer can't send
config.action_mailer.raise_delivery_errors = false
```

If you actually want to send mail while in development mode as part of debugging or ad-hoc testing, then you probably want to toggle this setting.

Xavier says...

I find it handy to set `config.action_mailer.perform_deliveries` = `false` in development. No delivery attempt is performed, but you can still see the mail in the log file to check it looks good, copy account activation URLs, etc.

1.4   Test Mode

Whenever you run Rails in test mode, that is, the value of the `RAILS_ENV` environment value is `test`, then the following settings are in effect (reproduced here for reference purposes):

```
# File: config/environments/test.rb
Example::Application.configure do
  # Settings specified here will take precedence over those
  # in config/environment.rb

  # The test environment is used exclusively to run your application's
  # test suite.  You never need to work with it otherwise.  Remember that
  # your test database is "scratch space" for the test suite and is wiped
  # and recreated between test runs.  Don't rely on the data there:
  config.cache_classes = true

  # Log error messages when you accidentally call methods on nil.
  config.whiny_nils = true

  # Show full error reports and disable caching
  config.consider_all_requests_local       = true
  config.action_controller.perform_caching = false
```

```
# Raise exceptions instead of rendering exception templates
config.action_dispatch.show_exceptions = false

# Disable request forgery protection in test environment
config.action_controller.allow_forgery_protection = false

# Tell Action Mailer not to deliver emails to the real world.
# The :test delivery method accumulates sent emails in the
# ActionMailer::Base.deliveries array.
config.action_mailer.delivery_method = :test

# Use SQL instead of Active Record's schema dumper when creating
# the test database. This is necessary if your schema can't be
# completely dumped by the schema dumper, like if you have
# constraints or database-specific column types
# config.active_record.schema_format = :sql

# Print deprecation notices to the stderr
config.active_support.deprecation = :stderr
end
```

Most people get by without ever needing to modify their test environment settings.

Custom environments

If necessary, you can create additional environments for your Rails app to run by cloning one of the existing environment files in the `config/environments` directory of your application. The most common use case for custom environments is in setting up additional production configurations, such as for staging and QA deployments. Do you have access to the production database from your development workstation? Then a triage environment might make sense. Use the normal environment settings for development mode, but point its database connection to a production database server. It's a potentially life-saving combination when you need to quickly diagnose issues in production.

1.5 Production Mode

Finally, production mode is what you want your Rails application running in whenever it is deployed to its hosting environment and serving public requests. There are a number of significant ways that production mode differs from the other modes, not least of which is the speed boost you get from not reloading all of your application classes for every request.

```
# File: config/environments/production.rb
Example::Application.configure do
  # Settings specified here will take precedence over those
  # in config/environment.rb
```

```
# The production environment is meant for finished, "live" apps.
# Code is not reloaded between requests
config.cache_classes = true

# Full error reports are disabled and caching is turned on
config.consider_all_requests_local        = false
config.action_controller.perform_caching = true

# Specifies the header that your server uses for sending files
config.action_dispatch.x_sendfile_header = "X-Sendfile"

# For nginx:
# config.action_dispatch.x_sendfile_header = 'X-Accel-Redirect'

# If you have no front-end server that supports something like
# X-Sendfile, just comment this out and Rails will serve the files

# See everything in the log (default is :info)
# config.log_level = :debug

# Use a different logger for distributed setups
# config.logger = SyslogLogger.new

# Use a different cache store in production
# config.cache_store = :mem_cache_store

# Disable Rails's static asset server
# In production, Apache or nginx will already do this
config.serve_static_assets = false

# Enable serving of images, stylesheets, and javascripts
# from an asset server
# config.action_controller.asset_host = "http://assets.example.com"

# Disable delivery errors, bad email addresses will be ignored
# config.action_mailer.raise_delivery_errors = false

# Enable threaded mode
# config.threadsafe!

# Enable locale fallbacks for I18n (makes lookups for any
# locale fall back to the I18n.default_locale when a translation
# can not be found)
config.i18n.fallbacks = true

# Send deprecation notices to registered listeners
config.active_support.deprecation = :notify
end
```

1.5.1 Asset Hosts

By default, Rails links to assets on the current host in the public folder,
but you can direct Rails to link to assets from a dedicated asset server. The
`config.action_controller.asset_host` setting is covered in detail in Chapter 10
in the Using Asset Hosts section.

1.5.2 Threaded Mode

Rails 2.2 introduced a thread-safe mode that, depending on your web server infrastructure, means you can handle more requests with fewer copies of Rails in memory, leading
to better server performance and higher utilization of multiple cores. Threadsafe operation is incompatible with development mode. Automatic dependency loading and class
reloading are automatically disabled when you call `config.threadsafe!`.

Threadsafe operation is a big deal for folks that run Rails on JRuby, since that
platform supports usage of multiple native threads across cores from a single operating
system process. Accordingly, one of the main authors of JRuby, Charles Nutter, published
this explanation of threadsafe mode on his blog:[7]

> Basically it means removing the single coarse-grained lock around every incoming request and
> replacing it with finer-grained locks around only those resources that need to be shared across
> threads. So for example, data structures within the logging subsystem have either been modified
> so they are not shared across threads, or locked appropriately to make sure two threads don't
> interfere with each other or render those data structures invalid or corrupt. Instead of a single
> database connection for a given Rails instance, there will be a pool of connections, allowing N
> database connections to be used by the M requests executing concurrently. It also means allowing
> requests to potentially execute without consuming a connection, so the number of live, active
> connections usually will be lower than the number of requests you can handle concurrently.

In the same blog post, Charles also eloquently explained why threadsafe operation
is significant even for green-thread[8] implementations of Ruby.[9]

> Thread-safe Rails will mean that an individual instance, even with green threads, can handle
> multiple requests at the same time. By "at the same time" I don't mean concurrently...green
> threads will never allow two requests to actually run concurrently or to utilize multiple cores.
> What I mean is that if a given request ends up blocking on IO, which happens in almost all

7. http://blog.headius.com/2008/08/qa-what-thread-safe-rails-means.html
8. http://en.wikipedia.org/wiki/Green_threads
9. Yehuda's take on the subject is essential reading http://yehudakatz.com/2010/08/14/threads-in-ruby-enough-already

Config

requests (due to REST hits, DB hits, filesystem hits and so on), Ruby will now have the option of scheduling another request to execute. Put another way, removing the coarse-grained lock will at least improve concurrency up to the "best" that green-threaded implementations can do, which isn't too bad.

To learn the practical implications of writing thread-safe application code, the extent of which exceed the scope of this book, make sure to study Pratik Naik's excellent (but foul-mouthed) analysis of the subject.[10]

1.6 Logging

Most programming contexts in Rails (models, controllers, view templates) have a `logger` attribute, which holds a reference to a logger conforming to the interface of `Log4r` or the default Ruby 1.8+ `Logger` class. Can't get a reference to `logger` somewhere in your code? The `Rails.logger` method references a logger that you can use anywhere.

It's really easy to create a new `Logger` in Ruby, as shown in the following example:

```
$ irb
> require 'logger'
=> true

irb(main):002:0> logger = Logger.new STDOUT
=> #<Logger:0x32db4c @level=0, @progname=nil, @logdev=
#<Logger::LogDevice:0x32d9bc ... >

> logger.warn "do not want!!!"
W, [2007-06-06T17:25:35.666927 #7303]  WARN -- : do not want!!!
=> true

> logger.info "in your logger, giving info"
I, [2007-06-06T17:25:50.787598 #7303]  INFO -- : in your logger, giving
your info
=> true
```

Typically, you add a message to the log using the logger whenever the need arises, using a method corresponding to the severity of the log message. The standard logger's severities are (in increasingly severe order):

debug Use the debug level to capture data and application state useful for debugging problems later on. This level is not usually captured in production logs.

---

10. http://m.onkey.org/2008/10/23/thread-safety-for-your-rails

info Use info level to capture informational messages. I like to use this log level for time-stamping non-ordinary events that are still within the bounds of good application behavior.

warn Use the warn level to capture things that are out of the ordinary and might be worth investigating. Sometimes I'll throw in a logged warning when guard clauses in my code keep a client from doing something they weren't supposed to do. My goal is to alert whoever's maintaining the application about a malicious user or bug in the user interface, as in the following example:

```
def create
  begin
    group.add_member(current_user)
    flash[:notice] = "Successfully joined #{scene.display_name}"
  rescue ActiveRecord::RecordInvalid
    flash[:error] = "You are already a member of #{group.name}"
    logger.warn "A user tried to join a group twice. UI should
                 not have allowed it."
  end

  redirect_to :back
end
```

error Use the error log level to capture information about error conditions that don't require a server restart.

fatal The worst-case imaginable has happened—your application is now dead and manual intervention is necessary to restart it.

1.6.1 Rails Log Files

The `log` folder of your Rails application holds three log files corresponding to each of the standard environments. Log files can grow very large over time. A rake task is provided for easily clearing the log files:

```
rake log:clear  # Truncates all *.log files in log/ to zero bytes
```

The contents of `log/development.log` are very useful while you're working. Many Rails coders leave a terminal window open with a continuous tail of the development log open while they're coding:

```
$ tail -f log/development.log

  User Load (0.5ms)   SELECT * FROM users WHERE (users.'id' = 1)
  CACHE (0.0ms)    SELECT * FROM users WHERE (users.'id' = 1)
```

All sorts of valuable information are available in the development log. For instance, every time you make a request, a bunch of useful information about it shows up in the log. Here's a sample from one of my projects.

```
Started GET "/user_photos/1" for 127.0.0.1 at 2007-06-06 17:43:13
  Processing by UserPhotosController#show as HTML
  Parameters: {"/users/8-Obie-Fernandez/photos/406"=>nil,
  "action"=>"show", "id"=>"406", "controller"=>"user_photos",
  "user_id"=>"8-Obie-Fernandez"}
  User Load (0.4ms)  SELECT * FROM users WHERE (users.'id' = 8)
  Photo Load (0.9ms) `SELECT * FROM photos WHERE (photos.'id' = 406
  AND (photos.resource_id = 8 AND photos.resource_type = 'User'))
  CACHE (0.0ms)   SELECT * FROM users WHERE (users.'id' = 8)
Rendered adsense/_medium_rectangle (1.5ms)
  User Load (0.5ms)   SELECT * FROM users WHERE (users.'id' = 8)
  LIMIT 1
  SQL (0.4ms)   SELECT count(*) AS count_all FROM messages WHERE
  (messages.receiver_id = 8 AND (messages.'read' = 0))
Rendered layouts/_header (25.3ms)
Rendered adsense/_leaderboard (0.4ms)
Rendered layouts/_footer (0.8ms)
Rendered photos/show.html.erb within layouts/application.html.erb (38.9ms)
Completed in 99ms (Views: 37.4ms | ActiveRecord: 12.3ms) with 200
```

This is a list of all the data items contained in that chunk of log output:

- The controller and action that were invoked
- The remote IP address of the computer making the request
- A timestamp indicating when the request happened
- The session ID associated with the request
- The hash of parameters associated with the request
- Database request information including the time and the SQL statement executed
- Query cache hit info including time and the SQL statement triggering results from the cache instead of a roundtrip to the database
- Rendering information for each template involved in rendering the view output and time consumed by each
- Total time used in completing the request with corresponding request-per-second figures
- Analysis of the time spent in database operations versus rendering
- The HTTP status code and URL of the response sent back to the client

1.6.2 Log File Analysis

A number of informal analyses can be easily performed using just the development log output and some common sense.

Performance One of the more obvious analyses would be a study of the performance of your application. The faster your requests execute, the more requests you can serve with a given Rails process. That's why performance figures are often expressed in terms of requests per second. Find the queries and rendering sections that are taking a long time and figure out why.

It's important to realize that the times reported by the logger are not super-accurate. In fact, they're wrong more often than not, if simply for the reason that it's very difficult to measure the timing of something from within itself. Add up the percentage of rendering and database times for any given request and it will not always be close to 100 percent.

However, despite not being accurate in a purely objective sense, the reported times are perfect for making subjective comparisons within the same application. They give you a way of gauging whether an action is taking longer than it used to, or whether it is relatively faster or slower than another action, and so on.

SQL queries Active Record not behaving as expected? The fact that SQL generated by Active Record is logged can often help you debug problems caused by complicated queries.

Identification of N+1 select problems Whenever you are displaying a record along with an associated collection of records, there's a chance that you will have a so-called N+1 select problem. You'll recognize the problem by a series of many SELECT statements, with the only difference being the value of the primary key.

For example, here's a snippet of some log output from a real Rails application showing an N+1 select issue in the way that FlickrPhoto instances are being loaded:

```
FlickrPhoto Load (1.3ms)   SELECT * FROM flickr_photos WHERE
(flickr_photos.resource_id = 15749 AND flickr_photos.resource_type =
'Place' AND (flickr_photos.'profile' = 1)) ORDER BY updated_at desc
LIMIT 1
FlickrPhoto Load (1.7ms)   SELECT * FROM flickr_photos WHERE
(flickr_photos.resource_id = 15785 AND flickr_photos.resource_type =
'Place' AND (flickr_photos.'profile' = 1)) ORDER BY updated_at desc
LIMIT 1
FlickrPhoto Load (1.4ms)   SELECT * FROM flickr_photos WHERE
(flickr_photos.resource_id = 15831 AND flickr_photos.resource_type =
```

```
'Place' AND (flickr_photos.'profile' = 1)) ORDER BY updated_at desc
LIMIT 1
```

and so on and so forth, for pages and pages of log output. Look familiar?

Luckily, each of those database queries is executing very quickly, around 0.0015 seconds each. That's because 1) MySQL is extraordinarily fast for small SELECT statements, and 2) my Rails process is on the same physical machine as the database.

Still, accumulate enough of those N queries and they add up quickly to eat away at performance. Absent the mitigating factors I mentioned, I would have a serious performance problem to address. The problem would be especially severe if the database was on a separate machine, giving me network latency to deal with on each of those queries.

N+1 select issues are not the end of the world. A lot of times all it takes is proper use of the includes method on a particular query to alleviate the problem.

Separation of concerns

A well-designed model-view-controller application follows certain protocols related to which logical tier does database operations (that would be the model) versus rendering tasks (the view). Generally speaking, you want your controller to cause the loading of all of the data that is going to be needed for rendering from the database. In Rails, it is accomplished by controller code that queries the model for needed data and makes that data available to the view.

Database access during rendering is usually considered a bad practice. Calling database methods directly from template code violates proper separation of concerns and is a maintainability nightmare.[11]

However, there are plenty of opportunities for implicit database access during view rendering to creep into your codebase, encapsulated by the model, and perhaps triggered by lazy loading of associations. Can we conclusively call it a bad practice? It's hard to say so definitively. There are cases (such as usage of fragment caching) where it makes sense to have database operations happening during view rendering.

Rails::Subscriber.colorize_logging

Tells Rails whether to use ANSI codes to colorize the logging statements. The colors make it much easier to read the logs (except on Windows) and may complicate matters if you use software like syslog. Defaults to true. Change to false if you view your logs with software that doesn't understand the ANSI color codes.

---

11. Practically every PHP application ever written has this problem.

Using alternate logging schemes

It's easy! Just assign a class compatible with Ruby's Logger to one of the various `logger` class variables, such as `ActiveRecord::Base.logger`. A quick hack based on the ability to swap loggers is one demonstrated by David at various events, including his keynote at Railsconf 2007. During a console session, assign a new `Logger` instance pointing to `STDOUT` to `ActiveRecord::Base.logger` in order to see the SQL being generated right in your console. Jamis has a complete write-up of the technique and more at `http://weblog.jamisbuck.org/2007/1/31/more-on-watching-activerecord`.

Here's a snippet of log output with the ANSI codes visible:

```
^[[4;36;1mSQL (0.0ms)^[[0m   ^[[0;1mMysql::Error: Unknown table
'expense_reports': DROP TABLE expense_reports^[[0m
  ^[[4;35;1mSQL (3.2ms)^[[0m   ^[[0mCREATE TABLE expense_reports ('id'
int(11) DEFAULT NULL auto_increment PRIMARY KEY, 'user_id' int(11))
```

Wilson says...

Almost nobody I meet seems to know how to display colorized logs in a pager. The `-R` option tells `less` to output "raw" control characters to the screen.

Syslog

UNIX-like systems have a system service called `syslog`. For various reasons, it might be a better choice for production logging of your Rails applications.

- Finer-grained control over logging levels and content.

- Consolidation of logger output for multiple Rails applications.

- If you're using remote syslog capabilities of many systems, consolidation of logger output for multiple Rails application servers is possible. Contrast with having to handle individual log files on each application server box separately.

You can use Eric Hodel's SyslogLogger* to interface your Rails application to `syslog`.

---

*`http://seattlerb.rubyforge.org/SyslogLogger`

Config

1.7 Conclusion

We've kicked off our Rails journey by covering Bundler in fairly good detail and then reviewing the different environments in which Rails executes and how it loads its dependencies, including your application code. An in-depth look at `application.rb` and its per-mode variants revealed how we can customize Rails behavior to our taste.

CHAPTER 2

Routing

I dreamed a thousand new paths. . . I woke and walked my old one.

—Chinese proverb

The routing system in Rails is the system that examines the URL of an incoming request and determines what action should be taken by the application. And it does a good bit more than that. Rails routing can be a bit of a tough nut to crack. But it turns out that most of the toughness resides in a small number of concepts. After you've got a handle on those, the rest falls into place nicely.

This chapter will introduce you to the principal techniques for defining and manipulating routes. The next chapter will build on this knowledge to explore the facilities Rails offers in support of writing applications that comply with the principles of Representational State Transfer (REST). As you'll see, those facilities can be of tremendous use to you even if you're not planning to scale the heights of REST theorization. Both chapters assume at least a basic knowledge of the Model-View-Controller (MVC) pattern and Rails controllers.

Some of the examples in these two chapters are based on a small auction application. The examples are kept simple enough that they should be comprehensible on their own. The basic idea is that there are auctions, and each auction involves auctioning off an item. There are users, and they submit bids. That's it.

The triggering of a controller action is the main event in the life cycle of a connection to a Rails application. So it makes sense that the process by which Rails determines which controller and which action to execute must be very important. That process is embodied in the routing system.

The routing system maps URLs to actions. It does this by applying rules that you specify using a special syntax in the `config/routes.rb` file. Actually it's just Ruby program code, but it uses special methods and parameters, a technique sometimes referred to as an internal Domain Specific Language (DSL). If you're using Rails generators, code gets added to the routes file automatically, and you'll get some reasonable behavior. But it doesn't take much work to write custom rules and reap the benefits of the flexibility of the routing system.

2.1 The Two Purposes of Routing

The routing system does two things: It maps requests to controller action methods, and it enables the dynamic generation of URLs for you for use as arguments to methods like `link_to` and `redirect_to`.

Each rule—or to use the more common term, route—specifies a pattern, which will be used both as a template for matching URLs and as a blueprint for creating them. The pattern can be generated automatically based on conventions, such as in the case of REST resources. Patterns can also contain a mixture of static substrings, forward slashes (mimicking URL syntax), and positional *segment key* parameters that serve as "receptors" for corresponding values in URLs.

A route can also include one or more hardcoded segment keys, in form of key/value pairs accessible to controller actions in a hash via the `params` method. A couple of keys (`:controller` and `:action`) determine which controller and action gets invoked. Other keys present in the route definition simply get stashed for reference purposes.

Putting some flesh on the bones of this description, here's a sample route:

```
match 'recipes/:ingredient' => "recipes#index"
```

In this example, you find:

- static string (`recipes`)
- slash (`/`)
- segment key (`:ingredient`)
- controller action mapping (`"recipes#index"`)

Routes have a pretty rich syntax—this one isn't by any means the most complex (nor the most simple)—because they have to do so much. A single route, like the one in this example, has to provide enough information both to match an existing URL and to manufacture a new one. The route syntax is engineered to address both of these processes.

2.2 The routes.rb File

Routes are defined in the file `config/routes.rb`, as shown (with some explanatory comments) in Listing 2.1. This file is created when you first create your Rails application and contains instructions about how to use it.

Listing 2.1 The default routes.rb file

```
Example::Application.routes.draw do
  # The priority is based upon order of creation:
  # first created -> highest priority.

  # Sample of regular route:
  # match 'products/:id' => 'catalog#view'

  # Keep in mind you can assign values other than :controller and :action

  # Sample of named route:
  # match 'products/:id/purchase' => 'catalog#purchase', :as => :purchase
  # This route can be invoked with purchase_url(:id => product.id)

  # Sample resource (maps HTTP verbs to controller actions automatically):
  # resources :products

  # Sample resource route with options:
  # resources :products do
  #   member do
  #     get :short
  #     post :toggle
  #   end
  #
  #   collection do
  #     get :sold
  #   end
  # end

  # Sample resource route with sub-resources:
  # resources :products do
  #   resources :comments, :sales
  #   resource :seller
  # end

  # Sample resource route with more complex sub-resources
  # resources :products do
  #   resources :comments
  #   resources :sales do
  #     get :recent, :on => :collection
  #   end
  # end
```

Routes

```
# Sample resource route within a namespace:
# namespace :admin do
#   # Directs /admin/products/* to Admin::ProductsController
#   # (app/controllers/admin/products_controller.rb)
#   resources :products
# end

# You can have the root of your site routed with "root"
# just remember to delete public/index.html.
# root :to => "welcome#index"

# See how all your routes lay out with "rake routes"

# This is a legacy wild controller route that's not
# recommended for RESTful applications.
# Note: This route will make all actions in every controller
# accessible via GET requests.
# match ':controller(/:action(/:id(.:format)))'
end
```

The whole file consists of a single call to the method `draw` of `Example::Application.routes`. That method takes a block, and everything from the second line of the file to the second-to-last line is the body of that block.

At runtime, the block is evaluated inside of an instance of the class `ActionDispatch::Routing::Mapper`. Through it you configure the Rails routing system.

The routing system has to find a pattern match for a URL it's trying to recognize or a parameters match for a URL it's trying to generate. It does this by going through the routes in the order in which they're defined; that is, the order in which they appear in `routes.rb`. If a given route fails to match, the matching routine falls through to the next one. As soon as any route succeeds in providing the necessary match, the search ends.

2.2.1 Regular Routes

The basic way to define a route is to supply a URL pattern plus a controller class/action method mapping string with the special `:to` parameter.

```
match 'products/:id', :to => 'products#show'
```

Since this is so common, a shorthand form is provided:

```
match 'products/:id' => 'products#show'
```

David has publicly commented on the design decision behind the Rails 3 shorthand form, when he said that it drew inspiration from two sources: [1]

> 1) the pattern we've been using in Rails since the beginning of referencing controllers as lowercase without the "Controller" part in :controller => "main" declarations and 2) the Ruby pattern of signaling that you're talking about an instance method by using #. The influences are even part mixed. Main#index would be more confusing in my mind because it would hint that an object called Main actually existed, which it doesn't. MainController#index would just be a hassle to type out every time. Exactly the same reason we went with :controller => "main" vs :controller => "MainController". Given these constraints, I think "main#index" is by far the best alternative...

While we're on this topic, note that the legacy way of supplying controller and action parameters prior to Rails 3 does not work anymore.

```
# DOES NOT WORK
match 'products/:id', :controller => "product", :action => "show"
```

The simplest routes

Sometimes you just want a 2-part URL mapping to a controller action along the lines of the classic Rails default route. The simplest kind of route definition in Rails 3 consists of a `match` method and a string.

```
match "/projects/status"
```

You can optionally include a placeholder for the format like

```
match "/projects/status(.:format)"
```

As you might be able to deduce, the examples above will route *any* type of HTTP request to the projects controller status action. However, if you know you'll be using only one HTTP verb then it's better to use its method instead of `match`, like this:

```
get "/projects/status"
post "/reports/publish"
```

2.2.2   URL Patterns

Keep in mind that there's no necessary correspondence between the number of fields in the pattern string, the number of segment keys, and the fact that every connection needs a controller and an action. For example, you could write a route like

```
match ":id" => "products#show"
```

---

1. Full comments at http://yehudakatz.com/2009/12/26/the-rails-3-router-rack-it-up

which would recognize a URL like

```
http://localhost:3000/8
```

The routing system would set `params[:id]` to 8 (based on the position of the `:id` segment key, which matches the position of 8 in the URL), and it would execute the `show` action of the `products` controller. Of course, this is a bit of a stingy route, in terms of visual information. On the other hand, the following example route contains a static string, `products/`, inside the URL pattern:

```
match 'products/:id' => 'products#show'
```

This string anchors the recognition process. Any URL that does not contain the static string `products/` in its leftmost slot will not match this route.

As for URL generation, static strings in the route simply get placed within the URL that the routing system generates. The URL generator uses the route's pattern string as the blueprint for the URL it generated. The pattern string stipulates the substring `products`.

As we go, you should keep the dual purpose of recognition/generation in mind, which is why it was mentioned several times so far. There are two principles that are particularly useful to remember:

- The same rule governs both recognition and generation. The whole system is set up so that you don't have to write rules twice. You write each rule once, and the logic flows through it in both directions.

- The URLs that are generated by the routing system (via `link_to` and friends) only make sense to the routing system. The resulting URL `http://example.com/products/19201`, contains not a shred of a clue as to what's supposed to happen when a user follows it—except insofar as it maps to a routing rule. The routing rule then provides the necessary information to trigger a controller action. Someone looking at the URL without knowing the routing rules won't know which controller and action the URL maps to.

2.2.3 Segment Keys

The URL pattern string can contain parameters (denoted with a colon) and referred to as *segment keys*. In the following route declaration, `:id` is a segment key.

```
match 'products/:id' => 'products#show'
```

When this route matches a request URL, the `:id` portion of the pattern acts as a type of matcher, and picks up the value of that segment. For instance, using the same example, the value of `id` for the following URL would be `4`: `http://example.com/products/4`

This route, when matched, will always take the visitor to the product controller's `show` action. You'll see techniques for matching controller and action based on segments of the URL shortly. The symbol `:id` inside the quoted pattern in the route is a segment key (that you can think of as a type of variable). Its job is to be latched onto by a value.

What that means in the example is that the value of `params[:id]` will be set to the string `"4"`. You can access that value inside your `products/show` action.

When you generate a URL, you have to supply values that will attach to the segment keys inside the URL pattern string. The simplest to understand (and original) way to do that is using a hash, like this:

```
link_to "Products",
  :controller => "products",
  :action => "show",
  :id => 1
```

As you probably know, it's actually more common nowadays to generate URLs using what are called *named routes*, versus supplying the controller and action parameters explicitly in a hash. However, right now we're reviewing the basics of routing.

In the call to `link_to`, we've provided values for all three parameters of the route. Two of them are going to match the hard-coded, segment keys in the route; the third, `:id`, will be assigned to the corresponding segment key in the URL pattern.

It's vital to understand that the call to `link_to` doesn't *know* whether it's supplying hard-coded or segment values. It just knows (or hopes!) that these three values, tied to these three keys, will suffice to pinpoint a route and therefore a pattern string, and therefore a blueprint for generating a URL dynamically.

Hardcoded parameters

It's always possible to insert additional hardcoded parameters into route definitions that don't have an effect on URL matching, but are passed along with the normal expected `params`.

```
match 'products/special' => 'products#show', :special => true
```

Mind you, I'm not suggesting that this example is a good practice. It would make more sense to me (as a matter of style) to point at a different action rather than inserting a clause. Your mileage may vary.

```
match 'products/special' => 'products#special'
```

2.2.4   Spotlight on the :id Field

Note that the treatment of the `:id` field in the URL is not magic; it's just treated as a value with a name. If you wanted to, you could change the rule so that `:id` was `:blah` but then you'd have to do the following in your controller action:

```
@product = Product.find(params[:blah])
```

The name `:id` is simply a convention. It reflects the commonness of the case in which a given action needs access to a particular database record. The main business of the router is to determine the controller and action that will be executed.

The `id` field ends up in the `params` hash, already mentioned. In the common, classic case, you'd use the value provided to dig a record out of the database:

```
class ProductsController < ApplicationController
  def show
    @product = Product.find(params[:id])
  end
end
```

2.2.5   Optional Segment Keys

Rails 3 introduces new routes syntax for defining optional parts of the URL pattern. The easiest way to illustrate it is using the new version of the *legacy wild controller route* as it exists at the bottom of a default `config/routes.rb` file:

```
match ':controller(/:action(/:id(.:format)))'
```

As of Rails 3, this route is commented out and remarks from the Rails team advise you not to use it. In previous versions of Rails, this was known as the *default route*, and could potentially open up every controller action that wasn't scoped as protected to GET requests.

Note that parentheses are used to define optional segment keys, kind of like what you would expect to see when defining optional groups in a regular expression.

2.2.6   Constraining Request Methods

It's possible (and often desirable) to limit the HTTP method used to access a route. You accomplish that using the `:via` parameter of the route:

```
match 'products/:id'  => 'products#show', :via => :get
```

Again, since this is a common thing to do, Rails provides a shorthand way of expressing this particular constraint, by replacing `match` with the HTTP method desired (get, post, etc.)

```
get 'products/:id'  => 'products#show'
post 'products' => 'products#create'
```

If, for some reason, you want to constrain a route to more than one HTTP method, you can pass :via an array of verb names.

```
match 'products/:id'  => 'products#show', :via => [:get, :post]
```

2.2.7 Redirect Routes

It's possible to code a redirect directly into a route definition, using the redirect method:

```
match "/foo", :to => redirect("/bar")
```

The argument to redirect can contain either a relative URL or a full URI.

```
match "/google", :to => redirect("http://google.com/")
```

The redirect method can also take a block, which receives the request params as its argument. This allows you to, for instance, do quick versioning of web service API endpoints.[2]

```
match "/api/v1/:api", :to =>
  redirect {|params| "/api/v2/#{params[:api].pluralize}" }
```

The redirect method also accepts an optional :status parameter.

```
match "/api/v1/:api", :to =>
  redirect(:status => 302) {|params| "/api/v2/#{params[:api].pluralize}" }
```

The redirect method returns a simple Rack endpoint, as we can see by examining its source code.

```
def redirect(*args, &block)
  options = args.last.is_a?(Hash) ? args.pop : {}

  path      = args.shift || block
  path_proc = path.is_a?(Proc) ? path : proc { |params| path % params }
  status    = options[:status] || 301

  lambda do |env|
    req = Request.new(env)

    params = [req.symbolized_path_parameters]
    params << req if path_proc.arity > 1
```

---

2. Examples drawn from Yehuda Katz's excellent blog post about generic actions in Rails 3 routes at http://yehudakatz.com/2009/12/20/generic-actions-in-rails-3/

```
    uri = URI.parse(path_proc.call(*params))
    uri.scheme ||= req.scheme
    uri.host   ||= req.host
    uri.port   ||= req.port unless req.standard_port?

    body = %(<html><body>You are being <a
href="#{ERB::Util.h(uri.to_s)}">redirected</a>.</body></html>)

    headers = {
      'Location' => uri.to_s,
      'Content-Type' => 'text/html',
      'Content-Length' => body.length.to_s
    }

    [ status, headers, [body] ]
  end
end
```

2.2.8 The Format Segment

Let's revisit the old default route again:

```
match ':controller(/:action(/:id(.:format)))'
```

The `.:format` at the end matches a literal dot and a `"format"` segment key after the id
field. That means it will match, for example, a URL like:

```
http://localhost:3000/products/show/3.xml
```

Here, `params[:format]` will be set to `xml`. The `:format` field is special; it has an effect
inside the controller action. That effect is related to a method called `respond_to`.[3]

The `respond_to` method allows you to write your action so that it will return different results, depending on the requested format. Here's a `show` action for the products
controller that offers either HTML or XML:

```
def show
  @product = Product.find(params[:id])
  respond_to do |format|
    format.html
    format.xml { render :xml => @product.to_xml }
  end
end
```

The `respond_to` block in this example has two clauses. The HTML clause just consists
of `format.html`. A request for HTML will be handled by the usual rendering of a view
template. The XML clause includes a code block; if XML is requested, the block will be
executed and the result of its execution will be returned to the client.

---

3. The `respond_to` method is full of quirks. Review them in the comments section of http://apidock.com/
rails/ActionController/MimeResponds/InstanceMethods/respond_to.

Here's a command-line illustration, using wget (slightly edited to reduce line noise):

```
$ wget http://localhost:3000/products/show/3.xml -O -
Resolving localhost... 127.0.0.1, ::1
Connecting to localhost|127.0.0.1|:3000... connected.
HTTP request sent, awaiting response... 200 OK
Length: 295 [application/xml]
<item>
  <created-at type="datetime">2007-02-16T04:33:00-05:00</created-at>
  <description>Keyboard</description>
  <id type="integer">3</id>
  <maker>Apple</maker>
  <modified-at type="datetime"></modified-at>
</item>
```

The .xml on the end of the URL results in respond_to choosing the *xml* branch, and the returned document is an XML representation of the product.

Requesting a format that is not included as an option in the respond_to block will not generate an exception. Rails will return a 406 Not Acceptable status, to indicate that it can't handle the request.

If you want to setup an *else* condition for your repond_to block, you can use the any method, which tells Rails to catch any other formats not explicitly defined.

```
def show
  @product = Product.find(params[:id])
  respond_to do |format|
    format.html
    format.xml { render :xml => @product.to_xml }
    format.any
  end
end
```

Just make sure that you explicitly tell any what to do with the request or have view templates corresponding to the formats you expect. Otherwise, you'll get a MissingTemplate exception.

```
ActionView::MissingTemplate (Missing template clients/index with
    {:handlers=>[:rhtml, :haml, :rxml, :erb, :builder, :rjs],
    :locale=>[:en], :formats=>[:json]}
```

2.2.9 Routes as Rack Endpoints

You'll see usage of the :to option in routes throughout this chapter. What's most interesting about :to is that its value is what's referred to as a *Rack endpoint*. To illustrate, consider the following simple example:

```
match "/hello", :to => proc {|env| [200, {}, ["Hello world"]] }
```

The router is very loosely coupled to controllers! The shorthand syntax (like `"items#show"`) relies on the `action` method of controller classes to return a Rack endpoint that executes the action requested.

```
>> ItemsController.action(:show)
=> #<Proc:0x01e96cd0@...>
```

This behavior means that adding a route that dispatches to a Sinatra[4] application is super-easy. Just point `:to => YourSinatraApp`. The Sinatra application class itself is a Rack endpoint.

```
class HelloApp < Sinatra::Base
  get "/" do
    "Hello World!"
  end
end


Example::Application.routes.draw do
  match "/hello", :to => HelloApp
end
```

2.2.10 **Accept** Header

You can also trigger a branching on `respond_to` by setting the `Accept` header in the request. When you do this, there's no need to add the `.:format` part of the URL. (However, note that out in the real world, it's difficult to get this technique to work reliably because of HTTP client/browser inconsistencies.)

Here's a `wget` example that does not specify an `.xml` format, but does set the `Accept` header to `application/xml`:

```
wget http://localhost:3000/items/show/3 -O - --header="Accept:
    text/xml"
Resolving localhost... 127.0.0.1, ::1
Connecting to localhost|127.0.0.1|:3000... connected.
HTTP request sent, awaiting response...
200 OK
Length: 295 [application/xml]
<item>
  <created-at type="datetime">2007-02-16T04:33:00-05:00</created-at>
  <description>Violin treatise</description>
  <id type="integer">3</id>
  <maker>Leopold Mozart</maker>
<medium>paper</medium>
  <modified-at type="datetime"></modified-at>
```

---

4. http://www.sinatrarb.com

```
    <year type="integer">1744</year>
</item>
```

The result is exactly the same as in the previous example.

2.2.11 Segment Key Constraints

Sometimes you want not only to recognize a route, but to recognize it at a finer-grained level than just what components or fields it has. You can do this through the use of the `:constraint` option (and possibly regular expressions).

For example, you could route all `show` requests so that they went to an error action if their `id` fields were non-numerical. You'd do this by creating two routes, one that handled numerical ids, and a fall-through route that handled the rest:

```
match ':controller/show/:id' => :show, :constraints => {:id => /\d+/}
match ':controller/show/:id' => :show_error
```

Implicit anchoring

The example constraint we've been using

```
:constraints => {:id => /\d+/}
```

seems like it would match `"foo32bar"`. It doesn't because Rails implicitly anchors it at both ends. In fact, as of this writing, adding explicit anchors `^` and `$` causes exceptions to be raised.

Apparently, it's so common to set constraints on the `:id` param, that Rails 3 lets you shorten our previous example to simply

```
match ':controller/show/:id' => :show, :id => /\d+/
match ':controller/show/:id' => :show_error
```

Regular expressions in routes can be useful, especially when you have routes that differ from each other only with respect to the patterns of their components. But they're not a full-blown substitute for data-integrity checking. A URL that matches a route with regular expressions could be like the vetting of Sarah Palin, not thorough enough.[5] You probably still want to make sure that the values you're dealing with are usable and appropriate for your application's domain.

From the example, you might conclude that `:constraints` checking applies to elements of the `params` hash. However, you can also check a grab-bag of other request

---

5. In 2008, American presidential candidate John McCain was widely mocked and later defeated, partly because of his ill-advised choice of running mate, the little-known Governor of Alaska, Sarah Palin.

attributes that return a string, such as `:subdomain` and `:referrer`. Matching methods of `request` that return numeric or boolean values are unsupported and will raise a somewhat cryptic exception during route matching.

```
# only allow users admin subdomain to do old-school routing
match ':controller/:action/:id' => :show, :constraints => {:subdomain =>
'admin'}
```

If for some reason you need more powerful constraints checking, you have full access to the `request` object, by passing a block or any other object that responds to `call` as the value of `:constraints` like:

```
# protect records with id under 100
match 'records/:id' => "records#protected",
  :constraints => proc {|req| req.params[:id].to_i < 100 }
```

2.2.12 The Root Route

At around line 50 of the default config/routes.rb (refer to Listing 2.1) you'll see

```
# You can have the root of your site routed with "root"
# just remember to delete public/index.html.
# root :to => "welcome#index"
```

What you're seeing here is the root route, that is, a rule specifying what should happen when someone connects to

```
http://example.com  # Note the lack of "/anything" at the end!
```

The root route says, "I don't want any values; I want nothing, and I already know what controller and action I'm going to trigger!"

In a newly generated `routes.rb` file, the root route is commented out, because there's no universal or reasonable default for it. You need to decide what this *nothing* URL should do for each application you write.

Here are some examples of fairly common empty route rules:

```
root :to => "welcome#index"
root :to => "pages#home"
root :to => "user_sessions#new"
```

Defining the empty route gives people something to look at when they connect to your site with nothing but the domain name. You might be wondering why you see something when you view a newly generated Rails application that still has its root route commented out.

The answer is that the public folder in the root of your app corresponds to the root-level URL, and the `public` directory in a newly generated Rails app contains an `index.html` file.

In fact, you can put any static content in the public directory hierarchy, matching the URL scheme that you come up with for your app, and the static content will be served up instead of routing rules triggering. Actually, the web server will serve up the content without involving Rails at all, which is why cached content ends up under the public directory. We'll cover caching in Chapter 10, "Action View."

A note on route order

Routes are consulted, both for recognition and for generation, in the order they are defined in `routes.rb`. The search for a match ends when the first match is found, meaning that you have to watch out for false positives.

2.3 Route Globbing

In some situations, you might want to grab one or more components of a route without having to match them one by one to specific positional parameters. For example, your URLs might reflect a directory structure. If someone connects to

```
/items/list/base/books/fiction/dickens
```

you want the `items/list` action to have access to all four remaining fields. But sometimes there might be only three fields:

```
/items/list/base/books/fiction
```

or five:

```
/items/list/base/books/fiction/dickens/little_dorrit
```

So you need a route that will match (in this particular case) everything after the second URI component. You define it by *globbing* the route with an asterisk.

```
match 'items/list/*specs', :controller => 'items', :action => 'list'
```

Now, the `products/list` action will have access to a variable number of slash-delimited URL fields, accessible via `params[:specs]`:

```
def list
  specs = params[:specs] # e.g, "base/books/fiction/dickens"
end
```

Globbing key-value pairs

Route globbing might provide the basis for a general mechanism for fielding ad hoc queries. Let's say you devise a URI scheme that takes the following form:

```
http://localhost:3000/items/q/field1/value1/field2/value2/...
```

Making requests in this way will return a list of all products whose fields match the values, based on an unlimited set of pairs in the URL.

In other words, `http://localhost:3000/items/q/year/1939/material/wood` could generate a list of all wood items made in 1939. The route that would accomplish this would be:

```
match 'items/q/*specs', :controller => "items", :action => "query"
```

Of course, you'll have to write a `query` action like this one to support the route:

```
def query
  @items = Item.all.where(Hash[params[:specs].split("/")])
  if @items.empty?
    flash[:error] = "Can't find items with those properties"
  end
  render :action => "index"
end
```

How about that square brackets class method on `Hash`, eh? It converts a one-dimensional array of key/value pairs into a hash! Further proof that in-depth knowledge of Ruby is a prerequisite for becoming an expert Rails developer.

2.4 Named Routes

The topic of named routes almost deserves a chapter of its own. In fact, what you learn here will feed directly into our examination of REST-related routing in Chapter 3.

The idea of naming a route is basically to make life easier on you, the programmer. There are no outwardly visible effects as far as the application is concerned. When you name a route, a new method gets defined for use in your controllers and views; the method is called `name_url` (with name being the name you gave the route), and calling the method, with appropriate arguments, results in a URL being generated for the route. In addition, a method called `name_path` also gets created; this method generates just the path part of the URL, without the protocol and host components.

2.4.1 Creating a Named Route

The way you name a route is by using the optional `:as` parameter in a rule:

```
match 'help'  => 'help#index', :as => 'help'
```

In this example, you'll get methods called `help_url` and `help_path`, which you can use wherever Rails expects a URL or URL components:

```
link_to "Help", help_path
```

And, of course, the usual recognition and generation rules are in effect. The pattern string consists of just the static string component `"help"`. Therefore, the path you'll see in the hyperlink will be

```
/help
```

When someone clicks on the link, the `index` action of the `help` controller will be invoked.

Xavier says...

You can test named routes in the console directly using the special `app` object.

```
>> app.clients_path
=> "/clients"

>> app.clients_url
=> "http://www.example.com/clients"
```

Named routes save you some effort when you need a URL generated. A named route zeros in directly on the route you need, bypassing the matching process that would be needed otherwise. That means you don't have to provide as much detail as you otherwise would, but you still have to provide values for any segment keys in the route's pattern string that cannot be inferred.

2.4.2   name_path vs. name_url

When you create a named route, you're actually creating at least two route helper methods. In the preceding example, those two methods are `help_url` and `help_path`. The difference is that the `_url` method generates an entire URL, including protocol and domain, whereas the `_path` method generates just the path part (sometimes referred to as an *absolute path* or a *relative URL*).

According to the HTTP spec, redirects should specify a URI, which can be interpreted (by some people) to mean a fully-qualified URL.[6] Therefore, if you want to be pedantic about it, you probably should always use the `_url` version when you use a named route as an argument to `redirect_to` in your controller code.

---

6. `http://www.w3.org/Protocols/rfc2616/rfc2616-sec10.html`

The `redirect_to` method works perfectly with the relative URLs generated by _path helpers, making arguments about the matter kind of pointless. In fact, other than redirects, permalinks, and a handful of other edge cases, it's the Rails way to use _path instead of _url. It produces a shorter string and the user agent (browser or otherwise) should be able to infer the fully qualified URL whenever it needs to do so, based on the HTTP headers of the request, a base element in the document, or the URL of the request.

As you read this book and as you examine other code and other examples, the main thing to remember is that `help_url` and `help_path` are basically doing the same thing. I tend to use the _url style in general discussions about named route techniques, but to use _path in examples that occur inside view templates (for example, with `link_to` and `form_for`). It's mostly a writing-style thing, based on the theory that the URL version is more general and the path version more specialized. In any case, it's good to get used to seeing both and getting your brain to view them as very closely connected.

Using literal URLs

You can, if you wish, hard-code your paths and URLs as string arguments to `link_to`, `redirect_to`, and friends. For example, instead of

```
link_to "Help", :controller => "main", :action => "help"
```

you can write

```
link_to "Help", "/main/help"
```

However, using a literal path or URL bypasses the routing system. If you write literal URLs, you're on your own to maintain them. (You can of course use Ruby's string interpolation techniques to insert values, if that's appropriate for what you're doing, but really stop and think about whether you are reinventing Rails functionality if you go down that path.)

2.4.3 What to Name Your Routes

As we'll learn in Chapter 3, the best way to figure out what names you should use for your routes is to follow REST conventions, which are baked into Rails and simplify things greatly. Otherwise, you'll need to think top-down; that is, think about what you want to write in your application code, and then create the routes that will make it possible.

Take, for example, this call to `link_to`

```
link_to "Auction of #{item.name}",
  :controller => "items",
  :action => "show",
  :id => item.id
```

The routing rule to match that path is (a generic route):

```
match "item/:id" => "items#show"
```

It sure would be nice to shorten that `link_to` code. After all, the routing rule already specifies the controller and action. This is a good candidate for a named route for items:

```
match "item/:id" => "items#show", :as => "item"
```

Lets improve the situation by introducing `item_path` in the call to `link_to`:

```
link_to "Auction of #{item.name}", item_path(:id => item.id)
```

Giving the route a name is a shortcut; it takes us straight to that route, without a long search and without having to provide a thick description of the route's hard-coded parameters.

2.4.4 Argument Sugar

In fact, we can make the argument to `item_path` even shorter. If you need to supply an id number as an argument to a named route, you can just supply the number, without spelling out the `:id` key:

```
link_to "Auction of #{item.name}", item_path(item.id)
```

And the syntactic sugar goes even further: You can and should provide objects and Rails will grab the id automatically.

```
link_to "Auction of #{item.name}", item_path(item)
```

This principle extends to other segment keys in the pattern string of the named route. For example, if you've got a route like

```
match "auction/:auction_id/item/:id" => "items#show", :as => "item"
```

you'd be able to call it like

```
link_to "Auction of #{item.name}", item_path(auction, item)
```

and you'd get something like this as your path (depending on the exact id numbers):

```
/auction/5/item/11
```

Here, we're letting Rails infer the ids of both an auction object and an item object, which it does by calling `to_param` on whatever non-hash arguments you pass into named route helpers. As long as you provide the arguments in the order in which their ids occur in the route's pattern string, the correct values will be dropped into place in the generated path.

2.4.5 A Little More Sugar with Your Sugar?

Furthermore, it doesn't have to be the id value that the route generator inserts into the URL. As alluded to a moment ago, you can override that value by defining a `to_param` method in your model.

Let's say you want the description of an item to appear in the URL for the auction on that item. In the `item.rb` model file, you would override `to_params`; here, we'll override it so that it provides a "munged" (stripped of punctuation and joined with hyphens) version of the description, courtesy of the `parameterize` method added to strings in Active Support.

```
def to_param
  description.parameterize
end
```

Subsequently, the method call `item_path(auction, item)` will produce something like

```
/auction/3/item/cello-bow
```

Of course, if you're putting things like `"cello-bow"` in a path field called `:id`, you will need to make provisions to dig the object out again. Blog applications that use this technique to create *slugs* for use in permanent links often have a separate database column to store the munged version of the title that serves as part of the path. That way, it's possible to do something like

```
Item.find_by_munged_description(params[:id])
```

to unearth the right item. (And yes, you can call it something other than `:id` in the route to make it clearer!)

Courtenay says...

Why shouldn't you use numeric IDs in your URLs? First, your competitors can see just how many auctions you create. Numeric consecutive IDs also allow people to write automated spiders to steal your content. It's a window into your database. And finally, words in URLs just look better.

2.5 Scoping Routing Rules

Rails gives you a variety of ways to bundle together related routing rules concisely. They're all based on usage of the `scope` method and its various shortcuts. For instance, let's say that you want to define the following routes for auctions:

```
match 'auctions/new' => 'auctions#new'
match 'auctions/edit/:id' => 'auctions#edit'
match 'auctions/pause/:id' => 'auctions#pause'
```

You could DRY up your `routes.rb` file by using the `scope` method instead:

```
scope :controller => :auctions do
  match 'auctions/new'      => :new
  match 'auctions/edit/:id'    => :edit
  match 'auctions/pause/:id' => :pause
end
```

Then you would DRY it up again by adding the `:path` argument to `scope`:

```
scope :path => '/auctions', :controller => :auctions do
  match 'new'     => :new
  match 'edit/:id'    => :edit
  match 'pause/:id' => :pause
end
```

2.5.1 Controller

The scope method accepts a `:controller` option (or it can interpret a symbol as its first argument to assume a controller). Therefore, the following two scope definitions are identical:

```
scope :controller => :auctions do
scope :auctions do
```

To make it more obvious what's going on, you can use the `controller` method instead of `scope`, in what's essentially syntactic sugar:

```
controller :auctions do
```

2.5.2 Path Prefix

The scope method accepts a `:path` option (or it can interpret a string as its first parameter to mean a path prefix). Therefore, the following two scope definitions are identical:

```
scope :path => '/auctions' do
scope '/auctions' do
```

2.5.3   Name Prefix

The scope method also accepts a `:as` option that affects the way that named route URL helper methods are generated. The route

```
scope :auctions, :as => 'admin' do
  match 'new' => :new, :as => 'new_auction'
end
```

will generate a named route URL helper method called `admin_new_auction_url`.

2.5.4   Namespaces

URLs can be grouped by using the `namespace` method, which is syntactic sugar that rolls up module, name prefix, and path prefix settings into one declaration. The implementation of the `namespace` method converts its first argument into a string, which is why in some example code you'll see it take a symbol.

```
namespace :auctions, :controller => :auctions do
  match 'new' => :new
  match 'edit/:id' => :edit
  match 'pause/:id' => :pause
end
```

2.5.5   Bundling Constraints

If you find yourself repeating similar segment key constraints in related routes, you can bundle them together using the `:constraints` option of the `scope` method:

```
scope :controller => :auctions, :constraints => {:id => /\d+/} do
  match 'edit/:id' => :edit
  match 'pause/:id' => :pause
end
```

It's likely that only a subset of rules in a given scope need constraints applied to them. In fact, routing will break if you apply a constraint to a rule that doesn't take the segment keys specified. Since you're nesting, you probably want to use the `constraints` method, which is just more syntactic sugar to tighten up the rule definitions.

```
scope :path => '/auctions', :controller => :auctions do
  match 'new' => :new
  constraints :id => /\d+/ do
    match 'edit/:id'    => :edit
    match 'pause/:id' => :pause
  end
end
```

To enable modular reuse, you may supply the `constraints` method with an object that
has a `matches?` method.

```
class DateFormatConstraint
  def self.matches?(request)
    request.params[:date] =~ /\A\d{4}-\d\d-\d\d\z/  # YYYY-MM-DD
  end
end

# in routes.rb
constraints(DateFormatConstraint) do
  match 'since/:date' => :since
end
```

In this particular example (`DateFormatConstraint`), if an errant or malicious user
input a badly formatted date parameter via the URL, Rails will respond with a 404
status instead of causing an exception to be raised.

2.6 Listing Routes

A handy route listing utility is included in all Rails projects as a standard rake task.
Invoke it by typing `rake routes` in your application directory. For example, here is
the output for a routes file containing just a single `resources :products` rule:

```
$ rake routes
products     GET    /products(.:format)        {:controller=>"products",
                                                :action=>"index"}

             POST   /products(.:format)        {:controller=>"products",
                                                :action=>"create"}

new_product  GET    /products/new(.:format)    {:controller=>"products",
                                                :action=>"new"}

product      GET    /products/:id(.:format)    {:controller=>"products",
                                                :action=>"show"}

             PUT    /products/:id(.:format)    {:controller=>"products",
                                                :action=>"update"}

             DELETE /products/:id(.:format)    {:controller=>"products",
                                                :action=>"destroy"}

edit_product GET /products/:id/edit(.:format)  {:controller=>"products",
                                                :action=>"edit"}
```

The output is a table with four columns. The first two columns are optional and contain
the name of the route and HTTP method constraint, if they are provided. The third
column contains the URL mapping string. Finally, the fourth column indicates the
controller and action method that the route maps to, plus constraints that have been
defined on that routes segment keys (if any).

Note that the routes task checks for an optional CONTROLLER environment variable

```
rake routes CONTROLLER=products
```

would only lists the routes related to ProductsController.

2.7 Conclusion

The first half of the chapter helped you to fully understand generic routing based on match rules and how the routing system has two purposes:

- Recognizing incoming requests and mapping them to a corresponding controller action, along with any additional variable receptors
- Recognizing URL parameters in methods such as link_to and matching them up to a corresponding route so that proper HTML links can be generated

We built on our knowledge of generic routing by covering some advanced techniques such as using regular expressions and globbing in our route definitions, plus the bundling of related routes under shared scope options.

Finally, before moving on, you should make sure that you understand how named routes work and why they make your life easier as a developer by allowing you to write more concise view code. As you'll see in the next chapter, once we start defining batches of related named routes, we're on the cusp of delving into REST.

## CHAPTER 3

REST, Resources, and Rails

Before REST came I (and pretty much everyone else) never really knew where to put stuff.

—Jonas Nicklas on the Ruby on Rails mailing list

With version 1.2, Rails introduced support for designing APIs consistent with the REST style. Representational State Transfer (REST) is a complex topic in information theory, and a full exploration of it is well beyond the scope of this chapter.[1] We'll touch on some of the keystone concepts, however. And in any case, the REST facilities in Rails can prove useful to you even if you're not a REST expert or devotee.

The main reason is that one of the inherent problems that all web developers face is deciding how to name and organize the resources and actions of their application. The most common actions of all database-backed applications happen to fit well into the REST paradigm.

3.1 REST in a Rather Small Nutshell

REST is described by its creator, Roy T. Fielding, as a network *architectural style*, specifically the style manifested in the architecture of the World Wide Web. Indeed, Fielding is not only the creator of REST but also one of the authors of the HTTP protocol itself. REST and the web have a very close relationship.

---

1. For those interested in REST, the canonical text is Roy Fielding's dissertation, which you can find at `http://www.ics.uci.edu/~fielding/pubs/dissertation/top.htm`. In particular, you'll probably want to focus on Chapters 5 and 6 of the dissertation, which cover REST and its relation to HTTP. You'll also find an enormous amount of information, and links to more, on the REST wiki at `http://rest.blueoxen.net/cgi-bin/wiki.pl`.

Fielding defines REST as a series of constraints imposed upon the interaction between system components. Basically, you start with the general proposition of machines that can talk to each other, and you start ruling some practices in and others out by imposing constraints that include (among others):

- Use of a client-server architecture
- Stateless communication
- Explicit signaling of response cacheability
- Use of HTTP request methods such as GET, POST, PUT, and DELETE

The World Wide Web allows for REST-compliant communication. It also allows for violations of REST principles; the constraints aren't always all there unless you put them there. As for this chapter, the most important thing you have to understand is that REST is designed to help you provide services using the native idioms and constructs of HTTP. You'll find, if you look for it, lots of discussion comparing REST to, for example, SOAP—the thrust of the pro-REST argument being that HTTP already enables you to provide services, so you don't need a semantic layer on top of it. Just use what HTTP already gives you.

One of the allures of REST is that it scales relatively well for big systems, like the web. Another is that it encourages—mandates, even—the use of stable, long-lived identifiers (URIs). Machines talk to each other by sending requests and responses labeled with these identifiers. Messages consist of representations (manifestations in text, XML, graphic format, and so on) of resources (high-level, conceptual descriptions of content) or simply HTTP headers.

Ideally at least, when you ask a machine for an XML representation of a resource— say, Romeo and Juliet—you'll use the same identifier every time and the same request metadata indicating that you want XML, and you'll get the same response. And if it's not the same response, there's a reason—like, the resource you're retrieving is a changeable one ("The current transcript for Student #3994," for example).

3.2 Resources and Representations

The REST style characterizes communication between system components (where a component is, say, a web browser or a server) as a series of requests to which the responses are representations of resources.

A resource, in this context, is a "conceptual mapping" (Fielding). Resources themselves are not tied to a database, a model, or a controller. Examples of resources include

- The current time of day
- A library book's borrowing history
- The entire text of *The Little Prince*
- A map of Jacksonville Beach
- The inventory of a store

A resource may be singular or plural, changeable (like the time of day) or fixed (like the text of *The Little Prince*). It's basically a high-level description of the thing you're trying to get hold of when you submit a request.

What you actually do get hold of is never the resource itself, but a representation of it. This is where REST unfolds onto the myriad content types and actual deliverables that are the stuff of the web. A resource may, at any given point, be available in any number of representations (including zero). Thus your site might offer a text version of *The Little Prince*, but also an audio version. Those two versions would be understood as the same resource, and would be retrieved via the same identifier (URI). The difference in content type—one representation vs. another—would be negotiated separately in the request.

3.3 REST in Rails

The REST support in Rails consists of methods to define resources in the routing system, designed to impose a particular style and order and logic on your controllers and, consequently, on the way the world sees your application. There's more to it than just a set of naming conventions (though there's that too). In the large scheme of things, the benefits that accrue to you when you use Rails's REST support fall into two categories:

- Convenience and automatic best practices for you
- A RESTful interface to your application's services for everyone else

You can reap the first benefit even if you're not concerned with the second. In fact, that's going to be our focus here: what the REST support in Rails can do for you in the realm of making your code nicer and your life as a Rails developer easier.

I don't mean to minimize the importance of REST itself, nor the seriousness of the endeavor of providing REST-based services. Rather, it's an expedient; we can't talk about everything, and this section of the book is primarily about routing and how to do it, so we're going to favor looking at REST in Rails from that perspective.

Getting back to practical matters, the focus of the rest of this chapter will be showing you how REST support works in Rails opening the door to further study and practice including the study of Fielding's dissertation and the theoretical tenets of REST. We won't cover everything here, but what we do cover will be onward compatible with the wider topic.

The story of REST and Rails starts with CRUD...

3.4 Routing and CRUD

The acronym CRUD (Create Read Update Delete) is the classic summary of the spectrum of database operations. It's also a kind of rallying cry for Rails practitioners. Because we address our databases through abstractions, we're prone to forget how simple it all is. This manifests itself mainly in excessively creative names for controller actions. There's a temptation to call your actions `add_item` and `replace_email_address` and things like that. But we needn't, and usually shouldn't, do this. True, the controller does not map to the database, the way the model does. But things get simpler when you name your actions after CRUD operations, or as close to the names of those operations as you can get.

The routing system does not force you to implement your app's CRUD functionality in any consistent manner. You can create a route that maps to any action, whatever the action's name. Choosing CRUD names is a matter of discipline. Except... when you use the REST facilities offered by Rails, it happens automatically.

REST in Rails involves standardization of action names. In fact, the heart of the Rails's REST support is a technique for creating bundles of named routes automatically—named routes that are bundled together to point to a specific, predetermined set of actions.

Here's the logic. It's good to give CRUD-based names to your actions. It's convenient and elegant to use named routes. The REST support in Rails gives you named routes that point to CRUD-based action names. Therefore, using the REST facilities gives you a shortcut to some best practices.

Shortcut hardly describes how little work you have to do to get a big payoff. If you put

```
resources :auctions
```

into your `config/routes.rb` file, you will have created four named routes, which, in a manner to be described in this chapter, connect to seven controller actions. And those actions have nice CRUD-like names, as you will see.

3.4.1 REST Resources and Rails

Like most of Rails, support for RESTful applications is "opinionated"; that is, it offers a particular way of designing a REST interface, and the more you play along, the more convenience you reap from it. Most Rails applications are database-backed, and the Rails take on REST tends to associate a resource very closely with an Active Record model, or a model/controller stack.

In fact, you'll hear people using the terminology fairly loosely. For instance, they'll say that they have created a *Book resource*. What they mean, in most cases, is that they have created a `Book` model, a book controller with a set of CRUD actions, and some named routes pertaining to that controller (courtesy of `resources :books`). You can have a `Book` model and controller, but what you actually present to the world as your resources, in the REST sense, exists at a higher level of abstraction: *The Little Prince*, borrowing history, and so on.

The best way to get a handle on the REST support in Rails is by going from the known to the unknown. In this case, from the topic of named routes to the more specialized topic of REST.

3.4.2 From Named Routes to REST Support

When we first looked at named routes, we saw examples where we consolidated things into a route name. By creating a route like

```
match 'auctions/:id' => "auction#show", :as => 'auction'
```

you gain the ability to use nice helper methods in situations like

```
link_to item.description, auction_path(item.auction)
```

The route ensures that a path will be generated that will trigger the `show` action of the auctions controller. The attraction of this kind of named route is that it's concise and readable.

Now, think in terms of CRUD. The named route `auction_path` is a nice fit for a `show` (the R in CRUD) action. What if we wanted similarly nicely named routes for the `create`, `update`, and `delete` actions?

Well, we've used up the route name `auction_path` on the `show` action. We could make up names like `auction_delete_path` and `auction_create_path` but those are cumbersome. We really want to be able to make a call to `auction_path` and have it mean different things, depending on which action we want the URL to point to.

We could differentiate between the singular (`auction_path`) and the plural (`auctions_path`). A singular URL makes sense, semantically, when you're doing something with a single, existing auction object. If you're doing something with auctions in general, the plural makes more sense.

The kinds of things you do with auctions in general include creating. The `create` action will normally occur in a form:

```
form_tag auctions_path
```

It's plural because we're not saying "perform an action with respect to a particular auction," but rather "with respect to the collection of auctions, perform the action of creation." Yes, we're creating one auction, not many. But at the time we make the call to our named route, `auctions_path`, we're addressing auctions in general.

Another case where you might want a plural named route is when you want an overview of all of the objects of a particular kind, or at least, some kind of general view, rather than a display of a particular object. This kind of general view is usually handled with an `index` action. These `index` actions typically load a lot of data into one or more variables, and the corresponding view displays it as a list or table (possibly more than one).

Here again, we'd like to be able to say:

```
link_to "Click here to view all auctions", auctions_path
```

Already, though, the strategy of breaking `auction_path` out into singular and plural has hit the wall: We've got two places where we want to use the plural named route. One is create; the other is index. But they're both going to look like

```
/auctions
```

How is the routing system going to know that when we use `auctions_path` as a link versus using it in a form that we mean the `create` action and not `index`? We need another qualifier, another flag, another variable on which to branch.

Luckily, we've got one.

3.4.3 Reenter the HTTP Verb

Form submissions are POSTs by default. Index actions are GETs. That means that we need to get the routing system to realize that

```
/auctions submitted in a GET request!
```

versus

```
/auctions submitted in a POST request!
```

are two different things. We also have to get the routing system to generate the same URL—/auctions—but with a different HTTP request method, depending on the circumstances.

This is what the REST facility of Rails routing does for you. It allows you to stipulate that you want /auctions routed differently, depending on the HTTP request method. It lets you define named routes with the same name, but with intelligence about their HTTP verbs. In short, it uses HTTP verbs to provide that extra data slot necessary to achieve everything you want to achieve in a concise way.

The way you do this is by using a special routing method: resources. Here's what it would look like for auctions:

```
resources :auctions
```

That's it. Making this one call inside routes.rb is the equivalent of defining four named routes. And if you mix and match those four named routes with a variety of HTTP request methods, you end up with seven useful—very useful—permutations.

3.5 The Standard RESTful Controller Actions

Calling resources :auctions involves striking a kind of deal with the routing system. The system hands you four named routes. Between them, these four routes point to seven controller actions, depending on HTTP request method. In return, you agree to use very specific names for your controller actions: index, create, show, update, destroy, new, edit.

It's not a bad bargain, since a lot of work is done for you and the action names you have to use are nicely CRUD-like.

Table 3.1 summarizes what happens. It's a kind of "multiplication table" showing you what you get when you cross a given RESTful named route with a given HTTP request method. Each box (the nonempty ones, that is) shows you, first, the URL that the route generates and, second, the action that gets called when the route is recognized. (The table lists _path methods rather than _url ones, but you get both.)

(The edit and new actions have unique named routes, and their URLs have a special syntax.)

Since named routes are now being crossed with HTTP request methods, you'll need to know how to specify the request method when you generate a URL, so that your GET'd clients_url and your POST'd clients_url don't trigger the same controller

Table 3.1 RESTful Routes Table Showing Helpers, Paths, and the Resulting Controller Action

Helper Method	GET	POST	PUT	DELETE
`client_path(client)`	/clients/1 show		/clients/1 update	/clients/1 destroy
`clients_path`	/clients index	/clients create		
`edit_client_ path(client)`	/clients/1/edit edit			
`new_client_path`	/clients/new new			

action. Most of what you have to do in this regard can be summed up in a few rules:

1. The default request method is GET.
2. In a `form_tag` or `form_for` call, the POST method will be used automatically.
3. When you need to (which is going to be mostly with PUT and DELETE operations), you can specify a request method along with the URL generated by the named route.

An example of needing to specify a DELETE operation is a situation when you want to trigger a `destroy` action with a link:

```
link_to "Delete", auction_path(auction), :method => :delete
```

Depending on the helper method you're using (as in the case of `form_for`), you might have to put the method inside a nested hash:

```
form_for "auction", :url => auction_path(auction),
        :html => { :method => :put } do |f|
```

That last example, which combined the singular named route with the PUT method, will result in a call to the `update` action when submitting the form (as per row 2, column 4 of Table 3.1). You don't normally have to program this functionality specifically, because as we'll see later in the book, Rails automatically figures out whether you need a POST or PUT if you pass an object to form helpers.

3.5.1   Singular and Plural RESTful Routes

As you may have noticed, some of the RESTful routes are singular; some are plural. The logic is as follows:

1. The routes for `show`, `new`, `edit`, and `destroy` are singular, because they're working on a particular resource.
2. The rest of the routes are plural. They deal with collections of related resources.

The singular RESTful routes require an argument, because they need to be able to figure out the id of the member of the collection referenced.

```
item_url(item)   # show, update, or destroy, depending on HTTP verb
```

You don't have to call the `id` method on `item`. Rails will figure it out (by calling `to_param` on the object passed to it).

3.5.2   The Special Pairs: new/create and edit/update

As Table 3.1 shows, `new` and `edit` obey somewhat special RESTful naming conventions. The reason for this has to do with `create` and `update`, and how `new` and `edit` relate to them.

Typically, `create` and `update` operations involve submitting a form. That means that they really involve two actions—two requests—each:

1. The action that results in the display of the form
2. The action that processes the form input when the form is submitted

The way this plays out with RESTful routing is that the `create` action is closely associated with a preliminary `new` action, and `update` is associated with `edit`. These two actions, `new` and `edit`, are really assistant actions: All they're supposed to do is show the user a form, as part of the process of creating or updating a resource.

Fitting these special two-part scenarios into the landscape of resources is a little tricky. A form for editing a resource is not, itself, really a resource. It's more like a *pre-resource*. A form for creating a new resource is sort of a resource, if you assume that being new—that is, nonexistent—is something that a resource can do, and still be a resource!

That line of reasoning might be a little too philosophical to be useful. The bottom line, as implemented in RESTful Rails, is the following: The `new` action is understood to be giving you a new, single (as opposed to plural) resource. However, since the logical verb for this transaction is GET, and GETting a single resource is already spoken for by the `show` action, `new` needs a named route of its own.

That's why you have to use

```
link_to "Create a new item", new_item_path
```

to get a link to the `items/new` action.

The `edit` action is understood not to be giving you a full-fledged resource, exactly, but rather a kind of edit *flavor* of the `show` resource. So it uses the same URL as `show`, but with a kind of modifier, in the form of `/edit`, hanging off the end, which is consistent with the URL form for `new`:

```
/items/5/edit
```

The corresponding named route is `edit_item_url(@item)`. As with `new`, the named route for `edit` involves an extra bit of name information, to differentiate it from the implied `show` of the existing RESTful route for GETting a single resource.

3.5.3 The PUT and DELETE Cheat

We have just seen how Rails routes PUT and DELETE requests. Some HTTP clients are able to use said verbs, but forms in web browsers can't be submitted using anything other than a POST. Rails provides a hack that is nothing to worry about, other than being aware of what's going on.

A PUT or DELETE request originating in a browser, in the context of REST in Rails, is actually a POST request with a hidden field called _method set to either `"put"` or `"delete"`. The Rails application processing the request will pick up on this, and route the request appropriately to the `update` or `destroy` action.

You might say, then, that the REST support in Rails is ahead of its time. REST components using HTTP should understand all of the request methods. They don't, so Rails forces the issue. As a developer trying to get the hang of how the named routes map to action names, you don't have to worry about this little cheat. And hopefully some day it won't be necessary any more. (HTML5 in particular adds PUT and DELETE as valid method attributes for forms.)

3.5.4 Limiting Routes Generated

It's possible to add `:except` and `:only` options to the call to `resources` in order to limit the routes generated.

```
resources :clients, :except => [:index]
resources :clients, :only => [:new, :create]
```

3.6 Singular Resource Routes

In addition to `resources`, there's also a singular (or *singleton*) form of resource routing: `resource`. It's used to represent a resource that only exists once in its given context.

A singleton resource route at the top level of your routes can be appropriate when there's only one resource of its type for the whole application, perhaps something like a per-user profile.

```
resource :profile
```

You get almost the full complement of resource routes, all except the collection route (index). Note that the method name `resource`, the argument to that method, and all the named routes generated are in the singular.

```
$ rake routes
      profile GET      /profile(.:format)       {:controller=>"profiles",
                                                  :action=>"show"}
              POST     /profile(.:format)       {:controller=>"profiles",
                                                  :action=>"create"}
              PUT      /profile(.:format)       {:controller=>"profiles",
                                                  :action=>"update"}
              DELETE   /profile(.:format)       {:controller=>"profiles",
                                                  :action=>"destroy"}
  new_profile GET      /profile/new(.:format)   {:controller=>"profiles",
                                                  :action=>"new"}
 edit_profile GET      /profile/edit(.:format)  {:controller=>"profiles",
                                                  :action=>"edit"}
```

It's assumed that you're in a context where it's meaningful to speak of *the profile*—the one and only—because there's a user to which the profile is scoped. The scoping itself is not automatic; you have to authenticate the user and retrieve the profile from (and/or save it to) the database explicitly. There's no real magic or mind-reading here; it's just an additional routing technique at your disposal if you need it.

3.7 Nested Resources

Let's say you want to perform operations on bids: create, edit, and so forth. You know that every bid is associated with a particular auction. That means that whenever you do anything to a bid, you're really doing something to an auction/bid pair—or, to look at it another way, an auction/bid nest. Bids are at the bottom of a drill-down hierarchical structure that always passes through an auction.

What you're aiming for here is a URL that looks like

```
/auctions/3/bids/5
```

What it does depends on the HTTP verb it comes with, of course. But the semantics of the URL itself are: the resource that can be identified as bid 5, belonging to auction 3.

Why not just go for `bids/5` and skip the auction? For a couple of reasons. First, the URL is more informative—longer, it's true, but longer in the service of telling you something about the resource. Second, thanks to the way RESTful routes are engineered in Rails, this kind of URL gives you immediate access to the auction id, via `params[:auction_id]`.

To created nested resource routes, put this in `routes.rb`:

```
resources :auctions do
  resources :bids
end
```

What that tells the mapper is that you want RESTful routes for auction resources; that is, you want `auctions_url`, `edit_auction_url`, and all the rest of it. You also want RESTful routes for bids: `auction_bids_url`, `new_auction_bid_url`, and so forth.

However, the nested resource command also involves you in making a promise. You're promising that whenever you use the bid named route helpers, you will provide a auction resource in which they can be nested. In your application code, that translates into an argument to the named route method:

```
link_to "See all bids", auction_bids_path(auction)
```

When you make that call, you enable the routing system to add the `/auctions/3` part before the `/bids` part. And, on the receiving end—in this case, in the action `bids/index`, which is where that URL points—you'll find the id of `auction` in `params[:auction_id]`. (It's a plural RESTful route, using GET. See Table 3.1 again if you forgot.)

You can nest to any depth. Each level of nesting adds one to the number of arguments you have to supply to the nested routes. This means that for the singular routes (`show`, `edit`, `destroy`), you need at least two arguments:

```
link_to "Delete this bid", auction_bid_path(auction, bid), :method =>
:delete
```

This will enable the routing system to get the information it needs (essentially `auction.id` and `bid.id`) in order to generate the route.

If you prefer, you can also make the same call using hash-style method arguments, but most people don't because it's longer code:

```
auction_bid_path(:auction => auction, :bid => bid)
```

3.7.1 RESTful Controller Mappings

Something we haven't yet explicitly discussed is how RESTful routes are mapped to a given controller. It was just presented as something that happens automatically, which in fact it does, based on the name of the resource.

Going back to our recurring example, given the following nested route:

```
resources :auctions do
  resources :bids
end
```

there are two controllers that come into play, the `AuctionsController` and the `BidsController`.

3.7.2 Considerations

Is nesting worth it? For single routes, a nested route usually doesn't tell you anything you wouldn't be able to figure out anyway. After all, a bid belongs to an auction.

That means you can access `bid.auction_id` just as easily as you can `params[:auction_id]`, assuming you have a bid object already.

Furthermore, the bid object doesn't depend on the nesting. You'll get `params[:id]` set to 5, and you can dig that record out of the database directly. You don't need to know what auction it belongs to.

```
Bid.find(params[:id])
```

A common rationale for judicious use of nested resources, and the one most often issued by David, is the ease with which you can enforce permissions and context-based constraints. Typically, a nested resource should only be accessible in the context of its parent resource, and it's really easy to enforce that in your code based on the way that you load the nested resource using the parent's Active Record association.

```
auction = Auction.find(params[:auction_id])
bid = auction.bids.find(params[:id]) # prevents auction/bid mismatch
```

If you want to add a bid to an auction, your nested resource URL would be

```
http://localhost:3000/auctions/5/bids/new
```

The auction is identified in the URL rather than having to clutter your new bid form data with hidden fields or resorting to non-RESTful practices.

3.7.3 Deep Nesting?

Jamis Buck is a very influential figure in the Rails community, almost as much as David himself. In February 2007, via his blog,[2] he basically told us that deep nesting was a bad thing, and proposed the following rule of thumb: Resources should never be nested more than one level deep.

That advice is based on experience and concerns about practicality. The helper methods for routes nested more than two levels deep become long and unwieldy. It's easy to make mistakes with them and hard to figure out what's wrong when they don't work as expected.

---

2. `http://weblog.jamisbuck.org/2007/2/5/nesting-resources`

Assume that in our application example, bids have multiple comments. We could nest comments under bids in the routing like this:

```
resources :auctions do
  resources :bids do
    resources :comments
  end
end
```

Instead, Jamis would have us do the following:

```
resources :auctions do
  resources :bids
end

resources :bids do
  resources :comments
end

resources :comments
```

Notice that each resource (except auctions) is defined twice, once in the top-level namespace, and one in its context. The rationale? When it comes to parent-child scope, you really only need two levels to work with. The resulting URLs are shorter and the helper methods are easier to work with.

```
auctions_path              # /auctions
auctions_path(1)           # /auctions/1
auction_bids_path(1)       # /auctions/1/bids
bid_path(2)                # /bids/2
bid_comments_path(3)       # /bids/3/comments
comment_path(4)            # /comments/4
```

I personally don't follow Jamis's guideline all the time in my projects, but I have noticed that limiting the depth of your nested resources helps with the maintainability of your codebase in the long run.

Courtenay says...

Many of us disagree with the venerable Jamis. Want to get into fisticuffs at a Rails conference? Ask people whether they believe routes should be nested more than one layer deep.

3.7.4 Shallow Routes

As of Rails 2.3 resource routes accept a `:shallow` option that helps to shorten URLs where possible. The goal is to leave off parent collection URL segments where they are not needed. The end result is that the only nested routes generated are for the `:index`, `:create`, and `:new` actions. The rest are kept in their own *shallow* URL context.

It's easier to illustrate than to explain, so let's define a nested set of resources and set `:shallow` to `true`:

```
resources :auctions, :shallow => true do
  resources :bids do
    resources :comments
  end
end
```

alternatively coded as follows (if you're block-happy)

```
resources :auctions do
  shallow do
    resources :bids do
      resources :comments
    end
  end
end
```

The resulting routes are:

```
                GET    /auctions(.:format)
      auctions  POST   /auctions(.:format)
   new_auction  GET    /auctions/new(.:format)
                GET    /auctions/:id(.:format)
                PUT    /auctions/:id(.:format)
       auction  DELETE /auctions/:id(.:format)
  edit_auction  GET    /auctions/:id/edit(.:format)
                GET    /auctions/:auction_id/bids(.:format)
  auction_bids  POST   /auctions/:auction_id/bids(.:format)
new_auction_bid GET    /auctions/:auction_id/bids/new(.:format)
                GET    /bids/:bid_id/comments(.:format)
  bid_comments  POST   /bids/:bid_id/comments(.:format)
new_bid_comment GET    /bids/:bid_id/comments/new(.:format
                GET    /comments/:id(.:format)
                PUT    /comments/:id(.:format)
       comment  DELETE /comments/:id(.:format)
  edit_comment  GET    /comments/:id/edit(.:format)
```

If you analyze the routes generated carefully, you'll notice that the nested parts of the URL are only included when they are needed to determine what data to display.

3.8 RESTful Route Customizations

Rails's RESTful routes give you a pretty nice package of named routes, mapped to useful, common, controller actions—the CRUD superset you've already learned about. Sometimes, however, you want to customize things a little more, while still taking advantage of the RESTful route naming conventions and the *multiplication table* approach to mixing named routes and HTTP request methods.

The techniques for doing this are useful when, for example, you've got more than one way of viewing a resource that might be described as *showing*. You can't (or shouldn't) use the `show` action itself for more than one such view. Instead, you need to think in terms of different perspectives on a resource, and create URLs for each one.

3.8.1 Extra Member Routes

For example, let's say we want to make it possible to retract a bid. The basic nested route for bids looks like this:

```
resources :auctions do
  resources :bids
end
```

We'd like to have a `retract` action that shows a form (and perhaps does some screening for retractability). The `retract` isn't the same as `destroy`; it's more like a portal to `destroy`. It's similar to `edit`, which serves as a form portal to `update`. Following the parallel with `edit`/`update`, we want a URL that looks like

```
/auctions/3/bids/5/retract
```

and a helper method called `retract_auction_bid_url`. The way you achieve this is by specifying an extra `member` route for the `bids`, as in Listing 3.1

Listing 3.1 Adding an extra member route

```
resources :auctions do
  resources :bids do
    member do
      get :retract
    end
  end
end
```

Then you can add a retraction link to your view using

```
link_to "Retract", retract_bid_path(auction, bid)
```

and the URL generated will include the `/retract` modifier. That said, you should probably let that link pull up a retraction form (and not trigger the retraction process itself!). The reason I say that is because, according to the tenets of HTTP, GET requests should not modify the state of the server; that's what POST requests are for.

So how do you trigger an actual retraction? Is it enough to add a `:method` option to `link_to`?

```
link_to "Retract", retract_bid_path(auction,bid), :method => :post
```

Not quite. Remember that in Listing 3.1 we defined the retract route as a `get`, so a POST will not be recognized by the routing system. The solution is to define an extra member route with `post`, like this:

```
resources :auctions do
  resources :bids do
    member do
      get :retract
      post :retract
    end
  end
end
```

If you're handling more than one HTTP verb with a single action, you should switch to using a single `match` declaration and a `:via` option, like this:

```
resources :auctions do
  resources :bids do
    member do
      match :retract, :via => [:get, :post]
    end
  end
end
```

Thanks to the flexibility of the routing system, we can tighten it up further using `match` with an `:on` option, like

```
resources :auctions do
  resources :bids do
    match :retract, :via => [:get, :post], :on => :member
  end
end
```

which would result in a route like this (output from `rake routes`):

```
retract_auction_bid  GET|POST
/auctions/:auction_id/bids/:id/retract(.:format)
{:controller => "bids", :action => "retract"}
```

REST

3.8.2   Extra Collection Routes

You can use the same routing technique to add routes that conceptually apply to an entire collection of resources:

```
resources :auctions do
  collection do
    match :terminate, :via => [:get, :post]
  end
end
```

In its shorter form:

```
resources :auctions do
  match :terminate, :via => [:get, :post], :on => :collection
end
```

This example will give you a `terminate_auctions_path` method, which will produce a URL mapping to the `terminate` action of the auctions controller. (A slightly bizarre example, perhaps, but the idea is that it would enable you to end all auctions at once.)

Thus you can fine-tune the routing behavior—even the RESTful routing behavior—of your application, so that you can arrange for special and specialized cases while still thinking in terms of resources.

3.8.3   Custom Action Names

Occasionally, you might want to deviate from the default naming convention for Rails RESTful routes. The `:path_names` option allows you to specify alternate name mappings. The example code shown changes the new and edit actions to Spanish-language equivalents.

```
resources :projects, :path_names => { :new => 'nuevo', :edit => 'cambiar'}
```

The URLs change (but the names of the generated helper methods do not).

```
new_report    GET      /reports/nuevo(.:format)
edit_report   GET      /reports/:id/cambiar(.:format)
```

3.8.4   Mapping to a Different Controller

You may use the `:controller` option to map a resource to a different controller than the one it would do so by default. This feature is occasionally useful for aliasing resources to a more natural controller name.

```
resources :photos, :controller => "images"
```

3.8.5   Routes for New Resources

The routing system has a neat syntax for specifying routes that only apply to new resources, ones that haven't been saved yet. You declare extra routes inside of a nested new block, like this:

```
resources :reports do
  new do
    post :preview
  end
end
```

The declaration above would result in the following route being defined.

```
preview_new_report POST    /reports/new/preview(.:format)
{:action=>"preview", :controller=>"reports"}
```

Refer to your new route within a view form by altering the default :url.

```
= form_for(report, :url => preview_new_report_path) do |f|
  ...
  = f.submit "Preview"
```

3.8.6   Considerations for Extra Routes

Referring to extra member and collection actions, David has been quoted as saying, "If you're writing so many additional methods that the repetition is beginning to bug you, you should revisit your intentions. You're probably not being as RESTful as you could be."

The last sentence is key. Adding extra actions corrupts the elegance of your overall RESTful application design, because it leads you away from finding all of the resources lurking in your domain.

Keeping in mind that real applications are more complicated than code examples in a reference book, let's see what would happen if we had to model retractions strictly using resources. Rather than tacking a retract action onto the BidsController, we might feel compelled to introduce a retraction resource, associated with bids, and write a RetractionController to handle it.

```
resources :bids do
  resource :retraction
end
```

RetractionController could now be in charge of everything having to do with retraction activities, rather than having that functionality mixed into BidsController. And if you think about it, something as weighty as bid retraction would eventually accumulate quite a bit of logic. Some would call breaking it out into its own controller proper separation of concerns or even just good object-orientation.

3.9 Controller-Only Resources

The word *resource* has a substantive, noun-like flavor that puts one in mind of database tables and records. However, a REST resource does not have to map directly to an Active Record model. Resources are high-level abstractions of what's available through your web application. Database operations just happen to be one of the ways that you store and retrieve the data you need to generate representations of resources.

A REST resource doesn't necessarily have to map directly to a controller, either, at least not in theory. You could, if you wanted to, provide REST services whose public identifiers (URIs) did not match the names of your controllers at all.

What all of this adds up to is that you might have occasion to create a set of resource routes, and a matching controller, that don't correspond to any model in your application at all. There's nothing wrong with a full resource/controller/model stack where everything matches by name. But you may find cases where the resources you're representing can be encapsulated in a controller but not a model.

An example in the auction application is the sessions controller. Assume a `routes.rb` file containing this line:

```
resource :session
```

It maps the URL `/session` to a `SessionController` as a singleton resource, yet there's no `Session` model. (By the way, it's properly defined as a singleton resource because from the user's perspective there is only one session.)

Why go the RESTful style for authentication? If you think about it, user sessions can be created and destroyed. The creation of a session takes place when a user logs in; when the user logs out, the session is destroyed. The RESTful Rails practice of pairing a `new` action and view with a `create` action can be followed! The user login form can be the session-creating form, housed in the template file such as `session/new.html.haml`

```
%h1 Log in
= form_for :user, :url => session_path do |f|
  %p
    = f.label :login
    = f.text_field :login
  %p
    = f.label :password
    = f.password_field :password
  %p
    = f.submit "Log in"
```

When the form is submitted, the input is handled by the `create` method of the sessions controller:

```
def create
  if user.try(:authorize, params[:user][:password])
    flash[:notice] = "Welcome, #{user.first_name}!"
    redirect_to home_url
  else
    flash[:error] = "Login invalid."
    redirect_to :action => "new"
  end
end

protected
def user
  @user ||= User.find_by_login(params[:user][:login])
end
```

Nothing is written to any database table in this action, but it's worthy of the name `create` by virtue of the fact that it creates a session. Furthermore, if you did at some point decide that sessions should be stored in the database, you'd already have a nicely abstracted handling layer.

It pays to remain open-minded, then, about the possibility that CRUD as an action-naming philosophy and CRUD as actual database operations may sometimes occur independently of each other; and the possibility that the resource-handling facilities in Rails might usefully be associated with a controller that has no corresponding model. Creating a session on the server isn't a REST-compliant practice, because REST mandates stateless transfers of representations of resources. But it's a good illustration of why, and how, you might make design decisions involving routes and resources that don't implicate the whole application stack.

Xavier says…

Whether sessions are REST-compliant or not depends on the session storage.

What REST disallows is not the idea of application state in general, but rather the idea of client state stored in the server. REST demands that your requests are complete. For example, putting an `auction_id` in a hidden field of a form or in its action path is fine. There is state in that request that the edit action wants to pass to the update action, and you dumped it into the page, so the next request to update a bid carries all that is needed. That's RESTful.

Now, using hidden fields and such is not the only way to do this. For example, there is no problem using a `user_id` cookie for authentication. Why? Because a cookie is part of a request. Therefore, I am pretty sure that cookie-based sessions are considered to be RESTful by the same principle. That kind of storage makes your requests self-contained and complete.

Sticking to CRUD-like action names is, in general, a good idea. As long as you're doing lots of creating and destroying anyway, it's easier to think of a user logging in as the creation of a session, than to come up with a whole new semantic category for it. Rather than the new concept of *user logs in*, just think of it as a new occurrence of the old concept, *session gets created*.

3.10 Different Representations of Resources

One of the precepts of REST is that the components in a REST-based system exchange representations of resources. The distinction between resources and their representations is vital.

As a client or consumer of REST services, you don't actually retrieve a resource from a server; you retrieve representations of that resource. You also provide representations: A form submission, for example, sends the server a representation of a resource, together with a request—for example, PUT—that this representation be used as the basis for updating the resource. Representations are the exchange currency of resource management.

3.10.1 The respond_to Method

The ability to return different representations in RESTful Rails practice is based on the `respond_to` method in the controller, which, as you've seen in the previous chapter, allows you to return different responses depending on what the client wants. Moreover, when you create resource routes you automatically get URL recognition for URLs ending with a dot and a `:format` parameter.

For example, assume that you have `resources :auctions` in your routes file and some `respond_to` logic in the `AuctionsController` like

```
def index
  @auctions = Auction.all
  respond_to do |format|
    format.html
    format.xml { render :xml => @auctions }
  end
end
```

which will let you to connect to this URL: `/auctions.xml`

The resource routing will ensure that the `index` action gets executed. It will also recognize the `.xml` at the end of the route and interact with `respond_to` accordingly, returning the XML representation.

There is also a more concise way of handling this now using the `respond_with` method.

```
class AuctionsController < ApplicationController
  respond_to :html, :xml, :json
  def index
    @auctions = Auction.all
    respond_with(@auctions)
  end
end
```

Here we've told our controller to respond to html, xml, and json so that each action will automatically return the appropriate content. When the request comes in, the responder would attempt to do the following given a `.json` extension on the URL:

- Attempt to render the associated view with a .json extension.
- If no view exists, call `to_json` on the object passed to `responds_with`.
- If the object does not respond to `to_json`, call `to_format` on it.

For nested and namespaced resources, simply pass all the objects to the `respond_to` method similar to the way you would generate a route.

```
respond_with(@user, :managed, @client)
```

Of course, all of this is URL recognition. What if you want to generate a URL ending in `.xml`?

3.10.2 Formatted Named Routes

Let's say you want a link to the XML representation of a resource. You can achieve it by passing an extra argument to the RESTful named route:

```
link_to "XML version of this auction", auction_path(@auction, :xml)
```

This will generate the following HTML:

```
<a href="/auctions/1.xml">XML version of this auction</a>
```

When followed, this link will trigger the XML clause of the `respond_to` block in the `show` action of the auctions controller. The resulting XML may not look like much in a browser, but the named route is there if you want it.

The circuit is now complete: You can generate URLs that point to a specific response type, and you can honor requests for different types by using `respond_to`. All told, the routing system and the resource-routing facilities built on top of it give you quite a set of powerful, concise tools for differentiating among requests and, therefore, being able to serve up different representations.

3.11 The RESTful Rails Action Set

Rails REST facilities, ultimately, are about named routes and the controller actions to which they point. The more you use RESTful Rails, the more you get to know each of the seven RESTful actions. How they work across different controllers (and different applications) is of course somewhat different. Still, perhaps because there's a finite number of them and their roles are fairly well-delineated, each of the seven tends to have fairly consistent properties and a characteristic *feel* to it.

We're going to take a look at each of the seven actions, with examples and comments. You'll encounter all of them again, particularly in Chapter 4, Working with Controllers, but here you'll get some backstory and start to get a sense of the characteristic usage of them and issues and choices associated with them.

3.11.1 Index

Typically, an index action provides a representation of a plural (or collection) resource. However, to be clear, not all resource collections are mapped to the index action. Your default index representations will usually be generic, although admittedly that has a lot to do with your application-specific needs. But in general, the index action shows the world the most neutral representation possible. A very basic index action looks like

```
class AuctionsController < ApplicationController
  def index
    @auctions = Auction.all
  end
end
```

The associated view template will display information about each auction, with links to specific information about each one, and to profiles of the sellers.

You'll certainly encounter situations where you want to display a representation of a collection in a restricted way. In our recurring example, users should be able to see a listing of all their bids, but may be you don't want users seeing other people's bids.

There are a couple of ways to do this. One way is to test for the presence of a logged-in user and decide what to show based on that. But that's not going to work here. For one thing, the logged-in user might want to see the more public view. For another, the more dependence on server-side state we can eliminate or consolidate, the better.

So let's try looking at the two bid lists, not as public and private versions of the same resource, but as different index resources. The difference can be reflected in the routing like:

```
resources :auctions do
  resources :bids do
    get :manage, :on => :collection
  end
end
resources :bids
```

We can now organize the bids controller in such a way that access is nicely layered, using filters only where necessary and eliminating conditional branching in the actions themselves:

```
class BidsController < ApplicationController
  before_filter :check_authorization, :only => :manage

  def index
    @bids = Bid.all
  end

  def manage
    @bids = auction.bids
  end

  protected

    def auction
      @auction ||= Auction.find(params[:auction_id])
    end

    def check_authorization
      auction.authorized?(current_user)
    end

end
```

There's now a clear distinction between /bids and /auctions/1/bids/manage and the role that they play in your application.

On the named route side, we've now got bids_url and manage_auction_bids_url. We've thus preserved the public, stateless face of the /bids resource, and quarantined as much stateful behavior as possible into a discrete member resource, /auctions/1/bids/manage. Don't fret if this mentality doesn't come to you naturally. It's part of the REST learning curve.

Lar says...

If they are truly different resources, why not give them each their own controllers? Surely there
will be other actions that need to be authorized and scoped to the current user.

3.11.2 Show

The RESTful `show` action is the singular flavor of a resource. That generally translates
to a representation of information about one object, one member of a collection. Like
`index`, `show` is triggered by a GET request.

A typical—one might say classic—`show` action looks like

```
class AuctionController < ApplicationController
  def show
    @auction = Auction.find(params[:id])
  end
end
```

You might want to differentiate between publicly available profiles, perhaps based on a
different route, and the profile of the current user, which might include modification
rights and perhaps different information.

As with index actions, it's good to make your show actions as public as possible and
offload the administrative and privileged views onto either a different controller or a
different action.

3.11.3 Destroy

Destroy actions are good candidates for administrative safeguarding, though of course it
depends on what you're destroying. You might want something like this to protect the
`destroy` action.

```
class ProductsController < ApplicationController
  before_filter :admin_required, :only => :destroy
```

A typical `destroy` action might look like

```
  def destroy
    product.destroy
    flash[:notice] = "Product deleted!"
    redirect_to products_url
  end
```

This approach might be reflected in a simple administrative interface like

```
%h1 Products
- products.each do |p|
  %p= link_to p.name, product_path(p)
  - if current_user.admin?
    %p= link_to "delete", product_path(p), :method => :delete
```

That delete link appears depending on whether current user is an admin.

With Rails 3, the UJS (Unobtrusive JavaScript) API greatly simplifies the HTML emitted for a `destroy` action, using CSS selectors to bind JavaScript to (in this case) the "delete" link. See Chapter 12, Ajax on Rails, for much more information about how it works.

`DELETE` submissions are dangerous. Rails wants to make them as hard as possible to trigger accidentally—for instance, by a crawler or bot sending requests to your site. So when you specify the `DELETE` method, JavaScript that submits a form is bound to your "delete" link, along with a `rel="nofollow"` attribute on the link. Since bots don't submit forms (and shouldn't follow links marked "nofollow"), this gives a layer of protection to your code.

3.11.4 New and Create

As you've already seen, the `new` and `create` actions go together in RESTful Rails. A "new resource" is really just an entity waiting to be created. Accordingly, the `new` action customarily presents a form, and `create` creates a new record, based on the form input.

Let's say you want a user to be able to create (that is, start) an auction. You're going to need

1. A `new` action, which will display a form
2. A `create` action, which will create a new `Auction` object based on the form input, and proceed to a view (`show` action) of that auction.

The `new` action doesn't have to do much. In fact, it has to do nothing. Like any empty action, it can even be left out. Rails will still figure out which view to render. However, your controller will need an auction helper method, like

```
protected

def auction
  @auction ||= current_user.auctions.build(params[:auction])
end
helper_method :auction
```

If this technique is alien to you, don't worry. We'll describe it in detail in Section 10.1.5.

A simplistic `new.html.haml` template might look like Listing 3.2.

Listing 3.2 A New Auction Form

```
%h1 Create a new auction
= form_for auction do |f|
  = f.label :subject
  = f.text_field :subject
  %br
  = f.label :description
  = f.text_field :description
  %br
  = f.label :reserve
  = f.text_field :reserve
  %br
  = f.label :starting_bid
  = f.text_field :starting_bid
  %br
  = f.label :end_time
  = f.datetime_select :end_time
  %br
  = f.submit "Create"
```

Once the information is filled out by a user, it's time for the main event: the `create` action. Unlike `new`, this action has something to do.

```
def create
  if auction.save
    redirect_to auction_url(auction), :notice => "Auction created!"
  else
    render :action => "new"
  end
end
```

3.11.5 Edit and Update

Like `new` and `create`, the `edit` and `update` actions go together: `edit` provides a form, and `update` processes the form input.

The form for editing a record appears similar to the form for creating one. (In fact, you can put much of it in a partial template and use it for both; that's left as an exercise for the reader.)

The `form_for` method is smart enough to check whether the object you pass to it has been persisted or not. If it has, then it recognizes that you are doing an edit and specifies a PUT method on the form.

3.12 Conclusion

In this chapter, we tackled the tough subject of using REST principles to guide the design of our Rails applications, mainly as they apply to the routing system and controller actions. We learned how the foundation of RESTful Rails is the `resources` method in your routes file and how to use the numerous options available to make sure that you can structure your application exactly how it needs to be structured.

By necessity, we've already introduced many controller-related topics and code examples in our tour of the routing and REST features. In the next chapter, we'll cover controller concepts and the Action Controller API in depth.

REST

CHAPTER 4

Working with Controllers

Remove all business logic from your controllers and put it in the model. (My) instructions are precise, but following them requires intuition and subtle reasoning.

—Nick Kallen

Like any computer program, your Rails application involves the flow of control from one part of your code to another. The flow of program control gets pretty complex with Rails applications. There are many bits and pieces in the framework, many of which execute each other. And part of the framework's job is to figure out, on the fly, what your application files are called and what's in them, which of course varies from one application to another.

The heart of it all, though, is pretty easy to identify: It's the controller. When someone connects to your application, what they're basically doing is asking the application to execute a controller action. Sure, there are many different flavors of how this can happen and edge cases where it doesn't exactly happen at all. But if you know how controllers fit into the application life cycle, you can anchor everything else around that knowledge. That's why we're covering controllers before the rest of the Rails APIs.

Controllers are the C in MVC. They're the first port of call, after the dispatcher, for the incoming request. They're in charge of the flow of the program: They gather information and make it available to the views.

Controllers are also very closely linked to views, more closely than they're linked to models. It's possible to write the entire model layer of an application before you create a single controller, or to have different people working on the controller and model layers who never meet or talk to each other. However, views and controllers are more tightly coupled to one another. They share a lot of information, and the names you choose for your variables in the controller will have an effect on what you do in the view.

In this chapter, we're going to look at what happens on the way to a controller action being executed, and what happens as a result. In the middle, we'll take a long look at how controller classes themselves are set up, particularly in regard to the many different ways that we can render views. We'll wrap up the chapter with a couple of additional topics related to controllers: filters and streaming.

4.1 Rack

Rack is a modular interface for handling web requests, written in Ruby, with support for many different web servers. It abstracts away the handling of HTTP requests and responses into a single, simple `call` method that can be used by anything from a plain Ruby script all the way to Rails itself.

```
Listing 2.1  HelloWorld as a Rack application
class HelloWorld
  def call(env)
    [200, {"Content-Type" => "text/plain"}, ["Hello world!"]]
  end
end
```

An HTTP request invokes the call method and passes in a hash of environment variables, akin to the way that CGI works. The call method should return a three-element array consisting of the status, a hash of response headers, and finally, the body of the request.

As of Rails 2.3, request handling was moved to Rack and the concept of middleware was introduced. Classes that satisfy Rack's call interface can be chained together as filters. Rack itself includes a number of useful filter classes that do things such as logging and exception handling.

Rails 3 was re-architected from the ground up to fully leverage Rack filters in a modular and extensible manner. A full explanation of Rails' Rack underpinnings are outside the scope of this book, especially since Rack does not really play a part in day-to-day development of applications. However, it is essential Rails 3 knowledge to understand that much of Action Controller is implemented as Rack middleware modules. Want to see which Rack filters are enabled for your Rails 3 application? There's a rake task for that!

```
$ rake middleware
use ActionDispatch::Static
use Rack::Lock
use ActiveSupport::Cache::Strategy::LocalCache
use Rack::Runtime
use Rails::Rack::Logger
use ActionDispatch::ShowExceptions
```

```
use ActionDispatch::RemoteIp
use Rack::Sendfile
use ActionDispatch::Callbacks
use ActiveRecord::QueryCache
use ActionDispatch::Cookies
use ActionDispatch::Session::CookieStore
use ActionDispatch::Flash
use ActionDispatch::ParamsParser
use Rack::MethodOverride
use ActionDispatch::Head
use Sass::Plugin::Rack
run Tae::Application.routes
```

What's Active Record query caching have to do with serving requests anyway?

```
module ActiveRecord
  class QueryCache

    ...

    def call(env)
      ActiveRecord::Base.cache do
        @app.call(env)
      end
    end
  end
end
```

Ahh, it's not that Active Record query caching has anything specifically to do with serving requests. It's that Rails 3 is designed in such a way that different aspects of its behavior are introduced into the request call chain as individual Rack middleware components or *filters*.

4.1.1   Configuring Your Middleware Stack

Your application object allows you to access and manipulate the Rack middleware stack during initialization, via `config.middleware` like

```
# application.rb

module Example
  class Application < Rails::Application
    ...
    # Rack::ShowStatus catches all empty responses the app it wraps and
    # replaces them with a site explaining the error.
    config.middleware.use Rack::ShowStatus
  end
end
```

Rack lobster

> As I found out trying to experiment with the hilariously-named `Rack::Lobster`, your custom Rack middleware classes need to have an explicit `initializer` method, even if they don't require runtime arguments.

The methods of `config.middleware` give you very fine-grained control over the order in which your middleware stack is configured. The `args` parameter is an optional hash of attributes to pass to the `initializer` method of your Rack filter.

`config.middleware.insert_after(existing_middleware, new_middleware, args)`

Adds the new middleware after the specified existing middleware in the middleware stack.

`config.middleware.insert_before (existing_middleware, new_middleware, args)`

Adds the new middleware before the specified existing middleware in the middleware stack.

`config.middleware.delete(middleware)`

Removes a specified middleware from the stack.

`config.middleware.swap(existing_middleware, new_middleware, args)`

Swaps a specified middleware from the stack with a new class.

`config.middleware.use(new_middleware, args)`

Takes a class reference as its parameter and just adds the desired middleware to the end of the middleware stack.

4.2 Action Dispatch: Where It All Begins

Controller and view code in Rails has always been part of its Action Pack framework. In Rails 3, dispatching of requests has been extracted into its own sub-component of Action Pack called Action Dispatch. It contains classes that interface the rest of the controller system to Rack.

4.2.1   Request Handling

The entry point to a request is an instance of `ActionDispatch::Routing::RouteSet`, the object on which you can call `draw` at the top of `config/routes.rb`.

The route set chooses the rule that matches, and calls its *Rack endpoint*. So a route like

```
match 'foo', :to => 'foo#index'
```

has a dispatcher instance associated to it, whose `call` method ends up executing

```
FooController.action(:index).call
```

As covered in Section 2.2.9 "Routes as Rack Endpoints", the route set can call any other type of Rack endpoint, like a Sinatra app, a redirect macro, or a bare lambda. In those cases, no dispatcher is involved.

All of this happens quickly, behind the scenes. It's unlikely that you would ever need to dig into the source code of Action Dispatch; it's the sort of thing that you can take for granted to just work. However, to really understand the Rails way, it is important to know what's going on with the dispatcher. In particular, it's important to remember that the various parts of your application are just bits (sometimes long bits) of Ruby code, and that they're getting loaded into a running Ruby interpreter.

4.2.2   Getting Intimate with the Dispatcher

Just for the purpose of learning, let's trigger the Rails dispatching mechanism manually. We'll do this little exercise from the ground up, starting with a new Rails application:

```
$ rails new dispatch_me
```

Now, create a single controller, with an `index` action:

```
$ cd dispatch_me/
$ rails generate controller demo index
    create  app/controllers/demo_controller.rb
     route  get "demo/index"
    invoke  erb
    create    app/views/demo
    create    app/views/demo/index.html.erb
    invoke  test_unit
    create    test/functional/demo_controller_test.rb
    invoke  helper
    create    app/helpers/demo_helper.rb
    invoke    test_unit
    create      test/unit/helpers/demo_helper_test.rb
```

If you take a look at `app/controllers/demo_controller.rb`, you'll see that it has an `index` action:

```
class DemoController < ApplicationController
  def index
  end
end
```

There's also a view template file, `app/views/demo/index.html.erb` with some place-holder language. Just to see things more clearly, let's replace it with something we will definitely recognize when we see it again. Replace the contents of `index.html.erb` with

```
Hello!
```

Not much of a design accomplishment, but it will do the trick.

Now that we've got a set of dominos lined up, it's just a matter of pushing over the first one: the dispatcher. To do that, start by firing up the Rails console from your Rails application directory.

```
$ rails console
Loading development environment.
>>
```

There are some variables from the web server that Rack expects to use for request processing. Since we're going to be invoking the dispatcher manually, we have to set those variables like this in the console (output ommited for brevity):

```
>> env = {}
>> env['REQUEST_METHOD'] = 'GET'
>> env['PATH_INFO'] = '/demo/index'
>> env['rack.input'] = StringIO.new
```

We're now ready to fool the dispatcher into thinking it's getting a request. Actually, it is getting a request. It's just that it's coming from someone sitting at the console, rather than from a web server:

```
>> ActionController::Dispatcher.new.call(env).last.body
=> "<!DOCTYPE html>\n<html>\n <head>\n <title>TAE</title>\n <link
href=\"/stylesheets/scaffold.css?1283099044\" media=\"screen\"
rel=\"stylesheet\" type=\"text/css\" />\n <script
src=\"/javascripts/prototype.js?1283098615\"
type=\"text/javascript\"></script>\n <script
src=\"/javascripts/effects.js?1283098615\"
type=\"text/javascript\"></script>\n <script
src=\"/javascripts/dragdrop.js?1283098615\"
type=\"text/javascript\"></script>\n <script
```

```
src=\"/javascripts/controls.js?1283098615\"
type=\"text/javascript\"></script>\n <script
src=\"/javascripts/rails.js?1283098615\"
type=\"text/javascript\"></script>\n
<script src=\"/javascripts/application.js?1283098615\"
type=\"text/javascript\"></script>\n <meta name=\"csrf-param\"
content=\"authenticity_token\"/>\n <meta name=\"csrf-token\"
content=\"Ot6XylwCEKlMn8K/QFkmeOPbjLxfGQLx6M4fA1Dvz+U=\"/>\n
</head>\n</html>\n<body>\n Hello!\n</body>\n"
```

If you want to see everything contained in the `ActionDispatch::Response` object returned from `call` then try the following code:

```
>> y ActionController::Dispatcher.new.last.call(env)
```

The handy `y` method formats its argument as a yaml string, making it a lot easier to understand. We won't reproduce the output here because it's huge.

So, we've executed the `call` method of a `Dispatcher` object and as a result, the `index` action got executed and the index template (such as it is) got rendered and the results of the rendering got wrapped in some HTTP headers and returned.

Just think: If you were a web server, rather than a human, and you had just done the same thing, you could now return that document, headers and "Hello!" and all, to a client.

You can follow the trail of bread crumbs even further by diving into the Rails source code, but for purposes of understanding the chain of events in a Rails request, and the role of the controller, the peek under the hood we've just done is sufficient.

Tim says...

Note that if you give Rack a path that resolves to a static file, it will be served directly from the web server without involving the Rails stack. As a result, the object returned by the dispatcher for a static file is different from what you might expect.

```
>> env['PATH_INFO'] ='/'

>> a = ActionController::Dispatcher.new.call(env).last
=> #<Rack::File:0x000001025fa4a8 @root="/Users/obie/work/tr3w_time_and
   _expenses/public", @path_info="/index.html", @path="/Users/obie/wor
   k/tr3w_time_and_expenses/public/index.html">

>> a.body
NoMethodError: undefined method `body' for #<Rack::File:0x000001025fa4a8>
```

Controllers

4.3 Render unto View...

The goal of the typical controller action is to render a view template—that is, to fill
out the template and hand the results, usually an HTML document, back to the server
for delivery to the client. Oddly—at least it might strike you as a bit odd, though not
illogical—you don't actually need to define a controller action, as long as you've got a
template that matches the action name.

You can try this out in under-the-hood mode. Go into `app/controller/demo_`
`controller.rb`, and delete the `index` action so that the file will look empty, like this:

```
class DemoController < ApplicationController
end
```

Don't delete `app/views/demo/index.html.haml`, and then try the console exercise
(`Dispatcher.dispatch` and all that) again. You'll see the same result.

By the way, make sure you reload the console when you make changes—it doesn't
react to changes in source code automatically. The easiest way to reload the console
is simply to type `reload!`. But be aware that any existing instances of Active Record
objects that you're holding on to will also need to be reloaded (using their individual
`reload` methods). Sometimes it's simpler to just exit the console and start it up again.

4.3.1 When in Doubt, Render

Rails knows that when it gets a request for the `index` action of the demo controller, what
really matters is handing something back to the server. So if there's no `index` action in
the controller file, Rails shrugs and says, "Well, let's just assume that if there were an
`index` action, it would be empty anyway, and I'd just render `index.html.haml`. So
that's what I'll do."

You can learn something from an empty controller action, though. Let's go back to
this version of the demo controller:

```
class DemoController < ApplicationController
  def index
  end
end
```

What you learn from seeing the empty action is that, at the end of every controller
action, if nothing else is specified, the default behavior is to render the template
whose name matches the name of the controller and action, which in this case means
`app/views/demo/index.html.haml`.

In other words, every controller action has an implicit `render` command in it. And `render` is a real method. You could write the preceding example like this:

```
def index
  render "demo/index"
end
```

You don't have to, though, because it's assumed that it's what you want, and that is part of what Rails people are talking about when they discuss *convention over configuration*. Don't force the developer to add code to accomplish something that can be assumed to be a certain way.

The `render` command, however, does more than just provide a way of telling Rails to do what it was going to do anyway.

4.3.2   Explicit Rendering

Rendering a template is like putting on a shirt: If you don't like the first one you find in your closet—the default, so to speak—you can reach for another one and put it on instead.

If a controller action doesn't want to render its default template, it can render a different one by calling the `render` method explicitly. Any template file in the `app/views` directory tree is available. (Actually, that's not exactly true. Any template on the whole system is available!) But why would you want your controller action to render a template other than its default? There are several reasons, and by looking at some of them, we can cover all of the handy features of the controller's `render` method.

4.3.3   Rendering Another Action's Template

A common reason for rendering an entirely different template is to redisplay a form, when it gets submitted with invalid data and needs correction. In such circumstances, the usual web strategy is to redisplay the form with the submitted data, and trigger the simultaneous display of some error information, so that the user can correct the form and resubmit.

The reason that process involves rendering another template is that the action that processes the form and the action that displays the form may be—and often are—different from each other. Therefore, the action that processes the form needs a way to redisplay the original (form) template, instead of treating the form submission as successful and moving on to whatever the next screen might be.

Controllers

Wow, that was a mouthful of an explanation. Here's a practical example:

```
class EventController < ActionController::Base
  def new
    # This (empty) action renders the new.html.haml template, which
    # contains the form for inputting information about the new
    # event record and is not actually needed.
  end

  def create
    # This method processes the form input. The input is available via
    # the params hash, in the nested hash keyed to :event
    @event = Event.new(params[:event])
    if @event.save
      flash[:notice] = "Event created!"
      # ignore the next line for now
      redirect_to :controller => "main"
    else
      render :action => "new" # doesn't execute the new method!
    end
  end
end
```

On failure, that is, if `@event.save` does not return `true`, we render the "new" template. Assuming `new.html.haml` has been written correctly, this will automatically include the display of error information embedded in the new (but unsaved) `Event` object. You've already seen this in some examples, as `f.error_messages`.

Note that the template itself doesn't "know" that it has been rendered by the `create` action rather than the `new` action. It just does its job: It fills out and expands and interpolates, based on the instructions it contains and the data (in this case, `@event`) that the controller has passed to it.

4.3.4 Rendering a Different Template Altogether

In a similar fashion, if you are rendering a template for a different action, it is possible to render any template in your application by calling `render` with a string pointing to the desired template file. The `render` method is very robust in its ability to interpret which template you're trying to refer to.

```
render :template => '/products/index.html.haml'
```

A couple of notes: It's not necessary to pass a hash with `:template`, because it's the default option. Also, in our testing, all of the following permutations worked identically when called from `ProductsController`:

```
render '/products/index.html.haml'
render 'products/index.html.haml'
render 'products/index.html'
render 'products/index'
render 'index'
render :index
```

The `:template` option only works with a path relative to the template root (`app/views`, unless you changed it, which would be extremely unusual).

Tim says...

> Use only enough to disambiguate. The content type defaults to that of the request and if you have two templates that differ only by template language, you're Doing It Wrong.

4.3.5 Rendering a Partial Template

Another option is to render a partial template (usually referred to simply as a *partial*). Usage of partial templates allows you to organize your template code into small files. Partials can also help you to avoid clutter and encourage you to break your template code up into reusable modules.

There are a few ways to trigger partial rendering. The first, and most obvious, is using the `:partial` option to explicitly specify a partial template. Rails has a convention of prefixing partial template file names with an underscore character, but you never include the underscore when referring to partials.

```
render :partial => 'product' # renders
app/views/products/_product.html.haml
```

Leaving the underscore off of the partial name applies, even if you're referring to a partial in a different directory from the controller that you're currently in!

```
render :partial => 'shared/product' # renders
app/views/shared/_product.html.haml
```

The second way to trigger partial rendering depends on convention. If you pass render `:partial` an object, Rails will use its class name to find a partial to render. You can even omit the `:partial` option, like in the following example code.

```
render :partial => @product
render @product
render 'product'
```

All three lines render the `app/views/products/_product.html.haml` template.

Partial rendering from a controller is mostly used in conjunction with Ajax calls that need to dynamically update segments of an already displayed page. The technique, along with generic use of partials in views, is covered in greater detail in Chapter 10, Action View.

4.3.6 Rendering Inline Template Code

Occasionally, you need to send the browser the result of translating a snippet of template code, too small to merit its own partial. I admit that this practice is contentious, because it is a flagrant violation of proper separation of concerns between the MVC layers.

Rails treats the inline code exactly as if it were a view template. The default type of view template processing is ERb, but passing an additional :type option allows you to choose Haml.

```
render :inline => "%span.foo #{@foo.name}", :type => "haml"
```

Courtenay says...

If you were one of my employees, I'd reprimand you for using view code in the controller, even if it is only one line. Keep your view-related code in the views!

4.3.7 Rendering Text

What if you simply need to send plain text back to the browser, particularly when responding to Ajax and certain types of web service requests?

```
render :text => 'Submission accepted'
```

Unfortunately, if you don't pass an additional :content_type option, Rails will default the response MIME type to text/html, rather than text/plain. The solution is to be explicit about what you want.

```
render :text => 'Submission accepted', :content_type => 'text/plain'
```

4.3.8 Rendering Other Types of Structured Data

The render command also accepts a series of (convenience) options for returning structured data such as JSON or XML. The content-type of the response will be set appropriately and additional options apply.[1]

---

1. Yehuda Katz has written an excellent description of how to register additional rendering options at http://www.engineyard.com/blog/2010/render-options-in-rails-3/

:json

JSON[2] is a small subset of JavaScript selected for its usability as a lightweight data-interchange format. It is mostly used as a way of sending data down to JavaScript code running in a rich web application via Ajax calls. Active Record has built-in support for conversion to JSON, which makes Rails an ideal platform for serving up JSON data, as in the following example:

```
render :json => @record
```

As long as the parameter responds to `to_json`, Rails will call it for you, which means you don't have to call it yourself with ActiveRecord objects.

Any additional options passed to `render :json` are also included in the invocation of `to_json`.

```
render :json => @projects, :include => :tasks
```

Additionally, if you're doing JSONP, you can supply the name of a callback function to be invoked in the browser when it gets your response. Just add a `:callback` option with the name of a valid JavaScript method.

```
render :json => @record, :callback => 'updateRecordsDisplay'
```

:xml

Active Record also has built-in support for conversion to XML, as in the following example:

```
render :xml => @record
```

As long as the parameter responds to `to_xml`, Rails will call it for you, which means you don't have to call it yourself with ActiveRecord objects.

Any additional options passed to `render :xml` are also included in the invocation of `to_xml`.

```
render :xml => @projects, :include => :tasks
```

We cover XML-related topics like this one extensively in Chapter 15, Active Resource.

4.3.9 Rendering Nothing

On rare occasions, you don't want to render anything at all. (To avoid a bug in Safari, rendering nothing actually means sending a single space character back to the browser.)

---

2. For more information on JSON go to `http://www.json.org/`.

```
render :nothing => true, :status => 401 # Unauthorized
```

It's worth noting that, as illustrated in this snippet, `render :nothing => true` is often used in conjunction with an HTTP status code.

4.3.10 Rendering Options

Most calls to the `render` method accept additional options. Here they are in alphabetical order.

`:content_type`

All content flying around the web is associated with a MIME type.[3] For instance, HTML content is labeled with a content-type of `text/html`. However, there are occasions where you want to send the client something other than HTML. Rails doesn't validate the format of the MIME identifier you pass to the `:content_type` option, so make sure it is valid.

`:layout`

By default, Rails has conventions regarding the layout template it chooses to wrap your response in, and those conventions are covered in detail in Chapter 10, Action View. The `:layout` option allows you to specify whether you want a layout template to be rendered if you pass it a boolean value, or the name of a layout template, if you want to deviate from the default.

```
render :layout => false     # disable layout template
render :layout => 'login'   # a template app/views/layouts is assumed
```

`:status`

The HTTP protocol includes many standard status codes[4] indicating a variety of conditions in response to a client's request. Rails will automatically use the appropriate status for most common cases, such as `200 OK` for a successful request.

The theory and techniques involved in properly using the full range of HTTP status codes would require a dedicated chapter, perhaps an entire book. For your convenience, Table 4.1 demonstrates some codes that I've occasionally found useful in my day-to-day Rails programming.

---

3. MIME is specified in five RFC documents, so it is much more convenient to point you to a rather good description of MIME provided by Wikipedia at `http://en.wikipedia.org/wiki/MIME`.
4. For a full list of HTTP status codes, consult the spec at `http://www.w3.org/Protocols/rfc2616/rfc2616-sec10.html`.

Table 4.1 Common HTTP status codes

Status Code	Description
200 OK	Everything is fine, and here is your content.
201 Created	A new resource has been created, and its location can be found in the Location HTTP response header.
307 Temporary Redirect	Occasionally, you need to temporarily redirect the user to a different action, perhaps while some long-running process is happening or while the account of a particular resource's owner is suspended.
The requested resource resides temporarily under a different URI.	This particular status code dictates that an HTTP response header named `Location` contain the URI of the resource that the client redirects to. Since the `render` method doesn't take a hash of response header fields, you have to set them manually prior to invoking `render`. Luckily, the `response` hash is in scope within controller methods, as in the following example:
| | ```
def paid_resource
  if current_user.account_expired?
    response.headers['Location'] =
      account_url(current_user)
    render :text => "Account expired",
:status => 307
  end
end
end
``` |
401 Unauthorized	Sometimes a user will not provide credentials to view a restricted resource or authentication and/or authorization will fail. Assuming using a Basic or Digest HTTP Authentication scheme, when that happens you should probably return a `401`.
403 Forbidden	I like to use `403` in conjunction with a short `render`
The server understood the request, but is refusing to fulfill it.	`:text` message in situations where the client has requested a resource that is not normally available via the web application's interface.
	In other words, the request appears to have happened via artificial means. A human or robot, for reasons innocent or guilty (it doesn't matter) is trying to trick the server into doing something it isn't supposed to do.

(continued)

Controllers
```

Table 4.1 Common HTTP status codes (Continued)

Status Code	Description
	For example, my current Rails application is public-facing and is visited by the GoogleBot on a daily basis. Probably due to a bug existing at some point, the URL `/favorites` was indexed. Unfortunately, `/favorites` is only supposed to be available to logged-in users. However, once Google knows about a URL it will keep coming back for it in the future. This is how I told it to stop:

```
def index
 return render :nothing => true,
  :status => 403 unless logged_in?
  @favorites = current_user.favorites.all
end
```

Status Code	Description
404 Not Found The server cannot find the resource you requested.	You may choose to use `404` when a resource of a specific given ID does not exist in your database (whether because it is an invalid ID or because the resource has been deleted). For example, "GET /people/2349594934896107" doesn't exist in our database at all, so what do we display? Do we render a show view with a flash message saying no person with that ID exists? Not in our RESTful world. A 404 would be better. Moreover, if we happen to use something like `acts_as_paranoid` and we know that the resource used to exist in the past, we could respond with `410 Gone`.
500 Internal Server Error	The server encountered an unexpected condition which prevented it from fulfilling the request. As you probably know by now, this is the status code that Rails serves up if you have an error in your code.
503 Service Unavailable The server is temporarily unavailable.	The 503 code comes in very handy when taking a site down for maintenance, particularly when upgrading RESTful web services. One of this book's reviewers, Susan Potter, shares the following suggestion:

Table 4.1 Common HTTP status codes (Continued)

Status Code	Description
	For my projects, I create a stub Rails application that responds with a 503 for each valid type of request that comes in. Clients of my services are usually services themselves or other applications, so this helps client developers that consume my web services know that this is a temporary blip and should be due to scheduled maintenance (and a good reminder for them to check the emails I sent them over the weekend instead of ignoring them).

4.4 Additional Layout Options

You can specify layout options at the controller class level if you want to reuse layouts for multiple actions.

```
class EventController < ActionController::Base
  layout "events", :only => [:index, :new]
  layout "global", :except => [:index, :new]
end
```

The `layout` method can accept either a String, Symbol, or boolean, with a hash of arguments after.

- `String` Determines the template name to use.
- `Symbol` Call the method with this name, which is expected to return a string with a template name.
- `true` Raises an argument error.
- `false` Do not use a layout.

The optional arguments are either `:only` or `:except` and expect an array of action names that should or should not apply to the layout being specified.

4.5 Redirecting

The life cycle of a Rails application is divided into requests. Rendering a template, whether the default one or an alternate one—or, for that matter, rendering a partial or some text or anything—is the final step in handling a request. Redirecting, however, means terminating the current request and asking the client to initiate a new one.

Look again at the example of the form-handling `create` method:

```
def create
  if @event.save
  flash[:notice] = "Event created!"
    redirect_to :action => "index"
  else
    render :action => "new"
  end
end
```

If the save operation succeeds, we store a message in the `flash` hash and `redirect_to` a completely new action. In this case, it's the `index` action. The logic here is that if the new `Event` record gets saved, the next order of business is to take the user back to the top-level view.

The main reason to redirect rather than just render a template after creating or editing a resource (really a POST action) has to do with browser reload behavior. If you didn't redirect, the user would be prompted to re-submit the form if they hit the back button or reload.

4.5.1 The **redirect_to** Method

The `redirect_to` method takes two parameters:

```
redirect_to(target, response_status = {})
```

The `target` parameter takes one of several forms.

Hash The URL will be generated by calling `url_for` with the argument provided.

```
redirect_to :action => "show", :id => 5
```

Active Record object The URL will be generated by calling `url_for` with the object provided, which should generate a named URL for that record.

```
redirect_to post
```

String starting with protocol like http:// Used directly as the target url for redirection.

```
redirect_to "http://www.rubyonrails.org"
redirect_to articles_url
```

String not containing a protocol The current protocol and host is prepended to the argument and used for redirection.

```
redirect_to "/"
redirect_to articles_path
```

:back Back to the page that issued the request. Useful for forms that are triggered from multiple places. Short-hand for `redirect_to(request.env["HTTP_REFERER"])` When using `redirect_to :back`, if there is no referrer set, a `RedirectBackError` will be raised. You may specify some fallback behavior for this case by rescuing `RedirectBackError`.

Sebastian says . . .

Which redirect is the right one? When you use Rails's `redirect_to` method, you tell the user agent (i.e., the browser) to perform a new request for a different URL. That response can mean different things, and it's why modern HTTP has four different status codes for redirection. The old HTTP 1.0 had two codes: 301 aka *Moved Permanently* and 302 aka *Moved Temporarily*.

A permanent redirect meant that the user agent should forget about the old URL and use the new one from now on, updating any references it might have kept (i.e., a bookmark or in the case of Google, its search databases). A temporary redirect was a *one-time only* affair. The original URL was still valid, but for this particular request the user agent should fetch a new resource from the redirection URL.

But there was a problem: If the original request had been a POST, what method should be used for the redirected request? For permanent redirects it was safe to assume the new request should be a GET, since that was the case in all usage scenarios. But temporary redirects were used both for redirecting to a view of a resource that had just been modified in the original POST request (which happens to be the most common usage pattern), and also for redirecting the entire original POST request to a new URL that would take care of it.

HTTP 1.1 solved this problem with the introduction of two new status codes: 303 meaning *See Other* and 307 meaning *Temporary Redirect*. A 303 redirect would tell the user agent to perform a GET request, regardless of what the original verb was, whereas a 307 would always use the same method used for the original request. These days, most browsers handle 302 redirects the same way as 303, with a GET request, which is the argument used by the Rails Core team to keep using 302 in `redirect_to`. A 303 status would be the better alternative, because it leaves no room for interpretation (or confusion), but I guess nobody has found it annoying enough to push for a patch.

If you ever need a 307 redirect, say, to continue processing a POST request in a different action, you can always accomplish your own custom redirect by assigning a path to `response.header["Location"]` and then rendering with `render : status => 307`.

Redirection happens as a "302 Moved" header unless otherwise specified. The `response_status` parameter takes a hash of arguments. The code can be specified by name or number, as in the following examples:

```
redirect_to post_url(@post), :status => :found
redirect_to :action=>'atom', :status => :moved_permanently
redirect_to post_url(@post), :status => 301
redirect_to :action=>'atom', :status => 302
```

Controllers

It is also possible to assign a flash message as part of the redirection. There are two special accessors for commonly used the flash names `alert` and `notice` as well as a general purpose `flash` bucket.

```
redirect_to post_url(@post), :alert => "Watch it, mister!"
redirect_to post_url(@post), :status=> :found, :notice => "Pay attention
to the road"
redirect_to post_url(@post), :status => 301, :flash => { :updated_post_id
=> @post.id }
redirect_to { :action=>'atom' }, :alert => "Something serious happened"
```

Courtenay says...

Remember that redirect and render statements don't magically halt execution of your controller action method. To prevent `DoubleRenderError`, consider explicitly calling `return` after `redirect_to` or render like this:

```
def show
  @user = User.find(params[:id])
  if @user.activated?
    render :action => 'activated' and return
  end
  ...
end
```

4.6 Controller/View Communication

When a view template is rendered, it generally uses data that the controller has pulled from the database. In other words, the controller gets what it needs from the model layer, and hands it off to the view.

The way Rails implements controller-to-view data handoffs is through instance variables. Typically, a controller action initializes one or more instance variables. Those instance variables can then be used by the view.

There's a bit of irony (and possible confusion for newcomers) in the choice of instance variables to share data between controllers and views. The main reason that instance variables exist is so that objects (whether `Controller` objects, `String` objects, and so on) can hold on to data that they don't share with other objects. When your controller action is executed, everything is happening in the context of a controller object—an instance of, say, `DemoController` or `EventController`. *Context* includes the fact that every instance variable in the code belongs to the controller instance.

When the view template is rendered, the context is that of a different object, an instance of `ActionView::Base`. That instance has its own instance variables, and does not have access to those of the controller object.

So instance variables, on the face of it, are about the worst choice for a way for two objects to share data. However, it's possible to make it happen—or make it appear to happen. What Rails does is to loop through the controller object's variables and, for each one, create an instance variable for the view object, with the same name and containing the same data.

It's kind of labor-intensive, for the framework: It's like copying over a grocery list by hand. But the end result is that things are easier for you, the programmer. If you're a Ruby purist, you might wince a little bit at the thought of instance variables serving to connect objects, rather than separate them. On the other hand, being a Ruby purist should also include understanding the fact that you can do lots of different things in Ruby—such as copying instance variables in a loop. So there's nothing really un-Ruby-like about it. And it does provide a seamless connection, from the programmer's perspective, between a controller and the template it's rendering.

Stephen says . . .

I'm a cranky old man, and dammit, Rails is wrong, wrong, wrong. Using instance variables to share data with the view sucks. If you want to see how my Decent Exposure library helps you avoid this horrible practice, skip ahead to Section 10.1.5.

4.7 Filters

Filters enable controllers to run shared pre and post processing code for its actions. These filters can be used to do authentication, caching, or auditing before the intended action is performed. Filter declarations are macro style class methods, that is, they appear at the top of your controller method, inside the class context, before method definitions. We also leave off the parentheses around the method arguments, to emphasize their declarative nature, like this:

```
before_filter :require_authentication
```

As with many other macro-style methods in Rails, you can pass as many symbols as you want to the filter method:

```
before_filter :security_scan, :audit, :compress
```

Or you can break them out into separate lines, like this:

```
before_filter :security_scan
before_filter :audit
before_filter :compress
```

In contrast to the somewhat similar callback methods of Active Record, you can't implement a filter method on a controller by adding a method named `before_filter` or `after_filter`.

You should make your filter methods `protected` or `private`; otherwise, they might be callable as public actions on your controller (via the default route).

Tim says...

In addition to `protected` and `private`, one can declare a method should never be dispatched with the more intention-revealing `hide_action`.

Importantly, filters have access to `request`, `response`, and all the instance variables set by other filters in the chain or by the action (in the case of `after` filters). Filters can set instance variables to be used by the requested action, and often do so.

4.7.1   Filter Inheritance

Controller inheritance hierarchies share filters downward. Your average Rails application has an `ApplicationController` from which all other controllers inherit, so if you wanted to add filters that are always run no matter what, that would be the place to do so.

```
class ApplicationController < ActionController::Base
  after_filter :compress
```

Subclasses can also add and/or skip already defined filters without affecting the superclass. For example, consider the two related classes in Listing 4.1, and how they interact.

Listing 4.1 A pair of cooperating before filters

```
class BankController < ActionController::Base
  before_filter :audit

  protected

  def audit
    # record this controller's actions and parameters in an audit log
  end

end
```

```
class VaultController < BankController
  before_filter :verify_credentials

  protected

  def verify_credentials
    # make sure the user is allowed into the vault
  end

end
```

Any actions performed on `BankController` (or any of its subclasses) will cause the `audit` method to be called before the requested action is executed. On the `VaultController`, first the `audit` method is called, followed by `verify_credentials`, because that's the order in which the filters were specified. (Filters are executed in the class context where they're declared, and the `BankController` has to be loaded before `VaultController`, since it's the parent class.)

If the audit method happens to call `render` or `redirect_to` for whatever reason, `verify_credentials` and the requested action are never called. This is called halting the filter chain.

4.7.2 Filter Types

A filter can take one of three forms: method reference (symbol), external class, or block. The first is by far the most common and works by referencing a protected method somewhere in the inheritance hierarchy of the controller. In the bank example in Listing 2.1, both `BankController` and `VaultController` use this form.

Filter Classes

Using an external class makes for more easily reused generic filters, such as output compression. External filter classes are implemented by having a static filter method on any class and then passing this class to the filter method, as in Listing 4.2. The name of the class method should match the type of filter desired (e.g., before, after, around).

Listing 4.2 An output compression filter

```
class OutputCompressionFilter
  def self.after(controller)
    controller.response.body = compress(controller.response.body)
  end
end
```

```
class NewspaperController < ActionController::Base
  after_filter OutputCompressionFilter
end
```

The method of the `Filter` class is passed the controller instance it is filtering. It gets full access to the controller and can manipulate it as it sees fit. The fact that it gets an instance of the controller to play with also makes it seem like feature envy, and frankly, I haven't had much use for this technique.

Inline Method

The inline method (using a block parameter to the filter method) can be used to quickly do something small that doesn't require a lot of explanation or just as a quick test.

```
class WeblogController < ActionController::Base
  before_filter do
    redirect_to new_user_session_path unless authenticated?
  end
end
```

The block is executed in the context of the controller instance, using `instance_eval`. This means that the block has access to both the request and response objects complete with convenience methods for params, session, template, and assigns.

4.7.3 Filter Chain Ordering

Using `before_filter` and `after_filter` appends the specified filters to the existing chain. That's usually just fine, but sometimes you care more about the order in which the filters are executed. When that's the case, you can use `prepend_before_filter` and `prepend_after_filter`. Filters added by these methods will be put at the beginning of their respective chain and executed before the rest, like the example in Listing 4.3.

Listing 4.3 An example of prepending before filters

```
class ShoppingController < ActionController::Base
  before_filter :verify_open_shop

class CheckoutController < ShoppingController
  prepend_before_filter :ensure_items_in_cart, :ensure_items_in_stock
```

The filter chain for the `CheckoutController` is now `:ensure_items_in_cart`, `:ensure_items_in_stock`, `:verify_open_shop`. So if either of the `ensure` filters halts execution, we'll never get around to seeing if the shop is open.

You may pass multiple filter arguments of each type as well as a filter block. If a block is given, it is treated as the last argument.

4.7.4 Around Filters

Around filters wrap an action, executing code both before and after the action that they wrap. They may be declared as method references, blocks, or objects with an around class method.

To use a method as an around_filter, pass a symbol naming the Ruby method. Use yield within the method to run the action.

For example, Listing 4.4 has an around filter that logs exceptions (not that you need to do anything like this in your application; it's just an example).

Listing 4.4 An around filter to log exceptions

```
around_filter :catch_exceptions

private

  def catch_exceptions
    yield
  rescue => exception
    logger.debug "Caught exception! #{exception}"
    raise
  end
```

To use a block as an around_filter, pass a block taking as args both the controller and the action parameters. You can't call yield from blocks in Ruby, so explicitly invoke call on the action parameter:

```
around_filter do |controller, action|
  logger.debug "before #{controller.action_name}"
  action.call
  logger.debug "after #{controller.action_name}"
end
```

Tim says...

> Since processing of filter blocks is done with instance_eval, you don't actually have to use the controller parameter in Rails 3. It's there for backward-compatibility reasons.

Controllers

To use a filter object with `around_filter`, pass an object responding to `:around`. With a filter method, yield to the block like this:

```
around_filter BenchmarkingFilter

class BenchmarkingFilter
  def self.around(controller)
    Benchmark.measure { yield }
  end
end
```

4.7.5 Filter Chain Skipping

Declaring a filter on a base class conveniently applies to its subclasses, but sometimes a subclass should skip some of the filters it inherits from a superclass:

```
class ApplicationController < ActionController::Base
  before_filter :authenticate
  around_filter :catch_exceptions
end

class SignupController < ApplicationController
  skip_before_filter :authenticate
end

class HackedTogetherController < ApplicationController
  skip_filter :catch_exceptions
end
```

4.7.6 Filter Conditions

Filters may be limited to specific actions by declaring the actions to include or exclude, using `:only` or `:except` options. Both options accept single actions (like `:only => :index`) or arrays of actions (`:except => [:foo, :bar]`).

```
class Journal < ActionController::Base
  before_filter :authorize, :only => [:edit, :delete]

  around_filter :except => :index do |controller, action_block|
    results = Profiler.run(&action_block)
    controller.response.sub! "</body>", "#{results}</body>"
  end

  private

  def authorize
    # Redirect to login unless authenticated.
  end
end
```

4.7.7 Filter Chain Halting

The `before_filter` and `around_filter` methods may halt the request before the body of a controller action method is run. This is useful, for example, to deny access to unauthenticated users. As mentioned earlier, all you have to do to halt the before filter chain is call `render` or `redirect_to`. After filters will not be executed if the before filter chain is halted.

Around filters halt the request unless the action block is called. If an around filter returns before yielding, it is effectively halting the chain and any after filters will not be run.

4.8 Verification

This official Rails verification plugin[5] provides a class-level method for specifying that certain actions are guarded against being called without certain prerequisites being met. It is essentially a special kind of `before_filter`.

An action may be guarded against being invoked without certain request parameters being set or without certain session values existing. When a verification is violated, values may be inserted into the flash and a redirection triggered. If no specific action is configured, verification failure will in a `400 Bad Request` response.

Note that these verifications are apart from the business rules expressed in your models. They do not examine the content of the session or the parameters nor do they replace model validations.

4.8.1 Example Usage

The following example prevents the `updates` action from being invoked unless the `privileges` key is present in `params`. The request will be redirected to the `settings` action if the verification fails.

```
verify :params => "privileges",
       :only => :update,
       :redirect_to => { :action => "settings" }
```

---

5. `rails plugin install git://github.com/rails/verification.git`

4.8.2 Options

The following options are valid parameters to the `verify` method.

:params A single key or an array of keys that must be present in the `params` hash in order for the action(s) to be safely called.

:session A single key or an array of keys that must be present in the `session` in order for the action(s) to be safely called.

:flash A single key or an array of keys that must be present in the `flash` in order for the action(s) to be safely called.

:method A single key or an array of keys that must match the current request method in order for the action(s) to be safely called. Valid keys are symbols like `:get` and `:post`.

:xhr Set to `true` or `false` to ensure that the request is coming from an Ajax call or not.

:add_flash A hash of name/value pairs that should be merged into the session‚Äôs flash if verification fails.

:add_headers A hash of name/value pairs that should be merged into the response‚Äôs headers hash if verification fails.

:redirect_to The parameters to be used when redirecting if verfication fails. You can redirect either to a named route or to the action in some controller.

:render The render parameters to be used if verification fails.

:only Only apply this verification to the actions specified in the array. (Single value permitted).

:except Do not apply this verification to the actions specified in the array (Single value permitted).

4.9 Streaming

Rails has built-in support for streaming binary content back to the browser, as opposed to its normal duties rendering view templates.

4.9.1 Via **render :text => proc**

The `:text` option of the `render` method optionally accepts a Proc object, which can be used to stream on-the-fly generated data to the browser or control page generation on a fine-grained basis. The latter should generally be avoided unless you know exactly what you're doing, as it violates the separation between code and content.

Two arguments are passed to the proc you supply, a `response` object and an `output` object. The `response` object is equivalent to the what you'd expect in the context of the controller, and can be used to control various things in the HTTP response, such as the `Content-Type` header. The output object is an writable IO-like object, so one can call `write` and `flush` on it.

The following example demonstrates how one can stream a large amount of on-the-fly generated data to the browser:

```
# Streams about 180 MB of generated data to the browser.
render :text => proc { |response, output|
  10_000_000.times do |i|
    output.write("This is line #{i}\n")
  end
}
```

Rails also supports sending buffers and files with two methods in the `ActionController::Streaming` module: `send_data` and `send_file`.

4.9.2 `send_data(data, options = {})`

The `send_data` method allows you to send textual or binary data in a buffer to the user as a named file. You can set options that affect the content type and apparent filename, and alter whether an attempt is made to display the data inline with other content in the browser or the user is prompted to download it as an attachment.

Options

The `send_data` method has the following options:

:filename Suggests a filename for the browser to use.

:type Specifies an HTTP content type. Defaults to `'application/octet-stream'`.

:disposition Specifies whether the file will be shown inline or downloaded. Valid values are `inline` and `attachment` (default).

status Specifies the status code to send with the response. Defaults to `'200 OK'`.

Usage Examples

Creating a download of a dynamically generated tarball:

```
send_data generate_tgz('dir'), :filename => 'dir.tgz'
```

Sending a dynamic image to the browser, like for instance a captcha system:

```
require 'RMagick'

class CaptchaController < ApplicationController

  def image
    # create an RMagic canvas and render difficult to read text on it
    ...

    img = canvas.flatten_images
    img.format = "JPG"

    # send it to the browser
    send_data img.to_blob, :disposition => 'inline', :type => 'image/jpg'
  end
end
```

4.9.3 `send_file(path, options = {})`

The `send_file` method sends an existing file down to the client using `Rack::Sendfile` middleware, which intercepts the response and replaces it with a webserver specific `X-Sendfile` header. The web server then becomes responsible for writing the file contents to the client instead of Rails. This can dramatically reduce the amount of work accomplished in Ruby and takes advantage of the web servers optimized file delivery code.[6]

Options

Here are the options available for `send_file`:

`:filename` suggests a filename for the browser to use. Defaults to `File.basename (path)`

`:type` specifies an HTTP content type. Defaults to `'application/octet-stream'`.

`:disposition` specifies whether the file will be shown inline or downloaded. Valid values are `'inline'` and `'attachment'` (default).

`:status` specifies the status code to send with the response. Defaults to `'200 OK'`.

`:url_based_filename` should be set to `true` if you want the browser to guess the filename from the URL, which is necessary for i18n filenames on certain browsers (setting `:filename` overrides this option).

---

6. More information, particularly about web server configuration available at `http://rack.rubyforge.org/doc/Rack/Sendfile.html`

There's also a lot more to read about `Content-*` HTTP headers[7] if you'd like to provide the user with additional information that Rails doesn't natively support (such as `Content-Description`).

Security Considerations

Note that the `send_file` method can be used to read any file accessible to the user running the Rails server process, so be extremely careful to sanitize[8] the `path` parameter if it's in any way coming from an untrusted users.

If you want a quick example, try the following controller code:

```
class FileController < ActionController::Base
  def download
    send_file(params[:path])
  end
end
```

Give it a route

```
match 'file/download' => 'file#download'
```

then fire up your server and request any file on your system:

```
$ curl http://localhost:3000/file/download?path=/etc/hosts
##
# Host Database
#
# localhost is used to configure the loopback interface
# when the system is booting.  Do not change this entry.
##
127.0.0.1       localhost
255.255.255.255 broadcasthost
::1             localhost
fe80::1%lo0     localhost
```

Be aware that your sent file may be cached by proxies and browsers. The `Pragma` and `Cache-Control` headers declare how the file may be cached by intermediaries. They default to require clients to validate with the server before releasing cached responses.[9]

Usage Examples

Here's the simplest example, just a simple zip file download:

```
send_file '/path/to.zip'
```

---

7. See the official spec at `http://www.w3.org/Protocols/rfc2616/rfc2616-sec14.html`.
8. Heiko Webers has an old, yet still useful write-up about sanitizing filenames at `http://www.rorsecurity.info/2007/03/27/working-with-files-in-rails/`.
9. See `http://www.mnot.net/cache_docs/` for an overview of web caching.

Courtenay says...

There are few legitimate reasons to serve static files through Rails. Unless you are protecting content, I strongly recommend you cache the file after sending it. There are a few ways to do this. Since a correctly configured web server will serve files in `public/` and bypass `rails`, the easiest is to just copy the newly generated file to the `public` directory after sending it:

```
public_dir = File.join(Rails.root, 'public', controller_path)
FileUtils.mkdir_p(public_dir)
FileUtils.cp(filename, File.join(public_dir, filename))
```

All subsequent views of this resource will be served by the web server. Alternatively, you can try using the `caches_page` directive, which will automatically do something similar for you. (Caching is covered comprehensively in Chapter 17.)

Sending a JPG to be displayed inline requires specification of the MIME content-type:

```
send_file '/path/to.jpg',
          :type => 'image/jpeg',
          :disposition => 'inline'
```

This will show a 404 HTML page in the browser. We append a `charset` declaration to the MIME type information:

```
send_file '/path/to/404.html,
          :type => 'text/html; charset=utf-8',
          :status => 404
```

How about streaming an FLV file to a browser-based Flash video player?

```
send_file @video_file.path,
          :filename => video_file.title + '.flv',
          :type => 'video/x-flv',
          :disposition => 'inline'
```

Regardless of how you do it, you may wonder why you would need a mechanism to send files to the browser anyway, since it already has one built in—requesting files from the `public` directory. Well, often a web application will front files that need to be protected from public access.[10] (Practically every porn site in existence!)

---

10. Ben Curtis writes up an excellent approach to securing downloads at `http://www.bencurtis.com/archives/2006/11/serving-protected-downloads-with-rails/`.

4.10 Conclusion

In this chapter, we covered some concepts at the very core of how Rails works: the dispatcher and how controllers render views. Importantly, we covered the use of controller action filters, which you will use constantly, for all sorts of purposes. The Action Controller API is fundamental knowledge, which you need to understand well along your way to becoming an expert Rails programmer.

Moving on, we'll leave Action Pack and head over to the other major component API of Rails: Active Record.

Controllers

CHAPTER 5

Working with Active Record

An object that wraps a row in a database table or view, encapsulates the database access, and adds domain logic on that data.

—Martin Fowler, *Patterns of Enterprise Architecture*

The Active Record pattern, identified by Martin Fowler in his seminal work, *Patterns of Enterprise Architecture*, maps one domain class to one database table, and one instance of that class to each row of that database. It is a simple approach that, while not perfectly applicable in all cases, provides a powerful framework for database access and object persistence in your application.

The Rails Active Record framework includes mechanisms for representing models and their relationships, CRUD (Create, Read, Update, and Delete) operations, complex searches, validation, callbacks, and many more features. It relies heavily on *convention over configuration*, so it's easy to use when you're creating a new database schema that can follow those conventions. However, Active Record also provides configuration settings that let you adapt it to work well with legacy database schemas that don't necessarily conform to Rails conventions.

According to Martin Fowler, delivering the keynote address at the inaugural Rails conference in 2006, Ruby on Rails has successfully taken the Active Record pattern much further than anyone imagined it could go. It shows you what you can achieve when you have a single-minded focus on a set of ideals, which in the case of Rails is simplicity.

5.1 The Basics

For the sake of completeness, let's briefly review the basics of how Active Record works. In order to create a new model class, the first thing you do is to declare it as a subclass of `ActiveRecord::Base`, using Ruby's class extension syntax:

```
class Client < ActiveRecord::Base
end
```

By convention, an Active Record class named `Client` will be mapped to the `clients` table. Rails understands pluralization, as covered in the section "Pluralization" in this chapter. Also by convention, Active Record will expect an `id` column to use as primary key. It should be an integer and incrementing of the key should be managed automatically by the database server when creating new records. Note how the class itself makes no mention of the table name, columns, or their datatypes.

Each instance of an Active Record class provides access to the data from one row of the backing database table, in an object-oriented manner. The columns of that row are represented as attributes of the object, using straightforward type conversions (i.e. Ruby strings for varchars, Ruby dates for dates, and so on), and with no default data validation. Attributes are inferred from the column definition pertaining to the tables with which they're linked. Adding, removing, and changing attributes and their types are done by changing the columns of the table in the database.

When you're running a Rails server in development mode, changes to the database schema are reflected in the Active Record objects immediately, via the web browser. However, if you make changes to the schema while you have your Rails console running, the changes will not be reflected automatically, although it is possible to pick up changes manually by typing `reload!` at the console.

Courtenay says...

Active Record is a great example of the Rails "Golden Path." If you keep within its limitations, you can go far, fast. Stray from the path, and you might get stuck in the mud. This Golden Path involves many conventions, like naming your tables in the plural form ("users"). It's common for new developers to Rails and rival web-framework evangelists to complain about how tables must be named in a particular manner, how there are no constraints in the database layer, that foreign keys are handled all wrong, enterprise systems must have composite primary keys, and more. Get the complaining out of your system now, because all these defaults are simply defaults, and in most cases can be overridden with a single line of code or a plugin.

5.2 Macro-Style Methods

Most of the important classes you write while coding a Rails application are configured using what I call macro-style method invocations (also known in some circles as a domain-specific language or DSL). Basically, the idea is to have a highly readable block of code at the top of your class that makes it immediately clear how it is configured.

Macro-style invocations are usually placed at the top of the file, and for good reason. Those methods declaratively tell Rails how to manage instances, perform data validation and callbacks, and relate with other models. Many of them do some amount of metaprogramming, meaning that they participate in adding behavior to your class at runtime, in the form of additional instance variables and methods.

5.2.1 Relationship Declarations

For example, look at the `Client` class with some relationships declared. We'll talk about associations extensively in Chapter 7, Active Record Associations, but all I want to do right now is to illustrate what I'm talking about when I say macro-style:

```
class Client < ActiveRecord::Base
  has_many :billing_codes
  has_many :billable_weeks
  has_many :timesheets, :through => :billable_weeks
end
```

As a result of those three `has_many` declarations, the `Client` class gains at least three new attributes, proxy objects that let you manipulate the associated collections interactively.

I still remember the first time I sat with an experienced Java programmer friend of mine to teach him some Ruby and Rails. After minutes of profound confusion, an almost visible light bulb appeared over his head as he proclaimed, "Oh! They're methods!"

Indeed, they're regular old method calls, in the context of the class object. We leave the parentheses off to emphasize the declarative intention. That's a style issue, but it just doesn't feel right to me with the parentheses in place, as in the following code snippet:

```
class Client < ActiveRecord::Base
  has_many(:billing_codes)
  has_many(:billable_weeks)
  has_many(:timesheets, :through => :billable_weeks)
end
```

When the Ruby interpreter loads `client.rb`, it executes those `has_many` methods, which, again, are defined as class methods of Active Record's `Base` class. They are executed in the context of the `Client` class, adding attributes that are subsequently available to `Client` instances. It's a programming model that is potentially strange to newcomers, but quickly becomes second nature to the Rails programmer.

5.2.2   Convention over Configuration

Convention over configuration is one of the guiding principles of Ruby on Rails. If we follow Rails conventions, very little explicit configuration is needed, which stands in stark contrast to the reams of configuration that are required to get even a simple application running in other technologies.

It's not that a newly bootstrapped Rails application comes with default configuration in place already, reflecting the conventions that will be used. It's that the conventions are baked into the framework, actually hard-coded into its behavior, and you need to override the default behavior with explicit configuration when applicable.

It's also worth mentioning that most configuration happens in close proximity to what you're configuring. You will see associations, validations, and callback declarations at the top of most Active Record models.

I suspect that the first explicit configuration (over convention) that many of us deal with in Active Record is the mapping between class name and database table, since by default Rails assumes that our database name is simply the pluralized form of our class name.

5.2.3   Setting Names Manually

The `set_table_name` and `set_primary_key` methods let you use any table and primary names youd like, but youll have to specify them explicitly in your model class. It's only a couple of extra lines per model, but on a large application it adds unnecessary complexity, so don't do it if you don't absolutely have to.

When you're not at liberty to dictate the naming guidelines for your database schema, such as when a separate DBA group controls all database schemas, then you probably don't have a choice. But if you have flexibility, you should really just follow Rails conventions. They might not be what you're used to, but following them will save you time and unnecessary headaches.

5.2.4   Legacy Naming Schemes

If you are working with legacy schemas, you may be tempted to automatically `set_table_name` everywhere, whether you need it or not. Before you get accustomed to doing that, learn the additional options available that might just be more DRY and make your life easier.

Let's assume you need to turn off table pluralization altogether; you would set the following attribute to your `config/application.rb`:

```
config.active_record.pluralize_table_names = false
```

There are various other useful attributes of `ActiveRecord::Base`, provided for configuring Rails to work with legacy naming schemes.

primary_key_prefix_type

Accessor for the prefix type that will be prepended to every primary key column name. If `:table_name` is specified, Active Record will look for `tableid` instead of `id` as the primary column. If `:table_name_with_underscore` is specified, Active Record will look for `table_id` instead of `id`.

table_name_prefix

Some departments prefix table names with the name of the database. Set this attribute accordingly to avoid having to include the prefix in all of your model class names.

table_name_suffix

Similar to prefix, but adds a common ending to all table names.

5.3 Defining Attributes

The list of attributes associated with an Active Record model class is not coded explicitly. At runtime, the Active Record model examines the database schema directly from the server. Adding, removing, and changing attributes and their type is done by manipulating the database itself via Active Record migrations.

The practical implication of the Active Record pattern is that you have to define your database table structure and make sure it exists in the database prior to working with your persistent models. Some people may have issues with that design philosophy, especially if they're coming from a background in top-down design.

The Rails way is undoubtedly to have model classes that map closely to your database schema. On the other hand, remember you can have models that are simple Ruby classes and do not inherit from `ActiveRecord::Base`. Among other things, it is common to use non-Active Record model classes to encapsulate data and logic for the view layer.

5.3.1 Default Attribute Values

Migrations let you define default attribute values by passing a `:default` option to the `column` method, but most of the time you'll want to set default attribute values at the model layer, not the database layer. Default values are part of your domain logic and should be kept together with the rest of the domain logic of your application, in the model layer.

A common example is the case when your model should return the string "n/a" instead of a nil (or empty) string for an attribute that has not been populated yet. Seems simple enough and it's a good way to learn how attributes exist at runtime.

To begin, let's whip up a quick spec describing the desired behavior.

```
describe TimesheetEntry do
  it "category should be 'n/a' if not available" do
    entry = TimesheetEntry.new
    entry.category.should == 'n/a'
  end
end
```

We run that test and it fails, as expected. Active Record doesn't provide us with any class-level methods to define default values for models declaratively. So it seems we'll have to create an explicit attribute accessor that provides a default value.

Normally, attribute accessors are handled magically by Active Record's internals, but in this case we're overriding the magic with an explicit getter. All we need to do is to define a method with the same name as the attribute and use Ruby's || operator, which will short-circuit if @category is not nil.

```
class TimesheetEntry < ActiveRecord::Base
  def category
    @category || 'n/a'
  end
end
```

Now we run the test and it passes. Great. Are we done? Not quite. We should test a case when the real category value should be returned. I'll insert an example with a not-nil category.

```
describe TimesheetEntry do
  it "should return category when available" do
    entry = TimesheetEntry.new(:category => "TR3W")
    entry.category.should == "TR3W"
  end

  it "should have a category of 'n/a' if not available" do
    entry = TimesheetEntry.new
    entry.category.should == 'n/a'
  end
end
```

Uh-oh. The first example fails. Seems our default 'n/a' string is being returned no matter what. That means that `@category` must not get set. Should we even know that it is getting set or not? It is an implementation detail of Active Record, is it not?

The fact that Rails does not use instance variables like `@category` to store the model attributes is in fact an implementation detail. But model instances have a couple of methods, `write_attribute` and `read_attribute`, conveniently provided by Active Record for the purposes of overriding default accessors, which is exactly what we're trying to do. Let's fix our `TimesheetEntry` class.

```ruby
class TimesheetEntry < ActiveRecord::Base
  def category
    read_attribute(:category) || 'n/a'
  end
end
```

Now the test passes. How about a simple example of using `write_attribute`?

```ruby
class SillyFortuneCookie < ActiveRecord::Base
  def message=(txt)
    write_attribute(:message, txt + ' in bed')
  end
end
```

Alternatively, both of these examples could have been written with the shorter forms of reading and writing attributes, using square brackets.

```ruby
class Specification < ActiveRecord::Base
  def tolerance
    self[:tolerance] || 'n/a'
  end
end

class SillyFortuneCookie < ActiveRecord::Base
  def message=(txt)
    self[:message] = txt + ' in bed'
  end
end
```

5.3.2 Serialized Attributes

One of Active Record's coolest features is the ability to mark a column of type `text` as being serialized. Whatever object (more accurately, graph of objects) you assign to that attribute will be stored in the database as YAML, Ruby's native serialization format.

Sebastian says…

TEXT columns usually have a maximum size of 64K and if your serialized attributes exceeds the size constraints, you'll run into a lot of errors. On the other hand, if your serialized attributes are that big, you might want to rethink what you're doing. At least move them into a separate table and use a larger column type if your server allows it.

One of the first thing that new Rails developers do when they discover the `serialize` declaration is to use it to store a hash of arbitrary objects related to user preferences. Why bother with the complexity of a separate preferences table if you can denormalize that data into the users table instead?

```
class User < ActiveRecord::Base
  serialize :preferences, Hash
end
```

The optional second parameter (used in the example) takes a class that limits the type of object that can be stored. The serialized object must be of that class on retrieval or `SerializationTypeMismatch` will be raised. Similarly to readonly attributes, access to the list of serialized attributes is handled through `serialized_attributes`.

The API does not give us an easy way to set a default value. That's unfortunate, because it would be nice to be able to assume that our preferences attribute is already initialized when we want to use it.

```
user = User.new
# the following line will raise NoMethodError unless preferences has a
default
user.preferences[:inline_help] = false
```

Unless a value has already been set for the attribute, it's going to be `nil`. You might be tempted to set a default YAML string for the serialized attribute at the database level, so that it's not `nil` when you're using a newly created object:

```
add_column :users, :preferences, :text, :default => "--- {}"
```

However, that approach won't work with MySQL 5.x, which ignores default values for binary and text columns. One possible solution is to overload the attribute's reader method with logic that sets the default value if it's nil.

```
def preferences
  read_attribute(:preferences) || write_attribute(:preferences, {})
end
```

I prefer this method over the alternative, using an `after_initialize` callback, because it incurs a small performance hit only when the preferences attribute is actually used and not at instantiation time of every single `User` object in your system.

5.4 CRUD: Creating, Reading, Updating, Deleting

The four standard operations of a database system combine to form a popular acronym: CRUD. It sounds somewhat negative, because as a synonym for *garbage* or *unwanted accumulation* the word *crud* in English has a rather bad connotation. However, in Rails circles, use of the word CRUD is benign. In fact, as in earlier chapters, designing your app to function primarily as RESTful CRUD operations is considered a best practice!

5.4.1 Creating New Active Record Instances

The most straightforward way to create a new instance of an Active Record model is by using a regular Ruby constructor, the class method new. New objects can be instantiated as either empty (by omitting parameters) or pre-set with attributes, but not yet saved. Just pass a hash with key names matching the associated table column names. In both instances, valid attribute keys are determined by the column names of the associated table—hence you can't have attributes that aren't part of the table columns.

You can find out if an Active Record object is saved by looking at the value of its id, or programmatically, by using the methods new_record? and persisted?:

```
>> c = Client.new
=> #<Client id: nil, name: nil, code: nil>
>> c.new_record?
=> true
>> c.persisted?
=> false
```

Active Record constructors take an optional block, which can be used to do additional initialization. The block is executed after any passed-in attributes are set on the instance:

```
>> c = Client.new do |client|
?> client.name = "Nile River Co."
>> client.code = "NRC"
>> end
=> #<Client id: 1, name: "Nile River Co.", code: "NRC">
```

Active Record has a handy-dandy create class method that creates a new instance, persists it to the database, and returns it in one operation:

```
>> c = Client.create(:name => "Nile River, Co.", :code => "NRC")
=> #<Client id: 1, name: "Nile River, Co.", code: "NRC" ...>
```

The create method takes an optional block, just like new.

5.4.2 Reading Active Record Objects

Finding an existing object by its primary key is very simple, and is probably one of the first things we all learn about Rails when we first pick up the framework. Just invoke find with the key of the specific instance you want to retrieve. Remember that if an instance is not found, a RecordNotFound exception is raised.

```
>> first_project = Project.find(1)
=>  #<Project id: 1 ...>
>> boom_client = Client.find(99)
ActiveRecord::RecordNotFound: Couldn't find Client with ID=99

>> all_clients = Client.all
=> [#<Client id: 1, name: "Paper Jam Printers", code: "PJP" ...>,
#<Client id: 2, name: "Goodness Steaks", code: "GOOD_STEAKS" ...>]

>> first_client = Client.first
=> #<Client id: 1, name: "Paper Jam Printers", code: "PJP" ...>
```

By the way, it is entirely common for methods in Ruby to return different types depending on the parameters used, as illustrated in the example. Depending on how find is invoked, you will get either a single Active Record object or an array of them.

For convenience, first, last and all also exist as syntactic sugar wrappers around the find method.

```
> Product.last
=> #<Product id: 1, name: "leaf", sku: nil, created_at: "2010-01-12
03:34:41", updated_at: "2010-01-12 03:34:41">
```

Finally, the find method also understands arrays of ids, and raises a RecordNotFound exception if it can't find all of the ids specified:

```
> Product.find([1, 2])
ActiveRecord::RecordNotFound: Couldn't find all Products with IDs (1,
 2) (found 1 results, but was looking for 2)
```

5.4.3 Reading and Writing Attributes

After you have retrieved a model instance from the database, you can access each of its columns in several ways. The easiest (and clearest to read) is simply with dot notation:

```
>> first_client.name
=> "Paper Jam Printers"
>> first_client.code
=> "PJP"
```

The private `read_attribute` method of Active Record, covered briefly in an earlier section, is useful to know about, and comes in handy when you want to override a default attribute accessor. To illustrate, while still in the Rails console, I'll go ahead and reopen the `Client` class on the fly and override the `name` accessor to return the value from the database, but reversed:

```
>> class Client < ActiveRecord::Base
>>   def name
>>      read_attribute(:name).reverse
>>   end
>> end
=> nil
>> first_client.name
=> "sretnirP maJ repaP"
```

Hopefully it's not too painfully obvious for me to demonstrate why you need `read_attribute` in that scenario. Recursion is a bitch, if it's unexpected:

```
>> class Client < ActiveRecord::Base
>> def name
>>    self.name.reverse
>> end
>> end
=> nil
>> first_client.name
SystemStackError: stack level too deep
        from (irb):21:in 'name'
>> class Client < ActiveRecord::Base from (irb):21:in 'name'
>> class Client < ActiveRecord::Base from (irb):24
```

As can be expected by the existence of a `read_attribute` method (and as we covered earlier in the chapter), there is also a `write_attribute` method that lets you change attribute values. Just as with attribute getter methods, you can override the setter methods and provide your own behavior:

```
class Project < ActiveRecord::Base
  # The description for a project cannot be changed to a blank string
  def description=(new_value)
    write_attribute(:description, new_value) unless new_value.blank?
  end
end
```

The preceding example illustrates a way to do basic validation, since it checks to make sure that a value is not blank before allowing assignment. However, as we'll see in Chapter 8, Validations, there are better ways to do this.

Active
Record

Hash Notation

Yet another way to access attributes is using the `[attribute_name]` operator, which lets you access the attribute as if it were a regular hash.

```
>> first_client['name']
=> "Paper Jam Printers"
>> first_client[:name]
=> "Paper Jam Printers"
```

String versus symbol

Many Rails methods accept symbol and string parameters interchangeably, and that is potentially very confusing. Which is more correct? The general rule is to use symbols when the string is a name for something, and a string when it's a value. You should probably be using symbols when it comes to keys of options hashes and the like.

The **attributes** Method

There is also an `attributes` method that returns a hash with each attribute and its corresponding value as returned by `read_attribute`. If you use your own custom attribute reader and writer methods, it's important to remember that `attributes` will not use custom attribute readers when accessing its values, but `attributes=` (which lets you do mass assignment) does invoke custom attribute writers.

```
>> first_client.attributes
=> {"name"=>"Paper Jam Printers", "code"=>"PJP", "id"=>1}
```

Being able to grab a hash of all attributes at once is useful when you want to iterate over all of them or pass them in bulk to another function. Note that the hash returned from `attributes` is not a reference to an internal structure of the Active Record object. It is copy, which means that changing its values will have no effect on the object it came from.

```
>> atts = first_client.attributes
=> {"name"=>"Paper Jam Printers", "code"=>"PJP", "id"=>1}
>> atts["name"] = "Def Jam Printers"
=> "Def Jam Printers"
>> first_client.attributes
=> {"name"=>"Paper Jam Printers", "code"=>"PJP", "id"=>1}
```

To make changes to an Active Record object's attributes in bulk, it is possible to pass a hash to the `attributes` writer.

5.4.4   Accessing and Manipulating Attributes Before They Are Typecast

The Active Record connection adapters, classes that implement behavior specific to databases, fetch results as strings. Rails then takes care of converting them to other datatypes if necessary, based on the type of the database column. For instance, integer types are cast to instances of Ruby's `Fixnum` class, and so on.

Even if you're working with a new instance of an Active Record object, and have passed in constructor values as strings, they will be typecast to their proper type when you try to access those values as attributes.

Sometimes you want to be able to read (or manipulate) the raw attribute data without having the column-determined typecast run its course first, and that can be done by using the *attribute*`_before_type_cast` accessors that are automatically created in your model.

For example, consider the need to deal with currency strings typed in by your end users. Unless you are encapsulating currency values in a currency class (highly recommended, by the way) you need to deal with those pesky dollar signs and commas. Assuming that our `Timesheet` model had a rate attribute defined as a `:decimal` type, the following code would strip out the extraneous characters before typecasting for the save operation:

```
class Timesheet < ActiveRecord::Base
  before_validation :fix_rate

  def fix_rate
    self[:rate] = rate_before_type_cast.tr('$,','')
  end
end
```

5.4.5   Reloading

The `reload` method does a query to the database and resets the attributes of an Active Record object. The optional options argument is passed to find when reloading so you may do, for example, `record.reload(:lock => true)` to reload the same record with an exclusive row lock. (See the section "Database Locking" later in this chapter.)

5.4.6   Cloning

Producing a copy of an Active Record object is done simply by calling `clone`, which produces a shallow copy of that object. It is important to note that no associations will get copied, even though they are stored internally as instance variables.

5.4.7 Dynamic Attribute-Based Finders

Since one of the most common operations in many applications is to simply query on one or two columns, Rails has an easy and effective way to do these queries without having to resort to `where`. They work thanks to the magic of Ruby's `method_missing` callback, which is executed whenever you invoke a method that hasn't been defined yet.

Dynamic finder methods begin with `find_by_` or `find_all_by_`, indicating whether you want a single value or array of results returned. The semantics are similar to calling the method `first` versus the `all` option.

```
>> City.find_by_name("Hackensack")
=> #<City id: 15942, name: "Hackensack", latitude: "40.8858330000",
longitude: "-74.0438890000", state: "NJ">

>> City.find_all_by_name("Atlanta").collect(&:state)
=> ["GA", "MI", "TX"]
```

It's also possible to use multiple attributes in the same find by separating them with "and", so you get finders like `Person.find_by_user_name_and_password` or even `Payment.find_by_purchaser_and_state_and_country`.

Dynamic finders have the benefits of being shorter and easier to read and understand. Instead of writing

```
Person.where("user_name = ? AND password = ?", user_name, password)
```

try writing[1]

```
Person.find_by_user_name_and_password(user_name, password)
```

You can customize dynamic finder calls by chaining them to the end of scopes or relations, however they must be the last call since they themselves return the actual results.

```
Payment.order("created_on).find_all_by_amount(50)
```

The same dynamic finder style can be used to create the object if it doesn't already exist. This dynamic finder is called with `find_or_create_by_` and will return the object if it already exists and otherwise creates it, then returns it.

```
> AreaCode.find_or_create_by_number_and_location_and_state "732",
"Central", "NJ"
 => #<AreaCode id: 6, number: "732", location: "Central", created_at:
"2010-09-19 20:11:37", updated_at: "2010-09-19 20:11:37", state: "NJ">
```

Use the `find_or_initialize_by_` finder if you want to return a new record without saving it first.

---

1. Well, slightly shorter in most cases.

```
>> AreaCode.find_or_initialize_by_number "551"
=> #<AreaCode id: nil, number: "551", location: nil, created_at: nil,
updated_at: nil, state: nil>
```

All of the `find_*` dynamic finder methods are incompatible with Arel and feel archaic in Rails 3, although they're still supported. The only type of dynamic finder that I use on any sort of regular basis is the convenient `find_or_create_by_`.

5.4.8 Dynamic Scopes

Dynamic scopes are similar to dynamic finders in that they operate via `method_missing`. Since they are based on Arel, they allow the kind of method chaining that is preferred in Rails 3.

```
>> AreaCode.find_all_by_state("NJ").order(:created_at)
NoMethodError: undefined method 'order' for #<Array:0x102e94f00>

>> AreaCode.scoped_by_state("NJ").order(:created_at)
=> [#<AreaCode id: 5, ...]
```

Since `method_missing` is costly in terms of execution performance, dynamic methods are created on the fly as needed. The following example picks up where the previous one left off, and shows that `scoped_by_state` is now a method on the `AreaCode` class, but `scoped_by_location`, which has not been invoked yet, is not.

```
>> AreaCode.methods.include? "scoped_by_state"
=> true
>> AreaCode.methods.include? "scoped_by_location"
=> false
```

5.4.9 Custom SQL Queries

The `find_by_sql` class method takes a SQL select query and returns an array of Active Record objects based on the results. Here's a barebones example, which you would never actually need to do in a real application:

```
>> Client.find_by_sql("select * from clients")
=> [#<Client id: 1, name: "Paper Jam Printers", code: "PJP" ...>,
#<Client id: 2, name: "Goodness Steaks", code: "GOOD_STEAKS" ...>]
```

I can't stress this enough: You should take care to use `find_by_sql` only when you really need it! For one, it reduces database portability. When you use Active Record's normal find operations, Rails takes care of handling differences between the underlying databases for you.

Note that Active Record already has a ton of built-in functionality abstracting SELECT statements. Functionality that it would be very unwise to reinvent. There are lots of cases where at first glance it might seem that you might need to use `find_by_sql`, but you actually don't. A common case is when doing a LIKE query:

```
>> Client.find_by_sql("select * from clients where code like 'A%'")
=> [#<Client id: 1, name: "Amazon, Inc" ...>]
```

Turns out that you can easily put that LIKE clause into a conditions option:

```
>> param = "A"
>> Client.where("code like ?", "#{param}%")
=> [#<Client id: 1, name: "Amazon, Inc" ...>]
```

Preventing SQL injection attacks

Under the covers, Rails sanitizes[2] your SQL code, provided that you parameterize your query. Active Record executes your SQL using the `connection.select_all` method, iterating over the resulting array of hashes, and invoking your Active Record's `initialize` method for each row in the result set.

What would this section's example look like un-parameterized?

```
>> Client.where("code like '#{params[:code]}%'")
=> [#<Client id: 1, name: "Amazon, Inc" ...>] # NOOOOO!
```

Notice the missing question mark as a variable placeholder. Always remember that interpolating user-supplied values into a SQL fragment of any type is very unsafe! Just imagine what would happen to your project if a malicious user called that unsafe find with `params[:code]` set to

```
"Amazon'; DELETE FROM users;'
```

This particular example might fail in your own experiments. The outcome is very specific to the type of database/driver that you're using. Some popular databases drivers may even have features that help to prevent SQL injection. I still think it's better to be safe than sorry.

The `count_by_sql` method works in a manner similar to `find_by_sql`.

```
>> Client.count_by_sql("select count(*) from clients")
=> 132
```

Again, you should have a special reason to be using it instead of the more concise alternatives provided by Active Record.

---

2. Sanitization prevents SQL injection attacks. For more information about SQL injection and Rails see http://www.rorsecurity.info/2007/05/19/sql-injection/.

5.4.10   The Query Cache

By default, Rails attempts to optimize performance by turning on a simple query cache. It is a hash stored on the current thread, one for every active database connection. (Most Rails processes will have just one.)

Whenever a `find` (or any other type of select operation) happens and the query cache is active, the corresponding result set is stored in a hash with the SQL that was used to query for them as the key. If the same SQL statement is used again in another operation, the cached result set is used to generate a new set of model objects instead of hitting the database again.

You can enable the query cache manually by wrapping operations in a `cache` block, as in the following example:

```
User.cache do
  puts User.first
  puts User.first
  puts User.first
end
```

Check your `development.log` and you should see the following entries:

```
User Load (1.0ms)   SELECT * FROM users LIMIT 1
CACHE (0.0ms)   SELECT * FROM users LIMIT 1
CACHE (0.0ms)   SELECT * FROM users LIMIT 1
```

The database was queried only once. Try a similar experiment in your own console without the `cache` block, and you'll see that three separate `User Load` events are logged.

Save and delete operations result in the cache being cleared, to prevent propagation of instances with invalid states. If you find it necessary to do so for whatever reason, call the `clear_query_cache` class method to clear out the query cache manually.

The active record context plugin

Rick Olson extracted a plugin from his popular Lighthouse application that allows you to easily seed the query cache with sets of objects that you know you will need. It's a powerful complement to Active Record's built-in caching support. Learn more about it at `http://activereload.net/2007/5/23/spend-less-time-in-the-database-and-more-time-outdoors`.

Logging

The log file indicates when data is being read from the query cache instead of the database. Just look for lines starting with CACHE instead of a Model Load.

```
Place Load (0.1ms)  SELECT * FROM places WHERE (places.id = 15749)
CACHE (0.0ms) SELECT * FROM places WHERE (places.id = 15749)
CACHE (0.0ms)  SELECT * FROM places WHERE (places.id = 15749)
```

Default Query Caching in Controllers
For performance reasons, Active Record's query cache is turned on by default for the processing of controller actions.

Limitations
The Active Record query cache was purposely kept very simple. Since it literally keys cached model instances on the SQL that was used to pull them out of the database, it can't connect multiple `find` invocations that are phrased differently but have the same semantic meaning and results.

For example, "select foo from bar where id = 1" and "select foo from bar where id = 1 limit 1" are considered different queries and will result in two distinct cache entries. The active_record_context plugin[3] by Rick Olson is an example of a query cache implementation that is a little bit smarter about identity, since it keys cached results on primary keys rather than SQL statements.

5.4.11 Updating

The simplest way to manipulate attribute values is simply to treat your Active Record object as a plain old Ruby object, meaning via direct assignment using `myprop=(some_value)`

There are a number of other different ways to update Active Record objects, as illustrated in this section. First, let's look at how to use the `update` class method of `ActiveRecord::Base`

```ruby
class ProjectController < ApplicationController
  def update
    Project.update(params[:id], params[:project])
    redirect_to projects_path
  end

  def mass_update
    Project.update(params[:projects].keys, params[:projects].values)
    redirect_to projects_path
  end
end
```

---

3. http://activereload.net/2007/5/23/spend-less-time-in-the-database-and-more-time-outdoors

The first form of `update` takes a single numeric id and a hash of attribute values, while the second form takes a list of ids and a list of values and is useful in scenarios where a form submission from a web page with multiple updateable rows is being processed.

The `update` class method does invoke validation first and will not save a record that fails validation. However, it returns the object whether or not the validation passes. That means that if you want to know whether or not the validation passed, you need to follow up the call to `update` with a call to `valid?`

```
class ProjectController < ApplicationController
  def update
    project = Project.update(params[:id], params[:project])
    if project.valid? # uh-oh, do we want to run validate again?
      redirect_to project
    else
      render 'edit'
    end
  end
end
```

A problem is that now we are calling `valid?` twice, since the `update` call also called it. Perhaps a better option is to use the `update_attributes` instance method:

```
class ProjectController < ApplicationController
  def update
    project = Project.find(params[:id])
    if project.update_attributes(params[:project])
      redirect_to project
    else
      render 'edit'
    end
  end
end
```

And of course, if you've done some basic Rails programming, you'll recognize that pattern, since it is used in the generated scaffolding code. The `update_attributes` method takes a hash of attribute values, and returns true or false depending on whether the save was successful or not, which is dependent on validation passing.

5.4.12   Updating by Condition

Active Record has another class method useful for updating multiple records at once: `update_all`. It maps closely to the way that you would think of using a SQL `update...where` statement. The `update_all` method takes two parameters, the set part of the SQL statement and the conditions, expressed as part of a where clause. The method returns the number of records updated.[4]

I think this is one of those methods that is generally more useful in a scripting context than in a controller method, but you might feel differently. Here is a quick example of how I might go about reassigning all the Rails projects in the system to a new project manager.

```
Project.update_all({:manager => 'Ron Campbell'}, :technology => 'Rails')
```

The update_all method also accepts string parameters, which allows you to lever-age the power of SQL!

```
Project.update_all("cost = cost * 3", "lower(technology) LIKE
'%microsoft%'")
```

5.4.13 Updating a Particular Instance

The most basic way to update an Active Record object is to manipulate its attributes directly and then call save. It's worth noting that save will insert a record in the database if necessary or update an existing record with the same primary key.

```
>> project = Project.find(1)
>> project.manager = 'Brett M.'
>> project.save
=> true
```

The save method will return true if it was successful or false if it failed for any reason. There is another method, save!, that will use exceptions instead. Which one to use depends on whether you plan to deal with errors right away or delegate the problem to another method further up the chain.

It's mostly a matter of style, although the non-bang save and update methods that return a boolean value are often used in controller actions, as the clause for an if condition:

```
class StoryController < ApplicationController def points
    story = Story.find(params[:id])
    if story.update_attribute(:points, params[:value])
      render :text => "#{story.name} updated"
    else
      render :text => "Error updating story points"
    end
  end
end
```

---

4. Microsoft's ADO library doesn't support reporting back the number of affected rows, so update_all does not work with the SQLServer adapter.

5.4.14   Updating Specific Attributes

The instance methods `update_attribute` and `update_attributes` take one key/
value pair or hash of attributes, respectively, to be updated on your model and saved to
the database in one operation.

The `update_attribute` method updates a single attribute and saves the record, but
updates made with this method are not subjected to validation checks! In other words,
this method allows you to persist an Active Record model to the database even if the full
object isn't valid. Callbacks are also skipped, but the `updated_at` is still bumped.

Lark says...

I feel dirty whenever I use `update_attribute`.

On the other hand, `update_attributes` is subject to validation checks and is often
used on update actions and passed the params hash containing updated values.

Courtenay says...

If you have associations on a model, Active Record automatically creates convenience methods for
mass assignment. In other words, a `Project` model that `has_many :users` will expose a
`user_ids` attribute writer, which gets used by its `update_attributes` method. This is an
advantage if you're updating associations with checkboxes, because you just name the checkboxes
`project[user_ids][]` and Rails will handle the magic. In some cases, allowing the user to
set associations this way would be a security risk. Definitely consider using `attr_accessible`
to prevent mass assignment whenever there's a possibility that your application will get abuse from
malicious users.

5.4.15   Convenience Updaters

Rails provides a number of convenience update methods in the form of `increment`,
`decrement`, and `toggle`, which do exactly what their names suggest with numeric and
boolean attributes. Each has a bang variant (such as `toggle!`) that additionally invokes
`update_attribute` after modifying the attribute.

5.4.16   Touching Records

There may be certain cases where updating a time field to indicate a record was viewed
is all you require, and Active Record provides a convenience method for doing so in the
form of `touch`. This is especially useful for cache autoexpiration, which is covered in
Chapter 17 "Caching and Performance."

Active
Record

Using this method on a model with no arguments updates the `updated_at` timestamp field to the current time without firing any callbacks or validation. If a timestamp attribute is provided it will update that attribute to the current time along with `updated_at`.

```
>> user = User.first
>> user.touch #=> sets updated_at to now.
>> user.touch(:viewed_at) # sets viewed_at and updated_at to now.
```

If a `:touch` option is provided to a belongs to relation, it will touch the parent record when the child is touched.

```
class User < ActiveRecord::Base
  belongs_to :client, :touch => true
end
```

```
>> user.touch #=> also calls user.client.touch
```

5.4.17 Controlling Access to Attributes

Constructors and update methods that take hashes to do mass assignment of attribute values are susceptible to misuse by hackers when they are used in conjunction with the `params` hash available in controller methods.

When you have attributes in your Active Record class that you want to protect from inadvertent or mass assignment, use one of the following two class methods to control access to your attributes:

The `attr_accessible` method takes a list of attributes that will be accessible for mass assignment. This is the more conservative choice for mass-assignment protection.

On the other hand, if you'd rather start from an all-open default and restrict attributes as needed, then use `attr_protected`. Attributes passed to this method will be protected from mass-assignment. Their assignment will simply be ignored. You will need to use direct assignment methods to assign values to those attributes, as illustrated in the following code example:

```
class Customer < ActiveRecord::Base
  attr_protected :credit_rating
end
```

```
customer = Customer.new(:name => "Abe", :credit_rating => "Excellent")
customer.credit_rating # => nil
```

```
customer.attributes = { "credit_rating" => "Excellent" }
customer.credit_rating # => nil
```

```
# and now, the allowed way to set a credit_rating
```

```
customer.credit_rating = "Average"
customer.credit_rating # => "Average"
```

5.4.18 Readonly Attributes

Sometimes you want to designate certain attributes as readonly, which prevents them from being updated after the parent object is created. The feature is primarily for use in conjunction with calculated attributes. In fact, Active Record uses this method internally for counter-cache attributes, since they are maintained with their own special SQL update statements.

The only time that readonly attributes may be set are when the object is not saved yet. The following example code illustrates usage of `attr_readonly`. Note the potential gotcha when trying to update a readonly attribute.

```
class Customer < ActiveRecord::Base
  attr_readonly :social_security_number
end

>> customer = Customer.new(:social_security_number => "130803020")
=> #<Customer id: 1, social_security_number: "130803020", ...>
>> customer.social_security_number
=> "130803020"
>> customer.save

>> customer.social_security_number = "000000000"  # Note, no error raised!
>> customer.social_security_number
=> "000000000"

>> customer.save
>> customer.reload
>> customer.social_security_number
=> "130803020"  # the original readonly value is preserved
```

The fact that trying to set a new value for a readonly attribute doesn't raise an error bothers my sensibilities, but I understand how it can make using this feature a little bit less code-intensive.

You can get a list of all readonly attributes via the method `readonly_attributes`.

5.4.19 Deleting and Destroying

Finally, if you want to remove a record from your database, you have two choices. If you already have a model instance, you can destroy it:

```
>> bad_timesheet = Timesheet.find(1)

>> bad_timesheet.destroy
```

```
=> #<Timesheet id: 1, user_id: "1", submitted: nil, created_at:
"2006-11-21 05:40:27", updated_at: "2006-11-21 05:40:27">
```

The `destroy` method will both remove the object from the database and prevent you from modifying it again:

```
>> bad_timesheet.user_id = 2
TypeError: can't modify frozen hash
```

Note that calling `save` on an object that has been destroyed will fail silently. If you need to check whether an object has been destroyed, you can use the `destroyed?` method.

You can also call `destroy` and `delete` as class methods, passing the id(s) to delete. Both variants accept a single parameter or array of ids:

```
Timesheet.delete(1)
Timesheet.destroy([2, 3])
```

The naming might seem inconsistent, but it isn't. The `delete` method uses SQL directly and does not load any instances (hence it is faster). The `destroy` method does load the instance of the Active Record object and then calls `destroy` on it as an instance method. The semantic differences are subtle, but come into play when you have assigned `before_destroy` callbacks or have dependent associations—child objects that should be deleted automatically along with their parent object.

5.5 Database Locking

Locking is a term for techniques that prevent concurrent users of an application from overwriting each other's work. Active Record doesn't normally use any type of database locking when loading rows of model data from the database. If a given Rails application will only ever have one user updating data at the same time, then you don't have to worry about it.

However, when more than one user may be accessing and updating the exact same data simultaneously, then it is vitally important for you as the developer to think about concurrency. Ask yourself, what types of collisions or race conditions could happen if two users were to try to update a given model at the same time?

There are a number of approaches to dealing with concurrency in database-backed applications, two of which are natively supported by Active Record: optimistic and pessimistic locking. Other approaches exist, such as locking entire database tables. Every approach has strengths and weaknesses, so it is likely that a given application will use a combination of approaches for maximum reliability.

5.5.1 Optimistic Locking

Optimistic locking describes the strategy of detecting and resolving collisions if they occur, and is commonly recommended in multi-user situations where collisions should be infrequent. Database records are never actually locked in optimistic locking, making it a bit of a misnomer.

Optimistic locking is a fairly common strategy, because so many applications are designed such that a particular user will mostly be updating with data that conceptually belongs to him and not other users, making it rare that two users would compete for updating the same record. The idea behind optimistic locking is that because collisions should occur infrequently, we'll simply deal with them only if they happen.

Implementation

If you control your database schema, optimistic locking is really simple to implement. Just add an integer column named lock_version to a given table, with a default value of zero.

```
class AddLockVersionToTimesheets < ActiveRecord::Migration

  def self.up
    add_column :timesheets, :lock_version, :integer, :default => 0
  end

  def self.down
    remove_column :timesheets, :lock_version
  end

end
```

Simply adding that `lock_version` column changes Active Record's behavior. Now if the same record is loaded as two different model instances and saved differently, the first instance will win the update, and the second one will cause an `ActiveRecord::StaleObjectError` to be raised.

We can illustrate optimistic locking behavior with a simple spec:

```
describe Timesheet do
  it "should lock optimistically" do
    t1 = Timesheet.create
    t2 = Timesheet.find(t1.id)

    t1.rate = 250
    t2.rate = 175

    t1.save.should be_true
    expect { t2.save }.to raise_error(ActiveRecord::StaleObjectError)
  end
end
```

The spec passes, because calling `save` on the second instance raises the expected `ActiveRecord::StaleObjectError` exception. Note that the `save` method (without the bang) returns false and does not raise exceptions if the save fails due to validation, but other problems such as locking in this case, can indeed cause it to raise exceptions.

To use a database column named something other than `lock_version` change the setting using `set_locking_column`. To make the change globally, add the following line to your `config/application.rb`:

```
config.active_record.set_locking_column = 'alternate_lock_version'
```

Like other Active Record settings, you can also change it on a per-model basis with a declaration in your model class:

```
class Timesheet < ActiveRecord::Base
  set_locking_column 'alternate_lock_version'
end
```

Handling `StaleObjectError`

Now of course, after adding optimistic locking, you don't want to just leave it at that, or the end user who is on the losing end of the collision would simply see an application error screen. You should try to handle the `StaleObjectError` as gracefully as possible.

Depending on the criticality of the data being updated, you might want to invest time into crafting a user-friendly solution that somehow preserves the changes that the loser was trying to make. At minimum, if the data for the update is easily re-creatable, let the user know why their update failed with controller code that looks something like the following:

```
def update
  timesheet = Timesheet.find(params[:id])
  timesheet.update_attributes(params[:timesheet])
  # redirect somewhere
rescue ActiveRecord::StaleObjectError
  flash[:error] = "Timesheet was modified while you were editing it."
  redirect_to [:edit, timesheet]
end
```

There are some advantages to optimistic locking. It doesn't require any special feature in the database, and it is fairly easy to implement. As you saw in the example, very little code is required to handle the `StaleObjectError`.

The main disadvantages to optimistic locking are that update operations are a bit slower because the lock version must be checked, and the potential for bad user experience, since they don't find out about the failure until after they've potentially lost data.

5.5.2 Pessimistic Locking

Pessimistic locking requires special database support (built into the major databases) and locks down specific database rows during an update operation. It prevents another user from reading data that is about to be updated, in order to prevent them from working with stale data.

Pessimistic locking works in conjunction with transactions as in the following example:

```
Timesheet.transaction do
  t = Timesheet.lock.first
  t.approved = true
  t.save!
end
```

It's also possible to call `lock!` on an existing model instance, which simply calls `reload(:lock => true)` under the covers. You wouldn't want to do that on an instance with attribute changes since it would cause them to be discarded by the reload. If you decide you don't want the lock anymore, you can pass `false` to the `lock!` method.

Pessimistic locking takes place at the database level. The SELECT statement generated by Active Record will have a FOR UPDATE (or similar) clause added to it, causing all other connections to be blocked from access to the rows returned by the select statement. The lock is released once the transaction is committed. There are theoretically situations (Rails process goes boom mid-transaction?!) where the lock would not be released until the connection is terminated or times out.

5.5.3 Considerations

Web applications scale best with optimistic locking, which as we've discussed doesn't really use any database-level locking at all. However, you have to add application logic to handle failure cases. Pessimistic locking is a bit easier to implement, but can lead to situations where one Rails process is waiting on another to release a database lock, that is, waiting and not serving any other incoming requests. Remember that Rails processes are typically single-threaded.

In my opinion, pessimistic locking should not be super dangerous as it is on other platforms, because in Rails we don't ever persist database transactions across more than a single HTTP request. In fact, it would be impossible to do that in a shared-nothing architecture. (If you're running Rails with JRuby and doing crazy things like storing Active Record object instances in a shared session space, all bets are off.)

A situation to be wary of would be one where you have many users competing for access to a particular record that takes a long time to update. For best results, keep your pessimistic-locking transactions small and make sure that they execute quickly.

5.6 Where Clauses

In mentioning Active Record's `find` method earlier in the chapter, we didn't look at the wealth of options available in addition to finding by primary key and the `first` and `all` methods. Note that this book covers a querying style that is new to Rails 3. Each method discussed here returns an `ActiveRecord::Relation` - a chainable object that is lazy evaluated against the database only when the actual records are needed.

5.6.1 `where(*conditions)`

It's very common to need to filter the result set of a find operation (just a SQL SELECT under the covers) by adding conditions (to the WHERE clause). Active Record gives you a number of ways to do just that with the `where` method.

The conditions parameter can be specified as a string or a hash. Parameters are automatically santized to prevent SQL-injection attacks.

Passing a hash of conditions will construct a where clause containing a union of all the key/value pairs. If all you need is equality, versus, say LIKE criteria, I advise you to use the hash notation, since it's arguably the most readable of the styles.

```
Product.where(:sku => params[:sku])
```

The hash notation is smart enough to create an IN clause if you associate an array of values with a particular key.

```
Product.where(:sku => [9400,9500,9900])
```

The simple string form can be used for statements that don't involve data originating outside of your app. It's most useful for doing LIKE comparsions, as well as greater-than/less-than and the use of SQL functions not already built into Active Record. If you do choose to use the string style, additional arguments to the `where` method will be treated as query variables to insert into the where clause.

```
Product.where('description like ? and color = ?', "%#{terms}%", color)
Product.where('sku in (?)', selected_skus)
```

Bind Variables

When using multiple parameters in the conditions, it can easily become hard to read exactly what the fourth or fifth question mark is supposed to represent. In those cases, you can resort to named bind variables instead. That's done by replacing the question marks with symbols and supplying a hash with values for the matching symbol keys as a second parameter.

```
Product.where("name = :name AND sku = :sku AND created_at > :date",
              :name => "Space Toilet", {:sku => 80800, :date =>
'2009-01-01'})
```

During a quick discussion on IRC about this final form, Robby Russell gave me the following clever snippet:

```
Message.where("subject LIKE :foo OR body LIKE :foo", :foo => '%woah%')
```

In other words, when you're using named placeholders (versus question mark characters) you can use the same bind variable more than once. Like, whoa!

Simple hash conditions like this are very common and useful, but they will only generate conditions based on equality with SQL's AND operator.

```
User.where(:login => login, :password => password).first
```

If you want logic other than AND, you'll have to use one of the other forms available.

Boolean Conditions

It's particularly important to take care in specifying conditions that include boolean values. Databases have various different ways of representing boolean values in columns. Some have native boolean datatypes, and others use a single character, often 1 and 0 or T and F (or even Y and N). Rails will transparently handle the data conversion issues for you if you pass a Ruby boolean object as your parameter:

```
Timesheet.where('submitted = ?', true)
```

Nil Conditions

Rails expert Xavier Noria reminds us to take care in specifying conditions that might be nil. Using a question mark doesn't let Rails figure out that a `nil` supplied as the value of a condition should probably be translated into IS NULL in the resulting SQL query.

Compare the following two find examples and their corresponding SQL queries to understand this common gotcha. The first example does not work as intended, but the second one does work:

```
>> User.where('email = ?', nil)
User Load (151.4ms)   SELECT * FROM users WHERE (email = NULL)
```

```
>> User.where(:email => nil)
User Load (15.2ms)   SELECT * FROM users WHERE (users.email IS NULL)
```

5.6.2 `order(*clauses)`

The `order` method takes one or more symbols (representing column names) or a fragment of SQL, specifying the desired ordering of a result set:

```
Timesheet.order('created_at desc')
```

The SQL spec defaults to ascending order if the ascending/descending option is omitted, which is exactly what happens if you use symbols.

```
Timesheet.order(:created_at)
```

Wilson says...

The SQL spec doesn't prescribe any particular ordering if no 'order by' clause is specified in the query. That seems to trip people up, since the common belief is that 'ORDER BY id ASC' is the default.

Random Ordering

The value of the `:order` option is not validated by Rails, which means you can pass any code that is understood by the underlying database, not just column/direction tuples. An example of why that is useful is when wanting to fetch a random record:

```
# MySQL
Timesheet.order('RAND()')

# Postgres
Timesheet.order('RANDOM()')

# Microsoft SQL Server
Timesheet.order('NEWID()')  # uses random uuids to sort

# Oracle
Timesheet.order('dbms_random.value').first
```

Remember that ordering large datasets randomly is known to perform terribly on most databases, particularly MySQL.

Tim says…

A clever, performant, and portable way to get a random record is to generate a random offset in Ruby.

```
Timsheet.limit(1).offset(rand(Timesheet.count)).first
```

5.6.3 `limit(number)` and `offset(number)`

The `limit` method takes an integer value establishing a limit on the number of rows to return from the query. The `offset` method, which must be chained to `limit`, specifies the number of rows to skip in the result set and is 0-indexed. (At least it is in MySQL. Other databases may be 1-indexed.) Together these options are used for paging results.

For example, a call to find for the second page of 10 results in a list of timesheets is:

```
Timesheet.limit(10).offset(10)
```

Depending on the particulars of your application's data model, it may make sense to always put some limit on the maximum amount of Active Record objects fetched in any one specific query. Letting the user trigger unbounded queries pulling thousands of Active Record objects into Rails at one time is a recipe for disaster.

5.6.4 `select(*clauses)`

By default, Active Record generates SELECT * FROM queries, but it can be changed if, for example, you want to do a join, but not include the joined columns. Or if you want to add calculated columns to your result set, like this:

```
>> b = BillableWeek.select("mon_hrs + tues_hrs as two_day_total").first
=> #<BillableWeek ...>
>> b.two_day_total
=> 16
```

Now, if you actually want to fully use objects with additional attributes that you've added via the `select` method, don't forget the * clause:

```
>> b = BillableWeek.select(:*, "mon_hrs + tues_hrs as
two_day_total").first
=> #<BillableWeek id: 1...>
```

Keep in mind that columns not specified in the query, whether by * or explicitly, will not be populated in the resulting objects! So, for instance, continuing the first example, trying to access `created_at` on b has unexpected results:

```
ActiveModel::MissingAttributeError: missing attribute: created_at
```

5.6.5 `from(*tables)`

The `from` method allows you to modify the table name(s) portion of the SQL statements generated by Active Record. You can provide a custom value if you need to include extra tables for joins, or to reference a database view.

Here's an example of usage from an application that features tagging:

```
def self.find_tagged_with(list)
  select("#{table_name}.*").
    from("#{table_name}, tags, taggings")
    where("#{table_name}.#{primary_key} = taggings.taggable_id
        and taggings.tag_id = tags.id
        and tags.name IN (?)",
        Tag.parse(list)])
end
```

(If you're wondering why `table_name` is used instead of a an explicit value, it's because this code is mixed into a target class using Ruby modules. That subject is covered in Chapter 9, Advanced Active Record.)

5.6.6 `group(*args)`

Specifies a GROUP BY SQL-clause to add to the query generated by Active Record. Generally you'll want to combine `:group` with the `:select` option, since valid SQL requires that all selected columns in a grouped SELECT be either aggregate functions or columns.

```
>> users = Account.select('name, SUM(cash) as money').group('name').all
=> [#<User name: "Joe", money: "3500">, #<User name: "Jane", money:
"9245">]
```

Keep in mind that those extra columns you bring back might sometimes be strings if Active Record doesn't try to typecast them. In those cases, you'll have to use `to_i` and `to_f` to explicitly convert the string to numeric types.

```
>> users.first.money > 1_000_000
ArgumentError: comparison of String with Fixnum failed
  from (irb):8:in '>'
```

5.6.7 `having(*clauses)`

If you need to perform a group query with a SQL HAVING clause, you use the `having` method

```
>> User.group("created_at").having(["created_at > ?", 2.days.ago])
=> [#<User name: "Joe", created_at: "2010-07-09 21:45:02">]
```

5.6.8 `includes(*associations)`

Active Record has the ability to eliminate "N+1" queries by letting you specify what associations to eager load using the `includes` method or option in your finders. Active Record will load those relationships with the minimum number of queries possible.

To eager load first degree associations, provide `includes` with an array of association names. When accessing these a database hit to load each one will no longer occur.

```
>> users = User.where(:login => "mack").includes(:billable_weeks)
=> [#<User login: "mack">]
>> users.first.billable_weeks.each { |week| puts week }
=> #<Week start_date: "2008-05-01 00:00:00">
```

For second degree associations, provide a hash with the array as the value for the hash key.

```
>> clients = Client.includes(:users => [:avatar])
=> [#<Client id: 1, name: "Hashrocket">]
```

You may add more inclusions following the same pattern.

```
>> Client.includes(
     :users => [:avatar, { :timesheets => :billable_weeks }]
   )
=> [#<Client id: 1, name: "Hashrocket">]
```

Similarly to `includes`, you may use `eager_load` or `preload` with the same syntax.

```
>> Client.eager_load(
     :users => [:avatar, { :timesheets => :billable_weeks }]
   )
=> [#<Client id: 1, name: "Hashrocket">]

>> Client.preload(
     :users => [:avatar, { :timesheets => :billable_weeks }]
   )
=> [#<Client id: 1, name: "Hashrocket">]
```

5.6.9 `joins`

The `joins` method can be useful when you're grouping and aggregating data from other tables, but you don't want to load the associated objects.

```
Buyer.select('buyers.id, count(carts.id) as cart_count').
    joins('left join carts on carts.buyer_id = buyers.id').
    group('buyers.id')
```

However, the most common usage of the `join` method is to allow you to eager-fetch additional objects in a single SELECT statement, a technique that is discussed at length in Chapter 7.

5.6.10 `readonly`

Chaining the `readonly` method marks returned objects as read-only. You can change
their attributes, but you won't be able to save them back to the database.

```
>> c = Comment.readonly.first
=> #<Comment id: 1, body: "Hey beeyotch!">
>> c.body = "Keep it clean!"
=> "Keep it clean!"
>> c.save
ActiveRecord::ReadOnlyRecord: ActiveRecord::ReadOnlyRecord
```

5.6.11 `exists?`

A convenience method for checking the existence of records in the database is included
in ActiveRecord as the aptly named `exists?` method. It takes similar arguments to
`find` and instead of returning records returns a boolean for whether or not the query
has results. Note that the `:conditions` key is not used here, only supply the conditions
themselves.

```
>> User.create(:login => "mack")
=> #<User id: 1, login: "mack">

>> User.exists?(1)
=> true
>> User.exists?(:login => "mack")
=> true
>> User.where(:login => "mack").exists?  # modern style
=> true
```

5.6.12 `arel_table`

For cases in which you want to generate custom SQL yourself through Arel, you may
use the `arel_table` method to gain access to the Table for the class.

```
>> users = User.arel_table
>> users.where(users[:login].eq("mack")).to_sql
=> "SELECT 'users'.'id', 'users'.'login' FROM 'users' WHERE
'users'.'login' = 'mack'"
```

You can consult the Arel documentation directly on how to construct custom queries
using its DSL.[5]

---

5. http://github.com/rails/arel/

5.7 Connections to Multiple Databases in Different Models

Connections are created via `ActiveRecord::Base.establish_connection` and retrieved by `ActiveRecord::Base.connection`. All classes inheriting from `ActiveRecord::Base` will use this connection. What if you want some of your models to use a different connection? You can add class-specific connections.

For example, let's say you need to access data residing in a legacy database apart from the database used by the rest of your Rails application. We'll create a new base class that can be used by models that access legacy data. Begin by adding details for the additional database under its own key in `database.yml`. Then call `establish_connection` to make `LegacyProjectBase` and all its subclasses use the alternate connection instead.

```
class LegacyProjectBase < ActiveRecord::Base
  establish_connection :legacy_database
  self.abstract_class = true
  ...
end
```

Incidentally, to make this example work with subclasses, you must specify `self.abstract_class = true` in the class context. Otherwise, Rails considers the subclasses of `LegacyProject` to be using single-table inheritance (STI), which we discuss at length in Chapter 9.

Xavier says…

You can easily point your base class to different databases depending on the Rails environment like this:

```
class LegacyProjectBase < ActiveRecord::Base
  establish_connection "legacy_#{Rails.env}"
  self.abstract_class = true
  ...
end
```

Then just add multiple entries to `database.yml` to match the resulting connection names. In the case of our example, `legacy_development`, `legacy_test`, etc.

The `establish_connection` method takes a string (or symbol) key pointing to a configuration already defined in `database.yml`. Alternatively, you can pass it a literal hash of options, although it's messy to put this sort of configuration data right into your model file instead of `database.yml`

```
class TempProject < ActiveRecord::Base
  establish_connection :adapter => 'sqlite3', :database => ':memory:'
  ...
end
```

Rails keeps database connections in a connection pool inside the `ActiveRecord::Base` class instance. The connection pool is simply a `Hash` object indexed by Active Record class. During execution, when a connection is needed, the `retrieve_connection` method walks up the class-hierarchy until a matching connection is found.

5.8   Using the Database Connection Directly

It is possible to use Active Record's underlying database connections directly, and sometimes it is useful to do so from custom scripts and for one-off or ad-hoc testing. Access the connection via the `connection` attribute of any Active Record class. If all your models use the same connection, then use the connection attribute of `ActiveRecord::Base`.

```
ActiveRecord::Base.connection.execute("show tables").all_hashes
```

The most basic operation that you can do with a connection is simply to `execute` a SQL statement from the `DatabaseStatements` module. For example, Listing 5.1 shows a method that executes a SQL file statement by statement.

Listing 5.1 Execute a SQL file line by line using active record's connection

```
def execute_sql_file(path)
  File.read(path).split(';').each do |sql|
    begin
ActiveRecord::Base.connection.execute(#{sql}\n") unless sql.blank?
    rescue ActiveRecord::StatementInvalid
      $stderr.puts "warning: #{$!}"
    end
  end
end
```

5.8.1   The DatabaseStatements Module

The `ActiveRecord::ConnectionAdapters::DatabaseStatements` module mixes a number of useful methods into the connection object that make it possible to work with the database directly instead of using Active Record models. I've purposely left out some of the methods of this module (such as `add_limit!` and `add_lock`) because they are used internally by Rails to construct SQL statements dynamically and I don't think they're of much use to application developers.

For the sake of readability in the select_examples below, assume that the connection object has been assigned to conn, like this:

```
conn = ActiveRecord::Base.connection
```

begin_db_transaction()

Begins a database transaction manually (and turns off Active Record's default autocommitting behavior).

commit_db_transaction()

Commits the transaction (and turns on Active Record's default autocommitting behavior again).

delete(sql_statement)

Executes a SQL DELETE statement provided and returns the number of rows affected.

execute(sql_statement)

Executes the SQL statement provided in the context of this connection. This method is abstract in the DatabaseStatements module and is overridden by specific database adapter implementations. As such, the return type is a result set object corresponding to the adapter in use.

insert(sql_statement)

Executes an SQL INSERT statement and returns the last autogenerated ID from the affected table.

reset_sequence!(table, column, sequence = nil)

Used in Oracle and Postgres; updates the named sequence to the maximum value of the specified table's column.

rollback_db_transaction()

Rolls back the currently active transaction (and turns on auto-committing). Called automatically when a transaction block raises an exception or returns false.

select_all(sql_statement)

Returns an array of record hashes with the column names as keys and column values as values.

Active
Record

```
conn.select_all("select name from businesses limit 5")
=> [{"name"=>"Hopkins Painting"}, {"name"=>"Whelan & Scherr"},
{"name"=>"American Top Security Svc"}, {"name"=>"Life Style Homes"},
{"name"=>"378 Liquor Wine & Beer"}]
```

select_one(sql_statement)

Works similarly to `select_all`, but returns only the first row of the result set, as a single Hash with the column names as keys and column values as values. Note that this method does not add a limit clause to your SQL statement automatically, so consider adding one to queries on large datasets.

```
>> conn.select_one("select name from businesses")
=> {"name"=>"New York New York Salon"}
```

select_value(sql_statement)

Works just like `select_one`, except that it returns a single value: the first column value of the first row of the result set.

```
>> conn.select_value("select * from businesses limit 1")
=> "Cimino's Pizza"
```

select_values(sql_statement)

Works just like `select_value`, except that it returns an array of the values of the first column in all the rows of the result set.

```
>> conn.select_values("select * from businesses limit 5")
=> ["Ottersberg Christine E Dds", "Bally Total Fitness", "Behboodikah,
Mahnaz Md", "Preferred Personnel Solutions", "Thoroughbred Carpets"]
```

update(sql_statement)

Executes the update statement provided and returns the number of rows affected. Works exactly like `delete`.

5.8.2   Other Connection Methods

The full list of methods available on `connection`, which returns an instance of the underlying database adapter, is fairly long. Most of the Rails adapter implementations define their own custom versions of these methods. That makes sense, since all databases have slight variations in how they handle SQL and very large variations in how they handle extended commands, such as for fetching metadata.

A peek at `abstract_adapter.rb` shows us the default method implementations:

. . .

```
# Returns the human-readable name of the adapter.   Use mixed case - one
# can always use downcase if needed.
def adapter_name
  'Abstract'
end

# Does this adapter support migrations?   Backend specific, as the
# abstract adapter always returns +false+.
def supports_migrations?
  false
end

# Does this adapter support using DISTINCT within COUNT?   This is
+true+
# for all adapters except sqlite.
def supports_count_distinct?
  true
end
```

. . .

In the following list of method descriptions and code samples, I'm accessing the connection of our sample time_and_expenses application in the Rails console, and again I've assigned `connection` to a local variable named `conn`, for convenience.

active?

Indicates whether the connection is active and ready to perform queries.

adapter_name

Returns the human-readable name of the adapter, as in the following example:

```
>> conn.adapter_name
=> "SQLite"
```

disconnect! and reconnect!

Closes the active connection or closes and opens a new one in its place, respectively.

raw_connection

Provides access to the underlying database connection. Useful for when you need to execute a proprietary statement or you're using features of the Ruby database driver that aren't necessarily exposed in Active Record. (In trying to come up with a code sample for this method, I was able to crash the Rails console with ease. There isn't much in the way of error checking for exceptions that you might raise while mucking around with `raw_connection`.)

supports_count_distinct?

Indicates whether the adapter supports using DISTINCT within COUNT in SQL statements. This is `true` for all adapters except SQLite, which therefore requires a workaround when doing operations such as calculations.

supports_migrations?

Indicates whether the adapter supports migrations.

tables

Produces a list of tables in the underlying database schema. It includes tables that aren't usually exposed as Active Record models, such as `schema_info` and `sessions`.

```
>> conn.tables
=> ["schema_info", "users", "timesheets", "expense_reports",
"billable_weeks", "clients", "billing_codes", "sessions"]
```

verify!(timeout)

Lazily verify this connection, calling `active?` only if it hasn't been called for `timeout` seconds.

5.9 Other Configuration Options

In addition to the configuration options used to instruct Active Record on how to handle naming of tables and primary keys, there are a number of other settings that govern miscellaneous functions. Set them in an initializer.

ActiveRecord::Base.default_timezone

Tells Rails whether to use `Time.local` (using `:local`) or `Time.utc` (using `:utc`) when pulling dates and times from the database. Defaults to `:local`

ActiveRecord::Base.schema_format

Specifies the format to use when dumping the database schema with certain default rake tasks. Use the `:sql` option to have the schema dumped as potentially database-specific SQL statements. Just beware of incompatibilities if you're trying to use the `:sql` option with different databases for development and testing. The default option is `:ruby`, which dumps the schema as an `ActiveRecord::Schema` file that can be loaded into any database that supports migrations.

`ActiveRecord::Base.store_full_sti_class`

Specifies whether Active Record should store the full constant name including namespace when using Single-Table Inheritance (STI), covered in Chapter 9, "Advanced Active Record".

5.10 Conclusion

This chapter covered the fundamentals of Active Record, the framework included with Ruby on Rails for creating database-bound model classes. We've learned how Active Record expresses the convention over configuration philosophy that is such an important part of the Rails way, and how to make settings manually, which override the conventions in place.

We've also looked at the methods provided by `ActiveRecord::Base`, the parent class of all persistent models in Rails, which include everything you need to do basic CRUD operations: Create, Read, Update, and Delete. Finally, we reviewed how to drill through Active Record to use the database connection whenever you need to do so.

In the following chapter, we continue our coverage of Active Record by learning about how related model objects interact via associations.

Active
Record

Active Record Migrations

Baby step to four o'clock. Baby step to four o'clock.

> —Bob Wiley, in the movie *What About Bob* (Touchstone Pictures, 1991)

It's a fact of life that the database schema of your application will evolve over the course of development. Tables are added, names of columns are changed, things are dropped—you get the picture. Without strict conventions and process discipline for the application developers to follow, keeping the database schema in proper lock-step with application code is traditionally a very troublesome job.

Migrations are the Rails way of helping you to evolve the database schema of your application (also known as its DDL) without having to drop and re-create the database each time you make a change. And not having to drop and recreate the database each time a change happens means that you don't lose your development data. That may or may not be that important, but is usually very convenient. The only changes made when you execute a migration are those necessary to move the schema from one version to another, whether that move is forward or backward in time.

Of course, being able to evolve your schema without having to recreate your databases and the loading/reloading of data is an order of magnitude more important once you're in production.

6.1 Creating Migrations

Rails provides a generator for creating migrations.

```
$ rails generate migration
Usage:
rails generate migration NAME [field:type field:type] [options]
```

At minimum, you need to supply descriptive name for the migration in CamelCase (or underscored_text, both work,) and the generator does the rest. Other generators, such as the model and scaffolding generators, also create migration scripts for you, unless you specify the `--skip-migration` option.

The descriptive part of the migration name is up to you, but most Rails developers that I know try to make it match the schema operation (in simple cases) or at least allude to what's going on inside (in more complex cases).

Note that if you change the classname of your migration to something that doesn't match its filename, you will get an `uninitialized constant` error when that migration gets executed.

6.1.1   Sequencing Migrations

Prior to Rails 2.1, the migrations were sequenced via a simple numbering scheme baked into the name of the migration file, and automatically handled by the migration generator. Each migration received a sequential number. There were many inconveniences inherent in that approach, especially in team environments where two developers could check in a migration with the same sequence number. Thankfully those issues have been eliminated by using timestamps to sequence migrations.

Migrations that have already been run are listed in a special database table that Rails maintains. It is named `schema_migrations` and only has one column:

```
mysql> desc schema_migrations;
+---------+--------------+------+-----+---------+-------+
| Field   | Type         | Null | Key | Default | Extra |
+---------+--------------+------+-----+---------+-------+
| version | varchar(255) | NO   | PRI | NULL    |       |
+---------+--------------+------+-----+---------+-------+
1 row in set (0.00 sec)
```

When you pull down new migrations from source control, `rake db:migrate` will check the `schema_migrations` table and execute all migrations that have not yet run (even if they have earlier timestamps than migrations that you've added yourself in the interim).

6.1.2   Irreversible Migrations

Some transformations are destructive in a manner that cannot be reversed. Migrations of that kind should raise an `ActiveRecord::IrreversibleMigration` exception in their `down` method. For example, what if someone on your team made a silly mistake and defined the telephone column of your clients table as an integer? You can change the column to a string and the data will migrate cleanly, but going from a string to an integer? Not so much.

```
def self.up
  # Phone number fields are not integers, duh!
  change_column :clients, :phone, :string
end

def self.down
  raise ActiveRecord::IrreversibleMigration
end
```

Getting back to the Migration API itself, here is the `20090124223305_create_clients.rb` file again, from earlier in the chapter, after adding a couple of column definitions for the `clients` table:

```
class CreateClients < ActiveRecord::Migration
  def self.up
    create_table :clients do |t|
      t.string :name
      t.string :code
      t.timestamps
    end
  end

  def self.down
    drop_table :clients
  end
end
```

As you can see in the example, migration directives happen within two class method definitions, `self.up` and `self.down`. If we go to the command line in our project folder and type `rake db:migrate`, the `clients` table will be created. Rails gives us informative output during the migration process so that we see what is going on:

```
$ rake db:migrate
== CreateClients: migrating ========================================
-- create_table(:clients)
   -> 0.0448s
== CreateClients: migrated (0.0450s) ===============================
```

Normally, only the code in the `up` method is run, but if you ever need to rollback to an earlier version of the schema, the `down` method specifies how to undo what happened in `up`.

   To execute a rollback, use the migrate task, but pass it a version number to rollback to, as in `rake db:migrate VERSION=20090124223305`.

6.1.3 `create_table`(name, options, & block)

The `create_table` method needs at minimum a name for the table and a block containing column definitions. Why do we specify identifiers with symbols instead of strings? Both will work, but symbols require one less keystroke.

The `create_table` method makes a huge, but usually true assumption that we want an autoincrementing, integer-typed, primary key. That is why you don't see it declared in the list of columns. If that assumption happens to be wrong, it's time to pass `create_table` some options in a hash.

For example, how would you define a simple join table consisting of two foreign key columns and not needing its own primary key? Just pass the `create_table` method an `:id` option set to `false`, as a boolean, not a symbol! It will stop the migration from autogenerating a primary key altogether:

```
create_table :ingredients_recipes, :id => false do |t|
  t.column :ingredient_id, :integer
  t.column :recipe_id, :integer
end
```

If all you want to do is change the name of the primary key column from its default of 'id', pass the `:id` option a symbol instead. For example, let's say your corporation mandates that primary keys follow the pattern tablename_id. Then the earlier example would look as follows:

```
create_table :clients, :id => :clients_id do |t|
  t.column :name, :string
  t.column :code, :string
  t.column :created_at, :datetime
  t.column :updated_at, :datetime
end
```

The `:force => true` option tells the migration to go ahead and drop the table being defined if it exists. Be careful with this one, since it will produce (possibly unwanted) data loss when run in production. As far as I know, the `:force` option is mostly useful for making sure that the migration puts the database in a known state, but isn't all that useful on a daily basis.

The `:options` option allows you to append custom instructions to the SQL CREATE statement and is useful for adding database-specific commands to your migration. Depending on the database you're using, you might be able to specify things such as character set, collation, comments, min/max sizes, and many other properties using this option.

The `:temporary => true` option specifies creation of a temporary table that will only exist during the current connection to the database. In other words, it only exists during the migration. In advanced scenarios, this option might be useful for migrating big sets of data from one table to another, but is not commonly used.

Sebastian says...

A little known fact is that you can remove old migration files (while still keeping newer ones) to keep the db/migrate folder to a manageable size. You can move the older migrations to a db/archived_migrations folder or something like that. Once you do trim the size of your migrations folder, use the rake db:reset task to (re)create your database from db/schema.rb and load the seeds into your current environment.

6.1.4 **change_table**(table_name, & block)

This basically works just like create_table and accepts the same kinds of column definitions.

6.1.5 API Reference

The following table details the methods that are available in the context of create_table and change_table methods within a migration class.

change(column_name, type, options = {})

Changes the column's definition according to the new options. The options hash optionally contains a hash with arguments that correspond to the options used when adding columns.

```
t.change(:name, :string, :limit => 80)
t.change(:description, :text)
```

change_default(column_name, default)

Sets a new default value for a column.

```
t.change_default(:qualification, 'new')
t.change_default(:authorized, 1)
```

column(column_name, type, options = {})

Adds a new column to the named table. Uses the same kind of options detailed in Section 6.1.6.

```
t.column(:name, :string)
```

Active
Record

Note that you can also use the short-hand version by calling it by type. This adds a column (or columns) of the specified type (string, text, integer, float, decimal, datetime, timestamp, time, date, binary, boolean).

```
t.string(:goat)
t.string(:goat, :sheep)
t.integer(:age, :quantity)
```

index(column_name, options = {})

Adds a new index to the table. The column_name parameter can be one symbol or an array of symbols referring to columns to be indexed. The name parameter lets you override the default name that would otherwise be generated.

```
# a simple index
t.index(:name)

# a unique index
t.index([:branch_id, :party_id], :unique => true)

# a named index
t.index([:branch_id, :party_id], :unique => true, :name =>
'by_branch_party')
```

belongs_to(*args) and references(*args)

These two methods are aliases to each other. They add a foreign key column to another model, using Active Record naming conventions. Optionally adds a _type column if the :polymorphic option is set to true.

```
create_table :accounts do
  t.belongs_to(:person)
end

create_table :comments do
  t.references(:commentable, :polymorphic => true)
end
```

remove(*column_names)

Removes the column(s) specified from the table definition.

```
t.remove(:qualification)
t.remove(:qualification, :experience)
```

remove_index(options = {})

Removes the given index from the table.

```
# remove the accounts_branch_id_index from the accounts table
t.remove_index :column => :branch_id

# remove the accounts_branch_id_party_id_index from the accounts table
t.remove_index :column => [:branch_id, :party_id]

# remove the index named by_branch_party in the accounts table
t.remove_index :name => :by_branch_party
```

remove_references(*args) and remove_belongs_to

Removes a reference. Optionally removes a `type` column.

```
t.remove_belongs_to(:person)
t.remove_references(:commentable, :polymorphic => true)
```

remove_timestamps

Here's a method that you will never use, unless you forgot to add timestamps in the `create_table` block and do it in a later migration. It removes the timestamp columns. (`created_at` and `updated_at`) from the table.

rename(column_name, new_column_name)

Renames a column. The old name comes first, a fact that I usually can't remember.

```
t.rename(:description, :name)
```

timestamps

Adds Active Record-maintained timestamp (`created_at` and `updated_at`) columns to the table.

```
t.timestamps
```

6.1.6 Defining Columns

Columns can be added to a table using either the `column` method, inside the block of a `create_table` statement, or with the `add_column` method. Other than taking the name of the table to add the column to as its first argument, the methods work identically.

```
create_table :clients do |t|
  t.column :name, :string
end

add_column :clients, :code, :string
add_column :clients, :created_at, :datetime
```

The first (or second) parameter obviously specifies the name of the column, and the second (or third) obviously specifies its type. The SQL92 standard defines fundamental data types, but each database implementation has its own variation on the standards.

If you're familiar with database column types, when you examine the preceding example it might strike you as a little weird that there is a database column declared as type `string`, since databases don't have string columns—they have char or varchars types.

Column Type Mappings

The reason for declaring a database column as type string is that Rails migrations are meant to be database-agnostic. That's why you could (as I've done on occasion) develop using Postgres as your database and deploy in production to Oracle.

A complete discussion of how to go about choosing the right data type for your application needs is outside the scope of this book. However, it is useful to have a reference of how migration's generic types map to database-specific types. The mappings for the databases most commonly used with Rails are in Table 6.1.

Each connection adapter class has a `native_database_types` hash which establishes the mapping described in Table 6.1. If you need to look up the mappings for a database not listed in Table 6.1, you can pop open the adapter Ruby code and find the `native_database_types` hash, like the following one inside the `PostgreSQLAdapter`

Table 6.1 Column Mappings for the Databases Most Commonly Used with Rails

Migration Type	MySQL	Postgres	SQLite	Oracle	Ruby Class
:binary	blob	bytea	blob	blob	String
:boolean	tinyint(1)	boolean	boolean	number(1)	Boolean
:date	date	date	date	date	Date
:datetime	datetime	timestamp	datetime	date	Time
:decimal	decimal	decimal	decimal	decimal	BigDecimal
:float	float	float	float	number	Float
:integer	int(11)	integer	integer	number(38)	Fixnum
:string	varchar(255)	character	varchar(255)	varchar2(255)	String
:text	text	clob(32768)	text	clob	String
:time	time	time	time	date	Time
:timestamp	datetime	timestamp	datetime	date	Time

class within `postgresql_adapter.rb`:

```
NATIVE_DATABASE_TYPES = {
  :primary_key => "serial primary key".freeze,
  :string      => { :name => "character varying", :limit => 255 },
  :text        => { :name => "text" },
  :integer     => { :name => "integer" },
  :float       => { :name => "float" },
  :decimal     => { :name => "decimal" },
  :datetime    => { :name => "timestamp" },
  :timestamp   => { :name => "timestamp" },
  :time        => { :name => "time" },
  :date        => { :name => "date" },
  :binary      => { :name => "bytea" },
  :boolean     => { :name => "boolean" },
  :xml         => { :name => "xml" }
}
```

Column Options

For many column types, just specifying type is not enough information. All column declarations accept the following options:

`:default => value`

Sets a default to be used as the initial value of the column for new rows. You don't ever need to explicitly set the default value to `null`. Just leave off this option to get a `null` default value. It's worth noting that MySQL 5.x ignores default values for binary and text columns.

`:limit => size`

Adds a size parameter to string, text, binary, or integer columns. Its meaning varies depending on the column type that it is applied to. Generally speaking, limits for string types refers to number of characters, whereas for other types it specifies the number of bytes used to store the value in the database.

`:null => false`

Makes the column required at the database level by adding a `not null` constraint.

Decimal Precision

Columns declared as type `:decimal` accept the following options:

`:precision => number`

Precision is the total number of digits in a number.

`:scale => number`

Scale is the number of digits to the right of the decimal point. For example, the number 123.45 has a precision of 5 and a scale of 2. Logically, the scale cannot be larger than the precision.

Note

Decimal types pose a serious opportunity for data loss during migrations of production data between different kinds of databases. For example, the default precisions between Oracle and SQL Server can cause the migration process to truncate and change the value of your numeric data. It's always a good idea to specify precision details for your data.

Column Type Gotchas

The choice of column type is not necessarily a simple choice and depends on both the database you're using and the requirements of your application.

:binary Depending on your particular usage scenario, storing binary data in the database can cause big performance problems. Active Record doesn't generally exclude any columns when it loads objects from the database, and putting large binary attributes on commonly used models will increase the load on your database server significantly. If you must put binary content in a commonly-used class, take advantage of the `select` method to only bring back the columns you need.

:boolean The way that boolean values are stored varies from database to database. Some use 1 and 0 integer values to represent true and false, respectively. Others use characters such as T and F. Rails handles the mapping between Ruby's `true` and `false` very well, so you don't need to worry about the underlying scheme yourself. Setting attributes directly to database values such as 1 or F may work correctly, but is considered an anti-pattern.

:datetime and :timestamp The Ruby class that Rails maps to `datetime` and `timestamp` columns is Time. In 32-bit environments, Time doesn't work for dates before 1902. Ruby's `DateTime` class does work with year values prior to 1902, and Rails falls back to using it if necessary. It doesn't use `DateTime` to begin for performance reasons. Under the covers, Time is implemented in C and is very fast, whereas `DateTime` is written in pure Ruby and is comparatively slow.

:time It's very, very rare that you want to use a `:time` datatype; perhaps if you're modeling an alarm clock. Rails will read the contents of the database as hour, minute, and second values, into a Time object with dummy values for the year, month, and day.

:decimal Older versions of Rails (prior to 1.2) did not support the fixed-precision :decimal type and as a result many old Rails applications incorrectly used :float datatypes. Floating-point numbers are by nature imprecise, so it is important to choose :decimal instead of :float for most business-related applications.

Tim says . . .

If you're using a float to store values which need to be precise, such as money, you're a jackass. Floating point calculations are done in binary rather than decimal, so rounding errors abound in places you wouldn't expect.

```
>> 0.1+0.2 == 0.3
=> false
>> BigDecimal('0.1') + BigDecimal('0.2') == BigDecimal('0.3')
=> true
```

:float Don't use floats to store currency values, or more accurately, any type of data that needs fixed precision. Since floating-point numbers are pretty much approximations, any single representation of a number as a float is probably okay. However, once you start doing mathematical operations or comparisons with float values, it is ridiculously easy to introduce difficult to diagnose bugs into your application.

:integer and :string There aren't many gotchas that I can think of when it comes to integers and strings. They are the basic data building blocks of your application, and many Rails developers leave off the size specification, which results in the default maximum sizes of 11 digits and 255 characters, respectively. You should keep in mind that you won't get an error if you try to store values that exceed the maximum size defined for the database column, which again, is 255 characters by default. Your string will simply get truncated. Use validations to make sure that user-entered data does not exceed the maximum size allowed.

:text There have been reports of text fields slowing down query performance on some databases, enough to be a consideration for applications that need to scale to high loads. If you must use a text column in a performance-critical application, put it in a separate table.

Custom Data Types

If use of database-specific datatypes (such as :double, for higher precision than :float) is critical to your project, use the config.active_record.schema_format = :sql setting in `config/application.rb` to make Rails dump schema information in native SQL DDL format rather than its own cross-platform compatible Ruby code, via the `db/schema.rb` file.

"Magic" Timestamp Columns

Rails does magic with datetime columns, if they're named a certain way. Active Record will automatically timestamp create operations if the table has columns named `created_at` or `created_on`. The same applies to updates when there are columns named `updated_at` or `updated_on`.

Note that `created_at` and `updated_at` should be defined as `datetime`, but if you use `t.timestamps` then you don't have to worry about what type of columns they are.

Automatic timestamping can be turned off globally, by setting the following variable in an initializer.

```
ActiveRecord::Base.record_timestamps = false
```

The preceding code turns off timestamps for all models, but `record_timestamps` is class-inheritable, so you can also do it on a case-by-case basis by setting `self.record_timestamps` to false at the top of specific model classes.

6.1.7 Command-line Column Declarations

You can supply name/type pairs on the command line when you invoke the migration generator and it will automatically insert the corresponding `add_column` and `remove_column` methods.

```
$ rails generate migration AddTitleBodyToPosts \
    title:string body:text published:boolean
```

This will create the `AddTitleBodyToPosts` in `db/migrate/20080514090912_add_title_body_to_posts.rb` with this in the up migration:

```
add_column :posts, :title, :string
add_column :posts, :body, :text
add_column :posts, :published, :boolean
```

And this in the down migration:

```
remove_column :posts, :published
remove_column :posts, :body
remove_column :posts, :title
```

6.2 Data Migration

So far we've only discussed using migration files to modify the schema of your database. Inevitably, you will run into situations where you also need to perform data migrations, whether in conjunction with a schema change or not.

6.2.1 Using SQL

In most cases, you should craft your data migration in raw SQL using the `execute` command that is available inside a migration class.

For example, say you had a `phones` table, which kept phone numbers in their component parts and later wanted to simplify your model by just having a `number` column instead. You'd write a migration similar to this one (only the `up` method is shown, for brevity):

```
class CombineNumberInPhones < ActiveRecord::Migration
  def self.up
    add_column :phones, :number, :string
    execute("update phones set number = concat(area_code, prefix,
                                               suffix)")
    remove_column :phones, :area_code
    remove_column :phones, :prefix
    remove_column :phones, :suffix
  end
end
```

The naive alternative to using SQL in the example above would be more lines of code and much, much slower.

```
Phone.find_each do |p|
  p.number = p.area_code + p.prefix + p.suffix
  p.save
end
```

In this particular case, you could use Active Record's `update_all` method to still do the data migration in one line.

```
Phone.update_all("set number = concat(area_code, prefix, suffix)")
```

However you might hit problems down the road as your schema evolves; as described in the next section, you'd want to declare an independent `Phone` model in the migration file itself. That's why I advise sticking to raw SQL whenever possible.

6.2.2 Migration Models

If you declare an Active Record model inside of a migration script, it'll be namespaced to that migration class.

```
class HashPasswordsOnUsers < ActiveRecord::Migration
  class User < ActiveRecord::Base
  end

  def self.up
    add_column :users, :hashed_password, :string
    User.find_each do |user|
      user.hashed_password = Digest::SHA1.hexdigest(user.password)
      user.save!
    end
    remove_column :users, :password
  end
end
```

Why not use just your application model classes in the migration scripts directly? As your schema evolves, older migrations that use model classes directly can and will break down and become unusable. Properly namespacing migration models prevent you from having to worry about name clashes with your application's model classes or ones that are defined in other migrations.

Durran says...

Note that Active Record caches column information on the first request to the database, so if you want to perform a data migration immediately after a migration you may run into a situation where the new columns have not yet been loaded. This is a case where using `reset_column_information` can come in handy. Simply call this class method on your model and everything will be reloaded on the next request.

6.3 `schema.rb`

The file `db/schema.rb` is generated every time you migrate and reflects the latest status of your database schema. You should never edit `db/schema.rb` by hand since this file is auto-generated from the current state of the database. Instead of editing this file, please use the migrations feature of Active Record to incrementally modify your database, and *then* regenerate this schema definition.

Note that this `schema.rb` definition is the authoritative source for your database schema. If you need to create the application database on another system, you should be using `db:schema:load`, not running all the migrations from scratch. The latter is a flawed and unsustainable approach (the more migrations you'll amass, the slower it'll run and the greater likelihood for issues).

It's strongly recommended to check this file into your version control system. First of all, it helps to have one definitive schema definition around for reference. Secondly, you can run `rake db:schema:load` to create your database schema from scratch without having to run all migrations. That's especially important considering that as your project evolves, it's likely that it will become impossible to run migrations all the way through from the start, due to code incompatibilities, such as renaming of classes named explicitly.

6.4 Database Seeding

The automatically created file `db/seeds.rb` is a default location for creating seed data for your database. It was introduced in order to stop the practice of inserting seed data in individual migration files, if you accept the premise that migrations should never be used for seeding example or base data required by your application. It is executed with the `rake db:seed` task (or created alongside the database when you run `rake db:setup`).

At its simplest, the contents of `seed.rb` is simply a series of `create!` statements that generate baseline data for your application, whether it's default or related to configuration. For example, let's add an admin user and some billing codes to our time and expenses app:

```
User.create!(:login => 'admin',
             :email => 'admin@tr3w.com',
             :password => '123', :password_confirmation => '123',
             :authorized_approver => true)

client = Client.create!(:name => 'Workbeast', :code => 'BEAST')
client.billing_codes.create!(:name => 'Meetings', :code => 'MTG')
client.billing_codes.create!(:name => 'Development', :code => 'DEV')
```

Why use the bang version of the create methods? Because otherwise you won't find out if you had errors in your seed file. An alternative would be to use `find_or_create_by` methods to make seeding idempotent.

```
c = Client.find_or_create_by_name_and_code!('Workbeast', 'BEAST')
c.billing_codes.find_or_create_by_name_and_code!('Meetings', 'MTG')
c.billing_codes.find_or_create_by_name_and_code!('Development', 'DEV')
```

Another common seeding practice worth mentioning is calling `delete_all` prior to creating new records, so that seeding does not generate duplicate records. This practice avoids the need for idempotent seeding routines and lets you be very secure about exactly what your database will look like after seeding.

```
User.delete_all
User.create!(:login => 'admin', ...

Client.delete_all
client = Client.create!(:name => 'Workbeast', ...
```

6.5 Database-Related Rake Tasks

The following rake tasks are included by default in boilerplate Rails projects.

db:create and db:create:all

Create the database defined in config/database.yml for the current `Rails.env` (Or create all of the local databases defined in config/database.yml in the case of `db:create:all`.)

db:drop and db:drop:all

Drops the database for the current `RAILS_ENV`. (Or drops all of the local databases defined in config/database.yml in the case of `db:drop:all`.)

db:forward and db:rollback

The `db:rollback` task moves your database schema back one version. Similarly, the `db:forward` task moves your database schema forward one version and is typically used after rolling back.

db:migrate

Applies all pending migrations. If a `VERSION` environment variable is provided, then `db:migrate` will apply pending migrations through the migration specified, but no further. The `VERSION` is specified as the timestamp portion of the migration file name. If the `VERSION` provided is older than the current version of the schema, then this task will actually rollback the newer migrations.

db:migrate:down

Invoked without a `VERSION`, this task will migrate all the way down the version list to an empty database, assuming that all your migrations are working correctly.

With a `VERSION`, this task will invoke the `down` method of the specified migration only. The `VERSION` is specified as the timestamp portion of the migration file name.

```
$ rake db:migrate:up VERSION=20100124181315
==  AddClientIdToUser: migrating ========================================
-- add_column(:users, :client_id, :integer)
   -> 0.0383s
==  AddClientIdToUser: migrated (0.0385s) ===============================
```

db:migrate:up

Invoked without a VERSION, this task will migrate up the version list, behaving the same as db:migrate.

With a VERSION, this task will invoke the up method of the specified migration only. The VERSION is specified as the timestamp portion of the migration file name.

```
$ rake db:migrate:down VERSION=20100124181315
==  AddClientIdToUser: reverting ========================================
-- remove_column(:users, :client_id)
   -> 0.0367s
==  AddClientIdToUser: reverted (0.0370s) ===============================
```

Tim says...

> The db:migrate:up and db:migrate:down tasks make for useful keybindings in migra-
> tions files. In Vim with rails.vim, for example, invoke :.Rake in a self.up or self.down
> method definition to invoke said task with the correct VERSION argument, or invoke it outside
> of both to invoke db:migrate:redo.

---

db:migrate:redo

Executes the down method of the latest migration file, immediately followed by its up method. This task is typically used right after correcting a mistake in the up method or to test that a migration is working correctly.

```
$ rake db:migrate:redo
==  AddTimesheetsUpdatedAtToUsers: reverting ============================
-- remove_column(:users, :timesheets_updated_at)
   -> 0.0853s
==  AddTimesheetsUpdatedAtToUsers: reverted (0.0861s) ===================

==  AddTimesheetsUpdatedAtToUsers: migrating ===========================
-- add_column(:users, :timesheets_updated_at, :datetime)
   -> 0.3577s
==  AddTimesheetsUpdatedAtToUsers: migrated (0.3579s) ===================
```

Active
Record

db:migrate:reset

Resets your database for the current environment using your migrations (as opposed to using `schema.rb`).

db:reset and db:setup

The `db:setup` creates the database for the current environment, loads the schema from `db/schema.rb`, then loads the seed data. It's used when you're setting up an existing project for the first time on a development workstation. The similar `db:reset` task does the same thing except that it drops and recreates the database first.

db:schema:dump

Create a `db/schema.rb` file that can be portably used against any DB supported by Active Record. Note that creation (or updating) of `schema.rb` happens automatically any time you migrate.

db:schema:load

Loads `schema.rb` file into the database for the current environment.

db:seed

Load the seed data from `db/seeds.rb` as described in this chapter's section Database Seeding.

db:structure:dump

Dump the database structure to a SQL file containing raw DDL code in a format corresponding to the database driver specified in `database.yml` for your current environment.

```
$ rake db:structure:dump

$ cat db/development_structure.sql
CREATE TABLE 'avatars' (
  'id' int(11) NOT NULL AUTO_INCREMENT,
  'user_id' int(11) DEFAULT NULL,
  'url' varchar(255) COLLATE utf8_unicode_ci DEFAULT NULL,
  PRIMARY KEY ('id')
) ENGINE=InnoDB DEFAULT CHARSET=utf8 COLLATE=utf8_unicode_ci;

...
```

I've rarely needed to use this task. It's possible that some Rails teams working in conjunction with DBAs that exercise strict control over their application's database schemas will need this task on a regular basis.

db:test:prepare

Check for pending migrations and load the test schema by doing a db:schema:dump followed by a db:schema:load.

This task gets used very often during active development whenever you're running specs or tests without using Rake. (Standard spec-related Rake tasks run db:test:prepare automatically for you.)

db:version

Returns the timestamp of the latest migration file that has been run. Works even if your database has been created from db/schema.rb, since it contains the latest version timestamp in it:

```
ActiveRecord::Schema.define(:version => 20100122011531)
```

6.6 Conclusion

This chapter covered the fundamentals of Active Record migrations. In the following chapter, we continue our coverage of Active Record by learning about how model objects are related to each other and interact via associations.

Active
Record

CHAPTER 7

Active Record Associations

Any time you can reify something, you can create something that embodies a concept, it gives you leverage to work with it more powerfully. That's exactly what's going on with `has_many:through`.

—Josh Susser

Active Record associations let you declaratively express relationships between model classes. The power and readability of the Associations API is an important part of what makes working with Rails so special.

This chapter covers the different kinds of Active Record associations available while highlighting use cases and available customizations for each of them. We also take a look at the classes that give us access to relationships themselves.

7.1 The Association Hierarchy

Associations typically appear as methods on Active Record model objects. For example, the method `timesheets` might represent the timesheets associated with a given `user`.

```
user.timesheets
```

However, people might get confused about the type of objects that are returned by association with these methods. This is because they have a way of masquerading as plain old Ruby objects and arrays (depending on the type of association we're considering). In the snippet, the `timesheets` method may appear to return an array of project objects.

The console will even confirm our thoughts. Ask any association collection what its return type is and it will tell you that it is an `Array`:

```
>> obie.timesheets.class
=> Array
```

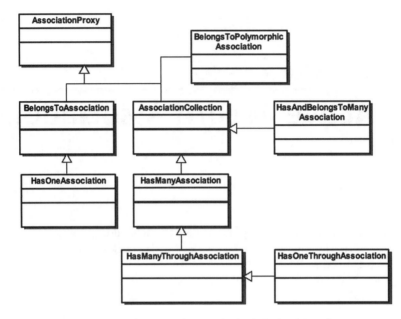

Figure 7.1   The Association proxies in their class hierarchy.

It's actually lying to you, albeit very innocently. Association methods for has_many associations are actually instances of HasManyAssociation, shown within its class hierarchy in Figure 7.1.

The parent class of all associations is AssociationProxy. It contains the basic structure and functionality of all assocation proxies. If you look near the top of its source code excerpted in Listing 7.1, you'll notice that it undefines a bunch of methods.

Listing 7.1   Excerpt from **lib/active_record/associations/association_proxy.rb**

```
instance_methods.each do |m|
  undef_method m unless m =~ /^(?:nil?|send|object_id|to_a)$|^__|proxy_/
end
```

As a result, most normal instance methods aren't actually defined on the proxy anymore, but are instead delegated to the target of the proxy via method_missing. That means that a call to timesheets.class returns the class of the underlying array rather than the proxy. You can prove that `timesheet` is actually a proxy by asking it if it responds to one of `AssociationProxy`'s public methods, such as `proxy_owner`:

```
>> obie.timesheets.respond_to? :proxy_owner
=> true
```

Fortunately, it's not the Ruby way to care about the actual class of an object. What messages an object responds to is a lot more significant.

The parent class of all `has_many` associations is AssociationCollection and most of the methods that it defines work similarly regardless of the options declared for the relationship. Before we get much further into the details of the association proxies, let's delve into the most fundamental type of association that is commonly used in Rails applications: the `has_many` / `belongs_to` pair, used to define one-to-many relationships.

7.2 One-to-Many Relationships

In our recurring sample application, an example of a one-to-many relationship is the association between the `User`, `Timesheet`, and `ExpenseReport` classes:

```
class User < ActiveRecord::Base
  has_many :timesheets
  has_many :expense_reports
end
```

Timesheets and expense reports should be linked in the opposite direction as well, so that it is possible to reference the `user` to which a timesheet or expense report belongs.

```
class Timesheet < ActiveRecord::Base
  belongs_to :user
end

class ExpenseReport < ActiveRecord::Base
  belongs_to :user
end
```

When these relationship declarations are executed, Rails uses some metaprogramming magic to dynamically add code to your models. In particular, proxy collection objects are created that let you manipulate the relationship easily. To demonstrate, let's play with these relationships in the console. First, I'll create a user.

```
>> obie = User.create :login => 'obie', :password => '1234',
:password_confirmation => '1234', :email => 'obiefernandez@gmail.com'
=> #<User...>
```

Now I'll verify that I have collections for timesheets and expense reports.

```
>> obie.timesheets
ActiveRecord::StatementInvalid: SQLite3::SQLException: no such column:
timesheets.user_id:
SELECT * FROM timesheets WHERE (timesheets.user_id = 1)
from /.../connection_adapters/abstract_adapter.rb:128:in `log'
```

As David might say, "Whoops!" I forgot to add the foreign key columns to the `timesheets` and `expense_reports` tables, so in order to go forward I'll generate a migration for the changes:

```
$ rails generate migration add_user_foreign_keys
      exists        db/migrate
      create        db/migrate/20100108014048_add_user_foreign_keys.rb
```

Then I'll open `db/migrate/20100108014048_add_user_foreign_keys.rb` and add the missing columns. (Using `change_table` would mean writing many more lines of code, so we'll stick with the traditional `add_column` syntax, which still works fine.)

```
class AddUserForeignKeys < ActiveRecord::Migration
  def self.up
    add_column :timesheets, :user_id, :integer
    add_column :expense_reports, :user_id, :integer
  end

  def self.down
    remove_column :timesheets, :user_id
    remove_column :expense_reports, :user_id
  end
end
```

Running `rake db:migrate` applies the changes:

```
$ rake db:migrate
(in /Users/obie/prorails/time_and_expenses)
== AddUserForeignKeys: migrating
===============================================
-- add_column(:timesheets, :user_id, :integer)
   -> 0.0253s
-- add_column(:expense_reports, :user_id, :integer)
   -> 0.0101s
== AddUserForeignKeys: migrated (0.0357s)
===============================================
```

Index associations for performance boost

Premature optimization is the root of all evil. Or something like that.[1] However, most experienced Rails developers don't mind adding indexes for foreign keys at the time that those are created. In the case of our migration example, you'd add the following statements.

```
add_index :timesheets, :user_id
add_index :expense_reports, :user_id
```

Loading of your associations (which is usually more common than creation of items) will get a big performance boost.

Now I should be able to add a new blank timesheet to my user and check `timesheets` again to make sure it's there:

```
>> obie = User.find(1)
=> #<User id: 1...>
>> obie.timesheets << Timesheet.new
=> [#<Timesheet id: 1, user_id: 1...>]
>> obie.timesheets
=> [#<Timesheet id: 1, user_id: 1...>]
```

Notice that the `Timesheet` object gains an `id` immediately.

7.2.1 Adding Associated Objects to a Collection

As you can deduce from the previous example, appending an object to a `has_many` collection automatically saves that object. That is, unless the parent object (the owner of the collection) is not yet stored in the database. Let's make sure that's the case using Active Record's `reload` method, which re-fetches the attributes of an object from the database:

```
>> obie.timesheets.reload
=> [#<Timesheet id: 1, user_id: 1...>]
```

There it is. The foreign key, `user_id`, was automatically set by the `<<` method. It takes one or more association objects to add to the collection, and since it flattens its argument list and inserts each record, `push` and `concat` behave identically.

---

1. See `http://www.acm.org/ubiquity/views/v7i24_fallacy.html`

In the blank timesheet example, I could have used the `create` method on the association proxy, and it would have worked essentially the same way:

```
>> obie.timesheets.create
=> #<Timesheet id: 1, user_id: 1...>
```

Even though at first glance << and `create` do the same thing, there are some important differences in how they're implemented that are covered in the following section.

7.2.2 Association Collection Methods

Association collections are basically fancy wrappers around a Ruby array, and have all of a normal array's methods. Named scopes and all of `ActiveRecord::Base`'s class methods are also available on association collections, including `find`, `order`, `where`, etc.

```
user.timesheets.where(:submitted => true).order('updated_at desc')
user.timesheets.late # assuming a scope :late defined on the Timesheet
class
```

The following methods of `AssociationCollection` are inherited by and available to association collections:

`<<(*records)` and `create(attributes = {})`
Both methods will add either a single associated object or many, depending on whether you pass them an array or not. However, << is transactional, and `create` is not.

Yet another difference has to do with association callbacks (covered in this chapter's options section for `has_many`). The << method triggers the `:before_add` and `:after_add` callbacks, but the `create` method does not.

Finally, the return value behavior of both methods varies wildly. The `create` method returns the new instance created, which is what you'd expect given its counterpart in `ActiveRecord::Base`. The << method returns the association proxy (ever masquerading as an array), which allows chaining and is also natural behavior for a Ruby array.

However, << will return `false` and not itself if any of the records being added causes the operation to fail. You shouldn't depend on the return value of << being an array that you can continue operating on in a chained fashion.

`all`
The `all` method exists here mostly for consistency, since normally if you wanted to operate on all records you would simply use the association itself.

any? and **many?**

The any? method behaves like its Enumerable counterpart if you give it a block, otherwise it's the opposite of empty? Its companion method many?, which is an ActiveSupport extension to Enumerable, returns true if the size of the collection is greater than one, or if a block is given, if two or more elements match the supplied criteria.

average(column_name, options = {})

Convenience wrapper for calculate(:average, ...)

build(attributes={}, & block)

Traditionally, the build method has corresponded to the new method of Active Record classes, except that it presets the owner's foreign key and appends it to the association collection in one operation. However, as of Rails 2.2, the new method has the same behavior and probably should be used instead of build.

```
user.timesheets.build(attributes)
user.timesheets.new(attributes) # same as calling build
```

One possible reason to still use build is that as a convenience, if the attributes parameter is an array of hashes (instead of just one) then build executes for each one. However, you would usually accomplish that kind of behavior using accepts_nested_attributes_for on the owning class, covered in Chapter 11, All About Helpers, in the section about fields_for.

calculate(operation, column_name, options = {})

Provides aggregate (:sum, :average, :minimum and :maximum) values within the scope of associated records. Covered in detail in Chapter 9, Advanced Active Record.

clear

Transactionally removes all records from this association by clearing the foreign key field (see delete). If the association is configured with the :dependent option set to :delete_all, then it calls delete_all. Similarly, if the :dependent option is set to :destroy_all, then the destroy_all method is invoked.

count(column_name=nil, options={})

Counts all associated records in the database. The first parameter, column_name gives you the option of counting on a column instead of generating COUNT(*) in the resulting SQL. If the :counter_sql option is set for the association, it will be used for the query, otherwise you can pass a custom value via the options hash of this method.

Active
Record

Assuming that no `:counter_sql` or `:finder_sql` options are set on the association, nor passed to `count`, the target class's count method is used, scoped to only count associated records.

`create(attributes, & block)` and `create!(attributes, & block)`

Instantiate a new record with its foreign key attribute set to the owner's id, add it to the association collection, and save it, all in one method call. The bang variant raises `Active::RecordInvalid` if saving fails, while the non-bang variant returns true or false, as you would expect it to based on the behavior of create methods in other places.

The owning record must be saved in order to use create, otherwise an `ActiveRecord::RecordNotSaved` exception is raised.

```
>> User.new.timesheets.create
ActiveRecord::RecordNotSaved: You cannot call create unless the parent is
saved
```

If a block is passed to `create` or `create!`, it will get yielded the newly created instance after the passed-in attributes are assigned, but before saving the record to the database.

`delete(*records)` and `delete_all`

The `delete` and `delete_all` methods are used to sever specified associations, or all of them, respectively. Both methods operate transactionally.

It's worth noting, for performance reasons, that calling `delete_all` first loads the entire collection of associated objects into memory in order to grab their ids. Then it executes a SQL UPDATE that sets foreign keys for all currently associated objects to nil, effectively disassociating them from their parent. Since it loads the entire association into memory, it would be ill-advised to use this method with an extremely large collection of associated objects.

Note

The names of the `delete` and `delete_all` methods can be misleading. By default, they don't delete anything from the database—they only sever associations by clearing the foreign key field of the associated record. This behavior is related to the `:dependent` option, which defaults to `:nullify`. If the association is configured with the `:dependent` option set to `:delete` or `:destroy`, then the associated records will actually be deleted from the database.

---

destroy(*records) and destroy_all

The `destroy` and `destroy_all` methods are used to remove specified associations from the database, or all of them, respectively. Both methods operate transactionally.

The `destroy_all` method takes no parameters; it's an all or nothing affair. When called, it begins a transaction and invokes `destroy` on each object in the association, causing them all to be deleted from the database with individual DELETE SQL statements. Again, there are load issues to consider if you plan to use this method with large association collections, since many objects will be loaded into memory at once.

empty?

Simply calls `size.zero?`

find(id)

Finds an associated record by `id`, a really common operation when dealing with nested RESTful resources. Raises `ActiveRecord::RecordNotFound` exception if either the id or foreign_key of the owner record is not found.

first(options)

Returns the first associated record. Wondering how Active Record figures out whether to go to the database instead of loading the entire association collection into memory?

```
def fetch_first_or_last_using_find?(args)
  args.first.kind_of?(Hash) ||
    !(loaded? ||
      @owner.new? ||
      @reflection.options[:finder_sql] ||
      @target.any? { |record| record.new? } ||
      args.first.kind_of?(Integer)
    )
end
```

Passing `first` an integer argument mimics the semantics of Ruby's `Array#first`, returning that number of records.

```
>> c = Client.first
=> #<Client id: 1, name: "Taigan", code: "TAIGAN", created_at: "2010-01-24
03:18:58", updated_at: "2010-01-24 03:18:58">
>> c.billing_codes.first(2)
=> [#<BillingCode id: 1, client_id: 1, code: "MTG", description:
"Meetings">,
#<BillingCode id: 2, client_id: 1, code: "DEV", description:
"Development">]
```

Active
Record

include?(record)

Checks to see if the supplied record exists in the association collection and that it still exists in the underlying database table.

last(options)

Returns the last associated record. Refer to description of first earlier in this section for more details—it behaves exactly the same except for the obvious.

length

Returns the size of the collection by loading it and calling size on the array.

maximum(column_name, options = {})

Convenience wrapper for calculate(:maximum, ...), covered in detail in Chapter 9, Advanced Active Record.

minimum(column_name, options = {})

Convenience wrapper for calculate(:minimum, ...), covered in detail in Chapter 9, Advanced Active Record.

new(attributes, & block)

Instantiate a new record with its foreign key attribute set to the owner's id, and add it to the association collection, in one method call.

replace(other_array)

Replaces the collection with other_array. Works by deleting objects that exist in the current collection, but not in other_array and inserting (using concat) objects that don't exist in the current collection, but do exist in other_array.

size

If the collection has already been loaded, or its owner object has never been saved, the size method simply returns the size of the current underlying array of associated objects. Otherwise, assuming default options, a SELECT COUNT(*) query is executed to get the size of the associated collection without having to load any objects. The query is bounded to the :limit option of the association, if there is any set.

Note that if there is a counter_cache option set on the association, then its value is used instead of hitting the database.

When you know that you are starting from an unloaded state and it's likely that there are associated records in the database that you will need to load no matter what, it's more efficient to use length instead of size.

Some association options, such as `:group` and `:uniq`, come into play when calculating size—basically they will always force all objects to be loaded from the database so that the resulting size of the association array can be returned.

sum(column_name, options = {})

Convenience wrapper for `calculate(:sum, ...)`, covered in detail in Chapter 9, Advanced Active Record.

uniq

Iterates over the target collection and populates a `Set` with the unique values present. Keep in mind that equality of Active Record objects is determined by identity, meaning that the value of the `id` attribute is the same for both objects being compared.

A warning about association names

> Don't create associations that have the same name as instance methods of `ActiveRecord::Base`. Since the association adds a method with that name to its model, it will override the inherited method and break things. For instance, `attributes` and `connection` would make really bad choices for association names.

7.3   The belongs_to Association

The `belongs_to` class method expresses a relationship from one Active Record object to a single associated object for which it has a foreign key attribute. The trick to remembering whether a class "belongs to" another one is considering which has the foreign key column in its database table.

Assigning an object to a `belongs_to` association will set its foreign key attribute to the owner object's id, but will not save the record to the database automatically, as in the following example:

```
>> timesheet = Timesheet.create
=> #<Timesheet id: 1409, user_id: nil...>
>> timesheet.user = obie
=> #<User id: 1, login: "obie"...>
>> timesheet.user.login
=> "obie"
>> timesheet.reload
=> #<Timesheet id: 1409, user_id: nil...>
```

Defining a `belongs_to` relationship on a class creates a method with the same name on its instances. As mentioned earlier, the method is actually a proxy to the related Active Record object and adds capabilities useful for manipulating the relationship.

7.3.1   Reloading the Association

Just invoking the asssociation method will query the database (if necessary) and return an instance of the related object. The method takes a `force_reload` parameter that tells Active Record whether to reload the related object, if it happens to have been cached already by a previous access.

In the following capture from my console, I look up a timesheet and take a peek at the `object_id` of its related user object. Notice that the second time I invoke the association via `user`, the `object_id` remains the same. The related object has been cached. However, passing `true` to the accessor reloads the relationship and I get a new instance.

```
>> ts = Timesheet.first
=> #<Timesheet id: 3, user_id: 1...>
>> ts.user.object_id
=> 27421330
>> ts.user.object_id
=> 27421330
>> ts.user(true).object_id
=> 27396270
```

7.3.2   Building and Creating Related Objects
via the Association

During the `belongs_to` method's metaprogramming it also adds factory methods for creating new instances of the related class and attaching them via the foreign key automatically.

The `build_association` method does not save the new object, but the `create_association` method does. Both methods take an optional hash of attribute parameters with which to initialize the newly instantiated objects. Both are essentially one-line convenience methods, which I don't find particularly useful. It just doesn't usually make sense to create instances in that direction!

To illustrate, I'll simply show the code for building a `User` from a `Timesheet` or creating a `Client` from a `BillingCode`, neither of which would ever happen in real code because it just doesn't make sense to do so:

```
>> ts = Timesheet.first
=> #<Timesheet id: 3, user_id: 1...>
```

```
>> ts.build_user
=> #<User id: nil, email: nil...>

>> bc = BillingCode.first
=> #<BillingCode id: 1, code: "TRAVEL"...>

>> bc.create_client
=> #<Client id: 1, name=>nil, code=>nil...>
```

You'll find yourself creating instances of belonging objects from the has_many side of the relationship much more often.

7.3.3 **belongs_to** Options

The following options can be passed in a hash to the belongs_to method.

:autosave => true

Whether to automatically save the owning record whenever this record is saved. Defaults to false.

:class_name

Assume for a moment that we wanted to establish another belongs_to relationship from the Timesheet class to User, this time modeling the relationship to the approver of the timesheet. You might start by adding an approver_id column to the timesheets table and an authorized_approver column to the users table via a migration. Then you would add a second belongs_to declaration to the Timesheet class:

```
class Timesheet < ActiveRecord::Base
  belongs_to :approver
  belongs_to :user
  ...
```

Active Record won't be able to figure out what class you're trying to link with just the information provided, because you've (legitimately) acted against the Rails convention of naming a relationship according to the related class. It's time for a :class_name parameter.

```
class Timesheet < ActiveRecord::Base
  belongs_to :approver, :class_name => 'User'
  belongs_to :user
  ...
```

:conditions

Rails allows us to add conditions to a relationship that must be satisfied in order for it to be valid. The :conditions option allows you to do just that, with the same syntax that is used when you add conditions to a find invocation. Assuming that I add an authorized_approver column to the users table, we'll make use of it here:

```
class Timesheet < ActiveRecord::Base
  belongs_to :approver,
             :class_name => 'User',
             :conditions => {:approver => true}
  ...
end
```

Now in order for the assignment of a user to the approver field to work, that user must be authorized. I'll go ahead and add test cases that both indicate the intention of my code and show it in action. I turn my attention to test/unit/timesheet_test.rb

```
require File.dirname(__FILE__) + '/../test_helper'

class TimesheetTest < ActiveSupport::TestCase
  def test_user_may_be_associated_as_approver
    sheet = Timesheet.create
    sheet.approver = User.create(:approver => true)
    assert_not_nil sheet.approver, "approver assignment failed"
  end
end
```

It's a good start, but I also want to make sure something happens to prevent the system from assigning a nonauthorized user to the approver field, so I add another test:

```
  def test_non_authorized_user_cannot_be_associated_as_approver
    sheet = Timesheet.create
    sheet.approver = User.create(:approver => false)
    assert sheet.approver.nil?, "approver assignment should have failed"
  end
```

I have my suspicions about the validity of that test, though, and as I half-expected, it doesn't really work the way I want it to work:

```
1) Failure:
test_non_authorized_user_cannot_be_associated_as_approver(TimesheetTest)
[./test/unit/timesheet_test.rb:16]:
approver assignment should have failed.
<false> is not true.
```

The problem is that Active Record (for better or worse, probably worse) allows me to make the invalid assignment. The :conditions option only applies during the query to get the association back from the database. I'll have some more work ahead of me to achieve the desired behavior, but I'll go ahead and prove out Rails's actual behavior by fixing my tests. I'll do so by passing `true` to the `approver` method's optional `force_reload` argument, which tells it to reload its target object:

```
def test_only_authorized_user_may_be_associated_as_approver
  sheet = Timesheet.create
  sheet.approver = User.create(:approver => true)
  assert sheet.save
  assert_not_nil sheet.approver(true), "approver assignment failed"
end

def test_non_authorized_user_cannot_be_associated_as_approver
  sheet = Timesheet.create
  sheet.approver = User.create(:approver => false)
  assert sheet.save
  assert sheet.approver(true).nil?, "approver assignment should fail"
end
```

Those two tests do pass, but note that I went ahead and saved the `sheet`, since just assigning a value to it will not save the record. Then, as mentioned, I took advantage of the `force_reload` parameter to make Rails reload `approver` from the database, and not just simply give me the same instance I originally assigned to it.

The lesson to learn is that `:conditions` on relationships never affect the assignment of associated objects, only how they're read back from the database. To enforce the rule that a timesheet approver must be authorized, you'd need to add a `before_save` callback to the `Timesheet` class itself. Callbacks are covered in detail at the beginning of Chapter 9, Advanced Active Record.

:counter_cache

Use this option to make Rails automatically update a counter field on the associated object with the number of belonging objects. The option value can be `true`, in which case the pluralized name of the belonging class plus `_count` is used, or you can supply your own column name to be used:

```
:counter_cache => true
:counter_cache => 'number_of_children'
```

If a significant percentage of your association collections will be empty at any given moment, you can optimize performance at the cost of some extra database storage by using counter caches liberally. The reason is that when the counter cache attribute is at zero, Rails won't even try to query the database for the associated records!

Note

The value of the counter cache column must be set to zero by default in the database! Otherwise the counter caching won't work at all. It's because the way that Rails implements the counter caching behavior is by adding a simple callback that goes directly to the database with an UPDATE command and increments the value of the counter. If you're not careful, and neglect to set a default value of 0 for the counter cache column on the database, or misspell the column name, the counter cache will still seem to work! There is a magic method on all classes with has_many associations called collection_count, just like the counter cache. It will return a correct count value based on the in-memory object, even if you don't have a counter cache option set or the counter cache column value is null!

In the case that a counter cache was altered on the database side, you may tell Active Record to reset a potentially stale value to the correct count via the class method reset_counters. It's parameters are the id of the object and a list of association names.

```
Timesheet.reset_counters(5, :weeks)
```

:dependent => :destroy or :delete

Specifies a rule that the associated owner record should be destroyed or just deleted from the database, depending on the value of the option. When triggered, :destroy will call the dependent's callbacks, whereas :delete will not.

Usage of this option *might* make sense in a has_one / belongs_to pairing. However, it is really unlikely that you want this behavior on has_many / belongs_to relationship; it just doesn't seem to make sense to code things that way. Additionally, if the owner record has its :dependent option set on the corresponding has_many association, then destroying one associated record will have the ripple effect of destroying all of its siblings.

:foreign_key => column_name

Specifies the name of the foreign key column that should be used to find the associated object. Rails will normally infer this setting from the name of the association, by adding _id to it. You can override the inferred foreign key name with this option if necessary.

```
# without the explicit option, Rails would guess administrator_id
belongs_to :administrator, :foreign_key => 'admin_user_id'
```

:include => [names_of_associations_to_eager_load]

Like all :include options, an optimization that takes a list of second-order association names (on the owning record) that should be eager-loaded when this object is loaded. In general, this technique is used to knock N+1 select operations down to N plus the number associations being included. It is rare to specify :include options on a belongs_to, rather than on the has_many side.

If necessary, due to conditions or orders referencing tables other than the main one, a SELECT statement with the necessary LEFT OUTER JOINS will be constructed on the fly so that all the data needed to construct a whole object graph is queried in one big database request.

With judicious use of :include and careful benchmarking, you can sometimes improve the performance of your application dramatically, mostly by eliminating N+1 queries. On the other hand, pulling lots of data from the database and instantiating large object trees can be very costly, so :include is no "silver bullet." As they say, your mileage may vary.

:inverse_of => name_of_has_association

Explicitly declares the name of the inverse association in a bidirectional relationship. Considered an optimization, use of this option allows Rails to return the same instance of an object no matter which side of the relationship it is accessed from.

Covered in detail in Section 7.4.1.

:select => clause

Replaces the SQL select clause that normally generated when loading this association, which usually takes the form table_name.*. Just additional flexibility that it normally never needed.

:polymorphic => true

Use the :polymorphic option to specify that an object is related to its association in a polymorphic way, which is the Rails way of saying that the type of the related object is stored in the database along with its foreign key. By making a belongs_to relationship polymorphic, you abstract out the association so that any other model in the system can fill it.

Polymorphic associations let you trade some measure of relational integrity for the convenience of implementation in child relationships that are reused across your application. Common examples are models such as photo attachments, comments, notes, line items, and so on.

Let's illustrate by writing a Comment class that attaches to its subjects polymorphically. We'll associate it to both expense reports and timesheets. Listing 7.2 has the schema information in migration code, followed by the code for the classes involved. Notice the :subject_type column, which stores the class name of the associated class.

Listing 7.2 Comment class using polymorphic belongs_to relationship

```
create_table :comments do |t|
  t.text :body
  t.references :subject, :polymorphic => true

  # references can be used as a shortcut for following two statements
  # t.integer :subject_id
  # t.string   :subject_type

  t.timestamps
end

class Comment < ActiveRecord::Base
  belongs_to :subject, :polymorphic => true
end

class ExpenseReport < ActiveRecord::Base
  belongs_to :user
  has_many :comments, :as => :subject
end

class Timesheet < ActiveRecord::Base
  belongs_to :user
  has_many :comments, :as => :subject
end
```

As you can see in the `ExpenseReport` and `Timesheet` classes of Listing 7.2, there is a corresponding syntax where you give Active Record a clue that the relationship is polymorphic by specifying `:as => :subject`. We haven't covered `has_many`'s options yet in this chapter, and polymorphic relationships have their own section in Chapter 9, Advanced Active Record.

`:primary_key => column_name`
You should never need to use this option, except perhaps with strange legacy database schemas. It allows you to specify a surrogate column on the owning record to use as the target of the foreign key, instead of the usual primary key.

`:readonly => true`
Locks down the reference to the owning record so that you can't modify it. Theoretically this might make sense in terms of constraining your programming contexts very

specifically, but I've never had a use for it. Still, for illustrative purposes, here is an example where I've made the user association on Timesheet readonly:

```
class Timesheet < ActiveRecord::Base
  belongs_to :user, :readonly => true
  ...

>> t = Timesheet.first
=> #<Timesheet id: 1, submitted: nil, user_id: 1...>

>> t.user
 => #<User id: 1, login: "admin"...>

>> t.user.save
ActiveRecord::ReadOnlyRecord: ActiveRecord::ReadOnlyRecord
```

:touch => true or column_name

"Touches" the owning record's updated_at timestamp, or a specific timestamp column specified by column_name, if it is supplied. Useful for caching schemes where timestamps are used to invalidate cached view content. The column_name option is particularly useful here, if you want to do fine-grained fragment caching of the owning record's view.

For example, let's set the foundation for doing just that with the User/Timesheet association:

```
$ rails generate migration AddTimesheetsUpdatedAtToUsers
timesheets_updated_at:datetime
      invoke      active_record
      create      db/migrate/20100124191217_add_timesheets_
                  updated_at_to_users.rb
$ rake db:migrate
==  AddTimesheetsUpdatedAtToUsers: migrating
==================================
-- add_column(:users, :timesheets_updated_at, :datetime)
   -> 0.0426s
==  AddTimesheetsUpdatedAtToUsers: migrated (0.0429s)
=========================

class Timesheet < ActiveRecord::Base
  belongs_to :user, :touch => :timesheets_updated_at
  ...
```

:validate => true

Defaults to false on belongs_to associations, contrary to its counterpart setting on has_many. Tells Active Record to validate the owner record, but only in circumstances where it would normally save the owning record, such as when the record is new and a save is required in order to get a foreign key value.

Tim says...

Use `validates_associated` if you want association validation outside of automatic saving.

7.4 The `has_many` Association

Just like it sounds, the `has_many` association allows you to define a relationship in which one model has many other models that belong to it. The sheer readability of code constructs such as `has_many` is a major reason that people fall in love with Rails.

The `has_many` class method is often used without additional options. If Rails can guess the type of class in the relationship from the name of the association, no additional configuration is necessary. This bit of code should look familiar by now:

```
class User < ActiveRecord::Base
  has_many :timesheets
  has_many :expense_reports
```

The names of the associations can be singularized and match the names of models in the application, so everything works as expected.

7.4.1 `has_many` Options

Despite the ease of use of `has_many`, there is a surprising amount of power and customization possible for those who know and understand the options available.

`:after_add => callback`

Called after a record is added to the collection via the `<<` method. Is not triggered by the collection's `create` method, so careful consideration is needed when relying on association callbacks. A lambda callback will get called directly, versus a symbol, which correlates to a method on the owning record, which takes the newly-added child as a parameter. It's also possible to pass an array of lambda or symbols.

Add callback method options to a `has_many` by passing one or more symbols corresponding to method names, or `Proc` objects. See Listing 7.3 in the `:before_add` option for an example.

:after_remove => callback

Called after a record has been removed from the collection with the delete method. A lambda callback will get called directly, versus a symbol, which correlates to a method on the owning record, which takes the newly-added child as a parameter. It's also possible to pass an array of lambda or symbols. See Listing 7.3 in the :before_add option for an example.

:as => association_name

Specifies the polymorphic belongs_to association to use on the related class. (See Chapter 9 for more about polymorphic relationships.)

:autosave => true

Whether to automatically save *all modified records* in an association collection when the parent is saved. Defaults to false, but note that normal Active Record behavior is to save *new* associations records automatically when the parent is saved.

:before_add => callback

Triggered when a record is added to the collection via the << method. (Remember that concat and push are aliases of <<.)

A lambda callback will get called directly, versus a symbol, which correlates to a method on the owning record, which takes the newly-added child as a parameter. It's also possible to pass an array of lambda or symbols.

Raising an exception in the callback will stop the object from getting added to the collection. (Basically, because the callback is triggered right after the type mismatch check, and there is no rescue clause to be found inside <<.)

Listing 7.3 A simple example of **:before_add** callback usage

```
has_many :unchangable_posts,
         :class_name => "Post",
         :before_add => :raise_exception

private

  def raise_exception(object)
    raise "You can't add a post"
  end
```

Active Record

Of course, that would have been a lot shorter code using a `Proc` since it's a one-liner. The `owner` parameter is the object with the association. The `record` parameter is the object being added.

```
has_many :unchangable_posts,
  :class_name => "Post",
  :before_add => Proc.new {|owner, record| raise "Can't do it!"}
```

One more time, with a lambda, which doesn't check the arity of block parameters:

```
has_many :unchangable_posts,
  :class_name => "Post",
  :before_add => lambda {raise "You can't add a post"}
```

:before_remove => callback

Called before a record is removed from a collection with the `delete` method. See `before_add` for more information. As with `:before_add`, raising an exception stops the remove operation.

```
class User < ActiveRecord::Base
  has_many :timesheets,
           :before_remove => :check_timesheet_destruction,
           :dependent => :destroy

  protected

  def check_timesheet_destruction(timesheet)
    if timesheet.submitted?
      raise TimesheetError, "Cannot destroy a submitted timesheet."
    end
  end
end
```

Note that this is a somewhat contrived example, because it violates my sense of good object-oriented principles. The `User` class shouldn't really be responsible for knowing when it's okay to delete a timesheet or not. The `check_timesheet_destruction` method would more properly be added as a `before_destroy` callback on the `Timesheet` class.

:class_name

The `:class_name` option is common to all of the associations. It allows you to specify, as a string, the name of the class of the association, and is needed when the class name cannot be inferred from the name of the association itself.

```
has_many :draft_timesheets, :class_name => 'Timesheet',
                            :conditions => { :submitted => false }
```

:conditions

The :conditions option is common to all of the associations. It allows you to add extra conditions to the Active Record-generated SQL query that bring back the objects in the association.

You can apply extra :conditions to an association for a variety of reasons. How about approval of comments?

```
has_many :comments, :conditions => { :approved => true }
```

Plus, there's no rule that you can't have more than one has_many association exposing the same two related tables in different ways. Just remember that you'll probably have to specify the class name too.

```
has_many :pending_comments, :class_name => 'Comment',
                            :conditions => { :approved => false }
```

:counter_sql

Overrides the Active Record–generated SQL query that would be used to count the number of records belonging to this association. Not necessarily needed in conjunction with the :finder_sql option, since Active Record will automatically generate counter SQL code based on the custom finder SQL statement.

As with all custom SQL specifications in Active Record, you must use single-quotes around the entire string to prevent premature interpolation. (That is, you don't want the string to get interpolated in the context of the class where you're declaring the association. You want it to get interpolated at runtime.)

```
has_many :things, :finder_sql => 'select * from things where id = #{id}'
```

:dependent => :delete_all

All associated objects are deleted in fell swoop using a single SQL command. Note: While this option is much faster than :destroy, it doesn't trigger any destroy callbacks on the associated objects—you should use this option very carefully. It should only be used on associations that depend solely on the parent object.

:dependent => :destroy

All associated objects are destroyed along with the parent object, by iteratively calling their destroy methods.

`:dependent => :nullify`

The default behavior when deleting a record with `has_many` associations is to leave those associated records alone. Their foreign key fields will still point at the record that was deleted. The `:nullify` option tells Active Record to nullify, or clear, the foreign key that joins them to the parent record.

`:extend => ExtensionModule`

Specifies a module with methods that will extend the association collection proxy. Used as an alternative to defining additional methods in a block passed to the `has_many` method itself. Discussed in the section "Association Extensions".

`:finder_sql => sql_statement`

Specifies a complete SQL statement to fetch the association. This is a possible way to load complex associations that depend on multiple tables for their data. It's also quite rare to need to go this route.

Count operations are done with a SQL statement based on the query supplied via the `:finder_sql` option. If Active Record has trouble with the transformation, it might be necessary to supply an explicit `:counter_sql` value also.

`:foreign_key => column_name`

Overrides the convention-based foreign key column name that would normally be used in the SQL statement that loads the association. Normally it would be the owning record's class name with `_id` appended to it.

`:group => sql_expression`

Adds a GROUP BY SQL clause to the queries used to load the contents of the association collection.

`:having => conditions`

Must be used in conjunction with `:group` and adds extra conditions to the resulting SQL query used to load the contents of the association collection.

`:include => associations`

Takes an array of second-order association names (as an array) that should be eager-loaded when this collection is loaded. As with the `:include` option on `belongs_to` associations, with judicious use of `:include` and careful benchmarking you can sometimes improve the performance of your application dramatically.

To illustrate, let's analyze how `:include` affects the SQL generated while navigating relationships. We'll use the following simplified versions of `Timesheet`, `BillableWeek`, and `BillingCode`:

```
class Timesheet < ActiveRecord::Base
  has_many :billable_weeks
end

class BillableWeek < ActiveRecord::Base
  belongs_to :timesheet
  belongs_to :billing_code
end

class BillingCode < ActiveRecord::Base
  belongs_to :client
  has_many :billable_weeks
end
```

First, I need to set up my test data, so I create a `timesheet` instance and add a couple of billable weeks to it. Then I assign a billable code to each billable week, which results in an object graph (with four objects linked together via associations).

Next I do a fancy one-line `collect`, which gives me an array of the billing codes associated with the timesheet:

```
>> Timesheet.find(3).billable_weeks.collect{ |w| w.billing_code.code }
=> ["TRAVEL", "DEVELOPMENT"]
```

Without the `:include` option set on the `billable_weeks` association of `Timesheet`, that operation cost me the following four database hits (copied from `log/development.log`, and prettied up a little):

```
Timesheet Load (0.3ms)  SELECT timesheets.* FROM timesheets WHERE
(timesheets.id = 3) LIMIT 1
BillableWeek Load (1.3ms)  SELECT billable_weeks.* FROM billable_weeks
WHERE (billable_weeks.timesheet_id = 3)
BillingCode Load (1.2ms)  SELECT billing_codes.* FROM billing_codes WHERE
(billing_codes.id = 7) LIMIT 1
BillingCode Load (3.2ms)  SELECT billing_codes.* FROM billing_codes WHERE
(billing_codes.id = 8) LIMIT 1
```

This demonstrates the so-called "N+1 select" problem that inadvertently plagues many systems. Anytime I need one billable week, it will cost me N select statements to retrieve its associated records. Now let's add :include to the billable_weeks association, after which the Timesheet class looks as follows:

```
class Timesheet < ActiveRecord::Base
  has_many :billable_weeks, :include => [:billing_code]
end
```

Simple! Rerunning our test statement yields the same results in the console:

```
>> Timesheet.find(3).billable_weeks.collect{ |w| w.billing_code.code }
=> ["TRAVEL", "DEVELOPMENT"]
```

But look at how different the generated SQL is:

```
Timesheet Load (0.4ms)  SELECT timesheets.* FROM timesheets WHERE
(timesheets.id
= 3) LIMIT 1
BillableWeek Load (0.6ms)  SELECT billable_weeks.* FROM billable_weeks
WHERE (billable_weeks.timesheet_id = 3)
BillingCode Load (2.1ms)  SELECT billing_codes.* FROM billing_codes WHERE
(billing_codes.id IN (7,8))
```

Active Record smartly figures out exactly which BillingCode records it will need and pulls them in using one query. For large datasets, the performance improvement can be quite dramatic!

It's generally easy to find N+1 select issues just by watching the log scroll by while clicking through the different screens of your application. (Of course, make sure that you're looking at realistic data or the exercise will be pointless.) Screens that might benefit from eager loading will cause a flurry of single-row SELECT statements, one for each record in a given association being used.

If you're feeling particularly daring (perhaps masochistic is a better term) you can try including a deep hierarchy of associations, by mixing hashes into your :include array, like in this fictional example from a bulletin board:

```
has_many :posts, :include => [:author, {:comments => {:author => :avatar
}}])
```

That example snippet will grab not only all the comments for a Post, but all their authors and avatar pictures as well. You can mix and match symbols, arrays and hashes in any combination to describe the associations you want to load.

The biggest potential problem with so-called "deep" includes is pulling too much data out of the database. You should always start out with the simplest solution that will work, then use benchmarking and analysis to figure out if optimizations such as eager-loading help improve your performance.

Wilson says...

Let people learn eager loading by crawling across broken glass, like we did. It builds character!

`:inverse_of => name_of_belongs_to_association`

Explicitly declares the name of the inverse association in a bidirectional relationship. Considered an optimization, use of this option allows Rails to return the same instance of an object no matter which side of the relationship it is accessed from.

Consider the following, using our recurring example, *without* usage of `inverse_of`.

```
>> user = User.first
>> timesheet = user.timesheets.first
=> <Timesheet id: 1, user_id: 1...>
>> timesheet.user.equal? user
=> false
```

If we add `:inverse_of` to the association objection on `User`, like

```
has_many :timesheets, :inverse_of => :user
```

then `timesheet.user.equal?` user will be `true`. Try something similar in one of your apps to see it for yourself.

Tim says...

With `:inverse_of` properly set, you'll still notice the following inconsistency:

```
>> timesheet.user.equal? timesheet.user
=> true
>> user.equal? timesheet.user
=> false
```

This is because `timesheet.user` is actually an association proxy, and `equal?` is quite the stickler for object identity.

```
>> user.equal? timesheet.user.proxy_target
=> true
```

`:limit => integer`

Appends a `LIMIT` clause to the SQL generated for loading this association. This option is potentially useful in capping the size of very large association collections. Use in conjunction with the `:order` option to make sure your grabbing the most relevant records.

:offset => integer

An integer determining the offset from where the rows should be fetched when loading the association collection. I assume this is here mostly for completeness, since it's hard to envision a valid use case.

:order => expression

Specifies the order in which the associated objects are returned via an "ORDER BY" sql fragment, such as `"last_name, first_name DESC"`.

:primary_key => column_name

Specifies a surrogate key to use instead of the owning record's primary key, whose value should be used when querying to fill the association collection.

:readonly => true

Sets all records in the association collection to read-only mode, which prevents saving them.

:select => expression

By default, this is `*` as in `SELECT * FROM`, but can be changed if you, for example, want to add additional calculated columns or "piggyback" additional columns from joins onto the associated object as its loaded.

:source and :source_type

Used exclusively as additional options to assist in using `has_many :through` associations with polymorphic `belongs_to`. Covered in detail later in this chapter.

:table_name => names

The `:table_name` option lets you override the table names (FROM clause) that will be used in SQL statements generated for loading the association.

:through => association_name

Creates an association collection via another association. See the section in this chapter entitled "`has_many :through`" for more information.

:uniq => true

Strips duplicate objects from the collection. Sometimes useful in conjunction with `has_many :through`.

:validate => false

In cases where the child records in the association collection would be automatically saved by Active Record, this option (true by default) dictates whether to ensure that they are valid. If you always want to check the validity of associated records when saving the owning record, then use `validates_associated :association_name`.

7.5 Many-to-Many Relationships

Associating persistent objects via a join table can be one of the trickier aspects of object-relational mapping to implement correctly in a framework. Rails has a couple of techniques that let you represent many-to-many relationships in your model. We'll start with the older and simpler `has_and_belongs_to_many` and then cover the newer `has_many :through`.

7.5.1 `has_and_belongs_to_many`

Before proceeding with this section, I must clear my conscience by stating that `has_and_belongs_to_many` is practically obsolete in the minds of many Rails developers, including the authors of this book. Use `has_many :through` instead and your life should be a lot easier. The section is preserved in this edition almost exactly as it appeared in the first, because it contains good techniques that enlighten the reader about nuances of Active Record behavior.

The `has_and_belongs_to_many` method establishes a link between two associated Active Record models via an intermediate join table. Unless the join table is explicitly specified as an option, Rails guesses its name by concatenating the table names of the joined classes, in alphabetical order and separated with an underscore.

For example, if I was using `has_and_belongs_to_many` (or `habtm` for short) to establish a relationship between `Timesheet` and `BillingCode`, the join table would be named `billing_codes_timesheets` and the relationship would be defined in the models. Both the migration class and models are listed:

```
class CreateBillingCodesTimesheets < ActiveRecord::Migration
  def self.up
    create_table :billing_codes_timesheets, :id => false do |t|
      t.references :billing_code, :null => false
      t.references :timesheet, :null => false
    end
  end
```

```
  def self.down
    drop_table :billing_codes_timesheets
  end
end

class Timesheet < ActiveRecord::Base
  has_and_belongs_to_many :billing_codes
end

class BillingCode < ActiveRecord::Base
 has_and_belongs_to_many :timesheets
end
```

Note that an `id` primary key is not needed, hence the `:id => false` option was passed
to the `create_table` method. Also, since the foreign key columns are both needed, we
pass them a `:null => false` option. (In real code, you would also want to make sure
both of the foreign key columns were indexed properly.)

Self-Referential Relationship

What about self-referential many-to-many relationships? Linking a model to itself via a
`habtm` relationship is easy—you just have to provide explicit options. In Listing 7.4, I've
created a join table and established a link between related `BillingCode` objects. Again,
both the migration and model class are listed:

Listing 7.4 Related billing codes

```
class CreateRelatedBillingCodes < ActiveRecord::Migration
  def self.up
    create_table :related_billing_codes, :id => false do |t|
      t.column :first_billing_code_id, :integer, :null => false
      t.column :second_billing_code_id, :integer, :null => false
    end
  end

  def self.down
    drop_table :related_billing_codes
  end
end

class BillingCode < ActiveRecord::Base
  has_and_belongs_to_many :related,
    :join_table => 'related_billing_codes',
    :foreign_key => 'first_billing_code_id',
    :association_foreign_key => 'second_billing_code_id',
    :class_name => 'BillingCode'
end
```

Bidirectional Relationships

It's worth noting that the `related` relationship of the `BillingCode` in Listing 7.4 is not bidirectional. Just because you associate two objects in one direction does not mean they'll be associated in the other direction. But what if you need to automatically establish a bidirectional relationship?

First let's write a spec for the `BillingCode` class to prove our solution. When we add bidirectional, we don't want to break the normal behavior, so at first my spec example establishes that the normal `habtm` relationship works:

```
describe BillingCode do
  let(:travel_code) { BillingCode.create(:code => 'TRAVEL') }
  let(:dev_code) { BillingCode.create(:code => 'DEV') }

  it "should have a working related habtm association" do
    travel_code.related << dev_code
    travel_code.reload.related.should include(dev_code)
  end
end
```

I run the spec and it passes. Now I can modify the example to prove that the bidirectional behavior that we're going to add works. It ends up looking very similar to the first example.

```
describe BillingCode do
  let(:travel_code) { BillingCode.create(:code => 'TRAVEL') }
  let(:dev_code) { BillingCode.create(:code => 'DEV') }

  it "should have a bidirectional habtm association" do
    travel_code.related << dev_code
    travel_code.reload.related.should include(dev_code)
    dev_code.reload.related.should include(travel_code)
  end
end
```

Of course, the new version fails, since we haven't added the new behavior yet. I'll omit the output of running the spec, since it doesn't tell us anything we don't know already.

Custom SQL Options

I'm not entirely happy with the approach we're going to take, since it involves bringing hand-coded SQL into my otherwise beautiful Ruby code. However, the Rails way is to use SQL when it makes sense to do so, and this is one of those cases. To get our bidirectional behavior, we'll use the `:insert_sql` option of `has_and_belongs_to_many` to override the normal SQL that Active Record would use to associate the related objects with each other.

Here's a neat trick so that you don't have to figure out the syntax of the INSERT statement from memory. Just copy and paste the normal INSERT statement that Rails uses. It's not too hard to find in log/test.log if you tail the file while running the spec we wrote in the previous section:

```
INSERT INTO related_billing_codes (first_billing_code_id,
second_billing_code_id) VALUES (1, 2)
```

Now we just have to tweak that INSERT statement so that it adds two rows instead of just one. You might be tempted to just add a semicolon and a second, full INSERT statement. That won't work, because it is invalid to stuff two statements into one using a semicolon. Try it and see what happens if you're curious.

After some quick googling, I found the following method of inserting multiple rows with one SQL statement that will work for Postgres, MySQL, and DB2 databases.[2] It is valid according to the SQL-92 standard, just not universally supported:

```
:insert_sql => 'INSERT INTO related_billing_codes
               (first_billing_code_id, second_billing_code_id)
               VALUES (#{id}, #{record.id}), (#{record.id}, #{id})'
```

There are some very important things to remember when trying to get custom SQL options to work. The first is to use single quotes around the entire string of custom SQL. If you were to use double quotes, the string would be interpolated in the context of the class where it is being declared, not at the time of your query like you need it to be.

Also, while we're on the subject of quotation marks and how to use them, note that when I copied the INSERT query over from my log, I ended up with backtick characters around the column names, instead of single quotes. Trying to use single-quotes around values instead of backtick characters will fail, because the database adapter will escape the quotes, producing invalid syntax. Yes, it's a pain in the neck—luckily you shouldn't need to specify custom SQL very often.

Another thing to remember is that when your custom SQL string is interpolated, it will happen in the context of the object holding the association. The object being associated will be made available as record. If you look closely at the code listing, you'll notice that to establish the bidirectional link, we just added two rows in the related_billing_codes table, one in each direction.

A quick spec run confirms that our :insert_sql approach did indeed work. Now we should also use the :delete_sql option to make sure that the relationship can be broken bidirectionally as well. Again, I'll drive the implementation in a BDD

---

2. http://en.wikipedia.org/wiki/Insert_(SQL)#Multirow_inserts

(Behavior-Driven Development)[3] fashion, adding the following example to the
BillingCode spec:

```
it "should remove bidirectional association on deletion" do
  travel_code.related << dev_code
  travel_code.related.delete(dev_code)

  travel_code.related(true).should_not include(dev_code)
  dev_code.related(true).should_not include(travel_code)
end
```

It's similar to the previous test method, except that after establishing the relationship,
it immediately deletes it. I expect that the first assertion will pass right away, but the
second should fail:

```
$ ruby spec/models/billing_code_spec.rb
.F

1) BillingCode - should remove bidirectional association on deletion
    Failure/Error: dev_code.related(true).should_not include(travel_code)
expected [#<BillingCode id: 7, client_id: nil, code: "TRAVEL",
description: nil>] not to include #<BillingCode id: 7, client_id: nil,
code: "TRAVEL", description: nil>
    # spec/models/billing_code_spec.rb:19
    # spec/models/billing_code_spec.rb:3

Finished in 0.067338 seconds
2 examples, 1 failures
```

Yep, just as expected. Let's take another peek at log/test.log and grab the SQL
DELETE clause that we'll work with:

```
DELETE FROM related_billing_codes WHERE first_billing_code_id = 1 AND
second_billing_code_id IN (2)
```

Hmph! This might be a little trickier than the insert. Curious about the IN operator, I take
a peek inside the active_record/associations/has_and_belongs_to_many_
association.rb file and find the following relevant method:

```
def delete_records(records)
  if sql = @reflection.options[:delete_sql]
    records.each { |r| @owner.connection.delete(interpolate_sql(sql, r)) }
  else
    relation = Arel::Table.new(@reflection.options[:join_table])
    relation.where(relation[@reflection.primary_key_name].eq(@owner.id).
```

---

3. http://blog.dannorth.net/introducing-bdd

```
and(Arel::Predicates::In.new(relation[@reflection.association_foreign_key],
                             records.map(&:id))
      )
    ).delete
  end
end
```

Whoops, in Rails 3 this method is certainly interesting, but not much help. The query is constructed using the new Arel API. Since what I was looking for is an indication of how to construct our SQL delete statement, I decide to just try winging it. It ends up looking like the :delete_sql option in the following snippet:

```
class BillingCode < ActiveRecord::Base
  has_and_belongs_to_many :related,
    :join_table => 'related_billing_codes',
    :foreign_key => 'first_billing_code_id',
    :association_foreign_key => 'second_billing_code_id',
    :class_name => 'BillingCode',
    :insert_sql => 'INSERT INTO related_billing_codes
                    (first_billing_code_id, second_billing_code_id)
                    VALUES (#{id}, #{record.id}), (#{record.id}, #{id})',
    :delete_sql => 'DELETE FROM related_billing_codes
                    WHERE (first_billing_code_id = #{id}
                      AND second_billing_code_id = #{record.id})
                    OR (first_billing_code_id = #{record.id}
                      AND second_billing_code_id = #{id})'
end
```

Another spec run and we confirm that it works as intended.

```
$ ruby spec/models/billing_code_spec.rb
..

Finished in 0.051355 seconds
2 examples, 0 failures
```

Extra Columns on **has_and_belongs_to_many** Join Tables

Rails won't have a problem with you adding as many extra columns as you want to habtm's join table. The extra attributes will be read in and added onto model objects accessed via the habtm association. However, speaking from experience, the severe annoyances you will deal with in your application code make it really unattractive to go that route.

What kind of annoyances? For one, records returned from join tables with additional attributes will be marked as read-only, because it's not possible to save changes to those additional attributes.

You should also consider that the way that Rails makes those extra columns of the join table available might cause problems in other parts of your codebase. Having extra attributes appear magically on an object is kind of cool, but what happens when you try to access those extra properties on an object that wasn't fetched via the `habtm` association? Kaboom! Get ready for some potentially bewildering debugging exercises.

Methods of the `habtm` proxy act just as they would for a `has_many` relationship. Similarly, `habtm` shares options with `has_many`; only its `:join_table` option is unique. It allows customization of the join table name.

To sum up, `habtm` is a simple way to establish a many-to-many relationship using a join table. As long as you don't need to capture additional data about the relationship, everything is fine. The problems with `habtm` begin once you want to add extra columns to the join table, after which you'll want to upgrade the relationship to use `has_many :through` instead.

"Real Join Models" and habtm

The Rails documentation advises readers that: "It's strongly recommended that you upgrade any [`habtm`] associations with attributes to a real join model." Use of `habtm`, which was one of the original innovative features in Rails, fell out of favor once the ability to create real join models was introduced via the `has_many :through` association.

Realistically, `habtm` is not going to be removed from Rails, for a couple of sensible reasons. First of all, plenty of legacy Rails applications need it. Second, `habtm` provides a way to join classes without a primary key defined on the join table, which is occasionally useful. But most of the time you'll find yourself wanting to model many-to-many relationships with `has_many :through`.

7.5.2 `has_many :through`

Well-known Rails guy and fellow cabooser Josh Susser is considered the expert on Active Record associations, even his blog is called has_many :through. His description of the `:through` association,[4] written back when the feature was originally introduced in Rails 1.1, is so concise and well-written that I couldn't hope to do any better. So here it is:

> The `has_many :through` association allows you to specify a one-to-many relationship indirectly via an intermediate join table. In fact, you can specify more than one such relationship via the same table, which effectively makes it a replacement for `has_and_belongs_to_many`.

---

4. `http://blog.hasmanythrough.com/articles/2006/02/28/association-goodness`

The biggest advantage is that the join table contains full-fledged model objects complete with primary keys and ancillary data. No more `push_with_attributes`; join models just work the same way all your other Active Record models do.

Join Models

To illustrate the `has_many :through` association, we'll set up a `Client` model so that it has many `Timesheet` objects, through a normal `has_many` association named `billable_weeks`.

```
class Client < ActiveRecord::Base
  has_many :billable_weeks
  has_many :timesheets, :through => :billable_weeks
end
```

The `BillableWeek` class was already in our sample application and is ready to be used as a join model:

```
class BillableWeek < ActiveRecord::Base
  belongs_to :client
  belongs_to :timesheet
end
```

We can also set up the inverse relationship, from timesheets to clients, like this.

```
class Timesheet < ActiveRecord::Base
  has_many :billable_weeks
  has_many :clients, :through => :billable_weeks
end
```

Notice that `has_many :through` is always used in conjunction with a normal `has_many` association. Also, notice that the normal `has_many` association will often have the same name on both classes that are being joined together, which means the `:through` option will read the same on both sides.

```
:through => :billable_weeks
```

How about the join model; will it always have two `belongs_to` associations? No.

You can also use `has_many :through` to easily aggregate `has_many` or `has_one` associations on the join model. Forgive me for switching to completely nonrealistic domain for a moment—it's only intended to clearly demonstrate what I'm trying to describe:

```
class Grandparent < ActiveRecord::Base
  has_many :parents
  has_many :grand_children, :through => :parents, :source => :children
end
```

```
class Parent < ActiveRecord::Base
  belongs_to :grandparent
  has_many   :children
end
```

For the sake of clarity in later chapters, I'll refer to this usage of `has_many :through` as aggregating.

Courtenay says...

We use `has_many :through` so much! It has pretty much replaced the old `has_and_belongs_to_many`, because it allows your join models to be upgraded to full objects.It's like when you're just dating someone and they start talking about the Relationship (or, eventually, Our Marriage). It's an example of an association being promoted to something more important than the individual objects on each side.

Usage Considerations and Examples

You can use nonaggregating `has_many :through` associations in almost the same ways as any other `has_many` associations. The limitations have to do with handling of unsaved records.

```
>> c = Client.create(:name => "Trotter's Tomahawks", :code => "ttom")
=> #<Client id: 5 ...>

>> c.timesheets << Timesheet.new
ActiveRecord::HasManyThroughCantAssociateNewRecords: Cannot associate
new records through 'Client#billable_weeks' on '#'. Both records must
have an id in order to create the has_many :through record associating
them.
```

Hmm, seems like we had a hiccup. Unlike a normal `has_many`, Active Record won't let us add an object to the `has_many :through` association if both ends of the relationship are unsaved records.

The `create` method saves the record before adding it, so it does work as expected, provided the parent object isn't unsaved itself.

```
>> c.save
=> true

>> c.timesheets.create
=> [#<Timesheet id: 2 ... > ]
```

The main benefit of `has_many :through` is that Active Record takes care of managing the instances of the join model for you. If we call `reload` on the `billable _weeks` association, we'll see that there was a billable week object created for us:

```
>> c.billable_weeks.reload
=> [#<BillableWeek id: 2, tuesday_hours: nil, start_date: nil,
timesheet_id: 2, billing_code_id:
nil, sunday_hours: nil, friday_hours: nil, monday_hours:
nil, client_id: 2, wednesday_hours:
nil, saturday_hours: nil, thursday_hours: nil>]
```

The `BillableWeek` object that was created is properly associated with both the client and the `Timesheet`. Unfortunately, there are a lot of other attributes (e.g., `start_date`, and the hours columns) that were not populated.

One possible solution is to use `create` on the `billable_weeks` association instead, and include the new `Timesheet` object as one of the supplied properties.

```
>> bw = c.billable_weeks.create(:start_date => Time.now,
                                :timesheet => Timesheet.new)
```

Aggregating Associations

When you're using `has_many :through` to aggregate multiple child associations, there are more significant limitations—essentially you can query to your hearts content using `find` and friends, but you can't append or create new records through them.

For example, let's add a `billable_weeks` association to our sample `User` class:

```
class User < ActiveRecord::Base
  has_many :timesheets
  has_many :billable_weeks, :through => :timesheets
  ...
```

The `billable_weeks` association aggregates all the billable week objects belonging to all of the user's timesheets.

```
class Timesheet < ActiveRecord::Base
  belongs_to :user
  has_many :billable_weeks, :include => [:billing_code]
  ...
```

Now let's go into the Rails console and set up some example data so that we can use the new `billable_weeks` collection (on `User`).

```
>> quentin = User.find :first
=> #<User id: 1, login: "quentin" ...>

>> quentin.timesheets
=> []
```

```
>> ts1 = quentin.timesheets.create
=> #<Timesheet id: 1 ...>

>> ts2 = quentin.timesheets.create
=> #<Timesheet id: 2 ...>

>> ts1.billable_weeks.create(:start_date => 1.week.ago)
=> #<BillableWeek id: 1, timesheet_id: 1 ...>

>> ts2.billable_weeks.create :start_date => 2.week.ago
=> #<BillableWeek id: 2, timesheet_id: 2 ...>

>> quentin.billable_weeks
=> [#<BillableWeek id: 1, timesheet_id: 1 ...>, #<BillableWeek id: 2,
timesheet_id: 2 ...>]
```

Just for fun, let's see what happens if we try to create a `BillableWeek` with a `User` instance:

```
>> quentin.billable_weeks.create(:start_date => 3.weeks.ago)
NoMethodError: undefined method user_id=' for #<BillableWeek:0x3f84424>
```

There you go... `BillableWeek` doesn't belong to a user, it belongs to a timesheet, so it doesn't have a `user_id` field.

Join Models and Validations

When you append to a non-aggregating `has_many :through` association with `<<`, Active Record will always create a new join model, even if one already exists for the two records being joined. You can add `validates_uniqueness_of` constraints on the join model to keep duplicate joins from happening.

This is what such a constraint might look like on our `BillableWeek` join model.

```
validates_uniqueness_of :client_id, :scope => :timesheet_id
```

That says, in effect: "There should only be one of each client per timesheet."

If your join model has additional attributes with their own validation logic, then there's another important consideration to keep in mind. Adding records directly to a `has_many :through` association causes a new join model to be automatically created with a blank set of attributes. Validations on additional columns of the join model will probably fail. If that happens, you'll need to add new records by creating join model objects and associating them appropriately through their own association proxy.

```
timesheet.billable_weeks.create(:start_date => 1.week.ago)
```

7.5.3 `has_many :through` Options

The options for `has_many :through` are the same as the options for `has_many`—remember that `:through` is just an option on `has_many`! However, the use of some of `has_many`'s options change or become more significant when `:through` is used.

First of all, the `:class_name` and `:foreign_key` options are no longer valid, since they are implied from the target association on the join model. The following are the rest of the options that have special significance together with `has_many :through`.

`:source => assocation_name`

The `:source` option specifies which association to use on the associated class. This option is not mandatory because normally Active Record assumes that the target association is the singular (or plural) version of the `has_many` association name. If your association names don't match up, then you have to set `:source` explicitly.

For example, the following code will use the `BillableWeek`'s `sheet` association to populate `timesheets`.

```
has_many :timesheets, :through => :billable_weeks, :source => :sheet
```

`:source_type => class_name`

The `:source_type` option is needed when you establish a `has_many :through` to a polymorphic `belongs_to` association on the join model. Consider the following example concerning clients and contacts:

```
class Client < ActiveRecord::Base
  has_many :client_contacts
  has_many :contacts, :through => :client_contacts
end

class ClientContact < ActiveRecord::Base
  belongs_to :client
  belongs_to :contact, :polymorphic => true
end
```

In this somewhat contrived example, the most important fact is that a `Client` has many `contacts`, through their polymorphic relationship to the join model, `ClientContact`. There isn't a `Contact` class; we just want to be able to refer to contacts in a polymorphic sense, meaning either a `Person` or a `Business`.

```
class Person < ActiveRecord::Base
  has_many :client_contacts, :as => :contact
end

class Business < ActiveRecord::Base
  has_many :client_contacts, :as => :contact
end
```

Now take a moment to consider the backflips that Active Record would have to perform in order to figure out which tables to query for a client's contacts. Remember that there isn't a contacts table!

```
>> Client.first.contacts
```

Active Record would theoretically need to be aware of every model class that is linked to the other end of the contacts polymorphic association. In fact, it cannot do those kinds of backflips, which is probably a good thing as far as performance is concerned:

```
>> Client.first.contacts
ArgumentError: /.../active_support/core_ext/hash/keys.rb:48:
in 'assert_valid_keys': Unknown key(s): polymorphic
```

The only way to make this scenario work (somewhat) is to give Active Record some help by specifying which table it should search when you ask for the contacts collection, and you do that with the source_type option naming the target class, symbolized, like this:

```
class Client < ActiveRecord::Base
  has_many :client_contacts
  has_many :people, :through => :client_contacts,
          :source => :contact, :source_type => :person

  has_many :businesses, :through => :client_contacts,
          :source => :contact, :source_type => :business
end
```

After the :source_type is specified, the association will work as expected, but sadly we don't get a general purpose contacts collection to work with, as it seemed might be possible at first.

```
>> Client.first.people.create!
=> [#<Person id: 1>]
```

If you're upset that you cannot associate `people` and `business` together in a contacts association, you could try writing your own accessor method for a client's contacts:

```
class Client < ActiveRecord::Base
  def contacts
    people_contacts + business_contacts
  end
end
```

Of course, you should be aware that calling that `contacts` method will result in at least two database requests and will return an `Array`, without the association proxy methods that you might expect it to have.

:uniq => true

The `:uniq` option tells the association to include only unique objects. It is especially useful when using `has_many :through`, since two different `BillableWeeks` could reference the same `Timesheet`.

```
>> client.first.timesheets.reload
[#<Timesheet id: 1...>, #<Timesheet id: 1...>]
```

It's not extraordinary for two distinct model instances of the same database record to be in memory at the same time—it's just not usually desirable.

```
class Client < ActiveRecord::Base
  has_many :timesheets, :through => :billable_weeks, :uniq => true
end
```

After adding the `:uniq` option, only one instance per record is returned.

```
>> client.find(:first).timesheets.reload
[#<Timesheet id: 1...>]
```

The implementation of `uniq` on `AssociationCollection` is a neat little example of how to build a collection of unique values in Ruby, using a `Set` and the `inject` method. It also proves that the record's primary key (and nothing else) is what's being used to establish uniqueness:

```
def uniq(collection = self)
  seen = Set.new
  collection.inject([]) do |kept, record|
    unless seen.include?(record.id)
      kept << record
      seen << record.id
    end
    kept
  end
end
```

7.6 One-to-One Relationships

One of the most basic relationship types is a one-to-one object relationship. In Active Record, we declare a one-to-one relationship using the has_one and belongs_to methods together. As in the case of a has_many relationship, you call belongs_to on the model whose database table contains the foreign key column linking the two records together.

7.6.1 `has_one`

Conceptually, has_one works almost exactly like has_many does, except that when the database query is executed to retrieve the related object, a LIMIT 1 clause is added to the generated SQL so that only one row is returned.

   The name of a has_one relationship should be singular, which will make it read naturally, for example: has_one :last_timesheet, has_one :primary_account, has_one :profile_photo, and so on. Let's take a look at has_one in action by adding avatars for our users.

```
class Avatar < ActiveRecord::Base
  belongs_to :user
end

class User < ActiveRecord::Base
  has_one :avatar
  # ... the rest of our User code ...
end
```

That's simple enough. Firing this up in rails console, we can look at some of the new methods that has_one adds to User.

```
>> u = User.first
>> u.avatar
=> nil

>> u.build_avatar(:url => '/avatars/smiling')
=> #<Avatar id: nil, url: "/avatars/smiling", user_id: 1>

>> u.avatar.save
=> true
```

As you can see, we can use build_avatar to build a new avatar object and associate it with the user. While it's great that has_one will associate an avatar with the user, it isn't really anything that has_many doesn't already do. So let's take a look at what happens when we assign a new avatar to the user.

```
>> u = User.first
>> u.avatar
=> #<Avatar id: 1, url: "/avatars/smiling", user_id: 1>

>> u.create_avatar(:url => '/avatars/frowning')
=> #<Avatar id: 2, url: "/avatars/4567", user_id: 1>

>> Avatar.all
=> [#<Avatar id: 1, url: "/avatars/smiling", user_id: nil>, #<Avatar id:
2, url:
"/avatars/4567", user_id: 1>]
```

The last line from that console session is the most interesting, because it shows that our initial avatar is now no longer associated with the user. Of course, the previous avatar was not removed from the database, which is something that we want in this scenario. So, we'll use the :dependent => :destroy option to force avatars to be destroyed when they are no longer associated with a user.

```
class User < ActiveRecord::Base
  has_one :avatar, :dependent => :destroy
end
```

With some additional fiddling around in the console, we can verify that it works as intended. In doing so, you might notice that Rails only destroys the avatar that was just removed from the user, so bad data that was in your database from before will still remain. Keep this in mind when you decide to add :dependent => :destroy to your code and remember to manually clear orphaned data that might otherwise remain.

Using **has_one** together with **has_many**

As I alluded to earlier, has_one is sometimes used to single out one record of significance alongside an already established has_many relationship. For instance, let's say we want to easily be able to access the last timesheet a user was working on:

```
class User < ActiveRecord::Base
  has_many :timesheets
  has_one  :latest_sheet, :class_name => 'Timesheet', :order =>
'created_at desc'
end
```

I had to specify a :class_name, so that Active Record knows what kind of object we're associating. (It can't figure it out based on the name of the association, :latest_sheet.)

When adding a has_one relationship to a model that already has a has_many defined to the same related model, it is not necessary to add another belongs_to method call to the target object, just for the new has_one. That might seem a little counterintuitive at first, but if you think about it, the same foreign key value is being used to read the data from the database.

`has_one` options

The options for `has_one` associations are similar to the ones for `has_many`. For your convenience, we briefly cover the most relevant ones here.

`:as`

Allows you to set up a polymorphic association; this is covered in Chapter 9.

`:class_name`

Allows you to specify the class this association uses. When you're doing `has_one :latest_timesheet, :class_name => 'Timesheet', :class_name => 'Timesheet'` specifies that `latest_timesheet` is actually the last `Timesheet` object in the database that is associated with this user. Normally, this option is inferred by Rails from the name of the association.

`:conditions`

Allows you to specify conditions that the object must meet to be included in the association. The conditions are specified the same as if you were using `ActiveRecord::Base#find`.

```
class User < ActiveRecord::Base
  has_one :manager, :class_name => 'Person',
                    :conditions => {:type => "manager"}
```

Here `manager` is specified as a person object that has `type = "manager"`. I tend to almost always use `:conditions` in conjunction with `has_one`. When Active Record loads the association, it's grabbing one of potentially many rows that have the right foreign key. Absent some explicit conditions (or perhaps an `:order` clause), you're leaving it in the hands of the database to pick a row.

`:dependent`

The `:dependent` option specifies how Active Record should treat associated objects when the parent object is deleted. (The default is to do nothing with associated objects, which will leave orphaned records in the database.) There are a few different values that you can pass, and they work just like the `:dependent` option of `has_many`. If you pass `:destroy` to it, you tell Rails to destroy the associated object when it is no longer associated with the primary object. Passing `:delete` will destroy the associated object without calling any of Rails's normal hooks. Finally, `:nullify` will simply set the foreign key values to `nil` so that the relationship is broken.

:order

Allows you to specify a SQL fragment that will be used to order the results. This is an especially useful option with `has_one` when trying to associate the latest of something or another.

```
class User < ActiveRecord::Base
  has_one :latest_timesheet,
          :class_name => 'Timesheet',
          :order => 'created_at desc'
end
```

7.7 Working with Unsaved Objects and Associations

You can manipulate objects and associations before they are saved to the database, but there is some special behavior you should be aware of, mostly involving the saving of associated objects. Whether an object is considered unsaved is based on the result of calling `new_record?`

7.7.1 One-to-One Associations

Assigning an object to a `belongs_to` association does not save the parent or the associated object.

Assigning an object to a `has_one` association automatically saves that object and the object being replaced (if there is one), so that their foreign key fields are updated. The exception to this behavior is if the parent object is unsaved, since that would mean that there is no foreign key value to set. If save fails for either of the objects being updated (due to one of them being invalid) the assignment operation returns false and the assignment is cancelled. That behavior makes sense (if you think about it), but it can be the cause of much confusion when you're not aware of it. If you have an association that doesn't seem to work, check the validation rules of the related objects.

7.7.2 Collections

Adding an object to `has_many` and `has_and_belongs_to_many` collections automatically saves it, unless the parent object (the owner of the collection) is not yet stored in the database.

If objects being added to a collection (via << or similar means) fail to save properly, then the addition operation will return `false`. If you want your code to be a little more explicit, or you want to add an object to a collection without automatically saving it, then you can use the collection's `build` method. It's exactly like `create`, except that it doesn't `save`.

Members of a collection are automatically saved or updated when their parent is saved or updated, unless `:autosave => false` is set on the association.

7.7.3   Deletion

Associations that are set with an `:autosave => true` option are also afforded the ability to have their records deleted when an inverse record is saved. This is to allow the records from both sides of the association to get persisted within the same transaction, and is handled through the `mark_for_destruction` method. Consider our `User` and `Timesheet` models again:

```
class User < ActiveRecord::Base
  has_many :timesheets, :autosave => true
end
```

If you would like to have a `Timesheet` destroyed when the `User` is saved, mark it for destruction.

```
user = User.where(:name => "Durran")
timesheet = user.timesheets.closed
timesheet.mark_for_destruction # => Flags timesheet
user.save # => The timesheet gets deleted
```

Since both are persisted in the same transaction, if the operation were to fail the database would not be in an inconsistent state. Do note that although the child record did not get deleted in that case, it *still* would be marked for destruction and any later attempts to save the inverse would once again attempt to delete it.

7.8   Association Extensions

The proxy objects that handle access to associations can be extended with your own application code. You can add your own custom finders and factory methods to be used specifically with a particular association.

For example, let's say you wanted a concise way to refer to an account's people by name. You might wrap the `find_or_create_by_first_name_and_last_name` method of a `people` collection in the following neat little package as shown in Listing 7.5.

Listing 7.5 An association extension on a people collection

```
class Account < ActiveRecord::Base

  has_many :people do
    def named(full_name)
      first_name, last_name = full_name.split(" ", 2)
      find_or_create_by_first_name_and_last_name(first_name, last_name)
    end
  end

end
```

Now we have a `named` method available to use on the `people` collection.

```
person = Account.first.people.named("David Heinemeier Hansson")
person.first_name # => "David"
person.last_name  # => "Heinemeier Hansson"
```

If you need to share the same set of extensions between many associations, you can use specify an extension module, instead of a block with method definitions. Here is the same feature shown in Listing 7.5, except broken out into its own Ruby module:

```
module ByNameExtension
  def named(full_name)
    first_name, last_name = full_name.split(" ", 2)
    find_or_create_by_first_name_and_last_name(first_name, last_name)
  end
end
```

Now we can use it to extend many different relationships, as long as they're compatible. (Our contract in the example consists of the `find_or_create_by_first_name_and_last_name` method.)

```
class Account < ActiveRecord::Base
  has_many :people, :extend => ByNameExtension
end

class Company < ActiveRecord::Base
  has_many :people, :extend => ByNameExtension
end
```

If you need to use multiple named extension modules, you can pass an array of modules to the `:extend` option instead of a single module, like this:

```
has_many :people, :extend => [ByNameExtension, ByRecentExtension]
```

In the case of name conflicts, methods contained in modules added later in the array supercede those earlier in the array.

Consider a class method instead

Unless you have a valid reason to reuse the extension logic with more than one type of model, you're probably better off leveraging the fact that class methods are automatically available on has_many associations.

```
class Person < ActiveRecord::Base
  belongs_to :account

  def self.named(full_name)
    first_name, last_name = full_name.split(" ", 2)
    find_or_create_by_first_name_and_last_name(first_name, last_name)
  end
end
```

7.9 The `AssociationProxy` Class

AssociationProxy, the parent of all association proxies (refer to Figure 7.1 if needed), contributes a handful of useful methods that apply to most kinds of associations and can come into play when you're writing association extensions.

`proxy_owner`, `proxy_reflection`, and `proxy_target`

References to the internal owner, reflection, and target attributes of the association proxy, respectively.

The proxy_owner method provides a reference to the parent object holding the association.

The proxy_reflection object is an instance of ActiveRecord::Reflection:: AssociationReflection and contains all of the configuration options for the association. That includes both default settings and those that were passed to the association method when it was declared.[5]

Finally, the proxy_target is the associated array (or associated object itself in the case of belongs_to and has_one).

It might not appear sane to expose these attributes publicly and allow their manipulation. However, without access to them it would be much more difficult to write advanced association extensions. The loaded?, loaded, target, and target= methods are public for similar reasons.

---

5. To learn more about how the reflection object can be useful, including an explanation on how to establish has_many :through associations via other has_many :through associations, check out the must-read article: http://www.pivotalblabs.com/articles/2007/08/26/ten-things-i-hate-about-proxy-objects-part-i

The following code sample demonstrates the use of `proxy_owner` within a `published_prior_to` extension method, originally contributed by Wilson Bilkovich:

```
class ArticleCategory < ActiveRecord::Base
  acts_as_tree

  has_many :articles do
    def published_prior_to(date, options = {})
      if proxy_owner.top_level?
        Article.where('published_at < ? and category_id = ?', date,
proxy_owner)
      else
        # self is the 'articles' association here so we inherit its scope
        self.all(options)
      end
    end
  end

def top_level?
    # do we have a parent, and is our parent the root node of the tree?
    self.parent && self.parent.parent.nil?
  end
end
```

The `acts_as_tree` Active Record plugin extension creates a self-referential association based on a `parent_id` column. The `proxy_owner` reference is used to check if the parent of this association is a "top-level" node in the tree.

reload and reset

The `reset` method puts the association proxy back in its initial state, which is unloaded (cached association objects are cleared). The `reload` method invokes `reset`, and then loads associated objects from the database.

7.10 Conclusion

The ability to model associations is what makes Active Record more than just a data-access layer. The ease and elegance with which you can declare those associations are what make Active Record more than your ordinary object-relational mapper.

In this chapter, we covered the basics of how Active Record associations work. We started by taking a look at the class hierarchy of associations classes, starting with `AssociationProxy`. Hopefully, by learning about how associations work under the hood, you've picked up some enhanced understanding about their power and flexibility.

Finally, the options and methods guide for each type of association should be a good reference guide for your day-to-day development activities.

CHAPTER **8**

Validations

I have bought this wonderful machine a computer. Now I am rather an authority on gods, so I identified the machine it seems to me to be an Old Testament god with a lot of rules and no mercy.

—Joseph Campbell

The Validations API in Active Model, along with its supplementary functionality in Active Record allows you to declaratively define valid states for your model objects. The validation methods hook into the life cycle of an Active Record model object and are able to inspect the object to determine whether certain attributes are set, have values in a given range, or pass any other logical hurdles that you specify.

In this chapter, we'll describe the validation methods available and how to use them effectively. We'll also explore how those validation methods interact with your model's attributes and how the built-in error-messaging system messages can be used effectively in your application's user interface to provide descriptive feedback.

Finally, we'll cover how to use Active Model's validation functionality in your own, non-Active Record classes.

8.1 Finding Errors

Validation problems are also known as (drumroll please...) errors! Every Active Record model object contains a collection of errors, accessible (unsurprisingly) as the `errors` attribute. It's an instance of the class `ActiveModel::Errors` that extends `ActiveSupport::OrderedHash`.

When a model object is valid, the `errors` collection is empty. In fact, when you call `valid?` on a model object, a series of steps to find errors is taken as follows (slightly simplified):

1. Clear the `errors` collection.
2. Run validations.
3. Return whether the model's `errors` collection is now empty or not.

If the `errors` collection ends up empty, the object is valid. In cases where you have to write actual validation logic yourself, you mark an object invalid by adding items to the `errors` collection using its `add` methods. Simple as that.

We'll cover the methods of the `Errors` class in some more detail later on. It makes more sense to look at the validation methods themselves first.

8.2 The Simple Declarative Validations

Whenever possible, you should set validations for your models declaratively by using one or more of the following class methods available to all Active Record classes. Unless otherwise noted, all of the `validates` methods accept a variable number of attributes, plus options. There are some options for these validation methods that are common to all of them, and we'll cover them at the end of the section.

8.2.1 `validates_acceptance_of`

Many web applications have screens in which the user is prompted to agree to terms of service or some similar concept, usually involving a check box. No actual database column matching the attribute declared in the validation is required. When you call this method, it will create virtual attributes automatically for each named attribute you specify. I see this validation as a type of syntax sugar since it is so specific to web application programming.

```
class Account < ActiveRecord::Base
  validates_acceptance_of :privacy_policy, :terms_of_service
end
```

You can use this validation with or without a boolean columns on the table backing your model. An attribute will be created if necessary. Choose to store the value in the database only if you need to keep track of whether the user accepted the term, for auditing or other reasons. Mind you, not accepting the term would prevent creation of the record, but it's good to know what is supported.

When the `validates_acceptance_of` validation fails, an error message is stored in the model object reading "attribute must be accepted."

The `:accept` option makes it easy to change the value considered acceptance. The default value is `"1"`, which matches the value supplied by check boxes generated using Rails helper methods.

```
class Cancellation < ActiveRecord::Base
  validates_acceptance_of :account_cancellation, :accept => 'YES'
end
```

If you use the preceding example in conjunction with a text field connected to the `account_cancellation` attribute, the user would have to type the word YES in order for the cancellation object to be valid.

8.2.2 `validates_associated`

This is used to ensure that *all* associated objects are valid on save. It works with any kind of association and is specific to Active Record (not Active Model.) We emphasize *all* because the default behavior of `has_many` associations is to ensure the validity of their *new* child records on save.

Suggestion

> You probably don't need to use this particular validation nowadays since `has_many` associations default to `:validate => true`. Additionally note that one of the implications of that default is that setting `:validate => true` carelessly on a `belongs_to` association can cause infinite loop problems.

A `validates_associated` on `belongs_to` will not fail if the association is `nil`. If you want to make sure that the association is populated and valid, you have to use `validates_associated` in conjunction with `validates_presence_of`.

Tim says...

> It's possible to get similar behavior by using a combination of the `:autosave` and `:validate` options on a `has_many`.

8.2.3 `validates_confirmation_of`

The `validates_confirmation_of` method is another case of syntactic sugar for web applications, since it is so common to include dual-entry text fields to make sure that the user entered critical data such as passwords and e-mail address correctly. This validation will create a virtual attribute for the confirmation value and compare the two attributes to make sure they match in order for the model to be valid.

Here's an example, using our fictional Account model again:

```
class Account < ActiveRecord::Base
  validates_confirmation_of :password
end
```

The user interface used to set values for the Account model would need to include extra text fields named with a _confirmation suffix, and when submitted, the value of those fields would have to match in order for this validation to pass. A simplified example of matching view code is provided.

```
= form_for account do |f|
  = f.label :login
  = f.text_field :login
  = f.label :password
  = f.password_field :password
  = f.label :password_confirmation
  = f.password_field :password_confirmation
  = f.submit
```

8.2.4 `validates_each`

The validates_each method is a little more free-form than its companions in the validation family in that it doesn't have a predefined validation function. Instead, you give it an array of attribute names to check, and supply a Ruby block to be used in checking each attribute's validity. Notice that parameters for the model instance (record), the name of the attribute as a symbol, and the value to check are passed as block parameters. The block function designates the model object as valid or not by merit of adding to its errors array or not. The return value of the block is ignored.

There aren't too many situations where this method is necessary, but one plausible example is when interacting with external services for validation. You might wrap the external validation in a faade specific to your application, and then call it using a validates_each block:

```
class Invoice < ActiveRecord::Base
  validates_each :supplier_id, :purchase_order do |record, attr, value|
    record.errors.add(attr) unless PurchasingSystem.validate(attr, value)
  end
end
```

8.2.5 `validates_format_of`

To use `validates_format_of`, you'll have to know how to use Ruby regular expressions.[1] Pass the method one or more attributes to check, and a regular expression as the (required) `:with` option. A good example, as shown in the Rails docs, is checking for a valid e-mail address format:

```
class Person < ActiveRecord::Base
  validates_format_of :email,
    :with => /\A([^@\s]+)@((?:[-a-z0-9]+\.)+[a-z]{2,})\Z/i
end
```

By the way, that example is totally not an RFC-compliant email address format checker.[2]

Courtenay says...

Regular expressions are awesome but can get very complex, particularly when validating domain names or email addresses. You can use `#{}` inside regular expressions, so split up your regex into chunks like this:

```
validates_format_of :name, :with =>
/^((localhost)|#{DOMAIN}|#{NUMERIC_IP})#{PORT}$/
```

Note

That expression is pretty straightforward and easy to understand. The constants themselves are not so easy to understand but easier than if they were all jumbled in together:

```
PORT = /(([:]\d+)?)/
DOMAIN = /([a-z0-9\-]+\.?)*([a-z0-9]{2,})\.[a-z]{2,}/
NUMERIC_IP =
/(?>(?:1?\d?\d|2[0-4]\d|25[0-5])\.){3}(?:1?\d?\d|2[0-4]\d|25[0-5])
(?:\/(?:[12]?\d|3[012]))|-(?>(?:1?\d?\d|2[0-4]\d|25[0-5])\.){3}
(?:1?\d?\d|2[0-4]\d|25[0-5]))?/
```

---

1. Check out the excellent http://rubular.com if you need help composing Ruby regular expressions.
2. If you need to validate email addresses try the plugin at http://code.dunae.ca/validates_email_format_of

Active Record

Lark says...

I'll take your readability Courtenay, and raise you test isolation. Your regular expression should
itself be in a constant so you can test it.

8.2.6 `validates_inclusion_of` and `validates_exclusion_of`

These methods take a variable number of attribute names and an `:in` option. When
they run, they check to make sure that the value of the attribute is included (or excluded,
respectively) in the enumerable object passed as the `:in` option.

The examples in the Rails docs are probably some of the best illustrations of their
use, so I'll take inspiration from them:

```
class Person < ActiveRecord::Base
  validates_inclusion_of :gender, :in => ['m','f'], :message => 'O RLY?'
  ...

class Account < ActiveRecord::Base
  validates_exclusion_of :login, :in => ['admin', 'root', 'superuser'],
                         :message => 'Borat says "Naughty, naughty!"'
  ...
```

Notice that in the examples I've introduced usage of the `:message` option, common
to all validation methods, to customize the error message constructed and added to the
`Errors` collection when the validation fails. We'll cover the default error messages and
how to effectively customize them a little further along in the chapter.

8.2.7 `validates_length_of`

The `validates_length_of` method takes a variety of different options to let you
concisely specify length constraints for a given attribute of your model.

```
class Account < ActiveRecord::Base
  validates_length_of :login, :minimum => 5
end
```

Constraint Options

The `:minimum` and `:maximum` options work as expected, but don't use them together.
To specify a range, use the `:within` option and pass it a Ruby range, as in the following
example:

```
class Account < ActiveRecord::Base
  validates_length_of :login, :within => 5..20
end
```

To specify an exact length of an attribute, use the `:is` option:

```
class Account < ActiveRecord::Base
  validates_length_of :account_number, :is => 16
end
```

Error Message Options

Rails gives you the ability to generate detailed error messages for `validates_length_of` via the `:too_long`, `:too_short`, and `:wrong_length` options. Use `{{count}}` in your custom error message as a placeholder for the number corresponding to the constraint.

```
class Account < ActiveRecord::Base
  validates_length_of :account_number, :is => 16,
                      :wrong_length => "should be {{count}} characters
long"
end
```

8.2.8 `validates_numericality_of`

The somewhat clumsily named `validates_numericality_of` method is used to ensure that an attribute can only hold a numeric value.

The `:only_integer` option lets you further specify that the value should only be an integral value and defaults to false.

```
class Account < ActiveRecord::Base
  validates_numericality_of :account_number, :only_integer => true
end
```

The `:even` and `:odd` options do what you would expect and are useful for things like, I don't know, checking electron valences. (Actually, I'm not creative enough to think of what you would use this validation for, but there you go.)

The following comparison options are also available:

- `:equal_to`

- `:greater_than`

- `:greater_than_or_equal_to`

- `:less_than`

- `:less_than_or_equal_to`

Infinity and Other Special Float Values

Interestingly, Ruby has the concept of infinity built-in. If you haven't seen infinity before, try the following in a console:

```
>> (1.0/0.0)
=> Infinity
```

`Infinity` is considered a number by `validates_numericality_of`. Databases (like PostgreSQL) with support for the IEEE 754 standard should allow special float values like `Infinity` to be stored. The other special values are positive infinity (+INF), negative infinity (−INF), and not-a-number (NaN). IEEE 754 also distinguishes between positive zero (+0) and negative zero (−0). NaN is used to represent results of operations that are undefined.

8.2.9 `validates_presence_of`

One of the more common validation methods, `validates_presence_of`, is used to denote mandatory attributes. This method checks whether the attribute is blank using the `blank?` method, defined on `Object`, which returns `true` for values that are `nil` or a blank string `""`.

```
class Account < ActiveRecord::Base
  validates_presence_of :login, :email, :account_number
end
```

A common mistake is to use `validates_presence_of` with a boolean attribute, like the backing field for a checkbox. If you want to make sure that the attribute is true, use `validates_acceptance_of` instead. The boolean value `false` is considered blank, so if you want to make sure that only `true` or `false` values are set on your model, use the following pattern:

```
validates_inclusion_of :protected, :in => [true, false]
```

Validating the Presence and/or Existence of Associated Objects

When you're trying to ensure that an association is present, pass `validates_presence_of` its foreign key attribute, not the association variable itself. Note that the validation will fail in cases when both the parent and child object are unsaved (since the foreign key will be blank).

Many developers try to use this validation with the intention of ensuring that associated objects actually exist in the database. Personally, I think that would be a valid use case for an actual foreign-key constraint in the database, but if you want to do the check in your Rails code then emulate the following example:

```
class Timesheet < ActiveRecord::Base
  belongs_to :user
  validates_presence_of :user_id
  validate :user_exists

  protected

  def user_exists
    errors.add(:user_id, "doesn't exist") unless User.exists?(user_id)
  end
end
```

Without a validation, if your application violates a database foreign key constraint, you will get an Active Record exception.

8.2.10 `validates_uniqueness_of`

The `validates_uniqueness_of` method, also exclusive to Active Record, ensures that the value of an attribute is unique for all models of the same type. This validation does not work by adding a uniqueness constraint at the database level. It does work by constructing and executing a query looking for a matching record in the database. If any record is returned when this method does its query, the validation fails.

```
class Account < ActiveRecord::Base
  validates_uniqueness_of :login
end
```

By specifying a `:scope` option, additional attributes can be used to determine uniqueness. You may pass `:scope` one or more attribute names as symbols (putting multiple symbols in an array).

```
class Address < ActiveRecord::Base
  validates_uniqueness_of :line_two, :scope => [:line_one, :city, :zip]
end
```

It's also possible to specify whether to make the uniqueness constraint case-sensitive or not, via the `:case_sensitive` option (ignored for nontextual attributes).

Tim says...

This validation is not foolproof because of a potential race condition between the SELECT query that checks for duplicates and the INSERT or UPDATE which persists the record. An Active Record exception could be generated as a result, so be prepared to handle that failure in your controller.

I recommend that you use a unique index constraint in the database if you absolutely must make sure that a column value is unique.

Enforcing Uniqueness of Join Models

In the course of using join models (with has_many :through), it seems pretty common to need to make the relationship unique. Consider an application that models students, courses, and registrations with the following code:

```
class Student < ActiveRecord::Base
  has_many :registrations
  has_many :courses, :through => :registrations
end

class Registration < ActiveRecord::Base
  belongs_to :student
  belongs_to :course
end

class Course < ActiveRecord::Base
  has_many :registrations
  has_many :students, :through => :registrations
end
```

How do you make sure that a student is not registered more than once for a particular course? The most concise way is to use validates_uniqueness_of with a :scope constraint. The important thing to remember with this technique is to reference the foreign keys, not the names of the associations themselves:

```
class Registration < ActiveRecord::Base
  belongs_to :student
  belongs_to :course

  validates_uniqueness_of :student_id, :scope => :course_id,
                          :message => "can only register once per course"
end
```

Notice that since the default error message generated when this validation fails would not make sense, I've provided a custom error message that will result in the expression: "Student can only register once per course."

Tim says . . .

Astute readers will notice that the validation was on student_id but the error message references "Student." Rails special cases this to do what you mean.

8.2.11 `validates_with`

All of the validation methods we've covered so far are essentially local to the class in which they are used. If you want to develop a suite of custom, reusable validation classes, then you need a way to apply them to your models, and that is what the `validates_with` method allows you to do.

To implement a custom validator, extend `ActiveRecord::Validator` and implement the `validate` method. The record being validated is available as `record` and you manipulate its `errors` hash to log validation errors.

The following examples, from Ryan Daigle's excellent post[3] on this feature, demonstrate a reusable email field validator:

```
class EmailValidator < ActiveRecord::Validator
  def validate()
    record.errors[:email] << "is not valid" unless
      record.email =~ /^([^@\s]+)@((?:[-a-z0-9]+\.)+[a-z]{2,})$/i
  end
end

class Account < ActiveRecord::Base
  validates_with EmailValidator
end
```

The example assumes the existence of an email attribute on the record. If you need to make your reusable validator more flexible, you can access validation options at runtime via the `options` hash, like this:

```
class EmailValidator < ActiveRecord::Validator
  def validate()
    email_field = options[:attr]
    record.errors[email_field] << "is not valid" unless
      record.send(email_field) =~
/^([^@\s]+)@((?:[-a-z0-9]+\.)+[a-z]{2,})$/i
  end
end

class Account < ActiveRecord::Base
  validates_with EmailValidator, :attr => :email
end
```

---

3. http://ryandaigle.com/articles/2009/8/11/what-s-new-in-edge-rails-independent-model-validators

8.2.12 RecordInvalid

Whenever you do so-called bang operations (such as `save!`) and a validation fails, you should be prepared to rescue `ActiveRecord::RecordInvalid`. Validation failures will cause `RecordInvalid` to be raised and its message will contain a description of the failures.

Here's a quick example from one of my applications that has pretty restrictive validations on its `User` model:

```
>> u = User.new
=> #<User ...>
>> u.save!
ActiveRecord::RecordInvalid: Validation failed: Name can't be blank,
Password confirmation can't be blank, Password is too short (minimum
is 5 characters), Email can't be blank, Email address format is bad
```

8.3 Common Validation Options

The following options apply to all of the validation methods.

8.3.1 `:allow_blank` and `:allow_nil`

In some cases, you only want to trigger a validation if a value is present, in other words the attribute is optional. There are two options that provide this functionality.

The `:allow_blank` option skips validation if the value is blank according to the `blank?` method. Similarly, the `:allow_nil` option skips the validation if the value of the attribute is `nil`; it only checks for `nil`, and empty strings `" "` are not considered nil, but they are considered blank.

8.3.2 `:if` and `:unless`

The `:if` and `:unless` options is covered in the next section, "Conditional Validation."

8.3.3 `:message`

As we've discussed earlier in the chapter, the way that the validation process registers failures is by adding items to the `Errors` collection of the model object being checked. Part of the error item is a specific message describing the validation failure. All of the validation methods accept a `:message` option so that you can override the default error message format.

```
class Account < ActiveRecord::Base
  validates_uniqueness_of :login, :message => "is already taken"
end
```

The default English locale file in Active Model defines most of the standard error message templates.

```
accepted: "must be accepted"
blank: "can't be blank"
confirmation: "doesn't match confirmation"
empty: "can't be empty"
equal_to: "must be equal to {{count}}"
even: "must be even"
exclusion: "is reserved"
greater_than: "must be greater than {{count}}"
greater_than_or_equal_to: "must be greater than or equal to {{count}}"
inclusion: "is not included in the list"
invalid: "is invalid"
less_than: "must be less than {{count}}"
less_than_or_equal_to: "must be less than or equal to {{count}}"
not_a_number: "is not a number"
odd: "must be odd"
too_long: "is too long (maximum is {{count}} characters)"
too_short: "is too short (minimum is {{count}} characters)"
wrong_length: "is the wrong length (should be {{count}} characters)"
```

The default messages only use the `count` variable for interpolation, where appropriate, but `model`, `attribute`, and `value` are always available.

```
validates_uniqueness_of :login, :message => "{{value}} is already
registered"
```

8.3.4 :on

By default, validations are run on save (both create and update operations). If you need to do so, you can limit a given validation to just one of those operations by passing the `:on` option either `:create` or `:update`.

Assuming that your application does not support changing login names, one good use for `:on => :create` might be in conjunction with `validates_uniqueness_of`, since checking uniqueness with a query on large datasets can be time-consuming.

```
class Account < ActiveRecord::Base
  validates_uniqueness_of :login, :on => :create
end
```

8.4 Conditional Validation

Since all validation methods are implemented via the Active Model Callback API, they also accept `:if` and `:unless` options, to determine at runtime (and not during the class definition) whether the validation needs to be run or not. The following three types of arguments can be supplied as an :if and :unless options:

Symbol The name of a method to invoke as a symbol. This is probably the most common option, and offers the best performance.

String A snippet of Ruby code to eval might be useful when the condition is really short, but keep in mind that eval'ing statements is relatively slow.

Proc A block of code to be instance_eval'd, so that self is the current record. Perhaps the most elegant choice for one-line conditionals.

```
validates_presence_of :approver, :if => lambda { approved? && !legacy?
}
```

8.4.1 Usage and Considerations

When does it make sense to use conditional validations? The answer is: whenever an object can be validly persisted in more than one state. A very common example involves the User (or Person) model, used for login and authentication.

```
validates_presence_of :password, :if => :password_required?
validates_presence_of :password_confirmation, :if => :password_required?
validates_length_of :password, :within => 4..40, :if=>:password_required?
validates_confirmation_of :password, :if => :password_required?
```

This code is not DRY (meaning that it is repetitive). You can refactor it to make it a little dryer using the with_options method that Rails mixes into Object.

```
with_options :if => :password_required? do |user|
  user.validates_presence_of :password
  user.validates_presence_of :password_confirmation
  user.validates_length_of :password, :within => 4..40
  user.validates_confirmation_of :password
end
```

All of the example validations check for the two cases when a (plaintext) password field should be required in order for the model to be valid.

```
def password_required?
  crypted_password.blank? || !password.blank?
end
```

The first case is if the crypted_password attribute is blank, because that means we are dealing with a new User instance that has not been given a password yet. The other case is when the password attribute itself is not blank; perhaps this is happening during an update operation and the user is attempting to reset her password.

8.4.2   Validation Contexts

Another way to accomplish conditional validation leverages support for *validation contexts*. Declare a validation and pass the name of an application-specific validation context as the value of the `:on` option. That validation will now only be checked when explicitly invoked using `record.valid?(context_name)`.

Consider the following example involving a report generation app. Saving a report without a name is fine, but publishing one without a name is not.

```
class Report < ActiveRecord::Base
  validates_presence_of :name, :on => :publish
end

class ReportsController < ApplicationController
  expose(:report)

  # POST /reports/1/publish
  def publish
    if report.valid? :publish
      redirect_to report, :notice => "Report published"
    else
      flash.now.alert = "Can't publish unnamed reports!"
      render :show
    end
  end
end
```

8.5   Short-form Validation

Rails 3 introduces a `validates` method that identifies an attribute and accepts options that correspond to the validators we've already covered in the chapter. Using `validates` can tighten up your model code nicely.

```
validates :login, :presence => true,
                  :format => { :with => /[A-Za-z0-9]+/,
                  :length => {:minimum => 3},
                  :uniqueness => true }
```

The following options are available for use with the `validates` method.

:acceptance => true Alias for `validates_acceptance_of`, typically used with checkboxes that indicate acceptance of terms. Supply additional options by replacing true with a hash.

```
validates :terms, :acceptance => { :message => 'You must accept terms.'
  }
```

:confirmation => true Alias for `validates_confirmation_of`, typically used to ensure that email and password confirmation fields match up correctly. Supply additional options by replacing `true` with a hash.

```
validates :email, :confirmation => { :message => 'Try again.' }
```

:exclusion => :in => [1,2,3] Alias for `validates_exclusion_of`.

:format => :with => /.*/ Alias for `validates_format_of`. If your only option is the regular expression, you can shorten the syntax further by making it the value like:

```
:format => /[A-Za-z0-9]+/
```

:inclusion => :in => [1,2,3] Alias for `validates_inclusion_of`.

:length => :minimum => 0, maximum => 1000 Alias for `validates_length_of`. If your only options are minimum and maximum lengths, you can shorten the syntax further by supplying a Ruby range as the value.

```
validates :login, :length => [3..20]
```

:numericality => true Alias for `validates_numericality_of`. Supply additional options by replacing `true` with a hash.

```
validates :quantity, :numericality => { :message => 'Supply a number.'
}
```

:presence => true Alias for `validates_presence_of`. Supply additional options by replacing `true` with a hash.

```
validates :login, :presence => { :message => 'How do you expect to
login?' }
```

:uniqueness => true Alias for `validates_uniqueness_of`. Supply additional options by replacing `true` with a hash.

```
validates :quantity, :uniqueness => { :message => "You're SOL on that
login choice, buddy!" }
```

8.6 Custom Validation Techniques

When the existing declarative validation macros are not enough for your application needs Rails gives you a few custom techniques.

8.6.1 Add Custom Validation Macros to Your Application

Rails 3 introduces the ability to add custom validation macros (available to all your model classes) by extending `ActiveModel::EachValidator`.

The following example is silly, but demonstrates the functionality nicely.

```
class ReportLikeValidator < ActiveModel::EachValidator
  def validate_each(record, attribute, value)
    unless value["Report"]
      record.errors.add attribute, 'does not appear to be a Report'
    end
  end
end
```

Now that your custom validator exists, it is available to use with the `validates` macro in your model.

```
class Report < ActiveRecord::Base
  validates :name, :report_like => true
end
```

The key `:report_like` is inferred from the name of the validator class, which in this case was `ReportLikeValidator`.

You can receive options via the `validates` method by adding an `initializer` method to your custom validator class. For example, let's make `ReportLikeValidator` more generic.

```
class LikeValidator < ActiveModel::EachValidator
  def initialize(options)
    @with = options[:with]
    super
  end

  def validate_each(record, attribute, value)
    unless value[@with]
      record.errors.add attribute, "does not appear to be like #{@with}"
    end
  end
end
```

Our model code would change to

```
class Report < ActiveRecord::Base
  validates :name, :like => {:with => "Report"}
end
```

8.6.2 Create a Custom Validator Class

This technique involves inheriting from `ActiveModel::Validator` and implementing a `validate` method that takes the record to validate.

I'll demonstrate with a really wicked example.

```
class RandomlyValidator < ActiveModel::Validator
  def validate(record)
    record.errors[:base] << "FAIL #1" unless first_hurdle(record)
    record.errors[:base] << "FAIL #2" unless second_hurdle(record)
    record.errors[:base] << "FAIL #3" unless third_hurdle(record)
  end

  private

  def first_hurdle(record)
    rand > 0.3
  end

  def second_hurdle(record)
    rand > 0.6
  end

  def third_hurdle(record)
    rand > 0.9
  end
end
```

Use your new custom validator in a model with the `validates_with` macro.

```
class Report < ActiveRecord::Base
  validates_with RandomlyValidator
end
```

8.6.3 Add a **validate** Method to Your Model

A `validate` instance method might be the way to go if you want to check the state of your object holistically and keep the code for doing so inside of the model class itself. (This is an older technique that I can't fully endorse; it adds complexity to your model class unnecessarily given how easy it is to create custom validator classes.)

For example, assume that you are dealing with a model object with a set of three integer attributes (`:attr1`, `:attr2`, and `:attr3`) and a precalculated total attribute (`:total`). The total must always equal the sum of the three attributes:

```
class CompletelyLameTotalExample < ActiveRecord::Base
  def validate
    if total != (attr1 + attr2 + attr3)
```

```
      errors[:total] << "The total doesn't add up!"
    end
  end
end
```

You can alternatively add an error message to the whole object instead of just a particular attribute, using the `:base` key, like this:

```
errors[:base] << "The total doesn't add up!"
```

Remember: The way to mark an object as invalid is to add to its `Errors` object. The return value of a custom validation method is not used.

8.7 Skipping Validations

The method `update_attribute` doesn't invoke validations, yet its companion method `update_attributes` does, a question that comes up quite often on the mailing list. Whoever wrote the API docs believes that this behavior is "especially useful for Boolean flags on existing records."

I don't know if that is entirely true or not, but I do know that it is the source of ongoing contention in the community. Unfortunately, I don't have much more to add other than some simple common-sense advice: Be very careful using the `update_attribute` method. It can easily persist your model objects in invalid states.

8.8 Working with the Errors Hash

Some methods are provided to allow you to add validation errors to the collection manually and alter the state of the `Errors` hash.

errors[:base] = msg

Adds an error message related to the overall object state itself and not the value of any particular attribute. Make your error messages complete sentences, because Rails does not do any additional processing of them to make them readable.

errors[:attribute] = msg

Adds an error message related to a particular attribute. The message should be a sentence fragment that reads naturally when prepended with the capitalized name of the attribute.

clear

As you might expect, the `clear` method clears the `Errors` collection.

Active Record

8.8.1   Checking for Errors

It's also possible to check the `Errors` object for validation failures on specific attributes
with a couple of methods, just using square brackets notation. An array is always returned;
an empty one when there aren't any validation errors for the attribute specified.

```
>> user.errors[:login]
=> ["zed is already registered"]
>> user.errors[:password]
=> []
```

8.9   Testing Validations with Shoulda

Even though validations are declarative code, if you're doing TDD then you'll want to
specify them before writing them. Luckily, Thoughtbot's Shoulda library[4] contains a
number of matchers designed to easily test validations.

```
describe Post do
    it { should validate_uniqueness_of :title }
    it { should validate_presence_of :body, :message => /wtf/ }
    it { should validate_presence_of :title }
    it { should validate_numericality_of :user_id }
end

describe User do
    it { should not_allow_values_for :email, "blah", "b lah" }
    it { should allow_values_for :email, "a@b.com", "asdf@asdf.com" }
    it { should ensure_length_in_range :email, 1..100 }
    it { should ensure_value_in_range :age, 1..100 }
    it { should not_allow_mass_assignment_of :password }
 end
```

8.10   Conclusion

In this (relatively speaking) short chapter, we covered the Active Record Validations API
in-depth. One of the most appealing aspects of Rails is how we can declaratively specify
the criteria for determining the validity of model objects.

---

4. `http://github.com/thoughtbot/shoulda`

Advanced Active Record

Active Record is a simple object-relational mapping (ORM) framework compared to other popular ORM frameworks, such as Hibernate in the Java world. Don't let that fool you, though: Under its modest exterior, Active Record has some pretty advanced features. To really get the most effectiveness out of Rails development, you need to have more than a basic understanding of Active Record—things like knowing when to break out of the one-table/one-class pattern, or how to leverage Ruby modules to keep your code clean and free of duplication.

In this chapter, we wrap up this book's comprehensive coverage of Active Record by reviewing callbacks, observers, single-table inheritance (STI), and polymorphic models. We also review a little bit of information about metaprogramming and Ruby domain-specific languages (DSLs) as they relate to Active Record.

9.1 Scopes

Scopes (or "named scopes" if you're old school) allow you define and chain query criteria in a declarative and reusable manner.

```
class Timesheet < ActiveRecord::Base
  scope :submitted, where(:submitted => true)
  scope :underutilized, where('total_hours < 40')
```

To declare a scope, use the `scope` class method, passing it a name as a symbol and some sort of query definition. If your query is known at load time, you can simply use Arel criteria methods like `where`, `order`, and `limit` to construct the definition as shown in the example. On the other hand, if you won't have all the parameters for your query until runtime, use a lambda as the second parameter. It will get evaluated whenever the scope is invoked.

251

```
class User < ActiveRecord::Base
  scope :delinquent, lambda { where('timesheets_updated_at < ?',
1.week.ago)}
```

Invoke scopes as you would class methods.

```
>> User.delinquent
=> [#<User id: 2, timesheets_updated_at: "2010-01-07 01:56:29"...>]
```

9.1.1   Scope Parameters

You can pass arguments to scope invocations by adding parameters to the lambda you use to define the scope query.

```
class BillableWeek < ActiveRecord::Base
  scope :newer_than, lambda { |date| where('start_date > ?', date) }
```

Then pass the argument to the scope as you would normally.

```
BillableWeek.newer_than(Date.today)
```

9.1.2   Chaining Scopes

One of the beauties of scopes is that you can chain them together to create complex queries from simple ones:

```
>> Timesheet.underutilized.submitted
=> [#<Timesheet id: 3, submitted: true, total_hours: 37 ...
```

Scopes can be chained together for reuse within scope definitions themselves. For instance, let's say that we always want to constrain the result set of underutilized to submitted timesheets:

```
class Timesheet < ActiveRecord::Base
  scope :submitted, where(:submitted => true)
  scope :underutilized, submitted.where('total_hours < 40')
```

9.1.3   Scopes and has_many

In addition to being available at the class context, scopes are available automatically on has_many association attributes.

```
>> u = User.find 2
=> #<User id: 2, login: "obie"...>

>> u.timesheets.size
=> 3
>> u.timesheets.underutilized.size
 => 1
```

9.1.4 Scopes and Joins

You can use Arel's `join` method to create cross-model scopes. For instance, if we gave our recurring example `Timesheet` a `submitted_at` date attribute instead of just a boolean, we could add a scope to `User` allowing us to see who is late on their timesheet submission.

```
scope :tardy, lambda {
  joins(:timesheets).
  where("timesheets.submitted_at <= ?", 7.days.ago).
  group("users.id")
}
```

Arel's `to_sql` method is useful for debugging scope definitions and usage.

```
>> User.tardy.to_sql
=> "SELECT users.* FROM users
    INNER JOIN timesheets ON timesheets.user_id = users.id
    WHERE (timesheets.submitted_at <= '2010-07-06 15:27:05.117700')
    GROUP BY users.id"  # query formatted nicely for the book
```

Note that as demonstrated in the example, it's a good idea to use unambiguous column references (including table name) in cross-model scope definitions so that Arel doesn't get confused.

9.1.5 Scope Combinations

Our example of a cross-model scope violates good object-oriented design principles: it contains the logic for determining whether or not a `Timesheet` is submitted, which is code that properly belongs in the `Timesheet` class. Luckily we can use Arel's merge method (aliased as `&`) to fix it. First we put the late logic where it belongs, in `Timesheet`:

```
scope :late, lambda { where("timesheet.submitted_at <= ?", 7.days.ago) }
```

Then we use our new `late` scope in `tardy`:

```
scope :tardy, lambda {
  joins(:timesheets).group("users.id") & Timesheet.late
}
```

If you have trouble with this technique, make absolutely sure that your scopes' clauses refer to fully qualified column names. (In other words, don't forget to prefix column names with tables.) The console and `to_sql` method is your friend for debugging.

9.1.6 Default Scopes

There may arise use cases where you want certain conditions applied to the finders for your model. Consider our timesheet application has a default view of open timesheets—we can use a default scope to simplify our general queries.

```
class Timesheet < ActiveRecord::Base
  default_scope :where(:status => "open")
end
```

Now when we query for our `Timesheets`, by default the open condition will be applied:

```
>> Timesheet.all.map(&:status)
=> ["open", "open", "open"]
```

Default scopes also get applied to your models when building or creating them, which can be a great convenience or a nuisance if you are not careful. In our previous example, all new `Timesheets` will be created with a status of "open."

```
>> Timesheet.new
=> #<Timesheet id: nil, status: "open">
>> Timesheet.create
=> #<Timesheet id: 1, status: "open">
```

You can override this behavior by providing your own conditions or scope to override the default setting of the attributes.

```
>> Timesheet.where(:status => "new").new
=> #<Timesheet id: nil, status: "new">
>> Timesheet.where(:status => "new").create
=> #<Timesheet id: 1, status: "new">
```

There may be cases where at runtime you want to create a scope and pass it around as a first class object leveraging your default scope. In this case, Active Record provides the `scoped` method.

```
>> timesheets = Timesheet.scoped.order("submitted_at DESC")
=> [#<Timesheet id: 1, status: "open"]
>> timesheets.where(:name => "Durran Jordan")
=> []
```

There's another approach to scopes that provides a sleeker syntax, `scoping`, which allows the chaining of scopes via nesting within a block.

```
>> Timesheet.order("submitted_at DESC").scoping do
>>    Timesheets.all
>> end
=> #<Timesheet id: 1, status: "open">
```

That's pretty nice, but what if we *don't* want our default scope to be included in our queries? In this case Active Record takes care of us through the `unscoped` method.

```
>> Timesheet.unscoped.order("submitted_at DESC")
=> [#<Timesheet id: 2, status: "submitted">]
```

Similarly to overriding our default scope with a relation when creating new objects, we can supply `unscoped` as well to remove the default attributes.

```
>> Timesheet.unscoped.new
=> #<Timesheet id: nil, status: nil>
```

9.1.7 Using Scopes for CRUD

You have a wide range of Active Record's CRUD methods available on scopes, which gives you some powerful abilities. For instance, let's give all our underutilized timesheets some extra hours.

```
>> u.timesheets.underutilized.collect(&:total_hours)
=> [37, 38]

>> u.timesheets.underutilized.update_all("total_hours = total_hours + 2")
=> 2

>> u.timesheets.underutilized.collect(&:total_hours)
=> [37, 38]  # whoops, cached result

>> u.timesheets(true).underutilized.collect(&:total_hours)
=> [39]  # results after telling association to reload
```

Scopes including a where clause using hashed conditions will populate attributes of objects built off of them with those attributes as default values. Admittedly it's a bit difficult to think of a plausible use case for this feature, but we'll show it in an example. First, we add the following scope to `Timesheet`:

```
scope :perfect, submitted.where(:total_hours => 40)
```

Now, building an object on the `perfect` scope should give us a submitted timesheet with 40 hours.

```
> Timesheet.perfect.build
 => #<Timesheet id: nil, submitted: true, user_id: nil, total_hours: 40
...>
```

As you've probably realized by now, the new Arel underpinnings of Active Record are tremendously powerful and truly elevate the Rails 3 platform.

9.2 Callbacks

This advanced feature of Active Record allows the savvy developer to attach behavior at a variety of different points along a model's life cycle, such as after initialization, before database records are inserted, updated or removed, and so on.

Callbacks can do a variety of tasks, ranging from simple things such as logging and massaging of attribute values prior to validation, to complex calculations. Callbacks can halt the execution of the life-cycle process taking place. Some callbacks can even modify the behavior of the model class on the fly. We'll cover all of those scenarios in this section, but first let's get a taste of what a callback looks like. Check out the following silly example:

```
class Beethoven < ActiveRecord::Base
  before_destroy :last_words

  protected

  def last_words
    logger.info "Friends applaud, the comedy is over"
  end
end
```

So prior to dying (ehrm, being `destroy`'d), the last words of the `Beethoven` class will always be logged for posterity. As we'll see soon, there are 14 different opportunities to add behavior to your model in this fashion. Before we get to that list, let's cover the mechanics of registering a callback.

9.2.1 Callback Registration

Overall, the most common way to register a callback method is to declare it at the top of the class using a typical Rails macro-style class method. However, there's a less verbose way to do it also. Simply implement the callback as a method in your class. In other words, I could have coded the prior example as follows:

```
class Beethoven < ActiveRecord::Base

  protected

  def before_destroy
    logger.info "Friends applaud, the comedy is over"
  end
end
```

This is a rare case of the less-verbose solution being bad. In fact, it is almost always preferable, dare I say it is the Rails way, to use the callback macros over implementing callback methods, for the following reasons:

- Macro-style callback declarations are added near the top of the class definition, making the existence of that callback more evident versus a method body potentially buried later in the file.

- Macro-style callbacks add callback methods to a queue. That means that more than one method can be hooked into the same slot in the life cycle. Callbacks will be invoked in the order in which they were added to the queue.

- Callback methods for the same hook can be added to their queue at different levels of an inheritance hierarchy and still work—they won't override each other the way that methods would.

- Callbacks defined as methods on the model are always called last.

9.2.2 One-Liners

Now, if (and only if) your callback routine is really short,[1] you can add it by passing a block to the callback macro. We're talking one-liners!

```
class Napoleon < ActiveRecord::Base
  before_destroy { logger.info "Josephine..." }
  ...
end
```

As of Rails 3, the block passed to a callback is executed via `instance_eval` so that its scope is the record itself (versus needing to act on a passed in record variable). The following example implements "paranoid" model behavior, covered later in the chapter.

```
class Account < ActiveRecord::Base
  before_destroy { update_attribute(:deleted_at, Time.now); false }
  ...
```

9.2.3 Protected or Private

Except when you're using a block, the access level for callback methods should always be protected or private. It should never be public, since callbacks should never be called from code outside the model.

---

1. If you are browsing old Rails source code, you might come across callback macros receiving a short string of Ruby code to be evaluated in the binding of the model object. That way of adding callbacks was deprecated in Rails 1.2, because you're always better off using a block in those situations.

Believe it or not, there are even more ways to implement callbacks, but we'll cover those techniques further along in the chapter. For now, let's look at the lists of callback hooks available.

9.2.4 Matched before/after Callbacks

In total, there are 14 types of callbacks you can register on your models! Twelve of them are matching `before/after` callback pairs, such as `before_validation` and `after_validation`. (The other two, `after_initialize` and `after_find`, are special, and we'll discuss them later in this section.)

List of Callbacks

This is the list of callback hooks available during a `save` operation. (The list varies slightly depending on whether you're saving a new or existing record.)

- `before_validation`
- `before_validation_on_create`
- `after_validation`
- `after_validation_on_create`
- `before_save`
- `before_create` (for new records) and `before_update` (for existing records)
- (Database actually gets an `INSERT` or `UPDATE` statement here)
- `after_create` (for new records) and `after_update` (for existing records)
- `after_save`

Delete operations have their own two callbacks:

- `before_destroy`
- (Database actually gets a `DELETE` statement here)
- `after_destroy` is called after all attributes have been frozen (read-only)

Additionally transactions have callbacks as well, for when you want actions to occur after the database is guaranteed to be in a permanent state. Note that only "after" callbacks exist here because of the nature of transactions—it's a bad idea to be able to interfere with the actual operation itself.

- `after_commit`

- `after_commit_on_create`

- `after_commit_on_update`

- `after_commit_on_destroy`

- `after_rollback`

- `after_rollback_on_create`

- `after_rollback_on_update`

- `after_rollback_on_destroy`

9.2.5   Halting Execution

If you return a boolean `false` (not `nil`) from a callback method, Active Record halts the execution chain. No further callbacks are executed. The `save` method will return `false`, and `save!` will raise a `RecordNotSaved` error.

Keep in mind that because the last expression of a Ruby method is returned implicitly, it is a pretty common bug to write a callback that halts execution unintentionally. If you have an object with callbacks that mysteriously fails to save, make sure you aren't returning `false` by mistake.

9.2.6   Callback Usages

Of course, the callback you should use for a given situation depends on what you're trying to accomplish. The best I can do is to serve up some examples to inspire you with your own code.

Cleaning Up Attribute Formatting with **before_validate_on_create**

The most common examples of using `before_validation` callbacks have to do with cleaning up user-entered attributes. For example, the following `CreditCard` class cleans up its `number` attribute so that false negatives don't occur on validation:

```
class CreditCard < ActiveRecord::Base

  ...

  def before_validation_on_create
    # Strip everything in the number except digits
    self.number = number.gsub(/[^0-9]/, "")
  end
end
```

Geocoding with `before_save`

Assume that you have an application that tracks addresses and has mapping features. Addresses should always be geocoded before saving, so that they can be displayed rapidly on a map later.[2]

As is often the case, the wording of the requirement itself points you in the direction of the `before_save` callback:

```
class Address < ActiveRecord::Base
  include GeoKit::Geocoders

  before_save :geolocate
  validates_presence_of :street, :city, :state, :zip
  ...

  def to_s
    "#{street} #{city}, #{state} #{zip}"
end

  protected

  def geolocate
    res = GoogleGeocoder.geocode(to_s)
    self.latitude = res.lat
    self.longitude = res.lng
  end
end
```

Before we move on, there are a couple of additional considerations. The preceding code works great if the geocoding succeeds, but what if it doesn't? Do we still want to allow the record to be saved? If not, we should halt the execution chain:

```
def geolocate
  res = GoogleGeocoder.geocode(to_s)
  return false if not res.success   # halt execution

  self.latitude = res.lat
  self.longitude = res.lng
end
```

The only problem remaining is that we give the rest of our code (and by extension, the end user) no indication of why the chain was halted. Even though we're not in a validation routine, I think we can put the `errors` collection to good use here:

```
def geolocate
  res = GoogleGeocoder.geocode(to_s)
```

---

2. I recommend the excellent GeoKit for Rails plugin available at `http://geokit.rubyforge.org/`.

```
  if res.success
    self.latitude = res.lat
    self.longitude = res.lng
  else
    errors[:base] << "Geocoding failed. Please check address."
    return false
  end
end
```

If the geocoding fails, we add a base error message (for the whole object) and halt execution, so that the record is not saved.

Exercise Your Paranoia with **before_destroy**

What if your application has to handle important kinds of data that, once entered, should never be deleted? Perhaps it would make sense to hook into Active Record's destroy mechanism and somehow mark the record as deleted instead?

The following example depends on the `accounts` table having a `deleted_at` datetime column.

```
class Account < ActiveRecord::Base

  ...

  def before_destroy
    update_attribute(:deleted_at, Time.now)
    false
  end

end
```

I chose to implement it as a callback method so that I am guaranteed it will execute last in the `before_destroy` queue. It returns `false` so that execution is halted and the underlying record is not actually deleted from the database.[3]

It's probably worth mentioning that there are ways that Rails allows you to unintentionally circumvent `before_destroy` callbacks:

- The `delete` and `delete_all` class methods of `ActiveRecord::Base` are almost identical. They remove rows directly from the database without instantiating the corresponding model instances, which means no callbacks will occur.

---

3. Real-life implementation of the example would also need to modify all finders to include `deleted_at` is NULL conditions; otherwise, the records marked deleted would continue to show up in the application. That's not a trivial undertaking, and luckily you don't need to do it yourself. There's a Rails plugin named ActsAsParanoid by Rick Olson that does exactly that, and you can find it at http://svn.techno-weenie.net/projects/plugins/acts_as_paranoid.

- Model objects in associations defined with the option `:dependent => :delete_all` will be deleted directly from the database when removed from the collection using the association's `clear` or `delete` methods.

Cleaning Up Associated Files with **after_destroy**

Model objects that have files associated with them, such as attachment records and uploaded images, can clean up after themselves when deleted using the `after_destroy` callback. The following method from Rick Olson's old AttachmentFu[4] plugin is a good example:

```
# Destroys the file.  Called in the after_destroy callback
def destroy_file
  FileUtils.rm(full_filename)
  ...
rescue
  logger.info "Exception destroying  #{full_filename ... }"
  logger.warn $!.backtrace.collect { |b| " > #{b}" }.join("\n")
end
```

9.2.7   Special Callbacks: **after_initialize** and **after_find**

The `after_initialize` callback is invoked whenever a new Active Record model is instantiated (either from scratch or from the database). Having it available prevents you from having to muck around with overriding the actual `initialize` method.

The `after_find` callback is invoked whenever Active Record loads a model object from the database, and is actually called before `after_initialize`, if both are implemented. Because `after_find` and `after_initialize` are called for each object found and instantiated by finders, performance constraints dictate that they can only be added as methods, and not via the callback macros.

What if you want to run some code only the first time that a model is ever instantiated, and not after each database load? There is no native callback for that scenario, but you can do it using the `after_initialize` callback. Just add a condition that checks to see if it is a new record:

```
def after_initialize
  if new?
    ...
  end
end
```

---

4. Get AttachmentFu at `http://svn.techno-weenie.net/projects/plugins/attachment_fu`.

In a number of Rails apps that I've written, I've found it useful to capture user preferences in a serialized hash associated with the `User` object. The `serialize` feature of Active Record models makes this possible, since it transparently persists Ruby object graphs to a text column in the database. Unfortunately, you can't pass it a default value, so I have to set one myself:

```
class User < ActiveRecord::Base
  serialize :preferences # defaults to nil
  ...

  protected

    def after_initialize
      self.preferences ||= Hash.new
    end
end
```

Using the `after_initialize` callback, I can automatically populate the `preferences` attribute of my user model with an empty hash, so that I never have to worry about it being `nil` when I access it with code such as `user.preferences[:show_help_text] = false`.

Ruby's metaprogramming capabilities combined with the ability to run code whenever a model is loaded using the `after_find` callback are a powerful mix. Since we're not done learning about callbacks yet, we'll come back to uses of `after_find` later on in the chapter, in the section "Modifying Active Record Classes at Runtime."

9.2.8 Callback Classes

It is common enough to want to reuse callback code for more than one object that Rails gives you a way to write callback classes. All you have to do is pass a given callback queue an object that responds to the name of the callback and takes the model object as a parameter.

Here's our paranoid example from the previous section as a callback class:

```
class MarkDeleted
  def self.before_destroy(model)
    model.update_attribute(:deleted_at, Time.now)
    return false
  end
end
```

The behavior of `MarkDeleted` is stateless, so I added the callback as a class method. Now you don't have to instantiate `MarkDeleted` objects for no good reason. All you do is pass the class to the callback queue for whichever models you want to have the mark-deleted behavior:

```
class Account < ActiveRecord::Base
  before_destroy MarkDeleted
  ...
end

class Invoice < ActiveRecord::Base
  before_destroy MarkDeleted
  ...
end
```

Multiple Callback Methods in One Class

There's no rule that says you can't have more than one callback method in a callback class. For example, you might have special audit log requirements to implement:

```
class Auditor
  def initialize(audit_log)
    @audit_log = audit_log
  end

  def after_create(model)
    @audit_log.created(model.inspect)
  end

  def after_update(model)
    @audit_log.updated(model.inspect)
  end

  def after_destroy(model)
    @audit_log.destroyed(model.inspect)
  end
end
```

To add audit logging to an Active Record class, you would do the following:

```
class Account < ActiveRecord::Base
  after_create Auditor.new(DEFAULT_AUDIT_LOG)
  after_update Auditor.new(DEFAULT_AUDIT_LOG)
  after_destroy Auditor.new(DEFAULT_AUDIT_LOG)
  ...
end
```

Wow, that's ugly, having to add three Auditors on three lines. We could extract a local variable called auditor, but it would still be repetitive. This might be an opportunity to take advantage of Ruby's open classes, the fact that you can modify classes that aren't part of your application.

Wouldn't it be better to simply say `acts_as_audited` at the top of the model that needs auditing? We can quickly add it to the `ActiveRecord::Base` class, so that it's available for all our models.

On my projects, the file where "quick and dirty" code like the method in Listing 9.1 would reside is `lib/core_ext/active_record_base.rb`, but you can put it anywhere you want. You could even make it a plugin (as detailed in Chapter 19, "Extending Rails with Plugins").

Listing 9.1 A quick-and-dirty "acts as audited" method

```
class ActiveRecord::Base
  def self.acts_as_audited(audit_log=DEFAULT_AUDIT_LOG)
    auditor = Auditor.new(audit_log)
    after_create auditor
    after_update auditor
    after_destroy auditor
  end
end
```

Now, the top of `Account` is a lot less cluttered:

```
class Account < ActiveRecord::Base
  acts_as_audited
```

Testability
When you add callback methods to a model class, you pretty much have to test that they're functioning correctly in conjunction with the model to which they are added. That may or may not be a problem. In contrast, callback classes are super-easy to test in isolation.

```
def test_auditor_logs_created
  (model = mock).expects(:inspect).returns('foo')
  (log = mock).expects(:created).with('foo')
  Auditor.new(log).after_create(model)
end
```

9.3 Calculation Methods

All Active Record classes have a `calculate` method that provides easy access to aggregate function queries in the database. Methods for `count`, `sum`, `average`, `minimum`, and `maximum` have been added as convenient shortcuts.

Options such as `conditions`, `:order`, `:group`, `:having`, and `:joins` can be passed to customize the query.

There are two basic forms of output:

Single aggregate value The single value is type cast to `Fixnum` for `COUNT`, `Float` for `AVG`, and the given column's type for everything else.

Grouped values This returns an ordered hash of the values and groups them by the `:group` option. It takes either a column name, or the name of a `belongs_to` association.

The following options are available to all calculation methods:

:conditions An SQL fragment like `"administrator = 1"` or `[ "user_name = ?", username ]`. See conditions in the intro to ActiveRecord::Base.

:include Eager loading, see Associations for details. Since calculations don't load anything, the purpose of this is to access fields on joined tables in your conditions, order, or group clauses.

:joins An SQL fragment for additional joins like `"LEFT JOIN comments ON comments.post_id = id"`. (Rarely needed). The records will be returned read-only since they will have attributes that do not correspond to the table's columns.

:order An SQL fragment like `"created_at DESC, name"` (really only used with `GROUP BY` calculations).

:group An attribute name by which the result should be grouped. Uses the `GROUP BY` SQL-clause.

:select By default, this is `*` as in `SELECT * FROM`, but can be changed if you, for example, want to do a join, but not include the joined columns.

:distinct Set this to true to make this a distinct calculation, such as `SELECT COUNT(DISTINCT posts.id) ...`

The following examples illustrate the usage of various calculation methods.

```
Person.calculate(:count, :all) # The same as Person.count

# SELECT AVG(age) FROM people
Person.average(:age)

# Selects the minimum age for everyone with a last name other than
'Drake'
Person.minimum(:age).where('last_name <> ?', 'Drake')
```

```
# Selects the minimum age for any family without any minors
Person.minimum(:age).having('min(age) > 17').group(:last_name)
```

9.3.1 `average(column_name, *options)`

Calculates the average value on a given column. The first parameter should be a symbol identifying the column to be averaged.

9.3.2 `count(column_name, *options)`

Count operates using three different approaches. Count without parameters will return a count of all the rows for the model. Count with a `column_name` will return a count of all the rows for the model with the supplied colum present. Lastly, count using :options will find the row count matched by the options used. In the last case you would send an options hash as the only parameter. 213

```
total_contacts = person.contacts.count(:from => "contact_cards")
```

Options are the same as with all other calculations methods with the additional option of :from which is by default the name of the table name of the class, however it can be changed to a different table name or even that of a database view. Remember that Person.count(:all) will not work because :all will be treated as a condition, you should use Person.count instead.

9.3.3 `maximum(column_name, *options)`

Calculates the maximum value on a given column. The first parameter should be a symbol identifying the column to be calculated.

9.3.4 `minimum(column_name, *options)`

Calculates the minimum value on a given column. The first parameter should be a symbol identifying the column to be calculated.

9.3.5 `sum(column_name, *options)`

Calculates a summed value in the database using SQL. The first parameter should be a symbol identifying the column to be summed.

9.4　Observers

The single responsibility principle is a very important tenet of object-oriented programming. It compels us to keep a class focused on a single concern. As you've learned in the previous section, callbacks are a useful feature of Active Record models that allow us to hook in behavior at various points of a model object's life cycle. Even if we pull that extra behavior out into callback classes, the hook still requires code changes in the model class definition itself. On the other hand, Active Record gives us a way to hook in to models that is completely transparent: Observers.

Here is the functionality of our old `Auditor` callback class as an observer of `Account` objects:

```
class AccountObserver < ActiveRecord::Observer
  def after_create(model)
    DEFAULT_AUDIT_LOG.created(model.inspect)
  end

  def after_update(model)
    DEFAULT_AUDIT_LOG.updated(model.inspect)
  end

  def after_destroy(model)
    DEFAULT_AUDIT_LOG.destroyed(model.inspect)
  end
end
```

9.4.1　Naming Conventions

When `ActiveRecord::Observer` is subclassed, it breaks down the name of the subclass by stripping off the "Observer" part. In the case of our `AccountObserver` in the preceding example, it would know that you want to observe the `Account` class. However, that's not always desirable behavior. In fact, with general-purpose code such as our `Auditor`, it's positively a step backward, so it is possible to overrule the naming convention with the use of the `observe` macro-style method. We still extend `ActiveRecord::Observer`, but we can call the subclass whatever we want and tell it explicitly what to observe using the `observe` method, which accepts one or more arguments.

```
class Auditor < ActiveRecord::Observer
  observe Account, Invoice, Payment

  def after_create(model)
    DEFAULT_AUDIT_LOG.created(model.inspect)
  end
```

```
  def after_update(model)
    DEFAULT_AUDIT_LOG.updated(model.inspect)
  end

  def after_destroy(model)
    DEFAULT_AUDIT_LOG.destroyed(model.inspect)
  end
end
```

9.4.2 Registration of Observers

If there weren't a place for you to tell Rails which observers to load, they would never get loaded at all, since they're not referenced from any other code in your application. Register observers with the following kind of code in an initializer:

```
# Activate observers that should always be running
ActiveRecord::Base.observers = Auditor
```

9.4.3 Timing

Observers are notified after the in-object callbacks are triggered.[5] It's not possible to act on the whole object from an observer without having the object's own callbacks executed first.

Durran says...

> For those of us who love to be organized, you can now put your observers in a separate directory under app if your heart desires. You won't need to perform custom loading anymore since Rails now loads all files under the app directory automatically.

9.5 Single-Table Inheritance (STI)

A lot of applications start out with a User model of some sort. Over time, as different kinds of users emerge, it might make sense to make a greater distinction between them. Admin and Guest classes are introduced, as subclasses of User. Now, the shared behavior can reside in User, and subtype behavior can be pushed down to subclasses. However, all user data can still reside in the users table—all you need to do is introduce a type column that will hold the name of the class to be instantiated for a given row.

---

5. https://rails.lighthouseapp.com/projects/8994/tickets/230 contains an interesting discussion about callback execution order.

To continue explaining single-table inheritance, let's turn back to our example of a recurring `Timesheet` class. We need to know how many `billable_hours` are outstanding for a given user. The calculation can be implemented in various ways, but in this case we've chosen to write a pair of class and instance methods on the `Timesheet` class:

```
class Timesheet < ActiveRecord::Base
  ...

  def billable_hours_outstanding
    if submitted?
      billable_weeks.map(&:total_hours).sum
    else
      0
    end
  end

  def self.billable_hours_outstanding_for(user)
    user.timesheets.map(&:billable_hours_outstanding).sum
  end

end
```

I'm not suggesting that this is good code. It works, but it's inefficient and that `if/else` condition is a little fishy. Its shortcomings become apparent once requirements emerge about marking a `Timesheet` as paid. It forces us to modify `Timesheet`'s `billable_hours_outstanding` method again:

```
def billable_hours_outstanding
  if submitted? && not paid?
    billable_weeks.map(&:total_hours).sum
  else
    0
  end
end
```

That latest change is a clear violation of the open-closed principle,[6] which urges you to write code that is open for extension, but closed for modification. We know that we violated the principle, because we were forced to change the `billable_hours_outstanding` method to accommodate the new `Timesheet` status. Though it may not seem like a large problem in our simple example, consider the amount of conditional code that will end up in the `Timesheet` class once we start having to implement functionality such as `paid_hours` and `unsubmitted_hours`.

---

6. `http://en.wikipedia.org/wiki/Open/closed_principle` has a good summary.

So what's the answer to this messy question of the constantly changing conditional? Given that you're reading the section of the book about single-table inheritance, it's probably no big surprise that we think one good answer is to use object-oriented inheritance. To do so, let's break our original `Timesheet` class into four classes.

```
class Timesheet < ActiveRecord::Base
  # non-relevant code ommitted

  def self.billable_hours_outstanding_for(user)
    user.timesheets.map(&:billable_hours_outstanding).sum
  end
end

class DraftTimesheet < Timesheet
  def billable_hours_outstanding
    0
  end
end

class SubmittedTimesheet < Timesheet
  def billable_hours_outstanding
    billable_weeks.map(&:total_hours).sum
  end
end
```

Now when the requirements demand the ability to calculate partially paid timesheets, we need only add some behavior to a `PaidTimesheet` class. No messy conditional statements in sight!

```
class PaidTimesheet < Timesheet
  def billable_hours_outstanding
    billable_weeks.map(&:total_hours).sum - paid_hours
  end
end
```

9.5.1   Mapping Inheritance to the Database

Mapping object inheritance effectively to a relational database is not one of those problems with a definitive solution. We're only going to talk about the one mapping strategy that Rails supports natively, which is single-table inheritance, called STI for short.

In STI, you establish one table in the database to holds all of the records for any object in a given inheritance hierarchy. In Active Record STI, that one table is named after the top parent class of the hierarchy. In the example we've been considering, that table would be named `timesheets`.

Hey, that's what it was called before, right? Yes, but to enable STI we have to add a type column to contain a string representing the type of the stored object. The following migration would properly set up the database for our example:

```
class AddTypeToTimesheet < ActiveRecord::Migration
  def self.up
    add_column :timesheets, :type, :string
  end

  def self.down
    remove_column :timesheets, :type
  end
end
```

No default value is needed. Once the type column is added to an Active Record model, Rails will automatically take care of keeping it populated with the right value. Using the console, we can see this behavior in action:

```
>> d = DraftTimesheet.create
>> d.type
=> 'DraftTimesheet'
```

When you try to find an object using the find methods of a base STI class, Rails will automatically instantiate objects using the appropriate subclass. This is especially useful in polymorphic situations, such as the timesheet example we've been describing, where we retrieve all the records for a particular user and then call methods that behave differently depending on the object's class.

```
>> Timesheet.find(:first)
=> #<DraftTimesheet:0x2212354...>
```

Sebastian says...

The word "type" is a very common column name and you might have plenty of uses for it not related to STI—which is why it's very likely you've experienced an ActiveRecord::SubclassNotFound error. Rails will read the "type" column of your Car class and try to find an "SUV" class that doesn't exist. The solution is simple: Tell Rails to use another column for STI with the following code:

```
set_inheritance_column "not_sti"
```

Note

Rails won't complain about the missing column; it will simply ignore it. Recently, the error message was reworded with a better explanation, but too many developers skim error messages and then spend an hour trying to figure out what's wrong with their models. (A lot of people skim sidebar columns too when reading books, but hey, at least I am doubling their chances of learning about this problem.)

9.5.2 STI Considerations

Although Rails makes it extremely simple to use single-table inheritance, there are a few caveats that you should keep in mind.

To begin with, you cannot have an attribute on two different subclasses with the same name but a different type. Since Rails uses one table to store all subclasses, these attributes with the same name occupy the same column in the table. Frankly, there's not much of a reason why that should be a problem unless you've made some pretty bad data-modeling decisions.

More importantly, you need to have one column per attribute on any subclass and any attribute that is not shared by all the subclasses must accept `nil` values. In the recurring example, `PaidTimesheet` has a `paid_hours` column that is not used by any of the other subclasses. `DraftTimesheet` and `SubmittedTimesheet` will not use the `paid_hours` column and leave it as null in the database. In order to validate data for columns not shared by all subclasses, you must use Active Record validations and not the database.

Third, it is not a good idea to have subclasses with too many unique attributes. If you do, you will have one database table with many null values in it. Normally, a tree of subclasses with a large number of unique attributes suggests that something is wrong with your application design and that you should refactor. If you have an STI table that is getting out of hand, it is time to reconsider your decision to use inheritance to solve your particular problem. Perhaps your base class is too abstract?

Finally, legacy database constraints may require a different name in the database for the `type` column. In this case, you can set the new column name using the class method `set_inheritance_column` in the base class. For the `Timesheet` example, we could do the following:

```
class Timesheet < ActiveRecord::Base
  set_inheritance_column 'object_type'
end
```

Now Rails will automatically populate the `object_type` column with the object's type.

9.5.3 STI and Associations

It seems pretty common for applications, particularly data-management ones, to have models that are very similar in terms of their data payload, mostly varying in their behavior and associations to each other. If you used object-oriented languages prior to Rails, you're probably already accustomed to breaking down problem domains into hierarchical structures.

Take for instance, a Rails application that deals with the population of states, counties, cities, and neighborhoods. All of these are places, which might lead you to define an STI class named `Place` as shown in Listing 9.2. I've also included the database schema for clarity:[7]

Listing 9.2 The places database schema and the place class

```
# == Schema Information
#
# Table name: places
#
#  id  :integer(11)  not null, primary key
#  region_id  :integer(11)
#  type  :string(255)
#  name  :string(255)
#  description  :string(255)
#  latitude  :decimal(20, 1)
#  longitude  :decimal(20, 1)
#  population  :integer(11)
#  created_at  :datetime
#  updated_at  :datetime

class Place < ActiveRecord::Base
end
```

`Place` is in essence an abstract class. It should not be instantiated, but there is no foolproof way to enforce that in Ruby. (No big deal, this isn't Java!) Now let's go ahead

---

7. For autogenerated schema information added to the top of your model classes, try Dave Thomas's annotate_ models plugin at `http://svn.pragprog.com/Public/plugins/`

and define concrete subclasses of `Place`:

```
class State < Place
  has_many :counties, :foreign_key => 'region_id'
end

class County < Place
  belongs_to :state, :foreign_key => 'region _id'
  has_many :cities, :foreign_key => 'region _id'
end

class City < Place
  belongs_to :county, :foreign_key => 'region _id'
end
```

You might be tempted to try adding a `cities` association to `State`, knowing that `has_many :through` works with both `belongs_to` and `has_many` target associations. It would make the `State` class look something like this:

```
class State < Place
  has_many :counties, :foreign_key => 'region_id'
  has_many :cities, :through => :counties
end
```

That would certainly be cool, if it worked. Unfortunately, in this particular case, since there's only one underlying table that we're querying, there simply isn't a way to distinguish among the different kinds of objects in the query:

```
Mysql::Error: Not unique table/alias: 'places': SELECT places.* FROM
places INNER JOIN places ON places.region_id = places.id WHERE
((places.region_id = 187912) AND ((places.type = 'County'))) AND
((places.`type` = 'City' ))
```

What would we have to do to make it work? Well, the most realistic would be to use specific foreign keys, instead of trying to overload the meaning of `region_id` for all the subclasses. For starters, the `places` table would look like the example in Listing 9.3.

Listing 9.3 The places database schema revised

```
# == Schema Information
#
# Table name: places
#
#  id  :integer(11)  not null, primary key
#  state_id  :integer(11)
#  county_id  :integer(11)
#  type  :string(255)
#  name  :string(255)
#  description  :string(255)
```

```
#   latitude   :decimal(20, 1)
#   longitude  :decimal(20, 1)
#   population :integer(11)
#   created_at :datetime
#   updated_at :datetime
```

The subclasses would be simpler without the `:foreign_key` options on the associations. Plus you could use a regular `has_many` relationship from `State` to `City`, instead of the more complicated `has_many :through`.

```
class State < Place
  has_many :counties
  has_many :cities
end

class County < Place
  belongs_to :state
  has_many :cities
end

class City < Place
  belongs_to :county
end
```

Of course, all those null columns in the places table won't win you any friends with relational database purists. That's nothing, though. Just a little bit later in this chapter we'll take a second, more in-depth look at polymorphic `has_many` relationships, which will make the purists positively hate you.

9.6 Abstract Base Model Classes

In contrast to single-table inheritance, it is possible for Active Record models to share common code via inheritance and still be persisted to different database tables. In fact, every Rails developer uses an abstract model in their code whether they realize it or not: `ActiveRecord::Base`.[8]

The technique involves creating an abstract base model class that persistent subclasses will extend. It's actually one of the simpler techniques that we broach in this chapter. Let's take the `Place` class from the previous section (refer to Listing 9.3) and revise it to

---

8. `http://m.onkey.org/2007/12/9/namespaced-models`

be an abstract base class in Listing 9.4. It's simple really—we just have to add one line of code:

Listing 9.4 The abstract place class

```
class Place < ActiveRecord::Base
  self.abstract_class = true
end
```

Marking an Active Record model abstract is essentially the opposite of making it an STI class with a type column. You're telling Rails: "Hey, I don't want you to assume that there is a table named `places`."

In our running example, it means we would have to establish tables for states, counties, and cities, which might be exactly what we want. Remember though, that we would no longer be able to query across subtypes with code like `Place.all`.

Abstract classes is an area of Rails where there aren't too many hard-and-fast rules to guide you—experience and gut feeling will help you out.

In case you haven't noticed yet, both class and instance methods are shared down the inheritance hierarchy of Active Record models. So are constants and other class members brought in through module inclusion. That means we can put all sorts of code inside `Place` that will be useful to its subclasses.

9.7 Polymorphic has_many Relationships

Rails gives you the ability to make one class `belong_to` more than one type of another class, as eloquently stated by blogger Mike Bayer:

> The "polymorphic association," on the other hand, while it bears some resemblance to the regular polymorphic union of a class hierarchy, is not really the same since you're only dealing with a particular association to a single target class from any number of source classes, source classes which don't have anything else to do with each other; i.e., they aren't in any particular inheritance relationship and probably are all persisted in completely different tables. In this way, the polymorphic association has a lot less to do with object inheritance and a lot more to do with aspect-oriented programming (AOP); a particular concept needs to be applied to a divergent set of entities which otherwise are not directly related. Such a concept is referred to as a cross-cutting concern, such as, all the entities in your domain need to support a history log of all changes to a common logging table. In the AR example, an Order and a User object are illustrated to both require links to an Address object.[9]

---

9. `http://techspot.zzzeek.org/?p=13`

In other words, this is not polymorphism in the typical object-oriented sense of the word; rather, it is something unique to Rails.

9.7.1 In the Case of Models with Comments

In our recurring Time and Expenses example, let's assume that we want both `BillableWeek` and `Timesheet` to have many comments (a shared `Comment` class). A naive way to solve this problem might be to have the `Comment` class belong to both the `BillableWeek` and `Timesheet` classes and have `billable_week_id` and `timesheet_id` as columns in its database table.

```
class Comment < ActiveRecord::Base
  belongs_to :timesheet
  belongs_to :expense_report
end
```

I call that approach is naive because it would be difficult to work with and hard to extend. Among other things, you would need to add code to the application to ensure that a `Comment` never belonged to both a `BillableWeek` and a `Timesheet` at the same time. The code to figure out what a given comment is attached to would be cumbersome to write. Even worse, every time you want to be able to add comments to another type of class, you'd have to add another nullable foreign key column to the comments table.

Rails solves this problem in an elegant fashion, by allowing us to define what it terms polymorphic associations, which we covered when we described the `:polymorphic => true` option of the `belongs_to` association in Chapter 7, Active Record Associations.

The Interface

Using a polymorphic association, we need define only a single `belongs_to` and add a pair of related columns to the underlying database table. From that moment on, any class in our system can have comments attached to it (which would make it commentable), without needing to alter the database schema or the `Comment` model itself.

```
class Comment < ActiveRecord::Base
  belongs_to :commentable, :polymorphic => true
end
```

There isn't a `Commentable` class (or module) in our application. We named the association `:commentable` because it accurately describes the interface of objects that will be associated in this way. The name :commentable will turn up again on the other side of the association:

```
class Timesheet < ActiveRecord::Base
  has_many :comments, :as => :commentable
end

class BillableWeek < ActiveRecord::Base
  has_many :comments, :as => :commentable
end
```

Here we have the friendly has_many association using the :as option. The :as marks this association as polymorphic, and specifies which interface we are using on the other side of the association. While we're on the subject, the other end of a polymorphic belongs_to can be either a has_many or a has_one and work identically.

The Database Columns

Here's a migration that will create the comments table:

```
class CreateComments < ActiveRecord::Migration
  def self.up
    create_table :comments do |t|
      t.text :body
      t.integer :commentable
      t.string       :commentable_type
    end
  end
end
```

As you can see, there is a column called commentable_type, which stores the class name of associated object. The Migrations API actually gives you a one-line shortcut with the references method, which takes a polymorphic option:

```
create_table :comments do |t|
  t.text :body
  t.references :commentable, :polymorphic => true
end
```

We can see how it comes together using the Rails console (some lines ommitted for brevity):

```
>> c = Comment.create(:text => "I could be commenting anything.")
>> t = TimeSheet.create
>> b = BillableWeek.create
>> c.update_attribute(:commentable, t)
=> true
>> "#{c.commentable_type}: #{c.commentable_id}"
=> "Timesheet: 1"
```

```
>> c.update_attribute(:commentable, b)
=> true
>> "#{c.commentable_type}: #{c.commentable_id}"
=> "BillableWeek: 1"
```

As you can tell, both the `Timesheet` and the `BillableWeek` that we played with in the
console had the same id (1). Thanks to the `commentable_type` attribute, stored as a
string, Rails can figure out which is the correct related object.

`has_many :through` and Polymorphics

There are some logical limitations that come into play with polymorphic associations.
For instance, since it is impossible for Rails to know the tables necessary to join through a
polymorphic association, the following hypothetical code, which tries to find everything
that the user has commented on, will not work.

```ruby
class Comment < ActiveRecord::Base
  belongs_to :user # author of the comment
  belongs_to :commentable, :polymorphic => true
end

class User < ActiveRecord::Base
  has_many :comments
  has_many :commentables, :through => :comments
end
```

```
>> User.first.comments
ActiveRecord::HasManyThroughAssociationPolymorphicError: Cannot have
a has_many :through association 'User#commentables' on the polymorphic
object 'Comment#commentable'.
```

If you really need it, `has_many :through` is possible with polymorphic associations,
but only by specifying exactly what type of polymorphic associations you want. To do
so, you must use the `:source_type` option. In most cases, you will also need to use the
`:source` option, since the association name will not match the interface name used for
the polymorphic association:

```ruby
class User < ActiveRecord::Base
  has_many :comments
  has_many :commented_timesheets, :through => :comments,
           :source => :commentable, :source_type => 'Timesheet'
  has_many :commented_billable_weeks, :through => :comments,
           :source => :commentable, :source_type => 'BillableWeek'
end
```

It's verbose, and the whole scheme loses its elegance if you go this route, but it works:

```
>> User.first.commented_timesheets
=> [#<Timesheet ...>]
```

9.8   Foreign-key Constraints

As we work toward the end of this book's coverage of Active Record, you might have noticed that we haven't really touched on a subject of particular importance to many programmers: foreign-key constraints in the database. That's mainly because use of foreign-key constraints simply isn't the Rails way to tackle the problem of relational integrity. To put it mildly, that opinion is controversial and some developers have written off Rails (and its authors) for expressing it.

There really isn't anything stopping you from adding foreign-key constraints to your database tables, although you'd do well to wait until after the bulk of development is done. The exception, of course, is those polymorphic associations, which are probably the most extreme manifestation of the Rails opinion against foreign-key constraints. Unless you're armed for battle, you might not want to broach that particular subject with your DBA.

9.9   Using Value Objects

In Domain Driven Design[10] (DDD), a distinction is drawn between Entity Objects and Value Objects. All model objects that inherit from ActiveRecord::Base could be considered Entity Objects in DDD. An Entity object cares about identity, since each one is unique. In Active Record uniqueness is derived from the primary key. Comparing two different Entity Objects for equality should always return false, even if all of its attributes (other than the primary key) are equivalent.

Here is an example comparing two Active Record Addresses:

```
>> home = Address.create(:city => "Brooklyn", :state => "NY")
>> office = Address.create(:city => "Brooklyn", :state => "NY")
>> home == office
=> false
```

In this case you are actually creating two new Address records and persisting them to the database, therefore they have different primary key values.

Value Objects on the other hand only care that all their attributes are equal. When creating Value Objects for use with Active Record you do not inherit from

---

10. http://www.domaindrivendesign.org/

`ActiveRecord::Base`. Instead you make them part of a parent model using the `composed_of` class method. This is a form of composition, called an Aggregate in DDD. The attributes of the Value Object are stored in the database together with the parent object and `composed_of` provides a means to interact with those values as a single object.

A simple example is of a Person with a single Address. To model this using composition, first we need a Person model with fields for the Address. Create it with the following migration:

```
class CreatePeople < ActiveRecord::Migration
  def self.up
    create_table :people do |t|
      t.string :name
      t.string :address_city
      t.string :address_state
    end
  end
end
```

The Person model looks like this:

```
class Person < ActiveRecord::Base
  composed_of :address, :mapping => [%w(address_city city),
%w(address_state state)]
end
```

We'd need a corresponding Address object which looks like this:

```
class Address
  attr_reader :city, :state

  def initialize(city, state)
    @city, @state = city, state
  end

  def ==(other_address)
    city == other_address.city && state == other_address.state
  end
end
```

Note that this is just a standard Ruby object that does not inherit from `ActiveRecord::Base`. We have defined reader methods for our attributes and are assigning them upon initialization. We also have to define our own == method for use in comparisons. Wrapping this all up we get the following usage:

```
>> gary = Person.create(:name => "Gary")
>> gary.address_city = "Brooklyn"
>> gary.address_state = "NY"
>> gary.address
=> #<Address:0x20bc118 @state="NY", @city="Brooklyn">
```

Alternately you can instantiate the address directly and assign it using the address accessor:

```
>> gary.address = Address.new("Brooklyn", "NY")
>> gary.address
=> #<Address:0x20bc118 @state="NY", @city="Brooklyn">
```

9.9.1   Immutability

It's also important to treat value objects as immutable. Don't allow them to be changed after creation. Instead, create a new object instance with the new value instead. Active Record will not persist value objects that have been changed through means other than the writer method.

The immutable requirement is enforced by Active Record by freezing any object assigned as a value object. Attempting to change it afterwards will result in a `ActiveSupport::FrozenObjectError`.

9.9.2   Custom Constructors and Converters

By default value objects are initialized by calling the `new` constructor of the value class with each of the mapped attributes, in the order specified by the `:mapping` option, as arguments. If for some reason your value class does not work well with that convention, `composed_of` allows a custom constructor to be specified.

When a new value object is assigned to its parent, the default assumption is that the new value is an instance of the value class. Specifying a custom converter allows the new value to be automatically converted to an instance of value class (when needed).

For example, consider the `NetworkResource` model with `network_address` and `cidr_range` attributes that should be contained in a `NetAddr::CIDR` value class.[11] The constructor for the value class is called create and it expects a CIDR address string as a parameter. New values can be assigned to the value object using either another `NetAddr::CIDR` object, a string or an array. The `:constructor` and `:converter` options are used to meet the requirements:

```
class NetworkResource < ActiveRecord::Base
  composed_of :cidr,
              :class_name => 'NetAddr::CIDR',
              :mapping => [ %w(network_address network), %w(cidr_range
bits) ],
              :allow_nil => true,
```

---

11. Actual objects from the NetAddr gem available at `http://netaddr.rubyforge.org`

```
              :constructor => Proc.new { |network_address, cidr_range|
NetAddr::CIDR.create("#{network_address}/#{cidr_range}") },
              :converter => Proc.new { |value|
NetAddr::CIDR.create(value.is_a?(Array) ? value.join('/') : value) }
end


# This calls the :constructor
network_resource = NetworkResource.new(:network_address => '192.168.0.1',
:cidr_range => 24)


# These assignments will both use the :converter
network_resource.cidr = [ '192.168.2.1', 8 ]
network_resource.cidr = '192.168.0.1/24'


# This assignment won't use the :converter as the value is already an
instance of the value class
network_resource.cidr = NetAddr::CIDR.create('192.168.2.1/8')


# Saving and then reloading will use the :constructor on reload
network_resource.save
network_resource.reload
```

9.9.3 Finding Records by a Value Object

Once a `composed_of` relationship is specified for a model, records can be loaded from the database by specifying an instance of the value object in the conditions hash. The following example finds all customers with `balance_amount` equal to 20 and `balance_currency` equal to `"USD"`:

```
Customer.where(:balance => Money.new(20, "USD"))
```

The Money Gem
A common approach to using `composed_of` is in conjunction with the money gem.[12]

```
class Expense < ActiveRecord::Base
  composed_of :cost,
  :class_name => "Money",
  :mapping => [%w(cents cents), %w(currency currency_as_string)],
  :constructor => Proc.new do |cents, currency|
    Money.new(cents || 0, currency || Money.default_currency)
  end
end
```

Remember to add a migration with the 2 columns, the integer `cents` and the string `currency` that money needs.

---

12. `http://github.com/FooBarWidget/money/`

```
class CreateExpenses < ActiveRecord::Migration
  def self.up
    create_table :expenses do |table|
      table.integer :cents
      table.string :currency
    end
  end
  def self.down
    drop_table :expenses
  end
end
```

Now when asking for or setting the cost of an item would use a `Money` instance.

```
>> expense = Expense.create(:cost => Money.new(1000, "USD"))
>> cost = expense.cost
>> cost.cents
=> 1000
>> expense.currency
=> "USD"
```

9.10 Modules for Reusing Common Behavior

In this section, we'll talk about one strategy for breaking out functionality that is shared between disparate model classes. Instead of using inheritance, we'll put the shared code into modules.

In the section "Polymorphic `has_many` Relationships," we described how to add a commenting feature to our recurring sample Time and Expenses application. We'll continue fleshing out that example, since it lends itself to factoring out into modules.

The requirements we'll implement are as follows: Both users and approvers should be able to add their comments to a `Timesheet` or `ExpenseReport`. Also, since comments are indicators that a timesheet or expense report requires extra scrutiny or processing time, administrators of the application should be able to easily view a list of recent comments. Human nature being what it is, administrators occasionally gloss over the comments without actually reading them, so the requirements specify that a mechanism should be provided for marking comments as "OK" first by the approver, then by the administrator.

Again, here is the polymorphic `has_many :comments, :as => :commentable` that we used as the foundation for this functionality:

```
class Timesheet < ActiveRecord::Base
  has_many :comments, :as => :commentable
end
```

```
class ExpenseReport < ActiveRecord::Base
  has_many :comments, :as => :commentable
end

class Comment < ActiveRecord::Base
  belongs_to :commentable, :polymorphic => true
end
```

Next we enable the controller and action for the administrator that list the 10 most recent comments with links to the item to which they are attached.

```
class Comment < ActiveRecord::Base
  scope :recent, order('created_at desc').limit(10)
end

class CommentsController < ApplicationController
  before_filter :require_admin, :only => :recent
  expose(:recent_comments) { Comment.recent }
end
```

Here's some of the simple view template used to display the recent comments.

```
%ul.recent.comments
  - recent_comments.each do |comment|
    %li.comment
      %h4= comment.created_at
      = comment.text
      .meta
        Comment on:
        = link_to comment.commentable.title, comment.commentable Yes, this
would result in N+1 selects.
```

So far, so good. The polymorphic association makes it easy to access all types of comments in one listing. In order to find all of the unreviewed comments for an item, we can use a named scope on the Comment class together with the comments association.

```
class Comment < ActiveRecord::Base
  scope :unreviewed, where(:reviewed => false)
end
```

```
>> timesheet.comments.unreviewed
```

Both `Timesheet` and `ExpenseReport` currently have identical `has_many` methods for comments. Essentially, they both share a common interface. They're commentable!

To minimize duplication, we could specify common interfaces that share code in Ruby by including a module in each of those classes, where the module contains the code common to all implementations of the common interface. So, mostly for the sake of example, let's go ahead and define a `Commentable` module to do just that, and include it in our model classes:

```
module Commentable
  has_many :comments, :as => :commentable
end

class Timesheet < ActiveRecord::Base
  include Commentable
end

class ExpenseReport < ActiveRecord::Base
  include Commentable
end
```

Whoops, this code doesn't work! To fix it, we need to understand an essential aspect of the way that Ruby interprets our code dealing with open classes.

9.10.1   A Review of Class Scope and Contexts

In many other interpreted OO programming languages, you have two phases of execution—one in which the interpreter loads the class definitions and says "this is the definition of what I have to work with," followed by the phase in which it executes the code. This makes it difficult (though not necessarily impossible) to add new methods to a class dynamically during execution.

In contrast, Ruby lets you add methods to a class at any time. In Ruby, when you type `class MyClass`, you're doing more than simply telling the interpreter to define a class; you're telling it to "execute the following code in the scope of this class."

Let's say you have the following Ruby script:

```
1   class Foo < ActiveRecord::Base
2     has_many :bars
3   end
4   class Foo < ActiveRecord::Base
5     belongs_to :spam
6   end
```

When the interpreter gets to line 1, you are telling it to execute the following code (up to the matching end) in the context of the `Foo` class object. Because the `Foo` class object doesn't exist yet, it goes ahead and creates the class. At line 2, we execute the statement `has_many :bars` in the context of the `Foo` class object. Whatever the `has_many` method does, it does right now.

When we again say class `Foo` at line 4, we are once again telling the interpreter to execute the following code in the context of the `Foo` class object, but this time, the interpreter already knows about class `Foo`; it doesn't actually create another class. Therefore, on line 5, we are simply telling the interpreter to execute the `belongs_to :spam` statement in the context of that same `Foo` class object.

In order to execute the `has_many` and `belongs_to` statements, those methods need to exist in the context in which they are executed. Because these are defined as class methods in `ActiveRecord::Base`, and we have previously defined class `Foo` as extending `ActiveRecord::Base`, the code will execute without a problem.

However, when we defined our `Commentable` module like this:

```
module Commentable
  has_many :comments, :as => :commentable
end
```

...we get an error when it tries to execute the `has_many` statement. That's because the `has_many` method is not defined in the context of the `Commentable` module object.

Given what we now know about how Ruby is interpreting the code, we now realize that what we really want is for that `has_many` statement to be executed in the context of the including class.

9.10.2 The `included` Callback

Luckily, Ruby's `Module` class defines a handy callback that we can use to do just that. If a `Module` object defines the method `included`, it gets run whenever that module is included in another module or class. The argument passed to this method is the module/class object into which this module is being included.

We can define an `included` method on our `Commentable` module object so that it executes the `has_many` statement in the context of the including class (`Timesheet`, `ExpenseReport`, and so on):

```
module Commentable
  def self.included(base)
    base.class_eval do
      has_many :comments, :as => :commentable
    end
  end
end
```

Now, when we include the Commentable module in our model classes, it will execute the `has_many` statement just as if we had typed it into each of those classes' bodies.

The technique is common enough, within Rails and plugins, that it was added as a first-class concept in the Rails 3 ActiveSupport API. The above example becomes shorter and easier to read as a result:

```
module Commentable
  extend ActiveSupport::Concern
  included do
    has_many :comments, :as => :commentable
  end
end
```

Whatever is inside of the `included` block will get executed in the class context of the class where the module is included.

```
has_many :comments, :as => :commentable, :extend => Commentable
```

Courtenay says...

There's a fine balance to strike here. Magic like `include Commentable` certainly saves on typing and makes your model look less complex, but it can also mean that your association code is doing things you don't know about. This can lead to confusion and hours of head-scratching while you track down code in a separate module. My personal preference is to leave all associations in the model, and extend them with a module. That way you can quickly get a list of all associations just by looking at the code.

9.11 Modifying Active Record Classes at Runtime

The metaprogramming capabilities of Ruby, combined with the `after_find` callback, open the door to some interesting possibilities, especially if you're willing to blur your perception of the difference between code and data. I'm talking about modifying the behavior of model classes on the fly, as they're loaded into your application.

Listing 9.5 is a drastically simplified example of the technique, which assumes the presence of a `config` column on your model. During the `after_find` callback, we get a handle to the unique singleton class[13] of the model instance being loaded. Then we execute the contents of the `config` attribute belonging to this particular `Account` instance, using Ruby's `class_eval` method. Since we're doing this using the singleton class for this instance, rather than the global `Account` class, other account instances in the system are completely unaffected.

---

13. I don't expect this to make sense to you, unless you are familiar with Ruby's singleton classes, and the ability to evaluate arbitrary strings of Ruby code at runtime. A good place to start is http://whytheluckystiff.net/articles/seeingMetaclassesClearly.html.

Listing 9.5 Runtime metaprogramming with **after_find**

```
class Account < ActiveRecord::Base

  ...

  protected

  def after_find
    singleton = class << self; self; end
    singleton.class_eval(config)
  end
end
```

I used powerful techniques like this one in a supply-chain application that I wrote for a large industrial client. A lot is a generic term in the industry used to describe a shipment of product. Depending on the vendor and product involved, the attributes and business logic for a given lot vary quite a bit. Since the set of vendors and products being handled changed on a weekly (sometimes daily) basis, the system needed to be reconfigurable without requiring a production deployment.

Without getting into too much detail, the application allowed the maintenance programmers to easily customize the behavior of the system by manipulating Ruby code stored in the database, associated with whatever product the lot contained.

For example, one of the business rules associated with lots of butter being shipped for Acme Dairy Co. might dictate a strictly integral product code, exactly 10 digits in length. The code, stored in the database, associated with the product entry for Acme Dairy's butter product would therefore contain the following two lines:

```
validates_numericality_of :product_code, :only_integer => true
validates_length_of       :product_code, :is => 10
```

9.11.1 Considerations

A relatively complete description of everything you can do with Ruby metaprogramming, and how to do it correctly, would fill its own book. For instance, you might realize that doing things like executing arbitrary Ruby code straight out of the database is inherently dangerous. That's why I emphasize again that the examples shown here are very simplified. All I want to do is give you a taste of the possibilities.

If you do decide to begin leveraging these kinds of techniques in real-world applications, you'll have to consider security and approval workflow and a host of other important concerns. Instead of allowing arbitrary Ruby code to be executed, you might feel compelled to limit it to a small subset related to the problem at hand. You might design a compact API, or even delve into authoring a domain-specific language (DSL), crafted specifically for expressing the business rules and behaviors that should be loaded dynamically. Proceeding down the rabbit hole, you might write custom parsers for your DSL that could execute it in different contexts—some for error detection and others for reporting. It's one of those areas where the possibilities are quite limitless.

9.11.2 Ruby and Domain-Specific Languages

My former colleague Jay Fields and I pioneered the mix of Ruby metaprogramming, Rails, and internal[14] domain-specific languages while doing Rails application development for clients. I still occasionally speak at conferences and blog about writing DSLs in Ruby.

Jay has also written and delivered talks about his evolution of Ruby DSL techniques, which he calls Business Natural Languages (or BNL for short[15]). When developing BNLs, you craft a domain-specific language that is not necessarily valid Ruby syntax, but is close enough to be transformed easily into Ruby and executed at runtime, as shown in Listing 9.6.

Listing 9.6 Example of business natural language

```
employee John Doe
compensate 500 dollars for each deal closed in the past 30 days
compensate 100 dollars for each active deal that closed more than
365 days ago
compensate 5 percent of gross profits if gross profits are greater than
1,000,000 dollars
compensate 3 percent of gross profits if gross profits are greater than
2,000,000 dollars
compensate 1 percent of gross profits if gross profits are greater than
3,000,000 dollars
```

The ability to leverage advanced techniques such as DSLs is yet another powerful tool in the hands of experienced Rails developers.

---

14. The qualifier internal is used to differentiate a domain-specific language hosted entirely inside of a general-purpose language, such as Ruby, from one that is completely custom and requires its own parser implementation.
15. Googling BNL will give you tons of links to the Toronto-based band Barenaked Ladies, so you're better off going directly to the source at `http://bnl.jayfields.com`.

9.12 Conclusion

With this chapter we conclude our coverage of Active Record. Among other things, we examined how callbacks and observers let us factor our code in a clean and object-oriented fashion. We also expanded our modeling options by considering single-table inheritance, abstract classes and Active Record's distinctive polymorphic relationships.

At this point in the book, we've covered two parts of the MVC pattern: the model and the controller. It's now time to delve into the third and final part: the view.

Courtenay says...

DSLs suck! Except the ones written by Obie, of course. The only people who can read and write most DSLs are their original authors. As a developer taking over a project, it's often quicker to just reimplement instead of learning the quirks and exactly which words you're allowed to use in an existing DSL. In fact, a lot of Ruby metaprogramming sucks, too. It's common for people gifted with these new tools to go a bit overboard. I consider metaprogramming, `self.included`, `class_eval`, and friends to be a bit of a code smell on most projects. If you're making a web application, future developers and maintainers of the project will appreciate your using simple, direct, granular, and well-tested methods, rather than monkeypatching into existing classes, or hiding associations in modules. That said, if you can pull it off ... your code will become more powerful than you can possibly imagine.

Action View

The very powerful and the very stupid have one thing in common. Instead of altering their views to fit the facts, they alter the facts to fit their views...which can be very uncomfortable if you happen to be one of the facts that needs altering.

—Doctor Who

Controllers are the skeleton and musculature of your Rails application. In which case, models form the heart and mind, and your view templates (based on Action View, the third major component of Rails) are your application's skin—the part that is visible to the outside world.

Action View is the Rails API for putting together the visual component of your application, namely the HTML and associated content that will be rendered in a web browser whenever someone uses your Rails application. Actually, in this brave new world of REST resources, Action View is involved in generating almost any sort of output you generate.

Action View contains a full-featured templating system based on a Ruby library named ERb. It takes data prepared by the controller layer and interleaves it with view code to create a presentation layer for the end user. It's also one of the first things you learn about Rails and part of the standard Ruby library. I much prefer a templating solution named Haml[1] and have used it all over the book for examples. I think Haml is such a superior choice over ERb, that this edition does not cover ERb at all.

In this chapter, we cover the fundamentals of the Action View framework, from effective use of partials, to the significant performance boosts possible via caching. If you

---

1. `http://haml-lang.com/`

need to learn Haml, the best resource is `http://haml-lang.com/` — the fundamentals of it are really easy — a comprehensive Haml reference is not included in this book.

10.1 Layouts and Templates

Rails has easy conventions for template usage, related to the location of templates with the Rails project directories.

The `app/views` directory contains subdirectories corresponding to the name of controllers in your application. Within each controller's view subdirectory, you place a template named to match its corresponding action.

The special `app/views/layout` directory holds layout templates, intended to be reusable containers for your views. Again, naming conventions are used to determine which templates to render, except that this time it is the name of the controller that is used for matching.

10.1.1 Template Filename Conventions

The filename of a template in Rails carries a lot of significance. Its parts, delimited with periods, correspond to the following information:

- name (usually maps to action)
- locale (optional)
- content type
- templating engine

10.1.2 Layouts

Action View decides which layout to render based on the inheritance hierarchy of controllers being executed. Most Rails applications have an `application.html.haml` file in their layout directory. It shares its name with the `ApplicationController`, which is typically extended by all the other controllers in an application; therefore it is picked up as the default layout for all views.

It is picked up, unless of course, a more specific layout template is in place, but quite often it makes sense to use just one application-wide template, such as the simple one shown in Listing 10.1.

Listing 10.1 A simple general-purpose application.html.haml layout template

```
!!!
%html
  %head
    %meta(http-equiv="Content-Type" content="text/html; charset=UTF-8")
    %title TR3W Time and Expenses Sample Application
    = stylesheet_link_tag 'scaffold', :media => "all"
  %body
    = yield
```

10.1.3 Yielding Content

The Ruby language's built-in `yield` keyword is put to good use in making layout and action templates collaborate. Notice the use of `yield` at the end of the layout template:

```
%body
  = yield
```

In this case, `yield` by itself is a special message to the rendering system. It marks where to insert the output of the action's rendered output, which is usually the template corresponding to that action.

You can add extra places in your layout where you want to be able to yield content, by including additional `yield` invocations—just make sure to pass a unique identifier as the argument. A good example is a layout that has left and right sidebar content (simplified, of course):

```
%body
  .left.sidebar
    = yield :left
  .content
    = yield
  .right.sidebar
    = yield :right
```

The `.content` div receives the main template markup generated. But how do you give Rails content for the left and right sidebars? Easy—just use the `content_for` method anywhere in your template code. I usually stick it at the top of the template so that it's obvious.

```
- content_for :left do
  %h2 Navigation
  %ul
    %li ...

- content_for :right do
```

```
%h2 Help
%p Lorem ipsum dolor sit amet, consectetur adipisicing elit...

%h1 Page Heading
%p ...
```

Besides sidebars and other types of visible content blocks, I suggest you yield for additional content to be added to the HEAD element of your page, as shown in Listing 10.2. It's a super-useful technique, because Internet Explorer can occasionally get very ill-tempered about SCRIPT tags appearing outside of the HEAD element.

Listing 10.2 Yielding additional head content

```
!!!
%html
  %head
    %meta(http-equiv="Content-Type" content="text/html; charset=UTF-8")
    %title TR3W Time and Expenses Sample Application
    = stylesheet_link_tag 'scaffold', :media => "all"
    = yield :head
  %body
    = yield
```

10.1.4 Conditional Output

One of the most common idioms you'll use when coding Rails views is to conditionally output content to the view. The most elementary way to control conditional output is to use if statements.

```
- if show_subtitle?
  %h2= article.subtitle
```

A lot of times you can use inline if conditions and shorten your code, since the = outputter doesn't care if you feed it a nil value. Just add a postfix if condition to the statement:

```
%h2= article.subtitle if show_subtitle?
```

Of course, there's a problem with the preceding example. The if statement on a separate line will eliminate the <h2> tags entirely, but the one-liner second example does not.

There are a couple of ways to deal with the problem and keep it a one-liner. First, there's the butt-ugly solution that I've occasionally seen in some Rails applications, which is the only reason why I'm mentioning it here!

```
= "<h2>#{h(article.subtitle)}</h2>".html_safe if show_subtitle?
```

A more elegant solution involves Rails' `content_tag` helper method, but admittedly a one-liner is probably not superior to its two-line equivalent in this case.

```
= content_tag('h2', article.subtitle) if show_subtitle?
```

Helper methods, both the ones included in Rails like `content_tag` and the ones that you'll write on your own, are your main tool for building elegant view templates. Helpers are covered extensively in Chapter 11, All About Helpers.

10.1.5 Decent Exposure

We've seen how layouts and yielding content blocks work, but other than that, how should data get from the controller layer to the view? During preparation of the template, instance variables set during execution of the controller action will be copied over as instance variables of the template context. Even though it's the standard way exposed by Rails documentation, sharing state via instance variables in controllers promotes close coupling with views.

Stephen Caudill's Decent Exposure gem[2] provides a declarative manner of exposing an interface to the state that controllers contain, thereby decreasing coupling and improving your testability and overall design.

When invoked, `expose` macro creates a method with the given name, evaluates the provided block and memoizes the result. This method is then declared as a `helper_method` so that views may have access to it and is made unroutable as an action. When no block is given, `expose` attempts to intuit which resource you want to acquire:

```
# Timesheet.find(params[:timesheet_id] || params[:id])
expose(:timesheet)
```

As the example shows, the symbol passed is used to guess the class name of the object you want to find—useful since almost every controller in a normal Rails uses this kind of code in the show, edit, update and destroy actions.

In a slightly more complicated scenario, you might need to find an instance of an object which doesn't map cleanly to a simple `find` method.

```
expose(:timesheet) { client.timesheets.find(params[:id]) }
```

In the RESTful controller paradigm, you'll again find yourself using this in show, edit, update, and destroy actions of nested resources.

---

2. http://github.com/voxdolo/decent_exposure

When the code has become long enough to surpass a single line (but still isn't appropriate to extract into a model method), use a do...end style of block, as in the following that uses all three styles:

```
expose(:client)

expose(:timesheet) { client.timesheets.find(params[:id]) }

expose(:timesheet_approval_presenter) do
  TimesheetApprovalPresenter.new(timesheet, current_user)
end
```

The previous example also demonstrates how expose declarations can depend on each other. In fact, proper use of expose should eliminate most model-lookup code from your actual controller actions.

At Hashrocket, use of Decent Exposure has proven so beneficial that it has completely replaced direct use of instance variables in controllers and views. The helper methods created by the expose macro are just referred to directly in the view.

10.1.6 Standard Instance Variables

More than just instance variables from the controller are copied over to the template. It's not a good idea to depend on some of the following objects directly, and especially not to use them to do data operations. Others are a standard part of most Rails applications.

assigns

Want to see everything that comes across the controller-view boundary? Throw = debug(assigns) into your template and take a look at the output. The assigns attribute is essentially internal to Rails and you should not use it directly in your production code.

base_path

Local filesystem path pointing to the base directory of your application where templates are kept.

controller

The current controller instance is made available via controller, before it goes out of scope at the end of request processing. You can take advantage of the controller's knowledge of its name (via the controller_name attribute) and the action that was just performed (via the action_name attribute), in order to structure your CSS more effectively.[3]

```
%body(class="#{controller.controller_name} #{controller.action_name}")
```

---

3. To learn more about identical functionality now included in a HAML helper visit http://vurl.me/WQH

That would result in a BODY tag looking something like this, depending on the action executed:

```
<body class="timesheets index">
```

Hopefully you already know that the C in CSS stands for cascading, which refers to the fact that class names cascade down the tree of elements in your markup code and are available for creation of rules. The trick is to automatically include the controller and action name as classnames of your body element, so that you can use them to customize look and feel of the page very flexibly later on in the development cycle. For example, here's how you would use the technique to vary the background of header elements depending on the controller path:

```
body.timesheets .header {
  background: url(../images/timesheet-bg.png) no-repeat left top
}

body.expense_reports .header {
  background: url(../images/expense-reports-bg.png) no-repeat left top
}
```

cookies

The cookies variable is a hash containing the user's cookies. There might be situations where it'd be okay to pull values out to affect rendering, but most of the time you'll be using cookies in your controller, not the view.

flash

The flash has popped up in larger code samples throughout the book so far, whenever you want to send the user a message from the controller layer, but only for the duration of the next request.

```
def create
  if user.try(:authorize, params[:user][:password])
    flash[:notice] = "Welcome, #{user.first_name}!"
    redirect_to home_url
  else
    flash[:alert] = "Login invalid."
    redirect_to :action => "new"
  end
end
```

A common Rails practice is to use flash[:notice] to hold benign notice messages, and flash[:alert] for communication of a more serious nature.

Action View

Note

It's so common to set `flash` notice and `alert` messages on redirects that in Rails 3 that they have been integrated as optional parameters of the `redirect_to` method.

```
def create
  if user.try(:authorize, params[:user][:password])
    redirect_to home_url, :notice => "Welcome, #{user.first_name}!"
  else
    redirect_to home_url, :alert => "Bad login"
  end
end
```

Special accessors for notices and alerts are included as helper methods on the flash object itself, since their use is so common.

```
def create
  if user.try(:authorize, params[:user][:password])
    flash.notice = "Welcome, #{user.first_name}!"
    redirect_to home_url
  else
    flash.alert = "Login invalid."
    redirect_to :action => "new"
  end
end
```

10.1.7 Displaying **flash** Messages

Personally, I like to conditionally output both `notice` and `alert` messages in `div` elements, right at the top of my layout, and use CSS to style them, as shown in Listing 10.3:

Listing 10.3 Standardized flash notice and error placement in application.html.haml

---

```
%html
  ...
  %body
    - if flash.notice
      .notice= flash.notice
    - if flash.alert
      .notice.alert= flash.alert

    = yield
```

The CSS for `.notice` defines most of the style for the element, and `.alert` overrides just the aspects that are different for alerts.

10.1.8 `flash.now`

Sometimes you want to give the user a flash message, but only for the current request. In fact, a common newbie Rails programming mistake is to set a flash notice and *not* redirect, thereby incorrectly showing a flash message on the following request.

It is possible to make flash cooperate with a render by using the `flash.now` method.

```
class ReportController < ActionController::Base
  def create
    if report.save
      flash.notice = "#{report.title} has been created."
      redirect_to report_path(report)
    else
      flash.now.alert = "#{@post.title} could not be created."
      render :action => "new"
    end
  end
end
```

The `flash.now` object also has `notice` and `alert` accessors, like its traditional counterpart.

logger

Have something to record for posterity in the logs while you're rendering the view? Use the `logger` method to get the view's `Logger` instance, the same as `Rails.logger`, unless you've changed it.

params

This is the same `params` hash that is available in your controller, containing the key/value pairs of your request. I'll occasionally use a value from the `params` hash directly in the view, particularly when I'm dealing with pages that are subject to filtering or row sorting.

```
%p
  Filter by month:
  = select_tag(:month_filter, options_for_select(@month_options,
params[:month_filter]))
```

It's very dangerous from a security perspective to put unfiltered parameter data into the output stream of your template. The following section, "Protecting the Integrity of Your View from User-Submitted Content," covers that topic in depth.

request and response

The HTTP `request` and `response` objects are exposed to the view, but other than for debugging purposes, I can't think of any reason why you would want to use them directly from your template.

Action View

session

The `session` variable is the user's session hash. There might be situations where it'd be okay to pull values out to affect rendering, but I shudder to think that you might try to set values in the session from the view layer. Use with care, and primarily for debugging, just like `request` and `response`.

10.2 Partials

A partial is a fragment of template code. The Rails way is to use partials to factor view code into modular chunks that can be assembled in layouts with as little repetition as possible. In older versions of Rails, the syntax for including a partial within a template started with `render :partial`, but now passing a string to `render` within your view will get interpreted to mean you want to render a partial. Partial template names must begin with an underscore, which serves to set them apart visually within a given view template directory. However, you leave the underscore out when you refer to them.

```
%h1 Details
= render 'details'
```

10.2.1 Simple Use Cases

The simplest partial use case is simply to extract a portion of template code. Some developers divide their templates into logical parts by using partial extraction. Sometimes it is easier to understand the structure of a screen if the significant parts are factored out of it. For instance, Listing 10.4 is a simple user registration screen that has its parts factored out into partials.

Listing 10.4 Simple user registration form with partials

```
%h1 User Registration
= error_messages_for :user
= form_for :user, :url => users_path do
  .registration
    .details.demographics
      = render 'details'
      = render 'demographics'
    .location
      = render 'location'
    .opt_in
      = render 'opt_in'
    .terms
      = render 'terms'
  %p= submit_tag 'Register'
```

While we're at it, let me pop open one of those partials. To conserve space, we'll take a look at one of the smaller ones, the partial containing the opt-in check boxes of this particular app. The source is in Listing 10.5; notice that its name begins with an underscore.

Listing 10.5 The opt-in partial in the file **app/views/users/_opt_in.html.haml**

```
%fieldset#opt_in
  %legend Spam Opt In
  %p
    = check_box :user, :send_event_updates
    Send me updates about events!
    %br
    = check_box :user, :send_site_updates
    Notify me about new services
```

Personally, I like partials to be entirely contained inside a semantically significant markup container. In the case of the opt-in partial in Listing 10.5, both check box controls are contained inside a single `fieldset` element, which I've given an `id` attribute. Following that rule, more as a loose guideline than anything else, helps me to mentally identify how the contents of this partial are going to fit inside the parent template. If we were dealing with other markup, perhaps outside of a form, I might choose to wrap the partial markup inside a well-identified `div` container, instead of a `fieldset`.

Why not include the `td` markup inside the partial templates? It's a matter of style—I like to be able to see the complete markup skeleton in one piece. In this case, the skeleton is the table structure that you see in Listing 10.4. If portions of that table were inside the partial templates, it would obfuscate the layout of the page. I do admit that this is one of those areas where personal style and preference should take precedence and I can only advise you as to what has worked for me, personally.

10.2.2 Reuse of Partials

Since the registration form is neatly factored out into its component parts, it is easy to create a simple edit form using some of its partials, as in Listing 10.6.

Listing 10.6 Simple user edit form reusing some of the same partials

```
%h1 Edit User
= form_for :user, :url => user_path(@user), :html => {:method => :put} do
  .settings
    .details
```

```
    = render :partial => 'details'
  .demographics
    = render :partial => 'demographics'
.opt_in
  = render :partial => 'opt_in'
%p= submit_tag 'Save Settings'
```

If you compare Listings 10.4 and 10.6, you'll notice that the structure of the table changed a little bit in the Edit form, and it has less content than the registration form. Perhaps the location is handled in greater detail on another screen, and certainly you don't want to require agreement of terms every time the user changes her settings.

10.2.3 Shared Partials

Until now, we've been considering the use of partials that reside in the same directory as their parent template. However, you can easily refer to partials that are in other directories, just by prefixing the directory name. You still leave off the underscore, which has always felt a little weird.

Let's add a `captcha` partial to the bottom of the registration form from Listing 10.4, to help prevent spammers from invading our web application:

```
...
  .terms
    = render :partial => 'terms'
  .captcha
    = render :partial => 'shared/captcha'
%p= submit_tag 'Register'
```

Since the `captcha` partial is used in various different parts of the application, it makes sense to let it reside in a shared folder rather than any particular view folder. However, you do have to be a little bit careful when you move existing template code into a shared partial. It's quite possible to inadvertently craft a partial that depends implicitly on where it's rendered.

For example, take the case of the Rails-talk mailing list member with a troublesome partial defined in `login/_login.html.haml`:

```
- form_tag do
  %fieldset
    %label
      Username:
      = text_field_tag :username, params[:username]
    %br
    %label
```

```
    Password:
    = password_field_tag :password, params[:password]
  %br
  = submit_tag "Login"
```

The login form submission worked when he rendered this partial as part of the login controller's `login` action ("the login page"), but not when it was included as part of the view for any other section of his website. The problem is that `form_tag` (covered in the next chapter) normally takes an optional action parameter telling it where to post its information. If you leave out the action, the form will post back to its current URL, which will vary for shared partials, depending on where they're being used from.

10.2.4   Passing Variables to Partials

Partials inherit the method exposed to their parent templates implicitly. That's why the form helpers used in the partials of Listings 10.4 and 10.6 work: They rely implicitly on an `user` method to be in scope. I feel it's fine to use this implicit sharing in some cases, particularly when the partials are tightly bound to their parent templates. It would be especially true in cases where the only reason you broke out a partial in the first place was to reduce the size and complexity of a particularly large template.

However, once you get into the practice of breaking out partial templates for reuse, depending on implicit context gets a lot more dicey. That's why Rails supports the passing of locally scoped variables to partial templates, as in the following snippet:

```
render 'shared/address', :form => form
```

The values of the optional hash are converted into locally scoped variables (no @ sign) in the partial. Listing 10.7 is a variation on the registration template. This time we're using the version of `form_for` that yields a block parameter representing the form to its form helper methods. We'll pass that form parameter on, too.

Listing 10.7   Simple user registration template passing form as local variable

```
%h1 User Registration
= form_for :user, :url => users_path do |form|
  = form.error_messages
  .registration
    .details.address.demographics
      = render 'details', :form => form
      = render 'shared/address', :form => form
  %p= form.submit 'Register'
```

And finally, in Listing 10.8 we have the shared address form.

Listing 10.8 A simple shared address partial using local variable

```
%fieldset.address
  %legend Address
  %p
    %label Street
    %br
    = form.text_area :street, :rows => 2, :cols => 40
  %p
    %label City
    %br
    = form.text_field :city
  %p
    %label State
    %br
    = form.text_field :state, :size => 2
  %p
    %label Zip
    %br
    = form.text_field :zip, :size => 15
```

The form helper methods, which we'll cover in Chapter 11, have a variation in which they are called on the `form` variable yielded by the `form_for` method. That is exactly what we passed on to these partials

The `local_assigns` Hash

If you need to check for the presence of a certain local variable in a partial, you need to do it by checking the `local_assigns` hash that is part of every template. Using `defined? variable` won't work because of the limitations of the rendering system.

```
- if local_assigns.has_key? :special
  = special
```

10.2.5 Rendering Collections

One of the best uses of partials is to render collections. Once you get into the habit of rendering collections with partials, you won't want to go back to the relative ugliness of cluttering your templates with `for` loops and `each`. When the `render` method gets an `Enumerable` as its first argument, it assumes that you want to render a collection of partials.

```
render entries
```

Simple and precise yet very dependent on a naming conventions. The objects being rendered are exposed to the partial template as a local variable named the same as the partial template itself. In turn the template should be named according to the class of the objects being rendered.

The partial corresponding to the last code snippet is named `_entry.html.haml` and gets a local variable named `entry`.

```
= div_for(entry) do
  = entry.description
  #{distance_of_time_in_words_to_now entry.created_at} ago
```

Rendering heterogeneous collections

Since the partial template used is based on the class of each item, you can easily render a heterogeneous collection of objects. This technique is particularly useful in conjunction with collections of STI subclasses.

If you want to override that behavior, then revert to the older partial syntax and specify the `:partial` and `:collection` options explicitly like

```
:partial => 'entry', :collection => @entries
```

The `partial_counter` Variable
There's another variable set for collection-rendered partials that doesn't get much attention. It's a 0-indexed counter variable that tracks the number of times the partial has gotten rendered. It's useful for rendering numbered lists of things. The name of the variable is the name of the partial, plus `_counter`.

```
= div_for(entry) do
  #{entry_counter}:#{entry.description}
  #{distance_of_time_in_words_to_now entry.created_at} ago
```

Sharing Collection Partials
If you wanted to use the same partial that you use with a collection, except with a single entry object, you'd have to pass it that single instance via the locals hash described in the preceding section, like this:

```
render 'entry', :entry => some_entry
```

Action View

10.2.6 Logging

If you take a look at your development log, you'll notice that it shows which partials have been rendered and how long they took.

```
Rendering template within layouts/application
Rendering listings/index
Rendered listings/_listing 0.6ms)
Rendered listings/_listing 0.3ms)
Rendered listings/_listing 0.2ms)
Rendered listings/_listing 0.2ms)
Rendered listings/_listing 0.2ms)
Rendered layouts/_login 2.4ms)
Rendered layouts/_header 3.3ms)
Rendered layouts/_footer 0.1ms)
```

10.3 Conclusion

In this chapter, we've covered the Action View framework with a detailed explanation of templating and how the Rails rendering system works. We've also covered the use of partials in-depth, since their use is essential for effective Rails programming.

Now it's time to cover the mechanism whereby you can inject a whole bunch of smarts into your view layer without cluttering up your templates: Helpers.

CHAPTER 11

All About Helpers

"Thank you for helping Helpers Helping the Helpless. Your help was very... helpful!"

—Mrs. Duong in the movie *The Weekenders*

Throughout the book so far, we've already covered some of the helper methods provided by Rails to help you assemble the user interface of your web application. This chapter lists and explains all of the helper modules and their methods, followed by instructions on effectively creating your own helpers.

Note

This chapter is essentially reference material. Although every effort has been made to make it readable straight through, you will notice that coverage of Action View's helper modules is arranged alphabetically, starting with `ActiveModelHelper` and ending with `UrlHelper`. Within each module's section, the methods are broken up into logical groups whenever appropriate.

Helpers

11.1 `ActiveModelHelper`

The `ActiveModelHelper` module contains helper methods for quickly creating forms from objects that follow Active Model conventions, starting with Active Record models. The `form` method is able to create an entire form for all the basic content types of a given record. However, it does not know how to assemble user-interface components for manipulating associations. Most Rails developers assemble their own forms from scratch using methods from `FormHelper`, instead of using this module. However, this module does contain some useful helper for reporting validation errors in your forms that you will use on a regular basis.

Note that as of Rails 3 you must install the following official plugin in order to use this module.

```
rails plugin install git://github.com/rails/dynamic_form.git
```

11.1.1 Reporting Validation Errors

The `error_message_on` and `error_messages_for` methods help you to add format-ted validation error information to your templates in a consistent fashion.

error_message_on(object, method, *options)

Returns a `div` tag containing the error message attached to the specified method on the object, if one exists. It's useful for showing validation errors inline next to the corresponding form field. The `object` argument of the method can be an actual object reference or a symbol corresponding to the name of an instance variable. The `method` should be a symbol corresponding to the name of the attribute on the object for which to render an error message.

The contents can be specialized with options for pre- and post-text and custom CSS class.

:prepend_text => string Fragment to prepend to error messages generated.

:append_text => string Fragment to append to error messages generated.

:css_class => class_name CSS class name for `div` generated wrapping the error message. Defaults to `formError`.

Use of this method is common when the user-interface requirements specify indi-vidual validation messages per input field of a form, as in the following real-life example:

```
.form_field
  .field_label
    %span.required *
    %label First Name
  .textual
    = form.text_field :first_name
    = form.error_message_on :first_name
```

As in the example, the `error_message_on` helper is most commonly accessed via the `form` block variable of `form_for` and its variants. When used via the `form` variable, you leave off the first argument (specifying the object) since it's implied.

error_messages_for(*params)

Returns a `div` tag containing all of the error messages for all of the objects held in instance variables identified as parameters.

```
= form_for @person do |form|
  = form.error_messages
  .textfield
  = form.label :name, "Name"
  = form.text_field :name
```

As in the example, the `error_message_for` helper is most commonly accessed via the `form` block variable of `form_for` and its variants. When used via the `form` variable, it is called `error_messages` and you leave off the first argument (specifying the object) since it's implied.

This method is used by Rails scaffolding, but rarely in real production applications. The Rails API documentation advises you to use this method's implementation as inspiration to meet your own requirements:

> This is a prepackaged presentation of the errors with embedded strings and a certain HTML structure. If what you need is significantly different from the default presentation, it makes plenty of sense to access the object.errors instance yourself and set it up. View the source of this method to see how easy it is.

We'll go ahead and reproduce the source of the method here with the warning that you should not try to use it as inspiration unless you have a good grasp of Ruby! On the other hand, if you have time to study the way that this method is implemented, it will definitely teach you a lot about the way that Rails is implemented, which is its own distinctive flavor of Ruby.

```
def error_messages_for(*params)
  options = params.extract_options!.symbolize_keys

  objects = Array.wrap(options.delete(:object) || params).map do |object|
    obj = instance_variable_get("@#{object}") unless
obj.respond_to?(:to_model)
    obj = convert_to_model(obj)
    if obj.class.respond_to?(:model_name)
      options[:object_name] ||= obj.class.model_name.human.downcase
    end
    obj
  end

  objects.compact!
  count = objects.inject(0) {|sum, object| sum + object.errors.count }
```

```ruby
  unless count.zero?
    html = {}
    [:id, :class].each do |key|
      if options.include?(key)
        value = options[key]
        html[key] = value unless value.blank?
      else
        html[key] = 'errorExplanation'
      end
    end
    options[:object_name] ||= params.first

    I18n.with_options :locale => options[:locale],
      :scope => [:errors, :template] do |locale|
      header_message = if options.include?(:header_message)
        options[:header_message]
      else
        locale.t :header, :count => count,
                        :model => options[:object_name].to_s.gsub('_', '
')
      end

      message = options.include?(:message) ? options[:message] :
locale.t(:body)

      error_messages = objects.sum do |object|
        object.errors.full_messages.map do |msg|
          content_tag(:li, ERB::Util.html_escape(msg))
        end
      end.join

      contents = ''
      contents << content_tag(options[:header_tag] ||
                              :h2, header_message) unless
header_message.blank?

      contents << content_tag(:p, message) unless message.blank?
      contents << content_tag(:ul, error_messages)

      content_tag(:div, contents, html)
    end
  else
    ''
  end
end
```

Later on in the chapter we'll talk extensively about writing your own helper methods.

11.1.2   Automatic Form Creation

The next couple of methods are used for automatic field creation by the scaffolding code. You can try using them too, but I suspect that their usefulness is somewhat limited in real applications.

form(name, options)

Returns an entire form with input tags and everything for a named model object. Here are the code examples given in the Rails API documentation, using a hypothetical `Post` object from a bulletin-board application as an example:

```
>> form("post")
=> <form action='/post/create' method='post'>
    <p>
      <label for="post_title">Title</label><br/>
      <input id="post_title" name="post[title]"
             size="30" type="text" value="Hello World" />
    </p>
    <p>
       <label for="post_body">Body</label><br/>
       <textarea cols="40" id="post_body" name="post[body]" rows="20">
         Back to the hill and over it again!
       </textarea>
    </p>
    <input type='submit' value='Create' />
  </form>
```

Internally, the method calls `record.new?` to infer whether the action for the form should be `create` or `update`. It is possible to explicitly specify the action of the form (and the value of the submit button along with it) by using the `:action` option.

If you need the form to have its `enctype` set to `multipart`, useful for file uploads, set the `options[:multipart]` to `true`.

You can also pass in an `:input_block` option, using Ruby's `Proc.new` idiom to create a new anonymous code block. The block you supply will be invoked for each content column of your model, and its return value will be inserted into the form.

```
.> form("entry", :action => "sign",
     :input_block => Proc.new { |record, column|
       "#{column.human_name}: #{input(record, column.name)}<br/>" })
=> <form action='/post/sign' method='post'>
     Message:
     <input id="post_title" name="post[title]" size="30"
            type="text" value="Hello World" /><br />
<input type='submit' value='Sign' />
   </form>
```

Helpers

That example's builder block, as it is referred to in the Rails API docs, uses the `input` helper method, which is also part of this module, and is covered in the next section of this chapter.

Finally, it's also possible to add additional content to the form by giving the call to `form` a block, as in the following snippet:

```
form("entry", :action => "sign") do |extra|
  extra << content_tag("b", "Department")
  extra << collection_select("department", "id", @departments, "id",
"name")
end
```

The block is yielded a string accumulator (named `extra` in the example), to which you append any additional content that you want to appear between the main input fields and the submit tag.

input(name, method, options)

The appropriately named `input` method takes some identifying information, and automatically generates an HTML input tag based on an attribute of an Active Record model. Going back to the `Post` example used in the explanation of `form`, here is the code snippet given in the Rails API docs:

```
>> input("post", "title")
=> <input id="post_title" name="post[title]" size="30"
         type="text" value="Hello World" />
```

To quickly show you the types of input fields generated by this method, I'll simply reproduce a portion of the code from the module itself:

```
def to_tag(options = {})
  case column_type
    when :string
      field_type = @method_name.include?("password") ? "password" : "text"
      to_input_field_tag(field_type, options)
    when :text
      to_text_area_tag(options)
    when :integer, :float, :decimal
      to_input_field_tag("text", options)
    when :date
      to_date_select_tag(options)
    when :datetime, :timestamp
      to_datetime_select_tag(options)
    when :time
      to_time_select_tag(options)
    when :boolean
      to_boolean_select_tag(options)
  end
end
```

11.1.3 Customizing the Way Validation Errors Are Highlighted

By default, when Rails marks a field in your form that failed a validation check, it does so by wrapping that field in a `div` element, with the class name `field_with_errors`. This behavior is customizable, since it is accomplished via a `Proc` object stored as a configuration property of the `ActionView::Base` class:

```
module ActionView
  class Base
    @@field_error_proc = Proc.new { |html_tag, instance|
      "<div class=\"field_with_errors\">#{html_tag}</div>"
    }
    cattr_accessor :field_error_proc
  end

  . . .
```

Armed with this knowledge, changing the validation error behavior is as simple as overriding Action View's `field_error_proc` attribute with your own custom `Proc`. I would suggest doing so in an initializer file.

In Listing 11.1, I changed the setting so that the input fields with validation errors are prefixed with a red ERR message.

Listing 11.1 Custom validation error display

```
ActionView::Base.field_error_proc =
  Proc.new do |html_tag,instance|
    %(<div style="color:red">ERR</div>) + html_tag
  end
```

Many people have suggested that it would have been a much better default solution to simply add a `field_with_errors` CSS class to the input tag itself, instead of wrapping it with an extra `div` tag. Indeed, that would have made many of our lives easier, since an extra `div` often breaks pixel-perfect layouts. However, since `html_tag` is already constructed at the time when the `field_error_proc` is invoked, it is not trivial to modify its contents.

There are some solutions out there that use regular expressions and modify the `html_tag` string, for instance this one, found at http://snippets.dzone.com/tag/field_error_proc:

```
ActionView::Base.field_error_proc = Proc.new do |html_tag, instance|
  error_style = "background-color: #ffff80"
  if html_tag =~ /<(input|textarea|select)[^>]+style=/
```

Helpers

```
    style_attribute = html_tag =~ /style=['"]/
    html_tag.insert(style_attribute + 7, "#{error_style}; ")
  elsif html_tag =~ /<(input|textarea|select)/
    first_whitespace = html_tag =~ /\s/
    html_tag[first_whitespace] = " style='#{error_style}' "
  end
  html_tag
end
```

Ugly! This is certainly an area of Action View that could use improvement.

11.2 `AssetTagHelper`

According to the Rails API docs, this module

> Provides methods for linking an HTML page together with other assets such as images, javascripts, stylesheets, and feeds. You can direct Rails to link to assets from a dedicated assets server by setting `ActionController::Base.asset_host` in your `environment.rb`. These methods do not verify the assets exist before linking to them.

The `AssetTagHelper` module includes some methods that you will use on a daily basis during active Rails development, particularly `image_tag`.

11.2.1 Head Helpers

Some of the helper methods in this module help you add content to the `head` element of your HTML document.

`auto_discovery_link_tag(type = :rss, url_options = {}, tag_options = {})`

Returns a link tag that browsers and newsreaders can use to autodetect an RSS or ATOM feed. The type can either be `:rss` (default) or `:atom`. Control the link options in `url_for` format using the `url_options`.

You can modify the `link` tag itself using the `tag_options` parameter:

`:rel` Specify the relation of this link; defaults to `"alternate"`.

`:type` Override MIME type (such as `"application/atom+xml"`) that Rails would otherwise generate automatically for you.

`:title` Specify the title of the link; defaults to a capitalized type.

Here are examples of usages of `auto_discovery_link_tag` as shown in the Rails API docs:

```
auto_discovery_link_tag # =>
  <link rel="alternate" type="application/rss+xml" title="RSS"
  href="http://www.curenthost.com/controller/action" />

auto_discovery_link_tag(:atom) # =>
  <link rel="alternate" type="application/atom+xml" title="ATOM"
  href="http://www.curenthost.com/controller/action" />

auto_discovery_link_tag(:rss, {:action => "feed"}) # =>
  <link rel="alternate" type="application/rss+xml" title="RSS"
  href="http://www.curenthost.com/controller/feed" />

auto_discovery_link_tag(:rss, {:action => "feed"}, {:title => "My
RSS"}) # =>
  <link rel="alternate" type="application/rss+xml" title="My RSS"
  href="http://www.curenthost.com/controller/feed" />
```

The Lesson of the Favorite Icon

Because of the options provided, you could theoretically use `auto_discovery_link_tag` to generate a `link` tag for a favorite icon, the little image that displays in the browser's address bar and bookmarks:

```
auto_discovery_link_tag('image/x-icon', 'favicon.ico',
  :rel => 'shortcut icon', :title => '') # =>
<link rel="shortcut icon" href="favicon.ico" type="image/x-icon" title="">
```

That said, there is very little reason, if any, to use the `auto_discovery_link_tag` to generate a favorite icon link in this way, because the Rails incantation is longer and more complicated than typing the HTML code! Neither is there anything dynamic about the construction of this tag that requires helper logic.

I made a point of including this example to reinforce the lesson that it is not necessarily the Rails way to use helpers to generate static markup that you could otherwise go ahead and write yourself.

`javascript_include_tag(*sources)`

Returns a `script` tag for each of the sources provided. You can pass in the filename (the `.js` extension is optional) of JavaScript files that exist in your `public/javascripts` directory for inclusion into the current page, or you can pass their full path, relative to your document root.

To include the Prototype and Scriptaculous JavaScript libraries in your application, pass `:defaults` as the source. When you're using `:defaults`, if an `application.js` file exists in your `public/javascripts` directory, it will be included as well. You can modify the attributes of the `script` tag by passing a hash as the last argument.

```
javascript_include_tag "xmlhr", :defer => 'defer' # =>
  <script type="text/javascript" src="/javascripts/xmlhr.js"
  defer="defer"></script>

javascript_include_tag "common.javascript", "/elsewhere/cools" # =>
  <script type="text/javascript"
src="/javascripts/common.javascript"></script>
  <script type="text/javascript" src="/elsewhere/cools.js"></script>

javascript_include_tag :defaults # =>
  <script type="text/javascript" src="/javascripts/prototype.js"></script>
  <script type="text/javascript" src="/javascripts/effects.js"></script>
  ...
  <script type="text/javascript"
src="/javascripts/application.js"></script>
```

javascript_path(source)

Computes the path to a JavaScript asset in the public/javascripts directory. If the source filename has no extension, `.js` will be appended. Full paths from the document root will be passed through. Used internally by `javascript_include_tag` to build the script path.

stylesheet_link_tag(*sources)

Returns a stylesheet `link` tag for the sources specified as arguments. If you don't specify an extension, `.css` will be appended automatically. Just like other helper methods that take a variable number of arguments plus options, you can pass a hash of options as the last argument and they will be added as attributes to the tag.

```
stylesheet_link_tag "style" # =>
  <link href="/stylesheets/style.css" media="screen"
        rel="Stylesheet" type="text/css" />

stylesheet_link_tag "style", :media => "all" # =>
  <link href="/stylesheets/style.css" media="all"
        rel="Stylesheet" type="text/css" />

stylesheet_link_tag "random.styles", "/css/stylish" # =>
  <link href="/stylesheets/random.styles" media="screen"
        rel="Stylesheet" type="text/css" />
  <link href="/css/stylish.css" media="screen"
        rel="Stylesheet" type="text/css" />
```

`stylesheet_path(source)`

Computes the path to a stylesheet asset in the `public/stylesheets` directory. If the source filename has no extension, `.css` will be appended. Full paths from the document root will be passed through. Used internally by `stylesheet_link_tag` to build the stylesheet path.

11.2.2 Asset Helpers

This module also contains a series of helper methods that generate asset-related markup. It's important to generate asset tags dynamically, because often assets are either packaged together or served up from a different server source than your regular content. Asset helper methods also timestamp your asset source urls to prevent browser caching problems.

Courtenay says...

The `image_tag` method makes use of the `image_path` method that we just covered earlier in the chapter. This helpful method determines the path to use in the tag. You can call a controller "image" and have it work as a resource, despite the seemingly conflicting name, because for its internal use, ActionView aliases the method to `path_to_image`.

`audio_path(source)`

Computes the path to an audio asset in the `public/audios` directory, which you would have to add yourself to your Rails project since it's not generated by default. Full paths from the document root will be passed through. Used internally by `audio_tag` to build the audio path.

`audio_tag(source, options = {})`

Returns an HTML 5 audio tag based on the `source` argument.

```
audio_tag("sound")  # =>
<audio src="/audios/sound" />
audio_tag("sound.wav")  # =>
   <audio src="/audios/sound.wav" />
audio_tag("sound.wav", :autoplay => true, :controls => true)  # =>
   <audio autoplay="autoplay" controls="controls" src="/audios/sound.wav"
/>
```

Helpers

image_path(source)

Computes the path to an image asset in the public/images directory. Full paths from the document root (beginning with a "/") will be passed through. This method is used internally by image_tag to build the image path.

```
image_path("edit.png")   # => /images/edit.png
image_path("icons/edit.png")   # => /images/icons/edit.png
image_path("/icons/edit.png")   # => /icons/edit.png
```

image_tag(source, options = {})

Returns an img tag for use in a template. The source parameter can be a full path or a file that exists in your public images directory. You can add additional arbitrary attributes to the img tag using the options parameter. The following two options are treated specially:

:alt If no alternate text is given, the filename part of the source is used, after being capitalized and stripping off the extension.

:size Supplied as widthxheight so "30x45" becomes the attributes width="30" and height="45". The :size option will fail silently if the value is not in the correct format.

```
image_tag("icon.png")   # =>
  <img src="/images/icon.png" alt="Icon" />

image_tag("icon.png", :size => "16x10", :alt => "Edit Entry")   # =>
  <img src="/images/icon.png" width="16" height="10" alt="Edit Entry" />

image_tag("/photos/dog.jpg", :class => 'icon')   # =>
  <img src="/photos/icon.gif" alt="Dog" class="icon"/>
```

video_path

Computes the path to an audio asset in the public/videos directory, which you would have to add yourself to your Rails project since it's not generated by default. Full paths from the document root will be passed through. Used internally by video_tag to build the video src path.

video_tag(sources, options = {})

Returns an HTML 5 video tag for the sources. If sources is a string, a single video tag will be returned. If sources is an array, a video tag with nested source tags for each source will be returned. The sources can be full paths or files that exists in your public videos directory.

You can add normal HTML video element attributes using the `options` hash. The `options` supports two additional keys for convenience and conformance:

`:poster` Set an image (like a screenshot) to be shown before the video loads. The path is calculated using `image_path`

`:size` Supplied as `widthxheight` in the same manner as `image_tag`.

```
video_tag("trailer")  # =>
  <video src="/videos/trailer" />

video_tag("trailer.ogg")  # =>
  <video src="/videos/trailer.ogg" />

video_tag("trail.ogg", :controls => true, :autobuffer => true)  # =>
    <video autobuffer="autobuffer" controls="controls"
    src="/videos/trail.ogg" />

video_tag("trail.m4v", :size => "16x10", :poster => "screenshot.png") # =>
    <video src="/videos/trailer.m4v" width="16" height="10"
           poster="/images/screenshot.png" />

video_tag(["trailer.ogg", "trailer.flv"]) # =>
    <video>
      <source src="trailer.ogg"/>
     <source src="trailer.flv"/>
    </video>
```

11.2.3 Using Asset Hosts

By default, Rails links to assets on the current host in the public folder, but you can direct Rails to link to assets from a dedicated asset server by setting `ActionController::Base.asset_host` in a configuration file, typically in `config/environments/production.rb` so that it doesn't affect your development environment. For example, you'd define `assets.example.com` to be your asset host this way:

```
config.action_controller.asset_host = "assets.example.com"
```

The helpers we've covered take that into account when generating their markup:

```
image_tag("rails.png")
  # => <img alt="Rails"
            src="http://assets.example.com/images/rails.png?1230601161" />

stylesheet_link_tag("application")
  # => <link
```

```
href="http://assets.example.com/stylesheets/application.css?1232285206"
   media="screen" rel="stylesheet" type="text/css" />
```

Browsers typically open at most two simultaneous connections to a single host, which means your assets often have to wait for other assets to finish download-ing. You can alleviate this by using a `%d` wildcard in the `asset_host`. For example, `"assets%d.example.com"`. If that wildcard is present Rails distributes asset requests among the corresponding four hosts "assets0.example.com", …, "assets3.example.com". With this trick browsers will open eight simultaneous connections rather than two.

```
image_tag("rails.png")
  # => <img alt="Rails"
src="http://assets0.example.com/images/rails.png?1230601161" />
stylesheet_link_tag("application")
  # => <link
href="http://assets2.example.com/stylesheets/application.css?1232285206"
media="screen" rel="stylesheet" type="text/css" />
```

To do this, you can either setup four actual hosts, or you can use wildcard DNS to CNAME the wildcard to a single asset host. You can read more about setting up your DNS CNAME records from your hosting provider. Note that this technique is purely a browser performance optimization and is not meant for server load balancing.[1]

Alternatively, you can exert more control over the asset host by setting `asset_host` to a proc like

```
config.action_controller.asset_host = Proc.new { |source|
  "http://assets#{rand(2) + 1}.example.com"
}
```

The example generates `http://assets1.example.com` and `http://assets2.example.com` randomly. This option is useful for example if you need fewer/more than four hosts, custom host names, etc. As you see the proc takes a `source` parameter. That's a string with the absolute path of the asset with any extensions and timestamps in place, for example `/images/rails.png?1230601161`.

```
config.action_controller.asset_host = Proc.new { |source|
  if source.starts_with?('/images')
    "http://images.example.com"
  else
    "http://assets.example.com"
  end
}
```

---

1. See `http://www.die.net/musings/page_load_time` for background information.

```
image_tag("rails.png")
  # => <img alt="Rails"
src="http://images.example.com/images/rails.png?1230601161" />

stylesheet_link_tag("application")
  # => <link
href="http://assets.example.com/stylesheets/application.css?1232285206"
media="screen" rel="stylesheet" type="text/css" />
```

Alternatively you may ask for a second parameter `request`, which is particularly useful for serving assets from an SSL-protected page. The example below disables asset hosting for HTTPS connections, while still sending assets for plain HTTP requests from asset hosts. If you don't have SSL certificates for each of the asset hosts this technique allows you to avoid warnings in the client about mixed media.

```
ActionController::Base.asset_host = Proc.new { |source, request|
  if request.ssl?
    "#{request.protocol}#{request.host_with_port}"
  else
    "#{request.protocol}assets.example.com"
  end
}
```

For easier testing and reuse, you can also implement a custom asset host object that responds to `call` and takes either one or two parameters just like the proc.

```
config.action_controller.asset_host = AssetHostingWithMinimumSsl.new(
  "http://asset%d.example.com", "https://asset1.example.com"
)
```

11.2.4 Using Asset Timestamps

By default, Rails appends an asset's timestamps to all asset paths. This allows you to set a cache-expiration date for the asset far into the future, but still be able to instantly invalidate it by simply updating the file (and hence updating the timestamp, which then updates the URL as the timestamp is part of that, which in turn busts the cache).

It's the responsibility of the web server you use to set the far-future expiration date on cache assets that you need to take advantage of this feature. Here's an example for Apache:

```
# Asset Expiration
ExpiresActive On
<FilesMatch "\.(ico|gif|jpe?g|png|js|css)$">
  ExpiresDefault "access plus 1 year"
</FilesMatch>
```

Also note that in order for this to work, all your application servers must return the same timestamps. This means that they must have their clocks synchronized. If one of them drifts out of sync, you'll see different timestamps at random and the cache won't work. In that case the browser will request the same assets over and over again even though they didn't change. You can use something like the Live HTTP Headers plugin for Firefox to verify that the cache is indeed working.

With the `cache_asset_timestamps` setting enabled, the asset tag helper methods will make fewer expensive file system calls. However, you will be prevented from modifying any asset files while the server is running. This setting defaults to true and you can modify it in an initializer with the following code:

```
config.action_view.cache_asset_timestamps = false
```

11.2.5 For Plugins Only

A handful of class methods in `AssetTagHelper` relate to configuration and are intended for use in plugins. You can find more details about these method in Chapter 19, "Extending Rails with Plugins."

- `register_javascript_expansion`

- `register_javascript_include_default`

- `register_stylesheet_expansion`

11.3 `AtomFeedHelper`

Provides an `atom_feed` helper to aid in generating Atom feeds in Builder templates.

```
atom_feed do |feed|
  feed.title("My great blog!")
  feed.updated(@posts.first.created_at)

  for post in @posts
    feed.entry(post) do |entry|
      entry.title(post.title)
      entry.content(post.body, :type => 'html')

      entry.author do |author|
        author.name("DHH")
      end
    end
  end
end
```

The options for `atom_feed` are:

:language Defaults to `"en-US"`.

:root_url The HTML alternative that this feed is doubling for. Defaults to `"/"` on the current host.

:url The URL for this feed. Defaults to the current URL.

:id The id for this feed. Defaults to `tag:#{request.host},#{options[:schema date]}:#{request.requesturi.split(".")[0]}`

:schema_date The date at which the tag scheme for the feed was first used. A good default is the year you created the feed. See `http://feedvalidator.org/docs/error/InvalidTAG.html` for more information. If not specified, 2005 is used (as an "I don't care" value).

:instruct Hash of XML processing instructions in the form `{target => {attribute => value, ...}}` or `{target => [{attribute => value, ...}, ]}`

Other namespaces can be added to the root element:

Listing 11.2 `app/views/posts/index.atom.builder`

```
atom_feed(
  'xmlns:app' => 'http://www.w3.org/2007/app',
  'xmlns:openSearch' => 'http://a9.com/-/spec/opensearch/1.1/'
) do |feed|
  feed.title("My great blog!")
  feed.updated((@posts.first.created_at))
  feed.tag!(openSearch:totalResults, 10)

  for post in @posts
    feed.entry(post) do |entry|
      entry.title(post.title)
      entry.content(post.body, :type => 'html')
      entry.tag!('app:edited', Time.now)

      entry.author do |author|
        author.name("DHH")
      end
    end
  end
end
```

Helpers

The Atom spec defines five elements that may directly contain xhtml content if
`:type => 'xhtml'` is specified as an attribute:

- `content`

- `rights`

- `title`

- `subtitle`

- `summary`

If any of these elements contain xhtml content, this helper will take care of the needed
enclosing div and an xhtml namespace declaration.

```
entry.summary :type => 'xhtml' do |xhtml|
 xhtml.p pluralize(order.line_items.count, "line item")
 xhtml.p "Shipped to #{order.address}"
 xhtml.p "Paid by #{order.pay_type}"
end
```

The `atom_feed` method yields an `AtomFeedBuilder` instance. Nested elements also
yield `AtomBuilder` instances.

11.4 CacheHelper

This module only contains one method, named `cache`. It is used to perform fragment
caching of blocks within templates, without caching the output of an entire action as a
whole. Rails also features page caching using the `caches_page` method of controllers,
where the entire output of an action is stored as a HTML file that the web server can
serve without going through the Action Pack.

In contrast, fragment caching is useful when certain elements of an action change
frequently or depend on complicated state, while other parts rarely change or can be
shared among multiple parties. The boundaries of a fragment to be cached are defined
within a view template using the `cache` helper method. The topic is covered in detail
in the caching section of Chapter 17, Caching.

11.5 CaptureHelper

One of the great features of Rails views is that you are not limited to rendering a single
flow of content. Along the way, you can define blocks of template code that should be
inserted into other parts of the page during rendering using `yield`. The technique is
accomplished via a pair of methods from the `CaptureHelper` module.

capture(& block)

The `capture` method lets you capture part of a template's output (inside a block) and assign it to an instance variable. The value of that variable can subsequently be used anywhere else on the template.

```
- message_html = capture do
  %div
    This is a message
```

I don't think that the `capture` method is that useful on its own in a template. It's a lot more useful when you use it in your own custom helper methods. It gives you the ability to write your own helpers that grab template content wrapped using a block. We cover that technique later on in this chapter in the section "Writing Your Own Helpers."

content_for(name, & block)

We mentioned the `content_for` method in Chapter 10 in the section "Yielding Content." It allows you to designate a part of your template as content for another part of the page. It works similarly to its sister method `capture` (in fact, it uses `capture` itself). Instead of returning the contents of the block provided to it, it stores the content to be retrieved using `yield` elsewhere in the template (or most commonly, in the surrounding layout).[2]

A common example is to insert *sidebar* content into a layout. In the following example, the link will not appear in the *flow* of the view template. It will appear elsewhere in the template, wherever `yield :navigation_sidebar` appears.

```
- content_for :navigation_sidebar do
  = link_to 'Detail Page', item_detail_path(item)
```

content_for?(name)

Using this method, you can check whether the template will ultimately yield any content under a particular name using the `content_for` helper method, so that you can make layout decisions earlier in the template. The following example clearly illustrates usage of this method, by altering the CSS class of the `body` element dynamically:

```
%body{:class => content_for?(:right_col) ? 'one-column' : 'two-column'}
  = yield
  = yield :right_col
```

---

2. For an interesting read on how yielding content and `contentfor` will probably change in Rails 3.1 because of the introduction of content flushing, see `http://yehudakatz.com/2010/09/07/automatic-flushing-the-rails-3-1-plan`

11.6 DateHelper

The `DateHelper` module is used primarily to create HTML `select` tags for different kinds of calendar data. It also features one of the longest-named helper methods, a beast peculiar to Rails, called `distance_of_time_in_words_to_now`.

Lark says...

I guess that helper method name was too much of a mouthful, since at some point it was aliased to `time_ago_in_words`.

11.6.1 The Date and Time Selection Helpers

The following methods help you create form field input tags dealing with date and time data. All of them are prepared for multiparameter assignment to an Active Record object. That's a fancy way of saying that even though they appear in the HTML form as separate input fields, when they are posted back to the server, it is understood that they refer to a single attribute of the model. That's some Rails magic for you!

date_select(object_name, method, options = {})
Returns a matched set of three `select` tags (one each for year, month, and day) preselected for accessing a specified date-based attribute (identified by the `method` parameter) on an object assigned to the template (identified by the `object_name` parameter).

It's possible to tailor the selects through the options hash, which accepts all the keys that each of the individual select builders do (like `:use_month_numbers` for `select_month`).

The `date_select` method also takes `:discard_year`, `:discard_month`, and `:discard_day` options, which drop the corresponding `select` tag from the set of three. Common sense dictates that discarding the month select will also automatically discard the day select. If the day is omitted, but not the month, Rails will assume that the day should be the first of the month.

It's also possible to explicitly set the order of the tags using the `:order` option with an array of symbols `:year`, `:month`, and `:day` in the desired order. Symbols may be omitted and the respective `select` tag is not included.

Passing `:disabled => true` as part of the options will make elements inaccessible for change (see Listing 11.3).

Listing 11.3 Examples of date_select

```
date_select("post", "written_on")

date_select("post", "written_on", :start_year => 1995,
                                   :use_month_numbers => true,
                                   :discard_day => true,
                                   :include_blank => true)

date_select("post", "written_on", :order => [:day, :month, :year])

date_select("user", "birthday",   :order => [:month, :day])
```

datetime_select(object_name, method, options = {})

Works exactly like date_select, except for the addition of hour and minute select tags. Seconds may be added with the option :include_seconds. Along with the addition of time information come additional discarding options: :discard_hour, :discard_minute, and :discard_seconds.

time_select(object_name, method, options = {})

Returns a set of select tags (one for hour, minute, and optionally second) preselected for accessing a specified time-based attribute (identified by method) on an object assigned to the template (identified by object_name). You can include the seconds with :include_seconds.

```
time_select("post", "sunrise")
time_select("post", "start_time", :include_seconds => true)
```

11.6.2 The Individual Date and Time Select Helpers

Sometimes you need just a particular element of a date or time, and Rails obliges you with a comprehensive set of individual date and time select helpers. In contrast to the date and time helpers that we just looked at, the following helpers are not bound to an instance variable on the page. Instead, they all take a date or time Ruby object as their first parameter. (All of these methods have a set of common options, covered in the following subsection.)

select_date(date = Date.today, options = {})

Returns a set of select tags (one each for year, month, and day) preselected with the date provided (or the current date). It's possible to explicitly set the order of the tags using the :order option with an array of symbols :year, :month, and :day in the desired order.

Helpers

`select_datetime(datetime = Time.now, options = {})`

Returns a set of `select` tags (one each for year, month, day, hour, and minute) preselected with the datetime. Optionally add a seconds field using the `:include_seconds => true` option. It's also possible to explicitly set the order of the tags using the `:order` option with an array of symbols `:year`, `:month`, and `:day`, `:hour`, `:minute`, and `:seconds` in the desired order. You can also add character values for the `:date_separator` and `:time_separator` options to control visual display of the elements (they default to `"/"` and `":"`).

`select_day(date, options = {})`

Returns a `select` tag with options for each of the days 1 through 31 with the current day selected. The date can also be substituted for an hour number. Override the field name using the `:field_name` option. It defaults to `day`. The `date` parameter may be substituted by a value from 1 to 31.

`select_hour(datetime, options = {})`

Returns a `select` tag with options for each of the hours 0 through 23 with the current hour selected. The `datetime` parameter can be substituted with an hour number from 0 to 23.

`select_minute(datetime, options = {})`

Returns a `select` tag with options for each of the minutes 0 through 59 with the current minute selected. Also can return a `select` tag with options by `minute_step` from 0 through 59 with the 00 minute selected. The `datetime` parameter can be substituted by a seconds value of 0 to 59.

`select_month(date, options = {})`

Returns a `select` tag with options for each of the months January through December with the current month selected. By default, the month names are presented as user options in the drop-down selection and the month numbers (1 through 12) are used as values submitted to the server.

It's also possible to use month numbers for the presentation instead of names, by setting `:use_month_numbers => true`. If you happen to want both numbers and names, set the `:add_month_numbers => true`. If you would prefer to show month names as abbreviations, set the `:use_short_month key => true`. Finally, if you want to use your own month names, set the value of the `:use_month_names key` in your options to an array of 12 month names.

```
# Will use keys like "January", "March"
select_month(Date.today)

# Will use keys like "1", "3"
select_month(Date.today, :use_month_numbers => true)

# Will use keys like "1 - January", "3 - March"
select_month(Date.today, :add_month_numbers => true)

# Will use keys like "Jan", "Mar"
select_month(Date.today, :use_short_month => true)

# Will use keys like "Januar", "Marts"
select_month(Date.today, :use_month_names => %w(Januar Februar
Marts ...))
```

Override the field name using the :field_name option. It defaults to month.

select_second(datetime, options = {})

Returns a select tag with options for each of the seconds 0 through 59 with the current second selected. The datetime parameter can either be a DateTime object or a second given as a number.

select_time(datetime, options = {})

Returns a set of HTML select tags (one for hour and minute). You can set :add_separator key to format the output.

select_year(date, options = {})

Returns a select tag with options for each of the 5 years on each side of the current year, which is selected. The five-year radius can be changed using the :start_year and :end_year options. Both ascending and descending year lists are supported by making :start_year less than or greater than :end_year. The date parameter can either be a Date object or a year given as a number.

```
# ascending year values
select_year(Date.today, :start_year => 1992, :end_year => 2007)

# descending year values
select_year(Date.today, :start_year => 2005, :end_year => 1900)
```

Helpers

11.6.3   Common Options for Date Selection Helpers

All of the select-type methods share a number of common options that are as follows:

- :discard_type   Set to true if you want to discard the type part of the select name. If set to true, the select_month method would use simply date (which can be overwritten using :prefix) instead of date[month].

- :field_name Allows you to override the natural name of a select tag (from day, minute, and so on).

- :include_blank Set to true if it should be possible to set an empty date.

- :prefix Overwrites the default prefix of date used for the names of the select tags. Specifying birthday would result in a name of birthday[month] instead of date[month] when passed to the select_month method.

- :use_hidden Set to true to embed the value of the datetime into the page as an HTML hidden input, instead of a select tag.

11.6.4   **distance_in_time** Methods with Complex Descriptive Names

Some distance_in_time methods have really long, complex descriptive names that nobody can ever remember without looking them up. Well, at least for the first dozen times or so you might not remember.

I find the following methods to be a perfect example of the Rails way when it comes to API design. Instead of going with a shorter and necessarily more cryptic alternative, the framework author decided to keep the name long and descriptive. It's one of those cases where a nonprogrammer can look at your code and understand what it's doing. Well, probably.

I also find these methods remarkable in that they are part of why people sometimes consider Rails part of the Web 2.0 phenomenon. What other web framework would include ways to humanize the display of timestamps?

distance_of_time_in_words(from_time, to_time = 0, include_seconds = false, options ={})
Reports the approximate distance in time between two Time or Date objects or integers as seconds. Set the include_seconds parameter to true if you want more detailed

approximations when the distance is less than 1 minute. The easiest way to show what this method does is via examples:

```
>> helper.distance_of_time_in_words(from_time, from_time + 50.minutes)
=> about 1 hour

>> helper.distance_of_time_in_words(from_time, from_time + 15.seconds)
=> less than a minute

>> helper.distance_of_time_in_words(from_time, from_time + 15.seconds,
true)
=> less than 20 seconds

>> helper.distance_of_time_in_words(from_time, 3.years.from_now)
=> about 3 years
```

The Rails API docs ask you to note that Rails calculates 1 year as 365.25 days.

distance_of_time_in_words_to_now(from_time, include_seconds = false)

Works exactly like `distance_of_time_in_words` except that the `to_time` is hard-coded to the current time. Usually invoked on `created_at` or `updated_at` attributes of your model, followed by the string `ago` in your template, as in the following example:

```
%strong= comment.user.name
%br
%small
  = distance_of_time_in_words_to_now(review.created_at)
  ago
```

11.7 DebugHelper

The `DebugHelper` module only contains one method, named `debug`. Output it in your template, passing it an object that you want dumped to YAML and displayed in the browser inside `PRE` tags. Useful for debugging during development, but not much else.

11.8 FormHelper

The `FormHelper` module provides a set of methods for working with HTML forms, especially as they relate to Active Record model objects assigned to the template. Its methods correspond to each type of HTML input fields (such as text, password, select, and so on) available. When the form is submitted, the value of the input fields are bundled into the `params` that is passed to the controller.

Helpers

There are two types of form helper methods. The types found in this module are meant to work specifically with Active Record model attributes, and the similarly named versions in the `FormTagHelper` module are not.

11.8.1 Creating Forms for Models

The core method of this helper is called `form_for`, and we covered it to some extent in Chapter 3, REST, Resources, and Rails. The helper method yields a `form` object, on which you can invoke input helper methods, omitting their first argument. Usage of `form_for` leads to succinct form code:

```
= form_for offer do |f|
  = f.label :version, 'Version'
  = f.text_field :version
  %br
  = f.label :author, 'Author'
  = f.text_field :author
```

The form_for block argument is a form builder object that carries the model. Thus, the idea is that:

```
= f.text_field :first_name
```

gets expanded to

```
= text_field :person, :first_name
```

If you want the resulting params hash posted to your controller to be named based on something other than the class name of the object you pass to `form_for`, you can pass an arbitrary symbol as the first argument and the actual record as the second argument:

```
= form_for :client, person, :url => { :action => "update" } do |f|
```

In that case, the following call to `text_field`

```
= f.text_field :first_name
```

would get expanded to

```
= text_field :client, :first_name, :object => person
```

form_for Options

In any of its variants, the rightmost argument to `form_for` is an optional hash of options:

:url The URL the form is submitted to. It takes the same fields you pass to `url_for` or `link_to`. In particular you may pass here a named route directly as well. Defaults to the current action.

:html Optional HTML attributes for the `form` tag.

:builder Optional form builder class (instead of `ActionView::Helpers::FormBuilder`)

Resource-oriented Style

The preferred way to use `form_for` is to rely on automated resource identification, which will use the conventions and named routes of that approach, instead of manually configuring the `:url` option.

For example, if `post` is an existing record to be edited, then the resource-oriented style:

```
= form_for post do |f|
```

is equivalent to

```
= form_for :post, post, :url => post_path(post),
  :html => { :method => :put, :class => "edit_post",
  :id => "edit_post_45" } do |f|
```

The `form_for` method also recognizes new records, by calling `new?` on the object you pass to it.

```
= form_for(Post.new) do |f|
```

expands to

```
= form_for :post, Post.new, :url => posts_path, :html => { :class =>
"new_post",
:id => "new_post" } do |f|
  ...
```

The individual conventions can be overriden by supplying an object argument plus `:url` and/or `:html` options.

```
= form_for(post, :url => super_post_path(post)) do |f|
```

You can create forms with namespaced routes by passing an array as the first argument, as in the following example, which would map to a `admin_post_url`:

```
= form_for([:admin, @post]) do |f|
```

This is the equivalent (old-school) version of `form_tag`, which doesn't use a yielded form object and explicitly names the object being used in the input fields:

```
- form_tag people_path do
  .field
    = label :person, :first_name
    = text_field :person, :first_name
  .field
    = label :person, :last_name
```

Helpers

```
  = text_field :person, :last_name
.buttons
  = submit_tag 'Create'
```

The first version has slightly less repetition (remember your DRY principle) and is almost always going to be more convenient as long as you're rendering Active Record objects.

Variables Are Optional

If you explicitly specify the object name parameter for input fields rather than letting them be supplied by the form, keep in mind that it doesn't have to match a *live* object instance in scope for the template. Rails won't complain if the object is not there. It will simply put blank values in the resulting form.

Rails-Generated Form Conventions

The HTML generated by the `form_for` invocations in the preceding example is characteristic of Rails forms, and follows specific naming conventions.

In case you're wondering, the `authenticity_token` hidden field with gibberish up near the top of the form has to do with protection against malicious cross-site request forgery (CSRF) attacks.

```html
<form action="/people" class="new_person" id="new_person" method="post">
  <div style="margin:0;padding:0;display:inline">
    <input name="authenticity_token" type="hidden"
           value="Zn9QZi/vK/QeNUByBlwU6xiRwTAqzD5b4TJNXgWW+9s=" />
  </div>
  <div class='field'>
    <label for="person_first_name">First name</label>
    <input id="person_first_name" name="person[first_name]"
           size="30" type="text" />
  </div>
  <div class='field'>
    <label for="person_last_name">Last name</label>
    <input id="person_last_name" name="person[last_name]"
           size="30" type="text" />
  </div>
  <div class='buttons'>
    <input id="person_submit" name="commit" type="submit" value="Create"
/>
  </div>
</form>
```

When this form is submitted, the `params` hash will look like the following example (using the format reflected in your development log for every request):

```
Parameters: {"commit"=>"Create", "action"=>"create",
"controller"=>"persons",
 "person"=> {"first_name"=>"William", "last_name"=>"Smith"}}
```

As you can see, the `params` hash has a nested `"person"` value, which is accessed using `params[:person]` in the controller. That's pretty fundamental Rails knowledge, and I'd be surprised if you didn't know it already. I promise we won't rehash much more basic knowledge after the following section.

Displaying Existing Values

If you were editing an existing instance of `Person`, that object's attribute values would have been filled into the form. That's also pretty fundamental Rails knowledge. What about if you want to edit a new model object instance, prepopulated with certain values? Do you have to pass the values as options to the input helper methods? No. Because the form helpers display the values of the model's attributes, it would simply be a matter of initializing the object with the desired values in the controller, as follows:

```
expose(:person) do
  if person_id = (params[:person_id] || params[:id])
    Person.find(person_id)
  else
    # Set default values that you want to appear in the form
    Person.new(:first_name => 'First', :last_name => 'Last')
  end
end
```

Because you're only using `new`, no record is persisted to the database, and your default values magically appear in the input fields.

Updating Multiple Objects at Once

That's all well and good for editing one object at a time. What if you want to edit multiple records at the same time? When the attribute name passed to `form_for` or individual input field helper methods contains a set of square brackets, the id for the object will be included in the autogenerated `name` and `id` attributes of the input tag.

I find this technique potentially challenging, on a couple of levels. First of all, we usually identify attribute names using symbols, but tacking a pair of square brackets onto a symbol (like `:name[]`) is invalid. We're forced to use a string to name the object instead:

```
= form_for "person[]" do |f|
  - for @person in people
    = f.text_field :name
```

Second, it generates HTML for the input tags looking something like

```
<input type="text" id="person_8_name" name="person[8][name]"
 value="Obie Fernandez"/>
```

The structure of the hash submitted to the controller is significantly different from what we're used to seeing. That nested `params` hash will now be three levels deep when it comes to the `"person"` and to make it more confusing, the ids of the objects are being used as has keys:

```
Parameters: {"person"=>{"8"=>{"name"=>"Obie Fernandez"},
                         "9"=>{"name"=>"Jodi Showers"}, ...}, ... }
```

Now the controller code to handle the form needs to change, or you're likely to see a stack trace like the following one:

```
NoMethodError (undefined method `8=' for #<User:0x8762174>)
```

The good news is that the way that you handle that nested hash structure in your controller's update method is probably one of the nicest examples of how Rails is well integrated across its MVC layers:

```
Person.update(params[:person].keys, params[:person].values)
```

Beautiful! This is the sort of harmony that makes the Rails way so enjoyable.

Square Brackets with New Records?

If you have a way of inserting HTML into your document dynamically, via JavaScript and/or Ajax techniques, you can leverage Rails' behavior with regard to empty square brackets. When you're using the square-brackets naming, Rails will happily generate HTML for new model objects that looks like

```
<input type="text" id="person__name" name="person[][name]"/>
```

If you were dynamically adding rows of child record entry forms to a parent form, you could replicate that convention easily. Just make sure the names of your input fields have the empty square brackets.

When you submit the form, the Rails request dispatcher will assume that the value of the `:person` key in the `params` hash is supposed to be an `Array`, and that is what you will have to deal with in the controller action as the value of `params[:person]`, an array!

Considering that the `create` class method of Active Record models takes an array or hashes to do multiple inserts, we have yet another one of those beautiful examples of Rails cross-framework harmony:

```
def add_people
  Person.create(params[:person])
  ...
end
```

However, there are some drawbacks to this technique, because it only works when all of the input fields in the `person` namespace have empty square brackets. Stick any other input fields on the same object without the empty square brackets, and Rack will barf:

```
TypeError (expected Hash (got Array) for param `person')
```

Indexed Input Fields

Okay, moving forward, here is a slightly more verbose and less magical way to define multiple sets of input fields. Use the `:index` option of the input field methods themselves. It allows you to explicitly provide an identifier that will be inserted into the field names, and in doing so opens up some interesting possibilities.

First, it lets you replicate the square brackets technique that we just discussed in the preceding section. For example, here's a set of name fields for a collection of people:

```
- for @person in @people
  = text_field :person, :name, :index => @person.id
...
```

The `id` attribute of the person will be inserted into the parameter hash in the way we've already discussed with the square brackets, and we'll get the same nesting behavior.

Now to make it more interesting, notice that the `:index` option is not picky about the type of identifier that you supply it, which makes it pretty useful for defining enumerated sets of records! That is exactly what sets it apart from the square-brackets technique, and I'm sure I need to explain it a little more.

Consider the template code in Listing 11.4, part of a basketball tournament application (or in a more generalized guise, any application that stores people in well-defined roles):

Listing 11.4 Basketball team entry form

```
= form_for :team do |f|
  %h2 Team Name
  Name: #{f.text_field :name}
  %br
  Coach: #{f.text_field :coach}

- %w(guard_1 guard_2 forward_1 forward_2 center).each do |role|
    %h3= role.humanize
    Name: #{text_field :players, :name, :index => role}
```

That code produces the following HTML output (simplified) when you run it:

```
<form method="post" action="/homepage/team">
  <h2>Team Name</h2>
```

```
  Name: <input id="team_name" type="text" size="30"
name="team[name]"/><br/>
  Coach: <input id="team_coach" type="text" size="30" name="team[coach]"/>
  <h3>Guard 1</h3>
  Name: <input id="players_guard_1_name" type="text" size="30"
  name="players[guard_1][name]"/>
  <h3>Guard 2</h3>
Name: <input id="players_guard_2_name" type="text" size="30"
  name="players[guard_2][name]"/>
  <h3>Forward 1</h3>
  Name: <input id="players_forward_1_name" type="text" size="30"
  name="players[forward_1][name]"/>
  <h3>Forward 2</h3>
  Name: <input id="players_forward_2_name" type="text" size="30"
  name="players[forward_2][name]"/>
  <h3>Center</h3>
  Name: <input id="players_center_name" type="text" size="30"
  name="players[center][name]"/>
</form>
```

Now when you submit that form (as I just did, using one of my favorite basketball teams of all time), your controller action would receive the following parameters hash. I took the liberty of formatting the log output nicely, to make sure the structure is clear:

```
Parameters: {"team"=>{
                "name"=>"Chicago Bulls",
                "coach"=>"Phil Jackson"},
             {"players"=> {
                "forward_1"=>{"name"=>"Scottie Pippen"},
                "forward_2"=>{"name"=>"Horace Grant"},
                "center"=>{"name"=>"Bill Cartwright"},
                "guard_1"=>{"name"=>"Michael Jordan"},
                "guard_2"=>{"name"=>"John Paxson"}}, ... }
```

I made it a point to give those text field inputs for the player's names and ages their own :players identifier, rather than linking them to the form's team object. You don't even need to worry about initializing an @players variable for the form to work. Form helper methods do not complain if the variable they're supposed to reflect is nil, provided you identify it using a symbol and not by passing the instance variable directly to the method.

For the sake of completeness, I'll give you some simplistic controller action code in Listing 11.5 that is capable of handling the form submission. Taking into account the nested parameters hash, we can take it apart in a loop based on params[:players].keys and do operations per role. Of course, this code assumes that the team has an instance method add_player(role, player), but I hope you get where I'm going with the example.

Listing 11.5 Controller action to create team

```
def create
  @team = Team.create(params[:team])
  params[:players].keys.each do |role|
    @team.add_player(role, Player.new(params[:players][role]))
  end
  ...
end
```

Faux Accessors

"Now hold on a second," you are probably saying to yourself. If our example `Team` model knew how to handle the setting of a `players` hash as part of its attributes, the controller code could be dramatically simpler. In fact, we could knock the meat of it down to just a couple of line (excluding error checking and redirection):

```
def create
  @team = Team.create(params[:team])
  @team.players = params[:players]
end
```

We'll use what Josh Susser called faux accessors[3]—setters that let you initialize parts of a model that aren't (database-backed) attributes. Our example `Team` model would need a `players` writer method that understood how to add those players to itself. Perhaps it would look like the example in Listing 11.6.

Listing 11.6 Adding writer methods that understand params hashes

```
class Team < ActiveRecord::Base
  has_many :positions
  has_many :players, :through => :positions

  def players=(players_hash)
    players_hash.keys.each do |role|
      positions.create(:role => role,
                       :player => Player.new(players_hash[role]))
    end
  end
end

class Position < ActiveRecord::Base
  belongs_to :player
```

---

3. Josh Susser tells you how to cheat and provide default values to non-column model attributes at http://blog.hasmanythrough.com/2007/1/22/using-faux-accessors-to-initialize-values.

```
    belongs_to :team
end

class Player < ActiveRecord::Base
  has_many :positions
  has_many :teams, :through => :positions
end
```

To recap, the `players=` writer method gets invoked as a result of calling `Team.create` with the full `params` hash structure, which includes a nested hash of `:players`. I must warn you that your mileage may, as they say, vary with this kind of technique. It's perfect for the example, with its `has_many :through` relationship connecting the `Team`, `Position`, and `Player` classes, but it may not be perfect for your domain model. The most important idea is to keep your mind open to the possibility of writing code that is this clean. It's the Rails way.

Courtenay says…

Hiding your code behind a method like this will make your code both simpler, and more powerful. You can now test this method in isolation, and can stub it in a controller spec. Stubbing in this case allows you to focus on testing the logic of the controller action, and not the behavior of the database.It also means you or another team member can change the implementation without breaking unrelated specs, and it keeps the database code where it belongs, in the model.

I've gotten us off on quite a tangent! We were talking about form helpers, so let's cover one more important aspect of them before moving forward.

11.8.2   How Form Helpers Get Their Values

A rather important lesson to learn about Rails form helper methods is that the value they display comes directly from the database prior to *meddling* by the developer. Unless you know what you're doing, you may get some unexpected results if you try to override the values to be displayed in a form.

Let's illustrate with a simple `LineItem` model, which has a decimal `rate` attribute (by merits of a `rate` column in its database table). We'll override its implicit rate accessor with one of our own:

```
class LineItem < ActiveRecord::Base
  def rate
    "A RATE"
  end
end
```

In normal situations, the overridden accessor is hiding access to the real rate attribute, as we can illustrate using the console.

```
>> li = LineItem.new
=> #<LineItem >
>> li.rate
=> "A RATE"
```

However, suppose you were to compose a form to edit line items using form helpers:

```
= form_for :line_item do |f|
  = f.text_field :rate
```

You would find that it works normally, as if that overridden `rate` accessor doesn't exist. The behavior is intentional, yet confusing enough that it has been reported multiple times as a bug.[4]

The fact is that Rails form helpers use special methods named `attribute_before_type_cast` (which are covered in Chapter 5, Working with Active Record). The preceding example would use the method `rate_before_type_cast`, and bypass the overriding method we defined.

11.8.3 Integrating Additional Objects in One Form

The `fields_for` helper method creates a scope around a specific model object like `form_for`, but doesn't create the form tags themselves. Neither does it have an actual HTML representation as a `div` or `fieldset`. The `fields_for` method is suitable for specifying additional model objects in the same form, particularly associations of the main object being represented in the form.

Generic Examples

The following simple example represents a person and its associated permissions.

```
= form_for person do |form| %>
  First name:
  = form.text_field :first_name
  Last name:
= form.text_field :last_name
.permissions
  = fields_for person.permission do |pf|
    = permission_fields.check_box :admin
    Admin
```

---

4. It's ancient history by now, but to read up on the "Form field helpers don't use object accessors at" http://dev.rubyonrails.org/ticket/2322.

Nested Attributes Examples

When the object belonging to the current scope has a nested attribute writer for a certain attribute, `fields_for` will yield a new scope for that attribute. This allows you to create forms that set or change the attributes of a parent object and its associations in one go.

Nested attribute writers are normal setter methods named after an association. The most common way of defining these writers is either by declaring `accepts_nested_attributes_for` in a model definition or by defining a method with the proper name, along the lines of the *faux accessors* described earlier in the chapter. For example: the attribute writer for the association `:address` is called `address_attributes=`.

Whether a one-to-one or one-to-many style form builder will be yielded depends on whether the normal reader method returns a single object or an `array` of objects. Consider a simple Ruby `Person` class which returns a single `Address` from its `address` reader method and responds to the `address_attributes=` writer method:

```ruby
class Person
  def address
    @address
  end

  def address_attributes=(attributes)
    # Process the attributes hash
  end
end
```

This model can now be used with a nested fields_for, like:

```ruby
= form_for person, :url => { :action => "update" } do |form|
  = form.fields_for :address do |address_fields|
    Street:
    = address_fields.text_field :street
    Zip code:
    = address_fields.text_field :zip_code
```

When address is already an association on a Person you can use `accepts_nested_attributes_for` to define the writer method for you, like:

```ruby
class Person < ActiveRecord::Base
  has_one :address
  accepts_nested_attributes_for :address
end
```

If you want to destroy the associated model through the form, you have to enable it first using the `:allow_destroy` option for `accepts_nested_attributes_for` like:

```
class Person < ActiveRecord::Base
  has_one :address
  accepts_nested_attributes_for :address, :allow_destroy => true
end
```

Now, when you use a checkbox form element specially named _destroy, with a value
that evaluates to true, the logic generated by accepts_nested_attribute_for will
destroy the associated model. (This is a super useful technique for list screens that allow
deletion of multiple records at once using checkboxes.)

```
= form_for person, :url => { :action => "update" } do |form|
  = person_form.fields_for :address do |address_fields|
    = address_fields.check_box :_destroy
    Delete this address
```

fields_for with One-to-Many Associations

Consider a Person class that returns an array of Project instances from the projects
reader method and responds to the projects_attributes= writer method:

```
class Person < ActiveRecord::Base
  def projects
    [@project1, @project2]
  end

  def projects_attributes=(attributes)
    # Process the attributes hash
  end
end
```

This model can now be used with a nested fields_for helper method in a form. The
block given to the nested fields_for call will be repeated for each instance in the
collection automatically:

```
= form_for person, :url => { :action => "update" } do |form|
  = form.fields_for :projects do |project_fields|
    .project
      Name:
      = project_fields.text_field :name
```

It's also possible to specify the instance to be used by doing the iteration yourself, which
is a refinement of the *square bracket* techniques that we discussed earlier. The symbol
passed to fields_for refers to the reader method of the parent object of the form, but
the second argument contains the actual object to be used for fields:

```
= form_for person, :url => { :action => "update" } do |form|
  - person.projects.select(&:active?).each do |project|
    = form.fields_for :projects, project do |project_fields|
```

Helpers

```
.project
  Name:
  = project_fields.text_field :name
```

Since `fields_for` also understands a collection as its second argument in that situation, you can shrink that last example to the following code. Just inline the projects collection:

```
= form_for person, :url => { :action => "update" } do |form|
  = form.fields_for :projects, projects.select(&:active?)do
|project_fields|
    .project
      Name:
      = project_fields.text_field :name
```

If, in our example, Person was an Active Record model and projects was one of its `has_many` associations, then you could use `accepts_nested_attributes_for` to define the writer method for you:

```
class Person < ActiveRecord::Base
  has_many :projects
  accepts_nested_attributes_for :projects
end
```

As with using `accepts_nested_attributes_for` with a `belongs_to` association, if you want to destroy any of the associated models through the form, you have to enable it first using the `:allow_destroy` option:

```
class Person < ActiveRecord::Base
  has_many :projects
  accepts_nested_attributes_for :projects, :allow_destroy => true
end
```

This will allow you to specify which models to destroy in the attributes hash by adding a boolean form element named _destroy

```
= form_for person do |form|
  = form.fields_for :projects do |project_fields| %>
    = project_fields.check_box :_destroy
    Delete this project
```

Saving Nested Attributes

Nested records are updated on save, even when the intermediate parent record is unchanged. For example, consider the following model code. [5]

---

5. See https://rails.lighthouseapp.com/projects/8994/tickets/4242-nested-child-only-updates-if-parent-changes for an explanation of the origin of this feature and example code.

```
class Project < ActiveRecord::Base
  has_many :tasks
  accepts_nested_attributes_for :tasks
end

class Task < ActiveRecord::Base
  belongs_to :project
  has_many :assignments
  accepts_nested_attributes_for :assignments
end

class Assignment < ActiveRecord::Base
  belongs_to :task
end
```

The following spec snippet illustrates nested saving:

```
# setup project, task and assignment objects...
project.update_attributes :name => project.name,
                          :tasks_attributes => [{
                            :id => task.id,
                            :name => task.name,
                            :assignments_attributes => [{
                              :id => assignment.id,
                              :name => 'Paul'
                            }]
                          }]

assignment.reload
assignment.name.should == 'Paul'
```

11.8.4 Customized Form Builders

Under the covers, the `form_for` method uses a class named `ActionView::Helpers::FormBuilder`. An instance of it is yielded to the form block. Conveniently, you can subclass it in your application to override existing or define additional form helpers.

For example, let's say you made a builder class to automatically add labels to form inputs when `text_field` is called. You'd enable it with the `:builder` option like:

```
= form_for person, :builder => LabelingFormBuilder do |f|
```

Instructions on making custom form builder classes would fill its own chapter, but luckily there are many open source examples to choose from on Github. If you're interested, check out the results of `http://github.com/search?type=Repositories&language=rb&q=form+builder`.

Helpers

11.8.5 Form Inputs

For each if these methods, there is a similarly named form builder method that omits the `object_name` parameter.

check_box(object_name, method, options = {}, checked_value = "1", unchecked_value = "0")

This helper gives you an extra hidden input field to ensure that a false value is passed even if the check box is unchecked.

```
>> check_box('timesheet', 'approved')
=> <input name="timesheet[approved]" type="hidden" value="0"/>
<input id="timesheet_approved" name="timesheet[approved]"
   type="checkbox" value="1"/>
```

email_field(object_name, method, options = {})

Creates an email input field. This method is otherwise identical to `text_field`.

file_field(object_name, method, options = {})

Creates a file upload field and automatically adds `:multipart => true` to the enclosing form. See `file_field_tag` for details.

hidden_field(object_name, method, options = {})

Creates a hidden field, with parameters similar to `text_field`.

label(object_name, method, text = nil, options = {})

Creates a label tag with the `for` attribute pointed at the specified input field.

```
>> label('timesheet', 'approved')
=> <label for="timesheet_approved">Approved</label>
>> label('timesheet', 'approved', 'Approved?')
=> <label for="timesheet_approved">Approved?</label>
```

Many of us like to link labels to input fields by nesting. (Many would say that's the correct usage of labels.) As of Rails 3 the `label` helper accepts a block so that nesting is possible and works as would be expected. As a result, instead of having to do this:

```
= f.label :terms, "<span>Accept #{link_to 'Terms', terms_path}</span>"
```

you can do the much more elegant and maintainable:

```
= f.label :terms do
  %span Accept #{link_to "Terms", terms_path}
```

number_field(object_name, method, options = {})

Creates a number input field. This method is otherwise identical to `text_field` with the following additional options:

:min The minimum acceptable value.

:max The maximum acceptable value.

:in A range specifying the `:min` and `:max` values.

:step The acceptable value granularity.

This field renders with a nil value by default for security reasons. If you want to pre-populate the user's password you can do something like

```
f.password_field(:password, :value => user.password)
```

password_field(object_name, method, options = {})

Creates a password input field. This method is otherwise identical to `text_field`, but renders with a nil value by default for security reasons. If you want to pre-populate the user's password you can do something like

```
f.password_field(:password, :value => user.password)
```

radio_button(object_name, method, tag_value, options = {})

Creates a radio button input field. Make sure to give all of your radio button options the same `name` so that the browser will consider them linked.

range_field(object_name, method, options = {})

Creates a range input field. This method is otherwise identical to `number_field`.

search_field(object_name, method, options = {})

Creates a search input field. This method is otherwise identical to `text_field`.

telephone_field(object_name, method, options = {})

Creates a telephone input field. This method is otherwise identical to `text_field` and is aliased as `phone_field`.

submit(value = nil, options = {})

Creates a submit button with the text value as the caption. The option `:disable_with` can be used to provide a name for disabled versions of the submit button.

text_area(object_name, method, options = {})

Creates a multiline text input field (the `textarea` tag). The `:size` option lets you easily specify the dimensions of the text area, instead of having to resort to explicit `:rows` and `:cols` options.

```
>> text_area "comment", "body", :size => "25x10"
=> <textarea name="comment[body]" id="comment_body" cols="25" rows="10">
</textarea>
```

text_field(object_name, method, options = {})

Creates a standard text input field.

11.9 FormOptionsHelper

The methods in the `FormOptionsHelper` module are all about helping you to work with HTML `select` elements, by giving you ways to turn collections of objects into `option` tags.

11.9.1 Select Helpers

The following methods help you to create `select` tags based on a pair of `object` and `attribute` identifiers.

collection_select(object, attribute, collection, value_method, text_method, options = {}, html_options = {})

Return both `select` and `option` tags for the given `object` and `attribute` using `options_from_collection_for_select` (also in this module) to generate the list of `option` tags from the `collection` parameter.

select(object, attribute, choices, options = {}, html_options = {})

Create a `select` tag and a series of contained `option` tags for the provided `object_name` and attribute. The value of the attribute currently held by the object (if any) will be selected, provided that the object is available (not nil). See `options_for_select` section for the required format of the choices parameter.

Here's a small example in which the value of @person.person_id is 1:

```
select("post", "person_id", Person.all.collect {|p|
[ p.name, p.id ] }, { :include_blank => true })
```

Executing that helper code would generate the following HTML output:

```
<select name="post[person_id]">
  <option value=""></option>
  <option value="1" selected="selected">David</option>
  <option value="2">Sam</option>
  <option value="3">Tobias</option>
</select>
```

If necessary, specify `:selected => value` to explicitly set the selection or `:selected => nil` to leave all options unselected. The `:include_blank => true` option inserts a blank `option` tag at the beginning of the list, so that there is no preselected value.

time_zone_select(object, method, priority_zones = nil, options = {}, html_options = {})

Return `select` and `option` tags for the given object and method, using `time_zone_options_for_select` to generate the list of `option` tags.

In addition to the `:include_blank` option documented in the preceding section, this method also supports a `:model` option, which defaults to `TimeZone`. This may be used by users to specify a different timezone model object. (See `time_zone_options_for_select` section for more information.)

11.9.2 Option Helpers

For all of the following methods, only `option` tags are returned, so you have to invoke them from within a select helper or otherwise wrap them in a `select` tag.

option_groups_from_collection_for_select(collection, group_method, group_label_method, option_key_method, option_value_method, selected_key = nil)

Returns a string of `option` tags, like `options_from_collection_for_select`, but surrounds them with OPTGROUP tags. The `collection` should return a subarray of items when calling `group_method` on it. Each group in the `collection` should return its own name when calling `group_label_method`. The `option_key_method` and `option_value_method` parameters are used to calculate `option` tag attributes.

It's probably much easier to show in an example than to explain in words.

```
>> html_option_groups_from_collection(@continents, "countries",
   "continent_name", "country_id", "country_name", @selected_country.id)
```

Helpers

This example could output the following HTML:

```
<optgroup label="Africa">
  <select>Egypt</select>
  <select>Rwanda</select>
  ...
</optgroup>
<optgroup label="Asia">
  <select>China</select>
  <select>India</select>
  <select>Japan</select>
  ...
</optgroup>
```

For the sake of clarity, here are the model classes reflected in the example:

```
class Continent
  def initialize(p_name, p_countries)
    @continent_name = p_name; @countries = p_countries
end

  def continent_name
    @continent_name
  end

  def countries
    @countries
  end
end

class Country
  def initialize(id, name)
    @id, @name = id, name
  end

  def country_id
    @id
  end

  def country_name
    @name
  end
end
```

options_for_select(container, selected = nil)

Accepts a container (hash, array, or anything else enumerable) and returns a string of
option tags.

Given a container in which the elements respond to first and last (such as a two-element array), the "lasts" serve as option values and the "firsts" as option text. It's not too hard to put together an expression that constructs a two-element array using the `map` and `collect` iterators.

For example, assume you have a collection of businesses to display, and you're using a select field to allow the user to filter based on the category of the businesses. The category is not a simple string; in this example, it's a proper model related to the business via a `belongs_to` association:

```
class Business < ActiveRecord::Base
  belongs_to :category
end

class Category < ActiveRecord::Base
  has_many :businesses

  def <=>(other)
    ...
  end
end
```

A simplified version of the template code for displaying that collection of businesses might look like:

```
- opts = businesses.map(&:category).collect{|c| [[c.name], [c.id]]}
= select_tag(:filter, options_for_select(opts, params[:filter]))
```

The first line puts together the `container` expected by `options_for_select` by first aggregating the `category` attributes of the `businesses` collection using `map` and the nifty `&:method` syntax supported by Rails. The second line generates the `select` tag using those options (covered later in the chapter). Realistically you want to massage that category list a little more, so that it is ordered correctly and does not contain duplicates:

```
... businesses.map(&:category).uniq.sort.collect {...
```

Particularly with smaller sets of data, it's perfectly acceptable to do this level of data manipulation in Ruby code. And of course, you probably don't want to ever shove hundreds or especially thousands of rows in a `select` tag, making this technique quite useful. Remember to implement the spaceship method in your model if you need it to be sortable by the `sort` method.

Also, it's worthwhile to experiment with eager loading in these cases, so you don't end up with an individual database query for each of the objects represented in the

Helpers

select tag. In the case of our example, the controller would populate the businesses collection using code like:

```
expose(:businesses) do
  Business.where(...).includes(:category)
end
```

Hashes are turned into a form acceptable to options_for_select automatically—the keys become *firsts* and values become *lasts*.

If selected parameter is specified (with either a value or array of values for multiple selections), the matching *last* or element will get the selected attribute:

```
>> options_for_select([["Dollar", "$"], ["Kroner", "DKK"]])
   <option value="$">Dollar</option>
   <option value="DKK">Kroner</option>

>> options_for_select([ "VISA", "MasterCard" ], "MasterCard")
   <option>VISA</option>
   <option selected="selected">MasterCard</option>

>> options_for_select({ "Basic" => "$20", "Plus" => "$40" }, "$40")
   <option value="$20">Basic</option>
   <option value="$40" selected="selected">Plus</option>

>> options_for_select([ "VISA", "MasterCard", "Discover" ],
                       ["VISA", "Discover"])
    <option selected="selected">VISA</option>
    <option>MasterCard</option>
    <option selected="selected">Discover</option>
```

A lot of people have trouble getting this method to correctly display their selected item. Make sure that the value you pass to selected matches the type contained in the object collection of the select; otherwise, it won't work. In the following example, assuming price is a numeric value, without the to_s, selection would be broken, since the values passed as options are all strings:

```
>> options_for_select({ "Basic" => "20", "Plus" => "40" }, price.to_s)
   <option value="20">Basic</option>
   <option value="40" selected="selected">Plus</option>
```

options_from_collection_for_select(collection, value_method, text_method, selected = nil)

Returns a string of option tags that have been compiled by iterating over the collection and assigning the result of a call to the value_method as the option value and the text_method as the option text. If selected is specified, the element returning a match on value_method will get preselected.

time_zone_options_for_select(selected = nil, priority_zones = nil, model = TimeZone)

Returns a string of `option` tags for pretty much any timezone in the world. Supply a `TimeZone` name as selected to have it preselected. You can also supply an array of `TimeZone` objects as `priority_zones`, so that they will be listed above the rest of the (long) list. `TimeZone.us_zones` is a convenience method that gives you a list of the U.S. timezones only.

The `selected` parameter must be either `nil`, or a string that names a `TimeZone` (covered in the Appendix A, ActiveSupport API Reference).

By default, the `model` is the `TimeZone` constant (which can be obtained in Active Record as a value object). The only requirement is that the `model` parameter be an object that responds to `all`, returning an array of objects representing timezones.

11.10 FormTagHelper

The following helper methods generate HTML form and input tags based on explicit naming and values, contrary to the similar methods present in `FormHelper`, which require association to an Active Record model instance. All of these helper methods take an `options` hash, which may contain special options or simply additional attribute values that should be added to the HTML tag being generated.

check_box_tag(name, value = "1", checked = false, options = {})

Creates HTML for a check box input field. Unlike its fancier cousin, `check_box` in `FormHelper`, this helper does not give you an extra hidden input field to ensure that a false value is passed even if the check box is unchecked.

```
>> check_box_tag('remember_me')
=> <input id="remember_me" name="remember_me" type="checkbox" value="1"/>

>> check_box_tag('remember_me', 1, true)
=> <input checked="checked" id="remember_me" name="remember_me"
   type="checkbox" value="1" />
```

email_field_tag(name, value = nil, options = {})

Creates an email input field. This method is otherwise identical to `text_field_tag`.

field_set_tag(legend = nil, options = nil, & block)

Wrap the contents of the given block in a `fieldset` tag and optinally give it a `legend` tag.

Helpers

`file_field_tag(name, options = {})`

Creates a file upload field. Remember to set your HTML form to multipart or file uploads will mysteriously not work:

```
- form_tag '/upload', :multipart => true do
  = label_tag :file, 'File to Upload'
  = file_field_tag :file
  = submit_tag
```

The controller action will receive a `File` object pointing to the uploaded file as it exists in a tempfile on your system. Processing of an uploaded file is beyond the scope of this book. If you're smart, you'll use Jonas Nicklas' excellent CarrierWave gem instead of reinventing the wheel.[6]

`form_tag(url_for_options = {}, options = {}, *parameters_for_url, & block)`

Starts a `form` tag, with its action attribute set to the URL passed as the `url_for_options` parameter. It is aliased as `start_form_tag`.

The `:method` option defaults to POST. Browsers handle HTTP GET and POST natively; if you specify "put," "delete," or any other HTTP verb is used, a hidden input field will be inserted with the name `_method` and a value corresponding to the `method` supplied. The Rails request dispatcher understands the `_method` parameter, which is the basis for the RESTful techniques you learned in Chapter 3.

The `:multipart` option allows you to specify that you will be including file-upload fields in the form submission and the server should be ready to handle those files accordingly.

```
>> form_tag('/posts')
=> <form action="/posts" method="post">

>> form_tag('/posts/1', :method => :put)
=> <form action="/posts/1" method="put">

>> form_tag('/upload', :multipart => true)
=> <form action="/upload" method="post" enctype="multipart/form-data">
```

You might note that all parameters to `form_tag` are optional. If you leave them off, you'll get a form that posts back to the URL that it came from—a quick and dirty solution that I use quite often when prototyping or experimenting. To quickly set up a

---

6. `https://github.com/jnicklas/carrierwave`

controller action that handles post-backs, just include an `if`/`else` condition that checks the request method, something like:

```
def add
  if request.post?
    # handle the posted params
    redirect_to :back
  end
end
```

Notice that if the request is a post, I handle the form `params` and then redirect back to the original URL (using `redirect_to :back`). Otherwise, execution simply falls through and would render whatever template is associated with the action.

hidden_field_tag(name, value = nil, options = {})

Creates a hidden field, with parameters similar to `text_field_tag`.

image_submit_tag(source, options = {})

Displays an image that, when clicked, will submit the form. The interface for this method is the same as its cousin `image_tag` in the `AssetTagHelper` module.

Image input tags are popular replacements for standard submit tags, because they make an application look fancier. They are also used to detect the location of the mouse cursor on click—the `params` hash will include x and y data.

label_tag(name, text = nil, options = {})

Creates a label tag with the `for` attribute set to `name`.

number_field_tag(name, value = nil, options = {})

Creates a number input field. This method is otherwise identical to `text_field_tag` with the following additional options:

:min The minimum acceptable value

:max The maximum acceptable value

:in A range specifying the `:min` and `:max` values

:step The acceptable value granularity

password_field_tag(name = "password", value = nil, options = {})

Creates a password input field. This method is otherwise identical to `text_field_tag`.

Helpers

radio_button_tag(name, value, checked = false, options = {})

Creates a radio button input field. Make sure to give all of your radio button options the same `name` so that the browser will consider them linked.

range_field_tag(name, value = nil, options = {})

Creates a range input field. This method is otherwise identical to `number_field_tag`.

search_field_tag(name, value = nil, options = {})

Creates a search input field. This method is otherwise identical to `text_field_tag`.

select_tag(name, option_tags = nil, options = {})

Creates a drop-down selection box, or if the :multiple option is set to true, a multiple-choice selection box. The `option_tags` parameter is an actual string of option tags to put inside the select tag. You should not have to generate that string explicitly yourself. Instead, use the helpers in `FormOptions` (covered in the previous section of this chapter), which can be used to create common select boxes such as countries, time zones, or associated records.

submit_tag(value = ''Save changes'', options = {})

Creates a submit button with the text value as the caption. The `option` `:disable_with` can be used to provide a name for disabled versions of the submit button.

telephone_field_tag(name, value = nil, options = {})

Creates a telephone input field. This method is otherwise identical to `text_field_tag` and is aliased as `phone_field_tag`.

text_area_tag(name, content = nil, options = {})

Creates a multiline text input field (the `textarea` tag). The `:size` option lets you easily specify the dimensions of the text area, instead of having to resort to explicit `:rows` and `:cols` options.

```
>> text_area_tag "body", nil, :size => "25x10"
=> <textarea name="body" id="body" cols="25" rows="10"></textarea>
```

text_field_tag(name, value = nil, options = {})

Creates a standard text input field.

11.11 JavaScriptHelper

Provides helper methods to facilitate inclusion of JavaScript code in your templates.

escape_javascript(javascript)
Escapes line breaks, single and double quotes for JavaScript segments.

javascript_tag(content, html_options={})
Outputs a `script` tag with the content inside. The `html_options` are added as tag attributes.

11.12 **NumberHelper**

This module provides assistance in converting numeric data to formatted strings suitable for displaying in your view. Methods are provided for phone numbers, currency, percentage, precision, positional notation, and file size.

human_size(size, precision=1)
Alias for `number_to_human_size`.

number_to_currency(number, options = {})
Formats a number into a currency string. You can customize the format in the options hash.

:precision Sets the level of precision, defaults to 2

:unit Sets the denomination of the currency, defaults to `"$"`

:separator Sets the separator between the units, defaults to `"."`

:delimiter Sets the thousands delimiter, defaults to `","`

```
>> number_to_currency(1234567890.50)
=> $1,234,567,890.50

>> number_to_currency(1234567890.506)
=> $1,234,567,890.51

>> number_to_currency(1234567890.506, :precision => 3)
=> $1,234,567,890.506

>> number_to_currency(1234567890.50, :unit => "&pound;",
=> :separator => ",", :delimiter => ""
=> &pound;1234567890,50
```

number_to_human_size(size, precision=1)
Formats the bytes in size into a more understandable representation. Useful for reporting file sizes to users. This method returns nil if size cannot be converted into a number. You can change the default precision of 1.

```
number_to_human_size(123)            => 123 Bytes
number_to_human_size(1234)           => 1.2 KB
number_to_human_size(12345)          => 12.1 KB
number_to_human_size(1234567)        => 1.2 MB
number_to_human_size(1234567890)     => 1.1 GB
number_to_human_size(1234567890123)  => 1.1 TB
number_to_human_size(1234567, 2)     => 1.18 MB
```

This method is also aliased as `human_size`.

number_to_percentage(number, options = {})

Formats a number as a percentage string. You can customize the format in the options hash.

:precision Sets the level of precision, defaults to 3

:separator Sets the separator between the units, defaults to `"."`

```
number_to_percentage(100)     => 100.000%
number_to_percentage(100, {:precision => 0})    => 100%
number_to_percentage(302.0574, {:precision => 2})    => 302.06%
```

number_to_phone(number, options = {})

Formats a number as a U.S. phone number. You can customize the format in the options hash.

:area_code Adds parentheses around the area code

:delimiter Specifies the delimiter to use, defaults to `"-"`

:extension Specifies an extension to add to the end of the generated number

:country_code Sets the country code for the phone number

```
number_to_phone(1235551234)                        #=> "123-555-1234"
number_to_phone(1235551234, :area_code => true) #=> "(123) 555-1234"
number_to_phone(1235551234, :delimiter => " ")  #=> "123 555 1234"
```

number_with_delimiter(number, delimiter=",", separator=".")

Formats a number with grouped thousands using a delimiter. You can customize the format using optional delimiter and separator parameters.

delimiter Sets the thousands delimiter, defaults to `","`

separator Sets the separator between the units, defaults to `"."`

```
number_with_delimiter(12345678)        #=> "12,345,678"
number_with_delimiter(12345678.05)     #=> "12,345,678.05"
number_with_delimiter(12345678, ".")   #=> "12.345.678"
```

number_with_precision(number, precision=3)

Formats a number with the specified level of precision. The default level of precision is 3.

```
number_with_precision(111.2345)        #=> "111.235"
number_with_precision(111.2345, 2)     #=> "111.24"
```

11.13 PrototypeHelper

PrototypeHelper has been heavily modified from what it was in earlier versions of Rails. It now primarily contains the implementation of RJS, covered in Section 12.2.

The following helper methods were removed and made available in an official Prototype Legacy Helper available at `http://github.com/rails/prototype_legacy_helper`.

- button_to_remote
- form_remote_for
- form_remote_tag
- link_to_remote
- observe_field
- observe_form
- periodically_call_remote
- remote_form_for
- submit_to_remote

Be aware that the functionality of the form_remote_for, form_remote_tag, link_to_remote, and remote_form_for methods remains partially supported using the :remote => true option on link and form helpers, as covered in Section 12.1.1.

11.14 RawOutputHelper

This is an extremely simple helper module, barely worth mentioning.

Helpers

raw(stringish)

Bypasses HTML sanitization, by calling `to_s`, then `html_safe` on the argument passed to it.

11.15 `RecordIdentificationHelper`

This module, which wraps the methods of `ActionController::RecordIdentifier`, encapsulates a number of naming conventions for dealing with records, like Active Record models or Active Resource models or pretty much any other type of model object that you want to represent in markup code (like HTML) and which has an `id` attribute. These patterns are then used to try to elevate the view actions to a higher logical level. For example, assume that you have `map.resources :posts` defined in your routes file, and code that looks like this in your view:

```
= div_for(post) do
  = post.body
```

The HTML for the `div` element would thus be rendered like:

```
<div id="post_45" class="post">
  What a wonderful world!
</div>
```

Notice the convention reflected in the `id` attribute. Now, for the controller, which has an Ajax-enabled `destroy` method. The idea is that it can be called to delete the record and make it disappear from the page without a reload operation:

```
def destroy
  post = Post.find(params[:id])
  post.destroy

  respond_to do |format|
    format.html { redirect_to :back }
    format.js do
      # Calls: new Effect.fade('post_45');
      render(:update) { |page| page[post].visual_effect(:fade) }
    end
  end
end
```

As the preceding example shows, you can stop caring to a large extent what the actual id of the model is (the `div` element holding the model information, that is). You just know that one is being assigned and that the subsequent calls in RJS expect that same naming convention and allow you to write less code if you follow it. You can find more information on this technique in Chapter 12.

dom_class(record_or_class, prefix = nil)

The DOM class convention is to use the singular form of an object or class.

```
dom_class(post)   # => "post"
dom_class(Person) # => "person"
```

If you need to address multiple instances of the same class in the same view, you can prefix the dom_class:

```
dom_class(post, :edit)   # => "edit_post"
dom_class(Person, :edit) # => "edit_person"
```

dom_id(record, prefix = nil)

The DOM id convention is to use the singular form of an object or class with the id following an underscore. If no id is found, prefix with new_ instead.

```
dom_id(Post.create) # => "post_42"
dom_id(Post.new)    # => "new_post"
```

If you need to address multiple instances of the same class in the same view, you can prefix the dom_id like: dom_id(Post.create, :edit) results in edit_post_42.

partial_path(record_or_class)

Returns plural/singular for a record or class, which is very useful for automatically rendering partial templates by convention.

```
partial_path(post)   # => "posts/post"
partial_path(Person) # => "people/person"
```

11.16 RecordTagHelper

This module is closely related to RecordIdentificationHelper in that it assists in creation of HTML markup code that follows good, clean naming conventions.

content_tag_for(tag_name, record, *args, & block)

This helper method creates an HTML element with id and class parameters that relate to the specified Active Record object. For instance, assuming @person is an instance of a Person class, with an id value of 123 then the following template code

```
= content_tag_for(:tr, @person) do
  %td= @person.first_name
  %td= @person.last_name
```

will produce the following HTML

```
<tr id="person_123" class="person">
  ...
</tr>
```

If you require the HTML `id` attribute to have a prefix, you can specify it as a third argument:

```
>> content_tag_for(:tr, @person, :foo) do ...
=> "<tr id=\"foo_person_123\" class=\"person\">..."
```

The `content_tag_for` helper also accepts a hash of options, which will be converted to additional HTML attributes on the tag. If you specify a `:class` value, it will be combined with the default class name for your object instead of replacing it (since replacing it would defeat the purpose of the method!).

```
>> content_tag_for(:tr, @person, :foo, :class => 'highlight') do ...
=> "<tr id=\"foo_person_123\" class=\"person highlight\">..."
```

div_for(record, *args, & block)

Produces a wrapper `div` element with `id` and `class` parameters that relate to the specified Active Record object. This method is exactly like `content_tag_for` except that it's hard-coded to output `div` elements.

11.17 SanitizeHelper

The SanitizeHelper module provides a set of methods for scrubbing text of undesired HTML elements. Rails 3 sanitizes and escapes html content by default, so this helper is really intended to assist with the inclusion of dynamic content into your views.

sanitize(html, options = {})

Encodes all tags and strip all attributes (not specifically allowed) from the `html` string passed to it. Also strips `href` and `src` tags with invalid protocols, particularly in an effort to to prevent abuse of `javascript:` attribute values.

```
= sanitize @article.body
```

With its default settings, the `sanitize` method does its best to counter known hacker tricks such as using unicode/ascii/hex values to get past the JavaScript filters.

You can customize the behavior of `sanitize` by adding or removing allowable tags and attributes using the `:attributes` or `:tags` options.

```
= sanitize @article.body, :tags => %w(table tr td), :attributes => %w(id
class style)
```

It's possible to add tags to the default allowed tags in your application by altering the value of `config.action_view.sanitized_allowed_tags` in an initializer. For instance, the following code adds support for basic HTML tables.

```
Rails::Initializer.run do |config|
  config.action_view.sanitized_allowed_tags = 'table', 'tr', 'td'
end
```

You can also remove some of the tags that are allowed by default.

```
Rails::Initializer.run do |config|
  config.after_initialize do
    ActionView::Base.sanitized_allowed_tags.delete 'div'
  end
end
```

Or change them altogether.

```
Rails::Initializer.run do |config|
  config.action_view.sanitized_allowed_attributes = 'id', 'class', 'style'
end
```

Sanitizing user-provided text does not guarantee that the resulting markup will be valid (conforming to a document type) or even well-formed. The output may still contain unescaped <, >, & characters that confuse browsers and adversely affect rendering.

sanitize_css(style)

Sanitizes a block of CSS code. Used by sanitize when it comes across a style attribute in HTML being sanitized.

strip_links(html)

Strips all link tags from text leaving just the link text.

```
strip_links('<a href="http://www.rubyonrails.org">Ruby on Rails</a>')
=> Ruby on Rails

strip_links('Please email me at <a
href="mailto:me@email.com">me@email.com</a>.')
=> Please email me at me@email.com.

strip_links('Blog: <a href="http://www.myblog.com/" class="nav"
target=\"_blank\">Visit</a>.')
=> Blog: Visit
```

Helpers

strip_tags(html)

Strips all tags from the `html` string, including comments. Its HTML parsing ability is limited by that of the html-scanner tokenizer built into Rails. [7]

```
strip_tags("Strip <i>these</i> tags!")
=> Strip these tags!

strip_tags("<b>Bold</b> no more!  <a href='more.html'>See more
here</a>...")
=> Bold no more!  See more here...

strip_tags("<div id='top-bar'>Welcome to my website!</div>")
=> Welcome to my website!
```

11.18 TagHelper

This module provides helper methods for generating HTML tags programmatically.

cdata_section(content)

Returns a CDATA section wrapping the given `content`. CDATA sections are used to escape blocks of text containing characters that would otherwise be recognized as markup. CDATA sections begin with the string `<![CDATA[` and end with (and may not contain) the string `]]>`.

content_tag(name, content = nil, options = nil, & block)

Returns an HTML block tag of type `name` surrounding the content. Add HTML attributes by passing an attributes hash as `options`. Instead of passing the content as an argument, you can also use a block to hold additional markup (and/or additional calls to `content_tag`) in which case, you pass your `options` as the second parameter.

Here are some simple examples of using `content_tag` without a block:

```
>> content_tag(:p, "Hello world!")
=> <p>Hello world!</p>

>> content_tag(:div, content_tag(:p, "Hello!"), :class => "message")
=> <div class="message"><p>Hello!</p></div>

>> content_tag("select", options, :multiple => true)
=> <select multiple="multiple">...options...</select>
```

---

7. You can examine the source code of the html-scanner yourself by opening up `actionpack/lib/action_controller/vendor/html-scanner/html/tokenizer.rb`

Here it is with content in a block (shown as template code rather than in the console):

```
- content_tag :div, :class => "strong" do
  Hello world!
```

The preceding code produces the following HTML:

```
<div class="strong"><p>Hello world!</p></div>
```

escape_once(html)

Returns an escaped version of HTML without affecting existing escaped entities.

```
>> escape_once("1 > 2 &amp; 3")
=> "1 &lt; 2 &amp; 3"

>> escape_once("&lt;&lt; Accept & Checkout")
=> "&lt;&lt; Accept &amp; Checkout"
```

tag(name, options = nil, open = false)

Returns an empty HTML tag of type name, which by default is XHTML compliant. Setting open to true will create an open tag compatible with HTML 4.0 and below. Add HTML attributes by passing an attributes hash to options.

The options hash is used with attributes with no value like (disabled and readonly), which you can give a value of true in the options hash. You can use symbols or strings for the attribute names.

```
>> tag("br")
=> <br />

>> tag("br", nil, true)
=> <br>

>> tag("input", { :type => 'text', :disabled => true })
=> <input type="text" disabled="disabled" />

>> tag("img", { :src => "open.png" })
=> <img src="open.png" />
```

Helpers

11.19 TextHelper

The methods in this module provide filtering, formatting, and string transformation capabilities.

auto_link(text, link = :all, href_options = {}, & block)

Turns all URLs and email addresses inside the `text` string into clickable links. The `link` parameter is used to optionally limit what should be linked; pass it `:email_addresses` or `:urls`. You can add HTML attributes to the generated links using `href_options`.

If for whatever reason you are unhappy with the way that Rails is turning your email addresses and URLs into links, you can supply a block to this method. Each address found is yielded and the return value of the block is used as the link text.

```
>> auto_link("Go to http://obiefernandez.com and say hello to
obie@obiefernandez.com")
=> "Go to <a
href="http://www.rubyonrails.org">http://www.rubyonrails.org</a>
and say hello to <a
href="mailto:obie@obiefernandez.com">obie@obiefernandez.com</a>"

>> auto_link("Welcome to my new blog at http://www.myblog.com/.  Please
email me at me@email.com.", :all, :target => '_blank') do |text|
    truncate(text, 15)
  end
=> "Welcome to my new blog at <a href=\"http://www.myblog.com/\"
target=\"_blank\">http://www.m...</a>.
Please email me at <a href=\"mailto:me@email.com\">me@email.com</a>."
```

concat(string, binding)

The preferred method of outputting text in your views is to use the `=` expression in Haml syntax, or the `<%= expression %>` in eRuby syntax. The regular puts and print methods do not operate as expected in an eRuby code block; that is, if you expected them to output to the browser. If you absolutely must output text within a non-output code block like `- expression` in Haml, or `<% expression %>` in eRuby, you can use the `concat` method. I've found that this method can be especially useful when combined with `capture` in your own custom helper method implementations.

The following example code defines a helper method that wraps its block content in a div with a particular css class.

```
def wrap(&block)
 concat(content_tag(:div, capture(&block), :class => "wrapped_content"))
end
```

You would use it in your template as follows:

```
- wrap do
  My wrapped content
```

current_cycle(name = "default")

Returns the current cycle string after a cycle has been started. Useful for complex table highlighting or any other design need which requires the current cycle string in more than one place.

```
- # Alternate background colors with coordinating text color
- [1,2,3,4].each do |item|
  %div(style="background-color:#{cycle('red', 'green', 'blue')}")
    %span(style="color:dark#{current_cycle}")= item
```

cycle(first_value, *values)

Creates a Cycle object whose to_s method cycles through elements of the array of values passed to it, every time it is called. This can be used, for example, to alternate classes for table rows. Here's an example that alternates CSS classes for even and odd numbers, assuming that the @items variable holds an array with 1 through 4:

```
%table
  - @items.each do |item|
    %tr{:class => cycle('even', 'odd')}
      %td= item
```

As you can tell from the example, you don't have to store the reference to the cycle in a local variable or anything like that; you just call the cycle method repeatedly. That's convenient, but it means that nested cycles need an identifier. The solution is to pass cycle a :name => cycle_name option as its last parameter. Also, you can manually reset a cycle by calling reset_cycle and passing it the name of the cycle to reset. For example, here is some data to iterate over:

```
# Cycle CSS classes for rows, and text colors for values within each row
@items = [{:first => 'Robert', :middle => 'Daniel', :last => 'James'},
          {:first => 'Emily', :last => 'Hicks'},
          {:first => 'June', :middle => 'Dae', :last => 'Jones'}]
```

And here is the template code. Since the number of cells rendered varies, we want to make sure to reset the colors cycle before looping:

```
- @items.each do |item|
  %tr{:class => cycle('even', 'odd', :name => 'row_class')}
    - item.values.each do |value|
      %td{:class => cycle('red', 'green', :name => 'colors')}
        = value
      - reset_cycle 'colors'
```

Helpers

excerpt(text, phrase, radius = 100, excerpt_string = "...")

Extracts an excerpt from text that matches the first instance of phrase. The radius expands the excerpt on each side of the first occurrence of phrase by the number of characters defined in radius (which defaults to 100). If the excerpt radius overflows the beginning or end of the text, the excerpt_string will be prepended/appended accordingly. If the phrase isn't found, nil is returned.

```
>> excerpt('This is an example', 'an', 5)
=> "...s is an examp..."

>> excerpt('This is an example', 'is', 5)
=> "This is an..."

>> excerpt('This is an example', 'is')
=> "This is an example"

>> excerpt('This next thing is an example', 'ex', 2)
=> "...next t..."

>> excerpt('This is also an example', 'an', 8, '<chop> ')
=> "<chop> is also an example"
```

highlight(text, phrases, highlighter = '<strong class="highlight">\1</strong>')

Highlights one or more phrases everywhere in text by inserting into a highlighter template. The highlighter can be specialized by passing highlighter as a single-quoted string with \1 where the phrase is to be inserted.

```
>> highlight('You searched for: rails', 'rails')
=> You searched for: <strong class="highlight">rails</strong>

>> highlight('You searched for: ruby, rails, dhh', 'actionpack')
=> You searched for: ruby, rails, dhh

>> highlight('You searched for: rails', ['for', 'rails'], '<em>\1</em>')
=> You searched <em>for</em>: <em>rails</em>

>> highlight('You searched for: rails', 'rails', "<a
href='search?q=\1'>\1</a>")
=> You searched for: <a href='search?q=rails>rails</a>
```

pluralize(count, singular, plural = nil)

Attempts to pluralize the singular word unless count is 1. If the plural is supplied, it will use that when count is > 1. If the ActiveSupport Inflector is loaded, it will use the `Inflector` to determine the plural form; otherwise, it will just add an "s" to the singular word.

```
>> pluralize(1, 'person')
=> "1 person"

>> pluralize(2, 'person')
=> "2 people"

>> pluralize(3, 'person', 'users')
=> "3 users"

>> pluralize(0, 'person')
=> "0 people"
```

reset_cycle(name = "default")

Resets a cycle (see the `cycle` method in this module) so that it starts cycling from its first element the next time it is called. Pass in a `name` to reset a named cycle.

simple_format(text)

Returns text transformed into HTML using simple formatting rules. Two or more consecutive newlines (\n\n) are considered to denote a paragraph and thus are wrapped in p tags. One newline (\n) is considered to be a line break and a br tag is appended. This method does not remove the newlines from the text.

strip_links(text)

Strips all link tags from text leaving just the link text.

```
>> strip_links('<a href="http://www.rubyonrails.org">Ruby on Rails</a>')
=> Ruby on Rails

>> strip_links('Please email me at <a
href="mailto:me@email.com">me@email.com</a>.')
=> Please email me at me@email.com.

>> strip_links('Blog: <a href="http://www.myblog.com/" class="nav"
target="_blank">Visit</a>.')
=> Blog: Visit
```

strip_tags(html)

Strips all HTML tags from the HTML, including comments. This uses the `html-scanner` tokenizer and so its HTML parsing ability is limited by that of `html-scanner`.

Helpers

```
>> strip_tags("Strip <i>these</i> tags!")
=> Strip these tags!

>> strip_tags("<b>Bold</b> no more!  <a href='more.html'>See more
here</a>...")
=> Bold no more!  See more here...

>> strip_tags("<div id='top-bar'>Welcome to my website!</div>")
=> Welcome to my website!
```

truncate(text, length = 30, truncate_string = "...")

If `text` is longer than `length`, `text` will be truncated to the length specified and the last three characters will be replaced with the `truncate_string`:

```
>> truncate("Once upon a time in a world far far away", 4)
=> "Once..."

>> truncate("Once upon a time in a world far far away")
=> "Once upon a time in a world f..."

>> truncate("And they found that many people were sleeping better.",
15, "... (continued)")
=> "And they found... (continued)"
```

word_wrap(text, line_width = 80)

Wraps the text into lines no longer than `line_width`. This method breaks on the first whitespace character that does not exceed `line_width` (which is 80 by default).

```
>> word_wrap('Once upon a time', 4)
=> "Once\nupon\na\ntime"

>> word_wrap('Once upon a time', 8)
=> "Once upon\na time"

>> word_wrap('Once upon a time')
=> "Once upon a time"

>> word_wrap('Once upon a time', 1)
=> "Once\nupon\na\ntime"
```

11.20 TranslationHelper and the I18n API

I18n stands for *internationalization* and the I18n gem that ships with Rails makes it easy to support multiple languages other than English in your Rails applications. When you internationalize your app, you do a sweep of all the textual content in your models and views that needs to be translated, as well as demarking data like currency and dates, which should be subject to localization.[8]

Rails provides an easy-to-use and extensible framework for translating your application to a single custom language other than English or for providing multi-language support in your application.

The process of *internationalization* in Rails involves the abstraction of strings and other locale-specific parts of your application (such as dates and currency formats) out of the codebase and into a locale file.

The process of *localization* means to provide translations and localized formats for the abstractions created during internationalization. In the process of *localizing* your application you'll probably want to do following three things:

- Replace or add to Rails's default locale

- Abstract strings used in your application into keyed dictionaries—e.g., flash messages, static text in your views, etc.

- Store the resulting dictionaries somewhere

Internationalization is a complex problem. Natural languages differ in so many ways (e.g., in pluralization rules) that it is hard to provide tools for solving all problems at once. For that reason the Rails I18n API focuses on:

- Providing support for English and similar languages by default

- Making it easy to customize and extend everything for other languages

As part of this solution, every static string in the Rails framework—e.g., Active Record validation messages, time and date formats—has been internationalized, so *localization* of a Rails application means *overriding* Rails defaults.

11.20.1   Localized Views

Before diving into the more complicated localization techniques, lets briefly cover a simple way to translate views that is useful for content-heavy pages. Assume you have a `BooksController` in your application. Your `index` action renders content in `app/views/books/index.html.haml` template. When you put a *localized variant* of

---

8. This section is an authorized remix of *The Complete Guide to Using I18n in Rails*, by Sven Fuchs and Karel Minarik, available at `http://guides.rails.info/i18n.html`.

that template such as `index.es.html.haml` in the same directory, Rails will recognize it as the appropriate template to use when the locale is set to `:es`. If the locale is set to the default, the generic `index.html.haml` view will be used normally.

You can make use of this feature when working with a large amount of static content that would be clumsy to maintain inside locale dictionaries. Just bear in mind that any changes to a template must be kept in sync with all of its translations.

11.20.2 `TranslationHelper` Methods

The following two methods are provided for use in your views and assume that I18n support is setup in your application.

`localize(*args)` aliased to `l`

Delegates to ActiveSupport's `I18n\#translate` method with no additional functionality. Normally you want to use `translate` instead.

`translate(key, options = {})` aliased to `t`

Delegates to ActiveSupport's `I18n\#translate` method, while performing two additional functions. First, it'll catch `MissingTranslationData` exceptions and turn them into inline spans that contain the missing key, such that you can see within your views when keys are missing.

Second, it'll automatically scope the key provided by the current partial if the key starts with a period. So if you call `translate(".foo")` from the `people/index.html.haml` template, you'll be calling `I18n.translate("people.index.foo")`. This makes it less repetitive to translate many keys within the same partials and gives you a simple framework for scoping them consistently. If you don't prepend the key with a period, nothing is converted.

11.20.3 I18n Setup

There are just a few simple steps to get up and running with I18n support for your application.

Following the *convention over configuration* philosophy, Rails will set up your application with reasonable defaults. If you need different settings, you can overwrite them easily.

Rails adds all `.rb` and `.yml` files from the `config/locales` directory to your translations load path, automatically.[9] The default `en.yml` locale in this directory contains a sample pair of translation strings:

```
en:
  hello: "Hello world"
```

This means, that in the `:en` locale, the key `hello` will map to the "Hello world" string.[10]

You can use YAML or standard Ruby hashes to store translations in the default (`Simple`) backend.

Unless you change it, the I18n library will use English (`:en`) as its default locale for looking up translations. Change the default in `config/application.rb` using code similar to:

```
config.i18n.default_locale = :de
```

Note

The i18n library takes a **pragmatic approach** to locale keys (after some discussion[11]), including only the *locale* ("language") part, like `:en`, `:pl`, not the *region* part, like `:en-US` or `:en-UK`, which are traditionally used for separating "languages" and "regional setting" or "dialects". Many international applications use only the "language" element of a locale such as `:cz`, `:th` or `:es` (for Czech, Thai, and Spanish). However, there are also regional differences within different language groups that may be important. For instance, in the `:en-US` locale you would have $ as a currency symbol, hereas in `:en-UK`, you would have £. Nothing stops you from separating regional and other settings in this way: you just have to provide full "English – United Kingdom" locale in a `:en-UK` dictionary. Rails I18n plugins such as Globalize2[12] may help you implement it.

11.20.4 Setting and Passing the Locale

If you want to translate your Rails application to a single language other than English, you can just set `default_locale` to your locale in `application.rb` as shown above

---

9. The translations load path is just a Ruby Array of paths to your translation files that will be loaded automatically and available in your application. You can pick whatever directory and translation file naming scheme makes sense for you.

10. Every string inside Rails is internationalized in this way, see for instance Active Record validation messages in the `activerecord/lib/active_record/locale/en.yml` file or time and date formats in the `activesupport/lib/active_support/locale/en.yml` file.

10. http://groups.google.com/group/rails-i18n/browse_thread/thread/14dede2c7dbe9470/80eec34395f64f3c?hl=en

11. http://github.com/joshmh/globalize2/tree/master

and it will persist through the requests. However, you probably want to provide support for more locales in your application, depending on the user's preference. In such cases, you need to set and pass the locale between requests. You can set the locale in a

---

Warning

You may be tempted to store the chosen locale in a *session* or a *cookie*. **Do not do so**. The locale should be transparent and a part of the URL. This way you don't break people's basic assumptions about the web itself: If you send a URL of some page to a friend, he or she should see the same page, same content.

`before_filter` in your `ApplicationController` like:

```
before_filter :set_locale
def set_locale
  # if params[:locale] is nil then I18n.default_locale will be used
  I18n.locale = params[:locale]
end
```

This approach requires you to pass the locale as a URL query parameter as in `http://example.com/books?locale=pt`. (This is, for example, Google's approach.)

Getting the locale from `params` and setting it accordingly is not the hard part of this techniqe. Including the locale parameter in every URL generated by your application *is* the hard part. To include an explicit option in every URL

```
= link_to books_url(:locale => I18n.locale)
```

would be tedious at best and impossible to maintain at worst.

A `default_url_options` method in `ApplicationController` is useful precisely in this scenario. It enables us to set defaults for `url_for` and helper methods dependent on it.

```
def default_url_options(options={})
  logger.debug "default_url_options is passed options:
#{options.inspect}\n"
  { :locale => I18n.locale }
end
```

Every helper method dependent on `url_for` (e.g., helpers for named routes like `root_path` or `root_url`, resource routes like `books_path` or `books_url`, etc.) will now automatically include the locale in the query string, like

```
http://localhost:3001/?locale=ja
```

Having the locale hang at the end of every path in your application can negatively impact readability of your URLs. Moreover, from an architectural standpoint, locales are a concept that live above other parts of your application domain and your URLs should probably reflect that.

You might want your URLs to look more like `www.example.com/en/books` (which loads the English locale) and `www.example.com/nl/books` (which loads the Netherlands locale). This is achievable with the same `default_url_options` strategy we just reviewed. You just have to set up your routes with a `path_prefix` option in this way:

```
# config/routes.rb
resources :books, :path_prefix => '/:locale'
```

Even with this approach, you still need to take special care of the root URL of your application. An URL like `http://localhost:3001/nl` will not work automatically, because the `map.root :controller => "dashboard"` declaration in your `routes.rb` doesn't take locale into account. After all, there should only be one "root" of your website.

A possible solution is to map a URL like:

```
# config/routes.rb
map.dashboard '/:locale', :controller => "dashboard"
```

Do take special care about the order of your routes, so this route declaration does not break other ones. It would be most wise to add it directly before the `map.root` declaration at the end of your routes file.

Warning

This solution has currently one rather big **downside**. Due to the `default_url_options` implementation, you have to pass the `:id` option explicitly, like `link_to 'Show', book_url(:id => book)` and not depend on Rails' magic in code like `link_to 'Show', book`. If this should be a problem, have a look at two plugins which simplify work with routes in this way: Sven Fuchs's routing_filter[13] and Raul Murciano's translate_routes[14]. Also make sure to read *How to encode the current locale in the URL*[15] in the Rails i18n Wiki.

Setting the Locale from the Domain Name

Another option you have is to set the locale from the domain name where your application runs. For example, we want `www.example.com` to load the English (or default) locale,

---

12. `http://github.com/svenfuchs/routing-filter/tree/master`
13. `http://github.com/raul/translate_routes/tree/master`
14. `http://rails-i18n.org/wiki/pages/how-to-encode-the-current-locale-in-the-url`

and www.example.es to load the Spanish locale. Thus the *top-level domain name* is used for locale setting. This has several advantages:

- The locale is a very *obvious* part of the URL
- People intuitively grasp in which language the content will be displayed
- It is very trivial to implement in Rails
- Search engines seem to like that content in different languages lives at different, inter-linked domains

You can implement it like this in your ApplicationController:

```
before_filter :set_locale

def set_locale
  I18n.locale = extract_locale_from_uri
end

# Get locale from top-level domain or return nil
def extract_locale_from_tld
  parsed_locale = request.host.split('.').last
  (available_locales.include? parsed_locale) ? parsed_locale  : nil
end
```

Try adding localhost aliases to your /etc/hosts file to test this technique.

```
127.0.0.1 application.com
127.0.0.1 application.it
127.0.0.1 application.pl
```

Setting the Locale from the Host Name

We can also set the locale from the subdomain in a very similar way inside of ApplicationController.

```
before_filter :set_locale

def set_locale
  I18n.locale = extract_locale_from_uri
end

def extract_locale_from_subdomain
  parsed_locale = request.subdomains.first
  (available_locales.include? parsed_locale) ? parsed_locale  : nil
end
```

11.20.5   Setting Locale from Client Supplied Information

In specific cases, it would make sense to set the locale from client-supplied information, i.e., not from the URL. This information may come for example from the users' prefered language (set in their browser), can be based on the users' geographical location inferred from their IP, or users can provide it simply by choosing the locale in your application interface and saving it to their profile. This approach is more suitable for web-based applications or services, not for websites. See the sidebar about *sessions, cookies,* and RESTful architecture.

Using **Accept-Language**

One source of client supplied information would be an `Accept-Language` HTTP header. People may set this in their browser[16] or other clients (such as `curl`).

A trivial implementation of setting locale based on the `Accept-Language` header in `ApplicationController` might be:

```
before_filter :set_locale

def set_locale
  I18n.locale = extract_locale_from_accept_language_header
  logger.debug "* Locale set to '#{I18n.locale}'"
end

private

def extract_locale_from_accept_language_header
  request.env['HTTP_ACCEPT_LANGUAGE'].scan(/^[a-z]{2}/).first
end
```

In real production environments, you should use much more robust code that the example above. Try plugins such as Iain Hecker's http_accept_language[17] or even Rack middleware such as Ryan Tomayko's locale.[18]

Using GeoIP (or Similar) Database

Yet another way of choosing the locale from client information would be to use a database for mapping the client IP to the region, such as GeoIP Lite Country.[19] The mechanics of the code would be very similar to the code above—you would need to query the database for the user's IP, and look up your prefered locale for the country/region/city returned.

---

16. http://www.w3.org/International/questions/qa-lang-priorities
17. http://github.com/iain/http_accept_language/tree/master
18. http://github.com/rtomayko/rack-contrib/blob/master/lib/rack/locale.rb
19. http://www.maxmind.com/app/geolitecountry

Helpers

User Profile

You can also provide users of your application with means to set (and possibly override) the locale in your application interface, as well. Again, mechanics for this approach would be very similar to the code above—you'd probably let users choose a locale from a dropdown list and save it to their profile in the database. Then you'd set the locale to this value using a `before_filter` in `ApplicationController`.

11.20.6 Internationalizing Your Application

After you've setup I18n support for your Ruby on Rails application and told it which locale to use and how to preserve it between requests, you're ready for the really interesting part of the process: actually internationalizing your application.

The Public I18n API

First of all, you should be acquainted with the I18n API. The two most important methods of the I18n API are

```
translate # Lookup text translations
localize  # Localize Date and Time objects to local formats
```

These have the aliases #t and #l so you can use them like

```
I18n.t 'store.title'
I18n.l Time.now
```

The Process

Take the following basic pieces of a simple Rails application as an example for describing the process.

```
# config/routes.rb
ActionController::Routing::Routes.draw do |map|
  map.root :controller => 'home', :action => 'index'
end

# app/controllers/home_controller.rb
class HomeController < ApplicationController
  def index
    flash[:notice] = "Welcome"
  end
end

# app/views/home/index.html.haml
%h1 Hello world!
%p.notice= flash[:notice]
```

The example has two strings that are currently hardcoded in English. To internationalize this code, we must replace those strings with calls to Rails's #t helper with a key that makes sense for the translation.

```
# app/controllers/home_controller.rb
class HomeController < ApplicationController
  def index
    flash[:notice] = t(:welcome_flash)
  end
end

# app/views/home/index.html.haml
%h1= t(:hello_world)
%p.notice= flash[:notice]
```

Now when you render this view, it will show an error message which tells you that the translations for the keys :hello_world and :welcome_flash are missing.

Rails adds a t (translate) helper method to your views so that you do not need to spell out I18n.t all the time. Additionally this helper will catch missing translations and wrap the resulting error message into a <span class="translation_missing">.

To make the example work you would add the missing translations into the dictionary files (thereby doing the localization part of the work):

```
# config/locale/en.yml
en:
  hello_world: Hello World
  welcome_flash: Welcome

# config/locale/pirate.yml
pirate:
  hello_world: Ahoy World
  welcome_flash: All aboard!
```

Note

You need to restart the server when you add or edit locale files.

You may use YAML (.yml) or plain Ruby (.rb) files for storing your translations. YAML is the prefered option among Rails developers. However, it has one big disadvantage. YAML is very sensitive to whitespace and special characters, so the application may not load your dictionary properly. Ruby files will crash your application on first request, so you may easily find what's wrong. (If you encounter any "weird issues" with YAML dictionaries, try putting the relevant portion of your dictionary into a Ruby file.)

Helpers

Adding Date/Time Formats

Okay! Now let's add a timestamp to the view, so we can demo the date/time localization feature as well. To localize the time format you pass the Time object to I18n.l or use Rails's #l helper method in your views.

```
# app/views/home/index.html.haml
%h1= t(:hello_world)
%p.notice= flash[:notice]
%p= l(Time.now, :format => :short)
```

And in our pirate translations file let's add a time format (it's already there in Rails's defaults for English):

```
# config/locale/pirate.yml
pirate:
  time:
    formats:
      short: "arrrround %H'ish"
```

The `rails-i18n` repository

There's a great chance that somebody has already done much of the hard work of translating Rails' defaults for your locale. See the rails-i18n repository at Github[20] for an archive of various locale files. When you put such file(s) in `config/locale/` directory, they will automatically be ready for use.

11.20.7 Organization of Locale Files

Putting translations for all parts of your application in one file per locale could be hard to manage. You can store these files in a hierarchy which makes sense to you.

For example, your `config/locale` directory could look like:

```
|-defaults
|---es.rb
|---en.rb
|-models
|---book
|-----es.rb
|-----en.rb
|-views
|---defaults
|-----es.rb
```

---

19. `http://github.com/svenfuchs/rails-i18n/tree/master/rails/locale`

```
|-----en.rb
|---books
|-----es.rb
|-----en.rb
|---users
|-----es.rb
|-----en.rb
|---navigation
|-----es.rb
|-----en.rb
```

This way, you can separate model and model attribute names from text inside views, and all of this from the "defaults" (e.g., date and time formats). Other stores for the i18n library could provide different means of such separation.

Note

The default locale loading mechanism in Rails does not load locale files in nested dictionaries, like we have here. So, for this to work, we must explicitly tell Rails to look further through settings in `config/application.rb`:

```
# config/application.rb
config.i18n.load_path += Dir[File.join(Rails.root, 'config', 'locales',
'**', '*.{rb,yml}')]
```

11.20.8 Looking Up Translations

Basic Lookup, Scopes and Nested Keys

Translations are looked up by keys which can be both Symbols or Strings, so these calls are equivalent:

```
I18n.t :message
I18n.t 'message'
```

The `translate` method also takes a `:scope` option which can contain one or more additional keys that will be used to specify a "namespace" or scope for a translation key:

```
I18n.t :invalid, :scope => [:activerecord, :errors, :messages]
```

This looks up the `:invalid` message in the Active Record error messages.

Additionally, both the key and scopes can be specified as dot-separated keys as in:

```
I18n.translate :"activerecord.errors.messages.invalid"
```

Thus the following four calls are equivalent:

```
I18n.t 'activerecord.errors.messages.invalid'
I18n.t 'errors.messages.invalid', :scope => :activerecord
I18n.t :invalid, :scope => 'activerecord.errors.messages'
I18n.t :invalid, :scope => [:activerecord, :errors, :messages]
```

Default Values

When a `:default` option is given, its value will be returned if the translation is missing:

```
I18n.t :missing, :default => 'Not here'
# => 'Not here'
```

If the `:default` value is a Symbol, it will be used as a key and translated. One can provide multiple values as default. The first one that results in a value will be returned.

E.g., the following first tries to translate the key `:missing` and then the key `:also_missing`. As both do not yield a result, the string "Not here" will be returned:

```
I18n.t :missing, :default => [:also_missing, 'Not here']
# => 'Not here'
```

Bulk and Namespace Lookup

To look up multiple translations at once, an array of keys can be passed:

```
I18n.t [:odd, :even], :scope => 'activerecord.errors.messages'
# => ["must be odd", "must be even"]
```

Also, a key can translate to a (potentially nested) hash of grouped translations. For instance, one can receive *all* Active Record error messages as a hash with:

```
I18n.t 'activerecord.errors.messages'
# => { :inclusion => "is not included in the list", :exclusion => ... }
```

View Scoped Keys

Rails implements a convenient way to reference keys inside of views. Assume you have the following local file:

```
es:
  books:
    index:
      title: "T\'{i}tulo"
```

You can reference the value of `books.index.title` inside of the `app/views/books/index.html.haml` template by prefixing the key name with a dot. Rails will automatically fill in the scope based on the identity of the view.

```
<%= t '.title' %>
```

Interpolation

In many cases you want to abstract your translations in such a way that variables can be interpolated into the translation. For this reason, the I18n API provides an interpolation feature.

All options besides `:default` and `:scope` that are passed to `translate` will be interpolated to the translation:

```
I18n.backend.store_translations :en, :thanks => 'Thanks {{name}}!'
I18n.translate :thanks, :name => 'Jeremy'
# => 'Thanks Jeremy!'
```

If a translation uses `:default` or `:scope` as an interpolation variable, an `I18n::ReservedInterpolationKey` exception is raised. If a translation expects an interpolation variable, but this has not been passed to `translate`, an `I18n::MissingInterpolationArgument` exception is raised.

Pluralization

In English there are only one singular and one plural form for a given string, e.g. "1 message" and "2 messages" but other languages have different grammars with additional or fewer plural forms[21]. Thus, the I18n API provides a flexible pluralization feature.

The `:count` interpolation variable has a special role in that it both is interpolated to the translation and used to pick a pluralization from the translations according to the pluralization rules defined by Unicode:

```
I18n.backend.store_translations :en, :inbox => {
  :one => '1 message',
  :other => '{{count}} messages'
}

>> I18n.translate :inbox, :count => 2
=> '2 messages'
```

The algorithm for pluralizations in `:en` is as simple as:

```
entry[count == 1 ? 0 : 1]
```

The translation denoted as `:one` is regarded as singular, versus any other value regarded as plural (including the count being zero).

If the lookup for the key does not return a Hash suitable for pluralization, an `I18n::InvalidPluralizationData` exception is raised.

---

21. http://www.unicode.org/cldr/data/charts/supplemental/language_plural_rules.html

11.20.9 How to Store Your Custom Translations

The `Simple` backend shipped with Active Support allows you to store translations in both plain Ruby and YAML format. A Ruby hash locale file would look like:

```
{
  :pt => {
    :foo => {
      :bar => "baz"
    }
  }
}
```

The equivalent YAML file would look like:

```
pt:
  foo:
    bar: baz
```

In both cases, the top level key is the locale. `:foo` is a namespace key and `:bar` is the key for the translation "baz".

Here is a real example from the Active Support `en.yml` translations YAML file:

```
en:
  date:
    formats:
      default: "%Y-%m-%d"
      short: "%b %d"
      long: "%B %d, %Y"
```

So, all of the following equivalent lookups will return the `:short` date format `"%B %d"`:

```
I18n.t 'date.formats.short'
I18n.t 'formats.short', :scope => :date
I18n.t :short, :scope => 'date.formats'
I18n.t :short, :scope => [:date, :formats]
```

Generally we recommend using YAML as a format for storing translations.

Translations for Active Record Models

You can use the methods `Model.human_name` and `Model.human_attribute_ name(attribute)` to transparently look up translations for your model and attribute names.

For example when you add the following translations:

```
en:
  activerecord:
    models:
      user: Dude
```

```
attributes:
  user:
    login: "Handle"
    # will translate User attribute "login" as "Handle"
```

`User.human_name` will return "Dude" and `User.human_attribute_name(:login)` will return "Handle".

Error Message Scopes

Active Record validation error messages can also be translated easily. Active Record gives you a couple of namespaces where you can place your message translations in order to provide different messages and translation for certain models, attributes, and/or validations. It also transparently takes single table inheritance into account.

This gives you quite powerful means to flexibly adjust your messages to your application's needs.

Consider a User model with a `validates_presence_of` validation for the name attribute like:

```
class User < ActiveRecord::Base
  validates_presence_of :name
end
```

The key for the error message in this case is `:blank`. Active Record will look up this key in the namespaces:

```
activerecord.errors.models.[model_name].attributes.[attribute_name]
activerecord.errors.models.[model_name]
activerecord.errors.messages
```

Thus, in our example it will try the following keys in this order and return the first result:

```
activerecord.errors.models.user.attributes.name.blank
activerecord.errors.models.user.blank
activerecord.errors.messages.blank
```

When your models are additionally using inheritance then the messages are looked up in the inheritance chain.

For example, you might have an Admin model inheriting from User:

```
class Admin < User
  validates_presence_of :name
end
```

Then Active Record will look for messages in this order:

```
activerecord.errors.models.admin.attributes.title.blank
activerecord.errors.models.admin.blank
```

Helpers

```
activerecord.errors.models.user.attributes.title.blank
activerecord.errors.models.user.blank
activerecord.errors.messages.blank
```

This way you can provide special translations for various error messages at different points in your models inheritance chain and in the attributes, models, or default scopes.

Error Message Interpolation

The translated model name, translated attribute name, and value are always available for interpolation.

So, for example, instead of the default error message `"can not be blank"` you could use the attribute name like `"Please fill in your {{attribute}}"`.

Translations for the Active Record **error_messages_for** Helper

If you are using the Active Record `error_messages_for` helper, you will want to add translations for it.

Rails ships with the following translations:

```
en:
  activerecord:
    errors:
      template:
        header:
          one:   "1 error prohibited this {{model}} from being saved"
          other: "{{count}} errors prohibited this {{model}} from being
saved"
        body:    "There were problems with the following fields:"
```

11.20.10 Overview of Other Built-In Methods that Provide I18n Support

Rails uses fixed strings and other localizations, such as format strings and other format information in a couple of helpers. Here's a brief overview.

Action View Helper Methods

- `distance_of_time_in_words` translates and pluralizes its result and interpolates the number of seconds, minutes, hours, and so on. See `datetime.distance_in_words`[22] translations.

---

[22]. http://github.com/rails/rails/blob/master/actionpack/lib/action_view/locale/en.yml#L51

Validation	with option	Message	interpolation
validates_confirmation_of	–	:confirmation	–
validates_acceptance_of	–	:accepted	–
validates_presence_of	–	:blank	–
validates_length_of	:within, :in	:too_short	count
validates_length_of	:within, :in	:too_long	count
validates_length_of	:is	:wrong_length	count
validates_length_of	:minimum	:too_short	count
validates_length_of	:maximum	:too_long	count
validates_uniqueness_of	–	:taken	–
validates_format_of	–	:invalid	–
validates_inclusion_of	–	:inclusion	–
validates_exclusion_of	–	:exclusion	–
validates_associated	–	:invalid	–
validates_numericality_of	–	:not_a_number	–
validates_numericality_of	:greater_than	:greater_than	count
validates_numericality_of	:greater_than_or_equal_to	:greater_than_or_equal_to	count
validates_numericality_of	:equal_to	:equal_to	count
validates_numericality_of	:less_than	:less_than	count
validates_numericality_of	:less_than_or_equal_to	:less_than_or_equal_to	count
validates_numericality_of	:odd	:odd	–
validates_numericality_of	:even	:even	–

Helpers

- `datetime_select` and `select_month` use translated month names for populating the resulting select tag. See `date.month_names`[23] for translations. `datetime_select` also looks up the order option from date.order[24] (unless you pass the option explicitly). All date selection helpers translate the prompt using the translations in the datetime.prompts[25] scope if applicable.

- The `number_to_currency`, `number_with_precision`, `number_to_percentage`, `number_with_delimiter`, and `number_to_human_size` helpers use the number format settings located in the number[26] scope.

Active Record Methods

- `human_name` and `human_attribute_name` use translations for model names and attribute names if available in the activerecord.models[27] scope. They also support translations for inherited class names (e.g., for use with STI) as explained in "Error message scopes".

- `ActiveRecord::Errors#generate_message` (which is used by Active Record validations but may also be used manually) uses `human_name` and `human_attribute_name`. It also translates the error message and supports translations for inherited class names as explained in "Error message scopes".

* `ActiveRecord::Errors#full_messages` prepends the attribute name to the error message using a separator that will be looked up from activerecord.errors.format.separator (and which defaults to `' '`).

Active Support Methods

- `Array#to_sentence` uses format settings as given in the `support.array` scope.

---

23. http://github.com/rails/rails/blob/master/activesupport/lib/active_support/locale/en.yml#L15

24. http://github.com/rails/rails/blob/master/activesupport/lib/active_support/locale/en.yml#L18

25. http://github.com/rails/rails/blob/master/actionpack/lib/action_view/locale/en.yml#L83

26. http://github.com/rails/rails/blob/master/actionpack/lib/action_view/locale/en.yml#L2

27. http://github.com/rails/rails/blob/master/activerecord/lib/active_record/locale/en.yml#L43

11.20.11 Exception Handling

In some contexts, you might want to I18n's default exception-handling behavior. For
instance, the default exception handling does not allow to catch missing translations
during automated tests easily. For this purpose, a different exception handler can be
specified. The specified exception handler must be a method on the I18n module. You
would add code similar to the following to your `spec_helper.rb` file or other kind of
initializer.

```
module I18n
  def just_raise_that_exception(*args)
    raise args.first
  end
end

I18n.exception_handler = :just_raise_that_exception
```

This would re-raise all caught exceptions including `MissingTranslationData`.

11.21 **UrlHelper**

This module provides a set of methods for making links and getting URLs that depend
on the routing subsystem, covered extensively in Chapters 2 and 3 of this book.

button_to(name, options = {}, html_options = {})

Generates a form containing a single button that submits to the URL created by the set
of options. This is the safest method to ensure that links that cause changes to your data
are not triggered by search bots or accelerators. If the HTML button does not work with
your layout, you can also consider using the `link_to` method (also in this module) with
the `:method` modifier.

The options hash accepts the same options as the `url_for` method (also part of this
module).

The generated FORM element has a class name of `button-to` to allow styling of the
form itself and its children. The `:method` and `:confirm` options work just like the
`link_to` helper. If no `:method` modifier is given, it defaults to performing a POST
operation. You can also disable the button by passing `:disabled => true`.

```
>> button_to "New", :action => "new"
=> "<form method="post" action="/controller/new" class="button-to">
     <div><input value="New" type="submit" /></div>
   </form>"

>> button_to "Delete Image", { :action => "delete", :id => @image.id },
```

Helpers

```
:confirm => "Are you sure?", :method => :delete
=> "<form method="post" action="/images/delete/1" class="button-to">
      <div>
        <input type="hidden" name="_method" value="delete" />
        <input onclick="return confirm('Are you sure?');" value="Delete"
type="submit" />
      </div>
    </form>"
```

current_page?(options)

Returns true if the current request URI was generated by the given options. For example, let's assume that we're currently rendering the /shop/checkout action:

```
>> current_page?(:action => 'process')
=> false

>>current_page?(:action => 'checkout') # controller is implied
=> true

>> current_page?(:controller => 'shop', :action => 'checkout')
=> true
```

link_to(name, options = {}, html_options = nil)

One of the fundamental helper methods. Creates a link tag of the given name using a URL created by the set of options. The valid options are covered in the description of this module's url_for method. It's also possible to pass a string instead of an options hash to get a link tag that uses the value of the string as the href for the link. If nil is passed as a name, the link itself will become the name.

:confirm => 'question?' Adds a JavaScript confirmation prompt with the question specified. If the user accepts, the link is processed normally; otherwise, no action is taken.

:popup => true Forces the link to open in a pop-up window. By passing true, a default browser window will be opened with the URL. You can also specify a string of options to be passed to JavaScript's window.open method.

:method => symbol Specify an alternative HTTP verb for this request (other than GET). This modifier will dynamically create an HTML form and immediately submit the form for processing using the HTTP verb specified (:post, :put, :delete, or other custom string like "HEAD", and so on).

Generally speaking, GET requests should be idempotent, that is, they do not modify the state of any resource on the server, and can be called one or many times without a problem. Requests that modify server-side resources or trigger dangerous actions like deleting a record should not usually be linked with a normal hyperlink, since search bots and so-called browser accelerators can follow those links while spidering your site, leaving a trail of chaos.

If the user has JavaScript disabled, the request will always fall back to using GET, no matter what :method you have specified. This is accomplished by including a valid href attribute. If you are relying on the POST behavior, your controller code should check for it using the post?, delete?, or put? methods of request.

As usual, the html_options will accept a hash of HTML attributes for the link tag.

```
= link_to "Help", help_widgets_path, :popup => true

= link_to "Rails", "http://rubyonrails.org/",
  :confirm => "Are you sure?"

= link_to "View", widget_path(@widget),
  :popup => ['new_window_name', 'height=300,width=600']

= link_to "Delete", widget_path(@widget),
  :confirm => "Are you sure?", :method => :delete
```

[Renders in the browser as...]

```
<a href="/widgets/help" onclick="window.open(this.href);return
false;">Help</a>

<a href="http://rubyonrails.org/" onclick="return confirm('Are you
sure?');">Rails</a>

<a href="/widgets/42" onclick="window.open(this.href,'new_window_name',
'height=300,width=600'); return false;">View</a>

<a href="/widgets/42" onclick="if (confirm('Are you sure?'))
{ var f = document.createElement('form'); f.style.display = 'none';
this.parentNode.appendChild(f); f.method = 'POST'; f.action =
this.href;var m = document.createElement('input');
m.setAttribute('type', 'hidden'); m.setAttribute('name', '_method');
m.setAttribute('value', 'delete'); f.appendChild(m);var s =
document.createElement('input'); s.setAttribute('type', 'hidden');
s.setAttribute('name', 'authenticity_token'); s.setAttribute('value',
'NerPwDh1oGUzH7681JDVvGgl3jzD/okzE8BxKQe175g='); 
f.appendChild(s);f.submit(); };return false;">Delete</a>
```

Helpers

link_to_if(condition, name, options = {}, html_options = {}, & block)

Creates a link tag using the same options as link_to if the condition is true; otherwise, only the name is output (or block is evaluated for an alternative value, if one is supplied).

link_to_unless(condition, name, options = {}, html_options = {}, & block)

Creates a link tag using the same options as link_to unless the condition is true, in which case only the name is output (or block is evaluated for an alternative value, if one is supplied).

link_to_unless_current(name, options = {}, html_options = {}, & block)

Creates a link tag using the same options as link_to unless the condition is true, in which case only the name is output (or block is evaluated for an alternative value, if one is supplied).

This method is pretty useful sometimes. Remember that the block given to link_to_unless_current is evaluated if the current action is the action given. So, if we had a comments page and wanted to render a "Go Back" link instead of a link to the comments page, we could do something like

```
link_to_unless_current("Comment", { :controller => 'comments',
    :action => 'new}) do
    link_to("Go back", { :controller => 'posts', :action => 'index' })
    end
```

mail_to(email_address, name = nil, html_options = {})

Creates a mailto link tag to the specified email_address, which is also used as the name of the link unless name is specified. Additional HTML attributes for the link can be passed in html_options.

The mail_to helper has several techniques for hindering email harvesters and customizing the email address itself by passing special keys to html_options:

:encode This key will accept the strings "javascript" or "hex". Passing "javascript" will dynamically create and encode the mailto: link and then eval it into the DOM of the page. This method will not show the link on the page if the user has JavaScript disabled. Passing "hex" will hex-encode the email_address before outputting the mailto: link.

:replace_at When the link name isn't provided, the email_address is used for the link label. You can use this option to obfuscate the email_address by substituting the @ sign with the string given as the value.

:replace_dot When the link name isn't provided, the email_address is used for the link label. You can use this option to obfuscate the email_address by substituting the "." in the email with the string given as the value.

:subject The subject line of the email.

:body The body of the email.

:cc Add cc recipients to the email.

:bcc Add bcc recipients to the email.

Here are some examples of usages:

```
>> mail_to "me@domain.com"
=> <a href="mailto:me@domain.com">me@domain.com</a>

>> mail_to "me@domain.com", "My email", :encode => "javascript"
=> <script type="text/javascript">eval(unescape('%64%6f%63...%6d%65'))
</script>

>> mail_to "me@domain.com", "My email", :encode => "hex"
=> <a href="mailto:%6d%65@%64%6f%6d%61%69%6e.%63%6f%6d">My email</a>

>> mail_to "me@domain.com", nil, :replace_at => "_at_", :replace_dot =>
"_dot_", :class => "email"
=> <a href="mailto:me@domain.com" class="email">me_at_domain_dot_com</a>

>> mail_to "me@domain.com", "My email", :cc => "ccaddress@domain.com",
:subject => "This is an example email"
=> <a href="mailto:me@domain.com?cc=ccaddress@domain.com&subject=This%20i
s%20an%20example%20email">My email</a>
```

url_for(options = {})

The url_for method returns a URL for the set of options provided and takes the same options as url_for in Action Controller.

Note that by default, the :only_path option is set to true so that you'll get the relative /controller/action instead of the fully qualified URL like http://example.com/controller/action. Note that as of Rails 3 url_for always returns unescaped strings.

Here is the complete list of options accepted by `url_for`:

:anchor Specifies an anchor name (`#anchor`) be appended to the end of the path

:only_path Specifies a relative URL (omitting the protocol, host name, and port)

:trailing_slash Adds a trailing slash, as in `"/archive/2005/"`. Note that this is currently not recommended since it breaks caching

:host Overrides the default (current) host if provided

:protocol Overrides the default (current) protocol if provided

:user Inline HTTP authentication (requires `:password` option)

:password Inline HTTP authentication (requires `:user` option)

:escape Determines whether the returned URL will be HTML-escaped

When you pass `url_for` a string, whether explicitly or via a named route helper method, it'll assume that it is an already formed URL and won't manipulate it. I'm mentioning this mostly for reference purposes; remember that you don't normally call `url_for` directly, but rather through other helper methods such as `link_to`.

```
>> url_for(timesheets_path)
=> "/timesheets"

>> url_for('http://cnn.com')
=> "http://cnn.com"
```

If you pass `url_for` a hash, it will do old-school URL generation with it, but only if it finds a *matching route definition* in `routes.rb`.

```
>> url_for(:controller => 'books', :action => 'find')
=> "/books/find"
```

Back in the day, URL generation of this type (controller/action) always worked because of the default route. Nowadays, most Rails applications have their default route turned off and using `url_for` with hashes is a lot less common. If you're a relative newcomer to Rails, it still makes sense to at least have a basic understanding of how this functionality works.

```
>> url_for(:controller => 'members', :action => 'login', :only_path =>
false, :protocol => 'https')
=> "https://www.railsapplication.com/members/login"
```

If some of the parameters of the route are missing from the call to `url_for`, it defaults to the current values for `:controller`, `:action`, and any other parameters required by the route and/or used in the current request.

For example, inside a `show` view for a template belonging to an auctions controller, you could create a link to the `edit` action like:

```
link_to "Edit auction", :action => "edit", :id => auction
```

Assuming that this view is only ever rendered by actions in the auctions controller, the current controller at the time of the rendering will always be auctions. Because there's no `:controller` specified in the URL hash, the generator will fall back on auctions, and based on the default route (`:controller/:action/:id`) or a matching resource route, it should come up with something like:

```
<a href="http://localhost:3000/auctions/edit/5">Edit auction</a>
```

The same is true of the action. If you don't supply an `:action` key, then the current action will be interpolated. Keep in mind, though, that it's pretty common for one action to render a template that belongs to another. So it's less likely that you'll want to let the URL generator fall back on the current action than on the current controller.

Redirecting Back

If you pass the magic symbol `:back` to any method that uses `url_for` under the covers (`redirect_to`, etc.) the contents of the `HTTP_REFERER` request header will be returned. (If a referer is not set for the current request, it will return `javascript:history.back()` to try to make the browser go back one page.)

```
>> url_for(:back)
=> "javascript:history.back()"
```

So-called *Polymorphic Paths*

If you pass an Active Record or Active Resource model instance instead of a hash to any method in the `UrlModule` that takes `url_for` parameters, you'll trigger generation of a path for that record's named route (assuming that one exists). For example, passing a `Timesheet` object instance will generate a `timesheet_path` route.

```
>> url_for(timesheet) # existing record
=> "/timesheets/5"
```

The lookup is based on the name of the class and is smart enough to call `new?` on the passed model to figure out whether to reference a collection or member route.

```
>> url_for(Timesheet.new)
=> "/timesheets"
```

If the object's route is nested within another route, you'll have to provide either a symbol designating the namespace that it's in and/or one or more other objects which are above it in the nesting hierarchy. (Make sure to use an array around your objects and symbols, so that the first argument is properly interpreted!)

```
>> url_for([client, Timesheet.new])
=> "/clients/1/timesheets"

>> url_for([:admin, Client.new])
=> "/admin/clients"
```

Somewhat confusingly, collection routes (even within namespaces) are accessed by prepending the name of the route to the front of the array, as in the following example:

```
>> url_for([:new, :admin, Client.new])
=> "/admin/clients/new"
```

11.22 Writing Your Own View Helpers

As you develop an application in Rails, you should be on the lookout for opportunities to refactor duplicated view code into your own helper methods. As you think of these helpers, you add them to one of the helper modules defined in the `app/helpers` folder of your application.

There is an art to effectively writing helper methods, similar in nature to what it takes to write effective APIs. Helper methods are basically a custom, application-level API for your view code. It is difficult to teach API design in a book form. It's the sort of knowledge that you gain by apprenticing with more experienced programmers and lots of trial and error. Nevertheless, in this section, we'll review some varied use cases and implementation styles that we hope will inspire you in your own application design.

11.22.1 Small Optimizations: The Title Helper

Here is a simple helper method that has been of use to me on many projects now. It's called `page_title` and it combines two simple functions essential to a good HTML document:

- Setting the `title` of the page in the document's `head`
- Setting the content of the page's `h1` element

This helper assumes that you want the `title` and `h1` elements of the page to be the same, and has a dependency on your application template. The code for the helper is in Listing 11.7 and would be added to `app/helpers/application_helper.rb`, since it is applicable to all views.

Listing 11.7 The `page_title` Helper

```
def page_title(name)
  content_for(:title) { name }
  content_tag("h1", name)
end
```

First it sets content to be yielded in the layout as `:title` and then it outputs an `h1` element containing the same text. I could have used string interpolation on the second line, such as `"<h1>#{name}</h1>"`, but it would have been sloppier than using the built-in Rails helper method `content_tag`.

My application template is now written to `yield :title` so that it gets the page title.

```
%html
  %head
    %title= yield :title
```

As should be obvious, you call the `page_title` method in your view template where you want to have an `h1` element:

```
- page_title "New User"
= error_messages_for :user
= form_for(:user, :url => users_path) do |f|
  ...
```

11.22.2 Encapsulating View Logic: The **photo_for** Helper

Here's another relatively simple helper. This time, instead of simply outputting data, we are encapsulating some view logic that decides whether to display a user's profile photo or a placeholder image. It's logic that you would otherwise have to repeat over and over again throughout your application.

The dependency (or contract) for this particular helper is that the user object being passed in has a `profile_photo` associated to it, which is an attachment model based on Rick Olson's old `attachment_fu` Rails plugin.[28] The code in Listing 11.8 should be easy enough to understand without delving into the details of `attachment_fu`. Since this is a code example, I broke out the logic for setting `src` into an `if`/`else` structure; otherwise, this would be a perfect place to use Ruby's ternary operator.

---

28. Nowadays most Rails developers use Paperclip (`https://github.com/thoughtbot/paperclip`) or CarrierWave (`https://github.com/jnicklas/carrierwave`) to model file attachments. Both are solid, so pick the one that matches your own style preference.

Listing 11.8 The `photo_for` helper encapsulating common view logic

```
def photo_for(user, size=:thumb)
  if user.profile_photo
    src = user.profile_photo.public_filename(size)
  else
    src = 'user_placeholder.png'
  end
  link_to(image_tag(src), user_path(user))
end
```

Tim says . . .

Luckily, the latest generation of attachment plugins such as Paperclip and CarrierWave use a NullObject pattern to alleviate the need for you to do this sort of thing.

11.22.3 Smart View: The **breadcrumbs** Helper

Lots of web applications feature user-interface concepts called breadcrumbs. They are made by creating a list of links, positioned near the top of the page, displaying how far the user has navigated into a hierarchically organized application. I think it makes sense to extract `breadcrumb` logic into its own helper method instead of leaving it in a layout template.

The trick to our example implementation (shown in Listing 11.9) is to use the presence of helper methods exposed by the controller, on a convention specific to your application, to determine whether to add elements to an array of breadcrumb links.

Listing 11.9 breadcrumbs Helper Method for a Corporate Directory Application

```
1 def breadcrumbs
2   return if controller.controller_name == 'home'

3   html = [link_to('Home', root_path)]

4   # first level
5   html << link_to(company.name, company) if respond_to? :company

6   # second level
7   html << link_to(department.name, department) if respond_to?
:department

8   # third and final level
9   html << link_to(employee.name, employee) if respond_to? :employee
```

```
10 html.join(' &gt; ').html_safe
11 end
```

Here's the line-by-line explanation of the code, noting where certain application-design assumptions are made:

On line 2, we abort execution if we're in the context of the application's `homepage` controller, since its pages don't ever need breadcrumbs. A simple return with no value implicitly returns `nil`, which is fine for our purposes. Nothing will be output to the layout template.

On line 3 we are starting to build an array of HTML links, held in the `html` local variable, which will ultimately hold the contents of our breadcrumb trail. The first link of the breadcrumb trail always points to the home page of the application, which of course will vary, but since it's always there we use it to initialize the array. In this example, it uses a named route called `root_path`.

After the `html` array is initialized, all we have to do is check for the presence of the methods returning objects that make up the hierarchy (lines 4 to 9). It is assumed that if a department is being displayed, its parent company will also be in scope. If an employee is being displayed, both department and company will be in scope as well. This is not just an arbitrary design choice. It is a common pattern in Rails applications that are modeled on REST principles and using nested resource routes.

Finally, on line 10, the array of HTML links is joined with the > character, to give the entire string the traditional breadcrumb appearance. The call to `html_safe` tells the rendering system that this is HTML code and we're cool with that—don't sanitize it!

11.23 Wrapping and Generalizing Partials

I don't think that partials (by themselves) lead to particularly elegant or concise template code. Whenever there's a shared partial template that gets used over and over again in my application, I will take the time to wrap it up in a custom helper method that conveys its purpose and formalizes its parameters. If appropriate, I might even generalize its implementation to make it more of a lightweight, reusable component. (Gasp!)

11.23.1 A `tiles` Helper

Let's trace the steps to writing a helper method that wraps what I consider to be a general-purpose partial. Listing 11.10 contains code for a partial for a piece of a user interface that is common to many applications, and generally referred to as a tile. It pairs a small thumbnail photo of something on the left side of the widget with a linked name and description on the right.

Tiles can also represent other models in your application, such as users and files. As I mentioned, tiles are a very common construct in modern user interfaces and operating systems. So let's take the cities tiles partial and transform it into something that can be used to display other types of data.

Listing 11.10 A tiles partial prior to wrapping and generalization

```
 1 %table.cities.tiles
 2  - cities.in_groups_of(columns) do |row|
 3    %tr
 4     - row.each do |city|
 5       %td[city]
 6         .left
 7           = image_tag(city.photo.url(:thumb))
 8         .right
 9           .title
10             = city.name
11           .description
12             = city.description
```

Note

I realize that it has become passé to use HTML tables, and I happen to agree that div-based layouts plus CSS are a lot more fun and flexible to work with. However, for the sake of simplicity in this example, and since the UI structure we're describing is tabular, I've decided to structure it using a table.

Explanation of the Tiles Partial Code

Since we're going to transform this city-specific partial into a generalized UI component, I want to make sure that the code we start with makes absolute sense to you first. Before proceeding, I'm going through the implementation line by line and explaining what everything in Listing 11.10 does.

Line 1 opens up the partial with a table element and gives it semantically significant CSS classes so that the table and its contents can be properly styled.

Line 2 leverages a useful Array extension method provided by ActiveSupport, called in_groups_of. It uses both of the local variables: cities and columns. Both will need to be passed into this partial using the :locals option of the render :partial method. The cities variable will hold the list of cities to be displayed, and columns is an integer representing how many city tiles each row should contain. A loop iterates over the number of rows that will be displayed in this table.

Line 3 begins a table row using the `tr` element.

Line 4 begins a loop over the tiles for each row to be displayed, yielding a `city` for each.

Line 5 opens a `td` element and uses Haml's *object reference* notation to autogenerate an `dom_id` attribute for the table cell in the style of `city_98`, `city_99`, and so on.

Line 6 opens a `div` element for the left side of the tile and has the CSS class name needed so that it can be styled properly.

Line 7 calls the `image_tag` helper to insert a thumbnail photo of the city.

Skipping along, lines 9–10 insert the content for the `.title` div element, in this case, the name and state of the city.

Line 12 directly invokes the `description` method.

Calling the Tiles Partial Code

In order to use this partial, we have to call `render :partial` with the two required parameters specified in the `:locals` hash:

```
render "cities/tiles", :cities => @user.cities, :columns => 3
```

I'm guessing that most experienced Rails developers have written some partial code similar to this and tried to figure out a way to include default values for some of the parameters. In this case, it would be really nice to not have to specify `:columns` all the time, since in most cases we want there to be three.

The problem is that since the parameters are passed via the `:locals` hash and become local variables, there isn't an easy way to insert a default value in the partial itself. If you left off the `:columns => n` part of your partial call, Rails would bomb with an exception about `columns` not being a local variable or method. It's not the same as an instance variable, which defaults to `nil` and can be used willy-nilly.

Experienced Rubyists probably know that you can use the `defined?` method to figure out whether a local variable is in scope or not, but the resulting code would be very ugly. The following code might be considered elegant, but it doesn't work![29]

```
columns = 3 unless defined? columns
```

29. If you want to know why it doesn't work, you'll have to buy the first book in this series: *The Ruby Way* ISBN: 0672328844

Helpers

Instead of teaching you how to jump through annoying Ruby idiom hoops, I'll show you how to tackle this challenge the Rails way, and that is where we can start discussing the helper wrapping techique.

Tim says...

Obie might not want to make you jump through Ruby idiom hoops, but I don't mind...

Write the Helper Method

First, I'll add a new helper method to the `CitiesHelper` module of my application, like in Listing 11.11. It's going to be fairly simple at first. In thinking about the name of the method, it occurs to me that I like the way that `tiled(cities)` will read instead of `tiles(cities)`, so I name it that way.

Listing 11.11 The CitiesHelper tiled method

```
module CitiesHelper
  def tiled(cities, columns=3)
    render "cities/tiles", :cities => cities, :columns => columns
  end
end
```

Right from the start, I can take care of that default `columns` parameter by giving the helper method parameter for columns a default value. That's just a normal feature of Ruby. Now instead of specifying the `render :partial` call in my view template, I can simply write = `tiled(cities)` which is considerably more elegant and terse. It also serves to decouple the implementation of the tiled city table from the view. If I need to change the way that the tiled table is rendered in the future, I just have to do it in one place: the helper method.

11.23.2 Generalizing Partials

Now that we've set the stage, the fun can begin. The first thing we'll do is move the helper method to the `ApplicationHelper` module so that it's available to all view templates. We'll also move the partial template file to `app/views/shared/_tiled_table.html.haml` to denote that it isn't associated with a particular kind of view and to more accurately convey its use. As a matter of good code style, I also do a sweep through the implementation and generalize the identifiers appropriately. The reference to `cities` on line 2 becomes `collection`. The block variable `city` on line 4 becomes `item`. Listing 11.12 has the new partial code.

Listing 11.12 Tiles partial code with revised naming

```
 1 %table.tiles
 2 - collection.in_groups_of(columns) do |row|
 3   %tr
 4     - row.each do |item|
 5       %td[item]
 6         .left
 7           = image_tag(item.photo.public_filename(:thumb))
 8         .right
 9           .title
10             = item.name
11           .description
12             = item.description
```

There's still the matter of a contract between this partial code and the objects that it is rendering. Namely, they must respond to the following messages: `photo`, `name`, and `description`. A survey of other models in my application reveals that I need more flexibility. Some things have names, but others have titles. Sometimes I want the description to appear under the name of the object represented, but other times I want to be able to insert additional data about the object plus some links.

Lambda: The Ultimate Flexibility

Ruby allows you to store references to anonymous methods (also known as *procs* or *lambdas*) and call them at will whenever you want.[30] Knowing this capability is there, what becomes possible? For starters, we can use lambdas to pass in blocks of code that will fill in parts of our partial dynamically.

For example, the current code for showing the thumbnail is a big problem. Since the code varies greatly depending on the object being handled, I want to be able to pass in instructions for how to get a thumbnail image without having to resort to big `if`/`else` statements or putting view logic in my model classes. Please take a moment to understand the problem I'm describing, and then take a look at how we solve it in Listing 11.13. Hint: The `thumbnail`, `link`, `title`, and `description` variables hold lambdas!

Helpers

---

30. If you're familiar with Ruby already, you might know that Proc.new is an alternate way to create anonymous blocks of code. I prefer lambda, at least in Ruby 1.9, because of subtle behavior differences. Lambda blocks check the arity of the argument list passed to them when call is invoked, and explicitly calling return in a lambda block works correctly.

Listing 11.13 Tiles partial code refactored to use lambdas

```
1  .left
2  = link_to thumbnail.call(item), link.call(item)
3  .right
4  .title
5  = link_to title.call(item), link.call(item)
6  .description
7  = description.call(item)
```

Notice that in Listing 11.13, the contents of the left and right `div` elements come from variables containing lambdas. On line 2 we make a call to `link_to` and both of its arguments are dynamic. A similar construct on line 5 takes care of generating the title link. In both cases, the first lambda should return the output of a call to `image_tag` and the second should return a URL. In all of these lambda usages, the `item` currently being rendered is passed to the lambdas as a block variable.

Wilson says...

Things like `link.call(item)` could potentially look even sassier as `link[item]`, except that you'll shoot your eye out doing it. (`Proc#[]` is an alias for `Proc#call`.)

The New Tiled Helper Method

If you now direct your attention to Listing 11.14, you'll notice that the `tiled` method is changed considerably. In order to keep my positional argument list down to a manageable size, I've switched over to taking a hash of options as the last parameter to the `tiled` method. This approach is useful and it mimics the way that almost all helper methods take options in Rails.

Default values are provided for all parameters, and they are all passed along to the partial via the `:locals` hash given to `render`.

Listing 11.14 The tiled collection helper method with lambda parameters

```
1  module ApplicationHelper

2  def tiled(collection, opts={})

3  opts[:columns] ||= 3

4  opts[:thumbnail] ||= lambda do |item|
5  image_tag(item.photo.url(:thumb))
6  end
```

```
 7   opts[:title]       ||= lambda {|item| item.to_s }

 8   opts[:description] ||= lambda {|item| item.description }

 9   opts[:link]        ||= lambda {|item| item }
10       render "shared/tiled_table",
11               :collection                 => collection,
12               :columns                  => opts[:columns],
13               :link              => opts[:link],
14               :thumbnail                => opts[:thumbnail],
15               :title               => opts[:title],
16               :description => opts[:description]
17   end
18  end
```

Finally, to wrap up this example, here's a snippet showing how to invoke our new `tiled` helper method from a template, overriding the default behavior for links:

```
tiled(cities, :link => lambda {|city| showcase_city_path(city)})
```

The `showcase_city_path` method is available to the lambda block, since it is a closure, meaning that it inherits the execution context in which it is created.

11.24 Conclusion

This very long chapter served as a thorough reference of helper methods, both those provided by Rails and ideas for ones that you will write yourself. Effective use of helper methods leads to more elegant and maintainable view templates. At this point, you should also have a good overview about how I18n support in Ruby on Rails works and are ready to start translating your project.

Before we fully conclude our coverage of Action Pack, (the name used to refer to Action Controller and Action View together), we'll jump into the world of Ajax and JavaScript. Arguably, one of the main reasons for Rails's continued popularity is its support for those two crucial technologies of Web 2.0.

This chapter is published under the Creative Commons Attribution-ShareAlike 3.0 license, `http://creativecommons.org/licenses/b-sa/3.0`

Helpers

CHAPTER 12

Ajax on Rails

Ajax isn't a technology. It's really several technologies, each flourishing in its own right, coming together in powerful new ways

—Jesse J. Garrett, who coined the term

Ajax is an acronym that stands for Asynchronous JavaScript and XML. It encompasses techniques that allow us to liven up web pages with behaviors that happen outside the normal HTTP request life cycle (without a page refresh).

Some example use-cases for Ajax techniques are

- "Type ahead" input suggestion, as in Google search
- Sending form data asynchronously
- Seamless navigation of web-presented maps, as in Google Maps
- Dynamically updated lists and tables, as in Gmail and other web-based email services
- Web-based spreadsheets
- Forms that allow in-place editing
- Live preview of formatted writing alongside a text input

Ajax is made possible by the `XMLHttpRequestObject` (or XHR for short), an API that is available in all modern browsers. It allows JavaScript code on the browser to exchange data with the server and use it to change the user interface of your application on the fly, without needing a page refresh. Working directly with XHR in a cross-browser-compatible way is difficult, to say the least, which is why the open-source ecosystem flourishes with Ajax JavaScript libraries.

Ajax

Incidentally, Ajax, especially in Rails, has very little to do with XML, despite its presence there at the end of the acronym. The payload of those asynchronous requests going back and forth to the server can be anything. Often it's just a matter of form parameters posted to the server, and receiving snippets of HTML back, for dynamic insertion into the page's DOM. Many times it even makes sense for the server to send back data encoded in a simple kind of JavaScript called JavaScript Object Notation (JSON).

It's outside the scope of this book to teach you the fundamentals of JavaScript and/or Ajax. It's also outside of our scope to dive into the design considerations of adding Ajax to your application, elements of which are lengthy and occasionally controversial. Proper coverage of those subjects would require a whole book and there are many such books to choose from in the marketplace. Therefore, the rest of the chapter will assume that you understand what Ajax is and why you would use it in your applications and that you have a basic understanding of JavaScript programming.

12.0.1   Changes in Rails 3

Since the First Edition of *The Rails Way*, the landscape has changed. jQuery (located at `http://jquery.com`) is the dominant JavaScript framework, due in part to its clean, unobtrusive API and its use of CSS selectors to obtain elements in the page. Prototype and Scriptaculous have their adherents but for day-to-day Ajax and Rails work, jQuery is the workhorse.

Josh says . . .

> Experience has shown us that if you want JavaScript code in your application, learn JavaScript and write it!

There is a declarative mechanism (where you write *what* you want, rather than *how* to do it) in Rails that ultimately generates JavaScript, the Unobtrusive JavaScript (UJS) API.

In Rails 3, the choice of JavaScript library to use in conjunction with Rails' Ajax helpers is yours, and you can choose either Prototype or jQuery (or any other library that has driver support for Rails).

12.0.2   Firebug

Firebug[1] is an extremely powerful extension for Firefox and a must-have tool for doing Ajax work. It lets you inspect Ajax requests and probe the DOM of the page extensively,

---

1. The first step to getting the Firebug plugin for Firefox is to visit `http://www.getfirebug.com`

even letting you change elements and CSS styles on the fly and see the results on your browser screen. It also has a very powerful JavaScript debugger that you can use to set watch expressions and breakpoints.

Firebug also has an interactive console, which allows you to experiment with JavaScript in the browser just as you would use `irb` in Ruby. In some cases, the code samples in this chapter are copied from the Firebug console, which has a >>> prompt.

As I've jokingly told many of my Ruby on Rails students when covering Ajax on Rails: "Even if you don't listen to anything else I say, use Firebug! The productivity gains you experience will make up for my fee very quickly."

If you're developing using Safari or Chrome, those fine browser have built-in development tools that mimic Firebug, but I still think the original is the best.

12.1   Unobtrusive JavaScript

The new Unobtrusive JavaScript (UJS) features in Rails provide a library-independent API for specifying Ajax actions. The Rails team has provided UJS implementations for both jQuery and Prototype, available under `http://github.com/rails/jquery-ujs` and `http://github.com/rails/prototype-ujs`, respectively.

Xavier says . . .

Prototype is the default JavaScript library used in Rails 3 and newly-generated applications use it to drive their Ajax UJS features. You can prevent the application generator from doing that by passing it `-J` or `--skip-prototype`. In that case `rails.js` is not generated, only `application.js`.

To use jQuery, just download the jQuery `rails.js` file into `public/javascripts`. Then add the following code to your layout's head section:

```
= javascript_include_tag
"http://ajax.googleapis.com/ajax/libs/jquery/1.4.1/jquery.min.js"
= javascript_include_tag 'rails'
```

Note that for our example we've hotlinked directly to the jQuery library provided free-of-charge by Google.

12.1.1   UJS Usage

One of the most dramatic changes caused by the move to UJS is the way that delete links are generated.

```
= link_to 'Delete', user_path(1), :method => :delete, :confirm => "Sure?"
```

Prior to Rails 3 the resulting HTML would look something like

```
<a href="/users/1" onclick="if (confirm('Sure?')) { var f =
document.createElement('form'); f.style.display = 'none';
this.parentNode.appendChild(f); f.method = 'POST'; f.action =
this.href;var m = document.createElement('input'); m.setAttribute('type',
'hidden'); m.setAttribute('name', '_method'); m.setAttribute('value',
'delete'); f.appendChild(m);f.submit(); };return false;">Delete</a>
```

Now, taking advantage of UJS techniques, it will look like

```
<a rel="nofollow" data-method="delete" data-confirm="Sure?" class="delete"
 href="/user/1">Delete</a>
```

What a difference! [2] Remote forms and link helpers also change due to UJS. Before Rails
3 you would write

```
remote_form_for(@user)
```

but now that changes to

```
form_for(@user, :remote => true)
```

Ajax links are now written as

```
link_to "More", more_user_details_path(@user), :remote => true
```

The above examples will append `data-remote="true"` attributes to the HTML output.

Also required for Rails UJS support is the `csrf_meta_tag`, which must be placed
in the head of the document and adds the `csrf-param` and `csrf-token` meta tags used
in dynamic form generation.

```
%head
  = csrf_meta_tag
```

12.2 Writing JavaScript in Ruby with RJS

Rails includes a feature called RJS, which generates blocks of JavaScript code based on
Ruby code. It allows you to manipulate a view from server side code and is used in
conjunction with Ajax requests.

The example code in this section adds instant searching of US telephone area codes
to the index view of an area codes resource. For your reference, the `AreaCode` model
has `number` and `location` attributes and looks like

---

2. Do be aware that Rails UJS requires JavaScript and HTML5 support in the browser.

```
class AreaCode < ActiveRecord::Base
  def to_s
    "#{number} #{location}"
  end
end
```

The `observe_field` method used in the following example is no longer a native part of Rails 3 and is not covered in this book. I don't think it's too difficult to figure out what it does. To use it you must install the official Prototype Legacy Helper plugin like this:

```
rails plugin install git://github.com/rails/prototype_legacy_helper
```

Our view features a simple table of area codes and a text field that is observed for changes.

```
%table
  - @area_codes.each do |area_code|
    %tr
      %td= link_to area_code.number, area_code
      %td= area_code.location
%hr
Area Code:
= text_field_tag 'number'
#area_code_results_message
%hr
#area_code_results

= observe_field 'number', :url => search_area_codes_path, :frequency =>
0.25, :with => 'number'
```

For that template to work, we'll need to add a collection route for searching area codes in `routes.rb`.

```
resources :area_codes do
  collection do
    post :search
  end
end
```

Now we'll use RJS in our `AreaCodesController` to update the page automatically as a result of searching.

```
def search
  respond_to do |format|
    format.js do
      number = params[:number]
      area_codes = AreaCode.where("number like ?", "%#{number}%")

      render(:update) do |page|
        page.replace_html 'area_code_results_message',
```

```
                         "Found #{area_codes.size} Results"
        if area_codes.empty?
          page.replace_html 'area_code_results', ''
        else
          page.replace_html 'area_code_results',
                            area_codes.map(&:to_s).join('<br/>')
        end
      end
    end
  end
end
```

The `replace_html` method of RJS replaces the inner HTML of the element identified in the first argument with the value of the second argument. We can use FireBug to see the JavaScript sent back to the browser in the response body.[3]

```
Element.update("area_code_results_message", "Found 41 Results");
Element.update("area_code_results", "301 - MD, W Maryland: Silver
Spring, Frederick, Camp Springs, Prince George's County (see
 240)\074br/\076302 - DE, Delaware\074br/\076303 - CO, Central
Colorado:Denver (see 970, also 720 overlay)\074br/\076...
```

The JavaScript generated uses the Prototype framework.

12.2.1 RJS Templates

It's a poor practice to combine controller and view logic in one place, which is exactly what we did when we used `render(:update)`. We can fix that by moving the RJS code out of the controller and into its own template named `search.js.rjs` with the following contents

```
if @area_codes.empty?
  page.replace_html 'area_code_results', ''
else
  page.replace_html 'area_code_results_message',
                    "Found #{@area_codes.size} Results"
  page.replace_html 'area_code_results',
                    @area_codes.map(&:to_s).join('<br/>')
end
```

---

3. Error handling code removed for clarity.

The controller action shrinks to just the logic that belongs there.

```
class AreaCodesController < ApplicationController
  def search
    @area_codes = AreaCode.where('number like ?', "#{params[:number]}%")
  end
end
```

The `respond_to` construct is gone, and we instead rely on Rails' default behavior of picking a view that matches the request. In other words, Rails will choose to serve JavaScript view to Ajax requests automatically.

Rails comes with a comprehensive selection of RJS methods described in the following sections.

12.2.2 `<<(javascript)`

This method will write raw JavaScript to the page. This is useful if we have a custom method in `application.js` that we want to call. For example:

```
// application.js
function my_method() {
  alert('my_method called');
}

// my_controllers.rb
class MyControllers < Application
  def show
    ...
    render :update do |page|
      page << 'my_method();'
    end
    ...
  end
end
```

12.2.3 `[](id)`

This returns a reference of the element identified by id in the DOM. Further calls can then be made on this element reference like `hide`, `show`, and so on. This behaves just like the `$(id)` construct in jQuery.

```
render :update do |page|
  page['my_div'].hide # same thing as $('my_div').hide
end
```

12.2.4 `alert(message)`

This will display a JavaScript alert with the given message:

```
render :update do |page|
  page.alert('Something is not right here')
end
```

12.2.5 `call(function, *arguments, & block)`

Calls the JavaScript function with the given arguments if any. If a block is given, a new JavaScript generator will be created and all generated JavaScript will be wrapped in a `function() { ... }` and passed as the class final argument.

```
// application.js
function my_method() {
  alert('my_method called');
}

// my_controllers.rb
class MyControllers < Application
  def show
    ...
    render :update do |page|
      page.call('my_method')
    end
    ...
  end
end
```

12.2.6 `delay(seconds = 1) ...`

This will execute the given block after the given number of seconds have passed.

```
render :update do |page|
  page.delay(5) {
    page.visual_effect :highlight, 'results_div', :duration => 1.5
  }
end
```

12.2.7 `draggable(id, options = {})`

This creates a draggable element.

12.2.8 `drop_receiving(id, options = {})`

Specifies an element that can act as a drop receiver for other elements that have been made draggable.

12.2.9 `hide(*ids)`

Hides the elements identified by the given DOM ids.

```
render :update do |page|
  page.hide('options_div')
  page.hide('options_form', 'options_message')
end
```

12.2.10 `insert_html(position, id, *options_for_render)`

Inserts HTML at the given position relative to the given element identified by the DOM id. Position can be any one of the values shown in Table 12.1.

The `options_for_render` can be either a string of HTML to insert or options passed to `render`.

```
render :update do |page|
  page.insert_html :after, 'my_div', '<br/><p>My Text</p>'
  page.insert_html :before, 'my_other_div', :partial => 'list_items'
end
```

12.2.11 `literal(code)`

This is used to pass a literal JavaScript expression as an argument to another JavaScript generator method. The returned object will have a `to_json` method that will evaluate to code.

Table 12.1 Options for `insert_html` Method

Parameter	Description
`:top`	HTML is inserted inside the element, before the element's existing content.
`:bottom`	HTML is inserted inside the element, after the element's existing content.
`:before`	HTML is inserted immediately preceding the element.
`:after`	HTML is inserted immediately following the element.

Ajax

12.2.12 `redirect_to(location)`

Causes the browser to redirect to the given location.

```
render :update do |page|
  page.redirect_to 'http://www.berlin.de'
end
```

12.2.13 `remove(*ids)`

Removes the given elements identified by the DOM ids.

12.2.14 `replace(id, *options_for_render)`

Replaces the entire element (not just its internal HTML) identified by the DOM id with either a string or render options set in `options_for_render`.

```
render :update do |page|
  page.replace 'my_div', '<div>Message</div>'
  page.replace 'my_div', :partial => 'entry'
end
```

12.2.15 `replace_html(id, *options_for_render)`

Replaces the internal HTML identified by the DOM id with either a string or render options set in `options_for_render`.

12.2.16 `select(pattern)`

Obtains a collection of element references by finding it through a CSS pattern. You can use standard jQuery enumerations with the returned collection.

```
render :update do |page|
  page.select('div.header p').first
  page.select('div.body ul li').each do |value|
    value.hide
  end
end
```

12.2.17 `show(*ids)`

Show the given hidden elements identified by the DOM ids.

12.2.18 `sortable(id, options = {})`

Creates a sortable list of elements. See `http://webtempest.com/sortable-list-in-ruby-on-rails-3-almost-unobtrusive-jquery` for a quick tutorial.

12.2.19 `toggle(*ids)`

Toggles the visibility of the elements identified by the ids. In other words, visible elements will become hidden and hidden elements will become visible.

12.2.20 `visual_effect(name, id = nil, options = {})`

This will start the named effect on the element identified by the DOM id. From RJS you can call `appear`, `fade`, `slidedown`, `slideup`, `blinddown`, and `blindup`. Each of these effects results in an element showing or hiding on the page. You can also call `toggle_appear`, `toggle_slide`, and `toggle_blind` to toggle the effect. For a complete list of visual effects, not just the displaying of elements, and options they take, consult the Scriptaculous documentation. To fade an element, we would do the following:

```
render :update do |page|
  page.visual_effect :fade, 'my_div'
end
```

12.3 Ajax and JSON

JavaScript Object Notation (JSON) is a simple way to encode JavaScript objects. It is also considered a language-independent data format, making it a compact, human-readable, and versatile interchange format. This is the preferred method of interchanging data between the web application code running on the server and any code running in the browser, particularly for Ajax requests.

Rails provides a `to_json` on every object, using a sensible mechanism to do so for every type. For example, `BigDecimal` objects, although numbers, are serialized to JSON as strings, since that is the best way to represent a `BigDecimal` in a language-independent manner. You can always customize the `to_json` method of any of your classes if you wish, but it should not be necessary to do so.

12.3.1 Ajax `link_to`

To illustrate an Ajax request, let's enable our Client controller to respond to JSON and provide a method to supply the number of draft timesheets outstanding for each client:

```
respond_to :html, :xml, :json

...
# GET /clients/counts
# GET /clients/counts.xml
```

Ajax

```
# GET /clients/counts.json
def counts
  respond_with(Client.all_with_counts, :root => 'clients') do |format|
    format.html { redirect_to clients_path }
  end
end
```

This uses the Client class method `all_with_counts` which returns an array of hashmaps:

```
def self.all_with_counts
  all.map do |client|
    { :id => client.id, :draft_timesheets_count =>
client.timesheets.draft.count }
  end
end
```

When GET /clients/counts is requested and the content type is JSON the response is:

```
[{"draft_timesheets_count":0, "id":20},
 {"draft_timesheets_count":1, "id":21}]
```

You will note in the code example that HTML and XML are also supported content types for the response, so it's up to the client to decide which format works best for them. We'll look at formats other than JSON in the next few sections.

In this case, our Client index view requests a response in JSON format:

```
- content_for :head do
  = javascript_include_tag 'clients.js'
...
%table#clients_list
...
  - for client in @clients
    %tr[client]
      %td= client.name
      %td= client.code
      %td.draft_timesheets_count= client.timesheets.draft.count
...
= link_to 'Update draft timesheets count', counts_clients_path, :remote =>
  true, 'data-type' => :json, :id => 'update_draft_timesheets'
```

Note

UJS probably should take the option `:data_type` and convert it to the HTML 5 attribute `data-type` when using jQuery, or explicitly specify the format in the URL when using Prototype. We'll be keeping a lookout for that behavior in future versions of Rails.

To complete the asynchronous part of this Ajax-enabled feature, we also need to add an event-handler to the UJS `ajax:success` event, fired when the Ajax call on the `update_draft_timesheets` element completes successfully. Here, jQuery is used to bind a JavaScript function to the event once the page has loaded. This is defined in `clients.js`:

```
$(function() {
  $("#update_draft_timesheets").bind("ajax:success", function(event,
data) {
    $(data).each(function() {
      var td = $('#client_' + this.id + ' .draft_timesheets_count')
      td.html(this.draft_timesheets_count);
    });
  });
});
```

In each row of the `clients` listing, the respective `td` with a class of `draft_timesheets_count` is updated in place with the values from the JSON response. There is no need for a page refresh and user experience is improved.

As an architectural constraint, this does require this snippet of JavaScript to have intimate knowledge of the target page's HTML structure and how to transform the JSON into changes on the DOM. This is a major reason why JSON is the best format for decoupling the presentation layer of your application or, more importantly, when the page is requesting JSON from another application altogether.

Sometimes, however, it may be desirable for the server to respond with a snippet of HTML which is used to replace a region of the target page.

12.4 Ajax and HTML

The Ruby classes in your Rails application will normally contain the bulk of that application's logic and state. Ajax-heavy applications can leverage that logic and state by transferring HTML, rather than JSON, to manipulate the DOM.

A web application may respond to an Ajax request with an HTML fragment, used to insert or replace an existing part of the page. This is most usually done when the transformation relies on complex business rules and perhaps complex state that would be inefficient to duplicate in JavaScript.

Let's say your application needs to display clients in some sort of priority order, and that order is highly variable and dependent on the current context. There could be a swag of rules dictating what order they are shown in. Perhaps it's that whenever a client has more than a number of draft timesheets, we want to flag that in the page.

Ajax

```
%td.draft_timesheets_count
  - if client.timesheets.draft.count > 3
    %span.drafts-overlimit WARNING!
    %br
  = client.timesheets.draft.count
```

Along with that, let's say on a Friday or Saturday we need to group clients by their *hottest spending day* so we can make ourselves an action plan for the beginning of the following week.

These are just two business rules that, when combined, are a bit of a handful to implement both in Rails and in JavaScript. Applications tend to have many more than just two rules combining and it quickly becomes prohibitive to implement those rules in JavaScript to transform JSON into DOM changes. That's particularly true when the page making the Ajax call is external and not one we've written.

We can opt to transfer HTML in the Ajax call and using JavaScript to update a section of the page with that HTML. Under one context, the snippet of HTML returned could look like

```
<tr id="client_22" class="client"></tr>
<tr>
  <td></td><td>Aardworkers</td><td>AARD</td><td>$4321</td>
  <td class="draft_timesheets_count">0</td>
</tr>
<tr id="client_23" class="client"></tr>
<tr>
  <td></td><td>Zorganization</td><td>ZORG</td><td>$9999</td>
  <td class="draft_timesheets_count">1</td>
</tr>
```

Whereas, in another context, it could look like

```
<tr>
  <td>Friday</td>
</tr>
<tr>
  <td>Saturday</td>
</tr>
<tr id="client_24" class="client"></tr>
<tr>
  <td></td><td>Hashrocket</td><td>HR</td><td>$12000</td>
  <td class="draft_timesheets_count">
    <span class="drafts-overlimit">WARNING!</span>
    5
  </td>
</tr>
<tr id="client_22" class="client"></tr>
<tr>
```

```
<td></td><td>Aardworkers</td><td>AARD</td><td>$4321</td>
<td class="draft_timesheets_count">0</td>
</tr>
```

The JavaScript event handler for the Ajax response then just needs to update the innerHTML of a particular HTML element to alter the page, without having to know anything about the business rules used to determine what the resulting HTML should be.

12.5 Ajax and JavaScript

The primary reason you want to work with a JavaScript response to an Ajax request is when it is for JSONP (JSON with Padding). JSONP *pads*, or wraps, JSON data in a call to a JavaScript function that exists on your page. You specify the name of that function in a callback query string parameter. Note that some public APIs may use something other than callback, but it has become the convention in Rails 3 and most JSONP applications.

Xavier says...

Although the Wikipedia entry[4] for Ajax does not specifically mention JSONP and the request is not XHR by Rails' definition, we'd like to think of it as Ajax anyways - it is after all asynchronous JavaScript.

JSONP is one technique for obtaining cross-domain data, avoiding the browser's *same-origin policy*. This introduces a pile of safety and security issues that are beyond the scope of this book. However, if you need to use JSONP the Rails 3 stack provides an easy way to handle JSONP requests (with Rack::JSONP) or make JSONP requests (with UJS and jQuery).

To respond to JSONP requests, activate the Rack JSONP module from the rack-contrib RubyGem in your environment.rb file:

```
class Application < Rails::Application
  require 'rack/contrib'
  config.middleware.use 'Rack::JSONP'
  ...
```

then, just use UJS to tell jQuery it's a JSONP call by altering the data-type to jsonp:

```
= link_to 'Update draft timesheets count', counts_clients_path, :remote =>
  true, 'data-type' => :jsonp, :id => 'update_draft_timesheets'
```

---

4. http://en.wikipedia.org/wiki/Ajax_(programming)

jQuery automatically adds the `?callback=` and random function name to the query string of the request URI. In addition to this it also adds the necessary `script` tags to our document to bypass the same-origin policy. Our existing event handler is bound to `ajax:success` so it is called with the data just like before. Now, though, it can receive that data from another web application.

jQuery also makes the request as if it is for JavaScript, so our Rails controller needs to `respond_to` `:js`. Unfortunately, the Rails 3 automatic rendering for JavaScript responses isn't there yet so we add a special handler for JavaScript in our controller:

```
respond_to :html, :xml, :json, :js
...

def counts
  respond_with(Client.all_with_counts, :root => 'clients') do |format|
    format.html { redirect_to clients_path }
    format.js { render :json => Client.all_with_counts.to_json, :root =>
'clients' }
  end
end
```

We still convert our data to JSON. The `Rack::JSONP` module then *pads* that JSON data in a call to the JavaScript function specified in the query string of the request. The response looks like this:

```
jsonp123456789([{"id":1,"draft_timesheets_count":0},
{"id":2,"draft_timesheets_count":1}])
```

When the Ajax response is complete, your Ajax event handler is called and the JSON data is passed to it as a parameter.

12.6 Conclusion

The success of Rails is often correlated to the rise of Web 2.0, and one of the factors linking Rails into that phenomenon is its baked-in support for Ajax. There are a ton of books about Ajax programming, including some that are specific to using Ajax and Rails together. It's a big subject, but an important enough part of Rails that we felt the need to include a quick introduction to it as part of this book.

CHAPTER 13

Session Management

I'd hate to wake up some morning and find out that you weren't you!

—Dr. Miles J. Binnell (Kevin McCarthy) in *Invasion of the Body Snatchers* (Allied Artists, 1956)

HTTP is a stateless protocol. Without the concept of a session (a concept not unique to Rails), there'd be no way to know that any HTTP request was related to another one. You'd never have an easy way to know who is accessing your application! Identification of your user (and presumably, authentication) would have to happen on each and every request handled by the server.[1]

Luckily, whenever a new user accesses our Rails application, a new session is automatically created. Using the session, we can maintain just enough server-side state to make our lives as web programmers significantly easier.

We use the word *session* to refer both to the time that a user is actively using the application, as well as to refer to the persistent hash data structure that we keep around for that user. That data structure takes the form of a hash, identified by a unique session id, a 32-character string of random hex numbers. When a new session is created, Rails automatically sends a cookie to the browser containing the session id, for future reference. From that point on, each request from the browser sends the session id back to the server, and continuity can be maintained.

The Rails way to design web applications dictates minimal use of the session for storage of stateful data. In keeping with the *share nothing* philosophy embraced by Rails, the proper place for persistent storage of data is the database, period. The bottom line is that the longer you keep objects in the user's session hash, the more problems you create

---

1. If you are really new to web programming and want a very thorough explanation of how web-based session management works, you may want to read the information available at `http://www.technicalinfo.net/papers/WebBasedSessionManagement.html`.

425

for yourself in trying to keep those objects from becoming stale (in other words, out of date in relation to the database).

This chapter deals with matters related to session use, starting with the question of what to put in the session.

13.1 What to Store in the Session

Deciding what to store in the session hash does not have to be super-difficult, if you simply commit to storing as little as possible in it. Generally speaking, integers (for key values) and short string messages are okay. Objects are not.

13.1.1 The Current User

There is one important integer that most Rails applications store in the session, and that is the `current_user_id`. Not the current user object, but its id. Even if you roll your own login and authentication code (which you shouldn't do), don't store the entire `User` (or `Person`) in the session while the user is logged in. (See Chapter 14, Login and Authentication, for more information about keeping track of the current user.) The authentication system should take care of loading the user instance from the database prior to each request and making it available in a consistent fashion, via a method on your `ApplicationController`. In particular, following this advice will ensure that you are able to disable access to given users without having to wait for their session to expire.

13.1.2 Session Use Guidelines

Here are some more general guidelines on storing objects in the session:

- They must be objects, serializable by Ruby's Marshal API, which excludes certain types of objects such as a database connection and other types of I/O objects.

- Large object graphs may exceed the size available for session storage. Whether this limitation is in effect for you depends on the session store chosen and is covered later in the chapter.

- Critical data should not be stored in the session, since it can be suddenly lost by the user ending his session (by closing the browser or clearing his or her cookies).

- Objects with attributes that change often should not be kept in the session.

- Modifying the structure of an object and keeping old versions of it stored in the session is a recipe for disaster. Deployment scripts should clear old sessions to prevent this sort of problem from occurring, but with certain types of session stores, such as the cookie store, this problem is hard to mitigate. The simple answer (again) is to just not keep anything except for the occasional id in the session.

13.2 Session Options

You used to be able to turn off the session, but as of Rails 3, applications that don't need sessions don't have to worry about them. Sessions are lazy-loaded, which means unless you access the session in a controller action, there is no performance implication.

13.3 Storage Mechanisms

The mechanism via which sessions are persisted can vary. Rails' default behavior is to store session data as cookies in the browser, which is fine for almost all applications. If you need to exceed the 4KB cookies storage limit inherent in using cookies, then you can opt for an alternative session store. But of course, you shouldn't be exceeding that limit, because you shouldn't be keeping much other than an id or two in the session.

There are also some potential security concerns around session-replay attacks involving cookies, which might push you in the direction of using an alternative session storage.

13.3.1 Active Record Session Store

The tools to switch over to storing sessions in the database are already built into Rails. The first step is to create the necessary migration, using a rake task provided for that very purpose, and run the migration to create the new table:

```
$ rake db:sessions:create
      invoke      active_record
      create      db/migrate/20100114005900_add_sessions_table.rb
$ rake db:migrate
==  AddSessionsTable: migrating
==========================================
-- create_table(:sessions)
   -> 0.0823s
-- add_index(:sessions, :session_id)
   -> 0.0301s
-- add_index(:sessions, :updated_at)
   -> 0.0280s
==  AddSessionsTable: migrated (0.1433s)
======================================
```

Session

The second (and final) step is to tell Rails to use the new sessions table to store sessions, via a setting in `config/initializers/session_store.rb`:

```
MyApplication::Application.config.session_store :active_record_store
```

That's all there is to it.

13.3.2 Memcache Session Storage

If you are running an extremely high-traffic Rails deployment, you're probably already leveraging `memcache` in some way or another. `memcache` is a remote-process memory cache that helps power some of the most highly trafficked sites on the Internet.

The `memcache` session storage option lets you use your `memcache` server as the repository for session data, and it is blazing fast. It's also nice because it has built-in expiration, meaning you don't have to expire old sessions yourself.

To use memcache, the first step is to modify Rails' default session settings in `config/initializers/session_store.rb`. At minimum, replace the contents of the file with the following:

```
MyApplication::Application.config.session_store :mem_cache_store
```

Note

The Ruby-based memcache client gem, located at `http://rubygems.org/gems/memcache-client` is supposed to ship with Rails. If your server startup crashes and complains that it can't find the memcache file to load, manually add `memcache_client` to your Gemfile. If you're feeling particularly geeky, you may try installing one of the memcache clients with native bindings, such as `http://github.com/ninjudd/memcache` or `http://blog.evanweaver.com/files/doc/fauna/memcached`.

The `session_store` method support options as well.

```
memcache_options = {
  :c_threshold => 10_000,
  :compression => true,
  :debug => false,
  :namespace => ":app-#{Rails.env}",
  :readonly => false,
  :urlencode => false
}

MyApplication::Application.config.session_store :mem_cache_store,
memcache_options
```

13.3.3 The Controversial CookieStore

In February 2007, core-team member Jeremy Kemper made a pretty bold commit to Rails. He changed the default session storage mechanism from the venerable `PStore` to a new system based on a `CookieStore`. His commit message summed it up well:

> Introduce a cookie-based session store as the Rails default. Sessions typically contain at most a user_id and flash message; both fit within the 4K cookie size limit. A secure hash is included with the cookie to ensure data integrity (a user cannot alter his user_id without knowing the secret key included in the hash). If you have more than 4K of session data or don't want your data to be visible to the user, pick another session store. Cookie-based sessions are dramatically faster than the alternatives.

I describe the `CookieStore` as controversial because of the fallout over making it the default session storage mechanism. For one, it imposes a very strict size limit, only 4K. A significant size constraint like that is fine if you're following the Rails way, and not storing anything other than integers and short strings in the session. If you're bucking the guidelines, well, you might have an issue with it.

OpenSSL Digests

Lots of people have complained about the inherent insecurity of storing session information, including the current user information on the user's browser. However, there are security measures in place that make the cookie store hard to crack open and exploit. For instance, you'd need to be able to compromise SHA1, which is somewhat difficult to do.

But let's say you want different security,[2] you can easily override the existing hashing code by setting it to any other digest provided by OpenSSL:

```
ActionController::Base.session_options[:digest] = SHA512
```

Replay Attacks

Another problem with cookie-based session storage is its vulnerability to replay attacks, which generated an enormous message thread on the rails-core mailing list. S. Robert

---

2. My fellow cabooser Courtenay wrote a great blog post about cookie session storage at `http://blog.caboo.se/articles/2007/2/21/new-controversial-default-rails-session-storage-cookies`.

James kicked off the thread[3] by describing a replay attack:

- Example:

    1. User receives credits, stored in his session.

    2. User buys something.

    3. User gets his new, lower credits stored in his session.

    4. Evil hacker takes his saved cookie from step 1 and pastes it back in his browser's cookie jar. Now he's gotten his credits back.

- This is normally solved using something called *nonce*. Each signing includes a once-only code, and the signer keeps track of all of the codes, and rejects any message with the code repeated. But that's very hard to do here, since there may be several app servers serving up the same application.

- Of course, we could store the nonce in the DB, but that defeats the entire purpose!

The short answer is: Do not store sensitive data in the session. Ever. The longer answer is that coordination of nonces across multiple servers would require remote process interaction on a per-request basis, which negates the benefits of using the cookie session storage to begin with.

The cookie session storage also has potential issues with replay attacks that let malicious users on shared computers use stolen cookies to log in to an application that the user thought he or she had logged out of. The bottom line is that if you decide to use the cookie session storage on an application with security concerns, please consider the implications of doing so carefully.

13.3.4 Cleaning Up Old Sessions

If you're using `ActiveRecordStore`, you can write your own little utilities for keeping the size of your session store under control. Listing 13.1 is a class that you can add to your `/lib` folder and invoke from the production console or a script whenever you need to do so.

---

3. If you want to read the whole thread (all 83 messages of it), simply search Google for "Replay attacks with cookie session." The results should include a link to the topic on the Ruby on Rails: Core Google Group.

Listing 13.1 SessionMaintenance class for cleaning up old sessions

```
class SessionMaintenance
 def self.cleanup(period = 24.hours.ago)
   session_store = ActiveRecord::SessionStore::Session
   session_store.destroy_all ['updated_at < ?', period]
 end
end
```

13.4 Cookies

This section is about using cookies, not the cookie session store. The cookie container, as it's known, looks like a hash, and is available via the `cookies` method in the scope of controllers. Lots of Rails developers use cookies to store user preferences and other small nonsensitive bits of data. Be careful not to store sensitive data in cookies because they can be read by users.

Contrary to what at least some developers might expect, the `cookies` container is not available by default in view templates or helpers. If you need to be able to access cookies in your helpers or views, there is a simple solution. Simply declare `cookies` to be a helper method:

```
class MyController < ActionController::Base
  helper_method :cookies
```

13.4.1 Reading and Writing Cookies

The cookie container is filled with cookies received along with the request, and sends out any cookies that you write to it with the response. Note that cookies are read by value, so you won't get the cookie object itself back, just the value it holds as a string (or as an array of strings if it holds multiple values).

To create or update cookies, you simply assign values using the brackets operator. You may assign either a single string value or a hash containing options, such as `:expires`, which takes a number of seconds before which the cookie should be deleted by the browser. Remember that Rails convenience methods for time are useful here:

```
# writing a simple session cookie
cookies[:list_mode] = "false"

# specifying options, curly brackets are needed to avoid syntax error
cookies[:recheck] = {:value => "false", :expires => 5.minutes.from_now}
```

Session

I find the `:path` options useful in allowing you to set options specific to particular sections or even particular records of your application. The `:path` option is set to `'1'`, the root of your application, by default.

The `:domain` option allows you to specify a domain, which is most often used when you are serving up your application from a particular host, but want to set cookies for the whole domain.

```
cookies[:login] = {:value => @user.security_token,
                   :domain => '.domain.com',
                   :expires => Time.now.next_year }
```

Cookies can also be written using the `:secure` option, and Rails will only ever transmit them over a secure HTTPS connection:

```
# writing a simple session cookie
cookies[:account_number] = { :value => @account.number, :secure => true }
```

Finally, you can delete cookies using the `delete` method:

```
cookies.delete :list_mode
```

Permanent Cookies
Writing cookies to the response via the `cookies.permanent` hash automatically gives them an expiration date 20 years in the future.

```
cookies.permanent[:remember_me] = current_user.id
```

Signed Cookies
Writing cookies to the response via the `cookies.signed` hash generates signed representations of cookies, to prevent tampering of that cookie's value by the end user. If a signed cookie was tampered with a `ActiveSupport::MessageVerifier::InvalidSignature` exception will be raised when that cookie is read in a subsequent request.

```
cookies.signed[:remember_me] = current_user.id
```

13.5 Conclusion

Deciding how to use the session is one of the more challenging tasks that faces a web application developer. That's why we put a couple of sections about it right in the beginning of this chapter. We also covered the various options available for configuring sessions, including storage mechanisms and methods for timing out sessions and the session life cycle. We also covered use of a closely related topic, browser cookies.

CHAPTER 14

Authentication

"Thanks goodness [sic], there's only about a billion of these because DHH doesn't think auth/auth [sic] belongs in the core."

—George Hotelling at http://del.icio.us/revgeorge/authentication

I bet every web app you've ever worked on has needed some form of user security, and some people assume it makes sense to include some sort of standard authentication functionality in a "kitchen-sink" framework such as Rails. However, it turns out that user security is one of those areas of application design that usually involves a bit more business logic than anyone realizes upfront.

David Heinemeier Hansson has clearly stated his opinions[1] on the matter, to help us understand why Rails does not include any sort of standard authentication mechanism:

> Context beats consistency. Reuse only works well when the particular instances are so similar that you're willing to trade the small differences for the increased productivity. That's often the case for infrastructure, such as Rails, but rarely the case for business logic, such as authentication and modules and components in general.

For better or worse, we need to either write our own authentication code or look outside of Rails core for a suitable solution. It's not too difficult to write your own authentication code, to the extent that it isn't that difficult to write anything in Rails. But why reinvent the wheel? That's not the Rails way!

As alluded to in the chapter quote, we have many different options out there to choose from. It seems that since authentication is one of the first features you add to a new application, it is also one of the first projects undertaken by many an aspiring plugin writer.

---

1. http://loudthinking.com/arc/2006_01.html

14.1 Authlogic

Authlogic[2] is a flexible, unobtrusive authentication framework for Ruby applications. It supports basic authentication with storage in a relational database out of the box, but can use other authentication means like OpenID or LDAP through the use of addons to the base framework.

14.1.1 Getting Started

Install Authlogic by adding the `Authlogic` gem to your application's `Gemfile`. There are no generators to run but there will be a few extra items that will need to be created in order to get Authlogic running properly.

14.1.2 Creating the Models

Depending on the model that you want to authenticate, you will need to create a corresponding session model for it. This pattern allows Authlogic to be flexible in what is authenticated and provides an easy mechanism for providing this functionality to multiple models in a single application.

For the purposes of our examples, we will have a `User` model that needs authentication. First we will create our `User` model and a corresponding `UserSession` model.

```
rails generate model user
rails generate model user_session
```

Then edit the `create_user` migration to add the columns that your application needs to satisfy its authentication requirements. Some columns are required by Authlogic, whereas others are optional but will get used if the framework sees that they exist.

The only required columns are `persistence_token` and either `login` or `email`, depending on your personal preference.

```
create_table :users do |t|
  # One must be defined, but it may be either
  t.string   :login,                :null => false
  t.string   :email,                :null => false

  # Required
  t.string   :persistence_token,    :null => false

  # Optional
  t.string   :crypted_password,     :null => false
```

---

2. `http://github.com/binarylogic/authlogic`

```
    t.string    :password_salt,        :null => false
    t.string    :single_access_token,  :null => false
    t.string    :perishable_token,     :null => false
    t.integer   :login_count,          :null => false, :default => 0
    t.integer   :failed_login_count,   :null => false, :default => 0
    t.datetime  :last_request_at
    t.datetime  :current_login_at
    t.datetime  :last_login_at
    t.string    :current_login_ip
    t.string    :last_login_ip
end
```

Next, set up your `User` and `UserSession` models, supplying them with optional configuration or use the defaults. The `UserSession` model will need to additionally provide a `to_key` method that returns an array with the session key in it.

```
class User < ActiveRecord::Base
  acts_as_authentic do |config|
    # Add custom configuration options here.
    config.crypto_provider = Authlogic::CryptoProviders::MD5
  end
end

class UserSession < Authlogic::Session::Base
  def to_key
    [session_key]
  end
end
```

14.1.3 Setting Up the Controllers

Authlogic handles the ability to login and logout through a controller that manages the session object for your authenticated model. In this case, we would create a `UserSessionsController` to handle this, as well as our `UsersController` to create our objects to authenticate.

```
rails generate controller user_sessions
rails generate controller users
```

In your `ApplicationController` you will need to provide access to the current user session and the current user, so that all of your controllers can access this information easily.

```
class ApplicationController < ActionController::Base
  helper_method :current_user_session, :current_user

  protected
  def current_user_session
```

```
    @current_user_session ||= UserSession.find
  end

  def current_user
    @current_user ||= current_user_session && current_user_session.user
  end
end
```

The UserSessionsController should respond to new, create, destroy in order
to leverage all basic login and logout functionality. The UsersController implementation will depend on your own application's requirements.

```
class UserSessionsController < ApplicationController
  def new
    @user_session = UserSession.new
  end

  def create
    @user_session = UserSession.new(params[:user_session])
    if @user_session.save
      redirect_to user_path(current_user)
    else
      render :action => :new
    end
  end

  def destroy
    current_user_session.destroy
    redirect_to new_user_session_path
  end
end
```

Make sure you've added the routes for the new controllers.

```
MyApp::Application.routes.draw do |map|
  resource :user_session
  resources :users
end
```

14.1.4 Controller, Limiting Access to Actions

Now that you are authenticating, you will want to control access to specific controller actions. A common pattern for handling this is through the use of filters in your controllers,
where the common checks reside in your ApplicationController.

```
class ApplicationController < ActionController::Base
  protected
  def authenticate
```

```
    unless current_user
      flash[:notice] = "You're not logged in captain."
      redirect_to new_user_session_path
      return false
    end
  end
end

class UserSessionsController < ApplicationController
  before_filter :authenticate, :only => :destroy
end
```

14.1.5 Configuration

Situations may arise where you want to configure the way Authlogic behaves to suit your individual application needs. This is handled by setting options in your authenticated model's Authlogic, `acts_as_authentic` block.

```
class User < ActiveRecord::Base
  acts_as_authentic do |config|
    config.logged_in_timeout = 20.minutes
    config.validate_email_field = false
  end
end
```

Authlogic has a wide range of configuration options, from setting password encryption algorithms to adding validation options to various fields that the framework uses internally. In addition to the options listed below, several additional ways to configure the validation options for various fields not listed. Please see Authlogic's documentation for details on how to configure those settings.

- `email_field`:
  Changes the name of the field that stores the email address.

- `validate_email_field`:
  Toggles whether email validation is on or off.

- `logged_in_timeout`:
  Sets the timeout to determine if the user is still signed in to the application.

- `login_field`:
  Change the name of the field that stores the login.

- `validate_login_field`:
  Toggles whether login validation is on or off.

- `check_passwords_against_database`:
  Sets if the object or database is queried when asking if a password is valid.

- `crypted_password_field`:
  Changes the name of the crypted_password field in the database.

- `crypto_provider`:
  Changes the encryption algorithm used on the password.

- `ignore_blank_passwords`:
  Allows ignoring password presence for new objects or when crypted passwords are blank.

- `password_salt_field`:
  Changes the name of the password_salt field in the database.

- `require_password_confirmation`:
  Sets whether password confirmation is required.

- `transition_from_crypto_providers`:
  Can be added if you initially stored passwords with a different algorithm.

- `disable_perishable_token_maintenance`:
  Turns off Authlogic's internal updating of the perishable token.

- `perishable_token_valid_for`:
  Specifies the length of time the perishable token is valid for.

- `act_like_restful_authentication`:
  Set this to true if you were previously using `restful_authentication` and want to make no code or database changes.

- `transition_from_restful_authentication`:
  Similar to acting like restful auth, this will resave user passwords with a new algorithm when the login.

- `maintain_sessions`:
  Tells Authlogic to use automatic session maintenance or not.

- `session_class`:
  If the session class cannot be inferred by the name, define it here.

- `change_single_access_token_with_password`:
  Allows for single access tokens to change when a user password is changed.

- `validations_scope`:
  Sets the scope of all validations, similar to `validates_uniqueness_of`.

14.1.6 Summary

Authlogic is a mature framework that's had plenty of use in the community. It is highly configurable and leaves the business logic of authentication in the hands of the application developer with very little code needed to implement it. It is easily extended and has a wide range of add-ons if you are looking to do different types of authentication, like OpenID or LDAP.

Authlogic is however tied to Active Record so if you are living on the edge with a non-relational store Authlogic will not work for you. Also, if you want to write almost no code at all and use a more standard solution (that can easily be extended to persist to multiple databases).

14.2 Devise

Devise[3] is a highly modular Rack-based authentication framework that sits on top of Warden. It has a robust feature set and leverages the use of Rails generators, and you only need to use what is suitable for your application.

14.2.1 Getting Started

Add the `devise` gem to your project's `Gemfile` and `bundle install`. Then you can generate the Devise configuration by running:

```
rails generate devise_install
```

This will create the initializer for devise, and an English version i18n YAML for Devise's messages. Devise will also alert you at this step to remember to do some mandatory Rails configuration if you have not done so already. This includes setting your default host for ActionMailer, setting up your root route, and making sure your flash messages will render in the application's default layout.

14.2.2 Modules

Adding authentication functionality to your models using Devise is based on the concept of adding different modules to your class, based on only what you need. The available modules for you to use are:

- `database_authenticatable`:
  Handles authentication of a user, as well as password encryption.

---

3. http://github.com/plataformatec/devise

- `confirmable:`
  Adds the ability to require email confirmation of user accounts.

- `lockable:`
  Can lock an account after *n* number of failed login attempts.

- `recoverable:`
  Provides password reset functionality.

- `registerable:`
  Alters user sign up to be handled in a registration process, along with account management.

- `rememberable:`
  Provides *remember me* functionality.

- `timeoutable:`
  Allows sessions to be expired in a configurable time frame.

- `token_authenticatable:`
  Allows sign in of a user based on single access tokens.

- `trackable:`
  Stores login counts, timestamps, and IP addresses.

- `validatable:`
  Adds customizable validations to email and password.

Knowing which modules you wish to include in your model is important for setting up your models, migrations, and configuration options later on.

14.2.3 Models

To set up authentication in a model, run the Devise generator for that model and then edit it. For the purpose of our examples, we will use the ever-so-exiting `User` model again.

```
rails generate devise User
```

This will create your model, a database migration, and route for your shiny new model. Devise will have given some default modules to use, which you will need to alter in your migration and model if you want to use different modules. In our example, we only use a subset of what is offered.

Our resulting database migration looks like

```
class DeviseCreateUsers < ActiveRecord::Migration
  def self.up
    create_table(:users) do |t|
      t.database_authenticatable :null => false
      t.confirmable
      t.recoverable
      t.rememberable
      t.timestamps
    end

    add_index :users, :email,                :unique => true
    add_index :users, :confirmation_token,   :unique => true
    add_index :users, :reset_password_token, :unique => true
  end

  def self.down
    drop_table :users
  end
end
```

We then modify our `User` model to mirror the modules we included in our migration.

```
class User < ActiveRecord::Base
  devise \
    :database_authenticatable,
    :confirmable,
    :recoverable,
    :rememberable

  attr_accessible \
    :email,
    :password,
    :password_confirmation
end
```

Now we're ready to `rake db:migrate` and let the magic happen.

14.2.4   Controllers

Devise provides some handy helper methods that can be used in your controllers to authenticate your model or get access to the currently signed-in person. For example, if you want to restrict access in a controller you may use one of the helpers as a `before_filter`.

```
class MeatProcessorController < ApplicationController
  before_filter :authenticate_user!
end
```

You can also access the currently signed-in user via the `current_user` helper method, or the current session via the `user_session` method. Use `user_signed_in?` if you want to check if the user had logged in without using the `before_filter`.

Thais says...

The helper methods are generated dynamically, so in the case where your authenticated models are named differently, use the model name instead of user in the examples. An instance of this could be with an Admin model—your helpers would be `current_admin`, `admin_signed_in?`, and `admin_session`.

14.2.5 Devise, Views

Devise is built as a Rails Engine, and comes with views for all of your included modules. All you need to do is write some CSS and you're off to the races. However, there may be some situations where you want to customize them, and Devise provides a nifty script to copy all of the internal views into your application.

```
rails generate devise_views
```

If you are authenticating more than one model and don't want to use the same views for both, just set the following option in your `config/initializers/devise.rb`:

```
config.scoped_views = true
```

14.2.6 Configuration

When you first set up Devise using `rails generate devise_install`, a `devise.rb` was tossed into your `config/initializers` directory. This initializer is where all the configuration for Devise is set, and it is already packed full of commented-out goodies for all configuration options with excellent descriptions for each option.

Durran says...

Using MongoDB as your main database? Under the general configuration section in the initializer switch the require of `active_record` to `mongoid` for pure awesomeness.

Devise comes with internationalization support out of the box and ships with English message Devise, internationalization definitions located in `config/locales/devise.en.yml`. (You'll see this was created after you ran the install generator at setup.) This file can be used as the template for Devise's messages in any other language by staying with the same naming convention for each file. Create a Chilean Spanish translation in `config/locales/devise.cl.yml` weon![4]

14.2.7 Extensions

There are plenty of third-party extensions out there for Devise that come in handy if you are authenticating using different methods.

- `cas_authenticatable`:
  Allows for single sign on using CAS.

- `facebook_connectable`:
  Provides support for authorizing through authenticating with Devise Facebook.[5]

- `imapable`:
  Adds authentication support through IMAP.

- `ldap_authenticatable`:
  Authenticates users using LDAP.

- `openid_authenticatable`:
  Provides authentication via OpenID.

- `rpx_connectable`:
  Adds support for using RPX authentication.

A complete list of extensions can be found at: `http://wiki.github.com/plataformatec/devise/3rd-party-extensions`

14.2.8 Summary

Devise is an excellent solution if you want a large number of standard features out of the box while writing almost no code at all. It has a clean and easy-understand API and can be used with little to no ramp-up time on any application.

14.3 Conclusion

We've covered the two most popular authentication frameworks for Rails at the moment, but there are plenty more out there to examine if these are not suited for your application. It's easy to even roll your own simple solution if basic authentication is all you need.

---

4. `http://www.urbandictionary.com/define.php?term=weon`
5. There are problems reported with this extension. Try `http://github.com/jerryluk/devise_oauth2_authenticatable` instead.

CHAPTER 15

XML and Active Resource

> Structure is nothing if it is all you got. Skeletons spook people if they try to walk around on their own. I really wonder why XML does not.
>
> —Erik Naggum

XML doesn't get much respect from the Rails community. It's *enterprisey*. In the Ruby world that other markup language YAML (YAML Ain't Markup Language) and data interchange format JSON (JavaScript Object Notation) get a heck of a lot more attention. However, use of XML is a fact of life for many projects, especially when it comes to interoperability with legacy systems. Luckily, Ruby on Rails gives us some pretty good functionality related to XML.

This chapter examines how to both generate and parse XML in your Rails applications, starting with a thorough examination of the to_xml method that most objects have in Rails.

15.1 The `to_xml` Method

Sometimes you just want an XML representation of an object, and Active Record models provide easy, automatic XML generation via the to_xml method. Let's play with this method in the console and see what it can do.

I'll fire up the console for my book-authoring sample application and find an Active Record object to manipulate.

```
>> User.find_by_login('obie')
 => #<User id: 8, login: "obie", email: "obie@tr3w.com", crypted_password:
 "4a6046804fc4dc3183ad9012fbfee91c85723d8c", salt:
"399754af1b01cf3d4b87da5478d82674b0438eb8", created_at: "2010-05-18
19:31:40", updated_at: "2010-05-18 19:31:40", remember_token: nil,
```

```
remember_token_expires_at: nil, authorized_approver: true, client_id: nil,
 timesheets_updated_at: nil>
```

There we go, a `User` instance. Let's see that instance as its generic model, XML representation.

```
>> User.find_by_login('obie').to_xml
=> "<?xml version=\"1.0\" encoding=\"UTF-8\"?>\n<user>\n
<authorized-approver type=\"boolean\">true</authorized-approver>\n
<salt>399754af1b01cf3d4b87da5478d82674b0438eb8</salt>\n  <created-at
type=\"datetime\">2010-05-18T19:31:40Z</created-at>\n
<crypted-password>4a6046804fc4dc3183ad9012fbfee91c85723d8c
</crypted-password>\n  <remember-token-expires-at type=\"datetime\"
nil=\"true\"></remember-token-expires-at>\n  <updated-at
type=\"datetime\">2010-05-18T19:31:40Z</updated-at>\n
<id type=\"integer\">8</id>\n  <client-id type=\"integer\"
nil=\"true\"></client-id>\n  <remember-token
nil=\"true\"></remember-token>\n  <login>obie</login>\n
<email>obie@tr3w.com</email>\n  <timesheets-updated-at type=\"datetime\"
nil=\"true\"></timesheets-updated-at>\n</user>\n"
```

Ugh, that's ugly. Ruby's `print`, formatted XML function might help us out here.

```
>> print User.find_by_login('obie').to_xml
<?xml version="1.0" encoding="UTF-8"?>
<user>
  <authorized-approver type="boolean">true</authorized-approver>
  <salt>399754af1b01cf3d4b87da5478d82674b0438eb8</salt>
  <created-at type="datetime">2010-05-18T19:31:40Z</created-at>
  <crypted-password>4a6046804fc4dc3183ad9012fbfee91c85723d8c
</crypted-password>
  <remember-token-expires-at type="datetime"
nil="true"></remember-token-expires-at>
  <updated-at type="datetime">2010-05-18T19:31:40Z</updated-at>
  <id type="integer">8</id>
  <client-id type="integer" nil="true"></client-id>
  <remember-token nil="true"></remember-token>
  <login>obie</login>
  <email>obie@tr3w.com</email>
  <timesheets-updated-at type="datetime"
nil="true"></timesheets-updated-at>
</user>
```

Much better! So what do we have here? Looks like a fairly straightforward serialized representation of our `User` instance in XML.

15.1.1 Customizing `to_xml` Output

The standard processing instruction is at the top, followed by an element name corresponding to the class name of the object. The properties are represented as subelements, with non-string data fields including a `type` attribute. Mind you, this is the default behavior, and we can customize it with some additional parameters to the `to_xml` method.

We'll strip down that XML representation of a user to just an email and login using the `only` parameter. It's provided in a familiar options hash, with the value of the `:only` parameter as an array:

```
>> print User.find_by_login('obie').to_xml(:only => [:email, :login])
<?xml version="1.0" encoding="UTF-8"?>
<user>
  <login>obie</login>
  <email>obie@tr3w.com</email>
</user>
```

Following the familiar Rails convention, the `only` parameter is complemented by its inverse, `except`, which will exclude the specified properties. What if I want my user's email and login as a snippet of XML that will be included in another document? Then let's get rid of that pesky instruction, too, using the `skip_instruct` parameter.

```
>> print User.find_by_login('obie').to_xml(:only => [:email, :login],
:skip_instruct => true)
<user>
  <login>obie</login>
  <email>obie@tr3w.com</email>
</user>
```

We can change the root element in our XML representation of `User` and the indenting from two to four spaces by using the `root` and `indent` parameters, respectively.

```
>> print User.find_by_login('obie').to_xml(:root => 'employee', :indent =>
 4)
<?xml version="1.0" encoding="UTF-8"?>
<employee>
    <authorized-approver type="boolean">true</authorized-approver>
    <salt>399754af1b01cf3d4b87da5478d82674b0438eb8</salt>
    <created-at type="datetime">2010-05-18T19:31:40Z</created-at>
    <crypted-password>4a6046804fc4dc3183ad9012fbfee91c85723d8c
</crypted-password>
    <remember-token-expires-at type="datetime"
nil="true"></remember-token-expires-at>
    <updated-at type="datetime">2010-05-18T19:31:40Z</updated-at>
    <id type="integer">8</id>
    <client-id type="integer" nil="true"></client-id>
    <remember-token nil="true"></remember-token>
    <login>obie</login>
    <email>obie@tr3w.com</email>
    <timesheets-updated-at type="datetime"
nil="true"></timesheets-updated-at>
</employee>
```

By default Rails converts CamelCase and underscore attribute names to dashes as in `created-at` and `client-id`. You can force underscore attribute names by setting the `dasherize` parameter to `false`.

```
>> print User.find_by_login('obie').to_xml(:dasherize => false, :only =>
[:created_at, :client_id])
<?xml version="1.0" encoding="UTF-8"?>
<user>
  <created_at type="datetime">2010-05-18T19:31:40Z</created_at>
  <client_id type="integer" nil="true"></client_id>
</user>
```

In the preceding output, the attribute type is included. This too can be configured using the `skip_types` parameter.

```
>> print User.find_by_login('obie').to_xml(:skip_types => true, :only =>
[:created_at, :client_id])
<?xml version="1.0" encoding="UTF-8"?>
<user>
  <created-at>2010-05-18T19:31:40Z</created-at>
  <client-id nil="true"></client-id>
</user>
```

15.1.2   Associations and `to_xml`

So far we've only worked with a base Active Record and not with any of its associations. What if we wanted an XML representation of not just a book but also its associated chapters? Rails provides the `:include` parameter for just this purpose. The `:include` parameter will also take an array or associations to represent in XML.

```
>> print User.find_by_login('obie').to_xml(:include => :timesheets)
<?xml version="1.0" encoding="UTF-8"?>
<user>
  <authorized-approver type="boolean">true</authorized-approver>
  <salt>399754af1b01cf3d4b87da5478d82674b0438eb8</salt>
  <created-at type="datetime">2010-05-18T19:31:40Z</created-at>
  <crypted-password>4a6046804fc4dc3183ad9012fbfee91c85723d8c
</crypted-password>
  <remember-token-expires-at type="datetime"
nil="true"></remember-token-expires-at>
  <updated-at type="datetime">2010-05-18T19:31:40Z</updated-at>
  <id type="integer">8</id>
  <client-id type="integer" nil="true"></client-id>
  <remember-token nil="true"></remember-token>
  <login>obie</login>
  <email>obie@tr3w.com</email>
  <timesheets-updated-at type="datetime"
nil="true"></timesheets-updated-at>
```

```
<timesheets type="array">
  <timesheet>
    <created-at type="datetime">2010-05-04T19:31:40Z</created-at>
    <updated-at type="datetime">2010-05-18T19:31:40Z</updated-at>
    <lock-version type="integer">0</lock-version>
    <id type="integer">8</id>
    <user-id type="integer">8</user-id>
    <submitted type="boolean">true</submitted>
    <approver-id type="integer">7</approver-id>
  </timesheet>
  <timesheet>
    <created-at type="datetime">2010-05-18T19:31:40Z</created-at>
    <updated-at type="datetime">2010-05-18T19:31:40Z</updated-at>
    <lock-version type="integer">0</lock-version>
    <id type="integer">9</id>
    <user-id type="integer">8</user-id>
    <submitted type="boolean">false</submitted>
    <approver-id type="integer" nil="true"></approver-id>
  </timesheet>
  <timesheet>
    <created-at type="datetime">2010-05-11T19:31:40Z</created-at>
    <updated-at type="datetime">2010-05-18T19:31:40Z</updated-at>
    <lock-version type="integer">0</lock-version>
    <id type="integer">10</id>
    <user-id type="integer">8</user-id>
    <submitted type="boolean">false</submitted>
    <approver-id type="integer" nil="true"></approver-id>
  </timesheet>
</timesheets>
</user>
```

Rails 3 has a much more useful to_xml method on core classes. Unlike Rails 2, arrays are easily serializable to XML, with element names inferred from the name of the Ruby type:

```
>> print ['cat', 'dog', 'ferret'].to_xml
<?xml version="1.0" encoding="UTF-8"?>
<strings type="array">
  <string>cat</string>
  <string>dog</string>
  <string>ferret</string>
</strings>
```

If you have mixed types in the array, this is also reflected in the XML output:

```
>> print [3, 'cat', 'dog', :ferret].to_xml
<?xml version="1.0" encoding="UTF-8"?>
<objects type="array">
  <object type="integer">3</object>
  <object>cat</object>
```

```
  <object>dog</object>
  <object type="symbol">ferret</object>
</objects>
```

To construct a more semantic structure, the `root` option on `to_xml` triggers more expressive element names:

```
>> print ['cat', 'dog', 'ferret'].to_xml(:root => 'pets')
<?xml version="1.0" encoding="UTF-8"?>
<pets type="array">
  <pet>cat</pet>
  <pet>dog</pet>
  <pet>ferret</pet>
</pets>
```

Ruby hashes are naturally representable in XML, with keys corresponding to element names, and their values corresponding to element contents. Rails automatically calls `to_s` on the values to get string values for them:

```
>> print({:owners => ['Chad', 'Trixie'], :pets => ['cat', 'dog',
'ferret'],
          :id => 123}.to_xml(:root => 'registry'))
<?xml version="1.0" encoding="UTF-8"?>
<registry>
  <pets type="array">
    <pet>cat</pet>
    <pet>dog</pet>
    <pet>ferret</pet>
  </pets>
  <owners type="array">
    <owner>Chad</owner>
    <owner>Trixie</owner>
  </owners>
  <id type="integer">123</id>
</registry>
```

JoshG says...

This simplistic serialization may not be appropriate for certain interoperability contexts, especially if the output must pass XML Schema (XSD) validation when the order of elements is often important. In Ruby 1.8.x, the Hash class does not order `keys` for enumeration. In Ruby 1.9.x, the Hash class uses insertion order. Neither of these may be adequate for producing output that matches an XSD. The section "The XML Builder" will discuss `Builder::XmlMarkup` to address this situation.

The `:include` option of `to_xml` is not used on `Array` and `Hash` objects.

15.1.3   Advanced **to_xml** Usage

By default, Active Record's to_xml method only serializes persistent attributes into XML. However, there are times when transient, derived, or calculated values need to be serialized out into XML form as well. For example, our User model has a method that returns only draft timesheets:

```
class User < ActiveRecord::Base
  ...
  def draft_timesheets
    timesheets.draft
  end
  ...
end
```

To include the result of this method when we serialize the XML, we use the :methods parameter:

```
>> print User.find_by_login('obie').to_xml(:methods => :draft_timesheets)
<?xml version="1.0" encoding="UTF-8"?>
<user>
  <id type="integer">8</id>
  ...
  <draft-timesheets type="array">
    <draft-timesheet>
      <created-at type="datetime">2010-05-18T19:31:40Z</created-at>
      <updated-at type="datetime">2010-05-18T19:31:40Z</updated-at>
      <lock-version type="integer">0</lock-version>
      <id type="integer">9</id>
      <user-id type="integer">8</user-id>
      <submitted type="boolean">false</submitted>
      <approver-id type="integer" nil="true"></approver-id>
    </draft-timesheet>
    <draft-timesheet>
      <created-at type="datetime">2010-05-11T19:31:40Z</created-at>
      <updated-at type="datetime">2010-05-18T19:31:40Z</updated-at>
      <lock-version type="integer">0</lock-version>
      <id type="integer">10</id>
      <user-id type="integer">8</user-id>
      <submitted type="boolean">false</submitted>
      <approver-id type="integer" nil="true"></approver-id>
    </draft-timesheet>
  </draft-timesheets>
</user>
```

We could also set the methods parameter to an array of method names to be called.

15.1.4   Dynamic Runtime Attributes

In cases where we want to include extra elements unrelated to the object being serialized, we can pass `to_xml` a block, or use the `:procs` option.

If we are using the same logic applied to different `to_xml` calls, we can construct lambdas ahead of time and use one or more of them in the `:procs` option. They will be called with `to_xml`'s option hash, through which we access the underlying `XmlBuilder`. (`XmlBuilder` provides the principal means of XML generation in Rails.

```
>> current_user = User.find_by_login('admin')
>> generated_at = lambda { |opts| opts[:builder].tag!('generated-at',
Time.now.utc.iso8601) }
>> generated_by = lambda { |opts| opts[:builder].tag!('generated-by',
current_user.email) }

>> print(User.find_by_login('obie').to_xml(:procs => [generated_at,
generated_by]))
<?xml version="1.0" encoding="UTF-8"?>
<user>
  ...
  <id type="integer">8</id>
  <client-id type="integer" nil="true"></client-id>
  <remember-token nil="true"></remember-token>
  <login>obie</login>
  <email>obie@tr3w.com</email>
  <timesheets-updated-at type="datetime"
nil="true"></timesheets-updated-at>
  <generated-at>2010-05-18T19:33:49Z</generated-at>
  <generated-by>admin@tr3w.com</generated-by>
</user>

>> print Timesheet.all.to_xml(:procs => [generated_at, generated_by])
<?xml version="1.0" encoding="UTF-8"?>
<timesheets type="array">
  <timesheet>
    ...
    <id type="integer">8</id>
    <user-id type="integer">8</user-id>
    <submitted type="boolean">true</submitted>
    <approver-id type="integer">7</approver-id>
    <generated-at>2010-05-18T20:18:30Z</generated-at>
    <generated-by>admin@tr3w.com</generated-by>
  </timesheet>
  <timesheet>
    ...
    <id type="integer">9</id>
    <user-id type="integer">8</user-id>
    <submitted type="boolean">false</submitted>
```

```
    <approver-id type="integer" nil="true"></approver-id>
    <generated-at>2010-05-18T20:18:30Z</generated-at>
    <generated-by>admin@tr3w.com</generated-by>
  </timesheet>
  <timesheet>
    ...
    <id type="integer">10</id>
    <user-id type="integer">8</user-id>
    <submitted type="boolean">false</submitted>
    <approver-id type="integer" nil="true"></approver-id>
    <generated-at>2010-05-18T20:18:30Z</generated-at>
    <generated-by>admin@tr3w.com</generated-by>
  </timesheet>
</timesheets>
```

Note that the :procs are applied to each top-level resource in the collection (or the single resource if the top level is not a collection). Use the sample application to compare the output with the output from the following:

```
>> print User.all.to_xml(:include => :timesheets, :procs => [generated_at,
   generated_by])
```

To add custom elements only to the root node, to_xml will yield an XmlBuilder instance when given a block:

```
>> print(User.all.to_xml { |xml| xml.tag! 'generated-by',
current_user.email })
<?xml version="1.0" encoding="UTF-8"?>
<users type="array">
  <user>...</user>
  <user>...</user>
  <generated-by>admin@tr3w.com</generated-by>
</users>
```

Unfortunately, both :procs and the optional block are hobbled by a puzzling limitation: The record being serialized is not exposed to the procs being passed in as arguments, so only data external to the object may be added in this fashion.

To gain complete control over the XML serialization of Rails objects, you need to override the to_xml method and implement it yourself.

15.1.5   Overriding `to_xml`

Sometimes you need to do something out of the ordinary when trying to represent data in XML form. In those situations, you can create the XML by hand.

```
class User < ActiveRecord::Base
  ...
  def to_xml(options = {})
    xml = options[:builder] || Builder::XmlMarkup.new(options)
    xml.instruct! unless options[:skip_instruct]
    xml.user do
      xml.tag!(:email, email)
    end
  end
  ...
end
```

This would give the following result:

```
>> print User.find(:first).to_xml
<?xml version="1.0" encoding="UTF-8"?>
<user><email>admin@tr3w.com</email></user>
```

Of course, you could just go ahead and use good Object Oriented design and use a class responsible for translating between your model and an external representation.

15.2 The XML Builder

`Builder::XmlMarkup` is the class used internally by Rails when it needs to generate XML. When `to_xml` is not enough and you need to generate custom XML, you will use `Builder` instances directly. Fortunately, the Builder API is one of the most powerful Ruby libraries available and is very easy to use, once you get the hang of it.

The API documentation says: "All (well, almost all) methods sent to an `XmlMarkup` object will be translated to the equivalent XML markup. Any method with a block will be treated as an XML markup tag with nested markup in the block."

That is a very concise way of describing how `Builder` works, but it is easier to understand with some examples, again taken from `Builder`'s API documentation. The `xm` variable is a `Builder::XmlMarkup` instance:

```
xm.em("emphasized") # => <em>emphasized</em>
xm.em { xm.b("emp & bold") }    # => <em><b>emph &amp; bold</b></em>

xm.a("foo", "href"=>"http://foo.org")
                            # => <a href="http://foo.org">foo</a>

xm.div { br }               # => <div><br/></div>

xm.target("name"=>"foo", "option"=>"bar")
                            # => <target name="foo" option="bar"/>

xm.instruct!                # <?xml version="1.0" encoding="UTF-8"?>
```

```
xm.html {                        # <html>
  xm.head {                      #   <head>
    xm.title("History")          #     <title>History</title>
  }                              #   </head>
  xm.body {                      #   <body>
    xm.comment! "HI"             #     <!-- HI -->
    xm.h1("Header")              #     <h1>Header</h1>
    xm.p("paragraph")            #     <p>paragraph</p>
  }                              #   </body>
}                                # </html>
```

A common use for `Builder::XmlBuilder` is to render XML in response to a request. Previously we talked about overriding `to_xml` on Active Record to generate our custom XML. Another way, though not as recommended, is to use an XML template.

We could alter our `UsersController` `show` method to use an XML template by changing it from:

```
def UsersController < ApplicationController ...
  def show
    @book = User.find(params[:id])
    respond_to do |format|
      format.html
      format.xml { render :xml => @user.to_xml }
    end
  end
end
```

to

```
def UsersController < ApplicationController ...
  def show
    @book = User.find(params[:id])
    respond_to do |format|
      format.html
      format.xml
    end
  end
end
```

Now Rails will look for a file called `show.xml.builder` in the `RAILS_ROOT/views/users` directory. That file contains `Builder::XmlMarkup` code like

```
xml.user {                              # <user>
  xml.email @user.email                 #   <email>...</email>
  xml.timesheets {                      #   <timesheets>
    @user.timesheets.each { |timesheet| #
```

```
      xml.timesheet {                      #       <timesheet>
        xml.draft timesheet.submitted?     #        <draft>true</draft>
      }                                    #       </timesheet>
    }                                      #
  }                                        #    </timesheets>
}                                          #  </user>
```

In this view, the variable `xml` is an instance of `Builder::XmlMarkup`. Just as in views, we have access to the instance variables we set in our controller, in this case `@user`. Using the `Builder` in a view can provide a convenient way to generate XML.

15.3 Parsing XML

Ruby has a full-featured XML library named REXML, and covering it in any level of detail is outside the scope of this book. If you have basic parsing needs, such as parsing responses from web services, you can use the simple XML parsing capability built into Rails.

15.3.1 Turning XML into Hashes

Rails lets you turn arbitrary snippets of XML markup into Ruby hashes, with the `from_xml` method that it adds to the `Hash` class.

To demonstrate, we'll throw together a string of simplistic XML and turn it into a hash:

```
>> xml = <<-XML
<pets>
  <cat>Franzi</cat>
  <dog>Susie</dog>
  <horse>Red</horse>
</pets>
XML

>> Hash.from_xml(xml)
 => {"pets"=>{"horse"=>"Red", "cat"=>"Franzi", "dog"=>"Susie"}}
```

There are no options for `from_xml`. You can also pass it an `IO` object:

```
>> Hash.from_xml(File.new('pets.xml'))
 => {"pets"=>{"horse"=>"Red", "cat"=>"Franzi", "dog"=>"Susie"}}
```

15.3.2 Typecasting

Typecasting is done by using a `type` attribute in the XML elements. For example, here's the auto-generated XML for a `User` object.

```
>> print User.first.to_xml
<?xml version="1.0" encoding="UTF-8"?>
<user>
  <authorized-approver type="boolean">true</authorized-approver>
  <salt>034fbec79d0ca2cd7d892f205d56ea95174ff557</salt>
  <created-at type="datetime">2010-05-18T19:31:40Z</created-at>
  <crypted-password>98dfc463d9122a1af0a5dc817601de437c69f365
</crypted-password>
  <remember-token-expires-at type="datetime"
nil="true"></remember-token-expires-at>
  <updated-at type="datetime">2010-05-18T19:31:40Z</updated-at>
  <id type="integer">7</id>
  <client-id type="integer" nil="true"></client-id>
  <remember-token nil="true"></remember-token>
  <login>admin</login>
  <email>admin@tr3w.com</email>
  <timesheets-updated-at type="datetime"
nil="true"></timesheets-updated-at>
</user>
```

As part of the `to_xml` method, Rails sets attributes called `type` that identify the class of the value being serialized. If we take this XML and feed it to the `from_xml` method, Rails will typecast the strings to their corresponding Ruby objects:

```
>> Hash.from_xml(User.first.to_xml)
=> {"user"=>{"salt"=>"034fbec79d0ca2cd7d892f205d56ea95174ff557",
"authorized_approver"=>true, "created_at"=>Tue May 18 19:31:40 UTC 2010,
"remember_token_expires_at"=>nil,
"crypted_password"=>"98dfc463d9122a1af0a5dc817601de437c69f365",
"updated_at"=>Tue May 18 19:31:40 UTC 2010, "id"=>7, "client_id"=>nil,
"remember_token"=>nil, "login"=>"admin", "timesheets_updated_at"=>nil,
"email"=>"admin@tr3w.com"}}
```

15.4 Active Resource

Web applications often need to serve users in front of web browsers and other systems via some API. Other languages accomplish this using SOAP or some form of XML-RPC, but Rails takes a simpler approach. In Chapter 3, REST, Resources, and Rails, we talked about building RESTful controllers and using `respond_to` to return different representations of resources. By doing so we could connect to `http://localhost:3000/auctions.xml` and get back an XML representation of all auctions in the system. We can now write a client to consume this data using Active Resource.

Active Resource is a standard part of the Rails framework. It has complete understanding of RESTful routing and XML representation, and is designed to look and feel much like Active Record.

15.4.1 List

The simplest Active Resource model would look something like this:

```
class Auction < ActiveResource::Base
  self.site = 'http://localhost:3000'
end
```

To get a list of auctions we would call its `all` method:

```
>> auctions = Auction.all
```

This will connect to `http://localhost:3000/auctions.xml`.

Active Resource can't automatically filter the resources like you would with Active Record's `where` method, but you can use `:params` to pass options to the server, which can then filter the results.

```
class AuctionsController < ApplicationController
  def index
    @auctions = Auction.where(params.except(:controller, :action,
:format))
    # ...
  end
end
```

And then from the consumer application, you might do:

```
>> auctions = Auction.all(:params => { :reserve => 100 })
```

This method, however, could easily become unmanageable, since in reality you would want to filter out unsupported params. A much better solution when you want to filter your results is to define a custom collection method on the server, and query against that instead.[1]

```
resource :auctions do
  collection do
    get :open
  end
end
```

---

1. Of course, that only works if you control both applications.

```
class AuctionsController < ApplicationController
  def open
    @auctions = Auction.open
    respond_to do |format|
      format.html
      format.xml { render :xml => @auctions }
    end
  end
end
```

It is then trivial to query this collection from Active Resource

```
>> Auction.all(:from => :open)
```

Active Resource also supports nested resource routes like this discussed in Chapter 3, "REST, Resources, and Rails,".

```
class Item < ActiveRecord::Base
  self.site = 'http://localhost:3000/auctions/:auction_id'
end
```

And now from your consumer application, you can pull back all of the items for an auction:

```
>> Item.all(:params => {:auction_id => 1})
```

15.4.2 Show

Finding specific resources with Active Resource follows the same pattern as retrieving a collection. To fetch the auction with the id 1986, for instance, we can do:

```
>> Auction.find(1986)
```

If instead we just want to get the first auction, we can do:

```
>> Auction.first
```

You should note that `Auction.first` is equivalent to calling `Auction.all.first` (i.e., it will load `http://localhost:3000/auctions.xml` and then call first on the returned collection).

If we wanted to find the newest Auction, we can do something similar to the `open` example, but with a `newest` method.

```
resource :auctions do
  collection do
    get :newest
  end
end
```

```
class AuctionsController < ApplicationController
  def newest
    @auction = Auction.order("created_at desc").first
    respond_to do |format|
      format.html
      format.xml { render :xml => @auction }
    end
  end
end
```

Now we can retrieve the newest auction.

```
>> Auction.find(:one, :from => :newest)
```

You need to remember that unlike with Active Record, `first` is not the same as `find(:one)`.

It's also important to understand how a request to a nonexistent item is handled. If we tried to access an item with an id of -1 (there isn't any such item), we would get an HTTP 404 status code back. This is exactly what Active Resource receives and raises a `ResourceNotFound` exception. Active Resource makes heavy use of the HTTP status codes as we'll see throughout this chapter.

15.4.3 Create

Active Resource is not limited to just retrieving data; it can also create it. If we wanted to place a new bid on an item via Active Resource, we would do the following:

```
>> Bid.create(:username => 'me', :auction_id => 3, :item_id => 6, :amount
=> 34.50)
```

This would HTTP POST to the URL:

`http://localhost:3000/auctions/3/items/6/bids.xml` with the supplied data. In our controller, the following would exist:

```
class BidController < ApplicationController
  ...
  def create
    @bid = Bid.new(params[:bid])
    respond_to do |format|
      if @bid.save
        flash[:notice] = 'Bid was successfully created.'
        format.html { redirect_to(@bid) }
        format.xml  { head :created, :location => @bid }
      else
        format.html { render :action => "new" }
        format.xml  { render :xml => @bid.errors, :status =>
:unprocessable_entity }
```

```
        end
      end
    end
    ...
end
```

If the bid is successfully created, the newly created bid is returned with an HTTP 201 status code and the Location header is set pointing to the location of the newly created bid. With the Location header set, we can determine what the newly created bid's id is. For example:

```
>> bid = Bid.create(:username => 'me', :auction_id => 3, :item_id => 6,
:amount => 34.50)
>> bid.id # => 12
>> bid.new? # => false
```

If we tried to create the preceding bid again but without a dollar amount, we could interrogate the errors.

```
>> bid = Bid.create(:username => 'me', :auction_id => 3, :item_id => 6)
>> bid.valid? # => false
>> bid.id # => nil
>> bid.new? # => true
>> bid.errors.class # => ActiveResource::Errors
>> bid.errors.size # => 1
>> bid.errors.on_base # => "Amount can't be blank"
>> bid.errors.full_messages # => "Amount can't be blank"
>> bid.errors[:amount] # => nil
```

In this case a new `Bid` object is returned from the `create` method, but it's not valid. If we try to see what its id is we also get a nil. We can see what caused the `create` to fail by calling the `ActiveResource#errors` method. This method behaves just like `ActiveRecord#errors` with one important exception. On `ActiveRecord` if we called `Errors#on`, we would get the error for that attribute. In the preceding example, we got a nil instead. The reason is that Active Resource, unlike Active Record, doesn't know what attributes there are. Active Record does a SHOW FIELDS FROM <table> to get this, but Active Resource has no equivalent. The only way Active Resource knows an attribute exists is if we tell it. For example:

```
>> bid = Bid.create(:username => 'me', :auction_id => 3, :item_id => 6,
:amount => nil)
>> bid.valid? # => false
>> bid.id # => nil
>> bid.new? # => true
>> bid.errors.class # => ActiveResource::Errors
>> bid.errors.size # => 1
>> bid.errors.on_base # => "Amount can't be blank"
```

```
>> bid.errors.full_messages # => "Amount can't be blank"
>> bid.errors[:amount] # => "can't be blank"
```

In this case we told Active Resource that there is an amount attribute through the `create` method. As a result we can now call `Errors#on` without a problem.

15.4.4 Update

Editing an Active Resource follows the same Active Record pattern.

```
>> bid = Bid.find(1)
>> bid.amount # => 10.50
>> bid.amount = 15.00
>> bid.save # => true
>> bid.reload

>> bid.amount # => 15.00
```

If we set the amount to nil, `ActiveResource.save` would return `false`. In this case we could interrogate `ActiveResource::Errors` for the reason, just as we would with `create`. An important difference between Active Resource and Active Record is the absence of the `save!` and `update!` methods.

15.4.5 Delete

Removing an Active Resource can happen in two ways. The first is without instantiating the Active Resource

```
>> Bid.delete(1)
```

The other way requires instantiating the Active Resource first:

```
>> bid = Bid.find(1)
>> bid.destroy
```

15.4.6 Headers

Active Resource allows for the setting of HTTP headers on each request too. This can be done in two ways. The first is to set it as a variable:

```
class Auctions < ActiveResource::Base
  self.site = 'http://localhost:3000'
  @headers = { 'x-flavor' => 'orange' }
end
```

This will cause every connection to the site to include the HTTP header: HTTP-X-FLAVOR: orange. In our controller, we could use the header value.

```
class AuctionController < ApplicationController
  def show
    @auction = Auction.find_by_id_and_flavor(params[:bid],
request.headers['HTTP_X_FLAVOR'])
    respond_to do |format|
      format.html
      format.xml { render :xml => @auction }
    end
  end
end
```

The second way to set the headers for an Active Resource is to override the headers method.

```
class Auctions < ActiveResource::Base
  self.site = 'http://localhost:3000'
  def self.headers
    { 'x-flavor' => 'orange' }
  end
end
```

15.4.7 Customizing URLs

Active Resource assumes RESTful URLs, but that doesn't always happen. Fortunately, you can customize the URL prefix and collection_name. Suppose we assume the following Active Resource class:

```
class OldAuctionSystem < ActiveResource::Base
  self.site = 'http://s60:3270'

  self.prefix = '/cics/'
  self.collection_name = 'auction_pool'
end
```

The following URLs will be used:

```
OldAuctionSystem.all          GET http://s60:3270/cics/auction_pool.xml
OldAuctionSystem.find(1)      GET http://s60:3270/cics/auction_pool/1.xml
OldAuctionSystem.             PUT http://s60:3270/cics/auction_pool/1.xml
find(1).save}
OldAuctionSystem.delete(1)}   DELETE http://s60:3270/cics/auction_pool/1.xml
OldAuctionSystem.             POST http://s60:3270/cics/auction_pool.xml
create(...)}
```

We could also change the element name used to generate XML. In the preceding Active Resource, a create of an OldAuctionSystem would look like the following in XML:

```
<?xml version=\"1.0\" encoding=\"UTF-8\"?>
  <OldAuctionSystem>
    <title>Auction A</title>
    ...
  </OldAuctionSystem>
```

The element name can be changed with

```
class OldAuctionSystem < ActiveResource::Base
  self.site = 'http://s60:3270'

  self.prefix = '/cics/'
  self.element_name = 'auction'
end
```

which will produce:

```
<?xml version=\"1.0\" encoding=\"UTF-8\"?>
<Auction>
  <title>Auction A</title>
  ...
</Auction>
```

One consequence of setting the `element_name` is that Active Resource will use the plural form to generate URLs. In this case it would be `'auctions'` and not `'OldAuctionSystems'`. To do this you will need to set the `collection_name` as well.

It is also possible to set the primary key field Active Resource uses with `self.primary_key`

```
class OldAuctionSystem < ActiveResource::Base
  self.site = 'http://s60:3270'

  self.primary_key = 'guid'
end
```

15.4.8 Hash Forms

The methods `find`, `create`, `save`, and `delete` correspond to the HTTP methods of GET, POST, PUT, and DELETE, respectively. Active Resource has a method for each of these HTTP methods, too. They take the same arguments as `find`, `create`, `save`, and `delete` but return a hash of the XML received.

```
>> bid = Bid.find(1)
>> bid.class # => ActiveResource::Base
>> bid_hash = Bid.get(1)
>> bid_hash.class # => Hash
```

15.5 Active Resource Authentication

Active Resource comes with support for both HTTP Basic and HTTP Digest Authentication, as well as SSL authentication using X.509 certificates. Each has various compromises of simplicity, strength, interoperability, and infrastructure/system-administration support needs.

As with most HTTP clients and servers, MD5 is the only hashing algorithm supported in HTTP Digest. This is the only algorithm mentioned by RFC 2617, but Rails supports the extended properties of the RFC that strengthen the protocol despite the hashing algorithm used.[2]

Other authentication mechanisms, like OAuth, CAS, and Kerberos, can be found in HTTP servers, middleware, Ruby gems, and Rails plugins.

15.5.1 HTTP Basic Authentication

When using Basic Authentication, the credentials are sent in plain text and as such can be easily snooped. For this reason, an HTTPS connection should be used when using Basic Authentication.

Here is a basic model class that consumes a RESTful service to obtain data, and specifies credentials for an authenticated connection to the service:

```
class MoneyTransfer < ActiveResource::Base
  self.site = 'https://localhost:3000/'
  self.user = 'administrator'
  self.password = 'secret'
end
```

You can also use URI-style credentials by putting them in the service's URL. This is particularly useful if you have a fully-qualified URL in a configuration file that has been supplied by the service provider:

```
class MoneyTransfer < ActiveResource::Base
  self.site = 'https://administrator:secret@localhost:3000/'
end
```

As soon as you supply any credential to the API, Active Resource will automatically attempt to authenticate on each connection. If the username and/or password is invalid, an `ActiveResource::ClientError` is generated and handled in the consuming application.

---

2. Over a period of years some weaknesses have come to light in MD5, and more recently SHA-1. But as of this writing those weaknesses have not led to exploits that are practical for breaching this kind of security.

15.5.2 HTTP Digest Authentication

Setting the `auth_type` tells Active Resource to use Digest Authentication.

```
class MoneyTransfer < ActiveResource::Base
  self.site = 'https://localhost:3000/'
  self.user = 'administrator'
  self.password = 'secret'
  self.auth_type = :digest
end
```

It's as simple as that! Rails takes care of the rest (pardon the pun).

Dealing with only a hashed value (HA1 being the hash of colon-separated username, authentication realm, and password) is good, as your password is never transmitted — except perhaps when you (re-)set it. However, if the repository storing the HA1 is compromised, passwords will have to be reset (even if it's just to the same password using a new secret or realm) as the HA1 could then be used by anyone to access your account on that server only. They still won't know your password or be able to use the HA1 within another authentication realm. As such, despite its many known limitations and interoperability issues, Digest is definitely a step above Basic.

15.5.3 Certificate Authentication

A type of public key authentication, you may also hear this referred to as "client-side certificate authentication" and, when used in conjunction with username/password credentials, is a form of two-factor authentication as it involves something you have (the certificate) and something you know (the credentials).

In this form of SSL-based authentication, the server provides its certificate as usual (creating the SSL connection), and then the client provides its certificate so that the server continues with the SSL session.

15.5.4 Proxy Server Authentication

Sometimes you may find your Active Resource model may need to access a service on another network that is only accessible through a proxy server on your network (a "forward" proxy). This is often the case in your development environment where you may have to access the Internet through a proxy server, or perhaps an intranet application that needs data from the Internet.

In particularly thrifty enterprise networks (where Internet access is actively discouraged), the proxy server may even require authentication. It is far better to work with the infrastructure teams to remove the need for proxy authentication from selected machines (like your development workstation, and the production server even more so), and preferably no explicit proxy at all.

JoshG says . . .

If the organization hasn't made it to the 90's yet with its Internet connectivity, or only trusts its information technologists as far as it can kick them, you may have bigger problems than configuring your Rails app.

To connect through your proxy server by providing it additional credentials either by providing a URI:

```
class Geocode < ActiveResource::Base
  self.site =
"http://maps.google.com/maps/api/geocode/json?address=#{@address}"
  self.proxy = URI::HTTP.build({:userinfo => 'apps:3x0du$', :host =>
'proxymuppets.smackaho.st', :port => 3470})
end
```

or using URI-style:

```
class Geocode < ActiveResource::Base
  self.site =
"http://maps.google.com/maps/api/geocode/json?address=#{@address}"
  self.proxy = 'http://apps:3x0du$@proxymuppets.smackaho.st:3470/'
end
```

15.5.5 Authentication in the Web Service Controller

On the other side of the connection, the RESTful service that our Active Resource model is consuming, we can use the authentication built-in to Rails:

```
class MoneyTransferController < ApplicationController
  USER_NAME, PASSWORD = 'administrator', 'secret'  #for example purpose
only

  before_filter :authenticate

  def create
    @money_transfer = MoneyTransfer.new(params[:money_transfer])
    respond_to do |format|
      if @money_transfer.save
        flash[:notice] = 'Money Transfer was successfully created.'
        format.html { redirect_to(@money_transfer) }
        format.xml  { head :created, :location => @money_transfer }
      else
        format.html { render :action => 'new' }
```

XML

```
      format.xml  { render :xml => @money_transfer.errors, :status =>
:unprocessable_entity}
        end
      end
  end


  private
    def authenticate
      authenticate_or_request_with_http_basic do |user_name, password|
        user_name == USER_NAME && password == PASSWORD #a very simple
authentication system with hard-coded username and password! Replace with
a lookup into some repository.
        end
      end
end
```

If the service is supporting HTTP Digest Authentication:

```
class MoneyTransferController < ApplicationController
  USER_NAME, PASSWORD = 'administrator', 'secret'  #for example purpose
only
  USERS = { USER_NAME => Digest::MD5::hexdigest([USER_NAME,
'ExampleAuthenticationRealm', PASSWORD].join(":")) } #for example purpose
only

  before_filter :authenticate

  def create
    @money_transfer = MoneyTransfer.new(params[:money_transfer])
    respond_to do |format|
      if @money_transfer.save
        flash[:notice] = 'Money Transfer was successfully created.'
        format.html { redirect_to(@money_transfer) }
        format.xml  { head :created, :location => @money_transfer }
      else
        format.html { render :action => 'new' }
        format.xml  { render :xml => @money_transfer.errors, :status =>
:unprocessable_entity}
        end
      end
  end


  private
    def authenticate
      authenticate_or_request_with_http_digest do |user_name|
        USERS[user_name]  #return HA1-style hashed password
      end
    end
end
```

The `authenticate_or_request_with_http_digest` method will first try to authenticate using a `HA1`-style digest password (which is what our example above uses). If that fails, it will attempt to hash a plain text password and match it against the hash in the request.

Initial authentication of client certificates is done by whatever in your HTTP stack that negotiates the SSL session (e.g. httpd, nginx), not in your Rails application.

Depending on your infrastructure technology, you may have access to additional environment variables like `SSL_CLIENT_CERT`, `REMOTE_USER`, `X-HTTP_AUTHORIZATION`. These can be used for deeper authentication (e.g., comparing a certificate's DN, email, and CN) and for authorization (to verify if an authenticated user is allowed to perform specific actions).

15.6 Conclusion

In practice, the `to_xml` and `from_xml` methods meet the XML handling needs for most situations that the average Rails developer will ever encounter. Their simplicity masks a great degree of flexibility and power, and in this chapter we attempted to explain them in sufficient detail to inspire your own exploration of XML handling in the Ruby world.

As a pair, the `to_xml` and `from_xml` methods also enabled the creation of a framework that makes tying Rails applications together using authenticated RESTful web services drop-dead easy. That framework is named Active Resource, and this chapter gave you a crash-course introduction to it.

CHAPTER 16

Action Mailer

It's a cool way to send emails without tons of code

—Jake Scruggs

Integration with email is a crucial part of most modern web application projects. Whether it's sign-up confirmations, password recovery, or letting users control their accounts via email, you'll be happy to hear that Rails offers great support for both sending and receiving email, thanks to its Action Mailer framework.

In this chapter, we'll cover what's needed to set up your deployment to be able to send and receive mail with the Action Mailer framework and by writing mailer models, the entities in Rails that encapsulate code having to do with email handling.

16.1 Setup

By default, Rails will try to send email via SMTP (port 25) of localhost. If you are running Rails on a host that has an SMTP daemon running and it accepts SMTP email locally, you don't have to do anything else in order to send mail. If you don't have SMTP available on localhost, you have to decide how your system will send email.

When not using SMTP directly, the main options are to use sendmail or to give Rails information on how to connect to an external mail server. Most organizations have SMTP servers available for this type of use, although it's worth noting that because of abuse many hosting providers have stopped offering shared SMTP service.

Most serious production deployments use third-party SMTP services that specialize in delivering automated email, avoiding user spam filters and blacklists.

16.2 Mailer Models

Assuming the mail system is configured, let's go ahead and create a mailer model that will contain code pertaining to sending and receiving a class of email. Rails provides a generator to get us started rapidly. Our mailer will send out a notices to any user of our sample application who is late entering their time.

```
$ rails generate mailer LateNotice
    create      app/mailers/late_notice.rb
    invoke      haml
    create      app/views/late_notice.text.html.haml
    invoke      rspec
    create      test/unit/late_notice_spec.rb
```

A view folder for the mailer is created at `app/views/late_notice` and the mailer itself is stubbed out at `app/mailers/late_notice.rb`:

```
class LateNotice < ActionMailer::Base
  default :from => "from@example.com"
end
```

Kind of like a default Active Record subclass, there's not much there at the start.

16.2.1 Preparing Outbound Email Messages

You work with Action Mailer classes by defining public mailer methods that correspond to types of emails that you want to send. Inside the public method, you assign any variables that will be needed by the email message template and then call the mail method, which is conceptually similar to the render method used in controllers.

Continuing with our example, let's write a `late_timesheet` mailer method that takes `user` and `week_of` parameters. Notice that it sets the basic information needed to send our notice email (see Listing 16.1).

Listing 16.1 Adding a mailer method

```
class LateNotice < ActionMailer::Base
  default :from => "system@timeandexpenses.com"

  def late_timesheet(user, week_of)
    @recipient = user.name
    @week = week_of
    attachments["image.png"] = File.read("/images/image.png")
    mail(
      :to => user.email,
```

```
            :subject => "[Time and Expenses] Timesheet notice"
        )
    end
end
```

Inside the method we've created we have access to a few methods to set up the message for delivery, including the `mail` method shown above:

attachments Allows you to add normal and inline file attachments to your message

```
attachments["myfile.zip"] = File.read("/myfile.zip")
attachments.inline["logo.png"] = File.read("/logo.png")
```

headers Allows you to supply a hash of custom email headers

```
headers("X-Author" => "Obie Fernandez")
```

mail Sets up the email that will get sent. It accepts a hash of headers that a `Mail::Message` will accept and allows an optional block. If no block is specified, views will be used to construct the email with the same name as the method in the mailer. If a block is specified these can be customized.

Note also the change of the default from address to one set up for our application. Here is a sample list of the headers that you can include in the hash passed to the mail method or in the default macro. In addition to these, you may pass any email header that is needed when sending, i.e., `{ "X-Spam" => value }`.

subject The subject line for the message.

to The recipient addresses for the message, either as a string (for a single address) or an array (for multiple addresses). Remember that this method expects actual address strings not your application's user objects.

```
users.map(&:email)
```

from Specifies the from address for the message as a string (required).

cc Specifies carbon-copy recipient (Cc:) addresses for the message, either as a string (for a single address) or an array for multiple addresses.

bcc Specifies blind recipient (Bcc:) addresses for the message, either as a string (for a single address) or an array for multiple addresses.

reply_to Sets the email for the reply-to header.

Mail

date An optional explicit sent on date for the message, usually passed `Time.now`. Will be automatically set by the delivery mechanism if you don't supply a value, and cannot be set using the default macro.

The `mail` method can either take a block or not if you want to do custom formats similar to Rails routes.

```
mail(:to => "user@example.com") do |format|
  format.text
  format.html
end
```

The body of the email is created by using an Action View template (regular Haml or ERb) that has the instance variables in the mailer available as instance variables in the template. So the corresponding body template for the mailer method in Listing 16.1 could look like

```
Dear #{@recipient},

Your timesheet for the week of #{@week} is late.
```

And if the recipient was Aslak, the email generated would look like this:

```
Date: Sun, 12 Dec 2004 00:00:00 +0100
From: system@timeandexpenses.com
To: aslak.hellesoy@gmail.com
Subject: [Time and Expenses] Late timesheet notice

Dear Aslak Hellesoy,

Your timesheet for the week of Aug 15th is late.
```

16.2.2 HTML Email Messages

To send mail as HTML, make sure your view template generates HTML and that the corresponding template name corresponds to the email method name. For our `late_timesheet` method this would be in `app/views/late_notice/late_timesheet.text.html.haml` (or `.erb`.) You can also override this template name in the `mail` block.

```
mail(:to => "user@example.com") do |format|
  format.text
  format.html { render "another_template" }
end
```

16.2.3   Multipart Messages

If a plain text and HTML template are present for a specific mailer action, the text template and the HTML template will both get sent by default as a multipart message. The HTML part will be flagged as alternative content for those email clients that support it.

Implicit Multipart Messages

As mentioned earlier in the chapter, multipart messages can also be used implicitly, without invoking the `part` method, because Action Mailer will automatically detect and use multipart templates, where each template is named after the name of the action, followed by the content type. Each such detected template will be added as separate part to the message.

For example, if the following templates existed, each would be rendered and added as a separate part to the message, with the corresponding content type. The same body hash is passed to each template.

- signup_notification.text.plain.haml

- signup_notification.text.html.haml

- signup_notification.text.xml.builder

- signup_notification.text.x-yaml.erb

16.2.4   Attachments

Including attachments in emails is relatively simple, just use the `attachments` method in your class.

```
class LateNotice < ActionMailer::Base
  def late_timesheet(user, week_of)
    @recipient = user.name
    attachments["image.png"] = File.read("/images/image.png")
    mail(
      :to => user.email,
      :from => "test@myapp.com",
      :subject => "[Time and Expenses] Timesheet notice"
    )
  end
end
```

If you wanted to attach the image inline, use `attachments.inline`.

```
attachments.inline["image.png"] = File.read("/images/image.png")
```

You can access this attachment in the template if need be via the , then calling `url` on that object for the image's relative content id (cid:) path. `image_tag` helper.

```
Dear #{@recipient},

Your timesheet is late, here's a photo depicting our sadness:

= image_tag attachments['image.png'].url, :alt => "Invoicing"
```

16.2.5 Generating URLs

Generating application URLs is handled through named routes or using the `url_for` helper. Since mail does not have request context like controllers do, the host configuration option needs to be set. The best practice for this is to define them in the corresponding environment configuration although it can be defined on a per mailer basis.

```
# config/environments/production.rb
config.action_mailer.default_url_options = { :host => 'accounting.com' }
```

In your mailer you can now generate your url. It is important to note that you cannot use the _path variation for your named routes since the must be rendered as absolute URLs.

```
class LateNotice < ActionMailer::Base
  def late_timesheet(user, week_of)
    @recipient = user.name
    @link = user_url(user)
    mail(
      :to => user.email,
      :from => "test@myapp.com",
      :subject => "[Time and Expenses] Timesheet notice"
    )
  end
end
```

When generating URLs through `url_for`, the controller and action also need to be specified. If you have provided a default host then the `:only_path` option must be provided to tell the helper to generate an absolute path.

```
= url_for(:controller => "users", :action => "update",
:only_path => false)
```

16.2.6 Mailer Layouts

Mailer layouts behave just like controller layouts. To be automatically recognized, they need to have the same name as the mailer itself. In our previous case, `layouts/late_notice.html.haml` would automatically be used for our HTML emails. You can also add custom layouts if your heart desires, either at the class level or as a render option.

```
class LateNotice < ActionMailer::Base
  layout "alternative"

  def late_timesheet(user, week_of)
    mail(:to => user.email) do |format|
      format.html { render :layout => "another" }
    end
  end
end
```

We've now talked extensively about preparing email messages for sending, but what about actually sending them to the recipients?

16.2.7   Sending an Email

Sending emails only involves getting a `Mail::Message` object from your mailer and delivering it.

```
aslak = User.find_by_name "Aslak Hellesoy"
message = LateNotice.late_timesheet(aslak, 1.week.ago)
message.deliver
```

16.3   Receiving Emails

To receive emails, you need to write a public method named `receive` on one of your application's `ActionMailer::Base` subclasses. It will take a `Mail::Message`[1] object instance as its single parameter. When there is incoming email to handle, you call an instance method named `receive` on your Mailer class. The raw email string is converted into a `Mail::Message` object automatically and your `receive` method is invoked for further processing. You don't have to implement the `receive` class method yourself, it is inherited from `ActionMailer::Base`.[2]

That's all pretty confusing to explain, but simple in practice. Listing 16.2 shows an example.

---

1. `http://github.com/mikel/mail`
2. If you're willing to depend on Google App Engine, you should investigate the innovative Remail gem at `http://github.com/maccman/remail` for an easy and powerful REST-based approach to solving the problem.

Listing 16.2 The simple MessageArchiver mailer class with a receive method

```
class MessageArchiver < ActionMailer::Base

  def receive(email)
    person = Person.find_by_email(email.to.first)
    person.emails.create(
      :subject => email.subject,
      :body => email.body
    )
  end
end
```

The `receive` class method can be the target for a Postfix recipe or any other mail-handler process that can pipe the contents of the email to another process. The `rails runner` command makes it easy to handle incoming mail:

```
rails runner 'MessageArchiver.receive(STDIN.read)'
```

That way, when a message is received, the `receive` class method would be fed the raw string content of the incoming email via `STDIN`.

16.3.1 Handling Incoming Attachments

Processing files attached to incoming email messages is just a matter of using the `attachments` attribute of `Mail::Message`, as in Listing 16.3. This example assumes that you have a `Person` class, with a `has_many` association to an `attachment_fu` object named `photos`.

```
class PhotoByEmail < ActionMailer::Base

  def receive(email)
    from = email.from.first
    person = Person.find_by_email(from)
    logger.warn("Person not found [#{from}]") and return unless person

    if email.has_attachments?
      email.attachments.each do |file|
        person.photos.create(:uploaded_data => file)
      end
    end
  end
end
```

There's not much more to it than that, except of course to wrestle with the configuration of your mail-processor (outside of Rails) since they are notoriously difficult to configure.[3] After you have your mail-processor calling the `rails runner` command correctly, add a `crontab` so that incoming mail is handled about every five minutes or so, depending on the needs of your application.

16.4 Server Configuration

Most of the time, you don't have to configure anything specifically to get mail sending to work, because your production server will have `sendmail` installed and Action Mailer will happily use it to send emails.

If you don't have sendmail installed on your server, you can try setting up Rails to send email directly via SMTP. The `ActionMailer::Base` class has a hash named `smtp_settings` (`server_settings` prior to Rails 2.0) that holds configuration information. The settings here will vary depending on the SMTP server that you use.

The sample (as shown in Listing 16.3) demonstrates the SMTP server settings that are available (and their default values). You'll want to add similar code to your `config/environment.rb` file:

Listing 16.3 SMTP settings for ActionMailer

```
ActionMailer::Base.smtp_settings = {
  :address => 'smtp.yourserver.com',   # default: localhost
  :port => 25,    # default: 25
  :domain => 'yourserver.com',    # default: localhost.localdomain
  :user_name => 'user',   # no default
  :password => 'password',   # no default
  :authentication => :plain   # :plain, :login or :cram_md5
}
```

16.5 Testing Email Content

Ben Mabey's `email_spec`[4] gem provides a nice way to test your mailers using RSpec. Add it to your Gemfile and first make the following additions to your `spec/spec_helper.rb`.

---

3. Rob Orsini, author of O'Reilly's Rails Cookbook recommends getmail, which you can get from `http://pyropus.ca/software/getmail`.
4. `http://github.com/bmabey/email-spec`

```
RSpec::Runner.configure do |config|
  config.include(EmailSpec::Helpers)
  config.include(EmailSpec::Matchers)
end
```

Mailer specs reside in `spec/mailers`, and `email_spec` provides convenience matchers for asserting that the mailer contains the right attributes.

- `reply_to`: Checks the reply-to value.

- `deliver_to`: Verifies the recipient.

- `deliver_from`: Assertion for the sender.

- `bcc_to`: Verifies the bcc.

- `have_subject`: Performs matching of the subject text.

- `include_email_with_subject`: Performs matching of the subject text in multiple emails.

- `have_body_text`: Match for text in the body.

- `have_header`: Check for a matching email header.

These matchers can then be used to assert that the generated email has the correct content included in it.

```
require "spec_helper"
describe InvoiceMailer do

  let(:invoice) do
    Invoice.new(:name => "Acme", :email => "joe@example.com")
  end

  let(:email) do
    InvoiceMailer.create_late(invoice)
  end

  it "delivers to the invoice email" do
    email.should deliver_to("joe@example.com")
  end

  it "contains the invoice name" do
    email.should have_body_text(/Acme/)
  end

  it "has a late invoice subject" do
    email.should have_subject(/Late Invoice/)
  end
end
```

If you're attempting to test whether or not the mailer gets called and sends the email, it is recommended to simply check via a mock that the deliver method got executed.

16.6 Conclusion

In this chapter, we learned how Rails makes sending and receiving email easy. With relatively little code, you can set up your application to send out email, even HTML email with inline graphics attachments. Receiving email is even easier, except perhaps for setting up mail-processing scripts and cron jobs. We also briefly covered the configuration settings that go in your application's environment specific configuration related to mail.

Mail

CHAPTER 17
Caching and Performance

Hard work never killed anybody, but why take the chance?

—Edgar Bergen (as Charlie McCarthy), 1903–1978

Historically Rails has suffered from an unfair barrage of criticisms over perceived weaknesses in scalability. Luckily, the continued success of Rails in ultra-high-traffic usage at companies such as Twitter and Groupon has made liars of the critics. Nowadays, you can make your Rails application very responsive and scalable with ease. The mechanisms used to squeeze maximum performance out of your Rails apps are the subject of this chapter.

View caching lets you specify that anything from entire pages down to fragments of the page should be captured to disk as HTML files and sent along by your web server on future requests with minimal involvement from Rails itself. ETag support means that in best-case scenarios, it's not even necessary to send any content at all back to the browser, beyond a couple of HTTP headers. Hard work may never have killed anyone, but make your Rails application work harder than it needs to, and you might kill your server!

17.1 View Caching

There are three types of view caching in Rails:

Page caching The output of an entire controller action is cached to disk, with no further involvement by the Rails dispatcher.

Action caching The output of an entire controller action is cached to disk, but the Rails dispatcher is still involved in subsequent requests, and controller filters are executed.

Fragment caching Arbitrary bits and pieces of your page's output can be cached to disk to save the time of having to render them in the future.

17.1.1 Caching in Development Mode?

I wanted to mention up front that caching is disabled in development mode. If you want to play with caching during development, you'll need to edit the following setting in the `config/environments/development.rb` file:

```
config.action_controller.perform_caching = false
```

Of course, remember to change it back before checking it back into your project repository, or you might face some very confusing errors down the road.[1]

17.1.2 Page Caching

The simplest form of caching is page caching, triggered by use of the `caches_page` macro-style method in a controller. It tells Rails to capture the entire output of the request to disk so that it is served up directly by the web server on subsequent requests without the involvement of the dispatcher. Nothing will be logged to the Rails log, nor will controller filters be triggered—absolutely nothing to do with Rails will happen, just like the static HTML files in your project's `public` directory.

17.1.3 Action Caching

By definition, if there's anything that has to change on every request or specific to an end user's view of that page, page caching is not an option. On the other hand, if all we need to do is run some filters that check conditions before displaying the page requested, the `caches_action` method will work. It's almost like page caching, except that controller filters are executed prior to serving the cached HTML file. That gives you the option to do some extra processing or even redirect if necessary.

Action caching is implemented with fragment caching (covered later in this chapter) and an `around_filter` (covered in Chapter 4, Working with Controllers). The cached action content is keyed based on the current host and the path, which means that it will still work even with Rails applications serving multiple subdomains using a DNS wildcard. Also, different representations of the same resource, such as HTML and XML, are treated like separate requests and cached separately.

Listing 17.1 (like most of the listings in this chapter) is taken from a blog application with public and private entries, so for default requests, we should run a filter that figures out whether the visitor is logged in and redirects them to the `public` action if necessary.

---

1. In his great screencast on the subject, Geoffrey Grosenbach suggests adding another environment mode to your project named `development_with_caching`, with caching turned on just for experimentation (`http://peepcode.com/products/page-action-and-fragment-caching`).

Listing 17.1 The EntriesController of lil_journal

```ruby
class EntriesController < ApplicationController
  before_filter :check_logged_in, :only => [:index]

  caches_page :public
  caches_action :index

  def public
    @entries = Entry.where(:private => false).limit(10)
    render :index
  end

  def index
    @entries = Entry.limit(10)
  end

  private

    def check_logged_in
      redirect_to :action => 'public' unless logged_in?
    end

end
```

The `public` action displays only the public entries and is visible to anyone, which makes it a candidate for page caching. However, since it doesn't require its own template, we just call `render :index` explicitly at the end of the `public` action.

Design Considerations

Knowing that your application will eventually require caching should influence your design decisions. Projects with optional authentication often have controller actions that are impossible to page or action-cache, because they handle both login states internally. That would have been the case in Listing 17.1 if we had written the `index` action to handle both public and private display:

```ruby
def index
  @entries = Entry.limit(10)
  @entries = @entries.where(:private => false) unless logged_in?
end
```

Most of the time, you won't have too many pages with completely static content that can be cached using `cache_page` or `cache_action`, and that's where fragment caching comes into play.

17.1.4 Fragment Caching

Users are accustomed to all sorts of dynamic content on the page, and your application layout will be filled with things like welcome messages and notification counts. Fragment caching allows us to capture parts of the rendered page on disk and serve them up on subsequent requests without needing to render their content again. The performance improvement is not as dramatic as with page or action caching, since the Rails dispatcher is still involved.

The `cache` Method

Fragment caching is by its very nature something that you specify in your view template rather than at the controller level. You do so using the `cache` method of Action View. It takes a block, which lets you wrap content that should be cached.

Once we log in to the sample application reflected in Listing 17.1, the header section should really display information about the logged-in user, so action-caching the index page is out of the question. We'll remove the `caches_action` directive from the `EntriesController`, but leave `cache_page` in place for the `public` action. Then we'll go into the `entries/index.html.haml` template and add fragment caching, as shown in Listing 17.2.

Listing 17.2 `entries/index.html.haml` template with fragment caching

```
= content_tag :h1, "#{@user.name}'s Journal"
- cache do
  = render :partial => 'entry', :collection => @entries
```

Easy as that—the HTML output of rendering the collection of entries is stored in the fragment cache associated with the `entries/index` page. That's fine if we're only caching one fragment of the page, but most of the time we'll need to give the fragment some extra identification.

Named Fragments

The `cache` method takes an optional `name` parameter. If you leave it blank, as we have in Listing 17.2, it caches its content keyed to the URL of its parent page. That's an acceptable solution as long as there is only one fragment on the page.

If we're caching more than one fragment on the page, we need to add an extra identifier, so that we don't suffer name collisions. Listing 17.3 is an enhanced version of the entries page, where we've added the display of recent comments in the sidebar.

Listing 17.3 The entries page with two fragment cache directives

```
= content_tag :h1, "#{@user.name}'s Journal"

- cache(:fragment => 'entries') do
  = render :partial => 'entry', :collection => @entries

- content_for :sidebar do
  - cache(:fragment => 'recent_comments') do
    = render :partial => 'comment', :collection => @recent_comments
```

After the code in Listing 17.3 is rendered, there will be two fragments stored in the cache, keyed as follows:

```
/entries/index?fragment=entries
/entries/index?fragment=recent_comments
```

The fact that Rails uses the page's URL scheme to key fragments in the cache is an elegant solution to a somewhat difficult problem. Consider, for instance, what would happen if you added pagination to the application and pulled up the second page of entries. Without further work, a pair of additional fragments would be correctly cached for future use:

```
/entries/index?page=2&fragment=entries
/entries/index?page=2&fragment=recent_comments
```

Note

Note that Rails uses the `url_for` mechanism to construct unique identifiers for fragments out of convenience. There's no requirement that your fragment keys correspond to actual working URLs in your application.

Global Fragments

Sometimes, you'll want to fragment-cache content that is not specific to a single URL of your application. To add globally keyed fragments to the cache, we'll again use the `name` parameter of the `cache` helper method, but this time we'll give it a string identifier instead of a hash.

To demonstrate, let's add a requirement that our sample application should display user statistics on every page. In Listing 17.4, we cache the stats partial for every user, using their name and a `"_stats"` suffix as the key.

Listing 17.4 The entries page with global user stats

```
= content_tag :h1, "#{@user.name}'s Journal"

- cache(:fragment => 'entries') do
  = render :partial => 'entry', :collection => @entries

- content_for :sidebar do
  - cache(@user.name + "_stats") do
    = render :partial => 'stats'
  - cache(:fragment => 'recent_comments') do
    = render :partial => 'comment', :collection => @recent_comments
```

Avoiding Extra Database Activity

Once you have fragments of your view cached, it no longer makes sense to do the database queries that supply those fragments with their data. After all, the results of those database queries will not be used again until the cached fragments are expired. The `fragment_exist?` method lets you check for the existence of cached content, and takes the same parameters that you used with the associated `cache` method.

Here's how we would modify the index action accordingly:

```
def index
  unless fragment_exist?(:fragment => 'entries')
    @entries = Entry.all.limit(10)
  end
end
```

Now the finder method will only get executed if the cache needs to be refreshed.

Tim says...

You wouldn't need to clutter your controller code with calls to `fragment_exist?` if you were using decent_exposure.[2]

17.1.5 Expiration of Cached Content

Whenever you use caching, you need to consider any and all situations that will cause the cache to become stale, out of date. Then you need to write code that sweeps away the old content, so to speak, making room for new content to be cached in its place.

---

2. `http://github.com/voxdolo/decent_exposure`

Expiring Pages and Actions

The expire_page and expire_action methods let you explicitly delete content from the cache, so that it is regenerated on the next request. There are various ways to identify the content to expire, but one of them is by passing a hash with url_for conventions used elsewhere in Rails. Listing 17.5 shows how we've added expiration to the create method of the entries controller.

Listing 17.5 The entries create action

```
1  def create
2    @entry = @user.entries.build(params[:entry])
3    if @entry.save
4      expire_page :action => 'public'
5      redirect_to entries_path(@entry)
6    else
7      render :action => 'new'
8    end
9  end
```

Notice how line 4 of Listing 17.5 explicitly expires the page associated with the public action. If you think about it, though, it's not only the create action that invalidates the cache. The update and destroy actions would invalidate it too.

In your applications, particularly when you're doing RESTful resources, remember that different representations of the same resource are treated like separate requests and cached separately. If you've cached the XML response of an action, you'll have to expire it by appending :format => :xml to the action specification.

Expiring Fragments

The sample app we've been considering also has cached fragments to clear out, using the expire_fragment method. Now the create action looks like:

Listing 17.6 The entries create action with fragment expiration

```
def create
  @entry = @user.entries.build(params[:entry])
  if @entry.save
    expire_page :action => 'public'
    expire_fragment(:fragment => 'entries')
    expire_fragment(:fragment => (@user.name + "_stats"))
    redirect_to entries_path(@entry)
  else
    render :action => 'new'
  end
end
```

Caching

There's actually a serious problem with the expiration routine that we wrote in Listing 17.6. Remember we said that the fragment caching of entries would work with pagination and that we'd have cached fragments keyed like `'/entries/index?page=2&fragment=entries'`

As a result, just doing `expire_fragment(:fragment => 'entries')` will only clear the first page from the cache. For that reason, the `expire_fragment` method understands regular expressions, and we'll need to use them in our code:

```
expire_fragment(%r{entries/.*})
```

There has to be a better way to handle invalidation than remembering to stick a bunch of complicated expiration statements in all your action methods. Also, since caching is a unique concern, it feels like something that should be applied in an aspect-oriented fashion instead of procedurally.

17.1.6 Automatic Cache Expiry with Sweepers

A `Sweeper` class is kind of like an `ActiveRecord Observer` object, except that it's specialized for use in expiring cached content. When you write a sweeper, you tell it which of your models to observe for changes, just as you would with callback classes and observers.

Listing 17.7 is a sweeper to keep the caching of our sample app's entries in order.

Listing 17.7 An entry sweeper

```
class EntrySweeper < ActionController::Caching::Sweeper
  observe Entry

  def expire_cached_content(entry)
    expire_page :controller => 'entries', :action => 'public'
    expire_fragment(%r{entries/.*})
    expire_fragment(:fragment => (entry.user.name + "_stats"))
  end

  alias_method :after_save, :expire_cached_content
  alias_method :after_destroy, :expire_cached_content

end
```

Once you have a `Sweeper` class (put it in your `app/models` directory), you need to tell your controller to use that sweeper in conjunction with its actions. Here's the top of the revised entries controller:

```
class EntriesController < ApplicationController

  before_filter :check_logged_in, :only => [:index]
  caches_page :public
  cache_sweeper :entry_sweeper, :only => [:create, :update, :destroy]


  ...
```

Like many other controller macros, the `cache_sweeper` method takes `:only` and
`:except` options. There's no need to bother the sweeper for actions that can't modify
the state of the application, so we do indeed include the `:only` option in our example.

Like the related `observers`, `sweepers` are not limited to observing just one model.
The main thing to remember if we go down that route is that our callback methods will
need to know how to handle all of them. Ruby's `case` statement may come in handy,
as shown in Listing 17.8, a full revision of the `EntrySweeper`, which may now observe
`Comment` as well as `Entry` objects.

Listing 17.8 The EntrySweeper revised to observe and handle both entries and comments

```
class EntrySweeper < ActionController::Caching::Sweeper
  observe Entry, Comment

  def expire_cached_content(record)
    expire_page :controller => 'entries', :action => 'public'
    expire_fragment(r%{entries/.*})

    user = case entry
      when Entry then record.user
      when Comment then record.entry.user
    end

    expire_fragment(:fragment => (user.name + "_stats"))
  end

  alias_method :after_save, :expire_cached_content
  alias_method :after_destroy, :expire_cached_content

end
```

The big gotcha with regular expression and `expire_fragment` is that it is not
supported with the most common caching service used on Rails production systems:
Memcached.

17.1.7   Cache Logging

If you've turned on caching during development, you can actually monitor the Rails log for messages about caching and expiration.

```
Processing Entries#index (for 127.0.0.1 at 2007-07-20 23:07:09) [GET]
  ...
Cached page: /entries.html (0.03949)

Processing Entries#create (for 127.0.0.1 at 2007-07-20 23:10:50) [POST]
  ...
Expired page: /entries.html (0.00085)
```

It's a good way to see whether your caching is actually working as expected.

17.1.8   Action Cache Plugin

The Action Cache plugin by Tom Fakes and Scott Laird is a recommended drop-in replacement for the built-in Rails caching facilities. It doesn't change the Caching API at all, only the underlying implementation.

```
rails plugin install http://craz8.com/svn/trunk/plugins/action_cache
```

These are the major features of the Action Cache plugin:

- Stores cached entries as YAML streams (instead of just HTML) so that the `Response` headers from the original response can be returned along with cached content.

- Adds a `last-modified` header to the response so that clients use a `get-if-modified` HTTP request. If the client already has cached content, sends a `304 Not Modified` response.

- Ensures that only requests with a `200 OK` status are cached. Otherwise, error pages and empty content can get stuck in the cache (and cause difficult-to-diagnose problems.)

- Allows developers to override Rails with their own implementation of cache key generation.

- Allows an action to specify an optional Time To Live value for a response, before cached content associated with the response will be automatically expired.

- Allows control over whether caching occurs for an action at runtime based on request parameters. (For instance, never cache content for site administrators.)

- A new method, `expire_all_actions`, clears out the entire action cache contents.

- Changes the `expire_action` implementation to actually use the `Regexp` fragment expiry call, causing all matching cache items to be cleared. For those of you using REST, and providing HTML, JS, and XML for the same action, all three will be expired when you expire one of them with code like `expire_action :controller => 'foo', :action => 'bar'`

17.1.9   Cache Storage

Unlike session data, fragment-cached data can grow to be quite large. Rails gives you three different options for cache storage:

`ActiveSupport::Cache::FileStore` Keeps the fragments on disk in the `cache_path`, which works well for all types of environments and shares the fragments for all the web server processes running off the same application directory.

`ActiveSupport::Cache::MemoryStore` Keeps the fragments in the memory, and can potentially consume an unacceptable amount of memory per process if you do not have a good expiration strategy. As of Rails 3, MemoryStore is now thread-safe.

`ActiveSupport::Cache::MemCacheStore` Keeps the fragments in a separate process using a proven cache server named `memcached`. General consensus at the time or writing suggests that `memcache` is the best option.

Configuration Example

The `:memory_store` option is enabled by default.

```
ActionController::Base.fragment_cache_store = :memory_store,
  :expire_in => 1.minute, :compress => true

ActionController::Base.fragment_cache_store = :file_store,
"/path/to/cache/directory"

ActionController::Base.fragment_cache_store = :mem_cache_store,
"localhost"
```

All cache stores take the following hash options as the last parameter:

- `expire_in`: Supply a time for items to be expired from the cache.

- `compress`: Specify to use compression or not.

- `compress_threshold`: Specify the threshold at which to compress, the default is 32k.

Caching

Note that most production Rails deployments use Passenger or Unicorn, which spawn new processes depending on application load. You will want to use a `MemCacheStore` or `FileStore` in these cases if you need the cache shared between processes.

Durran says...

> Using a key/value store in your application like Redis or Tokyo Cabinet? Check out `Moneta`[3] if you want to leverage it for your caching. Most supported databases are more than fast enough, and it has a very simple and easy to use API.

Limitations of File-Based Storage

As long as you're hosting your Rails application on a single server, setting up caching is fairly straightforward and easy to implement (of course, coding it is a different story).

If you think about the implications of running a cached application on a cluster of distinct physical servers, you might realize that cache invalidation is going to be painful. Unless you set up the file storage to point at a shared filesystem such as NFS or GFS, it won't work.

Manual Sweeping with **rake**

If you do choose file-based storage, you probably want to give yourself a way to manually clear your application's cached content. It's not difficult to do using Rake. Just add a file to the `lib/tasks` folder named `cache.rake`. You'll be creating a task similar to the one shown in Listing 17.9.

Listing 17.9 A **cache_sweeper** custom rake task

```
desc "Manually sweep the cache"
task :cache_sweeper do
  FileUtils.rm_rf Dir[File.join(Rails.root, "public", "entries*")] #pages
  FileUtils.rm_rf Dir[File.join(Rails.root, "tmp", "cache*")] #fragments
end
```

I used `entries` in the example task, but remember that you may have to add one or more of your own `FileUtils.rm_rf` statements corresponding to the pages that your application is caching.

---

3. http://github.com/wycats/moneta

As a final note, keep in mind, that it's common to use the `FileUtils.rm_rf` brute-force approach in sweepers instead of the `expire_*` methods, mostly because a lot of times it's just easier to blow away entire cached directories and let them be rebuilt as needed.

17.2 General Caching

Each of the caching mechanisms described in the previous section is actually using an implementation of an `ActiveSupport::Cache::Store`, covered in detail within Appendix A.

Rails always has a default cache store accessible via `Rails.cache`:

```
>> Rails.cache.write(:color, :red)
=> true
>> Rails.cache.read :color
=> :red
```

17.2.1 Eliminating Extra Database Lookups

One of the most common patterns of cache usage is to eliminate database lookups for commonly accessed data, using the cache's `fetch` method. For the following example, assume that your application's user objects are queried very often by id. The `fetch` method takes a block that is executed and used to populate the cache when the lookup *misses*, that is, a value is not already present.

```
class User < ActiveRecord::Base
  def self.fetch(id)
    Rails.cache.fetch("user_#{id}") { User.find(id) }
  end

  def after_save
    Rails.cache.write("user_#{id}", self)
  end

  def after_destroy
    Rails.cache.delete("city_#{id}")
  end
end
```

I opted to use my own key generation scheme in the example, because of the use of the `updated_at` attribute in the implementation of Active Record's `cache_key` method.

```
class ActiveRecord::Base
  def cache_key
    case
```

```
    when new?
      "#{self.class.model_name.cache_key}/new"
    when timestamp = self[:updated_at]

"#{self.class.model_name.cache_key}/#{id}-#{timestamp.to_s(:number)}"
    else
      "#{self.class.model_name.cache_key}/#{id}"
    end
  end
end
```

17.2.2 Initializing New Caches

We can also initialize a new cache directly, or through `ActiveSupport::Cache.`
`lookup_store` if we want to cache other objects in the application and not just the
views. Either one of these methods of creating a new cache takes the same expiration
and compression options as mentioned previously, and the same three stores exist as for
fragment caching: `FileStore`, `MemoryStore`, and `MemCacheStore`.

```
ActiveSupport::Cache::MemCacheStore.new(
  :expire_in => 5.seconds
)
ActiveSupport::Cache.lookup_store(
  :mem_cache_store, :compress => true
)
```

Once you have your cache object, you can read and write to it via its very simple
API and any Ruby object that can be serialized can be cached, including nils.

```
cache = ActiveSupport::Cache::MemoryStore.new
cache.write(:name, "John Doe")
cache.fetch(:name) # => "John Doe"
```

17.2.3 **fetch** Options

There are several options that can be passed to `fetch` in order to provide different types
of behavior for each of the different stores. Additional options than those listed here are
available based on the individual cache implementations.

- `:compress` Use compression for this request.

- `:expire_in` Tell an individual key in the cache to expire in *n* seconds.

- `:force` If set to true will force the cache to delete the supplied key.

- `:race_condition_ttl` Supply seconds as an integer and a block. When an item in the cache is expired for less than the number of seconds, its time gets updated and its value is set to the result of the block.

There are other available functions on caches, and options can be passed for the specific cache store implementation.

- `delete(name, options)` Delete a value for the key.
- `exist?(name, options)` Will return true if a value exists for the provided key.
- `read(name, options)` Get a value for the supplied key or return nil if none found.
- `read_multi(*names)` Return the values for the supplied keys as a hash of key/value pairs.
- `write(name, value, options)` Write a value to the cache.

17.3   Control Web Caching

Action Controller offers a pair of methods for easily setting HTTP 1.1 Cache-Control headers. Their default behavior is to issue a *private* instruction, so that intermediate caches (web proxies) must not cache the response. In this context, *private* only controls where the response may be cached and not the privacy of the message content.

The `public` setting indicates that the response may be cached by any cache or proxy and should never be used in conjunction with data served up for *a particular end user*.

Using `curl --head` we can examine the way that these methods affect HTTP responses. For reference, let's examine the output of a normal index action.

```
$ curl --head localhost:3000/reports
HTTP/1.1 200 OK
Etag: "070a386229cd857a15b2f5cb2089b987"
Connection: Keep-Alive
Content-Type: text/html; charset=utf-8
Date: Wed, 15 Sep 2010 04:01:30 GMT
Server: WEBrick/1.3.1 (Ruby/1.8.7/2009-06-12)
X-Runtime: 0.032448
Content-Length: 0
Cache-Control: max-age=0, private, must-revalidate
Set-Cookie: ...124cc92; path=/; HttpOnly
```

Don't get confused by the content length being zero. That's only because `curl --head` issues a HEAD request. If you're experimenting with your own Rails app, try `curl -v localhost:3000` to see all the HTTP headers plus the body content.

17.3.1 `expires_in(seconds, options = {})`

This method will overwrite an existing `Cache-Control` header.[4] Examples include

```
expires_in 20.minutes
expires_in 3.hours, :public => true
expires_in 3.hours, 'max-stale' => 5.hours, :public => true
```

Setting expiration to 20 minutes alters our reference output as follows:

```
Cache-Control: max-age=1200, private
```

17.3.2 `expires_now`

Sets a HTTP 1.1 Cache-Control header of the response to `no-cache` informing web proxies and browsers that they should not cache the response for subsequent requests.

17.4 ETags

The bulk of this chapter deals with caching content so that the server does less work than it would have to do otherwise, but still incurs the cost of transporting page data to the browser. The *ETags* scheme, where E stands for *entity*, allows you to avoid sending any content to the browser at all if nothing has changed on the server since the last time a particular resource was requested. A properly implemented ETags scheme is one of the most significant performance improvements that can be implemented on a high traffic website.[5]

Rendering automatically inserts the `Etag` header on *200 OK* responses, calculated as an MD5 hash of the response body. If a subsequent request comes in that has a matching `Etag`[6], the response will be changed to a *304 Not Modified* and the response body will be set to an empty string.

The key to performance gains is to short circuit the controller action and prevent rendering if you know that the resulting `Etag` is going to be the same as the one associated with the current request. I believe you're actually being a good Internet citizen by paying attention to proper use of ETags in your application. According to RFC 2616,[7] "the preferred behavior for an HTTP/1.1 origin server is to send both a strong entity tag and a Last-Modified value."

---

4. See `http://http://www.w3.org/Protocols/rfc2616/rfc2616-sec14.html#sec14.9` for more information.
5. Tim Bray wrote one of my favorite blog posts on the topic at `http://www.tbray.org/ongoing/When/200x/2008/08/14/Rails-ETags`.
6. `http://www.w3.org/Protocols/rfc2616/rfc2616-sec14.html#sec14.19`
7. `http://www.w3.org/Protocols/rfc2616/rfc2616-sec13.html#sec13.3.4`

Rails does not set a `Last-Modified` response header by default, so it's up to you to do so using one of the following methods.

17.4.1 `fresh_when(options)`

Sets `ETag` and/or `Last-Modified` headers and renders a `304 Not Modified` response if the request is already *fresh*. Freshness is calculated using the `cache_key` method of the object (or array of objects) passed as the `:etag` option.

For example, the following controller action shows a public article.

```
expose(:article)

def show
  fresh_when(:etag => article,
             :last_modified => article.created_at.utc,
             :public => true)
end
```

This code will only render the show template when necessary.

17.4.2 `stale?(options)`

Sets the `ETag` and/or `Last-Modified` headers on the response and checks them against the client request (using `fresh_when`). If the request doesn't match the options provided, the request is considered stale and should be generated from scratch.

You want to use this method instead of `fresh_when` if there is additional logic needed at the controller level in order to render your view.

```
expose(:article)

expose(:statistics) do
  article.really_expensive_operation_to_calculate_stats
end

def show
  if stale?(:etag => article,
            :last_modified => article.created_at.utc,
            :public => true)
    statistics  # decent_exposure memoizes the result
    respond_to do |format|
      ...
    end
  end
end
```

Caching

The normal rendering workflow is only triggered inside of the `stale?` conditional, if needed.

17.5 Conclusion

We've just covered a fairly complicated subject: Caching. Knowing how to use caching will really save your bacon when you work on Rails applications that need to scale. Indeed, developers of high-traffic Rails websites tend to see Rails as a fancy HTML generation platform with which to create content ripe for caching.

CHAPTER 18

RSpec

I do not think there is any thrill that can go through the human heart like that felt by the inventor as he sees some creation of the brain unfolding to success.

—Nikola Tesla

RSpec is a Ruby domain-specific language for specifying the desired behavior of Ruby code. Its strongest appeal is that RSpec scripts (or simply *specs*) can achieve a remarkable degree of readability, letting the authors express their intention with greater readability and fluidity than is achievable using `Test::Unit`'s methods and assertions.

`RSpec::Rails`, a drop-in replacement for the Rails testing subsystem supplies verification, mocking, and stubbing features customized for use with Rails models, controllers, and views. Since switching to RSpec I have never needed to touch `Test::Unit` for anything significant again. RSpec is simply that good.

18.1 Introduction

Since RSpec scripts are so readable, I can't really think of a better way of introducing you to the framework than to dive into an actual spec. Listing 18.1 is part of a real-world RSpec script defining the behavior of a `Payment` in a Hashrocket client project named Workbeast.com. As you're reading the spec, let the descriptions attached to the blocks of code come together to form sentences that describe the desired behavior.

Listing 18.1 Excerpt of Workbeast.com's timesheet spec

```
require 'spec_helper'

describe Timesheet do
  let(:timesheet) { Factory(:timesheet) }
```

501

```
describe "validation of hours worked" do
  it "fails without a number" do
    subject.hours_worked = 'abc'
    subject.should have(1).error_on(:hours_worked)
  end

  it "passes with a number" do
    subject.hours_worked = '123'
    subject.should have(0).errors_on(:hours_worked)
  end

end

context "when submitted" do
  it "sends an email notification to the manager" do
    Notifier.should_receive(:send_later).with(
      :deliver_timesheet_submitted, timesheet
    )
    timesheet.submit
  end

  it "notifies its opening" do
    timesheet.opening.should_not be_nil
    timesheet.opening.should_receive(:fill)
    timesheet.submit
  end

end
```

In the example, the fragment

```
describe Timesheet do
  let(:timesheet) { Factory(:timesheet) }

  describe "validation of hours worked" do
    it "fails without a number" do
      subject.hours_worked = 'abc'
      subject.should have(1).error_on(:hours_worked)
    end
```

... should be understood to mean "Timesheet validation of hours worked fails without a number."

RSpec scripts are collections of behaviors, which in turn have collections of examples. The `describe` method creates a `Behavior` object under the covers. The behavior sets the context for a set of specification examples defined with the `it` method, and you should pass a sentence fragment that accurately describes the context you're about to specify.

You can use RSpec to specify and test model and controller classes, as well as view templates, as individual units in isolation, like we did in Listing 18.1. RSpec is also used to create integration tests that exercise the entire Rails stack from top to bottom.

Listing 18.2 Excerpt of Workbeast.com's `search_colleagues` integration spec

```
describe "Search Colleagues" do
  let(:user) { Factory(:user, :name => 'Joe') }

  let(:public_user) do
    Factory(:user, :name => 'Pete', :privacy_level => 'Public')
  end

  let(:private_user) do
    Factory(:user, :name => 'Nancy', :privacy_level => 'Private')
  end

  before { login_as user }

  it "takes you to the search results page" do
    email_search_for(user, public_user.email)
    current_url.should == search_colleagues_path
  end

  it "doesn't return the current user" do
    email_search_for(user, user.email)
    response.body.should_not contain_text(user.name)
  end

  it "doesn't return private users" do
    email_search_for(@user, private_user.email)
    response.body.should_not contain_text(private_user.name)
  end

  context "when the user is not their colleague" do
    it "shows the 'Add colleague' button" do
      email_search_for(@user, Factory(:user).email)
      response.body.should have_tag('input[type=submit][value=?]',
                                    'Add as Colleague')
    end
  end

  def email_search_for(current_user, email)
    visit colleagues_path
    fill_in 'Search', :with => email
    click_button 'Search'
  end
end
```

RSpec

Use of methods such as `visit` and `fill_in`, as well as the checking the contents of objects such as `response.body`, hint at what this spec is doing: running your entire Rails application.

18.2 Basic Syntax and API

Let's run through some of the basic syntactical features of RSpec, which we've just encountered in the code listings. RSpec is essentially a domain-specific language for creating specifications. The following API methods form the vocabulary of the language.

18.2.1 `describe` and `context`

The `describe` and `context` methods are used to group together related examples of behavior. They are aliases, both taking a string description as their first argument and a block to define the context of their scope.

When writing model specs or anything that smacks of a unit test, you can pass a Ruby class as the first argument to `describe`. Doing so also creates an implicit subject for the examples, which we'll hold off on explaining for the moment. (If you're impatient, you can jump ahead in this section to the `subject` method heading.)

```
describe Timesheet do
  let(:timesheet) { Factory(:timesheet) }
```

18.2.2 `let(:name) {expression}`

The `let` method simplifies the creation of memoized attributes for use in your spec. *Memoized* means that the code block associated with the `let` is executed once and stored for future invocations, increasing performance. Use of `let` also allows you to lessen your dependence on instance variables, by creating a proper interface to the attributes needed in the spec.

So, why use the `let` method? Let's step through a typical spec coding session to understand the motivation. Imagine that you're writing a spec, and it all starts simply enough with a local `blog_post` variable.

```
describe BlogPost do
  it "does something" do
    blog_post = BlogPost.new :title => 'Hello'
    blog_post.should ...
  end
end
```

You continue on, writing another similar example, and you start to see some duplication. The `blog_post` creation is being done twice.

```
describe BlogPost do
  it "does something" do
    blog_post = BlogPost.new :title => 'Hello'
    blog_post.should ...
  end

  it "does something else" do
    blog_post = BlogPost.new :title => 'Hello'
    blog_post.should ...
  end
end
```

So, you refactor the instance creation into a before block, and start using an instance variable in the examples.

```
describe BlogPost do
  before do
    @blog_post = BlogPost.new :title => 'Hello'
  end

  it "does something" do
    @blog_post.should ...
  end

  it "does something else" do
    @blog_post.should ...
  end
end
```

And here comes the punchline: you replace the instance variables with a *variable* described by a let expression.

```
describe BlogPost do
  let(:blog_post) { BlogPost.new :title => 'Hello' }

  it "does something" do
    blog_post.should ...
  end

  it "does something else" do
    blog_post.should ...
  end
end
```

The advantages of using `let` are mostly in the realm of readability. One, it gets rid of all those instance variables and at-signs blotting your code. Two, gets rid of the `before` block, which arguably has no business setting up a bunch variables in the first place. And three, it shows you *who the players are.'* A set of `let` blocks at the top of an example group reads like a cast of characters in a playbill. You can always refer to it when you're deep in the code of an example.

18.2.3 `let!(:name) {expression}`

There are instances where the lazy evaluation of `let` will not suffice and you need the value memoized immediately. This is found often in cases of integration testing, and is where `let!` comes into play.

```
describe BlogPost do
  let(:blog_post) { BlogPost.create :title => 'Hello' }
  let!(:comment) { blog_post.comments.create :text => 'first post' }

  describe "#comment" do
    before do
      blog_post.comment("finally got a first post")
    end

    it "adds the comment" do
      blog_post.comments.count.should == 2
    end
  end
end
```

Since the comment block would never have been executed for the first assertion if you used a `let` definition, only one comment would have been added in this spec even though the implementation may be working. By using `let!` we ensure the initial comment gets created and the spec will now pass.

18.2.4 `before` and `after`

The `before` (and its reclusive cousin, `after`) methods are akin to the `setup` and `teardown` methods of xUnit frameworks like `Test::Unit`. They are used to set up the state as it should be prior to running an example, and if necessary, to clean up the state after the example has run. None of the example behaviors we've seen so far required an `after` block, because frankly, it's rare to need `after` in Rails programming.

Before and after code can be inserted in any `describe` or `context` blocks, and by default they execute for each `it` block that shares their scope.

18.2.5 `it`

The `it` method also takes a description plus a block, similar to `describe`. As mentioned, the idea is to complete the thought that was started in the `describe` method, so that it forms a complete sentence. Your assertions (aka expectations) will always happen within the context of an `it` block, and you should try to limit yourself to one expectation per `it` block.

```
context "when there are no search results" do
  before do
    email_search_for(user, '123')
  end

  it "shows the search form" do
    current_url.should == colleagues_url
  end

  it "renders an error message" do
    response.should have_tag('.error', 'No matching email addresses
found.')
  end
end
```

18.2.6 `specify`

The `specify` method is simply an alias of the `it` method. However, it's mainly used in a different construct to improve readability. Consider the following old-school RSpec example:

```
describe BlogPost do
  before { @blog_post = BlogPost.new :title => 'foo' }

  it "should not be published" do
    @blog_post.should_not be_published
  end
end
```

Note how the example says "should not be published" in plain English, and the Ruby code within says essentially the same thing: `@blog_post.should_not be_published` This is a situation where `specify` comes in handy. Examine a new-school example:

```
describe BlogPost do
  let(:blog_post) { BlogPost.new :title => 'foo' }
  specify { blog_post.should_not be_published }
end
```

RSpec

The English phrase has been removed, and the Ruby code has been move into a block passed to the `specify` method. Since the Ruby block already reads like English, there's no need to repeat yourself. Especially since RSpec automatically (which is pretty cool) generates English output by inspection. Here's what the specdoc output looks like:

```
BlogPost
- should not be published
```

18.2.7 **expect**

When you expect a method call to change a value or throw an exception, then `expect` is for you. Here's an example:

```
expect {
  BlogPost.create :title => 'Hello'
}.to change { BlogPost.count }.by(1)
```

This is just a more readable DSL-style version of the RSpec's older `lambda`-based syntax:

```
lambda {
  BlogPost.create :title => 'Hello'
}.should change { BlogPost.count }.by(1)
```

Simply put, `expect` is an alias of the `lambda` keyword and the `to` method is an alias of the `should` method.

Then comes the `change` matcher. This is where you inspect the attribute or value that you're interested in. In our example, we're making sure that the record was saved to the database, thus increasing the record count by 1.

There are a few different variations on the `change` syntax. Here's one more example, where we're more explicit about before and after values by further chaining `from` and `to` methods:

```
describe "#publish!" do
  let(:blog_post) { BlogPost.create :title => 'Hello' }

  it "updates published_on date" do
    expect {
      blog_post.publish!
    }.to change { blog_post.published_on }.from(nil).to(Date.today)
  end
end
```

Here the `published_on` attribute is examined both before and after invocation of the `expect` block. This style of change assertion comes in handy when you want to ensure a precondition of the value. Asserting `from` guarantees a known starting point.

Besides expecting changes, the other common expectation has to do with code that should generate exceptions:

```
describe "#unpublish!" do
  context "when brand new" do
    let(:blog_post) { BlogPost.create :title => 'Hello' }

    it "raises an exception" do
      expect {
        blog_post.unpublish!
      }.to raise_exception(NotPublishedError, /not yet published/)
    end
  end
end
```

In this example, we attempt to "unpublish" a brand-new blog post that hasn't been published yet. Therefore, we expect an exception to be raised.

18.2.8 `pending`

When you leave the block off of an example, RSpec treats it as pending.

```
describe GeneralController do
  describe "GET to index" do
    it "should be implemented eventually"
  end
end
```

RSpec prints out pending examples at the end of its run output, which makes it potentially useful for tracking work in progress.

```
Finished in 0.096941 seconds
1 example, 0 failures, 1 pending

Pending:
  GeneralController on GET to index should be successful
```

You can also explicitly create pending examples by inserting a call to the `pending` method anywhere inside of an example.

```
describe GeneralController do
  describe "on GET to index" do
    it "should be successful" do
      pending("not implemented yet")
    end
  end
end
```

RSpec

Interestingly, you can use `pending` with a block to keep broken code from failing your spec. However, if at some point in the future the broken code does execute without an error, the pending block will cause a failure.

```
describe BlogPost do
  it "defaults to rating of 3.0" do
    pending "implementation of new rating algorithm" do
      BlogPost.new.rating.should == 3.0
    end
  end
end
```

Pro-tip: You can make all examples in a group pending simply by calling `pending` once in the group's `before` block.

```
describe 'Veg-O-Matic' do
  before { pending }

  it 'slices' do
    # will not run, instead displays "slices (PENDING: TODO)"
  end

  it 'dices' do
    # will also be pending
  end

  it 'juliennes' do
    # will also be pending
  end
end
```

18.2.9 `should` and `should_not`

Rather than xUnit-style assertions, RSpec uses its own funky DSL syntax to do verification, based on a pair of methods called `should` and `should_not`. RSpec mixes them into the base Ruby `Object` class at runtime so that they are available on all objects. They expect to receive `Matcher` objects, generated using RSpec expectation syntax.

```
response.should have_tag('.error', 'No matching email addresses found.')
```

There are several ways to generate expectation matchers and pass them to `should` (and `should_not`):

```
receiver.should(matcher)                    # the simplest example
# Passes if matcher.matches?(receiver)

receiver.should == expected  # any value
```

```
# Passes if (receiver == expected)

receiver.should === expected #any value
# Passes if (receiver === expected)

receiver.should =~ regexp
# Passes if (receiver =~ regexp)
```

Tiger says...

> This is all fairly dry and academic, but stay with us because we've got plenty of real-world example
> in the next few sessions.

The process of learning to write expectations is probably one of the meatier parts of
the RSpec learning curve. One of the most common idioms is "should equal," akin to
`Test::Unit`'s `assert_equal` assertion.

18.2.10   Implicit Subject

Whether you know it or not, every RSpec example group has a *subject*. Think of it as *the
thing being described.* Let's start with an easy example:

```
describe BlogPost do
  it { should be_invalid }
end
```

By convention, the implicit subject here is a `BlogPost.new` instance. The `should` call
may look like it is being called *off of nothing.* But actually the call is delegated by the
example to the implicit subject. It's just as if you'd written the expression

```
BlogPost.new.should be_invalid
```

18.2.11   Explicit Subject

If the implicit subject of the example group doesn't quite do the job for you, you can
specify a subject explicitly. For example, maybe we need to tweak a couple of the blog
post's attributes on instantiation:

```
describe BlogPost do
  subject { BlogPost.new :title => 'foo', :body => 'bar' }
  it { should be_valid }
end
```

Here we have the same delegation story as with implicit subject. The `should be_valid`
call is delegated to the subject.

RSpec

You can also talk to the subject directly. For example, you may need to invoke a method off the subject to change object state:

```
describe BlogPost do
  subject { BlogPost.new :title => 'foo', :body => 'bar' }

  it "sets published timestamp" do
    subject.publish!
    subject.published?.should == true
  end
end
```

Here we call the `publish!` method off the subject. Mentioning `subject` directly is the way we get ahold of that `BlogPost` instance we set up. Finally, we assert that the `published?` boolean is true.

18.2.12 `its`

The `its` method works hand-in-hand with the fact that RSpec examples delegate to a subject. It can make your specs very compact and readable. Let's look at a quick example:

```
describe Array do
  its(:length) { should == 0 }
end
```

The implicit subject here is the `Array.new` instance. And the `length` call is made on that subject. Finally, the `should` call is made on that result of the `length` call.

That example was a bit simple, here's a meatier example that shows off what `its` can do:

```
describe BlogPost do
  subject do
    blog_post = BlogPost.new :title => 'foo', :body => 'bar'
    blog_post.publish!
    blog_post
  end

  it { should be_valid }
  its(:errors) { should be_empty }
  its(:title) { should == 'foo' }
  its(:body) { should == 'bar' }
  its(:published_on) { should == Date.today }
end
```

What's awesome is you still get the English translation of the Ruby code in the specdoc output:

```
BlogPost
- should be valid

BlogPost errors
- should be empty

BlogPost title
- should == "foo"

BlogPost body
- should == "bar"

BlogPost published_on
- should == Fri, 26 Mar 2010
```

18.3 Predicate Matchers

Thanks to `method_missing`, RSpec can support arbitrary predicates, that is, it understands that if you invoke something that begins with `be_`, then it should use the rest of the method name as an indicator of which predicate-style method to invoke the target object. (By convention, a predicate method in Ruby ends with a ? and should return the equivalent of `true` or `false`.) The simplest hard-coded predicate-style matchers are:

```
target.should be
target.should be_true
target.should be_false
target.should be_nil
target.should_not be_nil
```

Arbitrary predicate matchers can assert against any target, and even support parameters!

```
thing.should be                        # passes if thing is not nil or false
collection.should be_empty             # passes if target.empty?
target.should_not be_empty             # passes unless target.empty?
target.should_not be_under_age(16)     # passes unless target.under_age?(16)
```

As an alternative to prefixing arbitrary predicate matchers with `be_`, you may choose from the indefinite article versions `be_a_` and `be_an_`, making your specs read much more naturally:

```
"a string".should be_an_instance_of(String)
3.should be_a_kind_of(Fixnum)
3.should be_a_kind_of(Numeric)
3.should be_an_instance_of(Fixnum)
3.should_not be_instance_of(Numeric) #fails
```

The cleverness (madness?) doesn't stop there. RSpec will even understand `have_` prefixes as referring to predicates like `has_key?`:

```
{:foo => "foo"}.should have_key(:foo)
{:bar => "bar"}.should_not have_key(:foo)
```

RSpec has a number of expectation matchers for working with classes that implement module `Enumerable`. You can specify whether an array should include a particular element, or if a string contains a substring. This one always weirds me out when I see it in code, because my brain wants to think that include is some sort of language keyword meant for mixing modules into classes. It's just a method, so it can be overriden easily.

```
[1, 2, 3].should include(1)
[1, 2, 3].should_not include(4)
"foobar".should include("bar")
"foobar".should_not include("baz")
```

You get a slick bit of syntactic sugar for testing the length of collections:

```
[1, 2, 3].should have(3).items
```

What if you want to specify the length of a `has_many` collection? "Schedule.days.should have(3).items" is admittedly quite ugly. RSpec gives us some more sweetness here as well.

```
schedule.should have(3).days  # passes if schedule.days.length == 3
```

18.4 Custom Expectation Matchers

When you find that none of the stock expectation matchers provide a natural-feeling expectation, you can very easily write your own. All you need to do is write a Ruby class that implements the following two methods:

```
matches?(actual)
failure_message_for_should
```

The following methods are optional for your custom matcher class:

```
does_not_match?(actual)
failure_message_for_should_not
description
```

The example given in the RSpec API documentation is a game in which players can be in various zones on a virtual board. To specify that a player `bob` should be in zone 4, you could write a spec like

```
bob.current_zone.should eql(Zone.new("4"))
```

However, it's more expressive to say one of the following, using the custom matcher in Listing 18.3:

Listing 18.3 BeInZone custom expectation matcher class

```
bob.should be_in_zone(4) and bob.should_not be_in_zone(3)
class BeInZone
  def initialize(expected)
    @expected = expected
  end

  def matches?(target)
    @target = target
    @target.current_zone.eql?(Zone.new(@expected))
  end

  def failure_message_for_should
    "expected #{@target.inspect} to be in Zone #{@expected}"
  end

  def failure_message_for_should_not
    "expected #{@target.inspect} not to be in Zone #{@expected}"
  end
end
```

In addition to the matcher class you would need to write the following method so that it'd be in scope for your spec:

```
def be_in_zone(expected)
  BeInZone.new(expected)
end
```

This is normally done by including the method and the class in a module, which is then included in your spec:

```
describe "Player behaviour" do
  include CustomGameMatchers
  ...
end
```

Or you can include helpers globally in a `spec_helper.rb` file required from your spec file(s):

```
RSpec::Runner.configure do |config|
  config.include(CustomGameMatchers)
end
```

RSpec

18.4.1   Custom Matcher DSL

RSpec includes a DSL for easier definition of custom matchers. The DSL's directives
match the methods you implement on custom matcher classes. Just add code similar to
the following example in a file within the `spec/support` directory.

```
RSpec::Matchers.define :contain_text do |expected|
  match do |response_body|
    squished(response_body).include?(expected.to_s)
  end

  failure_message_for_should do |actual|
    "expected the following element's content to include
    #{expected.inspect}:\n\n#{response_text(actual)}"
  end

  failure_message_for_should_not do |actual|
    "expected the following element's content to not
    include #{expected.inspect}:\n\n#{squished(actual)}"
  end

  def squished(response_body)
    Webrat::XML.document(response_body).text.squish
  end
end
```

18.4.2   *Fluent* Chaining

You can create matchers that obey a fluent interface using the chain method:

```
RSpec::Matchers.define(:tip) do |expected_tip|
  chain(:on) do |bill|
    @bill = bill
  end

  match do |person|
    person.tip_for(@bill) == expected_tip
  end
end
```

This matcher can be used as follows:

```
describe Customer do
  it { should tip(10).on(50) }
end
```

In this way, you can begin to create your own fluent domain-specific languages for testing
your complex business logic in a very readable way.

18.5 Shared Behaviors

Often you'll want to specify similar behavior in multiple specs. It would be silly to type out the same code over and over. Fortunately, RSpec has a feature named shared behaviors that aren't run individually, but rather are included into other behaviors; they are defined using `shared_examples_for`.

```
shared_examples_for "a phone field" do
  it "has 10 digits" do
    Business.new(phone_field => '8004567890').should
      have(:no).errors_on(phone_field)
  end
end

shared_examples_for "an optional phone field" do
  it "handles nil" do
    business = Business.new phone_field => nil
    business.attributes[phone_field].should be_nil
  end
end
```

You can invoke a shared example using the `it_should_behave_like` method, in place of an `it`.

```
describe "phone" do
  let(:phone_field) { :phone }
  it_should_behave_like "a phone field"
end

describe "fax" do
  let(:phone_field) { :fax }
  it_should_behave_like "a phone field"
  it_should_behave_like "an optional phone field"
end
```

You can put the code for shared examples almost anywhere, but the default convention is to create a file named `spec/support/shared_examples.rb` to hold them.

18.6 RSpec's Mocks and Stubs

It's possible to use a number of mocking frameworks including Mocha, Flexmock, RR, and more. In our examples, however, we'll use RSpec's own mocking and stubbing facilities, which are almost the same and equally powerful. Mostly the method names vary.

Mock Objects

To create a mock object, you simply call the `mock` method anywhere in a spec, and give it a name as an optional parameter. It's a good idea to give mock objects a name if you will be using more than one of them in your spec. If you use multiple anonymous mocks, you'll probably have a hard time telling them apart if one fails.

```
echo = mock('echo')
```

Remember that you set expectations about what messages are sent to your mock during the course of your spec. Mocks will cause a spec to fail if their expectations are not met. To set an expectation on a mock, we invoke `should_receive` or `should_not_receive`.

```
echo.should_receive(:sound)
```

The chained method `with` is used to define expected parameters. If we care about the return value, we chain `and_return` at the end of the expectation or use a block.

```
echo.should_receive(:sound).with("hey").and_return("hey")
echo.should_receive(:sound).with("hey") { "hey" }
```

Null Objects

Occasionally you just want an object for testing purposes that accepts any message passed to it—a pattern known as null object. It's possible to make one using the `mock` method and the `:null_object` option.

```
null_object = mock('null', :null_object => true)
```

Stub Objects

You can easily create a stub object in RSpec via the `stub` factory method. You pass `stub` a name and default attributes as a hash.

```
yodeler = stub('yodeler', :yodels? => true)
```

The underlying implementation of mocks and stubs is the same in RSpec, although the semantic difference persists since mocks and stubs are meant to be used differently.[1]

By the way, there's no rule that the name parameter of a mock or stub needs to be a string. It's pretty typical to pass `mock` or `stub` a class reference corresponding to the real type of object.

```
yodeler = stub(Yodeler, :yodels? => true)
```

---

1. Confused about the difference between mocks and stubs? Read Martin Fowler's explanation at http://www.martinfowler.com/articles/mocksArentStubs.html.

Partial Mocking and Stubbing

You can use `stub` to install or replace methods on any object, not just mocks—a technique called partial mocking and stubbing.

```
describe "#grand_total" do
  it "is the sum of hourly total and billed expenses" do
    invoice.stubs(:hourly_total).returns(123.45)
    invoice.stubs(:billed_expenses).returns(543.21)
    invoice.grand_total.should == 666.66
  end
end
```

Even though RSpec's authors warn us about partial stubbing in their docs, the ability to do it is really useful in practice.

stub_chain

It's really common to find yourself writing some gnarly code when you rely on `stub` to spec behavior of nested method calls.[2] But, sometimes you need to stub methods *down a dot chain*, where one method is invoked on another method, which is itself invoked on another method, and so on. For example, you may need to stub out a set of recent, unpublished blog posts in chronological order, like `BlogPost.recent.unpublished.chronological`

Try to figure out what's going on in the following example. I bet it takes you more than a few seconds!

```
BlogPost.stub(:recent => stub(:unpublished => stub(
  :chronological => [stub, stub, stub])))
```

That example code can be factored to be more verbose, which makes it a little easier to understand, but is still pretty bad.

```
chronological = [stub, stub, stub]
unpublished = stub :chronological => chronological
recent = stub :unpublished => unpublished
BlogPost.stub :recent => recent
```

Luckily, Rspec gives you the `stub_chain` method, which understands exactly what you're trying to do here and dramatically simplifies the code needed:

```
BlogPost.stub_chain(:recent, :unpublished, :chronological).
  and_return([stub, stub, stub])
```

However, just because it's so easy to stub the chain, doesn't mean it's the right thing to do. The question to ask yourself is, "Why am I testing something related to methods so

---

2. ActiveRecord scopes are notoriously prone to causing this problem.

RSpec

deep down a chain? Could I move my tests down to that lower level?" Demeter would be proud.

18.7 Running Specs

Specs are executable documents. Each example block is executed inside its own object instance, to make sure that the integrity of each is preserved (with regard to instance variables, etc.).

If I run one of the Workbeast specs using the `rspec` command that should have been installed on my system by the RSpec gem, I'll get output similar to that of `Test::Unit`— familiar, comfortable, and passing. Just not too informative.

```
$ rspec spec/models/colleague_import_spec.rb
.........

Finished in 0.330223 seconds

9 examples, 0 failures
```

RSpec is capable of outputting results of a spec run in many formats. The traditional dots output that looks just like `Test::Unit` is called progress and, as we saw a moment ago, is the default. However, if we add the `-fs` command-line parameter to `rspec`, we can cause it to output the results of its run in a very different and much more interesting format, the specdoc format. It surpasses anything that Ruby's built-in `Test::Unit` is capable of doing on its own "out of the box."

```
$ rspec -fs spec/models/billing_code_spec.rb
BillingCode
  should have a bidirectional habtm association
  should remove bidirectional association on deletion

Finished in 0.066201 seconds
2 examples, 0 failures
```

Nice, huh? If this is the first time you're seeing this kind of output, I wouldn't be surprised if you drifted off in speculation about whether RSpec could help you deal with sadistic PHB-imposed[3] documentation requirements.

Having these sorts of self-documenting abilities is one of the biggest wins you get in choosing RSpec. It compels many people to work toward better spec coverage of their project. I also know from experience that development managers tend to really appreciate RSpec's output, even to the extent of incorporating it into their project deliverables.

---

3. Pointy-Haired Boss, as per Dilbert comic strips.

Besides the different formatting, there are all sorts of other command-line options available. Just type `rspec --help` to see them all.

That does it for our introduction to RSpec. Now we'll take a look at using RSpec with Ruby on Rails.

18.8   RSpec Rails Gem

The RSpec Rails gem provides four different contexts for specs, corresponding to the four major kinds of objects you write in Rails. Along with the API support you need to write Rails specs, it also provides code generators and a bundle of Rake tasks.

18.8.1   Installation

Assuming you have the `rspec-rails` gem bundled already, you should run the `rspec:install` generator provided to set up your project for use with RSpec.

```
$ rails generate rspec:install
     create  .rspec
     create  spec
     create  spec/spec_helper.rb
     create  autotest
     create  autotest/discover.rb
```

The generator will add the files and directories necessary to use RSpec with your Rails project.

RSpec and Rake

The `lib/tasks/rspec.rake` script sets the default Rake task to run all specs in your `/spec` directory tree. It also creates specific `rake spec` tasks for each of the usual spec directories.

```
$ rake -T spec
rake spec                # Run all specs in spec directory (excluding plugin
                           specs)
rake spec:controllers    # Run the code examples in spec/controllers
rake spec:helpers        # Run the code examples in spec/helpers
rake spec:lib            # Run the code examples in spec/lib
rake spec:mailers        # Run the code examples in spec/mailers
rake spec:models         # Run the code examples in spec/models
rake spec:rcov           # Run all specs with rcov
rake spec:requests       # Run the code examples in spec/requests
rake spec:routing        # Run the code examples in spec/routing
rake spec:views          # Run the code examples in spec/views
```

RSpec

If your project has a `config/database.yml` then the `rake spec` tasks will execute `rake db:test:prepare` as a dependency, to make sure that the schema of your development database is kept in sync. Keep in mind that this won't happen if you run a spec individually using the `rspec` command.

RSpec and Generators

RSpec ensures that other generators in your project are aware of it as your chosen test library. Subsequently it will be used for command-line generation of models, controllers, etc.

```
$ rails generate model Invoice
      invoke      active_record
      create      db/migrate/20100304010121_create_invoices.rb
      create      app/models/invoice.rb
      invoke      rspec
      create      spec/models/invoice_spec.rb
```

RSpec Options

The `.rspec` file contains a list of default command-line options. The generated file looks like

```
--color
--format progress
```

You can change it to suit your preference. I like my spec output in color, but usually prefer the more verbose output of `--format specdoc`.

Tim says...

> I go back and forth between preferring the dots of the `progress` format and the verbose output of the `specdoc` format. With the more verbose output and long spec suites, it's easy to miss if something failed if you look away from your screen. Specially on terminals with short buffers.

Here are some additional options that you might want to set in your `spec.opts`

```
-p, --profile    Enable profiling of examples w/output of top 10 slowest
examples
-b, --backtrace  Enable full backtrace
-d, --debug      Enable debugging
```

The RSpec Helper Script

As opposed to command-line options, major settings and configuration of your spec suite are kept in `spec/spec_helper.rb`, which is always required at the top of an RSpec spec.

A boilerplate copy is generated by default when you install RSpec into your project. Let's go through it section by section and cover what it does.

First of all, we ensure that the Rails environment is set to `test`. Remember that RSpec replaces the standard `TestUnit`-based suite that is generated by default for Rails apps.

```
ENV["RAILS_ENV"] ||= 'test'
```

Next the Rails environment and RSpec Rails are loaded up.

```
require File.dirname(__FILE__) + "/../config/environment" unless
defined?(Rails.root)
require 'rspec/rails'
```

RSpec has the notion of supporting files containing custom matchers and any other code that helps setup additional functionality for your spec suite, so it scans the `spec/support` directory to find those files, akin to Rails initializers.

```
# Requires supporting files with custom matchers and macros, etc,
# in ./support/ and its subdirectories.
Dir["#{File.dirname(__FILE__)}/support/**/*.rb"].each {|f| require f}
```

Finally, there is a block of configuration for your spec suite where you can set fixture paths, transaction options, and mocking frameworks.

```
Rspec.configure do |config|
  # == Mock Framework
  #
  # If you prefer to use mocha, flexmock or RR,
  # uncomment the appropriate line:
  #
  # config.mock_with :mocha
  # config.mock_with :flexmock
  # config.mock_with :rr
  config.mock_with :rspec

  # Remove this line if you're not using ActiveRecord
  # or ActiveRecord fixtures
  config.fixture_path = "#{::Rails.root}/spec/fixtures"

  # If you're not using ActiveRecord, or you'd prefer
  # not to run each of your examples within a transaction,
  # remove the following line or assign false instead of true.
  config.use_transactional_fixtures = true
end
```

RSpec

Traditionally a lot of extra helper methods were put into the `spec_helper` file, hence its name. However, nowadays it's generally easier to organize your additions in `spec/support` files, for the same reasons `config/initializers` can be easier to manage than sticking everything in `config/environment.rb`.

While we're on the subject, keep in mind that any methods defined at the top level of a support file will become global methods available from all objects, which almost certainly not what you want. Instead, create a module and mix it in, just like you'd do in any other part of your application.

```
module AuthenticationHelpers
  def sign_in_as(user)
    # ...
  end
end


Rspec.configure do |config|
  config.include AuthenticationHelpers
end
```

18.8.2 Model Specs

Model specs help you design and verify the domain model of your Rails application, both Active Record and your own classes. RSpec Rails doesn't provide too much special functionality for model specs, because there's not really much needed beyond what's provided by the base library. Let's generate a `Schedule` model and examine the default spec that is created along with it.

```
$ rails generate model Schedule name:string
      invoke    active_record
      create    db/migrate/20100304013800_create_schedules.rb
      create    app/models/schedule.rb
      invoke    rspec
      create    spec/models/schedule_spec.rb
```

The boilerplate `spec/models/schedule_spec.rb` looks like

```
require 'spec_helper'

describe Schedule do
  pending "add some examples to (or delete) #{__FILE__}"
end
```

Assume for example that our `Schedule` class has a collection of day objects.

```
class Schedule < ActiveRecord::Base
  has_many :days
end
```

Let's specify that we should be able to get a roll-up total of hours from schedule objects. Instead of fixtures, we'll mock out the `days` dependency.

```
require 'spec_helper'

describe Schedule do
  let(:schedule) { Schedule.new }

  it "should calculate total hours" do
    days = mock('days')
    days.should_receive(:sum).with(:hours).and_return(40)
    schedule.stub(:days).and_return(days)
    schedule.total_hours.should == 40
  end
end
```

Here we've taken advantage of the fact that association proxies in Rails are rich objects. Active Record gives us several methods for running database aggregate functions. We set up an expectation that `days` should receive the `sum` method with one argument—`:hours`—and return `40`. We can satisfy this specification with a very simple implementation:

```
class Schedule
  has_many :days

  def total_hours
    days.sum :hours
  end
end
```

A potential benefit of mocking the `days` proxy is that we no longer rely on the database[4] in order to write our specifications and implement the `total_hours` method, which will make this particular spec execute lightning fast.

On the other hand, a valid criticism of this approach is that it makes our code harder to refactor. Our spec would fail if we changed the implementation of `total_hours` to use `Enumerable#inject`, even though the external behavior doesn't change. Specifications are not only describing the visible behavior of objects, but the interactions between an object and its associated objects as well. Mocking the association proxy in this case lets us clearly specify how a `Schedule` should interact with its `Days`.

Leading mock objects advocates see mock objects as a temporary design tool. You may have noticed that we haven't defined the `Day` class yet. So another benefit of using

---

4. Well that's not quite true. Active Record still connects to the database to get the column information for `Schedule`. However, you could stub that information out as well to remove your dependency on the database completely.

mock objects is that they allow us to specify behavior in true isolation, and during design-time. There's no need to break our design rhythm by stopping to create the `Day` class and database table. This may not seem like a big deal for such a simple example, but for more involved specifications it is really helpful to just focus on the design task at hand. After the database and real object models exist, you can go back and replace the mock `days` with calls to the real deal. This is a subtle, yet very powerful message about mocks that is usually missed.

18.8.3 Mocked and Stubbed Models

The built-in helper method `mock_model` makes a mock object that pretends to be an ActiveRecord object. Its companion, `stub_model` makes a real model instance, but yells at you if and when you try an operation such as saving, which would connect to the database. (In other words, it's intended use in unit-test style specs.)

Ironically, one of the benefits of `stub_model` is that you don't have to be explicit about its attributes, because they are read from the database. You can get a similar effect using `mock_model(Foo).as_null_object`

The `mock_model` method creates mocks with autogenerated numeric ids and a number of certain common methods stubbed out:

id Returns an autogenerated primary key value

to_param Returns the `id` value as a URL-friendly string

new_record? Returns `false`

errors Returns an empty stub errors collection

is_a? Returns `true` if the parameter matches `model_class`

You should pass in any additional stubbed method values via the `stubs` hash argument or set them in a block using the yielded mock instance.

18.8.4 Controller Specs

RSpec gives you the ability to specify your controllers either in isolation from their associated views or together with them, as in regular Rails tests. According to the API docs:

> Controller Specs support running specs for Controllers in two modes, which represent the tension between the more granular testing common in TDD and the more high-level testing built into Rails. BDD sits somewhere in between: we want to achieve a balance between specs that are close

enough to the code to enable quick fault isolation and far enough away from the code to enable refactoring with minimal changes to the existing specs.

The controller class is passed to the `describe` method like

```
describe MessagesController do
```

An optional second parameter can provide additional information, or you can explicitly use the `controller_name` method inside a `describe` block to tell RSpec which controller to use.

```
describe "Requesting /messages using GET" do
  controller_name :messages
  fixtures :people
```

I typically group my controller examples by action and HTTP method. This example requires a logged-in user, so I stub my application controller's `current_person` accessor to return a fixture.

```
before(:each) do
  controller.stub!(:current_person, people(:quentin))
```

Next, I create a mock `Message` object using the `mock_model` method. I want this mock message to be returned whenever `Message.all` is called during the spec.

```
@message = mock_model(Message)
Message.stub!(:all).and_return([@message])
```

Now I can start specifying the behavior of actions (in this case, the `index` action). The most basic expectation is that the response should be successful, HTTP's 200 OK response code.

```
it "should be successful" do
  get :index
  response.should be_success
end
```

Additional expectations that should be done for most controller actions include the template to be rendered and variable assignment.

```
it "should render the index template " do
  get :index
  response.should render_template(:index)
end

it "should assign the found messages for the view" do
  get :index
  assigns[:messages].should include(@message)
end
```

RSpec

Previously we saw how to stub out a model's association proxy. Instead of stubbing the controller's `current_person` method to return an actual person from the database, we can have it return a mock person.

```
@mock_person = mock_model(Person, :name => "Quentin")
controller.stub!(:current_person).and_return @mock_person
```

Isolation and Integration Modes

By default, RSpec on Rails controller specs run in isolation mode, meaning that view templates are not involved. The benefit of this mode is that you can spec the controller in complete isolation of the view, hence the name. Maybe you can sucker someone else into maintaining the view specs?

That *sucker* comment is of course facetious. Having separate view specs is not as difficult as it's made out to be sometimes. It also provides much better *fault isolation*, which is a fancy way of saying that you'll have an easier time figuring out what's wrong when something fails.

If you prefer to exercise your views in conjunction with your controller logic inside the same controller specs, just as traditional Rails functional tests do, then you can tell RSpec on Rails to run in integration mode using the `render_views` macro. It's not an all-or-nothing decision. You can specify modes on a per-behavior basis.

```
describe "Requesting /messages using GET" do
  render_views
```

When you run integrated, the controller specs will be executed with view rendering turned on.

Specifying Errors

Ordinarily, Rails rescues exceptions that occur during action processing, so that it can respond with a 501 error code and give you that great error page with the stack trace and request variables, and so on. In order to directly specify that an action should raise an error, you have to override the controller's `rescue_action` method, by doing something like

```
controller.class.send(:define_method, :rescue_action) { |e| raise e }
```

If you don't mind checking that the response code was an error, you can just use the `be_an_error` predicate or `response_code` accessor of the `response` object:

```
it "should return an error in the header" do
  response.should be_an_error
end
```

```
it "should return a 501" do
  response.response_code.should == 501
end
```

Specifying Routes

One of Rails's central components is routing. The routing mechanism is the way Rails takes an incoming request URL and maps it to the correct controller and action. Given its importance, it is a good idea to specify the routes in your application. You can do this with by providing specs in the spec/routes directory and have two matchers to use, `route_to` and `be_routable`.

```
context "Messages routing" do

  it "routes /messages/ to messages#show" do
    { :get => "/messages/" }.should route_to(
      :controller => "messages",
      :action => "index"
    )
  end

  it "does not route an update action" do
    { :post => "/messages/" }.should_not be_routable
  end
end
```

18.8.5 View Specs

Controller specs let us integrate the view to make sure there are no errors with the view, but we can do one better by specifying the views themselves. RSpec will let us write a specification for a view, completely isolated from the underlying controller. We can specify that certain tags exist and that the right data is outputted.

Let's say we want to write a page that displays a private message sent between members of an internet forum. RSpec creates the `spec/views/messages` directory when we use the `rspec_controller` generator. The first thing we would do is create a file in that directory for the show view, naming it `show.html.haml_spec.rb`. Next we would set up the information to be displayed on the page.

```
describe "messages/show.html.haml" do
  before(:each) do
    @message = mock_model(Message, :subject => "RSpec rocks!")
    sender = mock_model(Person, :name => "Obie Fernandez")
    @message.stub!(:sender).and_return(sender)
    recipient = mock_model(Person, :name => "Pat Maddox")
@message.stub!(:recipient).and_return(recipient)
```

RSpec

If you want to be a little more concise at the cost of one really long line of code that you'll have to break up into multiple lines, you can create the mocks inline like:

```
describe "messages/show.html.haml " do
  before(:each) do
    @message = mock_model(Message,
      :subject => "RSpec rocks!",
      :sender => mock_model(Person, :name => "Obie Fernandez"),
      :recipient => mock_model(Person, :name => "Pat Maddox"))
```

Either way, this is standard mock usage similar to what we've seen before. Mocking the data used in views allows us to isolate the specification. If you're following our advice and using Decent Exposure to make data available to your view (instead of instance variables) then skip the following section and move on to Stubbing Helper Methods.

Assigning Instance Variables

We now need to assign the message to the view. The `rspec_on_rails` plugin gives us a familiar-looking `assigns` method, which you can treat as a hash.

```
assigns[:message] = @message
```

Fantastic! Now we are ready to begin specifying the view page. We'd like to specify that the message subject is displayed, wrapped in an `<h1>` tag. The `have_tag` expectation takes two arguments—the tag selector and the content within the tag.

```
it "should display the message subject" do
  render "messages/show"
  response.should have_tag('h1', 'RSpec rocks!')
end
```

HTML tags often have an ID associated with them. We would like our page to create a `<div>` with the ID `message_info` for displaying the sender and recipient's names. We can pass the ID to `have_tag` as well.

```
it "should display a div with id message_info" do
  render "messages/show"
  response.should have_tag('div#message_info')
end
```

What if we want to specify that the sender and recipient's names should appear in `<h3>` tags within the `div`?

```
it "should display sender and recipient names in div#message_info" do
  render "messages/show"
  response.should have_tag('div#message_info') do
    with_tag('h3#sender', 'Sender: Obie Fernandez')
    with_tag('h3#recipient', 'Recipient: Pat Maddox')
  end
end
```

Stubbing Helper Methods

Note that the view specs do not mix in helper methods automatically, in order to preserve isolation. If your view template code relies on helper methods, you need to mock or stub them out on the provided `template` object.

The decision to mock versus stub those helper methods should depend on whether they're an active player in the behavior you want to specify, as in the following example:

```
it "should truncate subject lines" do
    template.should_receive(:truncate).exactly(2).times
     render "messages/index"
    end
end
```

If you forget to mock or stub helper method calls, your spec will fail with a `NoMethodError`.

18.8.6 Helper Specs

Speaking of helpers, it's really easy to write specs for your custom helper modules. Just pass `describe` to your helper module and it will be mixed into a special `helper` object in the spec class so that its methods are available to your example code.

```
describe ProfileHelper do
  it "profile_photo should return nil if user's photos is empty" do
    user = mock_model(User, :photos => [])
    helper.profile_photo(user).should == nil
  end
end
```

It's worth noting that in contrast to view specs, all of the framework-provided `ActionView::Helper` modules are mixed into the `helper` object, so that they're available to your helper code. All dynamically generated routes helper methods are added too.

18.9 RSpec Tools

There are several open-source projects that enhance RSpec's functionality and your productivity or can be used in conjunction with RSpec and other testing libraries.

18.9.1 RSpactor

RSpactor[5] is an automated testing framework that runs your spec suite when files are modified. It has inotify, Libnotify, and Growl support, and is about as simple to run as they come.

---

5. `http://github.com/thibaudgg/rspactor`

18.9.2 watchr

Watchr[6] is a more configurable alternative to RSpactor in that it can monitor file modifications and trigger any user defined action. This is especially useful when using Cucumber in a project and you would like both your specs and features to run automatically when altered. Simply provide a Ruby script for watchr to load that defines what actions it should take on modification.

18.9.3 Spork

As your application grows, an automated test suite can start to slow down your workflow when writing specs at a frequent rate. This is due to the nature of Rails needing to load the environment for each spec run. Spork[7] alleviates this by loading the Rails environment only once and having the remaining specs use the preloaded environment in the DRb server.

18.9.4 Specjour

Specjour[8] is a tool aimed at lowering the run times of your entire spec suite. It distributes your specs over a LAN via Bonjour, running the specs in parallel on the number of workers it finds.

18.9.5 RCov

RCov is a code coverage tool for Ruby.[9] You can run it on a spec file to see how much of your production code is covered. It provides HTML output to easily tell what code is covered by specs and what isn't. You can RCov individually on a spec file, or the `rspec_on_rails` plugin provides the `spec:rcov` task for running all of your specs under RCov. The results are outputted into a directory named `coverage` and contain a set of HTML files that you can browse by opening `index.html` (as shown in Figure 18.2):

18.9.6 Heckle

Heckle is part of the Seattle Ruby Brigade's awesome collection of projects,[10] and is another code coverage tool. Instead of simply checking the scope of your tests, Heckle

---

6. `http://github.com/mynyml/watchr`
7. `http://github.com/timcharper/spork`
8. `http://github.com/sandro/specjour`
9. `http://eigenclass.org/hiki.rb?rcov`
10. `http://rubyforge.org/projects/seattlerb`

helps you measure the effectiveness of your specs. It dives into your code and scrambles things like variable values and `if` statements. If none of your specs break, you're missing a spec somewhere.

The current versions of RSpec have Heckle support built-in. Just experiment with the `--heckle` option and see what happens.

18.10 Conclusion

You've gotten a taste of the different testing experience that RSpec delivers. At first it may seem like the same thing as `Test::Unit` with some words substituted and shifted around. One of the key points of TDD is that it's about design rather than testing. This is a lesson that every good TDDer learns through lots of experience. RSpec uses a different vocabulary and style to emphasize that point. It comes with the lesson baked in so that you can attain the greatest benefits of TDD right away.

RSpec

Extending Rails with Plugins

Once again, when we come to the creation of things by people, the form this unfolding takes, always, is step by step to please yourself. We cannot perform the unfolding process without knowing how to please ourselves.

—Christopher Alexander

I doubt that many of us would still be programmers if we had to solve exactly the same problems repeatedly, day after day. Instead, we are always looking for ways to reapply existing solutions to the problems we encounter. Your code represents the abstract solution to a problem, and so you are often striving to either reuse this abstraction (albeit in slightly different contexts), or refine your solution so that it can be reused. Through reuse, you can save time, money, and effort, and give yourself the opportunity to focus on the interesting and novel aspects of the particular problem you're currently trying to solve. After all, it's coming up with interesting and novel solutions to problems that makes us really succeessful, not continually *reinventing the wheel.*

Even though the standard Ruby on Rails APIs are very useful, sooner or later you'll find yourself wishing for a particular feature not in Rails core or wishing that a bit of standard Rails behavior were different. That's where plugins come into play, and this book has already described many useful ones that you will use on a day-to-day basis.

This chapter covers the basic topics of extending Rails with plugins. We'll also supply you with basic information about writing your own Rails plugins.

19.1 The Plugin System

Rails 1.0 introduced a plugin system that lets developers easily add new functionality into the framework. An official mechanism makes it feasible to extract novel, useful features you've come up with in your individual applications and share those extracted solutions with other developers, as a single self-contained unit that is easy to maintain.

Plugins aren't only useful for sharing new features: Plugins are used to test alterations to the Rails framework itself. Almost any significant new piece of functionality or patch can be implemented as a plugin and road-tested easily by a number of developers before it is considered for inclusion in the core framework. Whether you find a bug in Rails and figure out how to fix it or you come up with a significant feature enhancement, you will want to put your code in a plugin for easy distribution and testing.

Of course, changing significant core behavior of the framework demands a solid understanding of how Rails works internally and is beyond the scope of this book. However, some of the techniques demonstrated will help you understand the way that Rails itself is implemented.

19.1.1 Plugins as RubyGems

All popular Rails plugins are published as RubyGems. To install, you just have to add them to your Gemfile and run `rake bundle`. David Heinemeier Hansson recommends that authors with popular, version-released plugins, and especially ones with dependencies, distribute their plugins as gems.

Interestingly, as of Rails 3, all the major component frameworks of Rails are essentially plugins themselves.

19.1.2 The Plugin Script

The `rails plugin install` command shouldn't be necessary very often anymore since popular plugins are now usually distributed as gems. Nonetheless, for legacy reasons we cover the plugin command here.

```
rails plugin install plugin_url
```

Note that it should be run from the root directory of the application you are developing and the URL must point to either a Git or Subversion repository.

```
$ rails plugin install git://github.com/mislav/will_paginate.git
Initialized empty Git repository in
/Users/obie/hashrocket/three/vendor/plugins/will_paginate/.git/
remote: Counting objects: 58, done.
remote: Compressing objects: 100% (55/55), done.
```

```
remote: Total 58 (delta 3), reused 26 (delta 0)
Unpacking objects: 100% (58/58), done.
From git://github.com/mislav/will_paginate
 * branch  HEAD  -> FETCH_HEAD
```

Checking the `vendor/plugins`, you can see that a directory named `will_paginate` has appeared. The plugin install command deletes the `.git` directory, so that you can add your new plugin easily to your own source control.

You also get an easy way to remove plugins, by name.

```
rails plugin remove plugin_name
```

Quite appropriately, this command performs the opposite of install: It removes the plugin from `vendor/plugins`:

```
$ rails plugin remove will_paginate
```

A quick inspection of your `vendor/plugins` directory shows that the `will_paginate` folder has indeed been removed completely. You can manually delete the plugin's directory, but running the `remove` command will also run the plugin's `uninstall.rb` script, if it has one.

19.2 Writing Your Own Plugins

At some point in your Rails career, you might find that you want to share common code among similar projects that you're involved with. Or if you've come up with something particularly innovative, you might wonder if it would make sense to share it with the rest of the world.

Rails makes it easy to become a plugin author. It even includes a plugin generator script that sets up the basic directory structure and files that you need to get started:

```
$ rails generate plugin my_plugin
      create        vendor/plugins/my_plugin
      create        vendor/plugins/my_plugin/init.rb
      create        vendor/plugins/my_plugin/install.rb
      create        vendor/plugins/my_plugin/MIT-LICENSE
      create        vendor/plugins/my_plugin/Rakefile
      create        vendor/plugins/my_plugin/README
      create        vendor/plugins/my_plugin/uninstall.rb
      create        vendor/plugins/my_plugin/lib
      create        vendor/plugins/my_plugin/lib/my_plugin.rb
      invoke        test_unit
      inside        vendor/plugins/my_plugin
      create        spec
      create        spec/plugins/my_plugin_test.rb
      create        spec/test_helper.rb
```

Plugins

The generator gives you the entire set of possible plugin directories and starter files, even including a /tasks folder for your plugin's custom rake tasks. The install.rb and uninstall.rb are optional one-time setup and teardown scripts that can do anything you want them to do. You don't have to use everything that's created by the plugin generator.

The two defining aspects of a plugin are the presence of the init.rb file and of a directory in the plugin called lib. If neither of these exists, Rails will not recognize that subdirectory of vendor/plugins as a plugin. In fact, many popular plugins consist only of an init.rb script and some files in lib.

19.2.1 The `init.rb` Hook

If you pop open the boilerplate init.rb file that Rails generated for you, you'll read a simple instruction.

```
# insert hook code here
```

Hook code means code that hooks into the Rails initialization routines. To see a quick example of hook code in action, just go ahead and generate a plugin in one of your projects and add the following line to its init.rb:

```
puts "Current Rails version: #{Rails::VERSION::STRING}"
```

Congratulations, you've written your first simple plugin. Run the Rails console and see:

```
$ rails console
Current Rails version: 3.0.pre
Loading development environment (Rails 3.0.pre)
>>
```

Code that's added to init.rb is run at startup. (That's any sort of Rails commands, including server, console, and runner.) Most plugins have their require statements in init.rb.

Initialization Variables

A few special variables are available to your code in init.rb:

name The name of your plugin ('my_plugin' in our simple example).

path The directory in which the plugin exists, which is useful in case you need to read or write nonstandard files in your plugin's directory.

config The configuration object created in environment.rb. (See Chapter 1, "Rails Environments and Configuration," as well as the online API docs for Rails:: Configuration to learn more about what's available via config.)

Our simple example is just that, simple. Most of the time you want a plugin to provide new functionality to the rest of your application or modify the Rails libraries in more interesting ways than printing out a version number on startup.

19.2.2 The `lib` Directory

The `lib` directory of your plugin is added to Ruby's load path before `init.rb` is run. That means that you can `require` your code without needing to jump through hoops specifying the load path:

```
require File.dirname(__FILE__) + '/lib/my_plugin' # unnecessary
```

Assuming your `lib` directory contains `my_plugin.rb`, your `init.rb` needs to read:

```
require 'my_plugin'
```

Simple. You can bundle any class or Ruby code in a plugin's lib folder and then load it in `init.rb` (or allow other developers to optionally load it an initializer) using Ruby's require statement. This is the simplest way to share Ruby code among multiple Rails applications.

It's typical for plugins to alter or enhance the behavior or existing Ruby classes. As a simple example, Listing 19.1 is the source of a plugin that gives ActiveRecord classes a square brackets operator for finding by id.

Listing 19.1 Adding [ ] to Active Record Classes

```
# in file vendor/plugins/my_plugin/my_plugin.rb

class ActiveRecord::Base
  def self.[](id)
    find(id)
  end
end
```

In addition to opening existing classes to add or modify behavior, there are at least three other ways used by plugins to extend Rails functionality:

- Mixins, which describes inclusion of modules into existing classes
- Dynamic extension through Ruby's callbacks and hooks such as `method_missing`, `const_missing`, and `included`
- Dynamic extension using runtime evaluation with methods such as `eval`, `class_eval`, and `instance_eval`

19.2.3 Extending Rails Classes

The way that we reopen the `ActiveRecord::Base` class in Listing 19.1 and simply add a method to it is simple, but most plugins follow a pattern used internally in Rails and split their methods into two modules, one each for class and instance methods. We'll go ahead and add a useful `to_param` instance method to all our ActiveRecord objects too.[1]

Let's rework `my_plugin` so that it follows that style. First, after requiring `'my_plugin'` in `init.rb`, we'll send an include message to the ActiveRecord class itself:

```
ActiveRecord::Base.send(:include, MyPlugin)
```

There's also another way of accomplishing the same result, which you might encounter when browsing through the source code of popular plugins[2]:

```
ActiveRecord::Base.class_eval do
  include MyPlugin
end
```

Now we need to write a `MyPlugin` module to house the class and instance variables with which we will extend `ActiveRecord::Base`. See Listing 19.2.

Listing 19.2 Extensions to ActiveRecord::Base

```
module MyPlugin
  extend ActiveSupport::Concern

  # extending ActiveSupport::Concern automatically does the following
  # def self.included(base)
  #   base.extend(ClassMethods)
  #   base.send(:include, InstanceMethods)
  # end

  module ClassMethods
    def [](id)
      find(id)
    end
  end

  module InstanceMethods
    def to_param
```

---

1. See `http://www.jroller.com/obie/entry/seo_optimization_of_urls_in` for an explanation of how smart use of the `to_param` method can help your search engine optimization efforts on public-facing websites.

2. Jay Fields has a good blog post about the motivations behind using the various types of code extension at `http://blog.jayfields.com/2007/01/class-reopening-hints.html`.

```
    has_name? ? "#{id}-#{name.gsub(/[^a-z0-9]+/i, '-')}" : super
  end

  private

  def has_name?
    respond_to?(:name) and persisted?
  end
  end
end
```

You can use similar techniques to extend controllers and views.[3] For instance, if you want to add custom helper methods available in all your view templates, you can extend Action View like this:

```
ActionView::Base.send(:include, MyPlugin::MySpecialHelper)
```

Now that we've covered the fundamentals of writing Rails plugins (init.rb and the contents of the lib directory), we can take a look at the other files that are created by the plugin generator script.

19.2.4 The **README** and **MIT-LICENSE** File

The first thing that developers do when they encounter a new plugin is to take a look in the README file. It's tempting to ignore this file, but at the very least, you should add a simple description of what the plugin does, for future reference. The README file is also read and processed by Ruby's RDoc tool, when you generate documentation for your plugin using the doc:: Rake tasks. It's worth learning some fundamentals of RDoc formatting if you want the information that you put in the README file to look polished and inviting later.

Rails is open-sourced under the extremely liberal and open MIT license, as are most of the popular plugins available. In his keynote address to Railsconf 2007, David announced that the plugin generator will auto-generate an MIT license for the file, to help to solve the problem of plugins being distributed without an open-source license. Of course, you can still change the license to whatever you want, but the MIT license is definitely considered the Rails way.

Plugins

---

3. Alex Young's http://alexyoung.org/articles/show/40/a_taxonomy_of_rails_plugins covers a variety of different kinds of Rails plugins, including a useful explanation of how to handle passed-in options for runtime-configuration.

19.2.5 The **install.rb** and **uninstall.rb** Files

This pair of files is placed in the root of the plugin directory along with init.rb and README. Just as the init.rb file can be used to perform a set of actions each time the server starts, these files can be used to ensure that prerequisites of your plugin are in place when the plugin is installed using the rails plugin install command and that your plugin cleans up after itself when it is uninstalled using rails plugin remove.

Installation

For example, you might develop a plugin that generates intermediate data stored as temporary files in an application. For this plugin to work, it might require a temporary directory to exist before the data can be generated by the plugin—the perfect opportunity to use install.rb. See Listing 19.3.

Listing 19.3 Creating a temporary directory during plugin installation

```
require 'fileutils'
FileUtils.mkdir_p File.join(Rails.root, 'tmp', 'my_plugin_data')
```

By adding these lines to your plugin's install.rb file, the directory tmp/my_plugin_data will be created in any Rails application in which the plugin is installed. This fire-once action can be used for any number of purposes, including but not limited to the following:

- Copying asset files (HTML, CSS, and so on) into the public directory

- Checking for the existence of dependencies (for example, RMagick)

- Installing other requisite plugins

- Displaying documentation (see Listing 19.4)

Listing 19.4 Outputting documentation

```
puts File.read(File.dirname(__FILE__)+'/README')
```

Removal

As mentioned, the rails plugin remove command checks for the presence of a file called uninstall.rb when removing a plugin. If this file is present, it will be evaluated just prior to the plugin files actually being deleted. Typically, this is useful for reversing any actions performed when the plugin was installed. This can be handy for removing any directories or specific data files that your plugin might have created when installed, or while the application was running.

Commonsense Reminder

What might not be so obvious about this scheme is that it isn't foolproof. Users of plugins often skip the installation routines without meaning to do so. Because plugins are distributed via source control, it is trivial to add a plugin to your project with a simple checkout:

```
$ git checkout git://github.com/mislav/will_paginate.git
vendor/plugins/will_paginate
```

Or perhaps a more common scenario is to add a plugin to your project by copying it over from another Rails project using the filesystem. (I know I've done just that many times.) Same situation applies to plugin removal—a developer that doesn't know any better might uninstall a plugin from his project simply by deleting its folder from the `vendor/plugins` directory, in which case the `uninstall.rb` script would never run.

If as a plugin writer you are concerned about making sure that your install and/or uninstall scripts are actually executed, it's probably worthwile to stress the point in your announcements to the community and within the plugin documentation itself, such as the README file.

19.2.6   Custom Rake Tasks

It is often useful to include Rake tasks in plugins. For example, if your plugin stores files in a temporary directory (such as `/tmp`), you can include a helpful task for clearing out those temporary files without having to dig around in the plugin code to find out where the files are stored. Rake tasks such as this should be defined in a `.rake` file in your plugin's tasks folder (see Listing 19.5).

Listing 19.5 A plugin's cleanup rake task

```
# vendor/plugins/my_plugin/tasks/my_plugin.rake

namespace :my_plugin do

  desc 'Clear out the temporary files'
  task :cleanup => :environment do
    Dir[File.join(Rails.root, 'tmp', 'my_plugin_data')].each do |f|
      FileUtils.rm(f)
    end
  end

end
```

Plugins

Rake tasks added via plugins are listed alongside their standard Rails brothers and sister when you run `rake -T` to list all the tasks in a project. (In the following snippet, I limited Rake's output by passing a string argument to use for matching task names):

```
$ rake -T my_plugin
rake my_plugin:cleanup   # Clear out the temporary files
```

19.2.7 The Plugin's **Rakefile**

Generated plugins get their own little Rakefile, which can be used from within the plugin's directory to run its tests and generate its RDoc documentation (see Listing 19.6).

Listing 19.6 A generated plugin rakefile

```
require 'rake/testtask'

desc 'Default: run unit tests.'
task :default => :test

desc 'Test the my_plugin plugin.'
Rake::TestTask.new(:test) do |t|
  t.libs << 'test'
  t.pattern = 'test/**/*_test.rb'
end
```

While we're on the subject, I'll also mention that Rails has its own default rake tasks related to plugins, and they're fairly self-explanatory:

```
$ rake -T plugin

rake doc:clobber_plugins        # Remove plugin documentation
rake doc:plugins # Generate docs for installed plugins
rake test:plugins               # Run the plugin tests in
                                  vendor/plugins/*/**/test
                                  (or specify with PLUGIN=name)
```

Before closing this section, let's make the distinction between a plugin's `Rakefile` and any `.rake` files in the `tasks` folder clear:

- Use Rakefile for tasks that operate on the plugin's source files, such as special testing or documentation. These must be run from the plugin's directory.

- Use `tasks/*.rake` for tasks that are part of the development or deployment of the application in which the plugin is installed. These will be shown in the output of `rake ‚ÄìT`, the list of all Rake tasks for this application.

19.2.8 Including Assets with Your Plugin

Sometimes when writing a plugin you will want to have additional resources available to the application, such as javascript or css, but you do not want installation to copy files all over the place. This can be handled in your plugin initializer via a few hooks provided by Action View.

For javascript, you will simply need to register a javascript expansion using `ActionView::Helpers::AssetTagHelper`. In the following example we add two javascript files from our plugin under the namespace `my_plugin`. Note that the source files in the plugin must also reside in `public/javascripts`.

```
ActionView::Helpers::AssetTagHelper.
  register_javascript_expansion :my_plugin => ["core", "ext"]
```

This javascript can then be loaded into the application through the standard javascript include tag, and passing the name defined by the plugin.

```
javascript_include_tag :my_plugin
```

Stylesheets are handled in a similar manner, with stylesheets needing to reside in your plugin's `public/stylesheets` directory.

```
ActionView::Helpers::AssetTagHelper.
  register_stylesheet_expansion :my_plugin => ["layouts", "forms"]
```

Once initialized the stylesheets can then be loaded using the stylesheet link tag in the application.

```
stylesheet_link_tag :my_plugin
```

19.2.9 Testing Plugins

Last but not least, the development of your plugin should be Test-Driven. Writing tests for plugins is for the most part identical to any testing in Rails or Ruby and for the most part the methods used to test both are the same. However, because plugins cannot often predict the exact environment in which they are run, they require extra precautions to ensure that the test behavior of your plugin code is isolated from the rest of the application.

There is a subtle distinction between running plugin tests using the global `test:plugins` rake task and via the plugin's own `Rakefile`. Although the former can test all installed plugins at the same time, the internal `Rakefile` can and should be exploited to add any specific tasks your plugin requires to be tested properly.

Techniques used in testing plugins properly include bootstrapping a separate database for testing plugins in complete isolation. This is particularly useful when a plugin augments ActiveRecord with additional functionality, because you need to test the new methods in a controlled environment, minimizing the interaction with other plugins and the application's own test data.

As you can imagine, testing of plugins is a lengthy topic that is primarily of interest to plugin authors. Unfortunately, I must leave further analysis of the subject out of this book for reasons of practicality and overall length.

19.2.10 Railties

Railties are classes that extend from `Rails::Railtie` and provide hooks into Rails initialization for add-on libraries. This is extremely useful for gems which want to seemlessly integrate with Rails.

Railties provide hooks for libraries to add the following functionality:

- Creating initializers
- Providing Rake tasks
- Adding generators
- Registering event subscribers (for logging)

To create a `Railtie`, create a class called `Railtie` in your project's namespace that inherits from `Rails::Railtie`. Make sure you require 'rails' and your own gem in the file as well.

```
require 'my_gem'
require 'rails'
module MyGem
  class Railtie < Rails::Railtie
  end
end
```

At this point you are ready to hook in. Methods defined on `Rails::Railtie` that can be used for configuration are:

initializer(&block) Execute the block on initialization, it yields to the application configuration object.

config Provides access to the global configuration object.

rake_tasks(&block) Loads rake tasks to be used by the application.

generators(&block) Require generators to be used by the application.

log_subscriber(name, subscriber) Register a custom log subscriber for your framework.

A more thorough example is

```
require 'my_gem'
require 'rails'
module MyGem
  class Railtie < Rails::Railtie

    initializer "setup" do
      # Some initialization code here, like setting up a
      # database connection.
    end

    initializer "verify setup" do
      config.after_initialize do
        # Do some verification on the setup.
      end
    end

    rake_tasks do
      load 'my_gem/railties/tasks.rake'
    end

    generators do
      require 'my_gem/rails/generators/my_generator'
    end

    log_subscriber :my_gem, MyGem::Railtie::Subscriber.new
  end
end
```

Note

Rails Engines are self-contained applications that can be packaged as gems and included in another Rails application. Devise (covered in Chapter 14) is an example of an engine and contains, among other things, its own configuration, routes, models, controllers, views and even generators.

The primary author of Devise, Jose Valim, has written one of the best descriptions of creating a Rails Engine at `https://gist.github.com/af7e572c2dc973add221#file_2_engine.rdoc`

19.3 Conclusion

You have now learned about all the basic aspects of Rails plugins. You learned how to install and remove them. You also learned the fundamentals of writing your own plugins, enough to at least get you started experimenting with them.

To cover everything related to Rails plugins would require its own book and would go beyond the needs of most Rails developers, so we did not cover testing plugins or the more advanced techniques employed by plugin developers. We also did not discuss topics related to the life of a plugin beyond its initial development.

For in-depth learning about extending Rails with plugins, I strongly recommend the Addison-Wesley publication *Rails Plugins* by James Adam, who is considered the world's top expert on the subject.

Background Processing

People count up the faults of those who keep them waiting.

—French Proverb

Users of modern websites have lofty expectations when it comes to application responsiveness – most likely they will expect behavior and speed similar to that of desktop applications. Proper user experience guidelines would dictate that no HTTP request/response cycle should take more than a second to execute however there will be actions that arise that simply cannot achieve this time constraint.

Tasks of this nature can range from simple, long running tasks due to network latency to more complex tasks that require heavy processing on the server. Examples of these actions could be sending an email or processing video, respectively. In these situations, it is best to have the actions execute asynchronously, so that the responsiveness of the application remains swift while the procedures run.

In this chapter these types of tasks are referred to as background jobs. They include any execution that is handled in a separate process from the Rails application. Rails and Ruby have several libraries and techniques for performing this work, most notably:

- Delayed Job
- Resque
- Rails Runner

This chapter will cover each of these tools, discussing the strengths and weaknesses of each one so that you may determine what is appropriate for your application.

20.1 Delayed Job

Delayed Job[1] is a robust background processing library that is essentially a highly configurable priority queue. It provides various approaches to handling asynchronous actions, including:

- Custom background jobs
- Permanently marked background methods
- Background execution of methods at runtime

By default Delayed Job relies on Active Record to store all queue related operations and requires a relational database to store job information. However, it can be configured to use other persistence frameworks, as well as other non-relational databases. Supported options are:

- DataMapper
- MongoMapper (for use with MongoDB)
- CouchREST (for use with CouchDB)

20.1.1 Getting Started

Add the `delayed_job` gem to your application's `Gemfile`, then run the generator to create your execution and migration scripts.

```
rails generate delayed_job
```

This will create the database migration that will need to be run to set up the `delayed_jobs` table in the database, as well as a script to run Delayed Job. If you are using MongoMapper or CouchREST as the persistence framework, you may run the command with a `--skip-migration` option supplied since no migration will be needed.

To change the default settings for Delayed Job, first add a `delayed_job.rb` in your `config/initializers` directory. Options then can be configured by calling various methods on `Delayed::Worker`, which include settings for changing the behavior of the queue with respect to tries, timeouts, maximum run times, sleep delays and other options.

---

1. http://github.com/collectiveidea/delayed_job

```
Delayed::Worker.backend = :mongo_mapper
Delayed::Worker.destroy_failed_jobs = false
Delayed::Worker.sleep_delay = 30
Delayed::Worker.max_attempts = 5
Delayed::Worker.max_run_time = 1.hour
Delayed::Worker.max_priority = 10
```

20.1.2   Creating Jobs

Delayed Job can create background jobs using 3 different techniques, and which one
you use depends on your own personal style.

The first option is to chain any method that you wish to execute asynchronously after
a call to `Object#delay`. This is good for cases where some common functionality needs
to execute in the background in certain situations, but is acceptable to run synchronously
in others.

```
# Execute normally
mailer.send_email(user)

# Execute asynchronously
mailer.delay.send_email(user)
```

The second technique is to tell Delayed Job to execute every call to a method in the
background via the `Object.handle_asynchronously` macro.

```
class Mailer
  def send_email(user)
    UserMailer.activation(user).deliver
  end
  handle_asynchronously :send_email
end
```

Durran says . . .

When using `handle_asynchronously`, make sure the declaration is after the method
definition, since Delayed Job uses `alias_method_chain` internally to set up the behavior.

Lastly, you may create a custom job by creating a separate Ruby object that only
needs to respond to `perform`. That job can then be run at any point by telling Delayed
Job to enqueue the action.

```
class EmailJob < Struct.new(:user_id)
  def perform
    user = User.find(@user_id)
    UserMailer.activation(user).deliver
  end
end
```

Background
Processing

```
# Enqueue a job with default settings
Delayed::Job.enqueue EmailJob.new(user.id)

# Enqueue a job with priority of 1
Delayed::Job.enqueue EmailJob.new(user.id, 1)

# Enqueue a job with priority of 0, starting tomorrow
Delayed::Job.enqueue EmailJob.new(user.id, 1, 1.day.from_now)
```

20.1.3 Running

To start up Delayed Job workers, use the delayed_job script created by the generator. This allows for starting a single worker or multiple workers on their own processes, and also provides the ability to stop all workers.

```
# Start a single worker
RAILS_ENV=staging script/delayed_job start

# Start multiple workers, each in a separate process
RAILS_ENV=production script/delayed_job -n 4 start

# Stop all workers
RAILS_ENV=staging script/delayed_job stop
```

Durran says...

Delayed Job workers generally have a lifecycle that is equivalent to an application deployment. Because of this, their memory consumption grows over time and may eventually have high swap usage, causing workers to become unresponsive. A good practice is to have a monitoring tool like God or monit watching jobs, and restarting them when their memory usage hits a certain point.

20.1.4 Summary

Delayed Job is an excellent choice when you want ease of setup, need to schedule jobs for later dates, or want to add priorities to jobs in your queue. It works well in situations where the total number of jobs is low and the tasks they execute are not long running or consume large amounts of memory.

Do note that if you are using Delayed Job with a relational database backend and have a large number of jobs, performance issues may arise due to the table locking the framework employs. Since jobs may have a long lifecycle, be wary of resource consumption due to workers not releasing memory once jobs are finished executing. Also where job execution can take a long period of time, higher priority jobs will still wait for the other jobs to complete before being processed. In these cases, using a non-relational backend such as MongoDB or potentially another library such as Resque may be advisable.

20.2   Resque

Resque[2] is a background processing framework that supports multiple queues and is optimized for handling extremely large numbers of jobs efficiently. It uses Redis for its persistent storage and comes with a Sinatra web application to monitor the queues and jobs.

Resque actions are Ruby objects or modules that respond to a `perform` class method. Jobs are stored in the database as JSON objects, and because of this only primitives can be passed as arguments to the actions. Resque also provides hooks into the worker and job lifecycles, as well as the ability to configure custom failure mechanisms.

Due to Resque's use of Redis as its storage engine, the overhead of job processing is unnoticable. It is currently the best performing background processing library for the feature set, and its parent/child forking architecture makes its resource consumption predictable and easily managed.

20.2.1   Getting Started

First in your `Gemfile` add the `resque` gem, then configure Resque by creating a Rails initializer and a `resque.yml` to store the configuration options. The YAML should be key/value pairs of environment name with the Redis host and port, and the initializer should load the YAML and set up the Redis options.

Configuring failure backends can also be done in the same manner Resque supports persistence to Redis or Hoptoad notifications out of the box, but custom backends can be easily created by inheriting from `Resque::Failure::Base`.

In config/resque.yml:

```
development: localhost:6379
staging:     localhost:6379
production:  localhost:6379
```

Background
Processing

---

2. `http://github.com/defunkt/resque`

The `config/initializers/resque.rb`:

```
require 'resque/failure/hoptoad'

rails_env = ENV['RAILS_ENV'] || 'development'
config = YAML.load_file(Rails.root.join 'config','resque.yml')
Resque.redis = config[rails_env]
Resque::Failure::Hoptoad.api_key = 'your-key-here'
Resque::Failure.backend = Resque::Failure::Hoptoad
```

20.2.2 Creating Jobs

Jobs in Resque are plain old Ruby objects that respond to a `perform` class method and define which queue they should be processed in. The simplest manner to define the queue is to set an instance variable on the job itself.

```
class EmailJob
  @queue = :communications

  class << self
    def perform(user_id)
      user = User.find(user_id)
      UserMailer.activation(user).deliver
    end
  end
end

# Enqueue the job
Resque.enqueue(EmailJob, user.id)
```

20.2.3 Hooks

Resque provides lifecycle hooks that can used to add additional behavior, for example adding an automatic retry for a failed job. There are two categories of hooks: worker hooks and job hooks.

The available worker hooks are `before_first_fork`, `before_fork`, and `after_fork`. Before hooks are executed in the parent process where the after hook executes in the child process. This is important to note since changes in the parent process will be permanent for the life of the worker, whereas changes in the child process will be lost when the job completes.

```
# Before the worker's first fork
Resque.before_first_fork do
  puts "Creating worker"
end
```

```
# Before every worker fork
Resque.before_fork do |job|
  puts "Forking worker"
end

# After every worker fork
Resque.after_fork do |job|
  puts "Child forked"
end
```

Job hooks differ slightly from worker hooks in that they are defined on the action classes themselves and are defined as class methods with the hook name as the prefix. The available hooks for jobs are: `before_perform`, `after_perform`, `around_perform`, and `on_failure`.

An example job that needs to retry itself automatically on failure, and logged some information before it started processing would look like:

```
class EmailJob
  class << self
    def perform(user_id)
      user = User.find(user_id)
      UserMailer.activation(user).deliver
    end

    def before_perform_log(*args)
      Logger.info "Starting Email Job"
    end

    def on_failure_retry(error, *args)
      Resque.enqueue self, *args
    end
  end
end
```

20.2.4 Plugins

Resque has a very good plugin ecosystem to provide it with additional useful features. Most plugins are modules that are included in your job classes, only to be used on specific jobs that need the extra functionality. Plugins of note are listed below and a complete list can be found at `http://wiki.github.com/defunkt/resque/plugins`.

- `resque-lock`: Allows for only a single instance of a job to be running at a time.
- `resque-retry`: Adds configurable retry and exponential backoff behavior for failed jobs.

Background
Processing

- `resque-restriction`: Provides configurable limits to job execution within given time frames.

- `resque-schedule`: Adds recurring jobs and the ability to schedule jobs in the future.

20.2.5 Running

Resque comes with two rake tasks that can be used to run workers, one to run a single worker for one or more queues the second to run multiple workers. Configuration options are supplied as environment variables when running the tasks and allow for defining the queue for the workers to monitor, logging verbosity, and the number or workers to start.

```
# Start 1 worker for the communications queue
QUEUE=communications rake environment resque:work

# Start 6 workers for the communications queue
QUEUE=communications COUNT=6 rake resque:workers

# Start 2 workers for all queues
QUEUE=* COUNT=2 rake resque:workers
```

Stopping jobs involves sending signals to the parent Resque workers, which then take the appropriate action on the child and themselves:

QUIT waits for the forked child to finish processing, then exists

TERM/INT immediately kills the child process and exits

USR1 immediately kills the child process, but leaves the parent worker running

USR2 finishes processing the child action, then waits for CONT before spawning another

CONT continues to start jobs again if it was halted by a USR2

20.2.6 Monitoring

One of the really nice features of Resque is the web interface that it ships with for monitoring your queues and jobs. It can run standalone or be mounted with your Rails application using `Rack::URLMap` in your app's `config.ru`.

To run standalone, simply run `resque-web` from the command line. If you prefer to mount with your Rails application, modify your `config.ru` to add the Resque server.

```
require "config/environment"
require "resque/server"

use Rails::Rack::LogTailer
use Rails::Rack::Static

run Rack::URLMap.new(
  "/" => ActionController::Dispatcher.new,
  "/resque" => Resque::Server.new
)
```

20.2.7 Summary

Resque is recommended where a large number of jobs are in play with potential unwanted memory growth. Completed child jobs release their memory on completing, so long-running workers do not have the negative effect on system resources that you could potentially have with other frameworks. It does not support priority queueing but does support multiple queues is advantageous when jobs can be categorized together and given pools of workers to run them.

With a Redis backend, Resque does not suffer from the potential database locking issues that can arise when using Delayed Job and has significantly better performance with respect to queue management.

Do note that Redis stores all of its data in memory, so if you are expecting a large amount of jobs but do not have a significant amount of RAM to spare, you may need to look at a different framework.

20.3 Rails Runner

Rails comes with a built-in tool for running tasks independent of the web cycle. The `rails runner` command simply loads the default Rails environment and then executes some specified Ruby code. Popular uses include:

- Importing batch external data
- Executing any (class) method in your models
- Running intensive calculations, delivering e-mails in batches, or executing scheduled tasks

    Usages involving `rails runner` that you should avoid at all costs are:

- Processing incoming e-mail
- Tasks that take longer to run as your database grows

Background Processing

20.3.1   Getting Started

For example, let us suppose that you have a model called Report. The Report model has a class method called `generate_rankings`, which you can call from the command line using

```
$ rails runner 'Report.generate_rankings'
```

Since we have access to all of Rails, we can even use the Active Record finder methods to extract data from our application.[3]

```
$ rails runner 'User.all.map(&:email).each {|e| puts e }'
charles.quinn@highgroove.com
me@seebq.com
bill.gates@microsoft.com
obie@obiefernandez.com
```

This example demonstrates that we have access to the User model and are able to execute arbitrary Rails code. In this case, we've collected some e-mail addresses that we can now spam to our heart's content. (Just kidding!)

20.3.2   Usage Notes

There are some things to remember when using `rails runner`. You must specify the production environment using the `-e` option; otherwise, it defaults to development. The `rails runner` help option tells us:

```
$ rails runner -h

Usage: rails runner [options] ('Some.ruby(code)' or a filename)
  -e, --environment=name    Specifies the environment for the runner
                            to operate in (test/development/ production)
                            Default: development
#!/usr/bin/env/path/to/script/railsrunner
```

Using `rails runner`, we can easily script any batch operations that need to run using `cron` or another system scheduler. For example, you might calculate the most popular or highest-ranking product in your e-commerce application every few minutes or nightly, rather than make an expensive query on every request:

```
$ rails runner ‚Äìe production 'Product.calculate_top_ranking'
```

A sample `crontab` to run that script might look like

```
0 */5 * * *   root   /usr/local/bin/ruby \
/apps/exampledotcom/current/script/rails runner -e production \
'Product.calculate_top_ranking'
```

---

3. Be careful to escape any characters that have specific meaning to your shell.

The script will run every five hours to update the `Product` model's top rankings.

20.3.3   Considerations

On the positive side, it doesn't get any easier and there are no additional libraries to install. That's about it.

As for negatives the `rails runner` process loads the entire Rails environment. For some tasks, particularly short-lived ones, that can be quite wasteful of resources. Also, nothing prevents multiple copies of the same script from running simultaneously, which can be catastrophically bad, depending on the contents of the script.

Wilson says . . .

Do not process incoming e-mail with `rails runner`. It's a Denial of Service attack waiting to happen. Use Fetcher (or something like it) instead: `http://slantwisedesign.com/rdoc/fetcher/`.

20.3.4   Summary

The Rails Runner is useful for short tasks that need to run infrequently, but jobs that require more heavy lifting, reporting, and robust failover mechanisms are best handled by other libraries.

20.4   Conclusion

Most web applications today will need to incorporate some form of asynchronous behavior, and we've covered some of the important libraries available when needing to implement background processing. There are many other frameworks and techniques available for handling this, so choose the solution that is right for your needs—just remember to never make your users wait.

Background
Processing

APPENDIX A
Active Model API Reference

Active Model is a Rails library containing various modules used in developing frameworks that need to interact with the Rails Action Pack library. This came about by extracting common functionality that was not persistence specific out of Active Record, so that 3rd party libraries did not have to copy code from Rails or monkey patch helpers in order to conform to the API.

Out of this extraction came extremely useful reusable functionality to developers of Rails compatible libraries, such as dirty attributes, validations, and serialization into JSON or XML. And simply by using these modules developers could be DRY and not need to rewrite what has already been done before.

Section headings reflect the name of the Class or Module where the API method is located and are organized in alphabetical order for easy lookup. Sub-sections appear according to the name of the Ruby file in which they exist within Active Model's `lib` directory. Finally, the sub-sub-sections are the API methods themselves.

A.1 AttributeMethods

`AttributeMethods` adds the ability for your class to have custom prefixes and suffixes on your methods. It is used by adding the definitions for the prefixes and suffixes, defining which methods on the object will use them, then implementing the common behavior for when those methods are called. An example implementation is as follows:

```
class Record
  include ActiveModel::AttributeMethods

  attribute_method_prefix 'reset_'
  attribute_method_suffix '_highest?'
  define_attribute_methods [ 'score' ]
```

Active
Model

561

```
  attr_accessor :score

  private
  def reset_attribute(attribute)
    send("#{attribute}=", nil)
  end

  def attribute_highest?(attribute)
    attribute > 1000 ? true : false
  end
end
```

A.1.1 `active_model/attribute_methods.rb`

`attribute_method_affix(*affixes)`

Defines a prefix and suffix that when used in conjuction with `define_attribute_methods` creates a instance method with the prefix and suffix wrapping the previous method name.

`attribute_method_prefix(*prefixes)`

Defines a prefix that when used in conjuction with `define_attribute_methods` creates a instance method with the prefix and the previous method name.

`attribute_method_suffix(*suffixes)`

Defines a suffix that when used in conjuction with `define_attribute_methods` creates a instance method with the suffix and the previous method name.

`attribute_methods_generated?`

Returns whether or not the dynamic attribute methods have been generated.

`define_attr_method(name, value = nil, & block)`

Defines an attribute method, which is a class method that replaces an existing method and prefixes the original method with `original_`. This is so the newmethod can access the original value.

`define_attribute_methods(*attr_names)`

Defines the methods that will get prefixed and suffixed.

`undefine_attribute_methods`

Removes all the attribute method definitions

A.2 Callbacks

`Callbacks` gives any class Active Record–style callbacks. It is used by defining the callbacks that the model will use, then in your model running the callbacks at the appropriate time. Once defined you have access to `before`, `after`, and `around` custom methods.

```
class Record
  extend ActiveModel::Callbacks

  define_model_callbacks :create
  define_model_callbacks :update, :destroy, :only => :before

  before_update :my_callback

  def save
    _run_update_callbacks do
      # Your save code here
    end
  end

  private
  def my_callback
    # Your callback code here
  end
end
```

A.2.1 `active_model/callbacks.rb`
`define_model_callbacks(*callbacks)`
Defines the callback hooks that can be used in the model, which will dynamically provide you with a `before`, `after`, and `around` hook for each name passed. Can optionally supply an `:only` option to specify which of those you want executed.

A.3 Conversion

`Conversion` is a simple module that when included gives the standard Rails conversion methods to your model. The only requirement for including this class is that your model contains a `persisted?` method and an `id` method.

A.3.1 `active_model/conversion.rb`
`to_model`
Returns self. If your model is not Active Model compliant, then override this method.

`to_key`
Will either return an array of primary key attributes or nil if the object is not persisted.

Active
Model

to_param

Will return a url friendly version of the primary or nil if the object is not persisted.

A.4 Dirty

Dirty is a powerful module that allows for tracking in your object what changes have been made to it since it was last initialized. It creates a handful of dynamic methods based on which attributes you define as attribute methods on your class, and requires that you also tell the attribute setters that they are being tracked for changes. (You can optionally also store previous changes each time your object is presisted as well.)

```
class User
  include ActiveModel::Dirty

  define_attribute_methods [:email]

  def email
    @email
  end

  def email=(value)
    email_will_change!
    @email = value
  end

  def save
    @previously_changed = changes
  end
end
```

In the example above, the following dynamic methods would then be available for checking the dirty state of the flagged field. (Assume user is an instance of the User class.)

```
# Returns an array of the old and new values
user.email_change

# Returns true if the value has changed
user.email_changed?

# Resets the attribute back to the original value
user.reset_email!

# Returns the old value of a changed field
user.email_was

# Flags an attribute that is will be changed
user.email_will_change!
```

A.4.1 `active_model/dirty.rb`

changed

Gets an array of fields whos values have changed on the object.

changed?

Returns whether or not the object's attributes have changed.

changed_attributes

Returns a Hash of the fields that have changed with their original values.

changes

Returns a Hash of changes, with the attribute names as the keys, and the values being an array of the old and new value for that field.

previous_changes

Returns a Hash of previous changes before the object was persisted, with the attribute names as the keys, and the values being an array of the old and new value for that field.

A.5 Errors

`Errors` is a class that provides a common interface for handling application error messages.

Note that in order for your object to be compatible with the `Errors` API with i18n and validations support, it needs to extend `ActiveModel::Naming`, `ActiveModel::Translations`, and include `ActiveModel::Validations`.

```
class User
  extend ActiveModel::Naming
  extend ActiveModel::Translations
  include ActiveModel::Validations

  attr_reader :errors

  def initialize
    @errors = ActiveModel::Errors.new(self)
  end
end
```

Active
Model

A.5.1 `active_model/errors.rb`

`[](attribute)`

Returns the errors for the supplied attribute as an array.

`[]=(attribute, error)`

Adds the provided error message to the attribute's errors.

`add(attribute, message = nil, options = {})`

Adds an error message for the supplied attribute. If no message is provided, `:invalid` is assumed. Options allowed are:

`:default` A default message for the error.

`add_on_blank(attributes, custom_message = nil)`

Adds an error message for each provided blank attribute name.

`add_on_empty(attributes, custom_message = nil)`

Adds an error message for each provided empty attribute name.

`count`

Returns the total number of error messages.

`each`

Iterates through the error keys, yielding the attribute and the errors for each.

`empty?`

Returns whether or not any errors exist.

`full_messages`

Returns all the error messages as an array.

`generate_message(attr, message = :invalid, options = {})`

Generates a translated error message for the supplied attribute. Messages are looked up via the following pattern: `models.MODEL.attributes.ATTRIBUTE.MESSAGE`. Options provided can be:

`:default` A default message for the error.

size

Returns the total number of error messages.

to_a

Returns an array of all the error messages, with the attribute name included in each.

to_xml

Returns the errors hash as XML.

A.6 Lint::Tests

You can check whether an object is compatible with the Active Model API by including `ActiveModel::Lint::Tests`. It contains assertions that tell you whether your object is fully compliant.

The tests only check compatibility. They do not attempt to determine the correctness of the returned values. For instance, you could implement `valid?` to always return true and the tests would still pass. It is up to you to ensure that the values are correct.

Objects you pass in are expected to return a compliant object from a call to `to_model`. Generally speaking, `to_model` just returns `self`.

A.7 MassAssignmentSecurity

`MassAssignmentSecurity` is a module that can be included to provided protected and accessible access to your attributes. Mass assignment is defined in Rails as any method or constructor that allows more than one value to be set at the same time. The methods provided in this module help prevent fields such as ids and passwords to get accidentally set through the likes of form submissions, etc.

```
User.new(:first_name => "Joe", :last_name => "Smith")
Account.create(:name => "Acme")
```

A.7.1 active_model/mass_assignment_ security.rb

attr_protected

Attributes defined as protected do not get their values set when a mass assignment method is called.

```
class User
  include ActiveModel::MassAssignmentSecurity
  attr_protected :id, :password
```

Active Model

```
    def attributes=(props)
      sanitize_for_mass_assignment(props).each do |key, value|
        send("#{key}=", value)
      end
    end
  end
end
```

attr_accessible

Defines a list of attributes that can be set via mass assignment, all others will be protected by default.

```
class User
  include ActiveModel::MassAssignmentSecurity
  attr_accessible :first_name, :last_name

  def attributes=(props)
    sanitize_for_mass_assignment(props).each do |key, value|
      send("#{key}=", value)
    end
  end
end
```

A.8 Name

Name extends String and wraps a bunch of logic around name information about your object so that it can be used with Rails.

How much name information could there be? Take a look at Name's constructor.

```
def initialize(klass, namespace = nil)
  super(klass.name)
  @unnamespaced = self.sub(/^#{namespace.name}::/, '') if namespace
  @klass = klass
  @singular = _singularize(self).freeze
  @plural = ActiveSupport::Inflector.pluralize(@singular).freeze
  @element = ActiveSupport::Inflector.underscore(ActiveSupport::Inflector.
  demodulize(self)).freeze
  @human = ActiveSupport::Inflector.humanize(@element).freeze
  @collection = ActiveSupport::Inflector.tableize(self).freeze
  @partial_path = "#{@collection}/#{@element}".freeze
  @param_key = (namespace ? _singularize(@unnamespaced)
: @singular).freeze
  @route_key = (namespace ? ActiveSupport::Inflector.pluralize(@param_key)
: @plural).freeze
end
```

All of this information is calculated and stored at initialization-time, presumably since it's used all over Rails.

A.8.1 `active_model/naming.rb`

collection

Returns an underscored plural version of the model name.

element

Returns an underscored version of the model name.

human

Returns a translated human readable version of the model name using I18n. The basic recipe is to capitalized the first word of the name.

```
BlogPost.model_name.human # => "Blog post"
```

partial_path

Returns `collection/element`.

plural

Returns a pluralized version of the model name.

singular

Returns a singularized version of the model name.

A.9 Naming

`Naming` is the module that you include in your class to get name type information for your model.

A.9.1 `active_model/naming.rb`

model_name

Returns an `ActiveModel::Name` for the object. Used by Action Pack to determine routing

A.10 Observer

`Observer` is the class to inherit from when creating your own observer to hook into the lifecycle of your models. In order for it to work properly, the model to observe must include `ActiveModel::Observing`, and the observers must be set up in an initializer or similar.

Active
Model

```
class LoggingObserver < ActiveModel::Observer
  observe :user, :admin

  def after_create(object)
    Rails.logger.info("#{object} created.")
  end
end
```

A.10.1 `active_model/observing.rb`

`observe(*models)`

Tells what models this observer observes. This is useful when the naming does not match the model name or multiple objects need to be observed. The models can be classes or symbols.

`observed_class`

Returns the default observed class.

`observe_class_inherited(subclass)`

Sets up the observer to watch subclasses of the observed model.

`observed_classes`

Returns an array of the classes this observer observes.

`update(observed_method, object)`

Calls the supplied method with the object as the args if the method exists.

A.11 `Observing`

`Observing` is a module to include in your models to set up observers in the lifecycle of your model. Observers are added to the class by calling the observers class method at some point in the application bootstrapping. An initializer would be a good fit for this.

```
class User
  include ActiveModel::Observing
end

User.observers = Logging
```

A.11.1 **active_model/observing.rb**

add_observer(observer)

Adds an instantiated observer to the class.

count_observers

Returns the number of observers the class has.

instantiate_observers

Instantiate each of the class' observers.

notify_observers(*args)

Iterates through all the class' observers and calls update on them.

observers

Get the observers for the class.

A.12 **Serialization**

Serialization is a module to include in your models when you want to represent your model as a serializable hash. You only need to define an attributes method and the rest is handled for you.

```
class User
  include ActiveModel::Serialization
  attr_accessor :first_name, :last_name

  def attributes
    { 'first_name' => @first_name, 'last_name' => @last_name }
  end
end
```

A.12.1 **active_model/serialization.rb**

serializable_hash(options = nil)

Returns the serializable hash representation of your model. Options provided can be of the following:

:except Do not include these attributes in the XML.

:methods Only include these methods in the XML.

:only Only include the supplied attributes.

Active
Model

A.13 Serializers::JSON

Serializers::JSON is a module to include in your models when you want to provide
a JSON representation of your object. It autmatically includes the Serialization
module and depends on the attributes and attributes= methods to be present.

```
class User
  include ActiveModel::Serializers::JSON
  attr_accessor :first_name, :last_name

  def attributes
    { 'first_name' => @first_name, 'last_name' => @last_name }
  end

  def attributes=(attrs)
    @first_name = attrs['first_name']
    @last_name = attrs['last_name']
  end
end
```

A.13.1 `active_model/serializers/json.rb`

`as_json(options = nil)`

Returns a hash to convert to JSON for the model attributes.

`from_json(json)`

Decodes the supplied JSON, sets the attributes on the model, and returns self.

A.14 Serializers::Xml

Serializers::Xml is a module to include in your models when you want to provide
an XML representation of your object. It automatically includes the Serialization
module and depends on the attributes and attributes= methods to be present.

```
class Pet
  include ActiveModel::Serializers::XML
  attr_accessor :name

  def attributes
    { 'name' => @name }
  end

  def attributes=(attrs)
    @name = attrs['name']
  end
end
```

A.14.1 `active_model/serializers/xml.rb`

`to_xml(options = {}, & block)`

Returns an XML representation of the object. Available options are:

:builder Supply a custom builder to generate the markup.

:except Do not include these attributes in the XML.

:indent Number of spaces to indent the XML.

:methods Only include these methods in the XML.

:namespace Set the XMLNS.

:only Only include the supplied attributes.

:skip_instruct Skip processing instructions.

:skip_types Skip typing.

:type Add a type to the XML tags.

`from_xml(xml)`

Decodes the supplied XML, sets the attributes on the model, and returns self.

A.15 Translation

`Translation` provides the ability to add internationalization support to your model

```
class User
  extend ActiveModel::Translation
end
```

A.15.1 `active_model/translation.rb`

`i18n_scope`

Returns :activemodel, you can override if you want a custom namespace.

`lookup_ancestors`

Gets all ancestors of this class that support i18n.

`human_attribute_name(attribute, options = {})`

Translates attribute names into a human readable format with options.

:default The default text for the attribute name.

Active Model

A.16 **Validations**

`Validations` adds a fully featured validations framework to your model. This includes the means to validate the following types of scenarios plus the ability to create custom validators.

Acceptance of a field.

Confirmation of a field.

Exclusion of a field from a set of values.

Format of a field against a regular expression.

Inclusion of a field in a set of values.

Length of a field.

Numericality of a field.

Presence of a field.

```
class User
  include ActiveModel::Validations

  attr_accessor :name

  validates_each :name do |record, attribute, value|
    record.errors.add(attribute, 'should be present') if value.nil?
  end
end
```

A.16.1 `active_model/validations.rb`

Note that available base options for validation macros that use options are as follows. If the specific validation has additional options they will be explained there. All options are supplied as a Hash, and are the last element of the first set of arguments to the macros.

`:allow_nil` Specify whether to validate nil attributes.

`:if` Only run if the supplied method or proc returns true.

`:on` Define when the validation will run.

`:unless` Only run if the supplied method or proc returns false.

attribute_method?(attribute)
Returns true if a method is defined for the supplied attribute.

errors
Get all the errors for the model.

invalid?(context = nil)

Checks if the object is invalid given the optional context.

valid?(context = nil)

Checks if the object is valid given the optional context.

validate(*args, & block)

Adds a single validation to the model. Can be a method name as a symbol or a block with options. Additional options are:

:allow_blank Specify whether to validate blank attributes.

validates_acceptance_of(*args)

Validates that a field was accepted.

```
validates_acceptance_of :terms, :on => :create
```

Additional Options:

:message An optional custom error message.

:accept Provide the value that is considered accepted.

validates_confirmation_of(*args)

Validates that a field was confirmed.

```
validates_confirmation_of :password, :message => "Please try again."
```

Additional Options:

:message An optional custom error message.

validates_each(*attrs, & block)

Validates each of the attribute names against the supplied block. Options are passed in as a Hash as the last element in the *attrs argument.

:allow_blank Specify whether to validate blank attributes.

validates_exclusion_of(*args)

Validates that a field does not have a value supplied in the list.

```
validates_exclusion_of :age, :in => 18..55
```

Active Model

Additional Options:

:in The list or range the check the value against.

:message An optional custom error message.

validates_format_of(*args)

Validates that a field conforms to the supplied format.

```
validates_format_of :phone, :with => /\A[\d\-\(\)\sx]+\z/
```

Additional Options:

:allow_blank Specify whether to validate blank attributes.

:with The regular expression to check if the format matches.

:without The regular expression to check that the format does not match.

:message An optional custom error message.

validates_inclusion_of(*args)

Validates that a field is a value supplied in the list.

```
validates_inclusion_of :state, :in => [ "CA", "NY" ]
```

Additional Options:

:allow_blank Specify whether to validate blank attributes.

:in The list or range the check the value against.

:message An optional custom error message.

validates_length_of(*args)

Validates that a field adheres to the supplied length limitations.

```
validates_length_of :name, :maximum => 48
```

Additional Options:

:allow_blank Specify whether to validate blank attributes.

:in Specify the range the length of the attribute can fall within.

:maximum Specify the maximum length of the attribute.

:message An optional custom error message.

:minimum Specify the minimum length of the attribute.

:tokenizer A block to define how the string should be broken up.

:too_long Define a custom message if the attribute is too long.

:too_short Define a custom message if the attribute is too short.

:within Specify the range the length of the attribute can fall within.

:wrong_length Define a custom message for an incorrect length.

validates_numericality_of(*args)
Validates that a field is numeric and optionally in a specified value range.

```
validates_numericality_of :score, :only_integer => true
```

Additional Options:

:equal_to Specify a value the field must be exactly.

:even Set that the value must be even.

:greater_than Specify a value the field must be greater than.

:greater_than_or_equal_to Specify a value the field must be greater than or equal to.

:less_than Specify a value the field must be less than.

:less_than_or_equal_to Specify a value the field must be less than or equal to.

:message An optional custom error message.

:odd Set that the value must be odd.

:only_integer Set whether the value has to be an integer.

validates_presence_of(*args)
Validates that a field is not blank.

```
validates_presence_of :dob
```

Additional Options:

:message An optional custom error message.

validates_with(*args, & block)
Validates with a supplied custom validator. The validator class must respond to validate and handle the options and error message addition internally.

```
class NameValidator < ActiveModel::Validator
  def validate(object)
    # Some validation logic here
  end
end
```

Active Model

```
class User
  include ActiveModel::Validations
  validates_with NameValidator, :on => :update
end
```

validators

Get all the validators being used by the class.

validators_on(attribute)

Get all the validators for a specific attribute.

A.17 Validator

Validator provides a class that custom validators can extend to seamlessly integrate into the ActiveModel::Validations API. It only requires that the new class defines a validate method.

A full explanation of how to use Validator and EachValidator is provided in Section 8.6 "Custom Validation Techniques".

```
class ScoreValidator < ActiveModel::Validator
  include ActiveModel::Validations

  def validate(object)
    # Perform validations and add errors here.
  end
end
```

A.17.1 active_model/validator.rb

kind

Returns the type of the validator, which is a symbol of the underscored class name without "Validator" included.

validate(record)

This method must be overwritten in the validator in order to actually handle the validation itself.

APPENDIX B

Active Support API Reference

Active Support is a Rails library containing utility classes and extensions to Ruby's built-in libraries. It usually doesn't get much attention on its own—you might even call its modules the supporting cast members of the Rails ensemble.

However, Active Support's low profile doesn't diminish its importance in day-to-day Rails programming. To ensure that this book is useful as an offline programming companion, here is a complete, enhanced version of the Rails Active Support API reference, supplemented in most cases with realistic example usages and commentary. As your reviewing the material in this appendix, note that many of the methods featured here are used primarily by other Rails libraries and are not particularly useful to application developers.

Section headings reflect the name of the Class or Module where the API method is located and are organized in alphabetical order for easy lookup. Sub-sections appear according to the name of the Ruby file in which they exist within Active Support's `lib` directory. Finally, the sub-sub-sections are the API methods themselves.

B.1 `Array`

The following methods provide additional functionality for accessing array elements.

B.1.1 `active_support/core_ext/array/access`

from(position)

Returns the tail of the array starting from the `position` specified. Note that the position is zero-indexed.

```
> %w(foo bar baz quux).from(2)
=> ["baz", "quux"]
```

to(position)

Returns the beginning elements of the array up to `position` specified. Note that the position is zero-indexed.

```
> %w(foo bar baz quux).to(2)
=> ["foo", "bar", "baz"]
```

second

Equivalent to calling `self[1]`.

```
> %w(foo bar baz quux).second
=> "bar"
```

third

Equivalent to `self[2]`.

fourth

Equivalent to `self[3]`.

fifth

Equivalent to `self[4]`.

forty_two

Equivalent to calling `self[41]`—a humorous addition to the API by David.

B.1.2 active_support/core_ext/array/ conversions

The following methods are used for converting Ruby arrays into other formats.

to_formatted_s(format = :default)

Two formats are supported, `:default` and `:db`. The `:default` format delegates to the normal `to_s` method for an array, which simply concatenates the contents into one mashed-up string.

```
> %w(foo bar baz quux).to_s
=> "foobarbazquux"
```

The much more interesting `:db` option returns `"null"` if the array is empty, or concatenates the `id` fields of its member elements into a comma-delimited string with code like this:

```
collect { |element| element.id }.join(",")
```

In other words, the `:db` formatting is meant to work with ActiveRecord objects (or other types of objects that properly respond to `id`).

```
> %w(foo bar baz quux).to_s(:db)
warning: Object#id will be deprecated; use Object#object_id
=> "20244090,20244080,20244070,20244060"
```

to_s
The `to_s` method of `Array` is aliased to `to_formatted_s`.

to_sentence(options = {})
Converts the array to a comma-separated sentence in which the last element is joined by a connector word.

```
>> %w(alcohol tobacco firearms).to_sentence
=> "alcohol, tobacco, and firearms"
```

The following options are available for `to_sentence`:

:connector The word used to join the last element in arrays with two or more elements (default: "and").

:skip_last_comma Set this option to `true` to return "a, b and c" instead of "a, b, and c."

to_xml(options = {}) |xml| ...
As covered in Chapter 15, XML and Active Resource, the `to_xml` method on `Array` can be used to create an XML collection by iteratively calling `to_xml` on its members, and wrapping the entire thing in an enclosing element. All of the array elements must respond to `to_xml`.

```
>> ["riding","high"].to_xml
RuntimeError: Not all elements respond to to_xml
```

The following example yields the `Builder` object to an optional block so that arbitrary markup can be inserted at the bottom of the generated XML, as the last child of the enclosing element.

```
{:foo => "foo", :bar => 42}.to_xml do |xml|
   xml.did_it "again"
end
```

outputs the following XML:

```
<?xml version="1.0" encoding="UTF-8"?>
<hash>
  <bar type="integer">42</bar>
```

Active
Support

```
  <foo>foo</foo>
  <did_it>again</did_it>
</hash>
```

The options for `to_xml` are:

:builder Defaults to a new instance of `Builder::XmlMarkup`. Specify explicitly if you're calling `to_xml` on this array as part of a larger XML construction routine.

:children Sets the name to use for element tags explicitly. Defaults to singularized version of the `:root` name by default.

:dasherize Whether or not to turn underscores to dashes in tag names (defaults to `true`).

:indent Indent level to use for generated XML (defaults to two spaces).

:root The tag name to use for the enclosing element. If no `:root` is supplied and all members of the array are of the same class, the dashed, pluralized form of the first element's class name is used as a default. Otherwise the default `:root` is `records`.

:skip_instruct Whether or not to generate an XML instruction tag by calling `instruct!` on `Builder`.

:skip_types Whether or not to include a `type="array"` attribute on the enclosing element.

B.1.3 `active_support/core_ext/array/extract_options`

Active Support provides a method for extracting Rails-style options from a variable-length set of argument parameters.

`extract_options!`

Extracts options from a variable set of arguments. It's a bang method because it removes and returns the last element in the array if it's a hash; otherwise, it returns a blank hash and the source array is unmodified.

```
def options(*args)
  args.extract_options!
end

>> options(1, 2)
=> {}

>> options(1, 2, :a => :b)
=> {:a=>:b}
```

B.1.4 `active_support/core_ext/array/grouping`

Methods used for splitting array elements into logical groupings.

`in_groups(number, fill_with = nil) |group| ...`

The `in_groups` method splits an array into a `number` of equally sized groups. If a `fill_with` parameter is provided, its value is used to pad the groups into equal sizes.

```
%w(1 2 3 4 5 6 7 8 9 10).in_groups(3) {|group| p group}
["1", "2", "3", "4"]
["5", "6", "7", nil]
["8", "9", "10", nil]

%w(1 2 3 4 5 6 7).in_groups(3, ' ') {|group| p group}
["1", "2", "3"]
["4", "5", " "]
["6", "7", " "]
```

In the special case that you don't want equally sized groups (in other words, no padding) then pass `false` as the value of `fill_with`.

```
%w(1 2 3 4 5 6 7).in_groups(3, false) {|group| p group}
["1", "2", "3"]
["4", "5"]
["6", "7"]
```

`in_groups_of(number, fill_with = nil) {|group| ...}`

Related to its sibling `in_groups`, the `in_groups_of` method splits an array into groups of the specified `number` size, padding any remaining slots. The `fill_with` parameter is used for padding and defaults to `nil`. If a block is provided, it is called with each group; otherwise, a two-dimensional array is returned.

```
>> %w(1 2 3 4 5 6 7).in_groups_of(3)
=> [[1, 2, 3], [4, 5, 6], [7, nil, nil]

>> %w(1 2 3).in_groups_of(2, ' ') {|group| puts group }
=> [[1, 2],[3, " "]]
```

Passing `false` to the `fill_with` parameter inhibits the fill behavior.

```
>> %w(1 2 3).in_groups_of(2, false) {|group| puts group }
=> [[1, 2][3]]
```

The `in_groups_of` method is particularly useful for batch-processing model objects and generating table rows in view templates.

split(value = nil, &block)

Divides an array into one or more subarrays based on a delimiting value:

```
[1, 2, 3, 4, 5].split(3)   #=> [[1, 2], [4, 5]]
```

or the result of an optional block:

```
(1..8).to_a.split { |i| i % 3 == 0 } # => [[1, 2], [4, 5], [7, 8]]
```

B.1.5 active_support/core_ext/array/ random_access

A convenience method for accessing a random element of an array.

sample

Returns a random element from the array.

```
>> [1, 2, 3, 4].sample
=> 3
>> [1, 2, 3, 4].sample
=> 1
```

Efficiently grabbing a random record from the database is covered under the heading, Random Ordering in Chapter 5, Working with Active Record.

B.1.6 active_support/core_ext/array/uniq_by

Two convenience methods used for deriving unique elements of an array.

uniq_by

Returns an unique array based on the criteria given as a proc. Can be used when you need to enhance or decorate Ruby's default uniq behavior.

```
>> [1, 2, 3, 4].uniq_by { |i| i.odd? }
=> [1, 2]
>> %w(Foo FOO fOO Bar BAR bAr bAR).uniq_by { |s| s.downcase }
=> ["Foo", "Bar"]
```

uniq_by!

Same behavior as uniq_by but modifies the array in place.

B.1.7 active_support/core_ext/array/wrap

This is a convenience method added to the Array class.

Array.wrap(object)

Wraps the object in an Array unless it's an Array. Converts the object to an Array using to_ary if it implements that. It differs with Array() in that it does not call to_a on the argument:

```
Array(:foo => :bar)       # => [[:foo, :bar]]
Array.wrap(:foo => :bar)  # => [{:foo => :bar}]

Array("foo\nbar")         # => ["foo\n", "bar"], in Ruby 1.8
Array.wrap("foo\nbar")    # => ["foo\nbar"]
```

B.1.8 active_support/core_ext/object/blank

blank?

Alias for empty?

B.1.9 active_support/core_ext/object/to_param

to_param

Calls to_param on all of its elements and joins the result with slashes. This is used by the url_for method in Action Pack.

```
>> ["riding","high","and","I","want","to","make"].to_param
=> "riding/high/and/I/want/to/make"
```

B.2 ActiveSupport::BacktraceCleaner

B.2.1 active_support/backtrace_cleaner

Many backtraces include too much information that's not relevant for the context. This makes it hard to find the signal in the backtrace and adds debugging time. With a custom BacktraceCleaner, you can setup filters and silencers for your particular context, so only the relevant lines are included.

If you want to change the setting of Rails's built-in BacktraceCleaner, to show as much as possible, you can call BacktraceCleaner.remove_silencers! in your console, specs or an application initializer. Also, if you need to reconfigure an existing BacktraceCleaner so that it does not filter or modify the paths of any lines of the backtrace, you can call BacktraceCleaner#remove_filters! These two methods will give you a completely untouched backtrace.

```
bc = ActiveSupport::BacktraceCleaner.new
bc.add_filter   { |line| line.gsub(Rails.root, '') }
```

```
bc.add_silencer { |line| line =~ /mongrel|rubygems/ }
bc.clean(exception.backtrace) # will strip the Rails.root prefix and
skip any lines from mongrel or rubygems
```

Inspired by the Quiet Backtrace gem by Thoughtbot.

B.3 ActiveSupport::Base64

Base64 provides utility methods for encoding and de-coding binary data using a base 64 representation. A base 64 representation of binary data consists entirely of printable US-ASCII characters. The Base64 module is included in Ruby 1.8, but has been removed in Ruby 1.9. Active Support will use Ruby's built-in Base64 library if it's available.

B.3.1 active_support/base64

Base64.encode64(data)

Encodes a string to its base 64 representation. Each 60 characters of output is separated by a newline character.

```
>> ActiveSupport::Base64.encode64("Original unencoded string")
=> "T3JpZ2luYWwgdW5lbmNvZGVkIHN0cmluZw==\n"
```

Base64.encode64s(data)

Encodes the value as base64 without the newline breaks. This makes the base64 encoding readily usable as URL parameters or memcache keys without further processing.

Base64.decode64(data)

Decodes a base 64 encoded string to its original representation.

```
>> ActiveSupport::Base64.decode64("T3JpZ2luYWwgdW5lbmNvZGVkIHN0cmluZw==")
=> "Original unencoded string"
```

B.4 ActiveSupport::BasicObject

A class with no predefined methods that behaves similarly to Builder's BlankSlate. Used for proxy classes and can come in handy when implementing domain-specific languages in your application code.

B.4.1 active_support/basic_object

The implementation of BasicObject is an interesting and common Ruby idiom, so it's reproduced here for your reference.

```
module ActiveSupport
  if defined? ::BasicObject
    # A class with no predefined methods that behaves similarly to
Builder's
    # BlankSlate. Used for proxy classes.
    class BasicObject < ::BasicObject
      undef_method :==
      undef_method :equal?

      # Let ActiveSupport::BasicObject at least raise exceptions.
      def raise(*args)
        ::Object.send(:raise, *args)
      end
    end
  else
    class BasicObject #:nodoc:
      instance_methods.each do |m|
        undef_method(m) if m.to_s !~ /(?:^__|^nil\?$|^send$|^object_id$)/
      end
    end
  end
end
```

B.5 ActiveSupport::Benchmarkable

Benchmarkable allows you to measure the execution time of a block in a template and records the result to the log.

B.5.1 active_support/benchmarkable

benchmark(message = "Benchmarking", options = {})

Wrap this block around expensive operations or possible bottlenecks to get a time reading for the operation. For example, let's say you thought your file processing method was taking too long; you could wrap it in a benchmark block.

```
benchmark "Process data files" do
  expensive_files_operation
end
```

That would add an entry like "Process data files (345.2ms)" to the log, which can then be used to compare timings when optimizing your code.

You may give an optional logger level as the :level option. Valid options are :debug, :info, :warn, and :error. The default level is :info.

```
benchmark "Low-level files", :level => :debug do
  lowlevel_files_operation
end
```

Finally, you can pass true as the third argument to silence all log activity inside the block. This is great for boiling down a noisy block to just a single statement:

```
benchmark "Process data files", :level => :info, :silence => true do
  expensive_and_chatty_files_operation
end
```

B.6 BigDecimal

B.6.1 active_support/core_ext/big_decimal/conversions

to_yaml

Emits the number without any scientific notation and without losing precision. Note that reconstituting YAML floats to native floats may lose precision.

```
>> bd = BigDecimal.new("8439487874978349874983473987.839723497347")
=> #<BigDecimal:269fabc,'0.8439487874 9783498749 8347349878 3972349734
7E29',44(48)>
>> bd.to_yaml
=> "--- 8439487874978349874983473987.839723497347\n"
```

B.6.2 active_support/json/encoding

A BigDecimal would be naturally represented as a JSON number. Most libraries, however, parse non-integer JSON numbers directly as floats. Clients using those libraries would get in general a wrong number and no way to recover other than manually inspecting the string with the JSON code itself.

That's why a JSON string is returned. The JSON literal is not numeric, but if the other end knows by contract that the data is supposed to be a BigDecimal, it still has the chance to post-process the string and get the real value.

as_json

Returns self.to_s.

B.7 ActiveSupport::BufferedLogger

The BufferedLogger class is Rails's built-in logger facility.

B.7.1 `active_support/buffered_logger`

Levels

The following levels are recognized by the logger, in order of increasing severity:

```
module Severity
  DEBUG   = 0
  INFO    = 1
  WARN    = 2
  ERROR   = 3
  FATAL   = 4
  UNKNOWN = 5
end
```

add(severity, msg)

The logger class uses meta-programming to wrap the `add` method in convenience methods named after the severity levels.

```
# equivalent to add(0, "foo")
logger.debug("foo")

# equivalent to add(3, "foo")
logger.error("bar")
```

auto_flushing=(period)

Sets the auto-flush period. Set to `true` to flush after every log message, to an integer to flush every N messages, or to `false`, `nil`, or `zero` to never auto-flush. If you turn auto-flushing off, be sure to regularly `flush` the log yourself. Otherwise you will quickly eat up all available memory.

close

Flushes the logger and closes the log (if supported), then sets its internal log reference to `nil`.

flush

Writes log messages buffered in memory to the log's IO stream (generally your application's log file.) Only needed when you turn auto-flushing off.

initialize(log, level = DEBUG)

You can change where the log is written by replacing the default logger in `application.rb`.

```
Rails.logger = ActiveSupport::BufferedLogger.new("mylogger.txt")
```

It won't work as expected in an initializer script, because the core frameworks are already loaded and have logger instances before the initializers.

The `initializer` code is versatile and understands filenames, paths or any other type of `IO` object, including `$stdout`, which allows you to do the following cool hack in your console:

```
>> ActiveRecord::Base.logger = ActiveSupport::BufferedLogger.new($stdout)
=> #<ActiveSupport::BufferedLogger...>

>> User.first
  SQL (1.1ms)    SELECT name
 FROM sqlite_master
 WHERE type = 'table' AND NOT name = 'sqlite_sequence'

  User Load (0.1ms)   SELECT "users".* FROM "users" LIMIT 1

=> nil
```

silence(temporary_level = ERROR)

Silences log items below the `temporary_level` severity for the duration of the block. Assuming that you're in a context, such as models or controllers, that have a `logger` method, you can use the `silence` method as follows:

```
logger.silence do
  really_chatty_operation
end
```

In other contexts, grab a reference to the logger via the `Rails.logger` method.

B.8 ActiveSupport::Cache::Store

This is an abstract cache store class. There are multiple cache store implementations, each having its own additional features. `MemCacheStore` is currently the most popular cache store for large production websites.

Some implementations may not support all methods beyond the basic cache methods of `fetch`, `write`, `read`, `exist?`, and `delete`.

`ActiveSupport::Cache::Store` can store any serializable Ruby object.

```
>> cache = ActiveSupport::Cache::MemoryStore.new
=> <#ActiveSupport::Cache::MemoryStore entries=0, size=0, options={}>
>> cache.read("city")
=> nil
>> cache.write("city", "Duckburgh")
=> true
```

```
>> cache.read("city")
=> "Duckburgh"
```

Keys are always translated into strings and are case-sensitive.

```
>> cache.read("city") == cache.read(:city)
=> true
```

When an object is specified as a key, its `cache_key` method will be called *if it is defined*. Otherwise, the `to_param` method will be called.

```
>> r = Report.first
=> #<Report id: 1, name: "Special", created_at: ...>
>> r.cache_key
=> "reports/1-20100829170518"
>> r.to_param
=> "1"
```

Hashes and Arrays can also be used as keys. The elements will be delimited by slashes and hash elements will be sorted by key so they are consistent.

```
>> cache.write ["USA","FL","Jacksonville"], "Obie"
=> true
>> cache.read "USA/FL/Jacksonville"
=> "Obie"
```

Nil values can be cached.

If your cache is on a shared infrastructure, you can define a namespace for your cache entries. If a namespace is defined, it will be prefixed on to every key. The namespace can be either a static value or a Proc. If it is a Proc, it will be invoked when each key is evaluated so that you can use application logic to invalidate keys.

```
cache.namespace = lambda { @last_mod_time }  # Set the namespace to a
variable
@last_mod_time = Time.now  # Invalidate the entire cache by changing
namespace
```

All caches support auto expiring content after a specified number of seconds. To set the cache entry time to live, you can either specify `:expires_in` as an option to the constructor to have it affect all entries or to the `fetch` or `write` methods for just one entry.

```
cache = ActiveSupport::Cache::MemoryStore.new(:expire_in => 5.minutes)
cache.write(key, value, :expire_in => 1.minute)  # Set a lower value for
one entry
```

Caches can also store values in a compressed format to save space and reduce time spent sending data. Since there is some overhead, values must be large enough to warrant compression. To turn on compression either pass `:compress => true` in the initializer or to `fetch` or `write`. To specify the threshold at which to compress values, set `:compress_threshold`. The default threshold is 32K.

cleanup(options = nil)
Cleanup the cache by removing expired entries. Not all cache implementations may support this method. Options are passed to the underlying cache implementation.

clear(options = nil)
Clear the entire cache. Not all cache implementations may support this method. You should be careful with this method since it could affect other processes if you are using a shared cache. Options are passed to the underlying cache implementation.

decrement(name, amount = 1, options = nil)
Decrement an integer value in the cache. Options are passed to the underlying cache implementation.

delete(name, options = nil)
Delete an entry in the cache. Returns `true` if there was an entry to delete. Options are passed to the underlying cache implementation.

delete_matched(matcher, options = nil)
Delete all entries whose keys match a pattern. Options are passed to the underlying cache implementation.

```
>> Rails.cache.write :color, :red
=> true
>> Rails.cache.read :color
=> :red
>> Rails.cache.delete_matched "c"
=> ["city", "color", "USA/FL/Jacksonville"]
>> Rails.cache.read :color
=> nil
```

exist?(name, options = nil)
Return `true` if the cache contains an entry with this name. Options are passed to the underlying cache implementation.

fetch(name, options = nil)
Fetches data from the cache, using the given key. If there is data in the cache with the given key, then that data is returned.

If there is no such data in the cache (a cache miss occurred), then `nil` will be returned. However, if a block has been passed, then that block will be run in the event of a cache miss. The return value of the block will be written to the cache under the given cache key, and that return value will be returned.

```
cache.write("today",  "Monday")
cache.fetch("today")  # => "Monday"

cache.fetch("city")   # => nil
cache.fetch("city") do
  "Duckburgh"
end
cache.fetch("city")   # => "Duckburgh"
```

You may also specify additional options via the options argument. Setting :force => true will force a cache miss:

```
cache.write("today",  "Monday")
cache.fetch("today", :force => true)  # => nil
```

Setting `:compress` will store a large cache entry set by the call in a compressed format.

Setting `:expires_in` will set an expiration time on the cache entry if it is set by call.

Setting `:race_condition_ttl` will invoke logic on entries set with an `:expires_in` option. If an entry is found in the cache that is expired and it has been expired for less than the number of seconds specified by this option and a block was passed to the method call, then the expiration future time of the entry in the cache will be updated to that many seconds in the and the block will be evaluated and written to the cache.

This is very useful in situations in which a cache entry is used very frequently under heavy load. The first process to find an expired cache entry will then become responsible for regenerating that entry while other processes continue to use the slightly out of date entry. This can prevent race conditions where too many processes are trying to regenerate the entry all at once. If the process regenerating the entry errors out, the entry will be regenerated after the specified number of seconds.

```
# Set all values to expire after one minute.
cache = ActiveSupport::Cache::MemoryCache.new(:expires_in => 1.minute)

cache.write("foo", "original value")
val_1 = nil
val_2 = nil
sleep 60
```

```
Thread.new do
  val_1 = cache.fetch("foo", :race_condition_ttl => 10) do
    sleep 1
    "new value 1"
  end
end

Thread.new do
  val_2 = cache.fetch("foo", :race_condition_ttl => 10) do
    "new value 2"
  end
end

# val_1 => "new value 1"
# val_2 => "original value"
# cache.fetch("foo") => "new value 1"
```

Other options will be handled by the specific cache store implementation. Internally, fetch calls read_entry, and calls write_entry on a cache miss. Options will be passed to the read and write calls.

For example, MemCacheStore's write method supports the :raw option, which tells the memcached server to store all values as strings. We can use this option with fetch too:

```
cache = ActiveSupport::Cache::MemCacheStore.new
cache.fetch("foo", :force => true, :raw => true) do
  :bar
end
cache.fetch("foo")  # => "bar"
```

increment(name, amount = 1, options = nil)
Increment an integer value in the cache. Options are passed to the underlying cache implementation.

options
Get the default options set when the cache was created.

read(name, options = nil)
Fetches data from the cache, using the given key. If there is data in the cache with the given key, then that data is returned. Otherwise, nil is returned. Options are passed to the underlying cache implementation.

read_multi(*names)

Read multiple values at once from the cache. Options can be passed in the last argument. Some cache implementation may optimize this method.

Returns a hash mapping the names provided to the values found.

```
>> cache.write :color, :red
=> true
>> cache.write :smell, :roses
=> true
>> cache.read_multi :color, :smell
=> {:color=>:red, :smell=>:roses}
```

write(name, value, options = nil)

Writes the given value to the cache, with the given key.

You may also specify additional options via the options argument. The specific cache store implementation will decide what to do with options.

B.9 ActiveSupport::Callbacks

Callbacks are hooks into the lifecycle of an object that allow you to trigger logic before or after an alteration of the object state. Mixing in this module allows you to define callbacks in your class.

For instance, assume you have the following code in your application:

```
class Storage
  include ActiveSupport::Callbacks

  define_callbacks :save
end

class ConfigStorage < Storage
  set_callback :save, :before, :saving_message
  def saving_message
    puts "saving..."
  end

  set_callback :save, :after do |object|
    puts "saved"
  end

  def save
    run_callbacks :save do
      puts "- running save callbacks"
    end
  end
end
```

Running the following code using

```
config = ConfigStorage.new
config.save
```

would output

```
saving...
- running save callbacks
saved
```

Note that callback defined on parent classes are inherited.

B.9.1 `active_support/callbacks`

The following methods are used to configure custom callbacks on your classes and are what Rails itself uses to create things such as `before_filter` in Action Pack and `before_save` in Active Record. Note that this is rather advanced functionality which you typically won't need in your day-to-day Rails programming.

`define_callbacks(*callbacks)`

Defines callbacks types for your custom class.

```
module MyOwnORM
  class Base
    define_callbacks :validate
  end
end
```

The following options determine the operation of the callback:

`:terminator` Indicates when a before filter is considered to be halted.

```
define_callbacks :validate, :terminator => "result == false"
```

In the example above, if any before validate callbacks return `false`, other callbacks are not executed. Defaults to `false`.

`:rescuable` By default, after filters are not executed if the given block or a `before_filter` raises an error. Supply `:rescuable => true` to change this behavior.

`:scope` Specifies which methods should be executed when a class is given as callback.

```
before_filter MyFilter
```

Assuming the callback has been defined with a `:kind` scope

```
define_callbacks :filters, :scope => [ :kind ]
```

then the method called will correspond to the type of the filter in the given class, which in this case, is before.

The :scope option can be supplied with multiple components, like this:

```
define_callbacks :validate, :scope => [ :kind, :name ]
```

A method named "#{kind}_#{name}" will be invoked in the given class. So before_validate will be called in the class below:

```
before_validate MyValidation
```

The :scope option defaults to :kind.

set_callback(name, *filter_list, &block)
Sets callbacks for a previously defined callback.

```
set_callback :save, :before,  :before_method
set_callback :save, :after,   :after_method, :if => :condition
set_callback :save, :around, lambda { |r| stuff; yield; stuff }
```

skip_callback(name, *filter_list, &block)
Skips a previously defined callback for a given type.

Callback conditions

When creating or skipping callbacks, you can specify conditions that are always the same for a given key. For instance, ActionPack converts :only and :except conditions into per-key conditions.

```
before_filter :authenticate, :except => "index"
```

becomes

```
dispatch_callback :before, :authenticate, :per_key => {:unless => proc
{|c| c.action_name == "index"}}
```

Per-Key conditions are evaluated only once per use of a given key. In the case of the above example, you would do:

```
run_callbacks(:dispatch, action_name) { ... dispatch stuff ... }
```

In that case, each action_name would get its own compiled callback method that took into consideration the per_key conditions. Introduction of this technique resulted in a large speed improvement for Action Pack.

B.10 Class

Rails extends Ruby's `Class` object with a number class methods that then become available on all other classes in the runtime, regardless of type.

B.10.1 `active_support/core_ext/class/attribute`

The following method allows for creation of attributes on Ruby classes.

`class_attribute(*attrs)`

Declares one or more class-level attributes whose value is inheritable and overwritable by subclasses and instances, like so:

```
class Base
  class_attribute :setting
end

class Subclass < Base
end

>> Base.setting = "foo"
=> "foo"

>> Subclass.setting
=> "foo"

>> Subclass.setting = "bar"
=> "bar"

>> Subclass.setting
=> "bar"

>> Base.setting
=> "foo"
```

This behavior matches normal Ruby method inheritance: Think of writing an attribute on a subclass as overriding the parent's reader method. Instances may overwrite the class value in the same way. (Note that the following code samples create anonymous classes to illustrate usage in a more concise fashion.)

```
klass = Class.new { class_attribute :setting }
object = klass.new

>> klass.setting = "foo
=> "foo"
```

```
>> object.setting = "bar"
=> "bar"

>> klass.setting
=> "foo"
```

To opt out of the instance writer method, pass :instance_writer => false.

```
klass = Class.new { class_attribute :setting, :instance_writer => false }
```

```
>> klass.new.setting
=> NoMethodError
```

The class_attribute method also works with singleton classes, as can be seen in the following example.

```
klass = Class.new { class_attribute :setting }
```

```
>> klass.singleton_class.setting = "foo"
=> "foo"
```

For convenience, a query method is defined as well, which allows you to see if an attribute has been set on a particular class instance.

```
klass = Class.new { class_attribute :setting }
```

```
>> klass.setting?
=> false
```

```
>> klass.setting = "foo"
=> "foo"
```

```
>> klass.setting?
=> true
```

B.10.2 active_support/core_ext/class/ attribute_accessors

This extends the class object with class and instance accessors for class attributes, just like the native attr* accessors for instance attributes.

cattr_accessor(*syms)

Creates both reader and writer methods for supplied method names syms.

```
class Person
  cattr_accessor :hair_colors
end
```

```
>> Person.hair_colors = [:brown, :black, :blonde, :red]

>> Person.new.hair_colors
=> [:brown, :black, :blonde, :red]
```

`cattr_reader(*syms)`

Creates class and instance reader methods for supplied method names `syms`.

`cattr_writer(*syms)`

Creates class and instance writer methods for supplied method names `syms`.

B.10.3 `active_support/core_ext/class/attribute_accessors`

This extends the class object with class and instance accessors for class attributes, just like the native `attr*` accessors for instance attributes.

B.10.4 `active_support/core_ext/class/delegating_attributes`

This is primarily for internal use by Rails.

`superclass_delegating_accessors(name, options = {})`

Generates class methods `name`, `name=`, and `name?`. These methods dispatch to the private `_name`, and `_name=` methods, making them overridable by subclasses.

If an instances should be able to access the attribute then pass `:instance_reader => true` in the options to generate a `name` method accessible to instances.

B.10.5 `active_support/core_ext/class/inheritable_attributes`

This allows attributes to be shared within an inheritance hierarchy, but where each descendant gets a copy of their parents' attributes, instead of just a pointer to the same. This means that the child can add elements to, for example, an array without those additions being shared with either their parent, siblings, or children, unlike the regular class-level attributes that are shared across the entire hierarchy.

The copies of inheritable parent attributes are added to subclasses when they are created, via the `inherited` hook. All reader methods accept `:instance_reader => true` option. All writer methods accept `:instance_writer => true` option. Accessor methods accept both options.

Like many other obscure corners of Active Support, these methods are primarily for internal use by Rails itself and some of them are no longer used internally by Rails 3. They are included here primarily for completeness and on the off chance that they could be useful in advanced application code or in libraries that depend on Active Support.

class_inheritable_accessor(*syms)

Creates class inheritable attribute accessor(s).

```
class FormBuilder
  class_inheritable_accessor :field_helpers
  ...
```

class_inheritable_array(*syms)

Creates class inheritable attribute(s) initialized to an empty array.

class_inheritable_hash(*syms)

Creates class inheritable attribute(s) initialized to an empty hash.

inheritable_attributes

Returns array of any class inheritable attributes that have been defined on a particular class instance.

```
>> ActiveRecord::Base.inheritable_attributes
=> {:nested_attributes_options=>{}, :default_scoping=>[],
:skip_time_zone_conversion_for_attributes=>[], :record_timestamps=>true,
:attribute_method_matchers=>...}
```

reset_inheritable_attributes

Clears class inheritable attributes that have been defined on a particular class instance.

B.10.6 active_support/core_ext/class/ subclasses

Provides methods that introspect the inheritance hierarchy of a class. Used extensively in Active Record.

subclasses

Returns an array with the names of the subclasses of `self` as strings.

```
Integer.subclasses # => ["Bignum", "Fixnum"]
```

descendents

Returns an array of all class objects found that are subclasses of `self`.

B.11 **ActiveSupport::Concern**

B.11.1 **active_support/concern**

The `Concern` module is only 29 lines of Ruby code, but it helps drive some of the most elegant code improvements in Rails 3. Using it, you can make your code more modular and have less dependency problems than ever before.

You use `Concern` to define common behavior that you want to mix into other application classes, or into Rails itself in the case of plugins.

A `Concern` module has three elements: the `included` block, `ClassMethods` module, and `InstanceMethods` module.

```
require 'active_support/concern'

module Foo
  extend ActiveSupport::Concern

  included do
    self.send(:do_something_in_mixin_class)
  end

  module ClassMethods
    def bar
      ...
    end
  end

  module InstanceMethods
    def baz
      ...
    end
  end
end
```

To use your custom `Concern` module, just mix it into a class.

```
class Widget
  include Foo
end
```

The `included` block will be triggered at inclusion time. Methods in `ClassMethods` will get added to `Widget` as class methods. Methods in `InstanceMethods` will get added to `Widget` as instance methods.

See `ActiveSupport::Configurable` for a good example of how `Concern` is used internally by Rails.

B.12 `ActiveSupport::Configurable`

This `Configurable` module is used internally by Rails to add configuration settings to `AbstractController::Base`. You can use it yourself to add configuration to your classes.

B.12.1 `active_support/configurable`

The implementation of `Configurable` is done as a `Concern` that is mixed into other classes.

config_accessor(*names)

Creates configuration properties accessible via class and instance contexts. The `names` parameter expects one or more symbols corresponding to property names.

```
module ActionController
  class Base < Metal
    config_accessor :assets_dir, :javascripts_dir, :stylesheets_dir
  end
end
```

B.13 Date

Active Support provides a wide array of extensions to Ruby's built-in date and time classes to simplify conversion and calculation tasks in simple-to-understand language.

B.13.1 `active_support/core_ext/date/acts_like`

Duck-types as a Date-like class. See `Object#acts_like?` for more explanation.

```
class Date
  def acts_like_date?
    true
  end
end
```

B.13.2 `active_support/core_ext/date/` `calculations`

The following methods enable the use of calculations with `Date` objects.

+(other) / -(other)

Rails extends the existing + and - operator so that a since calculation is performed when the other argument is an instance of ActiveSupport::Duration (the type of object returned by methods such as 10.minutes and 9.months).

```
>> Date.today + 1.day == Date.today.tomorrow
=> true
```

advance(options)

Provides precise Date calculations for years, months, and days. The options parameter takes a hash with any of these keys: :months, :days, :years.

```
>> Date.new(2006, 2, 28) == Date.new(2005, 2, 28).advance(:years => 1)
=> true
```

ago(seconds)

Converts Date to a Time (or DateTime if necessary) with the time portion set to the beginning of the day (0:00) and then subtracts the specified number of seconds.

```
>> Time.local(2005, 2, 20, 23, 59, 15) == Date.new(2005, 2, 21).ago(45)
=> true
```

at_beginning_of_day / at_midnight / beginning_of_day / midnight

Converts Date to a Time (or DateTime if necessary) with the time portion set to the beginning of the day (0:00).

```
>> Time.local(2005,2,21,0,0,0) == Date.new(2005,2,21).beginning_of_day
=> true
```

at_beginning_of_month / beginning_of_month

Returns a new DateTime representing the start of the month (1st of the month). Objects will have their time set to 0:00.

```
>> Date.new(2005, 2, 1) == Date.new(2005,2,21).beginning_of_month
=> true
```

at_beginning_of_quarter / beginning_of_quarter

Returns a new Date/DateTime representing the start of the calendar-based quarter (1st of January, April, July, and October). DateTime objects will have their time set to 0:00.

```
>> Date.new(2005, 4, 1) == Date.new(2005, 6, 30).beginning_of_quarter
=> true
```

at_beginning_of_week / beginning_of_week monday

Returns a new Date (or DateTime) representing the beginning of the week. (Calculation is Monday-based.)

```
>> Date.new(2005, 1, 31) == Date.new(2005, 2, 4).beginning_of_week
=> true
```

at_beginning_of_year / beginning_of_year

Returns a new Date/DateTime representing the start of the calendar year (1st of January). DateTime objects will have their time set to 0:00.

```
>> Date.new(2005, 1, 1) == Date.new(2005, 2, 22).beginning_of_year
=> true
```

at_end_of_month / end_of_month

Returns a new Date/DateTime representing the last day of the calendar month. DateTime objects will have their time set to 23:59:59.

```
>> Date.new(2005, 3, 31) == Date.new(2005,3,20).end_of_month
=> true
```

change(options)

Returns a new Date where one or more of the elements have been changed according to the options parameter.

The valid options are :year, :month, and :day.

```
>> Date.new(2007, 5, 12).change(:day => 1) == Date.new(2007, 5, 1)
=> true
```

```
>> Date.new(2007, 5, 12).change(:year => 2005, :month => 1) == Â
Date.new(2005, 1, 12)
=> true
```

Date.current

This is the preferred way to get the current date when your Rails application is timezone-aware. Returns Time.zone.today when config.time_zone is set, otherwise just returns Date.today.

end_of_day

Converts Date to a Time (or DateTime if necessary) with the time portion set to the end of the day (23:59:59).

```
>> Time.local(2005,2,21,23,59,59) == Date.new(2005, 2, 21).end_of_day
=> true
```

in(seconds) since(seconds)

Converts Date to a Time (or DateTime if necessary) with the time portion set to the beginning of the day (0:00) and then adds the specified number of seconds.

```
>> Time.local(2005, 2, 21, 0, 0, 45) == Date.new(2005, 2, 21).since(45)
=> true
```

last_month

Syntax sugar for months_ago(1).

last_year

Syntax sugar for years_ago(1).

months_ago(months)

Returns a new Date (or DateTime) representing the time a number of specified months ago.

```
>> Date.new(2005, 1, 1) == Date.new(2005, 3, 1).months_ago(2)
=> true
```

months_since(months)

Returns a new Date (or DateTime) representing the time a number of specified months into the past or the future. Supply a negative number of months to go back to the past.

```
>> Date.today.months_ago(1) == Date.today.months_since(-1)
=> true
```

next_month

Syntax sugar for months_since(1).

next_week(day = :monday)

Returns a new Date (or DateTime) representing the start of the given day in the following calendar week. Default day of the week may be overridden with a symbolized day name.

```
>> Date.new(2005, 3, 4) == Date.new(2005, 2, 22).next_week(:friday)
=> true
```

next_year

Syntax sugar for years_since(1).

Date.tomorrow

Convenience method that returns a new `Date` (or `DateTime`) representing the time one day in the future.

```
>> Date.new(2007, 3, 2) == Date.new(2007, 2, 28).tomorrow.tomorrow
=> true
```

years_ago(years)

Returns a new `Date` (or `DateTime`) representing the time a number of specified years ago.

```
>> Date.new(2000, 6, 5) == Date.new(2007, 6, 5).years_ago(7)
=> true
```

years_since(years)

Returns a new `Date` (or `DateTime`) representing the time a number of specified years into the future.

```
>> Date.new(2007, 6, 5) == Date.new(2006, 6, 5).years_since(1)
=> true
```

Date.yesterday

Convenience method that returns a new `Date` (or `DateTime`) representing the time one day ago.

```
>> Date.new(2007, 2, 21) == Date.new(2007, 2, 22).yesterday
=> true
```

B.13.3 active_support/core_ext/date/ conversions

The following methods facilitate the conversion of date data into various formats.

readable_inspect

Overrides the default inspect method with a human readable one.

```
>> Date.current
=> Wed, 02 Jun 2010
```

to_date

Used in order to keep `Time`, `Date`, and `DateTime` objects interchangeable in conversions.

to_datetime

Converts a `Date` object into a Ruby `DateTime` object. The time is set to beginning of day.

to_formatted_s(format = :default)

Converts a `Date` object into its string representation, according to the predefined formats in the `DATE_FORMATS` constant. (Aliased as `to_s`. Original `to_s` is aliased as `to_default_s`.)

The following hash of formats dictates the behavior of the `to_s` method.

```
DATE_FORMATS = {
  :short        => "%e %b",        # 2 Jun
  :long         => "%B %e, %Y",    # June  2, 2010
  :db           => "%Y-%m-%d",     # 2010-06-02
  :number       => "%Y%m%d",       # 20100602
  :long_ordinal => lambda { |date| # June 2nd, 2010
    date.strftime("%B #{ActiveSupport::Inflector.ordinalize(date.day)},
%Y") },
  :rfc822       => "%e %b %Y"      #  2 Jun 2010
}
```

to_time(timezone = :local)

Converts a `Date` object into a Ruby `Time` object; time is set to beginning of day. The time zone can be `:local` or `:utc`.

```
>> Time.local(2005, 2, 21) == Date.new(2005, 2, 21).to_time
=> true
```

If the `Date` object is a UTC time, Z is used as TZD. Otherwise `[+-]hh:mm` is used to indicate the hours offset.

xmlschema

Returns a string that represents the time as defined by XML Schema (also known as iso8601):

```
CCYY-MM-DDThh:mm:ssTZD
```

B.13.4 active_support/core_ext/date/freeze

`Date` memoizes some instance methods using metaprogramming to wrap the methods with one that caches the result in an instance variable.

If a `Date` instance is frozen but the memoized method hasn't been called, the first call will result in a frozen object error since the memo instance variable is uninitialized. The code in `freeze.rb` works around the issue by eagerly memoizing before freezing.

Ruby 1.9 uses a preinitialized instance variable so it's unaffected.

B.13.5 `active_support/json/encoding`

`as_json`

Returns `self` as a JSON string. The `ActiveSupport.use_standard_json_time_format` configuration setting determines whether the date string is delimited with dashes or not.

```
>> Date.today.as_json
=> "2010-06-03"
```

B.14 DateTime

The following methods extend Ruby's built-in `DateTime` class.

B.14.1 `active_support/core_ext/date_time/acts_like`

Duck-types as a DateTime-like class. See `Object#acts_like?` for more explanation.

```
class DateTime
  def acts_like_date?
    true
  end

  def acts_like_time?
    true
  endd
end
```

B.14.2 `active_support/core_ext/date_time/calculations`

The following methods permit easier use of `DateTime` objects in date and time calculations.

`<=>` `compare_with_coercion`

Layers additional behavior on `DateTime` so that `Time` and `ActiveSupport::TimeWithZone` instances can be compared with `DateTime` instances.

`at_beginning_of_day` `at_midnight` `beginning_of_day` `midnight`

Convenience methods that all represent the start of a day (00:00). Implemented simply as `change(:hour => 0)`.

advance(options)

Uses Date to provide precise Time calculations for years, months, and days. The options parameter takes a hash with any of the keys :months, :days, and :years.

ago(seconds)

Returns a new DateTime representing the time a number of seconds ago. The opposite of since.

change(options)

Returns a new DateTime where one or more of the elements have been changed according to the options parameter. The valid date options are :year, :month, :day. The valid time options are :hour, :min, :sec, :offset, and :start.

Date.current

Timezone-aware implementation of Time.now returns a DateTime instance.

end_of_day

Convenience method that represents the end of a day (23:59:59). Implemented simply as change(:hour => 23, :min => 59, :sec => 59).

future?

Tells whether the DateTime is in the future.

Date.local_offset

DateTime objects aren't aware of DST rules, so use a consistent non-DST offset when creating a DateTime with an offset in the local zone.

past?

Tells whether the DateTime is in the past.

seconds_since_midnight

Returns how many seconds have passed since midnight.

since(seconds)

Returns a new DateTime representing the time a number of seconds since the instance time. The opposite of ago.

utc

Returns a new DateTime with the offset set to 0 to represent UTC time.

utc?
Convenience method returns `true` if the `offset` is set to `0`.

utc_offset
Returns the offset value in seconds.

B.14.3   `active_support/core_ext/date_time/` `conversions`

The following methods permit conversion of `DateTime` objects (and some of their attributes) into other types of data.

Date.civil_from_format(utc_or_local, year, month=1, day=1, hour=0, min=0, sec=0)
Creates a datetime from the parameters provided. The `utc_or_local` parameter recognizes `:local` causing it to use the value of the `local_offset`.

formatted_offset(colon = true, alternate_utc_string = nil)
Returns the `utc_offset` as an `HH:MM` formatted string.

```
datetime = DateTime.civil(2000, 1, 1, 0, 0, 0, Rational(-6, 24))

>> datetime.formatted_offset
=> "-06:00"
```

The options provide for tweaking the output of the method by doing things like ommitting the colon character.

```
>> datetime.formatted_offset(false)
=> "-0600"
```

readable_inspect
Overrides the default inspect method with a human-readable one that looks like this:

```
Mon, 21 Feb 2005 14:30:00 +0000
```

to_date
Converts `self` to a Ruby `Date` object, discarding time data.

to_datetime
Returns `self` to be able to keep `Time`, `Date`, and `DateTime` classes interchangeable on conversions.

to_f

Converts self to a floating-point number of seconds since the Unix epoch. Note the limitations of this methods with dates prior to 1970.

```
>> Date.new(2000, 4,4).to_datetime.to_f
=> 954806400.0
>> Date.new(1800, 4,4).to_datetime.to_f
=> -5356627200.0
```

to_formatted_s(format=:default)

See the options on to_formatted_s of the Time class. The primary difference is the appending of the time information.

```
>> datetime.to_formatted_s(:db)
=> "2007-12-04 00:00:00"
```

to_i

Converts self to an integer number of seconds since the Unix epoch. Note the limitations of this methods with dates prior to 1970.

```
>> Date.new(2000, 4,4).to_datetime.to_i
=> 954806400
>> Date.new(1800, 4,4).to_datetime.to_i
=> -5356627200
```

to_time

Attempts to convert self to a Ruby Time object. Returns self if out of range of Ruby Time class. If self.offset is 0, will attempt to cast as a UTC time; otherwise, will attempt to cast in local timezone.

xmlschema

Converts datetime to an appropriate format for use in XML. The implementation is reproduced here for reference purposes:

```
strftime("%Y-%m-%dT%H:%M:%S%Z")
```

B.14.4 active_support/core_ext/date_time/zones

The following method allows conversion of a DateTime into a different time zone.

in_time_zone(zone = ::Time.zone)

Returns the simultaneous time in `Time.zone`

```
>> Time.zone = 'Hawaii'
>> DateTime.new(2000).in_time_zone
=> Fri, 31 Dec 1999 14:00:00 HST -10:00
```

This method is similar to `Time#localtime`, except that it uses the `Time.zone` argument as the local zone instead of the operating system's time zone. You can also pass it a string that identifies a TimeZone as an argument, and the conversion will be based on that zone instead. Allowable string parameters are operating-system dependent.

```
>> DateTime.new(2000).in_time_zone('Alaska')
=> Fri, 31 Dec 1999 15:00:00 AKST -09:00
```

B.14.5 **active_support/json/encoding**

as_json

Returns `self` as a JSON string. The `ActiveSupport.use_standard_json_time_format` configuration setting determines whether the output is formatted using `:xmlschema` or the following pattern:

```
strftime('%Y/%m/%d %H:%M:%S %z')
```

B.15 **ActiveSupport::Dependencies**

This module contains the logic for Rails' automatic classloading mechanism, which is what makes it possible to reference any constant in the Rails varied loadpaths without ever needing to issue a `require` directive.

This module extends itself, a cool hack that you can use with modules that you want to use elsewhere in your codebase in a functional manner:

```
module Dependencies
  extend self
  ...
```

As a result, you can call methods directly on the module constant, à la Java static class methods, like this:

```
>> ActiveSupport::Dependencies.search_for_file('person.rb')
=> "/Users/obie/work/tr3w_time_and_expenses/app/models/person.rb"
```

You shouldn't need to use this module in day-to-day Rails coding—it's mostly for internal use by Rails and plugins. On occasion, it might also be useful to understand the workings of this module when debugging tricky class-loading problems.

B.15.1 `active_support/dependencies/autoload`

Several of these attributes are set based on `Configuration` settings declared in your various environment files, as described in Chapter 1, Rails Environments and Configuration.

autoloaded_constants

An array of qualified constant names that have been loaded. Adding a name to this array will cause it to be unloaded the next time. `Dependencies` are cleared.

clear

Clears the list of currently loaded classes and removes unloadable constants.

constant_watch_stack

An internal stack used to record which constants are loaded by any block.

explicitly_unloadable_constants

An array of constant names that need to be unloaded on every request. Used to allow arbitrary constants to be marked for unloading.

history

The `Set` of all files ever loaded.

load_once_paths

The `Set` of directories from which automatically loaded constants are loaded only once. Usually consists of your plugin `lib` directories. All directories in this set must also be present in `load_paths`.

load_paths

The `Set` of directories from which Rails may automatically load files. Files under these directories will be reloaded on each request in development mode, unless the directory also appears in `load_once_paths`.

```
>> ActiveSupport::Dependencies.load_paths
=> ["/Users/obie/work/tr3w_time_and_expenses/app/controllers",
"/Users/obie/work/tr3w_time_and_expenses/app/helpers",
"/Users/obie/work/tr3w_time_and_expenses/app/models"...
```

loaded

The `Set` of all files currently loaded.

log_activity

Set this option to `true` to enable logging of `const_missing` and file loads. (Defaults to `false`.)

mechanism

A setting that determines whether files are loaded (default) or required. This attribute determines whether Rails reloads classes per request, as in development mode.

```
>> ActiveSupport::Dependencies.mechanism
=> :load
```

warnings_on_first_load

A setting that determines whether Ruby warnings should be activated on the first load of dependent files. Defaults to `true`.

associate_with(file_name)

Invokes `depend_on` with `swallow_load_errors` set to `true`. Wrapped by the `require_association` method of `Object`.

autoload_module!(into, const_name, qualified_name, path_suffix)

Attempts to autoload the provided module name by searching for a directory matching the expected `path suffix`. If found, the module is created and assigned to `into`'s constants with the name `+const_name+`. Provided that the directory was loaded from a reloadable base path, it is added to the set of constants that are to be unloaded.

autoloadable_module?(path_suffix)

Checks whether the provided `path_suffix` corresponds to an autoloadable module. Instead of returning a Boolean, the autoload base for this module is returned.

autoloaded?(constant)

Determines if the specified `constant` has been automatically loaded.

depend_on(file_name, swallow_load_errors = false)

Searches for the `file_name` specified and uses `require_or_load` to establish a new dependency. The `swallow_load_errors` argument specifies whether `LoadError` should be suppressed. Wrapped by the `require_dependency` method of `Object`.

load?

Returns `true` if `mechanism` is set to `:load`.

load_file(path, const_paths = loadable_constants_for_path(path))

Loads the file at the specified `path`. The `const_paths` is a set of fully qualified constant names to load. When the file is loading, `Dependencies` will watch for the addition of these constants. Each one that is defined will be marked as autoloaded, and will be removed when `Dependencies.clear` is next called.

If the second parameter is left off, `Dependencies` will construct a set of names that the file at `path` may define. See `loadable_constants_for_path` for more details.

load_once_path?(path)

Returns `true` if the specified `path` appears in the `load_once_path` list.

load_missing_constant(mod, const_name)

Loads the constant named `const_name`, which is missing from `mod`. If it is not possible to load the constant from `mod`, try its parent module by calling `const_missing` on it.

loadable_constants_for_path(path, bases = load_paths)

Returns an array of constants, based on a specified filesystem `path` to a Ruby file, which would cause `Dependencies` to attempt to load the file.

mark_for_unload(constant)

Marks the specified `constant` for unloading. The constant will be unloaded on each request, not just the next one.

new_constants_in(*descs, &block)

Runs the provided block and detects the new constants that were loaded during its execution. Constants may only be regarded as new once. If the block calls `new_constants_in` again, the constants defined within the inner call will not be reported in this one.

If the provided block does not run to completion, and instead raises an exception, any new constants are regarded as being only partially defined and will be removed immediately.

qualified_const_defined?(path)

Returns `true` if the provided constant path is `defined?`

qualified_name_for(parent_module, constant_name)

Returns a qualified path for the specified `parent_module` and `constant_name`.

remove_unloadable_constants!

Removes the constants that have been autoloaded, and those that have been marked for unloading.

require_or_load(file_name, const_path = nil)

Implements the main classloading mechanism. Wrapped by the `require_or_load` method of `Object`.

search_for_file(path_suffix)

Searches for a file in `load_paths` matching the provided `path_suffix`.

will_unload?(constant)

Returns `true` if the specified constant is queued for unloading on the next request.

B.16 ActiveSupport::Deprecation

The deprecate method provides Rails core and application developers with a formal mechanism to be able to explicitly state what methods are deprecated. (Deprecation means to mark for future deletion.) Rails will helpfully log a warning message when deprecated methods are called.

Deprecation.deprecate_methods(target_module, *method_names)

Pass the module and name(s) of the methods as symbols to deprecate.

Deprecation.silence(&block)

Silence deprecation warnings within the block.

B.17 ActiveSupport::Duration

Provides accurate date and time measurements using the `advance` method of `Date` and `Time`. It mainly supports the methods on `Numeric`, such as in this example:

```
1.month.ago # equivalent to Time.now.advance(:months => -1)
```

B.17.1 active_support/duration

+ (other)

Adds another `Duration` or a `Numeric` to this `Duration`. `Numeric` values are treated as seconds.

```
>> 2.hours + 2
=> 7202 seconds
```

- (other)

Subtracts another Duration or a Numeric to this Duration. Numeric values are treated as seconds.

```
>> 2.hours - 2
=> 7198 seconds
```

ago(time = Time.now)

Calculates a new Time or Date that is as far in the past as this Duration represents.

```
>> birth = 35.years.ago
=> Mon, 21 Apr 1975 00:48:43 UTC +00:00
```

from_now(time = Time.now)

Alias for since, which reads a little bit more naturally when using the default Time.now as the time argument.

```
>> expiration = 1.year.from_now
=> Thu, 21 Apr 2011 00:51:48 UTC +00:00
```

inspect

Calculates the time resulting from a Duration expression and formats it as a string appropriate for display in the console. (Remember that IRB and the Rails console automatically invoke inspect on objects returned to them. You can use that trick with your own objects.)

```
>> 10.years.ago
=> Sun Aug 31 17:34:15 -0400 1997
```

since(time = Time.now)

Calculates a new Time or Date that is as far in the future as this Duration represents.

```
>> expiration = 1.year.since(account.created_at)
```

until(time = Time.now)

Alias for ago. Reads a little more naturally when specifying a time argument instead of using the default value, Time.now.

```
>> membership_duration = created_at.until(expires_at)
```

B.18 **Enumerable**

Extensions to Ruby's built-in `Enumerable` module, which gives arrays and other types of collections iteration abilities.

B.18.1 **active_support/core_ext/enumerable**

The following methods are added to all `Enumerable` objects.

each_with_object(memo, &block)

Iterates over a collection, passing the current element and the `memo` to the block. Handy for building up hashes or reducing collections down to one object. Examples:

```
>>   %w(foo bar).each_with_object({}) { |str, hsh| hsh[str] = str.upcase }
=> {'foo' => 'FOO', 'bar' => 'BAR'}
```

Note: that you can't use immutable objects (like `numbers`, `true`, `false`, etc) as the `memo` argument. You would think the following returns 120, but since the memo is never changed, it does not.

    (1..5).each_with_object(1) }value, memo} memo *= value # => 1

group_by(&block)

Collects an enumerable into sets, grouped by the result of a block and ordered. Useful, for example, for grouping records by date like in the following example:

```
latest_transcripts.group_by(&:day).each do |day, transcripts|
puts "[#{day}] #{transcripts.map(&:class).join , }"
end
"[2006-03-01] Transcript"
"[2006-02-28] Transcript"
"[2006-02-27] Transcript, Transcript"
```

Rubys own `group_by` method is used in versions 1.9 and above.

index_by

Converts an enumerable to a hash, based on a block that identifies the keys. The most common usage is with a single attribute name:

```
>> people.index_by(&:login)
=> { "nextangle" => <Person ...>, "chad" => <Person ...>}
```

Use full block syntax (instead of the `to_proc` hack) to generate more complex keys:

```
>> people.index_by { |p| "#{p.first_name} #{p.last_name}" }
=> {"Chad Fowler" => <Person ...>, "David Hansson" => <Person ...>}
```

sum(default = 0, &block)

Calculates a sum from the elements of an enumerable, based on a block.

```
payments.sum(&:price)
```

Its easier to understand than Rubys clumsier inject method:

```
payments.inject { |sum, p| sum + p.price }
```

Use full block syntax (instead of the to_proc hack) to do more complicated calculations:

```
payments.sum { |p| p.price * p.tax_rate }
```

Also, sum can calculate results without the use of a block:

```
[5, 15, 10].sum # => 30
```

The default identity (a fancy way of saying, "the sum of an empty list") is 0. However, you can override it with anything you want by passing a default argument:

```
[].sum(10) { |i| i.amount } # => 10
```

index_by

Converts an enumerable to a hash, based on a block that identifies the keys. The most common usage is with a single attribute name:

```
>> people.index_by(&:login)
=> { "nextangle" => <Person ...>, "chad" => <Person ...>}
```

Use full block syntax (instead of the to_proc hack) to generate more complex keys:

```
>> people.index_by { |p| "#{p.first_name} #{p.last_name}" }
=> {"Chad Fowler" => <Person ...>, "David Hansson" => <Person ...>}
```

B.18.2 active_support/json/encoding

as_json

Returns self.to_a.

B.19 ERB::Util

B.19.1 active_support/core_ext/string/output_safety

html_escape(s)

A utility method for escaping HTML tag characters. This method is also aliased as h.

In your templates, use this method to escape any unsafe (often, anything user-submitted) content, like this:

```
=h @person.name
```

The method primarily escapes angle brackets and ampersands.

```
>> puts html_escape("is a > 0 & a < 10?")
=> is a &gt; 0 &amp; a &lt; 10?
```

json_escape(s)

A utility method for escaping HTML entities in JSON strings. This method is also aliased as j.

In your ERb templates, use this method to escape any HTML entities:

```
=j @person.to_json
```

The method primarily escapes angle brackets and ampersands.

```
puts json_escape("is a > 0 & a < 10?")
=> is a \u003E 0 \u0026 a \u003C 10?
```

B.20 FalseClass

B.20.1 active_support/core_ext/object/blank

blank?

Returns true.

B.20.2 active_support/json/encoding

as_json

Returns "false".

B.21 File

B.21.1 active_support/core_ext/file/atomic

Provides an atomic_write method to Ruby's File class.

atomic_write(file_name, temp_dir = Dir.tmpdir)

Writes to a file atomically, by writing to a temp file first and then renaming to the target file_name. Useful for situations where you need to absolutely prevent other processes or threads from seeing half-written files.

```
File.atomic_write("important.file") do |file|
  file.write("hello")
end
```

If your `temp` directory is not on the same filesystem as the file you're trying to write, you can provide a different temporary directory with the `temp_dir` argument.

```
File.atomic_write("/data/something.imporant", "/data/tmp") do |f|
  file.write("hello")
end
```

B.21.2 `active_support/core_ext/file/path`

Ensures that `to_path` is aliased to `path`.

B.22 Float
B.22.1 `active_support/core_ext/float/rounding`

Provides an `round` method to Ruby's `Float` class that accepts an optional `precision` parameter.

round(precision = nil)

Rounds the float with the specified precision.

```
>> x = 1.337
>> x.round
=> 1

>> x.round(1)
=> 1.3

>> x.round(2)
=> 1.34
```

B.23 Hash
B.23.1 `active_support/core_ext/hash/` `conversions`

Contains code that adds the ability to convert hashes to and from xml.

Hash.from_xml(xml)

Parses arbitrary strings of XML markup into nested Ruby arrays and hashes. Works great for quick-and-dirty integration of REST-style web services.

Here's a quick example in the console with some random XML content. The XML only has to be well-formed markup.

```
>> xml = %(<people>
  <person id="1">
    <name><family>Boss</family> <given>Big</given></name>
    <email>chief@foo.com</email>
  </person>
  <person id="2">
    <name>
     <family>Worker</family>
     <given>Two</given></name>
    <email>two@foo.com</email>
  </person>
</people>)
=> "<people>...</people>"

>> h = Hash.from_xml(xml)
=> {"people"=>{"person"=>[{"name"=>{"given"=>"Big", "family"=>"Boss"},
"id"=>"1", "email"=>"chief@foo.com"}, {"name"=>{"given"=>"Two",
"family"=>"Worker"}, "id"=>"2", "email"=>"two@foo.com"}]}}
```

Now you can easily access the data from the XML:

```
>> h["people"]["person"].first["name"]["given"] => "Big"
```

to_xml(options={})
Collects the keys and values of a hash and composes a simple XML representation.

```
>> print ({:greetings => {
            :english => "hello",
            :spanish => "hola"}}).to_xml

<?xml version="1.0" encoding="UTF-8"?>
<hash>
  <greetings>
    <english>hello</english>
    <spanish>hola</spanish>
  </greetings>
</hash>
```

B.23.2 `active_support/core_ext/hash/deep_merge`

deep_merge(other_hash)
Returns a new hash with `self` and `other_hash` merged recursively.

`deep_merge!(other_hash)`

Modifies `self` by merging in `other_hash` recursively.

B.23.3 `active_support/core_ext/hash/diff`

`diff(hash2)`

A method for getting the difference between one hash and another. Returns the difference between a hash and the one passed in as a parameter.

A quick example in the console:

```
>> {:a => :b}.diff({:a => :b})
=> {}
>> {:a => :b}.diff({:a => :c})
=> {:a=>:b}
```

B.23.4 `active_support/core_ext/hash/except`

`except(*keys)`

Returns a hash that includes everything but the given `keys`. This is useful for limiting a set of parameters to everything but a few known toggles.

```
person.update_attributes(params[:person].except(:admin))
```

If the receiver responds to `convert_key`, the method is called on each of the arguments. This allows `except` to play nice with hashes with indifferent access.

```
>> {:a => 1}.with_indifferent_access.except(:a)
=> {}

>> {:a => 1}.with_indifferent_access.except("a")
=> {}
```

`except!(*keys)`

Replaces the hash without the given keys.

B.23.5 `active_support/core_ext/hash/ indifferent_access`

`with_indifferent_access`

Returns an `ActiveSupport::HashWithIndifferentAccess` out of its receiver.

```
>> {:a => 1}.with_indifferent_access["a"]
=> 1
```

B.23.6 `active_support/core_ext/hash/keys`

Provides methods that operate on the keys of a hash. The `stringify` and `symbolize` methods are used liberally throughout the Rails codebase, which is why it generally doesn't matter if you pass option names as strings or symbols.

You can use `assert_valid_keys` method in your own application code, which takes Rails-style option hashes.

`assert_valid_keys(*valid_keys)`

Raises an `ArgumentError` if the hash contains any keys not specified in `valid_keys`.

```
def my_method(some_value, options={})
  options.assert_valid_keys(:my_conditions, :my_order, ...)
  ...
end
```

Note that keys are NOT treated indifferently, meaning if you use strings for keys but assert symbols as keys, this will fail.

```
>> { :name => "Rob", :years => "28" }.assert_valid_keys(:name, :age)
=> ArgumentError: Unknown key(s): years

>> { :name => "Rob", :age => "28" }.assert_valid_keys("name", "age")
=> ArgumentError: Unknown key(s): name, age

>> { :name => "Rob", :age => "28" }.assert_valid_keys(:name, :age)
=> nil #  passes, raises nothing
```

`stringify_keys`

Returns a new copy of the hash with all keys converted to strings.

`stringify_keys!`

Destructively converts all keys in the hash to strings.

`symbolize_keys and to_options`

Returns a new hash with all keys converted to symbols, as long as they respond to `to_sym`.

`symbolize_keys! and to_options!`

Destructively converts all keys in the hash to symbols.

B.23.7 `active_support/core_ext/hash/` `reverse_merge`

Allows for reverse merging where the keys in the calling hash take precedence over those in the `other_hash`. This is particularly useful for initializing an incoming option hash with default values like this:

```
def setup(options = {})
  options.reverse_merge! :size => 25, :velocity => 10
end
```

In the example, the default `:size` and `:velocity` are only set if the options passed in don't already have those keys set.

`reverse_merge(other_hash)`

Returns a merged version of two hashes, using key values in the `other_hash` as defaults, leaving the original hash unmodified.

`reverse_merge!(other_hash)` and `reverse_update`

Destructive versions of `reverse_merge`; both modify the original hash in place.

B.23.8 `active_support/core_ext/hash/slice`

`slice(*keys)`

Slices a hash to include only the given keys. This is useful for limiting an options hash to valid keys before passing to a method:

```
def search(criteria = {})
  assert_valid_keys(:mass, :velocity, :time)
end

search(options.slice(:mass, :velocity, :time))
```

If you have an array of keys you want to limit to, you should splat them:

```
valid_keys = [:mass, :velocity, :time]
search(options.slice(*valid_keys))
```

`slice!(*keys)`

Replaces the hash with only the given keys.

```
>> {:a => 1, :b => 2, :c => 3, :d => 4}.slice!(:a, :b)
=> {:c => 3, :d =>4}
```

B.23.9 `active_support/core_ext/object/` `to_param`

`to_param(namespace = nil)`

Converts a hash into a string suitable for use as a URL query string. An optional namespace can be passed to enclose the param names (see example below).

```
>> { :name => 'David', :nationality => 'Danish' }.to_param
=> "name=David&nationality=Danish"

>> { :name => 'David', :nationality => 'Danish' }.to_param('user')
=> "user[name]=David&user[nationality]=Danish"
```

B.23.10 `active_support/core_ext/object/` `to_query`

`to_query`

Collects the keys and values of a hash and composes a URL-style query string using ampersand and equal-sign characters.

```
>> {:foo => "hello", :bar => "goodbye"}.to_query
=> "bar=goodbye&foo=hello"
```

B.23.11 `active_support/json/encoding`
`as_json`

Returns `self` as a string of JSON.

B.23.12 `active_support/core_ext/object/blank`
`blank?`

Alias for `empty?`.

B.24 `HashWithIndifferentAccess`

A subclass of `Hash` used internally by Rails.

B.24.1 `active_support/hash_with_` `indifferent_access`

As stated in the source file:

> This class has dubious semantics and we only have it so that people can write `params[:key]` instead of `params['key']`.

B.25 ActiveSupport::Inflector:: Inflections

The Inflections class transforms words from singular to plural, class names to table names, modularized class names to ones without, and class names to foreign keys.

The default inflections for pluralization, singularization, and uncountable words are kept in activesupport/lib/active_support/inflections.rb and reproduced here for reference.

```
module ActiveSupport
  Inflector.inflections do |inflect|
    inflect.plural(/$/, 's')
    inflect.plural(/s$/i, 's')
    inflect.plural(/(ax|test)is$/i, '\1es')
    inflect.plural(/(octop|vir)us$/i, '\1i')
    inflect.plural(/(alias|status)$/i, '\1es')
    inflect.plural(/(bu)s$/i, '\1ses')
    inflect.plural(/(buffal|tomat)o$/i, '\1oes')
    inflect.plural(/([ti])um$/i, '\1a')
    inflect.plural(/sis$/i, 'ses')
    inflect.plural(/(?:([^f])fe|([lr])f)$/i, '\1\2ves')
    inflect.plural(/(hive)$/i, '\1s')
    inflect.plural(/([^aeiouy]|qu)y$/i, '\1ies')
    inflect.plural(/(x|ch|ss|sh)$/i, '\1es')
    inflect.plural(/(matr|vert|ind)(?:ix|ex)$/i, '\1ices')
    inflect.plural(/([m|l])ouse$/i, '\1ice')
    inflect.plural(/^(ox)$/i, '\1en')
    inflect.plural(/(quiz)$/i, '\1zes')

    inflect.singular(/s$/i, '')
    inflect.singular(/(n)ews$/i, '\1ews')
    inflect.singular(/([ti])a$/i, '\1um')
    inflect.singular(/((a)naly|(b)a|(d)iagno|(p)arenthe|(p)rogno|
(s)ynop|(t)he)ses$/i, '\1\2sis')
    inflect.singular(/(^analy)ses$/i, '\1sis')
    inflect.singular(/([^f])ves$/i, '\1fe')
    inflect.singular(/(hive)s$/i, '\1')
    inflect.singular(/(tive)s$/i, '\1')
    inflect.singular(/([lr])ves$/i, '\1f')
    inflect.singular(/([^aeiouy]|qu)ies$/i, '\1y')
    inflect.singular(/(s)eries$/i, '\1eries')
    inflect.singular(/(m)ovies$/i, '\1ovie')
    inflect.singular(/(x|ch|ss|sh)es$/i, '\1')
    inflect.singular(/([m|l])ice$/i, '\1ouse')
    inflect.singular(/(bus)es$/i, '\1')
    inflect.singular(/(o)es$/i, '\1')
    inflect.singular(/(shoe)s$/i, '\1')
    inflect.singular(/(cris|ax|test)es$/i, '\1is')
```

```
    inflect.singular(/(octop|vir)i$/i, '\1us')
    inflect.singular(/(alias|status)es$/i, '\1')
    inflect.singular(/^(ox)en/i, '\1')
    inflect.singular(/(vert|ind)ices$/i, '\1ex')
    inflect.singular(/(matr)ices$/i, '\1ix')
    inflect.singular(/(quiz)zes$/i, '\1')
    inflect.singular(/(database)s$/i, '\1')

    inflect.irregular('person', 'people')
    inflect.irregular('man', 'men')
    inflect.irregular('child', 'children')
    inflect.irregular('sex', 'sexes')
    inflect.irregular('move', 'moves')
    inflect.irregular('cow', 'kine')

    inflect.uncountable(%w(equipment information rice money species series
  fish sheep jeans))
  end
end
```

A singleton instance of `Inflections` is yielded by `Inflector.inflections`, which can then be used to specify additional inflection rules in an initializer.

```
ActiveSupport::Inflector.inflections do |inflect|
  inflect.plural /^(ox)$/i, '\1en'
  inflect.singular /^(ox)en/i, '\1'
  inflect.irregular 'octopus', 'octopi'
  inflect.uncountable "equipment"
end
```

New rules are added at the top. So in the example, the irregular rule for octopus will now be the first of the pluralization and singularization rules that are checked when an inflection happens. That way Rails can guarantee that your rules run before any of the rules that may already have been loaded.

B.25.1 `active_support/inflector/inflections`

This API reference lists the inflections methods themselves in the modules where they are actually used: `Numeric` and `String`. The `Inflections` module contains methods used for modifying the rules used by the inflector.

`clear(scope = :all))`

Clears the loaded inflections within a given `scope`. Give the `scope` as a symbol of the inflection type: `:plurals`, `:singulars`, `:uncountables`, or `:humans`.

```
ActiveSupport::Inflector.inflections.clear
ActiveSupport::Inflector.inflections.clear(:plurals)
```

human(rule, replacement)

Specifies a humanized form of a string by a regular expression rule or by a string mapping. When using a regular expression based replacement, the normal humanize formatting is called after the replacement. When a string is used, the human form should be specified as desired (example: "The name", not "the_name")

```
ActiveSupport::Inflector.inflections do |inflect|
  inflect.human /_cnt$/i, '\1_count'
  inflect.human "legacy_col_person_name", "Name"
end
```

inflections

Yields a singleton instance of `ActiveSupport::Inflector::Inflections` so you can specify additional inflector rules.

```
ActiveSupport::Inflector.inflections do |inflect|
  inflect.uncountable "rails"
end
```

irregular(singular, plural)

Specifies a new irregular that applies to both pluralization and singularization at the same time. The `singular` and `plural` arguments must be strings, not regular expressions. Simply pass the irregular word in singular and plural form.

```
ActiveSupport::Inflector.inflections do |inflect|
  inflect.irregular 'octopus', 'octopi'
  inflect.irregular 'person', 'people'
end
```

plural(rule, replacement)

Specifies a new pluralization rule and its replacement. The `rule` can either be a string or a regular expression. The `replacement` should always be a string and may include references to the matched data from the rule by using backslash-number syntax, like this:

```
ActiveSupport::Inflector.inflections do |inflect|
  inflect.plural /^(ox)$/i, '\1en'
end
```

singular(rule, replacement)

Specifies a new singularization rule and its replacement. The `rule` can either be a string or a regular expression. The `replacement` should always be a string and may include references to the matched data from the rule by using backslash-number syntax, like this:

```
ActiveSupport::Inflector.inflections do |inflect|
  inflect..singular /^(ox)en/i, '\1'
end
```

uncountable(*words)

Adds uncountable words that should not be inflected to the list of inflection rules.

```
ActiveSupport::Inflector.inflections do |inflect|
  inflect.uncountable "money"
  inflect.uncountable "money", "information"
```

B.25.2 `active_support/inflector/ transliteration`

transliterate(string, replacement = "?")

Replaces non-ASCII characters with an ASCII approximation, or if none exists, a replacement character which defaults to "?".

```
transliterate("øørskbing")
 # => "AEroskobing"
```

Default approximations are provided for Western/Latin characters, e.g, "ø", "ñ", "é", "ß", etc.

This method is I18n aware, so you can set up custom approximations for a locale. This can be useful, for example, to transliterate German's "ü" and "ö" to "ue" and "oe", or to add support for transliterating Russian to ASCII.

In order to make your custom transliterations available, you must set them as the <tt>i18n.transliterate.rule</tt> i18n key:

```
# Store the transliterations in locales/de.yml
i18n:
  transliterate:
    rule: ü
        : "ue" ö
        : "oe"

# Or set them using Ruby
I18n.backend.store_translations(:de, :i18n => {
  :transliterate => {
    :rule => {"ü"
        => "ue", "ö"
        => "oe"
    }
  }
})
```

The value for <tt>i18n.transliterate.rule</tt> can be a simple Hash that maps characters to ASCII approximations as shown above, or, for more complex requirements, a Proc:

```
I18n.backend.store_translations(:de, :i18n => {
  :transliterate => {
    :rule => lambda {|string| MyTransliterator.transliterate(string)}
  }
})
```

Now you can have different transliterations for each locale:

```
I18n.locale = :en
transliterate("Jürgen")
# => "Jurgen"

I18n.locale = :de
transliterate("Jürgen")
# => "Juergen"
```

parameterize(string, sep = '-')

Replaces special characters in a string so that it may be used as part of a "pretty" URL. This method replaces accented characters with their ASCII equivalents and discards all other non-ASCII characters by turning them into the string specified as sep. The method is smart enough to not double up separators. Leading and trailing separators are also removed.

```
class Person < ActiveRecord::Base
  def to_param
    "#{id}-#{name.parameterize}"
  end
end

>> @person = Person.find(1)
=> #<Person id: 1, name: "Donald E. Knuth">

>> helper.link_to(@person.name, person_path(@person))
=> <a href="/person/1-donald-e-knuth">Donald E. Knuth</a>
```

B.26 Integer

Extensions to Ruby's built-in Integer class.

B.26.1 `active_support/core_ext/integer/` `inflections`

ordinalize

Turns an integer into an ordinal string used to denote the position in an ordered sequence such as 1st, 2nd, 3rd, 4th.

```
1.ordinalize    # => "1st"
2.ordinalize    # => "2nd"
1002.ordinalize # => "1002nd"
1003.ordinalize # => "1003rd"
```

B.26.2 `active_support/core_ext/integer/` `multiple`

multiple_of?(number)

Returns `true` if the integer is a multiple of `number`.

```
9.multiple_of? 3 # => true
```

B.27 ActiveSupport::JSON

Rails includes support for three JSON (JavaScript Object Notation) backends:

- JSONGem (json)
- Yajl (yajl-ruby)
- Yaml

The `JSON` module adds JSON decoding and encoding support to Rails.

B.27.1 `active_support/json/decoding`

backend

Returns the selected JSON backend.

backend=(name)

Sets desired JSON backend.

decode(json)

Parses a JSON string or `IO` object and converts it into an object graph.

`with_backend(name, &block)`

Use an alternate JSON backend within the supplied `block`.

B.27.2 `active_support/json/encoding`

`encode(value, options = nil)`

Dumps object in JSON.

```
>> ActiveSupport::JSON.encode({:a => 1, :b => 2})
=> "{\"a\":1,\"b\":2}"
```

B.28 Kernel

Methods added to Ruby's `Kernel` class are available in all contexts.

B.28.1 `active_support/core_ext/kernel/ agnostics`

`` `(command) ``

Makes backticks behave (somewhat more) similarly on all platforms. On win32 `` `nonexistent_command` `` raises `Errno::ENOENT`, but on Unix, the spawned shell prints a message to stderr and sets `$?`.

B.28.2 `active_support/core_ext/kernel/ debugger`

`debugger`

Starts a debugging session if `ruby-debug` has been loaded. Use `rails server -- debugger` to start Rails with the debugger enabled.

B.28.3 `active_support/core_ext/kernel/ reporting`

`enable_warnings`

Sets `$VERBOSE` to true for the duration of the block provided and back to its original value afterward.

`silence_stream(stream)`

Silences any stream for the duration of the block provided.

```
silence_stream(STDOUT) do
puts 'This will never be seen'
end
puts 'But this will'
```

silence_warnings

Sets $VERBOSE to false for the duration of the block provided and back to its original value afterward.

suppress(*exception_classes)

Amethod that should be named swallow. Suppresses raising of any exception classes specified inside of the block provided. Use with caution.

B.28.4 active_support/core_ext/kernel/ requires

require_library_or_gem

Requires a library with fallback to RubyGems. Warnings during library loading are silenced to increase signal/noise for application warnings.

B.28.5 active_support/core_ext/kernel/ singleton_class

class_eval

Forces class_eval to behave like singleton_class.class_eval.

singleton_class

Returns the object's singleton class.

B.29 Logger

This section includes extensions to the built-in Ruby logger, accessible via the logger property in various Rails contexts such as Active Record models and controller classes. Always accessible via Rails.logger. Use of the logger is explained in Chapter 1.

To use the default log formatter as defined in the Ruby core, you need to set a formatter for the logger as in the following example:

```
logger.formatter = Formatter.new
```

You can then specify properties such as the datetime format, for example:

```
logger.datetime_format = "%Y-%m-%d"
```

B.29.1 `active_support/core_ext/logger`

`around_debug(start_message, end_message)` ...

Streamlines the all-too-common pattern of wrapping a few lines of code in comments that indicate the beginning and end of a routine, as follows:

```
logger.debug "Start rendering component (#{options.inspect}): "
result = render_component_stuff(...)
logger.debug "\n\nEnd of component rendering"
result
```

The same code would be written with `around_debug` like this:

```
around_debug "Start rendering component (#{options.inspect}):",
             "End of component rendering" do
  render_component_stuff(...)
end
```

`around_error, around_fatal, and around_info`

See as `around_debug` except with a different log-level.

`datetime_format`

Gets the current logging datetime format. Returns `nil` if the formatter does not support datetime formatting.

`datetime_format=(datetime_format)`

Sets the format string passed to `strftime` to generate the log's timestamp string.

`formatter`

Gets the current formatter. The Rails default formatter is a `SimpleFormatter`, which only displays the log message.

`silence(temporary_level = Logger::ERROR)`

Silences the logger for the duration of a block provided.

```
Rails.logger.silence do
  # some particularly verbose (or secret) operation
end
```

B.30 `ActiveSupport::MessageEncryptor`

`MessageEncryptor` is a simple way to encrypt values that get stored somewhere you don't trust.

The cipher text and initialization vector are base64 encoded and returned to you.

This can be used in situations similar to the `MessageVerifier`, but where you don't want users to be able to determine the value of the payload.

B.30.1 `active_support/message_encryptor`
`initialize(secret, cipher = 'aes-256-cbc')`
Creates a new instance of `MessageEncryptor`.

`encrypt(value)`
Encrypts `value`.

`decrypt(encrypted_messages)`
Decrypts `encrypted_message`.

B.31 ActiveSupport::MessageVerifier

`MessageVerifier` makes it easy to generate and verify signed messages to prevent tampering.

```
>> v = ActiveSupport::MessageVerifier.new("A_SECRET_STRING")
=> #<ActiveSupport::MessageVerifier:0x24af9f0 @secret="A_SECRET_STRING",
@digest="SHA1">

>> msg = v.generate([1, 2.weeks.from_now])
=> "BAhbB2kGVTogQWN0aXZlU3VwcG9ydDo6VGltZVdpdGhab25lWwh1Og..."

>> id, time = v.verify(msg)
=> [1, Thu, 17 Jun 2010 20:54:13 UTC +00:00]
```

This is useful for cases like remember-me tokens and auto-unsubscribe links where the session store isn't suitable or available.

B.31.1 `active_support/message_verifier`
`initialize(secret, digest = 'SHA1')`
Creates a new `MessageVerifier` with the supplied `secret` string and `digest`.

`generate(value)`
Generate a signed message.

```
cookies[:remember_me] = verifier.generate([user.id, 2.weeks.from_now])
```

verify(signed_message)

Verify a signed message.

```
id, time = @verifier.verify(cookies[:remember_me])
if time < Time.now
  self.current_user = User.find(id)
end
```

B.32 Module

This section covers extensions to Ruby's Module class, available in all contexts.

B.32.1 active_support/core_ext/module/ aliasing

alias_attribute(new_name, old_name)

This super-useful method allows you to easily make aliases for attributes, including their reader, writer, and query methods.

In the following example, the Content class is serving as the base class for Email using STI, but e-mails should have a subject, not a title:

```
class Content < ActiveRecord::Base
  # has column named 'title'
end

class Email < Content
  alias_attribute :subject, :title
end
```

As a result of the alias_attribute, you can see in the following example that the title and subject attributes become interchangeable:

```
>> e = Email.find(:first)

>> e.title
=> "Superstars"

>> e.subject
=> "Superstars"

>> e.subject?
=> true

>> e.subject = "Megastars"
=> "Megastars"

>> e.title
=> "Megastars"
```

alias_method_chain(target, feature)

Encapsulates the following common pattern:

```
alias_method :foo_without_feature, :foo
alias_method :foo, :foo_with_feature
```

With `alias_method_chain`, you simply do one line of code and both aliases are set up for you:

```
alias_method_chain :foo, :feature
```

Query and bang methods keep the same punctuation. The following syntax

```
alias_method_chain :foo?, :feature
```

is equivalent to

```
alias_method :foo_without_feature?, :foo?
alias_method :foo?, :foo_with_feature?
```

so you can safely chain `foo`, `foo?`, and `foo!`.

B.32.2 active_support/core_ext/module/ anonymous

anonymous?

Returns `true` if `self` does not have a name.

A module gets a name when it is first assigned to a constant. Either via the `module` or `class` keyword

```
module M
end

>> M.name
=> "M"

m = Module.new

>> m.name
=> ""
```

or by an explicit assignment

```
m = Module.new

>> M = m    # m gets a name here as a side-effect

>> m.name
=> "M"
```

B.32.3 `active_support/core_ext/module/` `attr_accessor_with_default`

`attr_accessor_with_default`
`(sym, default = nil, &block)`

Declares an attribute accessor with an initial default return value.

To give attribute `:age` the initial value `25`, you would write the following:

```
class Person
  attr_accessor_with_default :age, 25
end
```

To give attribute `:element_name` a dynamic default value, evaluated in scope of self, you would write

```
attr_accessor_with_default(:element_name) { name.underscore }
```

B.32.4 `active_support/core_ext/module/` `attr_internal`

`attr_internal`

Alias for `attr_internal_accessor`.

`attr_internal_accessor(*attrs)`

Declares attributes backed by internal instance variables names (using an `@_` naming convention). Basically just a mechanism to enhance controlled access to sensitive attributes.

For instance, `Object`'s `copy_instance_variables_from` will not copy internal instance variables.

`attr_internal_reader(*attrs)`

Declares an attribute reader backed by an internally named instance variable.

`attr_internal_writer(*attrs)`

Declares an attribute writer backed by an internally named instance variable.

B.32.5 `active_support/core_ext/module/` `attribute_accessors`

`mattr_accessor(*syms)`

Defines one or more module attribute reader and writer methods in the style of the native `attr*` accessors for instance attributes.

mattr_reader(*syms)

Defines one or more module attribute reader methods.

mattr_writer(*syms)

Defines one or more module attribute writer methods.

B.32.6 `active_support/core_ext/module/ delegation`

delegate(*methods)

Provides a delegate class method to easily expose contained objects' methods as your own. Pass one or more methods (specified as symbols or strings) and the name of the target object via the :to option (also a symbol or string). At least one method name and the :to option are required.

Delegation is particularly useful with Active Record associations:

```
class Greeter < ActiveRecord::Base
  def hello
    "hello"
  end

  def goodbye
    "goodbye"
  end
end

class Foo < ActiveRecord::Base
  belongs_to :greeter
  delegate :hello, :to => :greeter
end

Foo.new.hello   # => "hello"
Foo.new.goodbye # => NoMethodError: undefined method `goodbye' for
#<Foo:0x1af30c>
```

Multiple delegates to the same target are allowed:

```
class Foo < ActiveRecord::Base
  belongs_to :greeter
  delegate :hello, :goodbye, :to => :greeter
end

Foo.new.goodbye # => "goodbye"
```

Methods can be delegated to instance variables, class variables, or constants by providing them as a symbols:

```
class Foo
  CONSTANT_ARRAY = [0,1,2,3]
  @@class_array  = [4,5,6,7]

  def initialize
    @instance_array = [8,9,10,11]
  end
  delegate :sum, :to => :CONSTANT_ARRAY
  delegate :min, :to => :@@class_array
  delegate :max, :to => :@instance_array
end

Foo.new.sum # => 6
Foo.new.min # => 4
Foo.new.max # => 11
```

Delegates can optionally be prefixed using the `:prefix` option. If the value is `true`, the delegate methods are prefixed with the name of the object being delegated to.

```
Person = Struct.new(:name, :address)

class Invoice < Struct.new(:client)
  delegate :name, :address, :to => :client, :prefix => true
end

john_doe = Person.new("John Doe", "Vimmersvej 13")
invoice = Invoice.new(john_doe)
invoice.client_name    # => "John Doe"
invoice.client_address # => "Vimmersvej 13"
```

It is also possible to supply a custom prefix.

```
class Invoice < Struct.new(:client)
  delegate :name, :address, :to => :client, :prefix => :customer
end

invoice = Invoice.new(john_doe)
invoice.customer_name    # => "John Doe"
invoice.customer_address # => "Vimmersvej 13"
```

If the delegate object is `nil` an exception is raised, and that happens no matter whether `nil` responds to the delegated method. You can get a `nil` instead with the `:allow_nil` option.

```
class Foo
  attr_accessor :bar
  def initialize(bar = nil)
```

```
    @bar = bar
  end
  delegate :zoo, :to => :bar
end

Foo.new.zoo    # raises NoMethodError exception (you called nil.zoo)

class Foo
  attr_accessor :bar
  def initialize(bar = nil)
    @bar = bar
  end
  delegate :zoo, :to => :bar, :allow_nil => true
end

Foo.new.zoo    # returns nil
```

B.32.7 `active_support/core_ext/module/introspection`

`local_constants`

Returns the constants that have been defined locally by this object and not in an ancestor. This method is exact if running under Ruby 1.9. In previous versions it may miss some constants if their definition in some ancestor is identical to their definition in the receiver.

`local_constant_names`

Returns the names of the constants defined locally rather than the constants themselves.

`parent`

Returns the module that contains this one; if this is a root module, such as ::MyModule, then `Object` is returned.

```
>> ActiveRecord::Validations.parent
=> ActiveRecord
```

`parent_name`

Returns the name of the module containing this one.

```
>> ActiveRecord::Validations.parent_name
=> "ActiveRecord"
```

parents

Returns all the parents of this module according to its name, ordered from nested outwards. The receiver is not contained within the result.

```
module M
  module N
  end
end
X = M::N

>> M.parents
=> [Object]

>> M::N.parents
=> [M, Object]

>> X.parents
=> [M, Object]
```

B.32.8 active_support/core_ext/module/ synchronization

synchronize(*methods)

Synchronizes access around a method, delegating synchronization to a particular mutex. A mutex (either a Mutex, or any object that responds to synchronize and yields to a block) must be provided together with a :with option. The :with option should be a symbol or string, and can represent a method, constant, or instance or class variable.

```
class SharedCache
  @@lock = Mutex.new
  def expire
    ...
  end
  synchronize :expire, :with => :@@lock
end
```

It is used internally by Rails in various places including database connection pooling, the buffered logger, and generation of asset timestamps.

B.32.9 active_support/dependencies

const_missing(class_id)

The const_missing callback is invoked when Ruby can't find a specified constant in the current scope, which is what makes Rails autoclassloading possible. See the Dependencies module for more detail.

B.33 ActiveSupport::Multibyte::Chars

The chars proxy enables you to work transparently with multibyte encodings in the Ruby String class without having extensive knowledge about encoding.

B.33.1 active_support/multibyte/chars

A Chars object accepts a string upon initialization and proxies String methods in an encoding-safe manner. All the normal String methods are proxied through the Chars object, and can be accessed through the mb_chars method. Methods that would normally return a String object now return a Chars object so that methods can be chained together safely.

```
>> "The Perfect String".mb_chars.downcase.strip.normalize
=> "the perfect string"
```

Chars objects are perfectly interchangeable with String objects as long as no explicit class checks are made. If certain methods do explicitly check the class, call to_s before you pass Chars objects to them, to go back to a normal String object:

```
bad.explicit_checking_method("T".chars.downcase.to_s)
```

The default Chars implementation assumes that the encoding of the string is UTF-8. If you want to handle different encodings, you can write your own multibyte string handler and configure it through ActiveSupport::Multibyte.proxy_class

```
class CharsForUTF32
  def size
    @wrapped_string.size / 4
  end

  def self.accepts?(string)
    string.length % 4 == 0
  end
end

ActiveSupport::Multibyte.proxy_class = CharsForUTF32
```

Note that a few methods are defined on Chars instead of the handler because they are defined on Object or Kernel and method_missing (the method used for delegation) can't catch them.

<=> (other)

Returns −1, 0, or +1 depending on whether the Chars object is to be sorted before, equal to, or after the object on the right side of the operation. In other words, it works exactly as you would expect it to.

handler

Returns the proper handler for the contained string depending on $KCODE and the encoding of the string. This method is used internally by Rails to always redirect messages to the proper classes depending on the context.

method_missing(m, *a, & b)

Tries to forward all undefined methods to the designated handler. When a method is not defined on the handler, it sends it to the contained string instead. Also responsible for making the bang (!) methods destructive, since a handler doesn't have access to change an enclosed string instance.

split(*args)

Works just like the normal String's split method, with the exception that the items in the resulting list are Chars instances instead of String, which makes chaining calls easier.

```
'éCaf éôpriferl'.mb_chars.splité(//).map { |part| part.upcase.to_s } #=>
["CAF", " P", "ÔRIFERL"]
```

tidy_bytes(force = false)

Replaces all ISO-8859-1 or CP1252 characters by their UTF-8 equivalent resulting in a valid UTF-8 string.

Passing true will forcibly tidy all bytes, assuming that the string's encoding is entirely CP1252 or ISO-8859-1.

```
> "obie".mb_chars.tidy_bytes
=> #<ActiveSupport::Multibyte::Chars:0x25faa30 @wrapped_string="obie">
```

B.33.2 active_support/multibyte/unicode

Contains methods handling Unicode strings.

Unicode.compose_codepoints(codepoints)

Composes decomposed characters to the composed form.

Unicode.decompose_codepoints(type, codepoints)

Decomposes composed characters to the decomposed form. The type argument accepts :canonical or :compatability.

Unicode.g_pack(string)

Reverses operation of g_unpack

Unicode.g_unpack(string)

Unpacks the string at grapheme boundaries. Returns a list of character lists.

```
>> Unicode.g_unpack('ffff')
=> [[2325, 2381], [2359], [2367]]

>> Unicode.g_unpack('Café')
=> [[67], [97], [102], [233]]
```

Unicode.in_char_class?(codepoint, classes)

Detects whether the codepoint is in a certain character class. Returns true when it's in the specified character class and false otherwise. Valid character classes are: :cr, :lf, :l, :v, :lv, :lvt and :t.

Primarily used by grapheme cluster support.[1]

Unicode.normalize(string, form = nil)

Returns the KC normalization of the string by default. NFKC is considered the best normalization form for passing strings to databases and validations. The form specifies the form you want to normalize in and should be one of the following: :c, :kc, :d, or :kd. Default is form is stored in the ActiveSupport:: Multibyte.default_normalization_form attribute and is overridable in an initializer.

Unicode.reorder_characters(codepoints)

Re-orders codepoints so the string becomes canonical.

Unicode.u_unpack(string)

Unpacks the string at codepoints boundaries. Raises an EncodingError when the encoding of the string isn't valid UTF-8.

```
>> Unicode.u_unpack('Café')
=> [67, 97, 102, 233]
```

B.33.3 active_support/multibyte/utils

Contains methods for verifying the encoding of character strings.

---

[1]. http://unicode.org/reports/tr29/

`Multibyte.verify(string)`

Verifies the encoding of a string. Splits the string on character boundaries, which are determined based on $KCODE.

```
>> ActiveSupport::Multibyte.verify("obie")
=> true
```

`Multibyte.verify!(string)`

Verifies the encoding of a string. Splits the string on character boundaries, which are determined based on $KCODE. Raises an exception if it's not valid.

B.34 `NilClass`

Remembers that everything in Ruby is an object, even `nil`, which is a special reference to a singleton instance of the `NilClass`.

B.34.1 `active_support/core_ext/object/blank`

`blank?`
Returns `true`.

B.34.2 `active_support/json/encoding`

`as_json`
Returns `"null"`.

B.34.3 `active_support/whiny_nil`

Besides `blank?`, the extensions to `nil` try to raise more descriptive error messages, to help Rails newbies. The aim is to ensure that when developers pass `nil` to methods unintentionally, instead of `NoMethodError` and the name of some method used by the framework, they'll see a message explaining what type of object was expected. The behavior was named "whiny nil" as an inside joke.

Method missing magic is used to capture the method that was erroneously invoked on `nil`. The method name is looked up in a hash containing method names indexed to Rails classes, so that a helpful suggestion can be attempted.

If you've done any amount of Rails programming, you're probably familiar with the output of this error-helping process, as the description of a `NoMethodError`:

You have a nil object when you didn't expect it! You might have expected an instance of class_name. The error occurred while evaluating nil.method_name.

The whiny nil behavior can be controlled in the individual environment configurations with the following line:

```
config.whiny_nils = true
```

Rails has it set to true by default in development and test modes, and false in production mode.

NilClass.add_whiner(klass)

Specifies that klass should have whiny nil behavior. Active Support adds Array by default.

id

Raises a message along the lines of: Called id for nil, which would mistakenly be 4 -- if you really wanted the id of nil, use object_id.

B.35 ActiveSupport::Notifications

Notifications provides an instrumentation API for Ruby. To instrument an action in Ruby you just need to do:

```
ActiveSupport::Notifications.instrument(:render, :extra => :information)
do
  render :text => "Foo"
end
```

You can consume those events and the information they provide by registering a log subscriber. For instance, let's store all instrumented events in an array:

```
@events = []

ActiveSupport::Notifications.subscribe do |*args|
  @events << ActiveSupport::Notifications::Event.new(*args)
end

ActiveSupport::Notifications.instrument(:render, :extra => :information)
do
  render :text => "Foo"
end

event = @events.first
event.name       #=> :render
event.duration   #=> 10 (in miliseconds)
event.result     #=> "Foo"
event.payload    #=> { :extra => :information }
```

When subscribing to `Notifications`, you can pass a pattern, to only consume events that match the pattern:

```
ActiveSupport::Notifications.subscribe(/render/) do |event|
  @render_events << event
end
```

Notifications ships with a queue implementation that consumes and publish events to log subscribers in a thread. You can use any queue implementation you want.

B.36 Numeric

Extensions to Ruby's `Numeric` class.

B.36.1 active_support/core_ext/object/blank

blank?

Returns `false`.

B.36.2 active_support/json/encoding

as_json

Returns `self`.

encode_json

Returns `self.to_s`.

B.36.3 active_support/numeric/bytes

Enables the use of byte calculations and declarations, like `45.bytes + 2.6.megabytes`.

Constants

The following constants are defined in `bytes.rb`.

```
class Numeric
  KILOBYTE = 1024
  MEGABYTE = KILOBYTE * 1024
  GIGABYTE = MEGABYTE * 1024
  TERABYTE = GIGABYTE * 1024
  PETABYTE = TERABYTE * 1024
  EXABYTE  = PETABYTE * 1024
  ...
end
```

byte / bytes

Returns the value of self. Enables the use of byte calculations and declarations, like
45.bytes + 2.6.megabytes.

kilobyte / kilobytes

Returns self * 1024.

megabyte / megabytes

Returns self * 1024.kilobytes.

gigabyte / gigabytes

Returns self * 1024.megabytes.

terabyte / terabytes

Returns self * 1024.gigabytes.

petabyte / petabytes

Returns self * 1024.terabytes.

exabyte / exabytes

Returns self * 1024.petabytes.

B.36.4 `active_support/numeric/time`

Enables the use of time calculations and declarations, like 45.minutes + 2.hours +
4.years.

These methods use Time#advance for precise date calculations when using
from_now, ago, etc. as well as adding or subtracting their results from a Time object.
For example:

```
# equivalent to Time.now.advance(:months => 1)
1.month.from_now

# equivalent to Time.now.advance(:years => 2)
2.years.from_now

# equivalent to Time.now.advance(:months => 4, :years => 5)
(4.months + 5.years).from_now
```

While these methods provide precise calculation when used as in the examples above, care should be taken to note that this is not true if the result of 'months', 'years', etc is converted before use:

```
# equivalent to 30.days.to_i.from_now
1.month.to_i.from_now

# equivalent to 365.25.days.to_f.from_now
1.year.to_f.from_now
```

In such cases, Ruby's core `Date` and `Time` should be used for precision date and time arithmetic.

ago and until
Appends to a numeric time value to express a moment in the past.

```
10.minutes.ago
```

day / days
A duration equivalent to `self * 24.hours`.

fortnight / fortnights
A duration equivalent to `self * 2.weeks`.

from_now(time = Time.now) / since(time = Time.now)
An amount of time in the future, from a specified time (which defaults to `Time.now`).

hour / hours
A duration equivalent to `self * 3600.seconds`.

minute / minutes
A duration equivalent to `self * 60.seconds`.

month / months
A duration equivalent to `self * 30.days`.

second / seconds
A duration in seconds equal to `self`.

week / weeks
A duration equivalent to `self * 7.days`.

year / years

A duration equivalent to `self * 365.25.days`.

B.37 Object

Rails mixes quite a few methods into the `Object` class, meaning they are available via every other object at runtime.

B.37.1 `active_support/core_ext/object/acts_like`

`acts_like?(duck)`

A duck-type assistant method. For example, Active Support extends `Date` to define an `acts_like_date?` method, and extends `Time` to define `acts_like_time?`. As a result, we can do "x.acts_like?(:time)" and "x.acts_like?(:date)" to do duck-type-safe comparisons, since classes that we want to act like Time simply need to define an `acts_like_time?` method.

B.37.2 `active_support/core_ext/object/blank`

`blank?`

An object is blank if it's `false`, empty, or a whitespace string. For example, "", " ", `nil`, `[]`, and `{}` are blank.

This simplifies:

```
if !address.nil? && !address.empty?
```

to

```
unless address.blank?
```

`presence`

Returns object if it's `present?` otherwise returns `nil`. The expression `object.presence` is equivalent to `object.present? ? object : nil`

`present?`

An object is present if it's not blank.

This is handy for any representation of objects where blank is the same as not present at all. For example, this simplifies a common check for HTTP POST/query parameters:

```
state   = params[:state]   if params[:state].present?
country = params[:country] if params[:country].present?
region  = state || country || 'US'
```

becomes

```
region = params[:state].presence || params[:country].presence || 'US'
```

B.37.3 `active_support/core_ext/object/duplicable`

Most objects are cloneable, but not all. For example you can't dup +nil+:

```
nil.dup # => TypeError: can't dup NilClass
```

Classes may signal their instances are not duplicable removing dup and clone or raising exceptions from them. So, to dup an arbitrary object you normally use an optimistic approach and are ready to catch an exception, say:

```
arbitrary_object.dup rescue object
```

Rails dups objects in a few critical spots where they are not that arbitrary. That rescue is very expensive (like 40 times slower than a predicate), and it is often triggered.

That's why we hardcode the following cases and check duplicable? instead of using the rescue idiom.

duplicable?

Is it possible to safely duplicate this object? Returns false for nil, false, true, symbols, numbers, class and module objects, true otherwise.

B.37.4 `active_support/core_ext/object/instance_variables`

copy_instance_variables_from(object, exclude = [])

Copies the instance variables of object into self.

Instance variable names in the exclude array are ignored. If object responds to protected_instance_variables, then protected variables are also ignored.

In both cases, strings and symbols are understood, and they have to include the at sign.

```
class C
  def initialize(x, y, z)
    @x, @y, @z = x, y, z
  end

  def protected_instance_variables
    %w(@z)
  end
end

>> a = C.new(0, 1, 2)
>> b = C.new(3, 4, 5)

>> a.copy_instance_variables_from(b, [:@y])
# a is now: @x = 3, @y = 1, @z = 2
```

instance_values

Returns a hash that maps instance variable names without "@" to their corresponding values. Keys are strings both in Ruby 1.8 and 1.9.

```
class C
  def initialize(x, y)
    @x, @y = x, y
  end
end

C.new(0, 1).instance_values # => {"x" => 0, "y" => 1}
```

instance_variable_names

Returns an array of instance variable names including "@". They are strings both in Ruby 1.8 and 1.9.

```
class C
  def initialize(x, y)
    @x, @y = x, y
  end
end

C.new(0, 1).instance_variable_names # => ["@y", "@x"]
```

B.37.5 active_support/core_ext/object/
to_param

to_param

Alias of to_s.

B.37.6 `active_support/core_ext/object/`
   ## `with_options`

`with_options(options)`

An elegant way to refactor out common options.

```
class Post < ActiveRecord::Base
  with_options(:class_name => 'Comment', :order => 'id desc') do |post|
    post.has_many :approved, :conditions => ['approved = ?', true]
    post.has_many :unapproved, :conditions => ['approved = ?', false]
    post.has_many :all_comments
  end
end
```

B.37.7 `active_support/dependencies`

`load(file, *extras)`

Rails overrides Ruby's built-in `load` method to tie it into the `Dependencies` subsystem.

`require(file, *extras)`

Rails overrides Ruby's built-in `require` method to tie it into the `Dependencies` subsystem.

`require_association(file_name)`

Used internally by Rails. Invokes `Dependencies.associate_with (file_name)`.

`require_dependency(file_name)`

Used internally by Rails. Invokes `Dependencies.depend_on(file_name)`.

`require_or_load(file_name)`

Used internally by Rails. Invokes `Dependencies.require_or_load(file_name)`.

`unloadable(const_desc)`

Marks the specified constant as unloadable. Unloadable constants are removed each time dependencies are cleared.

Note that marking a constant for unloading need only be done once. Setup or init scripts may list each unloadable constant that will need unloading; constants marked in this way will be removed on every subsequent `Dependencies.clear`, as opposed to the first clear only.

The provided constant descriptor `const_desc` may be a (nonanonymous) module or class, or a qualified constant name as a string or symbol.

Returns `true` if the constant was not previously marked for unloading, `false` otherwise.

B.37.8 `active_support/json/encoding`
`to_json(options = nil)`
Dumps object in JSON (JavaScript Object Notation).

B.38 `ActiveSupport::OrderedHash`
B.38.1 `active_support/ordered_hash`

This is a hash implementation for Ruby 1.8.x that preserves the ordering of its elements, in contrast to normal Ruby hashes. (Ruby 1.9 hashes are ordered natively!) It's namespaced to prevent conflicts with other implementations, but you can assign it to a top-level namespace if you don't want to constantly use the fully qualified name:

```
OrderedHash = ActiveSupport::OrderedHash

>> oh = ActiveSupport::OrderedHash.new
=> []
>> oh[:one] = 1
=> 1
>> oh[:two] = 2
=> 2
>> oh[:three] = 3
=> 3
>> oh
=> [[:one, 1], [:two, 2], [:three, 3]]
```

B.39 `ActiveSupport::OrderedOptions`
B.39.1 `active_support/ordered_options`

A subclass of `OrderedHash` that adds a method-missing implementation so that hash elements can be accessed and modified using normal attribute semantics, dot-notation:

```
def method_missing(name, *args)
  if name.to_s =~ /(.*)=$/
    self[$1.to_sym] = args.first
  else
    self[name]
  end
end
```

B.40 ActiveSupport::Railtie

B.40.1 active_support/railtie

Contains Active Support's initialization routine for itself and the I18n subsystem.

If you're depending on Active Support outside of Rails, you should be aware of what happens in this Railtie in case you end up needing to replicate it in your own code.

```
module ActiveSupport
  class Railtie < Rails::Railtie
    config.active_support = ActiveSupport::OrderedOptions.new

    # Loads support for "whiny nil" (noisy warnings when methods are
invoked
    # on +nil+ values) if Configuration#whiny_nils is true.
    initializer "active_support.initialize_whiny_nils" do |app|
      require 'active_support/whiny_nil' if app.config.whiny_nils
    end

    # Sets the default value for Time.zone
    # If assigned value cannot be matched to a TimeZone, an exception will
 be raised.
    initializer "active_support.initialize_time_zone" do |app|
      require 'active_support/core_ext/time/zones'
      zone_default = Time.__send__(:get_zone, app.config.time_zone)

      unless zone_default
        raise \
          'Value assigned to config.time_zone not recognized.' +
          'Run "rake -D time" for a list of tasks for finding appropriate
time zone names.'
      end

      Time.zone_default = zone_default
    end
  end
end
```

B.41 Range

Extensions to Ruby's Range class.

B.41.1 active_support/core_ext/range/ blockless_step

step

Ruby's native Range#step (on most platforms) raises a LocalJumpError if you omit a block. Rails patches step to make it return an array if it's called without a block.

B.41.2 `active_support/core_ext/range/` `conversions`

`to_formatted_s(format = :default)`

Generates a formatted string representation of the range.

```
>> (20.days.ago..10.days.ago).to_formatted_s
=> "Fri Aug 10 22:12:33 -0400 2007..Mon Aug 20 22:12:33 -0400 2007"
>> (20.days.ago..10.days.ago).to_formatted_s(:db)
=> "BETWEEN '2007-08-10 22:12:36' AND '2007-08-20 22:12:36'"
```

B.41.3 `active_support/core_ext/range/` `include_range`

`include?(value)`

Extends the default `Range#include?` to support range comparisons.

```
>> (1..5).include?(1..5)
=> true

>> (1..5).include?(2..3)
=> true

>> (1..5).include?(2..6)
=> false
```

The native `include?` behavior is untouched.

```
>> ("a".."f").include?("c")
=> true

>> (5..9).include?(11)
=> false
```

B.41.4 `active_support/core_ext/range/` `include_range`

`overlaps?(other)`

Compares two ranges and sees if they overlap each other

```
>> (1..5).overlaps?(4..6)
=> true

>> (1..5).overlaps?(7..9)
=> false
```

B.42 Regexp

B.42.1 `active_support/core_ext/enumerable`

`sum(identity = 0)`

Optimizes range sum to use arithmetic progression if a block is not given and we have a range of numeric values.

B.42.2 `active_support/json/encoding`

`as_json`

Returns `self.to_s`.

B.43 ActiveSupport::Rescuable

The `Rescuable` module is a `Concern` that adds support for easier exception handling. Used within Rails primarily in controller actions, but potentially very useful in your own libraries too.

B.43.1 `active_support/rescuable`

`rescue_from(*klasses, &block)`

The `rescue_from` method receives a series of exception classes or class names, and a trailing `:with` option with the name of a method or a `Proc` object to be called to handle them. Alternatively a block can be given.

Handlers that take one argument will be called with the exception, so that the exception can be inspected when dealing with it.

Handlers are inherited. They are searched from right to left, from bottom to top, and up the hierarchy. The handler of the first class for which `exception.is_a?(klass)` returns `true` is the one invoked, if any.

Here's some example code taken from Action Controller.

```
class ApplicationController < ActionController::Base
  rescue_from User::NotAuthorized, :with => :deny_access
  rescue_from ActiveRecord::RecordInvalid, :with => :show_errors

  rescue_from 'MyAppError::Base' do |exception|
    render :xml => exception, :status => 500
  end

  protected
    def deny_access
      ...
    end
```

```
    def show_errors(exception)
      exception.record.new? ? ...
    end
end
```

B.44 **ActiveSupport::SecureRandom**

A secure random number generator interface.

This library is an interface for secure random number generator which is suitable for generating session key in HTTP cookies, etc.

It supports following secure random number generators.

- openssl

- /dev/urandom

- Win32

Note: This module is based on the SecureRandom library from Ruby 1.9, revision 18786, August 23 2008. It's 100 percent interface-compatible with Ruby 1.9's SecureRandom library.

```
# random hexadecimal string.
p SecureRandom.hex(10) #=> "52750b30ffbc7de3b362"
p SecureRandom.hex(10) #=> "92b15d6c8dc4beb5f559"
p SecureRandom.hex(11) #=> "6aca1b5c58e4863e6b81b8"
p SecureRandom.hex(12) #=> "94b2fff3e7fd9b9c391a2306"
p SecureRandom.hex(13) #=> "39b290146bea6ce975c37cfc23"

# random base64 string.
p SecureRandom.base64(10) #=> "EcmTPZwWRAozdA=="
p SecureRandom.base64(10) #=> "9b0nsevdwNuM/w=="
p SecureRandom.base64(10) #=> "KO1nIU+p9DKxGg=="
p SecureRandom.base64(11) #=> "l7XEiFja+8EKEtY="
p SecureRandom.base64(12) #=> "7kJSM/MzBJI+75j8"
p SecureRandom.base64(13) #=> "vKLJ0tXBHqQOuIcSIg=="

# random binary string.
p SecureRandom.random_bytes(10) #=> "\016\t{\370g\310pbr\301"
p SecureRandom.random_bytes(10) #=> "\323U\030TO\234\357\020\a\337"
```

B.44.1 **active_support/secure_random**

Note that all of the methods in this module will raise `NotImplementedError` if a secure random number generator is not available.

SecureRandom.base64(n = 16)

This method generates a random base64 string. The argument n specifies the length of the random length. The length of the result string is about 4/3 of n.

SecureRandom.hex(n = 16)

This method generates a random hex string. The argument n specifies the length of the random length. The length of the result string is twice of n.

SecureRandom.random_number(n = 0)

This method generates a random number. If an positive integer is given as n, then random_number returns an integer.

```
0 <= SecureRandom.random_number(n) < n
```

If 0 is given or an argument is not supplied then random_number returns a float.

```
0.0 <= SecureRandom.random_number() < 1.0
```

SecureRandom.random_bytes(n = 16)

This method generates a random binary string. The argument n specifies the length of the result string.

B.45 String

Extensions to Ruby's String class.

B.45.1 active_support/json/encoding

as_json

Returns self.

encode_json

Returns JSON escaped version of self.

B.45.2 active_support/core_ext/object/blank

blank?

Returns true if the string consists of only whitespace.

```
class String
  def blank?
    self !~ /\S/
  end
end
```

B.45.3 `active_support/core_ext/string/access`

`at(position)`

Returns the character at `position`, treating the string as an array (where 0 is the first character). Returns `nil` if the position exceeds the length of the string.

```
>> "hello".at(0)
=> "h"

>> "hello".at(4)
=> "o"

>> "hello".at(10)
=> ERROR if < 1.9, nil in 1.9
```

`blank?`

Returns the result of `empty?` (stripping whitespace, if needed).

`first(number)`

Returns the first `number` of characters in a string.

```
"hello".first     # => "h"
"hello".first(2)  # => "he"
"hello".first(10) # => "hello"
```

`from(position)`

Returns the remaining characters of a string from the `position`, treating the string as an array (where 0 is the first character). Returns `nil` if the position exceeds the length of the string.

```
"hello".at(0)  # => "hello"
"hello".at(2)  # => "llo"
"hello".at(10) # => nil
```

`last(number)`

Returns the last `number` of characters in a string.

```
"hello".last     # => "o"
"hello".last(2)  # => "lo"
"hello".last(10) # => "hello"
```

`to(position)`

Returns the beginning of the string up to the `position` treating the string as an array (where 0 is the first character). Doesn't produce an error when the `position` exceeds the length of the string.

Active Support

```
"hello".at(0)  # => "h"
"hello".at(2)   # => "hel"
"hello".at(10) # => "hello"
```

B.45.4 `active_support/core_ext/string/`
`acts_like`

Duck-types as a `String`-like class. See `Object#acts_like?` for more explanation.

```
class String
  def acts_like_time?
    true
  end
end
```

B.45.5 `active_support/core_ext/string/`
`conversions`

ord
Returns the codepoint of the first character of the string, assuming a single-byte character encoding:

```
"a".ord # => 97
"à".ord # => 224, in ISO-8859-1
```

This method is defined in Ruby 1.8 for Ruby 1.9 forward compatibility on these character encodings. It is forward compatible with Ruby 1.9 on UTF8 strings:

```
>> "a".mb_chars.ord
=> 97

>> "à".mb_chars.ord
=> 224 # in UTF8
```

Note that the 224 is different in both examples. In ISO-8859-1 "à" is represented as a single byte, 224. In UTF8 it is represented with two bytes, namely 195 and 160, but its Unicode codepoint is 224. If we call `ord` on the UTF8 string "à" the return value will be 195.

to_date
Uses `Date.parse` to turn a string into a `Date`.

to_datetime
Uses `Date.parse` to turn a string into a `DateTime`.

to_time(form = :utc)

Uses `Date.parse` to turn a string into a `Time` either using either `:utc` (default) or `:local`.

B.45.6 active_support/core_ext/string/ encoding

encoding_aware?

Returns `true` if `Encoding` is defined and `String` responds to `:encode`.

B.45.7 active_support/core_ext/string/exclude

exclude?(other)

The inverse of `include?`. Returns `true` if `self` does not include the `other` string.

B.45.8 active_support/core_ext/string/filters

squish

Returns the string, first removing all whitespace on both ends of the string, and then changing remaining consecutive whitespace groups into one space each.

```
>> %{ Multi-line
   string }.squish
=> "Multi-line string"

>> " foo    bar    \n  \t   boo".squish
=> "foo bar boo"
```

squish!

Performs a destructive squish. See `squish`.

truncate(length, options = {})

Truncates a given `text` after a given `length` if `text` is longer than `length`. The last characters will be replaced with the `:omission` (which defaults to "...") for a total length not exceeding `:length`.

Pass a `:separator` to truncate `text` at a natural break.

```
>> "Once upon a time in a world far far away".truncate(30)
=> Once upon a time in a worl...

>> "Once upon a time in a world far far away".truncate(30, :separator
=> ' ')
=> Once upon a time in a world...
```

```
>> "Once upon a time in a world far far away".truncate(14)
=> Once upon a...

>> "And they found that many people were sleeping better.".truncate(25,
:omission => "... (continued)")
=> And they f... (continued)
```

B.45.9 `active_support/core_ext/string/ inflections`

String inflections define new methods on the `String` class to transform names for different purposes.

For instance, you can figure out the name of a database from the name of a class:

```
>> "ScaleScore".tableize
=> "scale_scores"
```

If you get frustrated by the limitations of Rails inflections, try the most excellent Linguistics library by Michael Granger at `http://www.deveiate.org/projects/` Linguistics. It doesn't do all of the same inflections as Rails, but the ones that it does do, it does better. (See `titleize` for an example.)

`camelize(first_letter = :upper)`

By default, `camelize` converts strings to UpperCamelCase. If the argument to `camelize` is set to `:lower`, then `camelize` produces lowerCamelCase. Also converts "/" to "::", which is useful for converting paths to namespaces.

```
>> "active_record".camelize
=> "ActiveRecord"

>> "active_record".camelize(:lower)
=> "activeRecord"

>> "active_record/errors".camelize
=> "ActiveRecord::Errors"
>> "active_record/errors".camelize(:lower)
=> "activeRecord::Errors"
```

`classify`

Creates a class name from a table name; used by Active Record to turn table names to model classes. Note that the `classify` method returns a string and not a `Class`. (To convert to an actual class, follow `classify` with `constantize`.)

```
>> "egg_and_hams".classify
=> "EggAndHam"
```

```
>> "post".classify
=> "Post"
```

constantize

The `constantize` method tries to find a declared constant with the name specified in the string. It raises a `NameError` if a matching constant is not located.

```
>> "Module".constantize
=> Module

>> "Class".constantize
=> Class
```

dasherize

Replaces underscores with dashes in the string.

```
>> "puni_puni"
=> "puni-puni"
```

demodulize

Removes the module prefixes from a fully qualified module or class name.

```
>> "ActiveRecord::CoreExtensions::String::Inflections".demodulize
=> "Inflections"

>> "Inflections".demodulize
=> "Inflections"
```

foreign_key(separate_class_name_and_id_ with_underscore = true)

Creates a foreign key name from a class name.

```
"Message".foreign_key #=> "message_id"
"Message".foreign_key(false) #=> "messageid"
"Admin::Post".foreign_key #=> "post_id"
```

humanize

Capitalizes the first word of a string, turns underscores into spaces, and strips `_id`. Similar to the `titleize` method in that it is intended for creating pretty output.

```
"employee_salary" #=> "Employee salary"
"author_id" #=> "Author"
```

parameterize(sep = '-')

Replaces special characters in a string with `sep` string so that it may be used as part of a *pretty* URL.

pluralize

Returns the plural form of the word in the string.

```
"post".pluralize #=> "posts"
"octopus".pluralize #=> "octopi"
"sheep".pluralize #=> "sheep"
"words".pluralize #=> "words"
"the blue mailman".pluralize #=> "the blue mailmen"
"CamelOctopus".pluralize #=> "CamelOctopi"
```

singularize

The reverse of `pluralize`; returns the singular form of a word in a string.

```
"posts".singularize #=> "post"
"octopi".singularize #=> "octopus"
"sheep".singluarize #=> "sheep"
"word".singluarize #=> "word"
"the blue mailmen".singularize #=> "the blue mailman"
"CamelOctopi".singularize #=> "CamelOctopus"
```

tableize

Creates a plural and underscored database table name based on Rails conventions. Used by Active Record to determine the proper table name for a model class. This method uses the `pluralize` method on the last word in the string.

```
"RawScaledScorer".tableize #=> "raw_scaled_scorers"
"egg_and_ham".tableize #=> "egg_and_hams"
"fancyCategory".tableize #=> "fancy_categories"
```

titlecase

Alias for `titleize`.

titleize

Capitalizes all the words and replaces some characters in the string to create a nicer-looking title. The `titleize` method is meant for creating pretty output and is not used in the Rails internals.

```
>> "The light on the beach was like a sinus headache".titleize
=> "The Light On The Beach Was Like A Sinus Headache"
```

It's also not perfect. Among other things, it capitalizes words inside the sentence that it probably shouldn't, like "a" and "the." It also has a hard time with apostrophes:

```
>> "Her uncle's cousin's record albums".titleize
=> "Her Uncle'S Cousin'S Record Albums"
```

The Linguistics gem mentioned in the beginning of this section has an excellent proper_noun method that in my experience works much better than titleize:

```
>> "Her uncle's cousin's record albums".en.proper_noun
=> "Her Uncle's Cousin's Record Albums"
```

underscore

The reverse of camelize. Makes an underscored form from the expression in the string. Changes "::" to "/" to convert namespaces to paths.

```
"ActiveRecord".underscore #=> "active_record"
"ActiveRecord::Errors".underscore #=> active_record/errors
```

B.45.10 active_support/core_ext/string/ multibyte

Defines a mutibyte safe proxy for string methods.

mb_chars

In Ruby 1.8 and older mb_chars creates and returns an instance of ActiveSupport::Multibyte::Chars encapsulating the original string. A Unicode safe version of all the String methods are defined on the proxy class. If the proxy class doesn't respond to a certain method, it's forwarded to the encapsuled string.

```
>> name = 'Claus Müller'

>> name.reverse
=> "rell??M sualC"

>> name.length
=> 13

>> name.mb_chars.reverse.to_s
=> "ürellM sualC"
>> name.mb_chars.length
=> 12
```

In Ruby 1.9 and newer `mb_chars` returns `self` because `String` is (mostly) encoding aware. This means that it becomes easy to run one version of your code on multiple Ruby versions.

All the methods on the `Chars` proxy which normally return a string will return a `Chars` object. This allows method chaining on the result of any of these methods.

```
>> name.mb_chars.reverse.length
=> 12
```

The `Chars` object tries to be as interchangeable with `String` objects as possible: sorting and comparing between `String` and `Char` work like expected. The bang! methods change the internal string representation in the `Chars` object. Interoperability problems can be resolved easily with a `to_s` call.

For more information about the methods defined on the `Chars` proxy see `ActiveSupport::Multibyte::Chars`. For information about how to change the default `Multibyte` behavior see `ActiveSupport::Multibyte`.

is_utf8?(suffix)
Returns `true` if the string has UTF-8 semantics, versus strings that are simply being used as byte streams.

B.45.11 `active_support/core_ext/string/ output_safety`

html_safe
Returns an html-escaped version of `self`. See `ERB::Util#html_escape` for more information.

B.45.12 `active_support/core_ext/string/ starts_ends_with`

Provides `String` with additional condition methods.

starts_with?(prefix)
Returns `true` if the string starts with the specified `prefix`.

ends_with?(suffix)
Returns `true` if the string ends with the specified `suffix`.

B.45.13 `active_support/core_ext/string/xchar`

Requires the `fast_xs` gem[2], which provides C extensions for quickly escaping text.
Rails will automatically use `fast_xs` from either `Hpricot` or the gem version with the
bundled `Builder` package.

B.46 `ActiveSupport::StringInquirer`

Wrapping a string in this class gives you a prettier way to test for equality. The value
returned by `Rails.env` is wrapped in a `StringInquirer` object so instead of calling
this:

```
Rails.env == "production"
```

you can call this:

```
Rails.env.production?
```

This class is really simple, so you only really want to do this with strings that contain no
whitespace or special characters.

```
>> s = ActiveSupport::StringInquirer.new("obie")
=> "obie"
>> s.obie?
=> true
```

B.47 `Symbol`

Extensions to Ruby's `Symbol` class.

B.47.1 `active_support/json/encoding`
`as_json`
Returns `to_s` version of itself.

B.48 `ActiveSupport::Testing::Assertions`
B.48.1 `active_support/testing/assertions`

Rails adds a number of assertions to the basic ones provided with `Test::Unit`.

---

2. `http://fast-xs.rubyforge.org/`

assert_blank(object)

Test if an expression is blank. Passes if `object.blank?` is `true`.

```
assert_blank [] # => true
```

assert_present(object)

Tests if an expression is not blank. Passes if `object.present?` is `true`.

```
assert_present {:data => 'x' } # => true
```

assert_difference(expressions, difference = 1, message = nil, &block)

Tests whether a numeric difference in the return value of an expression is a result of what is evaluated in the yielded block. (Easier to demonstrate than to explain!)

The following example eval's the expression `Article.count` and saves the result. Then it yields to the block, which will execute the `post :create` and return control to the `assert_difference` method. At that point, `Article.count` is eval'd again, and the difference is asserted to be 1 (the default difference).

```
assert_difference 'Article.count' do
  post :create, :article => {...}
end
```

Any arbitrary expression can be passed in and evaluated:

```
assert_difference 'assigns(:article).comments(:reload).size' do
  post :create, :comment => {...}
end
```

Arbitrary difference values may be specified. The default is +1, but negative numbers are okay too:

```
assert_difference 'Article.count', -1 do
  post :delete, :id => ...
end
```

An array of expressions can also be passed in—each will be evaluated:

```
assert_difference [ 'Article.count', 'Post.count' ], +2 do
  post :create, :article => {...}
end
```

A error message can be specified:

```
assert_difference 'Article.count', -1, "Article should be destroyed" do
  post :delete, :id => ...
end
```

assert_no_difference(expressions, message = nil, &block)

Tests that the return value of the supplied expression does not change as a result of what is evaluated in the yielded block.

```
assert_no_difference 'Article.count' do
  post :create, :article => invalid_attributes
end
```

B.49 Time

Extensions to Ruby's built-in Time class.

B.49.1 active_support/json/encoding

as_json

Returns self as a JSON string. The ActiveSupport.use_standard_json_time_format configuration setting determines whether the output is formatted using :xmlschema or the following pattern:

```
%(#{strftime("%Y/%m/%d %H:%M:%S")} #{formatted_offset(false)})
```

B.49.2 active_support/core_ext/time/acts_like

Duck-types as a Time-like class. See Object#acts_like? for more explanation.

```
class Time
  def acts_like_time?
    true
  end
end
```

B.49.3 active_support/core_ext/time/ calculations

Contains methods that facilitate time calculations.

===(other)

Overriding case equality method so that it returns true for ActiveSupport::TimeWithZone instances.

+ (other)

Implemented by the plus_with_duration method. It allows addition of times like this:

```
expiration_time = Time.now + 3.days
```

- (other)

Implemented by the `minus_with_duration` method. It allows addition of times like this:

```
two_weeks_ago = Time.now - 2.weeks
```

advance(options)

Provides precise `Time` calculations. The `options` parameter takes a hash with any of the keys `:months`, `:days`, `:years`, `:hour`, `:min`, `:sec`, and `:usec`.

ago(seconds)

Returns a new `Time` representing the time a number of seconds into the past; this is basically a wrapper around the `Numeric` extension of the same name. For the best accuracy, do not use this method in combination with `x.months`; use `months_ago` instead!

at_beginning_of_day

Alias for `beginning_of_day`.

at_beginning_of_month

Alias for `beginning_of_month`.

at_beginning_of_week

Alias for `beginning_of_week`.

at_beginning_of_year

Alias for `beginning_of_year`.

at_end_of_day

Alias for `end_of_day`.

at_end_of_month

Alias for `end_of_month`.

at_end_of_week

Alias for `end_of_week`.

at_end_of_year

Alias for `end_of_year`.

beginning_of_day

Returns a new Time representing the "start" of the current instance's day, hard-coded to 00:00 hours.

beginning_of_month

Returns a new Time representing the start of the month (1st of the month, 00:00 hours).

beginning_of_quarter

Returns a new Time representing the start of the calendar quarter (1st of January, April, July, October, 00:00 hours).

beginning_of_week

Returns a new Time representing the "start" of the current instance's week, hard-coded to Monday at 00:00 hours.

beginning_of_year

Returns a new Time representing the start of the year (1st of January, 00:00 hours).

change(options)

Returns a new Time where one or more of the elements have been changed according to the options parameter. The valid date options are :year, :month, :day. The valid time options are :hour, :min, :sec, :offset, and :start.

Time.days_in_month(month, year = nil)

Returns the number of days in the given month. If a year is given, February will return the correct number of days for leap years. Otherwise, this method will always report February as having 28 days.

```
>> Time.days_in_month(7, 1974)
=> 31
```

end_of_day

Returns a new Time representing the end of the day (23:59:59).

end_of_month

Returns a new Time representing the end of the month (last day of the month, 00:00 hours).

last_month

Convenience method for months_ago(1).

last_year

Convenience method for `years_ago(1)`.

local_time(*args)

Wraps the class method `time_with_datetime_fallback` with `utc_or_local` argument set to `:local`.

monday

Alias for `beginning of_week`.

months_ago(months)

Returns a new `Time` representing the time a number of specified `months` into the past.

months_since(months)

The opposite of `months_ago`. Returns a new `Time` representing the time a number of specified `months` into the future.

next_month

Convenience method for `months_since(1)`.

next_year

Convenience method for `years_since(1)`.

seconds_since_midnight

Returns the number of seconds that have transpired since midnight.

since(seconds)

Returns a new `Time` representing the time a number of `seconds` into the future starting from the instance time. This method is basically a wrapper around the `Numeric` extension of the same name. For best accuracy, do not use this method in combination with `x.months`; use `months_since` instead!

time_with_datetime_fallback(utc_or_local, year, month=1, day=1, hour=0, min=0, sec=0, usec=0)

Returns a new `Time` if the requested year can be accommodated by Ruby's `Time` class. The range of the `Time` class is either 1970..2038 or 1902..2038, depending on the host system's architecture. Years outside the supported range will return a `DateTime` object.

tomorrow

Convenience method for `self.since(1.day)`.

utc_time(*args)

Wraps the class method `time_with_datetime_fallback` with `utc_or_local` argument set to `:utc`.

years_ago(years)

Returns a new `Time` representing the time a number of specified `years` into the past.

years_since(years)

The opposite of `years_ago`. Returns a new `Time` representing the time a number of specified `years` into the future.

yesterday

Convenience method for `self.ago(1.day)`.

B.49.4 `active_support/core_ext/time/ conversions`

Extensions to Ruby's `Time` class to convert time objects into different convenient string representations and other objects.

Date Formats

The `DATE_FORMATS` hash constant holds formatting patterns used by the `to_formatted_s` method to convert a `Time` object into a string representation:

```
DATE_FORMATS = {
  :db      => "%Y-%m-%d %H:%M:%S",
  :time    => "%H:%M",
  :short   => "%d %b %H:%M",
  :long    => "%B %d, %Y %H:%M",
  :long_ordinal => lambda { |time|
    time.strftime("%B #{time.day.ordinalize}, %Y %H:%M") },
  :rfc822  => "%a, %d %b %Y %H:%M:%S %z"
}
```

formatted_offset(colon = true, alternate_utc_string = nil)

Returns the UTC offset as an HH:MM formatted string.

```
Time.local(2000).formatted_offset         # => "-06:00"
Time.local(2000).formatted_offset(false)  # => "-0600"
```

to_date

Returns a new Date object based on a Time, discarding time data.

to_datetime

Returns a new DateTime object based on a Time, preserving the utc offset. Basically a wrapper around the DateTime.civil factory method:

```
DateTime.civil(year, month, day, hour, min, sec,
Rational(utc_offset,86400), 0)
```

to_formatted_s(format = :default)

Converts a Time object into a string representation. The :default option corresponds to the Time object's own to_s method.

```
>> time = Time.now
=> Thu Jan 18 06:10:17 CST 2007

>> time.to_formatted_s(:time)
=> "06:10:17"

>> time.to_s(:time)
=> "06:10:17"

>> time.to_formatted_s(:db)
=> "2007-01-18 06:10:17"

>> time.to_formatted_s(:number)
=> "20070118061017"

>> time.to_formatted_s(:short)
=> "18 Jan 06:10"

>> time.to_formatted_s(:long)
=> "January 18, 2007 06:10"

>> time.to_formatted_s(:long_ordinal)
=> "January 18th, 2007 06:10"

>> time.to_formatted_s(:rfc822)
=> "Thu, 18 Jan 2007 06:10:17 -0600"
```

to_time

Returns self.

B.49.5 `active_support/core_ext/time/marshal`

Pre-1.9 versions of Ruby have a bug with marshaling `Time` instances, where utc instances are unmarshalled in the local zone, instead of utc. Rails layers behavior on the `_dump` and `_load` methods so that utc instances can be flagged on dump, and coerced back to utc on load.

Ruby 1.9.2 adds `utc_offset` and zone to `Time`, but marshaling only preserves `utc_offset`. Rails preserves zone also, even though it may not work in some edge cases.

B.49.6 `active_support/core_ext/time/zones`

Extensions to `Time` having to do with support for time zones.

current

Returns `Time.zone.now` when `config.time_zone` is set, otherwise just returns `Time.now`.

use_zone(time_zone, &block)

Allows override of `Time.zone` locally inside supplied block; resets `Time.zone` to existing value when done.

```
>> Date.today
=> Wed, 02 Jun 2010

>> Time.use_zone(ActiveSupport::TimeZone['Fiji']) { Date.today }
=> Thu, 03 Jun 2010
```

zone

Returns the `TimeZone` for the current request, if this has been set (via `Time.zone=`). If `Time.zone>` has not been set for the current request, returns the `TimeZone` specified in `config.time_zone`.

zone=(time_zone)

Sets `Time.zone` to a `TimeZone` object for the current request/thread.

This method accepts any of the following:

- A Rails `TimeZone` object.

- An identifier for a Rails `TimeZone` object (e.g., "Eastern Time (US & Canada)", `-5.hours`).

- A `TZInfo::Timezone` object.

- An identifier for a `TZInfo::Timezone` object (e.g., "America/New_York").

Active Support

Here's an example of how you might set `Time.zone` on a per request basis. The code assumes that `current_user.time_zone` returns a string identifying the user's preferred `TimeZone`:

```
class ApplicationController < ActionController::Base
  before_filter :set_time_zone

  def set_time_zone
    Time.zone = current_user.time_zone
  end
end
```

B.50 `ActiveSupport::TimeWithZone`

A `Time`-like class that can represent a time in any time zone. Necessary because standard Ruby `Time` instances are limited to UTC and the system's <tt>ENV['TZ']</tt> zone.

You shouldn't ever need to create a `TimeWithZone` instance directly via `new`. Rails provides the methods `local`, `parse`, `at` and `now` on `TimeZone` instances, and `in_time_zone` on `Time` and `DateTime` instances, for a more user-friendly syntax.

```
>> Time.zone = 'Eastern Time (US & Canada)'
=> 'Eastern Time (US & Canada)'

>> Time.zone.local(2007, 2, 10, 15, 30, 45)
=> Sat, 10 Feb 2007 15:30:45 EST -05:00

>> Time.zone.parse('2007-02-01 15:30:45')
=> Sat, 10 Feb 2007 15:30:45 EST -05:00

>> Time.zone.at(1170361845)
=> Sat, 10 Feb 2007 15:30:45 EST -05:00

>> Time.zone.now
=> Sun, 18 May 2008 13:07:55 EDT -04:00

>> Time.utc(2007, 2, 10, 20, 30, 45).in_time_zone
=> Sat, 10 Feb 2007 15:30:45 EST -05:00
```

See `Time` and `ActiveSupport::TimeZone` for further documentation of these methods.

`TimeWithZone` instances implement the same API as Ruby Time instances, so that Time and `TimeWithZone` instances are interchangable.

```
>> t = Time.zone.now
=> Sun, 18 May 2008 13:27:25 EDT -04:00
```

```
>> t.class
=> ActiveSupport::TimeWithZone

>> t.hour
=> 13

>> t.dst?
=> true

>> t.utc_offset
=> -14400

>> t.zone
=> "EDT"

>> t.to_s(:rfc822)
=> "Sun, 18 May 2008 13:27:25 -0400"

>> t + 1.day
=> Mon, 19 May 2008 13:27:25 EDT -04:00

>> t.beginning_of_year
=> Tue, 01 Jan 2008 00:00:00 EST -05:00

>> t > Time.utc(1999)
=> true

>> t.is_a?(Time)
=> true
```

B.51 ActiveSupport::TimeZone

The TimeZone class serves as a wrapper around TZInfo::Timezone instances. It allows Rails to do the following:

- Limit the set of zones provided by TZInfo to a meaningful subset of 142 zones

- Retrieve and display zones with a friendlier name (e.g., "Eastern Time (US & Canada)" instead of "America/New_York")

- Lazily load TZInfo::Timezone instances only when they're needed

- Create ActiveSupport::TimeWithZone instances via TimeZone's local, parse, at and now methods.

If you set `config.time_zone` in an initializer, you can access this `TimeZone` object via `Time.zone`:

```
config.time_zone = "Eastern Time (US & Canada)"

Time.zone        # => #<TimeZone:0x514834...>
Time.zone.name   # => "Eastern Time (US & Canada)"
Time.zone.now    # => Sun, 18 May 2008 14:30:44 EDT -04:00
```

B.51.1 `active_support/values/time_zone`

The version of `TZInfo` bundled with Active Support only includes the definitions necessary to support the zones defined by the `TimeZone` class. If you need to use zones that aren't defined by `TimeZone`, you'll need to install the `TZInfo` gem. If a recent version of the gem is installed locally, this will be used instead of the bundled version.

`<=> (other)`

Compares this timezone to the parameter. The two are compared first based on their offsets, and then by name.

`TimeZone[] (arg)`

Locates a specific timezone object. If the argument is a string, it is interpreted to mean the name of the timezone to locate.

```
>> TimeZone['Dublin']
=> #<TimeZone:0x3208390 @name="Dublin", @utc_offset=0>
```

If it is a numeric value it is either the hour offset, or the second offset, of the timezone to find. (The first one with that offset will be returned.)

Returns `nil` if no such timezone is known to the system.

`TimeZone.all`

Returns an array of all 142 `TimeZone` objects. There are multiple `TimeZone` objects per timezone (in many cases) to make it easier for users to find their own timezone.

```
>> ActiveSupport::TimeZone.all
=> [#<ActiveSupport::TimeZone:0x551c34...
```

`TimeZone.create(name, offset)`

Creates a new `TimeZone` instance with the given name and offset.

```
>> ActiveSupport::TimeZone.create("Atlanta", -5.hours)
=> #<ActiveSupport::TimeZone:0x26c3a48 @current_period=nil, @tzinfo=nil,
@utc_offset=-18000 seconds, @name="Atlanta">
```

TimeZone.find_tzinfo(name)
Returns a TZInfo instance matching the specified name.

formatted_offset(colon = true)
Returns the offset of this timezone as a formatted string, in the format HH:MM. If the offset is zero, this method will return an empty string. If colon is false, a colon will not be inserted into the output.

initialize(name, utc_offset = nil, tzinfo = nil)
Creates a new TimeZone object with the given name and offset. The offset is the number of seconds that this time zone is offset from UTC (GMT). Seconds were chosen as the offset unit because that is the unit that Ruby uses to represent time zone offsets (see Time#utc_offset). The tzinfo parameter can be explicitly passed in, otherwise the name will be used to find it: TimeZone.find_tzinfo(name)

now
Returns Time.now adjusted to this timezone.

```
>> Time.now
=> Fri Aug 31 22:39:58 -0400 2007
>> TimeZone['Fiji'].now
=> Sat Sep 01 14:40:00 UTC 2007
```

TimeZone.seconds_to_utc_offset (seconds, colon = true)
Assumes self represents an offset from UTC in seconds (as returned from Time#utc_offset) and turns this into an +HH:MM formatted string.

```
TimeZone.seconds_to_utc_offset(-21_600) # => "-06:00"
```

to_s
Returns a textual representation of this timezone.

```
TimeZone['Dublin'].to_s  #=> "(GMT) Dublin"
```

today

Returns the current date in this timezone.

```
>> Date.today.to_s
=> "2007-08-31"
>> TimeZone['Fiji'].today.to_s
=> "2007-09-01"
```

TimeZone.us_zones

A convenience method for returning a collection of `TimeZone` objects for timezones in the United States.

```
>> TimeZone.us_zones.map(&:name)
=> ["Hawaii", "Alaska", "Pacific Time (US & Canada)", "Arizona",
"Mountain Time (US & Canada)", "Central Time (US & Canada)", "Eastern
Time (US & Canada)", "Indiana (East)"]
```

B.52 ActiveSupport::TrueClass
B.52.1 active_support/core_ext/object/blank
blank?

Returns `false`.

B.52.2 active_support/json/encoding
as_json

Returns `"true"`.

B.53 ActiveSupport::XmlMini

The `XmlMini` module contains code that allows Rails to serialize/deserialize and parse XML using a number of different libraries.

- JDOM (requires JRuby)
- LibXML (fast native XML parser)
- Nokogiri (requires Nokogiri gem)
- ReXML

B.53.1 **active_support/xml_mini**

If you're doing anything of significance with XML in your application, you should definitely use the super-fast native `libxml` parser. Install the binaries (instructions vary depending on platform) then the Ruby binding:

```
gem 'libxml-ruby', '=0.9.7'
```

Set XmlMini to use `libxml` in `application.rb` or an initializer.

```
XmlMini.backend = 'LibXML'
```

Constants

The TYPE_NAMES constant holds a mapping of Ruby types to their representation when serialized as XML.

```
TYPE_NAMES = {
  "Symbol"     => "symbol",
  "Fixnum"     => "integer",
  "Bignum"     => "integer",
  "BigDecimal" => "decimal",
  "Float"      => "float",
  "TrueClass"  => "boolean",
  "FalseClass" => "boolean",
  "Date"       => "date",
  "DateTime"   => "datetime",
  "Time"       => "datetime",
  "Array"      => "array",
  "Hash"       => "hash"
}
```

The FORMATTING constant holds a mapping of lambdas that define how Ruby values are serialized to strings for representation in XML.

```
FORMATTING = {
  "symbol"   => Proc.new { |symbol| symbol.to_s },
  "date"     => Proc.new { |date| date.to_s(:db) },
  "datetime" => Proc.new { |time| time.xmlschema },
  "binary"   => Proc.new { |binary|
ActiveSupport::Base64.encode64(binary) },
  "yaml"     => Proc.new { |yaml| yaml.to_yaml }
}
```

The PARSING constant holds a mapping of lambdas used to deserialize values stored in XML back into Ruby objects.

```
  PARSING = {
    "symbol"      => Proc.new { |symbol|  symbol.to_sym },
    "date"        => Proc.new { |date|    ::Date.parse(date) },
```

```ruby
    "datetime"      => Proc.new { |time|    ::Time.parse(time).utc rescue
::DateTime.parse(time).utc },
    "integer"       => Proc.new { |integer| integer.to_i },
    "float"         => Proc.new { |float|   float.to_f },
    "decimal"       => Proc.new { |number|  BigDecimal(number) },
    "boolean"       => Proc.new { |boolean| %w(1
true).include?(boolean.strip) },
    "string"        => Proc.new { |string|  string.to_s },
    "yaml"          => Proc.new { |yaml|    YAML::load(yaml) rescue yaml },
    "base64Binary"  => Proc.new { |bin|
ActiveSupport::Base64.decode64(bin) },
    "binary"        => Proc.new { |bin, entity| _parse_binary(bin, entity)
},
    "file"          => Proc.new { |file, entity| _parse_file(file, entity)
}
  }

  PARSING.update(
    "double"   => PARSING["float"],
    "dateTime" => PARSING["datetime"]
  )
```

Index

Method Index

Addison
Wesley

REGISTER

THIS PRODUCT

informit.com/register

Register the Addison-Wesley, Exam Cram, Prentice Hall, Que, and Sams products you own to unlock great benefits.

To begin the registration process, simply go to **informit.com/register** to sign in or create an account. You will then be prompted to enter the 10- or 13-digit ISBN that appears on the back cover of your product.

Registering your products can unlock the following benefits:

- Access to supplemental content, including bonus chapters, source code, or project files.
- A coupon to be used on your next purchase.

Registration benefits vary by product. Benefits will be listed on your Account page under Registered Products.

About InformIT — **THE TRUSTED TECHNOLOGY LEARNING SOURCE**

INFORMIT IS HOME TO THE LEADING TECHNOLOGY PUBLISHING IMPRINTS Addison-Wesley Professional, Cisco Press, Exam Cram, IBM Press, Prentice Hall Professional, Que, and Sams. Here you will gain access to quality and trusted content and resources from the authors, creators, innovators, and leaders of technology. Whether you're looking for a book on a new technology, a helpful article, timely newsletters, or access to the Safari Books Online digital library, InformIT has a solution for you.

informIT.com

THE TRUSTED TECHNOLOGY LEARNING SOURCE

Addison-Wesley | Cisco Press | Exam Cram
IBM Press | Que | Prentice Hall | Sams

SAFARI BOOKS ONLINE

informIT.com
THE TRUSTED TECHNOLOGY LEARNING SOURCE

LearnIT at InformIT

Looking for a book, eBook, or training video on a new technology? Seeking timely and relevant information and tutorials? Looking for expert opinions, advice, and tips? **InformIT has the solution.**

- Learn about new releases and special promotions by subscribing to a wide variety of newsletters.
  Visit **informit.com/newsletters**.

- Access FREE podcasts from experts at **informit.com/podcasts**.

- Read the latest author articles and sample chapters at **informit.com/articles**.

- Access thousands of books and videos in the Safari Books Online digital library at **safari.informit.com**.

- Get tips from expert blogs at **informit.com/blogs**.

Visit **informit.com/learn** to discover all the ways you can access the hottest technology content.

Are You Part of the IT Crowd?

Connect with Pearson authors and editors via RSS feeds, Facebook, Twitter, YouTube, and more! Visit **informit.com/socialconnect**.